HANDBOOK OF RESEARCH ON COMPARATIVE HUMAN RESOURCE MANAGEMENT

Handbook of Research on Comparative Human Resource Management

Edited by

Chris Brewster

Henley Business School, University of Reading, UK

Wolfgang Mayrhofer

WU Wien (Vienna University of Economics and Business), Austria

Edward Elgar
Cheltenham, UK • Northampton, MA, USA

Published by
Edward Elgar Publishing Limited
The Lypiatts
15 Lansdown Road
Cheltenham
Glos GL50 2JA
UK

Edward Elgar Publishing, Inc.
William Pratt House
9 Dewey Court
Northampton
Massachusetts 01060
USA

A catalogue record for this book
is available from the British Library

Library of Congress Control Number: 2009941089

MIX
Paper from
responsible sources
FSC® C018575

ISBN 978 1 84720 726 5 (cased)

Typeset by Servis Filmsetting Ltd, Stockport, Cheshire
Printed and bound by MPG Books Group, UK

Contents

Contributors

Phil Almond, De Montfort University, UK

Christine Bischoff, Society, Work and Development Institute (SWOP), University of Witwatersrand, South Africa

María Jesús Belizón Cebada, IESE Business School, Spain

Tanya Bondarouk, University of Twente, The Netherlands

Paul Boselie, Tilburg University, The Netherlands

Anna Bos-Nehles, University of Twente, The Netherlands

Peter Boxall, University of Auckland, New Zealand

Julia Brandl, University of Innsbruck, Austria

Chris Brewster, University of Reading, UK

Pawan Budhwar, Aston University, UK

David G. Collings, National University of Ireland, Galway, Ireland

Ngan Collins, RMIT University, Australia

Gwendolyn M. Combs, University of Nebraska-Lincoln, USA

Françoise Dany, EMLYON Business School, France

Anabella Davila, EGADE Business School, Tecnologico de Monterrey, Mexico

Philippe Debroux, Soka University, Japan

Peter J. Dowling, La Trobe University, Australia

Ina Ehnert, Université Catholique de Louvain (UCL), Belgium

Marta M. Elvira, IESE Business School, Spain

Allen D. Engle Sr., Eastern Kentucky University, USA

Elaine Farndale, Pennsylvania State University, USA / Tilburg University, The Netherlands

Marion Festing, ESCP Europe, Germany

Steve Frenkel, University of New South Wales, Australia

Barry Gerhart, University of Wisconsin-Madison, USA

Maria C. Gonzalez, University of Oviedo, Spain

Wes Harry, Cass Business School, UK

Shigeaki Hayashi, Tokyo Institute of Technology, Japan

Jason Huang Heh, National Sun Yat-sen University, Taiwan

Noreen Heraty, University of Limerick, Ireland

Susan E. Jackson, Rutgers University, USA and Lorange Institute of Business, Zurich, Switzerland

Keith Jackson, University of London, UK

Toru Kiyomiya, Seinan Gakuin University, Japan

Alain Klarsfeld, Toulouse Business School, France

Mila Lazarova, Simon Fraser University, Canada

Yih-teen Lee, IESE Business School, Spain

David Lepak, Rutgers University, USA

Christopher Mabey, University of Birmingham, UK

Wolfgang Mayrhofer, WU Wien (Vienna University of Economics and Business), Austria

Kamel Mellahi, University of Sheffield, UK

Snejina Michailova, University of Auckland, New Zealand

Dana Minbaeva, Copenhagen Business School, Denmark

Michael J. Morley, University of Limerick, Ireland

Werner Nienhüser, University of Duisburg-Essen, Germany

Irene Nikandrou, Athens University of Economics and Business, Greece

Jaap Paauwe, Tilburg University, The Netherlands

Leda Panayotopoulou, Athens University of Economics and Business, Greece

Tuomo Peltonen, Tampere University of Technology, Finland

Andrew Pendleton, University of York, UK

practices made by the size of the organisation and the sector (or sectors) in which it operates. More recently, HRM researchers have become aware of the differences in the subject between nations and have argued that this is a matter not only of differences in practice but also in differences in the way that the subject is thought about: its meaning and its purpose. Even if we accept that the purpose of HRM should be improving the performance of the firm, Gerhart has argued, 'it seems unlikely that one set of HRM practices will work equally well no matter what the context' (Gerhart, 2005: 178).

Much of the new thinking and innovation in HRM continues to come from the USA, the origin of the concept. Originating from the United States, concepts and ideas about HRM have followed the 'Gulf Stream . . . drifting in from the USA and hitting the UK first, then crossing the Benelux countries . . . and Germany and France and proceeding finally to southern Europe' (DeFidelto & Slater, 2001: 281). And then, usually later, to the rest of the world. The hegemony of the US model is such that many universities and business schools as well as consultancies around the world use US teaching materials, US teaching methods and US text-books and case studies, more or less ignoring HRM in the local environment around them. Like many others, we believe this is an error. HRM does not operate the same way in every country. The idea that human resource management varies around the world is by no means new, but much HRM commentary either ignores that fact or assumes that countries that do HRM differently are 'lagging behind'. Human Resource Management of the 'best practice' variety may not even be that common in the United States, but it looks and feels very different elsewhere in the world.

Against the backdrop of contextual differences and the more dynamic view of changes over time, comparative HRM is concerned with understanding and explaining differences between contexts as constituted by countries and analysing how much changes over time, in particular through the process of globalisation, leading to a harmonisation of HRM across the world, and how far countries retain their distinctive national flavour.

In the view of Clark et al. (1999), 20 years of research into international and comparative HRM left the subject 'running on the spot'. The problems include the lack of conceptual analysis of the topic and limited coverage of various parts of the world. In the years since then there have been significant attempts to remedy this situation and the time is now right to summarise those attempts and perhaps to stimulate others to move from running on the spot to making real progress.

This chapter introduces both the subject of comparative HRM and this

Handbook. We attempt to identify the establishment of the subject and its boundaries; we explore levels of analysis of comparative HRM; perspectives for studying it; and we address the issue of whether globalisation is making such an analysis increasingly irrelevant as societies converge. Then we outline the shape and content of the book. We note some theoretical and empirical issues in comparative HRM, the way that these affect particular elements of HRM and the way that different regions think differently about the topic: a framework for the *Handbook*.

THE ESTABLISHMENT OF COMPARATIVE HRM AND ITS BOUNDARIES

The classic texts marking the origin of HRM identified, respectively, four (employee influence, human resource flow, reward systems and work systems in Beer et al., 1984) or five (selection, performance, appraisal, rewards and development in Fombrun et al., 1984) areas which can be used to analyse HRM. The unstated implication was that these areas can be used in any organisation, anywhere in the world. Most universities and business schools tend to teach a very similar version of HRM to that outlined in the famous books.

In reality there has been little agreement about the meaning of the term 'human resource management'. We are not the first to note the confusion surrounding the concept (see, as early examples, Boxall, 1992; Goss, 1994; Guest, 1990; Storey, 1992). Conceptually, a range of definitions of human resource management is possible: from an almost etymological analysis at one end to a clearly normative perspective at the other. Within this range two broad categories can be discerned:

- HRM as a subject area, exploring processes by which an organisation deals with the labour it needs to perform its functions and encompassing, therefore, traditional definitions of personnel management (including manpower planning, resourcing, training and development, etc. and, importantly for us here, industrial relations) and also subcontracting, outsourcing and similar arrangements for utilising human resources even when not employed within the organisation.
- HRM as a contribution to organisational (usually business) effectiveness. In many cases this usage has defined itself as strategic HRM (see e.g. Armstrong, 2008; Boxall & Purcell, 2008; Brewster et al., 2011; Hendry & Pettigrew, 1990; Schuler, 1992 ; Schuler & Jackson, 2007; Torrington et al., 2008).

Whereas the first kind of focus concentrates upon identifying and studying either the whole relationship between people at work and their organisations or a particular aspect of it, the latter one is focused on the activities of management and the practices that management can adopt to improve efficiency and effectiveness. Arguably, a contributory reason for these different approaches to the topic are similar to the basic argument of comparative HRM: it is perhaps little wonder that researchers, based in a different institutional and cultural context, with different historical antecedents of research perspectives and different practical problems to explain, have different views of what is central to the topic.

The developing stream of work in comparative HRM has its roots in different traditions: the industrial relations tradition, the growth of international business as a fact and a subject of study, and the equally fast-growing topic of international HRM.

There has been an input from the industrial relations tradition. In Europe and Australasia, particularly, many of the earlier researchers and teachers in human resource management moved into the field from industrial relations studies. Industrial relations vary markedly from country to country and this has traditionally been an area of study much concerned with nationally comparative issues, for example: Why is union membership so much higher in some countries than in others? Why do different consultation structures apply in different countries? The embeddedness of industrial relations in its national context was a given, so it was natural for the specialists who moved across from that field to take a more comparative view of the closely linked subject of human resource management.

The study of various aspects of the management of multinational corporations (MNCs; see, for example, Rugman & Collinson, 2008; Shenkar & Luo, 2008) concentrated on the advantages conferred by operating across countries. Differences between countries were either an inevitable background or regarded as an additional difficulty for MNCs wanting to benefit from doing business across national borders. There was also an assumption that MNCs invariably created change – and convergence, often assumed to be to an American model – in the host countries of their subsidiaries. This thinking has developed considerably in recent years and the literature has become much more aware of national differences.

The international HRM tradition of research has been summarised as having three distinct streams of discussion (Dowling, 1999): one considers individuals working abroad and more recently other forms of working such as self-initiated stays abroad (see, for example, Benson & Marshall, 2008; Dickmann et al., 2008b; Haslberger & Brewster, 2009; Jokinen et al., 2008; Mayrhofer et al., 2007; Takeuchi et al., 2005); a second stream looking at various aspects of HRM in companies operating across national borders, specifically the HRM problems of MNCs (for an excellent summary of the latest research position in that stream, see Stahl & Björkman, 2011); and a third stream of research analysing HRM in the light of national, cultural and regional differences – comparative HRM.

Comparative HRM now has a firmly established place within HRM (see, for example, the contributions on comparative HRM in overview works on HRM/international HRM such as Collings & Wood, 2009; Harzing & Pinnington, 2011; Sparrow, 2009). Starting in the 1990s, early works described the differences between societies and explored the theoretical foundations of the subject (e.g. Begin, 1992; Boxall, 1995; Brewster & Tyson, 1991; Hegewisch & Brewster, 1993). Since then the balance of the discussion has changed from a primarily descriptive perspective to a more explanatory angle looking into 'why' and 'how', i.e. the reasons for and the processes leading to commonalities and differences in HRM between different countries and cultures, in particular also looking at developments over time (Brewster et al., 2004; Mayrhofer et al., 2011a). Some of the theoretical underpinnings and conceptual approaches to the topic are summarised in later chapters of this handbook. An increased knowledge about the specifics of management across borders, including knowledge of how human resource management issues are handled in various countries (Dickmann et al., 2008a), has become a prominent issue for social scientists as it has become a key issue for all kinds of managers.

LEVELS OF ANALYSIS OF HRM

Many of the seminal management and HRM texts are written as if the analysis applies at all levels, something one can call 'false universalism' (Rose, 1991). This is a major problem in relation to the literature from the United States. The cultural hegemony of US teaching and publishing, particularly in the leading US and 'international' journals, means that these texts are often utilised by readers and students in other countries. US-based literature searches, now all done on computers, of course, tend to privilege texts in English and texts in the US-based journals and texts in the universalist tradition (Brewster, 1999a, b). For analysts and practitioners elsewhere with interests in different sectors, countries and so on, many of these descriptions and prescriptions fail to meet their reality and a more context sensitive analysis is necessary.

Comparative HRM strives to provide such analyses. In its simplest form, HRM in two different countries is compared and contrasted at a merely descriptive level. In a broader sense the criteria for comparison, derived from theoretical reasoning or closely linked to observable phenomena, go far beyond that to explore clusters of countries, or to challenge the national boundaries concept. Cultural groups do not always coincide with national borders. Hence studies such as that by Dewettinck et al. (2004) who compare the way people are managed in the Walloon and Flemish parts of Belgium (with France and the Netherlands) would be claimed as comparative HRM texts. While basically using comparative in this broad sense, the majority of comparative HRM contributions do deal with differences across nations, culture clusters and world regions.

When looking at HRM from a comparative angle, a key question concerns the levels of HRM (Kochan et al., 1992; Locke et al., 1995). It implies decisions on how to conceive of the differences in HRM systems and approaches and then choosing an appropriate perspective. A telescope analogy has been proposed as useful in this context (Brewster, 1995). Changing the focus on a telescope provides the viewer with ever more detail and the ability to distinguish ever-finer differences within the big picture than can be seen with the naked eye. None of the chosen perspectives are wrong or inaccurate, but some are more useful for some purposes than for others. HRM can be conceived of in this way. In HRM there are universals, for example, the need for organisations to attract, deploy, assess, train and pay workers; there are some things that are shared within regions; some that are distinctive for certain nations; some that are unique to certain sectors; in many ways each organisation or even each section of an organisation is different; and there are some factors that are unique to each individual manager and employee. Each perspective sharpens the focus on some aspects but, inevitably, blurs others. The many (within country) studies that (accurately) find differences between sectors within a country, for example, have been extended to studies of particular sectors across countries with the implicit (but inaccurate) assumption that there will be more differences between the sectors than between the countries. Hence, when discussing comparative HRM it is important to take into account the chosen perspective and to be aware of the missing complexity. Many commentators either state, or imply by omission, that their analysis is universal. Comparative HRM challenges that view.

This book adopts a mid-level position, concentrating upon comparative HRM at the country and country cluster level. As with the telescope metaphor, this picture is no more nor less accurate than the others: it just helps us to understand some things more clearly.

CONVERGENCE AND DIVERGENCE

Given that there are differences between countries and regions at this level, one intriguing area of research explores whether the process of globalisation – so significant in other subjects – applies to comparative HRM. The globalisation literature has even argued that the increasing political importance of supra-national bodies such as the EU, global efforts to reduce trade barriers and the burgeoning power of MNCs heralds the end of nation states (Ohmae, 1995).

Catchwords exemplify this, for example, the global village where political, time-related and geographical boundaries have little importance (McLuhan & Powers, 1989), the McDonaldisation of society, where the fast-food chain serves as a unifying role model for a form of rationalisation spreading globally and permeating all realms of day-to-day interaction and personal identity (Ritzer, 1993), or the flat world where Friedman (Friedman, 2007b) argues that technology is making the world increasingly homogeneous.

In the subject of our attention, are countries in fact becoming more alike in the way that they think about and practice HRM so that the differences between them will be of diminishing importance? Are the differences static or, more sensibly and assuming that no social systems will remain completely static, what is the direction of movement – or are different units of analysis (aspects of HRM, for example, or policy and practice) heading in different directions, are they becoming more or less alike? Contributions to answering these questions – often labelled within the frame of convergence and divergence – come from theoretical, methodological and empirical sources.

Much attention has been focused on how MNCs are changing local HRM practices by importing successful practices across national borders. In the general management literature there have been clear voices raised in favour of the globalisation thesis (Friedman, 2007a; Kidger, 1991). Galbraith contended that modern man's 'area of decision is, in fact, exceedingly small' and that 'the imperatives of organization, technology and planning operate similarly, and . . . to a broadly similar result, on all societies' (1967: 336). Likewise, Kerr et al. (1960) postulated that the logics of industrialisation produce common values, beliefs and systems of organisation despite different ideologies, politics and cultures. Management consultancies, business schools, and professional bodies tend to favour the 'one best way' (usually the US way, Smith & Meiksins, 1995) leading to a convergence of rhetoric at least. MNCs are a key channel for such diffusion practices, attempting to enforce common policies, usually headquarters policies, across their systems and often enforcing even the language in which employees communicate (e.g. Björkman & Piekkari, 2009; Freely & Harzing, 2003; Piekkari, 2006). Recent research (Farndale et al., 2008) finds that whilst MNC subsidiaries do on average manage their human resources differently from other organisations in the same country, they are not very different.

There have also been voices arguing that for both institutional (Amable, 2003; Hall & Soskice, 2001; Whitley, 1999) and cultural reasons (Hofstede, 1980; House et al., 2004) convergence is unlikely. There are also arguments that emphasise the simultaneous occurrence of both converging and diverging trends (Crouch & Streeck, 1997; Inkeles, 1998).

These arguments can be applied to human resource management too. Questions concern whether the actions of MNCs reduce national differences in HRM and the balance between the extent to which foreign organisations bring new practices into a country compared to the extent to which they adjust to local practices (Quintanilla & Ferner, 2003). It has been argued that this will vary with a number of factors, most importantly with: the kind of business system or market economy the MNC operates in; the country of origin of the MNCs; the type of organisation, i.e. foreign-owned MNCs, domestic-owned MNCs and domestic organisations; and with the impact of context on MNCs operating under these different conditions (Almond & Ferner, 2006; Farndale et al., 2008; Gooderham et al., 1999). So the question of convergence of HRM practices is a live one.

From a methodological perspective, it is essential to have a clear understanding about what convergence and divergence actually mean. Some studies have claimed to find convergence from a single point in time analysis (e.g. Chen et al., 2005). Clearly, what they have found are similarities, but not convergence, which requires a coming together over time.

To be clearer about this, two major forms of convergence have been suggested (Mayrhofer et al., 2002). Final convergence exists when units of analysis are becoming more alike, i.e. they share a development towards a common end point, implying a decrease in differences between countries. Of course, this does not imply that this endpoint of total similarity will ever be reached. Directional convergence countries share the same trend, i.e. they go in the same direction, regardless of their initial starting level and any common endpoint.

From an empirical perspective, hard evidence of long-term development in HRM is scarce. Arguably the best data in this area stems from Cranet, a research network dedicated to a trend study about developments in the area of HRM in public and private organisations with more than 200 employees. Since 1989 there have been seven survey-rounds in currently more than 50 countries worldwide, with an emphasis on Europe (see Brewster & Hegewisch, 1994; Brewster et al., 2000). Detailed evidence is available for developments in Europe (see the overview in Brewster et al., 2004, and a more detailed analysis in Mayrhofer et al., 2011b). Results from a rigorous statistical analysis of the data show that in Europe many aspects of HRM show directional convergence, i.e. the trends are the same. Thus, there are increases in most countries most of the time in such issues as the professionalisation of the HRM function, the use of more sophisticated recruitment and selection systems, the use of contingent rewards and the extent of communication with employees. However, contrary to the received wisdom in the universalistic texts, there is no sign of common trends in the size of the HRM department (see also Brewster et al., 2006) nor in training and development, which is given high priority in many countries but seems to remain the first area for cuts when finances become tight. The evidence is summarised as follows: 'from a directional convergence point of view, there seems to be a positive indication of convergence. However, when one looks at the question from a final convergence point of view, the answer is no longer a clear positive. None of the HRM practices converge' (Mayrhofer et al., 2004: 432).

It seems clear that the evidence supports those who would argue, for various reasons, that globalisation might not be taking place in the clear, straightforward way of 'making things more similar'. Hence, the broader issue of factors explaining similarities and differences between HRM in different countries and their development becomes crucial and constitutes a core element of comparative HRM.

UNITS OF ANALYSIS

Comparative HRM research usually focuses on individual and collective actors of various kinds as well as the respective structures and processes linked with these actors, all of them in different countries, cultures or regions (Brewster & Mayrhofer, 2009). The degree of social complexity constitutes a useful main differentiation criterion in order to group these actors according to different analytical levels. Actors are characterised by low social complexity if the emerging social relationships within these actors are either non-existent as in the case of individuals or have comparatively little complexity, e.g. in face-to-face groups. However, collective actors such as countries or supra-national units show high social complexity. A complex fabric of social relationships constitutes their internal environment.

Looking back to the early 1990s, an analysis of published comparative HRM research reveals that country-, organisation- and individual-level analyses dominate the scene. Reflecting the view of Clark et al. 10 years earlier, extensive research in peer-reviewed articles published in the years from 1990 to 2005 (Mayrhofer & Reichel, 2009) showed that comparative HRM was typically empirical rather than conceptual; focused on country, organisation or individual as the primary units of analysis; used cross-sectional 'snapshot' rather than longitudinal, i.e. panel or trend study, designs; and focused on comparison of one or more sets of HRM practices, e.g. recruitment procedures, and/or HRM configuration such as strategic orientation or size of the HRM department rather than the link between HRM and some kind of output like satisfaction, performance or commitment. Overall, early comparative HRM research put an emphasis on actors and respective processes and structures at a low to medium level of social complexity. Typical blind spots were networks of organisations and supra-national actors. Moreover the research tended to be focused on a very limited number of countries and regions of the world. More recent work has attempted to address some of these issues as we note below.

How has the research been changing to meet such critiques? We argue that there are three areas where we can see developments There has been progress in understanding the theoretical and methodological frameworks that can be applied to comparative HRM; in exploring different tasks and themes in HRM from a comparative viewpoint; and in the range of countries and regions about which we have information on the way that they understand and practice HRM. These three areas form the main sections of this book.

OUTLINE OF THE BOOK

Part I: Theoretical and Conceptual Issues

The first section of the book contains chapters that examine some of the theoretical and conceptual issues, and some of the research problems, that arise in comparative HRM. In itself we believe that this is somewhat unusual – perhaps unique – and a distinguishing feature of the book. We are aware, of course, that size limitations, and the perspective of the editors, mean that it is impossible to cover all such issues, but we believe that this first attempt to bring such issues together provides the reader with a good starting point for anyone doing research in the field.

At the more general socio-economic level, there are **institutional explanations** for national differences. An interest in comparative capitalisms (Deeg & Jackson, 2008) was sparked by the fall of the Berlin Wall and the realisation that the Central and Eastern European states had not one but different models that they could follow. Some of these (for example,

Hall & Soskice, 2001; and, specifically in HRM, Gooderham et al., 1999) have been one-dimensional and limited to simple dichotomies, contrasting Anglo-Saxon style free-market capitalism with varieties where there is greater state intervention and co-ordinated markets. However, there have also been analyses (Amable, 2003; Hollingsworth & Boyer, 1997; Whitley, 1999) that develop a more nuanced version, noting the differences in Japanese management, or between the Nordic countries and those of southern Europe. More recently these insights have been extended to human resource management specifically (Brookes, Brewster, & Wood, 2005; Farndale et al., 2008; Goergen et al., 2009a, b; Tregaskis & Brewster, 2006; Wood et al., 2009). Chapter 2 by Geoffrey Wood, Alexandros Psychogios, Leslie T. Szamosi and David G. Collings explores these issues.

But institutional variations are not the only explanator: are differences between nations sustained 'because a wider formal system of laws, agreements, standards and codes exist[s]' . . . or because 'people find it repulsive, unethical or unappealing to do otherwise' (Sorge, 2004: 118)? In other words (Brewster, 2004), is the explanation institutional or cultural? The literature on culture is focused on the values that people have and the relationships between them. It would be extraordinary if this did not impact on human resource management and **cultural differences and their link to HRM** are addressed in detail in Chapter 3 in this volume by B. Sebastian Reiche, Yih-teen Lee and Javier Quintanilla.

Chapter 4 by Tuomo Peltonen and Eero Vaara explores **a more critical approach** to HRM and comparative HRM, arguing that HRM has been bedevilled by a series of assumptions based around a US neo-liberal paradigm that has either ignored or hidden key issues like conflicts of interest and power relationships. They argue that the challenges to such approaches implicit in the notion of comparative, nationally embedded HRM, would be strengthened by a closer relationship with theories that already tangentially, at least, discuss these debates: global labour process theory, postcolonial analysis and transnational feminism.

The next chapter focuses on some of the methodological issues in comparative HRM research. Chapter 5 is a closely argued analysis by Ingo Weller and Barry Gerhart of some of the difficulties inherent in analysing and understanding the large-scale surveys that have been used in comparative HRM research. Using the example of Hofstede's cultural studies, they show how care needs to be taken in interpreting the results of such studies.

Part II: HRM Tasks and Themes

The second section of the book, which though perhaps not unique is also unusual, examines tasks and themes in HRM from a comparative

on the subject of the chapter, **financial participation**. They explore the antecedents and the incidence of profit sharing and a variety of forms of employee share ownership: why are they so different between countries? They give some detailed analysis of the embeddedness of financial participation in a number of developed countries. They conclude that that legislative and fiscal frameworks account for much of the variation but go on to ask the deeper question of what lies behind those differences.

Financial participation has some resonances with the subject of Chapter 16, **performance management**. Paul Boselie, Elaine Fandale and Jaap Paauwe draw on some of their own research to argue that this popular and topical subject is worthy of definitional and conceptual analysis as well as the prescriptive approach that is so often taken. They show the development of the subject over time and argue that there are international trends in the way it is being used. They conclude that although differences in the meaning and use of performance management can be distinguished between countries, this is one area of HRM where a clear trend and perhaps final convergence are visible.

In Chapter 17, which reviews the subject of **diversity**, Alain Klarsfeld, Gwendolyn M. Combs, Lourdes Susaeta and María Jesús Belizón Cebada show how this sometimes controversial topic has been differently understood, applied to different groups within the workforce and managed very differently in different national contexts. The authors run quickly through the history of diversity management and its development through legislative provision. They examine the range and depth of legislation in detail and show how different clusters of countries have adopted separate approaches. Finally, they examine the effects of such legislation and management action and show that where managements have embraced the topic it has had a positive effect for both the organisations and the individuals employed.

Chapter 18 explores the issue of **e-HRM**, the relatively new packages being offered by a number of organisations to employers to allow them to manage significant aspects of their HRM electronically. Huub J. M. Ruël and Tanya Bondarouk draw on their own research as well as that of others to show how this fairly new field is one that has been relatively well-served by researchers. The impact of e-HRM, particularly in larger organisations, may be only just becoming apparent. The likelihood is that its impact will be ever more strongly felt and that there will be an ever larger divide between electronic and non-electronic HRM, within organisations as much as between them. Pointing out that e-HRM research has largely ignored the cross-national element, these authors develop a model approach to such research requirements.

Part III: Regional Perspectives

The third section of the *Handbook* examines regional perspectives and provides, we believe, the widest coverage of any book available. Both the institutional literature and the cultural literature have developed clusters of countries that have obvious implications for HRM. The varieties of capitalism literature explored in Chapter 2 has different categorisations, dividing Europe into more categories and leaving much of the rest of the world apart from the Anglo-Saxon states and Japan and Korea untouched. The cross-cultural literature explored in Chapter 3 has a rather different, and often more comprehensive, but still partial, categorisation. More specifically, attempts have been made to examine comparative HRM in particular regions (see, for example, Brewster et al., 2004; Brewster et al., 1992; or even in sub-regions, e.g. Brewster & Larsen, 2000).

Inevitably, our ambition to cover the world has not been fully realised; there are countries missing. Even so, trying to do so has forced our contributors to generalise and to combine insights and data on countries that could have been, in a different context, described and analysed separately. We wish that there had been space to do otherwise, because this inevitably means that individual countries are subject to broad statements that do not capture the full complexity of their situation and the differences between them. Yet, we believe that the gains from having this unique global coverage outweigh those concerns.

There are many categorisations of regions: the International Labour Office, for example, (ILO Employment Development Report, 2007) divided the world into: Developed Economies and European Union; Central and Eastern Europe (non–EU) and Commonwealth of Independent States (CIS); East Asia; South-East Asia and the Pacific; South Asia; Latin America and the Caribbean; Middle East and North Africa; sub-Saharan Africa. In this book we have taken a broadly geographical focus, linking adjacent countries (though with a few exceptions), with the intention of covering as much of the world as possible.

We have asked our contributors, in each case the chapter is written by an individual from or a team including people from that region, to focus on what makes the ways of thinking about HRM in their region unique rather than just showing ways in which practices differ. Some of them have, perhaps, found this easier than others. It depends on authors, of course, but there does seem to be an indication that those regions culturally furthest from the US model find it easier to show how in, for example, China or Japan what serves the shareholders best in the short-term is not necessarily seen as good HRM; there is greater on-going responsibility for employees and their families as a key element of HRM.

Chapter 19 by Susan E. Jackson, Randall S. Schuler, Dave Lepak and Ibraiz Tarique starts the examination of regions by considering HRM in **North America** – the land where the subject began. They explore current HRM issues on that continent such as competence and values or the enhanced role of shareholders in relation to other stakeholders and suggest the need for an integrative framework to understand developments there. They emphasise recent developments such as employee privacy, workplace diversity, performance management and individual performance based pay

In Chapter 20 Anabella Davila and Marta Elvira consider the southern parts of the Americas and show how differently HRM is conceived of and practiced there. They emphasise the importance of a wider view of stakeholder analysis for understanding human resource management in **Latin America**. They draw some fascinating examples of how this would work from the existing literature and note the importance of the voices of those not normally heard in these countries.

In Chapter 21 Christine Bischoff and Geoffrey Wood also try to summarise HRM across most of a whole continent: in this case **sub-Saharan Africa**. Attempting to establish a business systems model for the region, they note the gap between the extensive laws and the capacity for individuals or unions to enforce them, the prevalence of short-termism and the way that the autocratic, low-skilled African model is ameliorated by paternalism. They make a plea for more work in what is generally a 'blind spot' in comparative HRM research.

The rest of **north Africa and the Middle East** are examined in Chapter 22 by Pawan Budhwar and Kamel Mellahi. Again, they point to the paucity of research into HRM in the region and the difficulty of access to reliable information. They stress the importance of Islam but also caution against under-estimating the diversity within the region. The problems of unemployment and a growing population will be handled more easily in some countries than in others.

In Chapter 23 Wolfgang Mayrhofer, Chris Brewster and Paul Sparrow explore the varied countries of **Europe**, arguing that HRM research in that continent often takes a wider and more critical view than is common elsewhere. A stakeholder perspective is more common than a shareholder one and governments, and the supra-national government of the European Union, are more likely to be involved in and to constrain or support HRM. Examples of the type and range of practices in different European countries are given to illustrate the arguments.

On the borders of Europe lie **Russia and the Transition States**, those countries that used to be part of the Union of Soviet Socialist Republics. HRM in that context is explored in Chapter 24 by Michael J. Morley,

Dana Minbaeva and Snejina Michailova. One key question focuses on the extent to which Western-dominated theories and practices are applicable to Central and Eastern Europe (CEE) and Former Soviet Union (FSU) countries and whether we see a unique regional approach to HRM emerging or whether there is evidence of a hybrid system, combining western and regional elements. The authors provide empirical evidence from a broad range of sources, showing idiosyncratic elements of HRM in CEE and FSU as well as common characteristics.

Chapter 25 examines HRM in the **Indian subcontinent**. Written by Pawan Budhwar, and Arup Varma, the chapter points out the importance of the geographical and socio-economic context, noting particularly the issues of emigration and economic liberalisation. On the basis of a review of the relevant literature they conclude that the region faces issues of coping with diversity and with rapid change. In the circumstances it is not surprising that the forms of HRM in the region are still developing.

Chapter 26, by Ngan Collins, Ying Zhu and Malcolm Warner, examines three other Asian countries – the **Asian communist states** of the People's Republic of China, Viet Nam and North Korea, a group of countries that might be said to span the full range of economic success. These countries are in transition with on-going reforms, though the authors except little-researched North Korea from this. This is a region of low wages, though that is changing fast in China. Unlike most other chapters this one includes a section on the governmental perspective and the role of government, in negotiation with enterprises, is emphasised throughout.

Chapter 27 is by Philippe Debroux, Wes Harry, Hayashi Shigeaki, Huang Heh Jason, Keith Jackson and Kiyomiya Toru and considers the view of HRM in the countries that were the first **Asian success stories**: Japan, Taiwan and South Korea. They show the importance of history and the fact that the late development of capitalism in these countries gave them some advantages. They also show, through careful analysis of each country in turn, how the culture of these countries and their considerable work ethic contributed to their success. Finally, they outline some of the challenges that these countries face.

The last word, in Chapter 28, the final chapter, is given to Peter Boxall and Steve Frenkel, who outline HRM in **Australia and New Zealand**. Drawing on their own research as well as that of others they outline the nature of HRM in the Antipodes and the distinctions between the two countries. They emphasis the way that the region fits into the Anglo-Saxon HRM paradigm, though there is a larger focus here on industrial relations issues and controversies over employment legislation than is found in most other regions.

CONCLUSIONS

Overall, research in comparative HRM shows that beyond some universals, there are substantial differences in the meaning and practice of HRM in different countries. There are clear regional differences between, say, the patterns of contingent employment, anti-unionism and the role of the HRM department in the United States, Japan and Europe. And, going back to the focus-pulling analogy of the telescope, within each regional bloc different sub-regional patterns can be distinguished, reflecting the wider discussion about business systems and varieties of capitalism. Below the sub-regional level there is clearly in existence a set of broad, relatively inert distinctions between the various national contexts of human resource management that makes any universalistic models problematic. The idiosyncratic national institutional settings are so variable that no common model is likely to emerge for the foreseeable future. Any discussion of issues of comparative HRM must necessarily, therefore, be equivocal: it will require more careful nuance than has been the case in much of the writing about HRM.

Comparative HRM is inevitably a complex subject. A full understanding requires drawing on a wide range of possible explanators. The current state of theory and its capacity to analyse important questions of comparative HRM is perhaps the key unresolved issue characterising existing comparative HRM research. So far, the theoretical efforts are not coherent and only partly able to explain observed differences and commonalities. Whilst it may be unsatisfactory for the field of comparative HRM research – and, indeed, we would argue, for much of management and cross-cultural research – to have so many different explanations of the commonalities and differences in HRM between countries, cultures and regions, it is almost certainly too ambitious to call for a meta-theory uniting the differing perspectives.

Comparative HRM research challenges the 'one best way' prescriptions so widely propounded, and requires the rethinking of many theoretical approaches to HRM. In turn, that has important implications for practitioners. The growth in the number, reach and power of MNCs means that they play a central role in the globalisation process (Meyer, 2000). In international human resource management the standardisation/differentiation dilemma of MNCs is well understood (see, for example, Brewster, 2002; Sparrow et al., 2004; Stahl & Björkman, 2011). Whilst there may be some signs of convergence, the differences in meaning, policies and practices around the world remain strong. Increasingly, we will find it difficult to understand either international or comparative HRM as separate topics. Some understanding of each is needed in order to understand the other.

HRM is the managerial function that most specifically depends on the respective institutional arrangements and other factors closely linked to the nation state (Rosenzweig & Nohria, 1994). Unlike other production factors, such as finance, which, though not independent of national legislative and other institutional influences are arguably much more open to global developments, human resources are prone to local variation. The management of people is open to soft factors such as national culture, societal values or local traditions as well as hard factors such as labour market regimes, legal regulations or demographic patterns.

Managers in each country operate within a national institutional context and a shared set of cultural assumptions. Neither institutions nor cultures change quickly and rarely in ways that are the same as other counties. It follows that managers within one country behave in a way that is noticeably different from managers in other countries. More importantly, change is path-dependent and organisations are to an extent locked into their respective national institutional settings. Hence, even when change does occur it can be understood only in relation to the specific social context in which it occurs (Maurice et al., 1986). Even superficially universal principles, such as profit or efficiency, may be interpreted differently in different countries (Hofstede et al., 2002).

There are increasing numbers of researchers excited by the field of comparative Human Resource Management and increasing amounts of work being done in the area. That inevitably means increasing debates about meaning and outcomes. We look forward to the expansion of these debates in the years to come.

REFERENCES

Almond, P. & Ferner, A. (eds) 2006. *American Multinationals in Europe*. New York: Oxford University Press.

Amable, B. 2003. *The Diversity of Modern Capitalism*. Oxford: Oxford University Press.

Armstrong, M. 2008. *Strategic Human Resource Management: A Guide to Action*. London: Kogan Page.

Beer, M., Spector, B., Lawrence, P. R., Mills, D. Q. & Walton, R. E. 1984. *Managing Human Assets*. New York: The Free Press.

Beer, M., Spector, B., Lawrence, P. R., Mills, D. Q. & Walton, R. E. 1985. *Human Resource Management*. New York and London: Free Press.

Begin, J. P. 1992. Comparative human resource management (HRM): a systems perspective. *International Journal of Human Resource Management*, 3: 379–408.

Benson, P. & Marshall, P. 2008. Is expatriation good for my career? The impact of expatriate assignments on perceived and actual career outcomes. *International Journal of International Human Resource Management*, 19(9): 1636–1653.

Björkman, A. & Piekkari, R. 2009. Language and subsidiary control: an empirical test. *Journal of International Management*, 15(1): 105–117.

Boxall, P. 1995. Building the theory of comparative HRM. *Human Resource Management Journal*, 5(5): 5–17.

ILO 2007. *Employment development report.* Geneva, International Labour Organization.

Jokinen, T., Brewster, C. & Suutari, V. 2008. Career capital during international work experiences: contrasting self-initiated expatriate experiences and assigned expatriation. *International Journal of Human Resource Management*, **19**(6): 981–1000.

Kerr, C., Dunlop, J., Harbison, F. & Myers, C. 1960. *Industrialism and Industrial Man.* Cambridge, MA: Harvard University Press.

Kidger, P. J. 1991. The emergence of international human resource management. *International Journal of Human Resource Management*, **2**(2): 149–163.

Kochan, T. A., Dyer, L. & Batt, R. 1992. International human resource management studies: a framework for future research. In D. Lewin, O. S. Mitchell & P. D. Sherer (eds), *Research Frontiers in Industrial Relations and Human Resources.* Madison, WI: Industrial Relations Research Association, pp. 309–337.

Locke, R., Piore, M. & Kochan, T. 1995. Introduction. In R. Locke, T. Kochan & M. Piore (eds), *Employment Relations in a Changing World Economy.* Cambridge, MA: MIT Press, pp. i–xviii.

Maurice, M., Sellier, F. & Silvestre, J. 1986. *The Social Foundations of Industrial Power.* Cambridge, MA: MIT Press.

Mayrhofer, W., Brewster, C., Morley, M. J. & Ledolter, J. 2011b. Hearing a different drummer? Convergence of human resource management in Europe: a longitudinal analysis. *Human Resource Management Review*, **21**(1): 50–67.

Mayrhofer, W., Meyer, M., Steyrer, J. & Langer, K. 2007. Can expatriation research learn from other disciplines? The case of international career habitus. *International Studies of Management & Organization*, **37**(3): 89–107.

Mayrhofer, W., Morley, M. & Brewster, C. 2004. Convergence, stasis, or divergence? In C. Brewster, W., Mayrhofer & M. Morley (eds), *Human Resource Management in Europe. Evidence of Convergence?* London: Elsevier/Butterworth-Heinemann, pp. 417–436.

Mayrhofer, W., Müller-Camen, M., Ledolter, J., Strunk, G. & Erten, C. 2002. The diffusion of management concepts in Europe: conceptual considerations and longitudinal analysis. *Journal of Cross-Cultural Competence & Management*, **3**: 315–349.

Mayrhofer, W. & Reichel, A. 2009. Comparative analysis of HR. In P. R. Sparrow (ed.), *Handbook of International Human Resource Management: Integrating People, Process, and Context.* Chichester: Wiley, pp. 41–62.

McLuhan, M. H. & Powers, B. R. 1989. The global village: transformations in world life and media in the 21st century. New York: Oxford University Press.

Meyer, J. W. 2000. Globalization: sources and effects on national states and societies. *International Sociology*, **15**: 233–248.

Ohmae, K. 1995. *The End of the Nation State: The Rise of Regional Economies.* New York: Free Press.

Piekkari, R. 2006. Language effects in MNCs: a review from an IHRM perspective. In G. K. Stahl & I. Björkman (eds), *Handbook of Research in International Human Resource Management.* Cheltenham, UK: Edward Elgar, pp. 536–550.

Quintanilla, J. & Ferner, A. 2003. Multinationals and human resource management: between global convergence and national identity. *International Journal of Human Resource Management*, **14**(3): 363–368.

Ritzer, G. 1993. *The McDonaldization of Society.* Thousand Oaks, CA: Pine Forge Press.

Rose, M. J. 1991. Comparing forms of comparative analysis. *Political Studies*, **39**: 446–462.

Rosenzweig, P. M. & Nohria, N. 1994. Influences on human resource development practices in multinational corporations. *Journal of International Business Studies*, **25**(1): 229–251.

Rugman, A. M. & Collinson, S. 2008. *International Business*, 5th edn. Harlow, UK: Pearson Education.

Schuler, R. & Jackson, S. 2007. *Strategic Human Resource Management.* Oxford: Blackwell.

Schuler, R. S. 1992. Strategic human resource management: linking the people with the strategic needs of the business. *Organizational Dynamics*, **21**(1): 18–32.

Shenkar, O. & Luo, Y. 2008. *International Business.* Los Angeles: Sage Publications.

Smith, C. & Meiksins, P. 1995. System, Society and Dominance Effects in Cross-National Organisational Analysis. *Work, Employment and Society*, **9**(2): 241–267.

Sorge, A. 2004. Cross-national differences in human resources and organization. In A.-W. Harzing, & J. van Ruysseveldt (eds), *International Human Resource Management*. London: Sage Publications, pp. 117-140.

Sparrow, P., Brewster, C. & Harris, H. 2004. *Globalizing Human Resource Management*. London: Routledge.

Sparrow, P. & Hiltrop, J. M. 1994. European human resource management in transition. London: Prentice Hall.

Sparrow, P. R. (ed.) 2009. *Handbook of International Human Resource Management: Integrating People, Process, and Context*. Chichester, UK: Wiley.

Stahl, G. & Björkman, I. 2011. *Handbook of Research in International HRM*, 2nd edn. Cheltenham, UK: Edward Elgar

Storey, J. 1992. *Developments in the Management of Human Resources: An Analytical Review*. Oxford: Blackwell.

Takeuchi, R., Wang, M. & Marinova, S. V. 2005. Antecedents and consequences of workplace strain during expatriation: a cross-sectional and longitudinal investigation. *Personnel Psychology*, **58**(4): 925–948.

Torrington, D., Hall, L. & Taylor, S. 2008. *Fundamentals of Human Resource Management: Managing People at Work*. Harlow, UK: Pearson Education.

Tregaskis, O. & Brewster, C. 2006. Converging or diverging? A comparative analysis of trends in contingent employment practice in Europe over a decade. *Journal of International Business Studies*, **37**(1): 111–126.

Whitley, R. 1999. *Divergent Capitalisms: The Social Structuring and Change of Business Systems*. Oxford: Oxford University Press.

Wood, G. T., Croucher, C., Brewster, C., Collings, G. C. & Brooks, M. 2009. Varieties of firm: complementarity and bounded diversity. *Journal of Economic Issues*, **43**(1): 241–260.

2 Institutional approaches to comparative HRM

Geoffrey Wood, Alexandros Psychogios, Leslie T. Szamosi and David G. Collings

This chapter introduces the principal traditions of socio-economic think-ing on institutions, and the relationship between institutions and the uti-lisation, role and impact of people within the firm. The finance literature – and more broadly speaking, economic institutionalism – is dominated by rational–hierarchical approaches that see institutions primarily as provid-ers of incentives or disincentives to rational actors (North, 1990; Powell & Di Maggio, 1991; Shleifer & Vishny, 1997). An abiding concern of much of this literature relates to property rights, and the extent to which they are protected in different contexts: strong rights for owners are seen as a prerequisite of competitiveness (Djankov et al., 2003: 596). The heterodox socio-economic literature can be divided into three key traditions: the varieties of capitalism literature, business systems theory and regulationist thinking. An emerging fourth approach seeks to accord greater atten-tion to the effects of social action. What the heterodox tradition has in common is that it makes no assumptions as to the relationship between strong property and weak employee rights, on the one hand, and economic efficiency on the other. Rather, it is held that, within specific regulatory contexts, complementarities may result in strong employee rights contrib-uting not only to greater economic efficiency, but also broader stakeholder well-being.

It is recognised that the use of the concept 'HRM' may not be fully appropriate in comparing and contrasting different strands of institution-alist thinking, as much of the latter literature concerns itself not only with the management of people, but how people impact on (even 'manage') the organisation, and the relationship between a firm's people and the deployment and utilisation of technology. Hence, this chapter compares and contrasts different approaches to institutions to what may be broadly termed work and employment relations: wherever possible, this is linked to what is more narrowly defined as HRM.

INSTITUTIONS, WORK AND EMPLOYMENT: RATIONAL–HIERARCHICAL APPROACHES

There is a range of different ways in which the impact of institutions on the practice of HRM (and vice versa) may be understood. Whilst the rational choice approach focuses on the actions of rational profit seeking individuals, which, it is assumed, will operate most effectively in the absence of regulatory restraints, developments of this tradition have taken on board the possible effects of institutions. In a classic 1990 study, North argued that embedded property rights would make for more optimal economic outcomes. His approach, which emphasises the relationship between organisation and their environments, broadly resonates with new institutionalism.

Although new institutionalism has many faces and indeed has taken on a number of guises, its central tenets remain consistent (Scott, 1987). The underlying thesis of the approach is that advances in technology and communications are creating a less differentiated world order, where differences in management practices that had been perpetuated by geographic isolation of businesses are superseded by the logic of technology: hence it predicts convergence in management practices globally (Kidger, 1991). Organisations have a tendency to copy what is done elsewhere in an attempt to gain legitimacy or the support of external agencies within a society (Strauss & Hanson, 1997). Thus it emphasises the influence of the societal or cultural environment on organisations (DiMaggio & Powell, 1983; Meyer & Rowan, 1977). In order to ensure their survival, organisations must respond to rationalised and institutionalised expectations emanating from their environment and adopt expected management practices and organisational structures (Meyer & Rowan, 1977). So firms operating in the same regulatory environment will adopt similar HRM practices, a process referred to as 'isomorphism' (Kostova & Roth, 2002). This isomorphic process may be mimetic (firms copy practices associated with success), coercive (firms are forced to do certain things), or normative (firms do what is considered to be the 'right thing' to do in particular environment) (DiMaggio & Powell, 1983).

Institutionalisation has been defined as the 'process by which social processes, obligations, or actualities come to take on a rule-like status in social thought and action' (Meyer & Rowan, 1977: 341). At earlier stages of adaptation, functional or technical criteria may be key determinants of adoptions of innovations, the importance of these determinants however becomes weaker over time (Tolbert & Zucker, 1983). The decision to conform to a set of institutionalised practices is premised on the expectation that organisations are rewarded for doing so through increased legitimacy, resources or survival capabilities rather than simply because they are taken for granted or 'constitute reality' (Meyer and Rowan, 1977). In other words, there are some external incentives that inform the organisation's decision to adopt the practices. In theorising how a practice becomes institutionalised Tolbert and Zucker (1996) identify a three-stage process of institutionalisation. Firstly, in the pre-institutionalised stage, there is limited knowledge about a practice or process and few adaptors of it. As diffusion of the practice increases and it begins to gain normative acceptance, it becomes semi-institutionalised. Finally, at the last stage, full-institutionalisation, the practice becomes 'taken for granted by members of a social group as efficacious and necessary' (Tolbert & Zucker, 1996: 179). A further distinction relates to the extent to which policies are internalised (Kostova & Roth, 2002) vis-à-vis mere 'ceremonial adoption', reflecting a lack of belief or commitment to practices or structures resulting in loose coupling between the practices and day-to-day activity. Internalisation is hypothesised to be a function of the belief that the practice is valuable; whereas when actors do not perceive the practice to be valuable ceremonial adoption is more likely.

But, what is the relationship between context and HRM practice? And, what is really important in defining particular contexts?

A substantive component of the literature related to the impact of institutions on HRM practice has retained North's (1990) emphasis on property rights. For example, Shleifer and Vishny (1997) argue that, as only shareholders have sunk funds into the organisation, the objectives of the organisation should primarily be the maximisation of returns. Indeed, it has been argued that improving the terms and conditions of employment lessens managerial accountability to shareholders: as employees gain more rights, this restrains the ability of managers to act autonomously, and hence to act as effective agents of owners (Roe, 2003).

Political ideology and HR practice
Roe (2003) suggests that, above all, it is government ideology that will determine the relative position of employees vis-à-vis owners. In countries with right-wing governments, owner rights are likely to be stronger and worker rights weaker: this will allow managers to act more effectively in the interests of owners. However, this process should be qualified: there is a degree of path dependence, which can be traced back to the underlying structures of the national economy at a formative stage, in addition to formal rules and regulations which may be adjusted according to the government of the day (Bebchuk & Roe, 1999). Path dependency also represents a product of the manner in which vested interests operate; they suggest that, for example, if employee rights are stronger, employees will resist deregulation even if this may result in greater efficiency (Bebchuk & Roe, 1999).

What does this translate to in practical HRM terms? Roe (2003) suggests that managers and workers, if not subject to the control of shareholders, have a vested interest in retaining and expanding job provision, the former for reasons of empire building, and the latter for security. Similarly, wage rates are likely to be inflated under such circumstances. In contrast, where owner rights are stronger, human resources can be deployed instrumentally: surplus labour can readily be shed, wages are restrained, and what is commonly termed 'hard' HRM techniques (e.g. focused performance appraisals, narrowly defined performance-based pay) can be deployed. A central drawback with this approach is that it assumes that such techniques, and – more broadly speaking – strong owner rights, are more efficient, whilst the evidence is rather more mixed. Countries that have been particularly successful in incrementally innovative high value added manufacturing are associated with high levels of employee rights, making for an environment conducive to mutual trust and effective human capital development. It is worth noting that, in the run up to the 2008 financial crisis, whilst commonly dismissed by neo-liberals as an uncompetitive basket-case, Germany remained the world's biggest exporter (even larger than China). Again, a close scrutiny of OECD data from 2000 to 2008 reveals that many countries with strong levels of employee rights (e.g. the Nordic countries) have outperformed deregulated liberal markets such as the United States and the United Kingdom (OECD, 2007).

Legal traditions and HR practice
A second strand of thinking within this tradition believes that it is the legal tradition that will mould corporate governance and, hence, HRM practice. La Porta et al. (1997) argue that common law countries (e.g. the United States and the UK) are associated with stronger owner rights and weaker employee ones. On the one hand, a long tradition of legal precedents has made for clearly defined owner rights and effective mechanisms to ensure that companies are governed in a manner that is in the latter's interest. In contrast, in civil law countries, employer rights are weaker. Given weaker investor protection, there will be a lower degree of formal separation of ownership from control (La Porta et al., 1997; 1998). In addition, employee rights are likely to be stronger in such contexts (Djankov et al., 2003). In civil law countries, labour legislation tends to be more comprehensive, making individual employees and unions more confident of their rights. In common law countries, labour legislation tends to be of the broad brushstroke variety, which is fleshed out by case law. In practice, this means that individual employees will have to make greater use of litigation, a highly risky process with uncertain outcomes, with the firm having a greater pool of resources (i.e. capital and legal expertise) at

its disposal during a dispute. In terms of practical work and employment relations, this means that firms in civil law countries will find it much more difficult to shed labour; from a neo-liberal perspective, this may generate greater 'inefficiencies'. Again, firms will face greater constraints on their ability to deploy labour power, resulting in a greater degree of codetermination.

Interestingly, as with Roe (2003), La Porta et al., (1997, 1998) see the relationship between employer and employee rights as a zero-sum game: if the one side has more rights (and is more powerful) the other side will be less so (Djankov et al., 2003). This viewpoint can be contrasted with more optimistic strands of the HRM literature that suggest that employers and employees can mutually benefit from a situation that combines a focus on the 'bottom line' (i.e. shareholder value), with cooperative paradigms in the workplace (Kochan & Osterman, 1994).

Electoral systems and HR practice
Another strand of the rational–hierarchical literature that explores the relationship between institutions and workplace practice looks at the effects of electoral systems. Pagano and Volpin (2005) argue that employees will have weaker, and employers stronger, rights in first-past-the-post electoral systems, such as found in the United States and the UK. The reason is that such systems result in clear governing majorities (even if the electoral verdict was more mixed), allowing governments to concentrate on promoting shareholder value (and, hence, a particular trajectory of economic growth), unhampered by pressures posed by interest groupings. In contrast, in proportional representation countries (such as continental Europe), coalition governments are more common, giving interest groupings (such as unions) more influence. In practical workplace terms, this may result in unions having stronger legal rights, forcing firms to adopt more pluralist employment relations policies, centring on the collective representation of employees via collective bargaining or works councils. Some evidence supports these arguments: it is worth noting that two countries that formerly had first-past-the-post electoral systems – Ireland and New Zealand – have gradually drifted towards adopting elements of neo-corporatism following on electoral reforms that have infused aspects of proportional representation.

Summarising Rational Incentive Approaches

Key similarities in these approaches can be summarised as in Figure 2.1. As noted earlier, whilst divided as to specific institutional causes, rational–hierarchical approaches assumed that the relationship between owner and

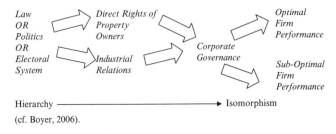

Hierarchy ─────────────────────────→ Isomorphism

(cf. Boyer, 2006).

Figure 2.1   Rational choice accounts of institutional setting, property owners and outcomes

worker rights is a zero-sum game. Where owner rights are stronger, this will make for HRM policies that are more 'bottom line' orientated, characterised by individually orientated performance evaluation and reward systems, and low security of tenure. Where they are weaker, worker (and union) rights will invariably be stronger: this will make for stronger job security (and hence lower staff turnover rates) which will make, from a neo-liberal perspective, firms less numerically flexible. At the same time, managerial (and owner) power will be diluted through co-determinist structures for employee representation in the workplace, which could encompass both collective bargaining and works councils.

Although it could be assumed that light regulation in other areas would make for 'diffuse diversity', rational–hierarchical approaches suggest that uniformities in practice are likely to emerge and persist even in heavily deregulated liberal markets, reflecting both the existence of efficient best practices and an isomorphic process imposing commonalities based on practical efficiencies and shared rules (Boyer, 2006). Table 2.1 further illustrates differences and similarities.

Critique of the Rational Approach

Beyond the above arguments of the rational approach, several researchers agree that isomorphic tendencies in HRM practices, whilst emerging from globalisation pressures, vary in different national contexts (Fotopoulou et al., 2007; Ramírez & Mabey, 2005). Katz and Darbishire (2000) identify what they term converging divergences. The countries they examined (United States, UK, Australia, Germany, Japan, Sweden, Italy) were found to converge not towards one universal type of employment system but towards four patterns of work practices. The implementation of these work practices in different countries suggested that variations existed. The researchers surmised that, although globalisation and internationalisation

Table 2.1   Variations in rational–hierarchical approaches

Theory characteristic	Roe	Pagano & Volpin	La Porta et al.
Determines strength of non-owner stakeholders	Government policy and ideology	Electoral system	Legal System
Measure	Left or right wing governments	Proportional representation (PR) or first past the post	Common or civil law
Path dependence	Only one optimal trajectory possible	Limited number of alternatives Electoral systems rarely changed	Path dependence
Predictions – Shareholder rights	Property owners stronger under right wing governments	Property owners stronger under majoritarian systems	Property owners stronger under common law
Predictions – Employee rights	Right-wing governments are likely to make for weaker employee rights, and hence, fewer constraints on corporate governance	First-past-the-post electoral systems are likely to make for weaker employee rights, and hence, fewer constraints on corporate governance	Common-law systems are likely to make for weaker employee rights, and hence, fewer constraints on corporate governance
Number of optimal arrangements	One	One	One

Source: Based on Goergen et al. (2008).

seem to be the pressures fostering a general converging trend in employment systems, the existence of national deviations indicate that national forces play a substantial role in determining managerial practices. Similar conclusions can be drawn from Edwards and Kuruvilla's (2005) critique of HRM strategies of multinational corporations (MNCs). The need of MNCs to be responsive to the local peculiarities is explained by the prevalence of interdependencies between organisational politics and national institutional frameworks in various national contexts.

Emphasising European countries, we can argue that, although the European Monetary Union effort includes neo-liberalising tendencies, these countries seem to present divergent outcomes (Hay, 2004; Psychogios et al., 2007). Mayrhofer and Brewster (1996) concluded that despite a certain similarity of trends in the application of HRM practices among European countries, national differences hold back the emergence of a European HRM model. Even in the case of MNCs, different business systems of the host countries influence the way business strategies and managerial practices are developed, despite headquarter pressures (Lane, 1998).

More recent evidence by Tregaskis and Brewster (2006) suggests that there is no actual proof that global competitive pressures alone lead to a convergence in HRM practices. In their comparative analysis of trends in contingent employment practice in five European countries, they identify the role of national institutional systems as a powerful force contributing to the formation of employment practices. These national systems are inevitably linked with country-specific microeconomic conditions such as industrial relations traditions and government policy. Overall, they argue that despite the convergence pressures of the European Union, countries continue to resist certain employment practices due to pre-existing systems.

Similarly, based on the Cranet survey (including 22 countries), Brewster et al., (2008) concluded that the global dissemination of best practices does not seem to exist, at least in the HRM field. Although there is some evidence of similar global practices there is a lack of strong evidence of a common global HRM archetype. In another study concerning the examination of HRM practices in European firms, Gooderham et al. (1999) admitted that, despite the fact that their findings supported rational approaches in terms of mimetic processes, they failed to examine the impact of national institutional barriers. Moreover, they suggested that more focus should be placed on regulative and political pressures as well as on cognitive processes.

The above arguments lead to the development of another school of thought emphasising the importance of variation of capitalistic contexts in HRM integration.

THE VARIETIES OF THE CAPITALISM RELATIONSHIP

The 'relationship' approaches within the varieties of capitalism (VoC) literature do not see owner dominance as necessarily resulting in superior organisational and macroeconomic outcomes, given that the inputs of other social actors contribute to the emergence and persistence of

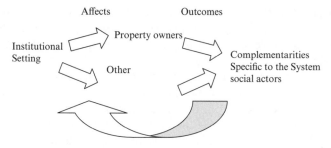

Figure 2.2   Alternative accounts of institutional setting, social outcomes and outcomes: a complementarity perspective

combinations of complementarities that may be beneficial to a large component of society (see Figure 2.2). Nor is the relationship a linear one, with hierarchy making for isomorphism: rather institutions themselves evolve as a result of practices by social actors (Boyer, 2006; Hall & Soskice, 2001).

Recent developments and extensions of the finance literature have examined the issue of complementarity. For Gordon and Roe (2004: 16), complementarity is where practices fit together, mutually increasing the overall system benefits; this means that practices that are objectively 'inferior' may persist if they can generate overall benefits. Hence, a problem with systemic change may be that existing complementarities may be jettisoned, with no assurances that better complementarities may replace them.

Heterodox Accounts

If a number of different institutions and practices are found clustered together, this would suggest coherence and complementarity (Boyer, 2006). Proponents of the shareholder model focus on a single hierarchical set of relations; those who question the superiority of the shareholder model would argue that alternative sets of relationships may make for alternative complementarities (Boyer, 2006). In other words, even if owners are weaker, firms and/or other stakeholders and, indeed, the economy at large may do equally as well (if not better) than when owner rights are stronger.

A further question is the issue of sustainability. Rational choice incentives approaches suggest that systemic inertia, imposed by non-rational social relations – superstitions and their modern counterparts (e.g. worker rights) – may lock a system onto a sub-optimal path (see North, 1990). The VoC literature suggests that, whilst institutional arrangements are subject to development and adjustment over time, there is a similar degree of path dependence, but that this is often positive: social actors know how the system works, lowering transaction costs, and making the retention of the existing order viable, even if it is operating sub-optimally (see Marsden, 1999; Whitley, 1999).

To summarise, firstly, particular institutional designs may be seen as encouraging owners and managers to make optimal choices: a particular hierarchy imposes isomorphism (Boyer, 2006). Alternatively, it can be argued that there is no single set of optimal choices: rather rules and practices may be combined in different ways to bring about different types of complementarity: in other words, a system may work nearly (or equally) as well as another; there is no single 'best' way of doing things, as would be suggested by the rational choice model. Finally, institutions may evolve on a linear path dependent way, or be prone to periodic restructuring and redesign in response to ad hoc systemic crises.

The Varieties of Capitalism Approach

The ascendancy of right-wing governments into power in both Britain and the United States in the 1980s led to increasingly confident neo-liberals questioning the viability of more regulated economies in continental Western Europe and Japan. The fact that such economies continued to out-perform liberal markets economies such as Britain and the United States through much of the 1980s did little to deter them. These attacks intensified when, during the late 1990s and the early 2000s, liberal markets outperformed Germany and Japan. The fact that more regulated Scandinavian countries performed even better than liberal markets during these years, and Germany and Japan not very much worse (OECD, 2007), was ignored by these commentators.

It was partially in reaction to this that the influential VoC literature emerged (Dore, 2000; Hall & Soskice, 2001; Lincoln & Kalleberg, 1990). This literature draws on both the structuralist sociology of Talcott Parsons (1951) and the political economy of Karl Polanyi (1957). In his classic account of institutions, firms and practice, Dunlop (1975) argued that what firms did reflected their wider social context. Formal political frameworks, and the nature of socialisation, located economic transactions in the context of rights and obligations: within the firm, this means that industrial relations (and HRM) will tend to follow certain patterns in specific contexts. This could aid in generating greater levels of predictability and trust, allowing for better outcomes for individual actors than were this not the case (Dunlop, 1975). Similarly, Bendix (1956) argued that, rather than through autocratic owner power, firms may work better through softer more cooperative ways of doing things, promoted by wider institutional realities.

Central to the varieties of capitalism thesis is a distinction between the above-mentioned liberal market economies (LMEs) and the cooperative market economies (CMEs) of continental north-western Europe ('Rhineland' and Scandinavia) and the Far East (Japan and Korea). Within the former, shareholders are more powerful and, within the latter, other stakeholders share power (Dore, 2000). Whilst this may not sound that much different from rational–hierarchical approaches, a defining feature of the VoC literature is that it saw LMEs as no 'better' in terms of organisational performance and macro-economic outcomes than CMEs; implicit, however, is that they were worse in many respects (cf. Dore, 2000; Lincoln & Kalleberg, 1990).

The persistent difference between LMEs and CMEs economies reflects institutional features such as the nature of labour market institutions, the degree of financial intermediation, the severity of competition policy (Boyer, 2005) and the organisation of education and training (Boyer, 2005; Psychogios et al., 2007). More specifically, CMEs are characterised by high employment, security and strong employee rights, while in LMEs the pressure to prioritise short-term shareholder interests affects employment relationships and leads to low employment security and weaker employee rights (Dore, 2000).

This difference reflects the VoC literature's conception of institutions themselves, and its take on the nature of complementarity and of path dependence. The rational–hierarchical literature primarily views institutions as providers of incentives and disincentives to rational actors. In contrast, the VoC literature sees them as webs of relationships, linking together social actors: in short, in any context, 'economic man' is bounded and constrained. Whilst institutions are concentrated at the state level, reflected in formal law and societal conventions, they enmesh and bind together economic and non-economic associations and individuals.

Institutions are likely to persist if complementarities are present: that is if one works better through the presence of another (Hall & Soskice, 2001: 18). For example, banking regulations and the operation of financial markets may encourage more 'patient' investor behaviour. This may be complementary to labour market institutions characterised by a high degree of protection of employment rights. This may mean that owners are not only under less short-term pressure to maximise profits but also cannot easily make workers redundant in the event of a downturn. This should encourage human capital development, which is likely to be good both for employees and the long-term future of the firm. In such contexts, firms will have a workforce with a high degree of organisation specific skills, and the knowledge base of the firm will be preserved: this will be particularly good for incrementally innovative areas of economic activity,

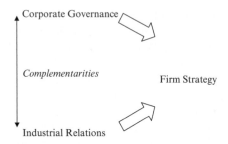

Source: Goergen, et al. (2008); Jackson (2005: 378).

Figure 2.3   *Corporate governance and HR: a complementarity perspective corporate governance*

such as high value added manufacturing (Thelen, 2001). Here, two institutional features working together yield greater benefits than they might have had on their own (cf. Boyer, 2006). Social compromises are likely to take place and continue through the operation of complementarities: trade-offs and concessions are likely to occur if they will result in a disproportionately 'good' pay-off (see Figure 2.3).

There is little doubt that such an approach adds much to our understanding of why national economies are, and remain, different: specific configurations encourage firms to take on ways of doing things in a wide range of areas that are likely to harness systemic complementarities (Hall & Soskice, 2001: 18). Clusters of practices are, hence, likely to emerge and persist within individual national regulatory contexts. Rational–hierarchical approaches argue that, as deregulated economies are more efficient, they would be more likely to supplant others. In contrast, the VoC literature holds that distinct national developmental paths will develop and emerge: hence, path dependence, with national systems evolving but remaining distinct.

Critique of the VoC Approach

There are two major criticisms that can be levelled against this approach. The first is that some critics have suggested that the VoC literature is overly functionalist (Streeck, 2005). In other words, it assumes that institutional features work together in such a way as to make for overall systemic functionality. Further, institutional features will be introduced to strengthen and broaden existing complementarities; however, it can be argued that complementarities need not always be the product of functioning institutional components: rather, complementarities may

compensate for institutional weaknesses (Crouch, 2005a). For example, Crouch argues that the German vocational training system provides industry specific skills, allowing individual employees to move within a particular industry: this may encourage a greater degree of job mobility than may otherwise have been the case, countering any negative effects that would be associated with high levels of job security (Crouch, 2005b: 360-2). In other words, not all complementarities are synergies (Deeg, 2005: 2–5); indeed, some may flow from dysfunctional systemic features, such as the operation of a military industrial complex in the United States, which has nonetheless had some positive spin-offs in the high technology sector. The range of permutations in the operation of complementarities is summarised in Figure 2.4.

It can be argued that these two types of economic systems are not as coherent as they are presented in the VoC literature (Hollingsworth, 2006). National coherence along regional lines is questioned as substantial differences are observed in the internal workings of countries, for example, south and north Italy (Whitley, 1999). Similarly, Deakin et al., (2006) surmise that there are differences in corporate governance and employee relationships between countries belonging to LMEs; they argue that there is not a uniform HRM paradigm that dominates these economies, further implying that the LME model might not be useful as a uniform model.

The dichotomy approach has been criticised as over simplistic and static (Boyer, 2005). Amable (2003) explains that most researchers adopt the LME–CME dichotomous classification, at least as an initial approximation, as LMEs present quite distinctive characteristics compared to other countries. Hollingsworth (2006: 71) suggests that that there should be a shift of emphasis from trying to construct types of systems towards a deeper analysis of institutional change within and across various capitalisms, and that systems and societies should be conceptualised 'in a continuous state of flux'. Crouch, (2005b) argues that dichotomy approaches are fixed over time, despite the fact that their contribution in terms of their focus on the firm, as an actor of economic success, is recognised. In addition, Hollingsworth (2006) suggests that these kinds of typologies make systems appear as if they have a static nature, while in reality they evolve continuously.

Responding to the Critiques

VoC theorists counter that both LMEs and CMEs are indeed continuously changing; they just do not converge, despite the 'liberalising reforms' of the last decades (Hall & Thelen, 2006). Despite evidence of internal diversity, survey evidence points to the persistence of widespread packages

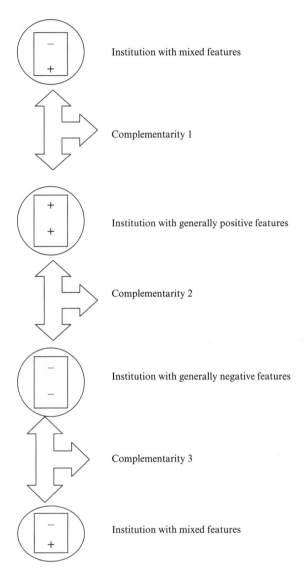

Figure 2.4   Institutional complementarity and diversity

of practices in LMEs and CMEs such that the dichotomy can provide a theoretical basis for comparison (Brewster et al., 2007). In addition, in most cross-national studies on issues such as HRM policies, the clear difference that exists is indeed that between Anglo-Saxon or LMEs and CMEs, as Hall and Soskice (2001) suggested (Boyer, 2005).

VoC theorists also recognise the existence of other political economies that do not correspond either to LMEs or CMEs (Fotopoulou et al., 2007) and suggest that each economy has specific competencies affecting firm and government policies (Hall & Soskice, 2001). Hall and Thelen (2006), for instance, have recognised a third set of economies found in Southern Europe, called 'mixed market economies' including countries such as France and Spain.

Finally, in terms of internal diversity, there is the argument that while a variety of practices may exist in a particular national setting that limits uniformity, there is the possibility that certain sets of practices might prevail in particular regions or industries (Brewster et al., 2006). For example, Japanese evidence points to increasing variations in practice, with two new hybrid models of corporate governance and organisational practices emerging to supplement the traditional coordinated paradigm (Jackson, 2009). Similarly, in looking at the case of continental Europe, Deeg (2009) argues that 'a relatively small number of firms have shifted to a new institutional context consisting of common international institutions and practices, while the large majority of firms continue to operate in a more slowly evolving set of domestic institutions or rules.' This growing diversity may undermine the basis of the established CME model, although it is unlikely that this will result in seamless convergence with the LME paradigm (Deeg, 2009).

BUSINESS SYSTEMS THEORY

A development and extension of the VoC literature is the business systems approach. Business systems are:

> distinctive patterns of economic organisation that vary in their degree and mode of authoritative co-ordination of economic activities, and in the organisation of, and interconnections between, owners, managers, experts and other employees. (Whitley, 1999: 33)

Hence, business systems represent ways of regulating market relations, making possible everyday economic exchange relationships through imitation, administrative structures, and social and network ties (Pedersen & Thomsen, 1999: 44). Business systems approaches share the VoC literature's central concern with the nature of complementarity. From a business systems perspective, complementarities result not only from economic experimentation but also from innovations by organisations constantly seeking new advantages; similarly, old complementarities are likely to be subject to constant modification and renewal (Morgan, 2007: 136).

In contrast to the VoC literature, business systems theory places the firm at the centre of this web of relationships. In practical terms, this means that a lot more explicit attention is accorded to the HRM effects of institutions.

The degree to which managers are autonomous (vis-à-vis capital markets, owners and providers of credit), the power of unions and the extent to which employees can impact on what firms do reflects the degree to which, in a particular context, managers and workers can have common interests and establish particular work and employment relations practices (Whitley, 1999). The latter can be divided into two broad categories. Firstly, there is the degree of employer–employee interdependence (Whitley, 1999). The latter can be defined as both a product of security of tenure, and the extent to which each side has committed resources to continuing the relationship (Whitley, 1999). From the employee's point of view this would include developing one's organisation specific skills, while from the firm's point of view the focus is on the degree of spending on training particularly focused on long-term skills and capability development. Secondly, there is the degree of delegation to employees. This may range from advanced forms of delegation (e.g. via collective bargaining – here managers agree to share through negotiation to a greater or lesser degree decision making regarding the nature of the employment contract) and works councils, to weaker, more consultative forms of delegation (e.g., through quality circles). Empirical research by Brewster et al., (2008) has confirmed the strong relationship between national context, and variations in the degree of both delegation and interdependence. In liberal markets employer–employee interdependence will be lower (weaker job security and less emphasis on long term human capital development), as will delegation to employees (collective representation of employees will be similarly weaker, than in more cooperative varieties of capitalism) (Brewster et al., 2007; Whitley, 1999).

If the first major difference between the VOC literature and business systems theory is the fact that the latter is more firm-orientated, the second major difference is the number of systemic archetypes: Whitley (1999) has identified six archetypical business systems. Table 2.2 summarises their key features.

Wood and Frynas (2006) identify a seventh business system archetype, the segmented business system, which can be found in tropical Africa. Within such systems, unions are likely to be weak, and only encountered in a few 'pockets' of relatively stable employment: a large proportion of jobs are in the informal sector, where there is little prospect of unionism. Moreover, a tradition of patriarchal management is further likely to mitigate against meaningful delegation. Given intense cost-based competition

Table 2.2 National business system archetypes

Type Form	Fragmented	Co-ord. Industrial District	Compart-mentalised	State Organised	Collaborative	Highly Co-Ordinated
Examples	Hong Kong	Italy	US, UK, New Zealand, Australia	Post-War South Korea	Sweden, Austria, Norway	Japan
Ownership Co-Ordination Owner Control	Direct	Direct	Market	Direct	Alliance	Alliance
Ownership integration of production chain/sectors	Low	Low	High	Some to high	High/limited	Some/Limited
Non-Ownership Co-Ordination Alliance co-ord of production chains/sectors	Low	Limited/Low	Low	Low	Limited/low	High/some
Collaboration between competing firms	Low	Some	Low	Low	High	High
Work and Employment Relations Delegation to employees	Low	Some	Low	Low	Some	High
Interdependence between managers and workers	Low	Some	Low	Low	High	Considerable

Source: Brookes et al. (2005; based on Whitley, 1999: 41–44).

43

from abroad, firms are likely to be under pressure to cut short-term costs leading to weak job security. Whilst extensive labour legislation may be in place, enforcement is likely to be poor. Finally, national skills training systems are likely to face crises of funding, leading to poor skills bases, and a large pool of poorly skilled job seekers and issues related to the level of human capital available. Again, this would make for very low levels of employer–employee interdependence: labour would be in a poor bargaining position, and very easily shed (Wood & Frynas, 2006).

The literature on comparative capitalism has, as yet, accorded only limited attention to the case of China, which, arguably, is not a capitalist country. However, what is clear is that China is following a distinct trajectory, balancing communism and capitalism and regional diversity with focused state intervention. As is the case with other export-dependent economies, China faces the challenges of developing domestic consumer demand to insulate the country against fluctuations in international demand, the return of protectionism to the global agenda, and currency volatilities. Above all, it is clear that China is still in a transition, with institutional arrangements continuing to be subject to redesign.

Regulation Approaches

Drawing on the radical political economy tradition, regulation theory explores the role of institutions in stabilising and providing the basis for periods of economic growth, always on a spatially and temporarily confined basis (Jessop, 2001). Central to regulationist thinking is the notion that it is the role of institutions to provide both rules and informal norms that encourage firms and other social actors to behave in a particular way. Regulationist thinking assumes that, in turn, social actors will impact institutions, and on each other: institutional interaction is a similar dynamic process. This situation can be summarised as in Figure 2.5.

Thus, regulation theory begins from a very different starting point to both the VoC literature and business systems theory. Rather than being path dependent, institutional innovations and experiments have foreseen and unforeseen consequences in relation to firm level behaviour: this may or may not result in a period of strong firm and macroeconomic performance (Boyer, 2006). Hence, national evolution is non-linear, uneven, and episodic: systems will not function in an optimal manner for more than a few decades, followed on by a period of crisis, innovation and experimentation that, in turn, may provide the foundations for a new period of growth (Hollingsworth, 2006; Jessop, 2001).

Furthermore, whilst sharing the VoC and business systems theory's emphasis on national variations in institutional configurations,

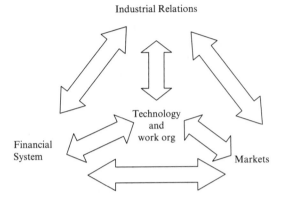

Figure 2.5   Industrial relations, markets and the financial system

contemporary regulationist thinking suggests that institutions are nested at regional, industrial, national and supra-national levels: the fact that institutions may be particularly concentrated at the national level does not detract from the importance of concentrations of institutions at other levels (Boyer & Hollingsworth, 1997). For example, the European Union has encouraged not only the opening of markets, but also the adoption of common labour practices in a range of areas. The latter would range from anti-discriminatory measures to the introduction of consultative mechanisms (e.g. European Works Councils in pan-European firms). Likewise, national and regional governments, and clusters of local firms, may work together (or even in opposition) in promoting specific regional development initiatives, which may reinforce sub-national particularism (Hudson, 2006): for example, rising imbalances between the north and the south, led to specific regional development policies being promoted in North Eastern England.

Regional specificity may not necessarily be the only result of governmental interventions. Firms may seek to exploit the opportunities provided by local markets to produce specialised goods and services, resulting in sub-national modes of organisation coexisting with what happens nationwide (Collinge, 2001: 184). Given the tendency for different segments of capital to band together, it might seem that there will be a greater diversity within liberal market economies. Divergent parcels of interests may coalesce on sectoral lines, particularly in relatively diverse social systems: there will always be industries with approaches towards the deployment of technology and to work and employment relations that will differ along national norms (Hollingsworth & Boyer, 1997: 270).

Regulationist accounts link the dominance of specific forms of work organisation with particular modes of regulation: for example, in the Fordist era, national governments promoted policies aimed at supporting mass production and consumption. The crisis of this model in the 1970s led to a number of alternative regulatory experiments (Jessop, 2001). In practical organisational terms this translated into a broad range of alternative production paradigms, distinguished by variations in employee rights and responsibilities and differences in the development and deployment of skills and technologies.

Reflecting its progressive origins, regulationist thinking suggests that the mediation of owner power provided the basis of the golden age of economic growth in the 1950s and 1960s and that a similar – or even greater – degree of mediation may be necessary to ensure future prosperity. This would suggest paradigms for work and employment relations that formally entrench worker rights on a collective basis, and the use of technology in a manner that promotes efficiency and imparts a dignity to working life. This does not mean that regulation theory is utopian: it recognises that there are strong pressures in the opposite direction. For example, an emphasis on short-term returns in shareholder dominant models will enrich a few key actors, entrenching such approaches, even if they are proven to be dysfunctional in the long term. Likewise, waves of opportunistic experiments may do little to promote long-term growth (or more inclusive work and employment relations), but may assist in further directing resources to the economically powerful (cf. Wolfson, 2003).

Synthetic Approaches

Over the years there have been numerous attempts to combine institutional theories with those of social action, most notably those of Norbert Elias and Anthony Giddens (see Giddens, 1991). To Sorge (2005), institutions are bound together by social actions. At the same time, social actions break down the partitions that define these same institutions. Hence, social actions both sustain the present order and change it (Sorge, 2005: 55). At the level of the firm, social actors have considerable room to innovate in a manner that may be independent of national government policy, even if the key actors are broadly supportive of the latter (Sorge, 2005: 188); so institutions are both rigid and fluid, and national contexts diverse. New areas of activity may emerge and old ones be reconfigured. This will make not only for dominant HRM paradigms within national contexts, but also the existence of a wide range of alternative ones. And even clearly definable sets of HRM practices (e.g. high involvement ones organised on collective lines) may vary greatly in both form and effect. Whilst a highly insightful account, a limitation of Sorge's analysis is the difficulties it poses in terms of effectively analyzing and comparing work and employment practices across national boundaries, and, indeed, clearly defining what really makes HRM at the firm level.

Conclusion

We begin our conclusion with a caveat. The institutional literature is a diverse and developing one, and it is not possible within a short review to do full justice to a wide range of alternative, often conflicting, paradigms. Many are somewhat vague as to what the HRM implications really are of specific alternative institutional archetypes.

At the same time, a number of clearly defined intellectual traditions are identifiable, all of which make some clear assumptions as to the role of the employee within the firm. Rational–hierarchical approaches see owner and employee rights as a zero-sum game: they would suggest that strong owner and weak employee rights are likely to maximise organisational efficiency. This would translate into the promotion of HRM paradigms characterised by weak security of tenure and individually orientated per-formance appraisal and reward systems. In contrast, heterodox accounts would argue that more cooperative HRM approaches are likely to help underpin strong organisational performance in specific industries and regulatory contexts; however, whilst the VoC and business systems lit-erature emphasises the embedded and path dependent nature of national institutional configurations and firm practices, regulationist accounts would point to their temporarily confined, fragile and contested nature. The global financial crisis that began in 2008 highlighted the limitations of a LME-style shareholder value orientated model; an excessive concentra-tion on short term shareholder value led to uncontrollable speculation and a lack of attention to developing sustainable methods of wealth creation.

Although neo-liberals have never been overly troubled by facts, a growing consensus is emerging on the need for more and better regula-tion, balancing shareholder returns with the need for greater account-ability in the interests of society at large. Meanwhile, export-reliant CME economies have themselves been hit by a global decline of consumer demand. However, as the complementarities generated in such contexts have proved better at supporting 'real' economic activity, they should be better equipped to benefit from any recovery. Nonetheless, whilst the prospects of a convergence to a LME model may have receded, there is as yet insufficient evidence of any move towards convergence in the direction of greater coordination either on the European social democratic model, or a new paradigm.

REFERENCES

Amable, B. 2003. *The Diversity of Modern Capitalism*. Oxford: Oxford University Press.

Bebchuk, L. & Roe, M. 1999. A theory of path dependence of corporate ownership and governance. *Stanford Law Review*, **52**: 127–170.

Bendix, R. 1956. *Work and Authority in Industry*. New York: John Wiley.

Boyer, R. 2005. How and why capitalism differ. *Economy and Society*, **34**(4): 509–557.

Boyer, R. 2006. How do institutions cohere and change? In G. Wood & P. James (eds), *Institutions and Working Life*. Oxford: Oxford University Press, pp. 13–61.

Boyer, R. & Hollingsworth, J. R. 1997. From national embeddedness to spatial and institutional nestedness. In J. R. Hollingsworth, & R. Boyer (eds), *Contemporary Capitalism: The Embeddedness of Institutions*. Cambridge: Cambridge University Press, pp. 433-484.

Brewster, C., Wood, G. & Brookes, M. 2006. Varieties of capitalism and varieties of firms. In G. Wood, & P. James (eds), *Institutions, Production and Working Life*. Oxford: Oxford University Press.

Brewster, C., Wood, G., Croucher, R. & Brookes, M. 2007. Collective and individual voice: convergence in Europe? *International Journal of Human Resource Management*, **18**(7): 1246–1262.

Brewster, C., Wood, G. & Brookes, M. 2008. Similarity, isomorphism, or duality? Recent survey evidence on the human resource management policies of multinational corporations. *British Journal of Management*, **19**(4): 320–342.

Brookes, M., Brewster, C. & Wood, G. 2005. Social relations, firms and societies: a study in institutional embeddedness. *International Sociology*, **20**(4): 403–426.

Collinge, C. 2001. Self organisation of society by scale. In B. Jessop (ed.), *Regulation Theory and the Crisis of Capitalism Volume 4: Development and Extensions*. Cheltenham, UK: Edward Elgar.

Crouch, C. 2005a. Models of capitalism. *New Political Economy*, **10**(4): 439–456.

Crouch, C. 2005b. Three meanings of complementarity. *Socio-Economic Review*, **3**(2): 359–363.

Deakin, S., Hobbs, R., Konzelmann, S. & Wilkinson, F. 2006. Anglo-American corporate governance and the employment relationship: a case to answer? *Socio-Economic Review*, **4**(1): 155–174.

Deeg, R. 2005. Complementary and institutional change: how useful a concept. Social Science Research Centre, Vol. 21. Discussion Paper SP II. Berlin.

Deeg, R. 2009. The rise of internal capitalist diversity? Changing patterns of finance and corporate governance in Europe. *Economy and Society*, **38**(3), 552–579.

DiMaggio, P. J. & Powell, W. W. 1983. The Iron Cage revisited: institutional isomorphism and collective rationality in organisational fields. *American Sociological Review*, **48**(2): 147–160.

Djankov, S., Glaeser, E., La Porta, R. et al. 2003. The new comparative economics. *Journal of Comparative Economics*, **31**(4): 595–619.

Dore, R. 2000. *Stock Market Capitalism: Welfare Capitalism*. Cambridge: Cambridge University Press.

Dunlop, J. 1975. Political systems and industrial relations. In B. Barrett, E. Rhodes & J. Beishon (eds), *Industrial Relations and Wider Society*. London: Collier Macmillan.

Edwards, T. & Kuruvilla, S. 2005. International HRM: national business systems, organisational politics and the international division of labour in MNCs. *The International Journal of Human Resource Management*, **16**(1): 1–21.

Fotopoulou, D., Psychogios, A. & Wood, G. 2007. Issues and challenges in knowledge transfer of Anglo-Saxon management models and concepts in non-Anglo-Saxon business Environments. 2nd Annual South East European Doctoral Conference. Thessaloniki, Greece.

Giddens, A. 1991. *Modernity and Self-identity: Self and Society in the Late Modern Age*. Cambridge: Polity Press.

Goergen, M., Wood, G. & Brewster, C. 2008. *Corporate Governance Regimes and Employment Relations in Europe*. Sheffield, UK: University of Sheffield Management School.

Gooderham, P., Nordhaug, O. & Ringdal, K. 1999. Institutional and rational determinants of organisational practices: human resource management in European firms. *Administrative Science Quarterly*, **44**(2): 507–531.

Gordon, J. & Roe, M. 2004. Introduction. In J. Gordon & M. Roe (eds), *Convergence and Persistence in Corporate Governance*. Cambridge: Cambridge University Press.

Hall, P. & Soskice, D. 2001. An introduction to varieties of capitalism. In P. Hall & D. Soskice (eds), *Varieties of Capitalism: The Institutional Foundations of Competitive Advantage*. Oxford: Oxford University Press, pp. 1–68.

Hall, P. & Thelen, K. 2006. Institutional change in varieties of capitalism, Europeanists Conference. Chicago.

Hay, C. 2004. Common trajectories, variable paces, divergent outcomes? Models of European capitalism under conditions of complex economic interdependence. *Review of International Political Economy*, **11**(2): 231–262.

Hollingsworth, J. R. 2006. Advancing our understanding of capitalism with Niels Bohr's thinking about complementarity. In G. T. Wood & P. James (eds), *Institutions, Production and Working Life*. Oxford: Oxford University Press.

Hollingsworth, J. R. & Boyer, R. 1997. Coordination of economic actors and social systems of production. In J. R. Hollingsworth & R. Boyer (eds), *Contemporary Capitalism: The Embeddedness of Institutions*. Cambridge: Cambridge University Press.

Hudson, R. 2006. The production of institutional complementarity? The case of North East England. In G. Wood & P. James (eds), *Institutions and Working Life*. Oxford: Oxford University Press.

Jackson, G. 2005. *Reforming Stakeholder Models: Comparing Germany and Japan*. London: DTI Eco.

Jackson, G. 2009. The Japanese firm and its diversity. *Economy and Society*, **38**(3): 605–628.

Jessop, B. 2001. Series preface. In B. Jessop (ed.), *The Parisian Regulation School. Regulation Theory and the Crisis of Capitalism Volume 1*. Cheltenham, UK: Edward Elgar, pp. ix–xxiii.

Katz, H. & Darbishire, O. 2000. *Converging Divergences: Worldwide Changes in Employment Systems*. New York: Cornell University Press.

Kidger, P. J. 1991. The emergence of international human resource management. *International Journal of Human Resource Management*, **2**(2): 149–163.

Kochan, T. & Osterman, P. 1994. *The Mutual Gains Enterprise*. Boston, MA: Harvard Business School Press.

Kostova, T. & Roth, K. 2002. Adoption of an organisational practice by subsidiaries of multinational corporations: institutional and relational effects. *Academy of Management Journal*, **45**(1): 215–233.

La Porta, R., Lopez-de-Silanes, F., Shleifer, A. & Vishny, R. 1997. Legal determinants of finance. *Journal of Finance*, **52**(3): 1131–1150.

La Porta, R., Lopez-de-Silanes, F., Shleifer, A. & Vishny, R. 1998. Law and finance. *Journal of Political Economy*, **106**(6): 1113–1155.

Lane, C. 1998. European companies between globalisation and localisation: a comparison of internationalisation strategies of British and German MNCs. *Economy and Society*, **27**(4): 462–485.

Lincoln, J. & Kalleberg, A. 1990. *Culture, control and commitment: a study of work organisation in the United States and Japan*. Cambridge: Cambridge University Press.

Marsden, D. 1999. A Theory of Employment Systems. Oxford: OUP.

Mayrhofer, W. & Brewster, C. 1996. In praise of ethnocentricity: expatriate policies in European multinationals. *International Executive*, **38**(6): 749–778.

Meyer, J. W. & Rowan, B. 1977. Institutional organisations: formal structure as myth and ceremony. *American Journal of Sociology*, **83**(2): 340–363.

Morgan, G. 2007. National business systems research: process and prospects. *Scandinavian Journal of Management*, **23**(2): 127–145.

North, D. C. 1990. *Institutions, Institutional Change and Economic Performance.* Cambridge: Cambridge University Press.

OECD. 2007. *Country Statistical Profiles.* Paris: OECD.

Pagano, M. & Volpin, P. 2005. The political economy of corporate governance. *American Economic Review*, **95**(4): 1005–1030.

Parsons, T. 1951. *The Social System.* Glencoe: Free Press.

Pedersen, T. & Thomsen, S. 1999. Business systems and corporate governance. *International Studies of Management & Organisation*, **29**(2): 42–59.

Polanyi, K. 1957. *The Great Transformation.* Boston, MA: Beacon Press.

Powell, W. & Di Maggio, P. 1991. *The New Institutionalism in Organisational Analysis.* Chicago: University of Chicago Press.

Psychogios, A., Fotopoulou, D. & Wood, G. 2007. A Londoner in Athens: transferring Anglo-Saxon management knowledge to non-Anglo-Saxon business systems, 23rd EGOS Colloquium: Beyond Waltz – Dances of Individuals and Organisation. Vienna University of Economics and Business Administration.

Ramírez, M., & Mabey, C. 2005. A labour market perspective on management training and development in Europe. *International Journal of Human Resource Management*, **16**(3): 291–310.

Roe, M. 2003. *Political Determinants of Corporate Governance.* Oxford: Oxford University Press.

Scott, W. R. 1987. The adolescence of institutional theory. *Administrative Sciences Quarterly*, **32**(4): 493–511.

Shleifer, A., & Vishny, R. 1997. A survey of corporate governance. *Journal of Finance*, **52**(2): 737–783.

Sorge, A. 2005. *The Global and the Local: Understanding the Dialectics of Business Systems.* Oxford: Oxford University Press.

Strauss, G. & Hanson, M. 1997. Review article: American anti-management theories of organisation: a critique of paradigm proliferation. *Human Relations*, **50**(9): 1426–1429.

Streeck, W. 2005. Rejoinder: on terminology, functionalism, (historical) institutionalism and liberalisation. socio-economic review, **5**(3): 577–587.

Thelen, K. 2001. Varieties of labor politics in the developed democracies. In P. A. Hall & D. Soskice (eds), *Varieties of Capitalism: The Institutional Foundations of Comparative Advantage.* Oxford: Oxford University Press.

Tolbert, P. S. & Zucker, L. G. 1983. Institutional sources of change in the formal structure of organisations: the diffusion of civil service reform, 1880–1935. *Administrative Science Quarterly*, **28**(1): 22–39.

Tolbert, P. S. & Zucker, L. G. 1996. The institutionalisation of institutional theory. In S. Clegg, C. Hardy & W. R. Nord (eds), *Handbook of Organisation Studies.* London: Sage.

Tregaskis, O. & Brewster, C. 2006. Converging or diverging? A comparative analysis of trends in contingent employment practice in Europe over a decade. *Journal of International Business Studies*, **37**(1): 111–126.

Whitley, R. 1999. *Divergent Capitalisms: The Social Structuring and Change of Business Systems.* Oxford: Oxford University Press.

Wolfson, M. 2003. Neoliberalism and the social structure of accumulation. *Review of Radical Political Economics*, **35**(3): 255–263.

Wood, G. & Frynas, G. 2006. The institutional basis of economic failure: anatomy of the segmented business system. *Socio-economic Review*, **4**(2): 239–277.

3 Cultural perspectives on comparative HRM

B. Sebastian Reiche, Yih-teen Lee and Javier Quintanilla

Over the past few decades, increased globalisation of business transactions, the emergence of new markets such as the BRIC countries (Brazil, Russia, India and China) as well as more intense competition among organisations at the domestic and international level alike have been associated with an increased interest in and need for comparative human resource management (HRM) studies (Budhwar & Sparrow, 2002a). As a result, a growing number of conceptual (Aycan, 2005; Edwards & Kuruvilla, 2005) and empirical studies (Bae et al., 1998; Budhwar & Sparrow, 2002b; Easterby-Smith et al., 1995) have addressed the configuration of HRM in different national contexts.

The literature has developed different frameworks to analyse and explain how historical evolution, social institutions and different national cultures can influence firm behaviour in general and HRM in particular. One line of inquiry builds on path dependency arguments and claims that a firm's historical development shapes its extant organisational features such as the configuration of assets and capabilities, the dispersal of responsibilities, the prevailing management style and organisational values (Bartlett & Ghoshal, 1998). This administrative heritage leads an organisation to adopt specific structures and behaviours. A second strand of literature takes an institutional perspective and investigates the social and institutional determinants that underlie the logic of organising business enterprises and their competitive behaviour in different national contexts. A systematic emphasis for understanding the permanent interaction between firms and markets, on the one hand, and other socio-economic institutions, on the other, has been conceptualised in terms of national industrial orders (Lane, 1994) and national business systems (Whitley, 1991, 1992).

In contrast, the cultural perspective has concentrated its attention on the cultural distinctiveness of practices, beliefs and values shared by a community. Culture and values are associated with the national culture of a country as boundaries that allow interaction and socialisation within them. Scholars have analysed the influence of these national cultural values, attitudes and behaviours on business and management styles (Hofstede, 1980; Laurent, 1986; Trompenaars & Hampden-Turner, 1997). At the same time, the movement of people across national borders and the preservation of particular groups with specific idiosyncratic customs, together with differences in social and economic experiences, highlight that subcultures can co-exist in many countries.

In this chapter, we focus on the cultural approaches to comparative HRM, examining how cultural values and norms shape managerial choices across national contexts and how these may, in turn, explain differences in HRM. In a first step, we review conceptualisations of culture and consider the main cultural frameworks applied in comparative research on HRM. We also explain the sources for these national effects and describe mechanisms through which culture influences the design of HRM. In a second step, we review specific areas of HRM that are subject to the influence of culture, placing a particular focus on four key HRM functions. In a third step, we concentrate on multinational companies (MNCs) as carriers of culture that promote the flow and adaptation of culturally imbued HRM practices. Finally, we reflect critically on the limitations of the cultural perspectives on comparative HRM and we conclude with directions for future research.

THE ROLE OF CULTURE IN HUMAN RESOURCE MANAGEMENT

The study of the effect of culture on the design, implementation and experience of HRM policies and practices is not only limited to national cultural differences but also encompasses individual (Stone et al., 2007) and organisational (Aycan et al., 2000) cultural variation. However, in this chapter we will focus on the role of national cultural differences. In the following sections, we will first define the concept of culture and review major cultural frameworks that have been adopted to examine national cultural differences in HRM. Subsequently, we discuss sources and mechanisms through which culture is thought to impact on the design and implementation of HRM policies and practices.

Defining Culture

Implicit to the concept of cultural effect is the notion that societies are considered to vary in terms of the arrangements which their institutions and organisations are composed of, and that these variations reflect their distinctive traditions, values, attitudes and historical experiences.

In this regard, culture can be defined as the 'crystallisation of history in the thinking, feeling and acting of the present generation' (Hofstede, 1993: 5). Bartlett and Ghoshal (1998) also suggest that the history, infrastructure, resources and culture of a nation state permeate all aspects of life within a given country, including the behaviour of managers in its national organisations. Accordingly, traditional national cultural values affect managerial processes and organisational behaviours, which, in turn, affect economic performance. It has been common to conceptualise and measure culture through various value dimensions (Hofstede, 1980; Schwartz, 1994; Trompenaars & Hampden-Turner, 1997). Although reducing the concept of culture to a limited number of value dimensions is not without criticism, this approach allows for comparability across cultural studies and is able to provide valid measures for a highly elusive construct.

Cultural Frameworks in Comparative HRM

An important strand of the cultural perspective is based on Hofstede's (1980) conceptualisation of four distinct cultural value dimensions. The four dimensions he postulates in his examination of dominant value patterns across countries include power distance, uncertainty avoidance, individualism/collectivism and masculinity/femininity. Hofstede suggests that cultural patterns are rooted in the value systems of substantial groupings of the population and that they stabilise over long periods in history. These notions are useful in analysing and understanding managerial behaviour and reactions. Specifically, as cultural differences are embedded in managers' frames of reference and ways of thinking they reinforce particular values and guide managerial actions and choices. In short, all national cultural factors can be regarded as potential influences on how managers make decisions and perform their roles. Nevertheless, Hofstede has been highly criticised (d'Iribarne, 1991, McSweeney, 2002) not only for the limited number of dimensions, which fail to capture the richness of national environments, and his insistence that national cultural features persist over time but also because his dimensions essentially are statistical constructs based on clusters of responses without in-depth understanding of the underlying processes.

Another important contribution to the understanding of cultural differences concentrates its attention on the difference between low context and high context societies (Hall, 1976). Hall describes context as the information that surrounds an event. In high context societies, the situation, the external environment and non-verbal cues are crucial in the communication process. Examples of high context cultures are Japan as well as Arab and southern European societies, where the meaning of communication is mainly derived from paralanguage, facial expressions, setting and timing (Boyacigiller & Adler, 1991). Low context cultures, in contrast, appreciate more clear, explicit and written forms of communication. Anglo-Saxon and northern European countries are examples of low context societies. The implications of these different cultural contexts for managerial attitudes and organisational behaviour are evident. However, this approach fits much better with a generic concept of culture, in the sense of a broad cultural community such as Arab, Latin or Chinese, than with the constrained boundaries of a nation state, where individual and organisational diversity allows for a pluralistic coexistence of both low and high context.

The work of Kluckhohn and Strodtbeck (1961) offers another useful framework to understand cultural differences. Viewing culture as a set of assumptions and deep-level values regarding relationships among humans and between humans and their environments, Kluckhohn and Strodtbeck proposed four basic value orientations, which can be further divided into sub-dimensions to capture the complex cultural variations across societies. The major orientations in their model are human nature (evil, mixed, good), human–environment relationship (subjugation, harmony, dominant), social relation with people (hierarchical, collateral, individual), human activity (being, becoming, doing) and time sense (past, present, future). The cultural orientation framework has been adopted by researchers to explain variations of HRM practices across countries (e.g. Aycan et al., 2007; Nyambegera et al., 2000; Sparrow & Wu, 1998). However, this framework has been applied less frequently to comparative HRM research than that of Hofstede, due to its complexity and the existence of certain overlaps between the two models.

Building on the framework of Hofstede (1980) and Kluckhohn and Strodtbeck (1961), the recent development of the GLOBE project (House et al., 2004) offers a rather comprehensive nine-dimension framework to explain cultural similarities and differences. Moreover, by further differentiating each value into 'as it is' and 'as it should be', this framework allows researchers to investigate cultural variations and their impacts on managerial practices in a more refined way. As this framework starts to be integrated into research practice and establishes an accumulated body of knowledge, its future application in cross-cultural research promises to shed additional light on exploring differences and similarities in HRM across countries.

Finally, mainly drawing on the work of Parsons and Shils (1951), Trompenaars and Hampden-Turner's (1997) framework of value dilemmas also enjoys a high popularity in the teaching of cultural differences.

However, its adaptation in scientific research remains limited due to concerns of conceptual and methodological ambiguities.

More recent research has added additional cultural dimensions for studying the effect of culture on the design and implementation of HRM policies and practices (Aycan et al., 2000; Aycan et al., 1999). For example, the dimension of paternalism concerns the extent to which a society encourages and accepts that individuals with authority provide care, guidance and protection to their subordinates. Subordinates in paternalistic societies, in turn, are expected to show loyalty and deference to their superiors. In contrast, fatalism refers to the belief of societal members that the outcomes of their actions are not fully controllable.

Sources and Mechanisms of Cultural Influences on HRM

In the process of understanding how national cultural features influence organisations in general and HRM in particular, scholars highlight the fact that the cultural environment is not external to organisations but rather permeates them. Crozier (1963: 307), for example, argues that the mechanisms of social control 'are closely related to the values and patterns of social relations', as manifested within organisations. Similarly, Scott (1983: 16) points out that 'the beliefs, norms, rules and understandings are not just 'out there' but additionally 'in here'. Participants, clients, constituents all participate in and are carriers of the culture. This means that organisations and environmental culture interpenetrate. This process of interpenetration highlights several sources of cultural influences on the design and implementation of HRM policies and practices.

First, national culture is thought to shape its members' basic assumptions (Hofstede, 1983; Kluckhohn & Strodtbeck, 1961). Individuals who take on managerial positions in a particular culture are thus socialised along similar values and beliefs (Van Maanen & Schein, 1979) and will form similar views about the managerial role itself as well as the relevance of and choice between alternative organisational practices.

Second, the enduring character of culture continuously helps to socialise new generations of members and reinforce the predominant cultural values and norms (Child & Kiesser, 1979) which, in turn, influence the preference individuals have for particular HRM policies and practices (Sparrow & Wu, 1998) and the degree to which these policies and practices will function effectively within a given cultural system. Accordingly, while the 'what' aspects of HRM (which instruments to adopt in order to achieve HRM outcomes) may be universal across cultures, the 'how' question that determines the particular configuration and design of a specific instrument and the extent to which a desired outcome is reached will be culture-specific (Tayeb, 1995).

Third, according to social cognition theory, individual cognition is strongly influenced by one's cultural background (Abramson et al., 1996; Bandura, 2001). Specifically, culture may influence the way in which individuals 'scan, select, interpret and validate information from the environment in order to identify, prioritise and categorise issues' (Budhwar & Sparrow, 2002b: 603). In other words, culture is a powerful determinant in how human performance problems are perceived and how their solutions in the form of employee development interventions are created, implemented and evaluated. As a lens, cultural frames colour both the design and implementation of HRM in that specific socio-cultural context. In particular, cultural values and norms will shape the way in which people assess justice rules and criteria (Fischer, 2008; Morris et al., 1999). Because ensuring fairness/justice is one of the key concerns of HRM, the culture-bounded appreciation of justice will, in turn, influence how key HRM practices such as recruitment, appraisal, compensation and promotion are designed and implemented in a specific society.

Fourth, culture may be considered to cast a certain influence on creating the social institutions in a society, which subsequently provide value frameworks for individuals in these socio-cultural settings to learn which behaviours and opinions are rewarded and which are punished. For example, cultures may encompass idiosyncratic social elites or pressure groups (Keesing, 1974). The existence of such groups may make the implementation of specific HRM policies and practices politically and socially unacceptable (Budhwar & Sparrow, 2002a). Although it is generally recognised that the relationship between culture and institutions is reciprocal and that no clear consensus has been reached about which should precede which, the influence of culture on HRM through its impact on institutions is also considered as an important mechanism.

Existing research has also considered the level at which HRM is affected by culture. In general, scholars agree that whereas HRM philosophies may entail culturally universal traits, it is the specific HRM practices that are culture-bound and thus show variation across cultures (Teagarden & Von Glinow, 1997). For example, in their study of British and Indian firms Budhwar and Sparrow (2002a) show that even despite a convergence in the desire among Indian and British HR managers to integrate HRM with business strategy, they differ in the underlying logic of implementing this integration. In the following section, we therefore examine the implementation of different HRM policies and practices across cultures in more detail.

CULTURAL DIFFERENCES IN NATIONAL HRM PRACTICES

Scholars have studied the design and implementation of HRM policies and practices across a wide range of cultural contexts, including China (Warner, 2008), Korea (Bae & Lawler, 2000), Singapore (Barnard & Rodgers, 2000), Hong Kong (Ngo et al., 1998), Kenya (Nyambegera et al., 2000) and Oman (Aycan et al., 2007). In addition, existing studies have compared HRM systems across different cultural contexts such as the United States, Canada and the Philippines (Galang, 2004), the United States, Japan and Germany (Pudelko, 2006), East Asia (Zhu et al., 2007), Australia, Indonesia, Malaysia and Hong Kong (Mamman et al., 1996), the UK and China (Easterby-Smith et al., 1995), Turkey, Germany and Spain (Özcelik & Aydinli, 2006), China and the Netherlands (Verburg et al., 1999), China, Japan and South Korea (Rowley et al., 2004), the UK and India (Budhwar & Khatri, 2001; Budhwar & Sparrow, 2002b) and China and Taiwan (Warner & Zhu, 2002). Despite the multitude of cultural contexts that are examined, the studies generally focus on similar dimensions of HRM. Our following discussion is framed along cultural differences in HRM with regard to four key HRM practices: recruitment and selection, compensation and benefits, performance appraisal, and training and development.

Recruitment and Selection

Existing research has shown recruitment, selection and retention practices to be culture-bound. First, the underlying selection criteria have been found to differ across cultures. Based on a review of extant literature, Aycan (2005) suggests that recruitment and selection in cultures high on performance orientation or universalism are based on hard criteria such as job-related knowledge and technical skills whereas cultures that are low on performance orientation, oriented towards ascribed status or particularistic tend to favour soft criteria such as relational skills or social class affiliation.

Second, there is also evidence that the recruitment and selection strategy differs across cultures. For example, collectivist cultures seem to prefer the use of internal labour markets in order to promote loyalty to the firm (Budhwar & Khatri, 2001). In collectivist societies it is often also difficult for externally recruited candidates to enter the strong social networks within the organisation and cope with resistance following their appointment, especially in cases where an internal candidate has been supported (Björkman & Lu, 1999).

Third, selection methods are likely to be culture-bound. Evidence suggests that cultures high on uncertainty avoidance tend to use more types of selection tests, use them more extensively, conduct more interviews and monitor their processes in more detail, thus suggesting a greater desire to collect objective data for making selection decisions (Ryan et al., 1999). Cultures high on performance orientation or universalism will also employ more standardised and job-specific selection methods (Aycan, 2005). Finally, practices concerning the retention of staff in short-term oriented cultures tend to focus on transactional employment relationships and be more responsive in nature. In contrast, retention practices in long-term oriented cultures entail a more preventive character and centre on relational employment needs (Reiche, 2008).

Compensation and Benefits

Evidence also suggests that compensation and benefit schemes need to be tailored to different cultural settings. A key dimension refers to the basis upon which employees are compensated. Specifically, the literature differentiates between job-based and skill- or person-based pay systems (Lawler, 1994). In this vein, performance-oriented or universalistic cultures are likely to devise compensation systems that are based on formal, objective and systematic assessments of the relative value of a job within the organisation. In contrast, in high power-distance or particularistic cultures pay systems will be influenced by subjective decisions from top management and will focus on the person rather than the job itself (Aycan, 2005). There is also evidence for cultural variation concerning the accepted level of performance-based rewards. For example, high power-distance and fatalistic cultures tend to have lower performance-reward contingencies (Aycan et al., 2000). In addition, Schuler and Rogovsky (1998) showed that high uncertainty-avoidance cultures prefer seniority- and skill-based reward systems given their inherent predictability whereas low uncertainty-avoidance cultures place a stronger focus on individual performance-based pay. Similarly, they found that employee share options and stock ownership plans are more widespread in low power-distance cultures.

Compensation systems also differ considerably between individualist and collectivist cultures. While pay-for-performance schemes are very common in individualist cultures, collectivist societies tend to use group-based reward allocation and reveal lower overall pay dispersion (Easterby-Smith et al., 1995; Schuler & Rogovsky, 1998). Finally, there are also different cultural preferences for indirect pay components. Huo and Von Glinow (1995) discovered a relatively greater use of flexible benefit plans, workplace child-care practices, maternity leave programmes and career break schemes in the collectivist context of China, while Schuler and Rogovsky (1998) found these practices to be less important in masculine cultures.

Performance Appraisal

The process of evaluating employee performance usually comprises three distinct stages: (1) preparation for the appraisal process, which concerns the performance criteria and goals to be assessed, (2) the appraisal method or process, as well as (3) the content of the performance evaluation (Milliman et al., 1998). Concerning the preparation stage, evidence suggests that individualistic societies tend to emphasise personal achievement in the appraisal whereas collectivist cultures highlight group-based achievement (Miller et al., 2001). In a study on performance appraisal in Hungary, Kovach (1995) showed that fatalistic cultures, in which individuals perceive work outcomes to be beyond their influence, tend to accept performance below expectations as long as the focal individual displays effort and willingness. Furthermore, low power-distance and universalistic cultures are also more likely to stress task-related competencies and outcomes (Aycan, 2005).

There is support for the notion that culture also has a bearing on the process of conducting performance appraisal. For example, evidence suggests that feedback quality and relational quality between supervisor and subordinate tend to be higher for matched collectivist–collective and individualist–individual dyadic relationships than for mismatched dyads (Van de Vliert et al., 2004). In general, researchers emphasise that evaluation based on direct feedback is more prevalent in individualist cultures whereas collectivist societies focus on indirect, subtle, relationship-oriented and personal forms of feedback (Hofstede, 1998). Similarly, direct, explicit and formal processes of appraisal are more widespread in low-context cultures (Milliman et al., 1998). Moreover, low power-distance cultures appear to use more participative and egalitarian forms of performance appraisal whereas members of high power-distance cultures tolerate autocratic assessment styles that do not require them to openly express their perspectives in the appraisal review (Snape et al., 1998).

Finally, there is also some indication that the topics and issues discussed during the performance appraisal are likely to vary across cultures. Individualistic cultures are considered to place a stronger focus on discussing employees' potential for future promotion based on task performance whereas collectivist societies concentrate on seniority-based promotion decisions (Milliman et al., 1998). However, empirical evidence supporting this notion is inconsistent. For example, Snape et al. (1998) found that the content of performance appraisal in Hong Kong companies was more strongly geared towards reward and punishment, and less towards training and development compared to British firms. This suggests that other factors may play a role and that cultural dimensions are likely to interact in influencing the design and implementation of HRM practices in different cultural contexts.

Training and Development

A last set of HRM policies and practices concerns training and development. Cultural variation exists both with regard to the importance of training and development as well as with regard to the content and methods of training. First, there is evidence that fatalistic cultures perceive training and development as less relevant for organisations given the prevalent assumption that employees have limited abilities that cannot easily be enhanced (Aycan et al., 2000). Second, individual learning styles are inherently culture-bound (Harvey, 1997; Yamazaki, 2005) and therefore call for a different design and delivery of training across cultures. For example, high power-distance cultures generally prefer one-way over participative delivery of training and education courses in which the instructor is perceived to possess sufficient authority. In these cultures, organisations tend to employ senior managers rather than external trainers as instructors in order to ensure a high level of credibility and trust (Wright et al., 2002). Furthermore, it is found that cultural values such as high uncertainty avoidance and low assertiveness drive managers to pursue internal, systematic and long-term orientations in personnel development (Reichel et al., 2009).

Existing research on cultural variations in the design and implementation of other HRM practices, such as HR planning and job analysis, has attracted very little attention (Aycan, 2005). Overall, it has to be acknowledged that not all HRM practices possess the same level of culture-specificity. Indeed, practices such as recruitment and selection or training are likely to be less culture-bound than practices such as career development, performance appraisal and reward allocation, since the latter deal with interpersonal relationships rather than technology (Evans & Lorange, 1990; Verburg et al., 1999) and are thus more embedded within the cultural fabric of the local context.

MULTINATIONALS AS INTER-CULTURAL AGENTS

One of the most relevant implications of comparative HRM research is to provide managers, particularly those working in MNCs, with specific guidelines concerning how to design and implement an effective HRM system when their business operation enters into different cultural contexts. This notion has generated controversial yet critical topics of discussion in comparative HRM, such as the debate on localisation versus standardisation, and the process of transferring HRM policies and practices across nations.

Localisation Versus Standardisation Debate

In the presence of cultural differences, one critical challenge that HR managers in MNCs face is how to maintain a consistent global HRM system while, at the same time, responding sensitively to local cultural norms. Implicit to this standardisation versus localisation (or integration versus responsiveness) debate is the more fundamental assumption about whether a set of universally valid best practices can be identified, irrespective of the cultural context (also known as the convergence versus divergence debate; see Pudelko & Harzing, 2007). If best practices do exist, it makes sense to identify them and transfer them to different parts of the world. Whereas various authors have proclaimed the existence of international HRM best practices (e.g. Von Glinow et al., 2002), other scholars refute this idea and argue that practices need to be closely adapted to the local context in order to be effective (e.g. Marchington & Grugulis, 2000; Newman & Nollen, 1996). From the latter perspective, the congruence between management practices and national culture is so critical that local responsiveness may become an inevitable task.

Transfer of HR Practices

In general, there is a strong temptation for MNCs to transfer their HRM policies and practices to various other countries, either from the headquarters (i.e. country-of-origin effect) or from a third country which has set the standard of global best practices (i.e. dominance effect; Pudelko & Harzing, 2007). Scholars subscribing to the culturalist approach maintain that it could be very difficult, if not impossible, to transfer HRM practices between two countries with different national cultures (Beechler & Yang, 1994). For instance, implementing an individualistic HRM system (e.g. merit-based promotion) in a collectivist culture may encounter difficulties (Ramamoorthy & Carroll, 1998). In the same vein, national cultural distance has been considered as an indicator to predict the transferability of HRM systems across countries (Kogut & Singh, 1988; Liu, 2004; Shenkar, 2001).

Despite the existence of fierce debates about the cross-cultural transfer of HRM practices, scholars generally agree that (1) it is necessary to distinguish between HRM policies and HRM practices, and (2) although some HRM policies may be similar across MNC subsidiaries, the actual practices are more prone to respond to local norms and display differences across cultures (Khilji, 2003; Tayeb, 1998).

LIMITATIONS OF THE CULTURAL PERSPECTIVE

While an increasing number of studies have investigated the role of national culture in shaping local HRM policies and practices, this perspective is not without criticism on both conceptual and empirical fronts. An important risk of culturalist approaches is the tendency to over-simplify national cultures and construct cross-cultural comparative analysis based on exaggerated cultural stereotypes. As Child and Kiesser (1979: 269) have indicated, a methodological problem of using cultural variables is that these have not been incorporated into 'a model which systematically links together the analytical levels of context, structure, role and behaviour'.

Often, it is also difficult to distinguish clearly between cultural values and institutional arrangements. Traditionally, scholars have tried to blend and probe the relationship between them. Dore (1973) points out how institutions are created or perpetuated by powerful actors following their interests and cultural orientations. Likewise, Hofstede (1980, 1993) argues that culture reflects institutions. More specifically, Whitley (1992) also acknowledges strong cultural features within his dominant contingency institutional perspective, arguing that institutions include cultural attitudes. He identified two main groups of major institutions – background and proximate – which constrain and guide the behaviour of organisations. Whereas background institutions entail trust relations, collective loyalties, individualism and authority relations, proximate institutions comprise the political, financial and labour systems, and so forth. As Whitley (1992: 269) points out, 'background institutions may be conceived as predominantly "cultural"'.

Another weakness of the culturalist approach is the lack of a priori theorising in existing research (Schaffer & Riordan, 2003). Rather than explicitly incorporating culture into their underlying theoretical framework, researchers frequently explain observed differences only *ex post*. With few exceptions (e.g. Aycan et al., 1999) studies do not sufficiently explain how and why, i.e. through which sources and mechanisms, culture affects the design and implementation of HRM. Similarly, by using the nation state as a proxy for culture, research risks not capturing all relevant sub-cultural differences that may influence HRM (Ryan et al., 1999). The example of the literature on choice of entry-mode suggests that an almost blind reliance on an overly simplistic measure of cultural distance may not only lead to inconsistent results but also overlooks more subtle cultural factors that may play a role (Harzing, 2004). We would encourage more research to focus on within-culture variation when studying cultural preferences for HRM policies and practices (e.g. Aycan et al., 2007).

Comparative cross-cultural research is plagued by a variety of methodological problems (Tsui et al., 2007) that may reduce the researcher's ability to draw valid conclusions about relevant differences in the design, implementation and, in particular, the perception of HRM policies and practices across cultures. As Galang (2004) points out, comparative HRM studies need to not only ensure functional and conceptual invariance of the underlying practices of interest but also pay attention to the metric and linguistic equivalence of their measures. Moreover, there is a lack of studies applying multilevel models in investigating culture's impacts on HRM policies and practices. Scholars should strive to include a larger number of countries in their study to insure that a full range of the predictor variable distribution (i.e. cultural values) is covered (Milliman et al., 1998), which, in turn, would allow researchers to attribute the variations in HRM systems found across countries to cultural differences in a more convincing way.

By over-relying on the dimensional models of culture (e.g. Hofstede), studies adopting a culturalist approach also suffer from the weaknesses inherited in those models, particularly when culture is not directly measured but scores of cultural dimensions reported in the cultural models are applied. In other words, if the cultural scores are flawed in the first place, the analyses using these scores may also be contaminated, thus rendering the conclusions suspicious. Furthermore, the coverage of culture in comparative HRM may also be constrained by the original cultural models. Therefore, while there are abundant cases studying the United States and West European countries, accompanied by Japan and some emerging economies in Asia and Latin America, the African, Middle East and Arabic world is still largely absent in the current body of literature.

Finally, even if culture is actually measured in the studies, a huge risk of confusion of levels still persists. It is not rare that researchers fail to align their level of theory, measurement and analysis, thus committing various types of multilevel fallacies (Klein et al., 1994; Vijver et al., 2008). Scholars may measure 'cultural values' at the individual level but make inferences at the organisational or country level variables. Consequently, some of the results reported by this culturalist line of research should be considered with caution.

CONCLUSION

In this chapter, we discussed how cultural values and norms shape managerial choices across national contexts and how these may, in turn, explain differences in HRM. While this approach certainly deserves merit as shown by the growing number of empirical studies and conceptual debate, it is clear that national cultural factors can only serve as one among several determinants that influence the design and implementation of HRM policies and practices across different contexts. Subsequent research would greatly benefit from expanding the scope of the cultural perspective to entail additional factors. In this vein, our review serves as a modest starting point to organise a future research agenda.

REFERENCES

Abramson, N., Keating, R. & Lane, H. W. 1996. Cross-national cognitive process differences: a comparison of Canadian, American and Japanese Managers. *Management International Review*, **36**: 123–148.

Aycan, Z. 2005. The interplay between cultural and institutional/structural contingencies in human resource management practices. *International Journal of Human Resource Management*, **16**(7): 1083–1119.

Aycan, Z., Al-Hamadi, A. B., Davis, A. & Budhwar, P. 2007. Cultural orientations and preferences for HRM policies and practices: the case of Oman. *International Journal of Human Resource Management*, **18**(1): 11–32.

Aycan, Z., Kanungo, R. N., Mendonca, M., Yu, K., Deller, J. & Stahl, G. 2000. Impact of culture of human resource management practices: a 10-country comparison. *Applied Psychology*, **49**(1): 192–221.

Aycan, Z., Kanungo, R. N. & Sinha, J. B. P. 1999. Organizational culture and human resource management practices: the model of culture fit. *Journal of Cross-Cultural Psychology*, **30**(4): 501–526.

Bae, J., Chen, S.-J. & Lawler, J. J. 1998. Variations in human resource management in Asian countries: MNC home-country and host-country effects. *International Journal of Human Resource Management*, **9**(4): 653–670.

Bae, J. & Lawler, J. J. 2000. Organisational and HRM Strategies in Korea: impact on firm performance in an emerging economy. *Academy of Management Journal*, **43**(3): 502–517.

Bandura, A. 2001. Social cognitive theory: an agentic perspective. *Annual Review of Psychology*, **52**: 1–26.

Barnard, M. E. & Rodgers, R. A. 2000. How are internally oriented HRM policies related to high-performance work practices? Evidence from Singapore. *International Journal of Human Resource Management*, **11**(6): 1017–1046.

Bartlett, C. A. & Ghoshal, S. 1998. *Managing across Borders: The Transnational Solution*, 2nd edn. Boston, MA: Harvard Business School Press.

Beechler, S. & Yang, J. Z. 1994. The transfer of Japanese-style management to American subsidiaries: contingencies, constraints, and competencies. *Journal of International Business Studies*, **25**(3): 467–491.

Björkman, I. & Lu, Y. 1999. The management of human resources in Chinese–Western Joint ventures. *Journal of World Business*, **34**(3): 306–325.

Boyacigiller, N. A. & Adler, N. J. 1991. The parochial dinosaur: organizational science in a global context. *Academy of Management Review*, **16**(2): 262–290.

Budhwar, P. & Khatri, N. 2001. A comparative study of HR practices in Britain and India. *International Journal of Human Resource Management*, **12**(5): 800–826.

Budhwar, P. & Sparrow, P. R. 2002a. An integrative framework for understanding cross-national human resource management practices. *Human Resource Management Review*, **12**(3): 377–403.

Budhwar, P. S. & Sparrow, P. R. 2002b. Strategic HRM trough the cultural looking glass: mapping the cognition of British and Indian managers. *Organization Studies* (Walter de Gruyter GmbH & Co.KG), **23**(4): 599–638.

Child, J. & Kiesser, A. 1979. Organizational and managerial roles in British and West German companies: an examination of the culture-free thesis. In J. Cornelis & D. Hickson (eds), *Organizations Alike and Unlike: International and Inter-institutional Studies in the Sociology of Organizations*. London: Routledge & Kegan Paul, pp. 251–271.

Crozier, M. 1963. *The Bureaucratic Phenomenon*. Chicago: University of Chicago.

d'Iribarne, P. 1991. *The Usefulness of an Ethnographic Approach to International Comparisons of the Functioning of Organizations*. Vienna: EGOS Colloquium.

Dore, R. 1973. *British Factory, Japanese Factory: The Origins of National Diversity in Industrial Relations*. Los Angeles: University of California Press.

Easterby-Smith, M., Malina, D. & Yuan, L. 1995. How culture-sensitive is HRM? A comparative analysis of practice in Chinese and UK companies. *International Journal of Human Resource Management*, **6**(1): 31–59.

Edwards, T., & Kuruvilla, S. 2005. International HRM: national business systems, organizational politics and the international division of labour in MNCs. *The International Journal of Human Resource Management*, **16**(1): 1–21.

Evans, P. & Lorange, P. 1990. Two logics behind human resource management. In J. Evans, Y. Doz & A. Laurent (eds), *Human Resource Management in International Firms*. New York: St. Martins Press, pp. 144–161.

Fischer, R. 2008. Organizational justice and reward allocation. In P. B. Smith, M. F. Peterson & D. C. Thomas (eds), *The Handbook of Cross-Cultural Management Research*. London: Sage Publications.

Galang, M. C. 2004. The transferability question: comparing HRM practices in the Philippines with the US and Canada. *International Journal of Human Resource Management*, **15**(7): 1207–1233.

Hall, E. T. 1976. *Beyond Culture*. New York: Anchor Press/Doubleday.

Harvey, M. 1997. 'Inpatriation' training: the next challenge for international human resource management. *International Journal of Intercultural Relations*, **21**(3): 393–428.

Harzing, A.-W. 2004. The role of culture in entry-mode studies: from neglect to myopia? In J. L. C. Cheng & M. A. Hitt (eds), *Advances in International Management*, Vol. 15. Oxford: Elsevier JAI, pp. 75–127.

Hofstede, G. 1980. *Culture's Consequences: International Differences in Work-Related Values*. Beverly Hills: Sage Publications.

Hofstede, G. 1983. The cultural relativity of organizational practices and theories. *Journal of International Business Studies*, **14**(2): 75–89.

Hofstede, G. 1993. Intercultural conflict and synergy in Europe: management in Western Europe. In D. J. Hickson (ed.), *Society, Culture and Organization in Twelve Nations: 1–8*. New York: de Gruyter.

Hofstede, G. 1998. Think locally, act globally: cultural constraints in personnel management. *Management International Review*, **38**(Special Issue 2): 7–26.

House, R. J., Hanges, P. J., Javidan, M., Dorfman, P. W. & Gupta, V. 2004. *Leadership, Culture, and Organizations: The GLOBE Study of 62 Societies*. London: Sage Publications.

Huo, Y. P. & Von Glinow, M. A. 1995. On transplanting human resource practices to China: a culture-driven approach. *International Journal of Manpower*, **16**(9): 3–11.

Keesing, R. M. 1974. Theories of culture. *Annual Review of Anthropology*, 3: 73–97.

Khilji, S. E. 2003. To adapt or not to adapt: exploring the role of national culture in HRM: a study of Pakistan. *International Journal of Cross Cultural Management*, **3**(1): 109–132.

Klein, K. J., Dansereau, F. & Hall, R. J. 1994. Levels issues in theory development, data collection, and analysis. *The Academy of Management Review*, **19**(2): 195–229.

Kluckhohn, F. & Strodtbeck, F. 1961. *Variations in Value Orientations*. Evanston, IL: Row-Peterson.

Kogut, B. & Singh, H. 1988. The effect of national culture on the choice of entry mode. *Journal of International Business Studies*, **19**(3): 411–432.

Kovach, R. C. 1995. Matching assumptions to environment in the transfer of management practices: performance appraisal in Hungary. *International Studies of Management & Organization*, **24**(4): 83–99.

Lane, C. 1994. Industrial order and the transformation of industrial relations: Britain, Germany and France compared. In R. Hyman & A. Ferner (eds), *New Frontiers in European Industrial Relations*. Oxford: Blackwell, pp. 167–196.

Laurent, A. 1986. The cross-cultural puzzle of international human resource management. *Human Resource Management*, **25**(1): 91–102.

Lawler, E. E. 1994. From job-based to competency-based organizations. *Journal of Organizational Behavior*, **15**(1): 3–15.

Liu, W. 2004. The cross-national transfer of HRM practices in MNCs: an integrative research model. *International Journal of Manpower*, **25**(6): 500–517.

Mamman, A., Sulaiman, M. & Fadel, A. 1996. Attitudes to pay systems: an exploratory study within and across cultures. *International Journal of Human Resource Management*, **7**(1): 101–121.

Marchington, M. & Grugulis, I. 2000. 'Best practice' human resource management: perfect opportunity or dangerous illusion? *International Journal of Human Resource Management*, **11**(6): 1104–1124.

McSweeney, B. 2002. Hofstede's model of national cultural differences and their consequences: a triumph of faith – a failure of analysis. *Human Relations*, **55**(1): 89–118.

Miller, J. S., Hom, P. W. & Gomez-Mejia, L. R. 2001. The high cost of low wages: does maquiladora compensation reduce turnover. *Journal of International Business Studies*, **32**(3): 585–595.

Milliman, J., Nason, S., Gallagher, E., Huo, P., Von Glinow, M. A. & Lowe, K. B. 1998. The impact of national culture on human resource management practices: the case of performance appraisal. In J. L. C. Cheng & R. B. Peterson (eds), *Advances in International Comparative Management*, Vol. 12. Greenwich, CT: JAI Press, pp. 157–183.

Morris, M. W., Leung, K., Ames, D., & Lickel, B. 1999. Views from inside and outside: integrating emic and etic insights about culture and justice judgment. *Academy of Management Review*, **24**(4): 781–796.

Newman, K. L. & Nollen, S. D. 1996. Culture and congruence: the fit between management practices and national culture. *Journal of International Business Studies*, **27**(4): 753–779.

Ngo, H. Y., Turban, D., Lau, C. M. & Lui, S. Y. 1998. Human resource practices and firm performance of multinational corporations: influences of country origin. *International Journal of Human Resource Management*, **9**(4): 632–652.

Nyambegera, S. M., Sparrow, P. R. & Daniels, K. 2000. The impact of cultural value orientations on individual HRM preferences in developing countries: lessons from Kenyan organizations. *International Journal of Human Resource Management*, **11**(4): 639–663.

Özcelik, A. O. & Aydinli, F. 2006. Strategic role of HRM in Turkey: a three-country comparative analysis. *Journal of European Industrial Training*, **30**(4): 310–327.

Parsons, T. & Shils, E. A. 1951. *Towards a General Theory of Action*. Cambridge, MA: Harvard University Press.

Pudelko, M. 2006. A comparison of HRM systems in the USA, Japan and Germany in their socio-economic context. *Human Resource Management Journal*, **16**(2): 123–153.

Pudelko, M. & Harzing, A.-W. 2007. Country-of-origin, localization, or dominance effect? An empirical investigation of HRM practices in foreign subsidiaries. *Human Resource Management*, **46**(4): 535–559.

Ramamoorthy, N. & Carroll, S. 1998. Individualism/collectivism orientations and reactions toward alternative human resource management practices. *Human Relations*, **51**(5): 571–588.

Reiche, B. S. 2008. The configuration of employee retention practices in multinational corporations' foreign subsidiaries. *International Business Review*, **17**(6): 676–687.

Reichel, A., Mayrhofer, W. & Chudzikowski, K. 2009. Human resource development in Austria: a cultural perspective of management development. In C. D. Hansen & Y. T. Lee (eds), *The Cultural Contexts of Human Resource Development*. Hampshire, UK: Palgrave Macmillan.

Rowley, C., Benson, J. & Warner, M. 2004. Towards an Asian model of human resource management? A comparative analysis of China, Japan and South Korea. *International Journal of Human Resource Management*, **15**(4): 917–933.

Ryan, A. M., McFarland, L., Baron, H. & Page, R. 1999. An international look at selection practices: nation and culture as explanations for variability in practice. *Personnel Psychology*, **52**(2): 351–391.

Schaffer, B. S. & Riordan, C. M. 2003. A review of cross-cultural methodologies for organizational research: a best-practices approach. *Organizational Research Methods*, **6**(2): 169–215.

Schuler, R. S. & Rogovsky, N. 1998. Understanding compensation practice variations across firms: the impact of national culture. *Journal of International Business Studies*, **29**(1): 159–177.

Schwartz, S. H. 1994. Beyond individualism / collectivism: new cultural dimensions of values. In K. Uichol, C. Kagitçibasi, H. C. Triandis & G. Yoon (eds), Individualism and collectivism: theory, method and applications. Thousand Oaks, CA: Sage Publications.

Scott, W. R. 1983. The organizations of environments: network, cultural, and historical elements. In J. W. Meyer & W. R. Scott (eds), *Organizational Environments: Ritual and Rationality*. Beverly Hills, CA: Sage Publications, pp.155–175.

Shenkar, O. 2001. Cultural distance revisited: towards a more rigorous conceptualization and measurement of cultural differences. *Journal of International Business Studies*, **32**(3): 519–535.

Snape, E., Thompson, D., Yan, F. K. & Redman, T. 1998. Performance appraisal and culture: practice and attitudes in Hong Kong and Great Britain. *International Journal of Human Resource Management*, **9**(5): 841–861.

Sparrow, P. R. & Wu, P. C. 1998. Does national culture really matter? Predicting HRM preferences of Taiwanese employees. *Employee Relations*, **20**(1): 26–56.

Stone, D. L., Stone-Romero, E. F. & Lukaszewski, K. M. 2007. The impact of cultural values on the acceptance and effectiveness of human resource management policies and practices. *Human Resource Management Review*, **17**(2): 152–165.

Tayeb, M. 1995. The competitive advantage of nations: the role of HRM and its socio-cultural context. *International Journal of Human Resource Management*, **6**(3): 588–605.

Tayeb, M. 1998. Transfer of HRM practices across cultures: an American company in Scotland. *International Journal of Human Resource Management*, **9**: 332–358.

Teagarden, M. B. & Von Glinow, M. A. 1997. Human resource management in cross-cultural contexts: emic practices versus etic philosophies. *Management International Review*, **37**(Special Issue 1): 7–20.

Trompenaars, F. & Hampden-Turner, C. 1997. *Riding the Waves of Culture, Understanding Cultural Diversity in Business.* London: McGraw-Hill.

Tsui, A. S., Nifadkar, S. S. & Ou, A. Y. 2007. Cross-national, cross-cultural organizational behavior research: advances, gaps, and recommendations. *Journal of Management*, **33**(3): 426–478.

Van de Vliert, E., Shi, K., Sandeers, K., Wang, Y. & Huang, X. 2004. Chinese and Dutch interpretations of supervisory feedback. *Journal of Cross-Cultural Psychology*, **35**(4): 417–435.

Van Maanen, J. & Schein, E. H. 1979. Towards a theory of organizational socialization. In B. M. Staw (ed.), *Research in Organizational Behavior*, Vol. 1. Greenwich, CT: JAI Press, pp. 209–264.

Verburg, R. M., Drenth, P. J. D., Koopman, P. L., Muijen, J. J. V. & Wang, Z. M. 1999. Managing human resources across cultures: a comparative analysis of practices in industrial enterprises in China and the Netherlands. *International Journal of Human Resource Management*, **10**(3): 391–410.

Vijver, F. J. R., Hemert, D. A. & Poortinga, Y. H. 2008. Conceptual issues in multilevel models. In F. J. R. Vijver, D. A. Hemert & Y. H. Poortings (eds), *Multilevel Analysis of Individuals and Cultures*. New York: Erlbaum.

Von Glinow, M. A., Drost, E. A. & Teagarden, M. B. 2002. Converging on IHRM best practices: lessons learned from a globally distributed consortium on theory and practice. *Human Resource Management*, **41**(1): 123–140.

Warner, M. 2008. Reassessing human resource management 'with Chinese' characteristics: an overview. *International Journal of Human Resource Management*, **19**(5): 771–801.

Warner, M., & Zhu, Y. 2002. Human resource management 'with Chinese characteristics': a comparative study of the People's Republic of China and Taiwan. *Asia Pacific Business Review*, **9**(2): 21–42.

Whitley, R. 1991. The societal construction of business systems in East Asia. *Organization Studies*, **12**(1): 1–28.

Whitley, R. 1992. Societies, firms and markets: the social structuring of business systems. In R. Whitley (ed.), *European Business Systems. Firms and Markets in Their National Contexts*. London: Sage Publications, pp. 5–45.

Wright, P., Szeto, W. F. & Cheng, L. T. W. 2002. Guanxi and professional conduct in China: a management development perspective. *International Journal of Human Resource Management*, **13**(1): 156–182.

Yamazaki, Y. 2005. Learning styles and typologies of cultural differences: a theoretical and empirical comparison. *International Journal of Intercultural Relations*, **29**(5): 521–548.

Zhu, Y., Warner, M. & Rowley, C. 2007. Human resource management with 'Asian' characteristics: a hybrid people-management system in East Asia. *International Journal of Human Resource Management*, **18**(5): 745–768.

4 Critical approaches to comparative HRM
Tuomo Peltonen and Eero Vaara

Comparative HRM occupies an important position in the scholarship of international human resource management (IHRM) (Brewster, 1999; Brewster & Hegewisch, 1994; Brewster et al., 2004; Clark & Pugh, 2000; Dickmann et al., 2008). This is because it adopts a 'broader' view of the human resource practices and strategies than the mainstream approaches in IHRM research (cf. Keating & Thompson, 2004). By 'broader' we mean that it takes seriously the recent calls for more societally embedded organisational research as evidenced by the widespread use of neo-institutional theory (Drori et al., 2006; Granovetter, 1985; Scott, 2001), national business systems approach (Morgan et al., 2001; Quack et al., 2000; Whitley, 2002; Whitley & Kristensen, 1996;) and cross-cultural perspectives in management studies in general (Hall & Soskice, 2001; Maurice & Sorge, 2000). Thus, comparative research is prone to look into the wider societal issues and problems in its description and explanation of organisational and working life phenomena.

The comparative stance has demonstrated the limits of the HRM theories and models derived from the institutional realities of the North American context. The individualised approach to employment relations and people management has its roots in the US institutional environment where the unions are relatively weak and where there is a strong belief in the potency of the free markets in the organisation of labour relations. In contrast, the Continental European system has traditionally been organised along corporatist lines, with strong trade union membership and a tradition of collective bargaining. The European system, with its more regulative and representative character, has put more weight on the societal level agreements and on the active role of the government. At the same time, it is important to note that the HR environments in developing countries tend to lack even the most basic institutional frameworks that are taken for granted in the mainstream HRM literature (cf. Jackson, 2004). For example trade unions are banned completely in some Asian countries, whereas in Africa one can find societies where the informal or grey job market dominates the whole economy. With these kinds of insights, comparative HRM research has successfully demonstrated that what we take as the universal model of HRM is in reality a local North American approach transferred into the rest of the world as 'best practice'. Given the recent debates on the ethical shortcomings and societal irrelevance of Americanised management practices and theories (Dore, 2000; Ghoshal, 2005; Mintzberg, 2004; Pfeffer & Fong, 2005), this is a timely message.

While we acknowledge the advances made in comparative studies, we want to push this approach even further in terms of its ability to connect with and apply critical perspectives. We draw from the critical theories and methodologies that have been put forth by the critical management studies movement. In particular, we offer global labour process theory, postcolonial analysis and transnational feminism as perspectives that can further advance the comparative approach to IHRM. Even though some scholars have already used and developed such ideas, a great deal can and needs to be done to map out and examine the various problematic aspects of IHRM in our globalising world.

The next section provides an overview of comparative HRM research and its contributions. This is followed by a look at the globalisation of employment management as a manifestation of neoliberal economic and societal policies and practices. The fourth section discusses critical management studies as a fruitful approach to organisations and organisational research. The fifth section focuses on global labour process theory, postcolonial analysis and transnational feminism, which are explained and illustrated in the following section. A brief concluding section wraps up our argument and suggests some avenues for further research.

COMPARATIVE HRM AS A 'BROADER' VIEW ON THE HUMAN RESOURCE MANAGEMENT PHENOMENA

Comparative HRM as a field of study focuses on the national-institutional differences in human resource practices, strategies and systems. Originally contained within the emerging study of international human resource management, it has in recent years developed into an independent area in its own right. According to Brewster (1999, 2007), comparative HRM relies on a distinct research paradigm that sets it apart from the mainstream US human resource management discipline. The US scholars tend to view HRM from a universalist perspective, treating HRM as a general phenomenon that exists irrespective of the institutional environment where it is practised. Comparative HRM, instead, insists that human resource management practices are best understood as societal phenomena, shaped by the institutional, cultural and political contexts of their occurrence. Brewster (2007) argues that a contextualist paradigm in comparative HRM makes a crucial difference in many respects.

These include a more critical stance towards the 'goodness' of the North American conception of HRM as manipulation of individual employees and employment contracts, incorporation of industrial relations issues and trade union topics into the conception of HRM, and a willingness to look at HRM from a national, EU or even global world systems level of analysis. The different realities of contexts such as the European welfare states as well as the Asian and African developing economies all need to be accounted for in search of a more accurate picture of human resource management worldwide (Jackson, 2004).

Comparative HRM differs from the mainstream human resource study also in terms of methodological preferences (Brewster, 1999, 2007). Comparative HRM seeks to understand individual national contexts and the way in which HRM is organised in each particular country. It is not interested in the discovery of general laws and causal mechanisms in HRM, but in gaining sensitivity for the locally contingent circumstances surrounding the particular forms and approaches to labour management. The focus on the particular is also reflected in the tendency to rely on the insights of empirical data in theory development. Comparative HRM seeks to develop new theories and understandings of the HRM outcomes without any strong commitment to a priori models and theories of human resource management. It is inductive rather than deductive in its methodology. Empirical data used in comparative HRM is often a combination of quantitative and qualitative materials, used heuristically to reach a deeper understanding of the different forms of HRM and how they are shaped in various institutional-national contexts (Keating & Thompson, 2004). Overall, comparative HRM has (tried to) set itself apart from the positivist-deductive methodology that has dominated HRM research in the North American field, with an interest in developing a non-managerialist theory of HRM as embedded in the variety of institutional and socio-political contexts and relations.

However, comparative HRM has not made explicit its standing vis-à-vis the various theoretical issues that preoccupy organisation and management studies as a branch of social science. Using the classical outline of organisational theoretical paradigms by Burrell and Morgan (Burrell & Morgan, 1979), it is not clear whether comparative HRM is committed to consensus sociology characterised by a unitarist conception of work organisations, to conflict theories that approach organisations as sites of structural contradictions and tensions, or to some other position. At times it seems to agree with the neo-Marxist and other radical views on the continuing presence of a power asymmetry between managers and workers, but this is not systematically noted nor made explicit. Comparative HRM seems also to hesitate between objective and interpretative positions with regard to epistemology and methods. While it is keen to stress the use of qualitative data in making sense of organising HRM, it also tends to resort to quantitative survey studies of national forms of HRM (e.g. the Cranet survey). Given the broad range of different epistemological alternatives to objectivist approaches to methodology (Morgan & Smircich, 1980), comparative HRM lands in a fairly conventional area within organisational inquiry. These limitations become apparent if we take a closer look at globalisation of HRM as a manifestation of the spread of neoliberal capitalism to new areas around the world.

Globalisation and Neoliberal Capitalism

The spread of the individualised, market-based employment systems is one of the key interests in comparative HRM. The rise of contingent work, flexible working patterns and new organisational forms are manifestations of what Sennett (2006) calls the 'culture of new capitalism'. According to Sennett (2006, 1998), late modern capitalism is characterised by a shift from bureaucratic organisations and stable careers to flexible networks and contingent employment. The assumption that an employee is committed to one corporation for the whole of his or her working life is no longer valid; instead, workers are left largely to rely on their own devices as free agents seeking jobs in the constantly changing economic situations. Employees are treated as entrepreneurs, who are responsible for their own employment. As Bauman (2000) has noted, ours is the era of 'liquid modernity' in which capital is globally mobile and seeks to guarantee the best possible returns at the same time as labour continues to stay tied to its local communal contexts. As we now know, in spring 2009, the neoliberal experiment of unregulated international financial markets has ended in a major economic crisis. The promise of the finance-driven economy to bring prosperity to all through continuous growth has turned out to be an extremely one-sided and ethically questionable arrangement. The continuously shifting organisational and economic contexts made it difficult to build coherent working lives already before the financial crisis. Now, as the economic problems have spread from banking to other sectors, it is the workers who have the carry the burden of unsuccessful policies in the form of lay-offs. The underlying dynamics of neoliberal capitalism has come more visible, producing a wave of anger and protest against what is considered as an essentially flawed approach to organisation of economy and work (Wikipedia, 2009).

At the same time, however, organisational control has intensified its grip over the empowered employees. The market model of employment relations has not displaced managerial control in organisations. The emerging organisational model is akin to a rationally controlled network, envisioned as a lean, managerially diluted and dispersed network of individual employees. Kunda and Ailon (2005; cf. Barley & Kunda, 1992) call this the Market Rationalist ideology that has connections to the classical Taylorist and Fordist techniques of managerial control. Employees constitute minuscule 'business units' that are analysed, measured and managed just like any other economic entities. Rational managerial techniques developed for financial accounting are applicable to human individuals, a development that has made work in large organisations highly competitive, short-term oriented and instrumental.

Global capitalism has institutionalised uncertainty to an extent that it can be regarded as one of the most acute problems facing working life today. While HRM scholars have noted this change, they have been unable to fully describe the human and social consequences of market-based human resource strategies. The notions of boundaryless careers and transactional psychological contracts refer to transformations in the world of work, but they have not been sufficient to illuminate the full scale of human experiences brought about by the 'HRMist' employment models. In a similar way, studies examining the global convergence or divergence of HRM practices have tended to look at the surface patterns and structural manifestations of contingent labour instead of elucidating the social meanings and lived experiences of workers, professionals and managers worldwide (cf. Hassard et al., 2007).

Let us exemplify this with a reference to our own immediate working environment as Finnish academic employees. Finland is typically portrayed in the comparative studies as following the Nordic model of HRM (Lilja, 1998; Lindeberg et al., 2004). This includes a high trade union organisation rate, comparatively strong government presence in business regulation and the tradition of collective bargaining processes. Yet the recent changes in private and public organisations suggest a rapid 'Anglo-Americanisation' of economic systems and industrial relations (cf. Tainio & Lilja, 2002). Collective bargaining is in crisis and precarious employment on the rise. In the public sector, traditional bureaucratic careers are being demolished in favour of flexible arrangements typical of the New Economy. As part of that shift, universities are undergoing profound reforms that touch the very essence of academic values such as the impartiality of professors guaranteed by their status as tenured civil servants. We have already witnessed a salary reform that has moved academic remuneration towards individualistic, performance-related compensation. Organisational and individual performance is measured and appraised more frequently than before. The latest reform involves a change in the employment type of the academics who are to be attached in the future to the universities through standard employee contracts instead of being treated as civil servants. This implies a profound change in the nature and organisation of academic work but also manifests a broader transformation in the traditionally corporatist industrial relations system that has prevailed in Finland for the past decades. Stable labour market structures and communal values are being replaced by the principles of flexibility and short term profitability. Yet it is fair to note that while we see Finnish development as an example of the degradation of contemporary working life, people in extra-European countries often suffer from more acute problems. The core human rights such as the freedom to join trade unions are not within the reach of employees in many emerging economies. Without the social safety net, employees in those countries are much more vulnerable to external changes: for example the current economic crisis seems to hit worst the poorest nations and their citizens. To make better sense of these types of global shifts, and their human and social consequences for the employees, it is useful to take a closer look at the insights offered by critical management studies.

Critical Management Studies

Critical management studies (CMS) have become a legitimate approach within management and organisation studies. Following openings such as the paradigm analysis of organisational studies by Burrell and Morgan (1979), CMS has expanded during the last 20 years in the form of special conferences (International Critical Management Studies Conference), interest groups (the CMS Division at the American Academy of Management) and scholarly outlets. The roots of CMS lay in three discussions: labour process theory (LPT), critical theory (CT) and also some forms of postmodernist or poststructuralist theorising. LPT is a more materialist approach to the structuring of organisational hierarchies under the forces of late modern capitalism. Its main argument, the so-called deskilling thesis, was originally formulated by Braverman (1974). According to Braverman, the advances in modern people management techniques have not delivered autonomy and self-fulfilment for the employees of the modern corporation, but, instead, have sedimented and intensified the clash between the capitalist interests and the working conditions of organisational labour. Modern management strategies strip away individual creativity and dignity, providing the employees with monotonous tasks that are detached from their own personal aspirations. According to Braverman's deskilling thesis, work is degraded under monopoly capitalism because of an inexorable tendency for the conception or planning of work to be separated from its execution. Conception is concentrated in an ever-smaller section of the workforce, while most workers are reduced to executing tasks conceived by others. In the LPT view, this Taylorist division of labour makes work meaningless for the majority of organisational employees.

CT is a more humanistic stream of radical theorising. Its roots lay in the so-called Frankfurt School and the work of scholars such as Adorno, Marcuse and Habermas. CT is interested in the one-dimensionality of our cultural beliefs and in the ways in which ideological constructions serve the interests of the powerful, or capital. The work of Habermas (1972, 1984) has been pivotal in guiding the research on organisational culture and communication towards a critical agenda. According to Habermas (1984), the realm of work has been estranged from its self-realising and dialogic potentials, and has, instead, transformed into dispassionate activity with no connection to the deeper social and communicative needs of the employees. Organisational life takes on an instrumental outlook as the members resort to external motivations and markers of personal attachment. Also, communication is restricted to ideologically acceptable discourses and the free flow of debate is blocked by the accumulation of power and authority to the hands of the few, such as professional managers. Disciplines and scientific articulations of organisational management such as those contained within human resource management can be seen as manifestations of the broader ideological milieu where prevailing forms of understanding are shaped by the structures of power (Alvesson & Willmott, 1996). All this takes place in a world of conflicting interests between the privileged and those excluded from the benefits of contemporary capitalism. In addition, CT is keen to restore some of the emancipatory potential of the alienated employees and organisations in order to help them to better address their own interests and how they could be articulated in the corporate decision making and communication (Alvesson & Deetz, 2006).

The CMS movement has also been inspired by various postmodernist and poststructuralist theories and methodologies, especially by the work of Foucault, Deleuze, Derrida and Bourdieu. Foucault's discourse analysis has been particularly influential, as it has provided means to examine and elucidate how managerial and organisational phenomena are structured and governed by specific discourses. His ideas have also been very useful in highlighting how subjectivities and identities are constructed in contemporary organisations. Foucauldian critical analysis of institutional practices aims to uncover the techniques and relations of power implicit in the constitution of organisational objects and subjects. Given the interest of Foucault on educational and psychological practices (Foucault, 1977, 1978), it is understandable that human resources management has received a wealth of attention in the recent debates inspired by poststructuralist theory. As to HRM, this perspective has been reflected in critical analyses of HRM practices and discourses and their implications (Barratt, 2003; Legge, 1989; McKinlay & Starkey, 1998; Townley, 1993).

In an attempt to develop a generalised research agenda for the CMS community, Alvesson and Willmott (2003) introduce five general themes that define the theoretical and epistemological approach taken by critical management scholars:

1. Developing a non-objective view of management techniques and processes: management techniques such as those practised in HRM (selection, assessment, career development) are not merely technical procedures as they are deeply implicated in constructing the social realities and relations in the workplaces. Formal techniques are subjective or reality constituting in the same way as informal social practices.
2. Exposing asymmetrical power relations: organisations are micro-cosms that enact and reproduce wider power structures. Critical inquiry is motivated to expose and challenge the privileged position of corporate elites such as top managerial classes. Ideas like the division of labour between the strategic apex and the rest of the organisation are seen as political constellations that sustain inequality between different occupational or social groups.
3. Counteracting discursive closure: rational management practices are often taken for granted and not openly debated. Critical management studies aims to break up the communicative closures and to prompt democratic dialogue between the various stakeholders.
4. Revealing the partiality of shared interests: organisational goals and corporate decisions are often legitimised as being in the interest of the whole organisation or economy. However, a critical perspective reveals that shared interests often represent the aspirations of a limited clique (top managers, economic elite, state elite) instead of being declarations of negotiated intentions of a wider set of viewpoints.
5. Appreciating the centrality of language and communicative action: language is a socio-historical realm that carries, reproduces and transforms social realities and relations in and around organisations. Linguistic or discursive focus serves as a bridge between the issues related to power, class and ideology and the local construction of social meanings in organisational life.

We subscribe to these ideas, and wish to present specific critical perspectives as fruitful avenues to further these interests in the context of comparative HRM.

Critical Perspectives on Comparative HRM

Having introduced a critical approach to management studies, we turn our attention back to comparative HRM. As noted, there is a need to account for and analyse the spread of new employment practices and organisational forms, associated with the emerging hegemony of neoliberal policies across countries and regions. This type of critical agenda could be informed and further developed by three theoretical and methodological approaches, namely global labour process theory, postcolonial discourse analysis and transnational feminism. We will introduce their respective theoretical and methodological assumptions next (see Table 4.1).

Global Labour Process Theory

Global labour process theory (GLPT) is an application of the main tenets of labour process theory to the globalising economy and working life. Whereas the traditional LPT research has tended to focus on nation-states and their organisation and management of work, Global LPT takes a more explicitly global or transnational look. The aim is to analyse how deskilling and related phenomena appear in contexts other than those researched in the United States and British studies of labour processes and management. With multinational corporations extending their operations to non-Western countries and the Anglo-American liberal market economy occupying a dominant role in the worldwide structuring of societies and organisations, it is of interest to test the deskilling hypothesis in new national and cultural environments. The GLPT research is particularly interested in analysing whether there is an emerging convergence of employment management practices and organisational forms. The focus is on the adoption of neo-Fordist and neo-Taylorist HRM practices that manifest the intensification of managerial control. Unlike the more inductive convergence–divergence debates, GLPT takes as its starting point the deskilling hypothesis originally introduced by Braverman and subsequently empirically studied and theoretically elaborated by a number of organisational scholars. However, GLPT is slightly more attuned to the contemporary theorising that takes into account the role of agency and subjectivity in the organising of social relations at work (Knights & Willmott, 1989). In this regard, it departs from the 'orthodox' LPT and its structuralistic assumptions about social and organisational life that have tended to neglect the role of subjective experiences and interpretations. This can also be seen in the methodology: GLPT uses qualitative methods such as field studies and organisational cases to complement the more broad-brush approaches such as surveys. At the same time, however,

Table 4.1 Three critical perspectives on comparative human resource management

	Global Labour Process Theory	Postcolonial Discourse Analysis	Transnational feminism
Background influences	Labour Process theory: Braverman 1974 Reconstructed Labour Process theory: Willmott & Knights, 1989	Discourse analysis: Foucault (1977, 1978) Postcolonial theory: Saïd (1978), Bhabha (1994), Spivak (1987), Young (2001)	Feminist theories Postcolonial theory: (Spivak, 1987) Transnational feminism: Mohanty (2004)
Focus	Global convergence of management of work	Institutional-cultural differences between West and non-West (as constructed in practices and discourses)	Divisions of labour and social relations between men and women in globalising world, and differences in them
Research questions	How global convergence links to the spread of capitalist principles and practices Is there a trend towards deskilling around the world? Are emerging economies adapting neo-Fordist or neo-Taylorist management methods?	What are the underlying assumptions about West and non-West in comparative HRM? How are West and non-West represented in discourses of comparative management research and practice?	How are workplace and social relations organised between men and women in global capitalism in different locations? How do Western conceptions of Third World women reproduce domination and subjugation?

	Are there national variations in the adoption of neo-Fordist techniques? How are employees across the world experiencing new organisational forms and management practices?	What are the implications of the identities of the West and the non-West to the structuring of power? What kinds of practices are being legitimised with reference to colonial identities and rhetoric?	Are there alternative discourses that allow one to go beyond simplified categories of 'gender' and 'Third World'? What role do HRM practices and discourses play in reproducing particular identities and subjectivities?
Epistemology	Objectivist/realist	Subjectivist/constructionist	Subjectivist/constructionist
Ontology	Structural	Relational	Structural and relational
Methods	Field work, organisational case studies National comparisons	Discourse analysis Critical reading of canonical texts Case studies	Discourse analysis Activism
Exemplary studies	Hassard et al. (2006)	Westwood (2001) Vaara et al. (2005)	Mohanty (2004)

GLPT is inclined to adopt a more realist stance on epistemology than some of the alternative interpretative and poststructuralist perspectives.

GLPT is to our mind perhaps best exemplified by the studies of a British team of Hassard, Morris and McCann. Their empirical research has studied the changing work and organisation patterns in a variety of national contexts, including UK, United States, Germany, Japan and China. Empirical data for the research programme has been drawn from organisational case studies of large and mid-sized companies undergoing major restructurings. Qualitative material includes interviews with senior and HRM management, as well as with employees from a variety of levels. In some cases, field studies are complemented with macro-data from surveys and economic statistics. Methodologically, Hassard et al. advocate a middle of the road position, which tries to get closer to the lived experiences and personal meanings of the employees without losing sight of the contextual and political structures affecting the organisation of working life in modern companies. Their approach can be seen as a response to the critiques of traditional structural theories that they ignore the role of subjectivity in the actualisation and reproduction of social structures (Giddens, 1979, 1984; Knights & Willmott, 1989). In short, the aim is to provide a counterweight to the under-socialised accounts of the mainstream international and comparative management research while at the same time arguing for a realist reading of the employee informants' narratives.

Research studies have revealed the structuring of work and human resource management against the continuing capitalist accumulation of surplus value in the globalised modernity. In their study of Japanese middle managers, Morris, Hassard and McCann (2006; McCann et al., 2004) found that the Japanese management culture, famous for its focus on lifetime employment, strong corporate culture and seniority-based hierarchy, shows signs of moving towards an Anglo-American model of individualised employment terms and flatter hierarchies. Management layers have been reduced in many companies to comply with the post-bureaucratic ideal celebrated in the market ideologies of the new organisational forms, although elements of the more stable hierarchies have remained. Similarly, companies have been forced to abandon the tradition of lifetime employment as restructurings have led to redundancies and early retirement arrangements. Career moves and reward system have become more individualised and competitive instead of following the traditional Japanese emphasis on seniority and collective unity.

In comparison, the middle managers in a number of UK corporations seem to have experienced a more direct transformation. McCann, Morris and Hassard (2008) report that the middle managers interviewed all reported increasing workloads and pace of change. Many companies have cut their workforces, including also middle management, and the remaining employees have faced longer working hours, intensifying monitoring of their performance as well as tightening competition over the shrinking vacancies at the top management level. To some extent, the restructurings have meant constant re-skilling of the individual competencies of the employees but this has come with the price of having to lead ever more dispersed and fragmented teams and projects. Recent changes have often led to serious cases of stress and even deep burnout among middle managers continuing in their jobs after downsizings and restructurings.

The main argument from these studies is that although the changes among the UK and Japanese middle managers are not structurally similar, there is a remarkable similarity in the way recent work and HRM related transformations are experienced at the employee level. Hassard and his colleagues refer to the influence of the neoliberal ideology that has led to organisational arrangements such as the demolition of the internal labour market, rise of performance-related pay, reduced job security and increased work hours, all implemented in the name of international competitiveness. Although the factual statistical labour data does not always support the argument that changes they identify are widespread, the subjective experiences and the way middle managers and other employees interpret their situation give rise to global convergence. Insofar as employees in a variety of national-institutional contexts construct their own organisational environment as highly individualised, competitive and uncertain, the global convergence of employment management becomes produced as an enduring reality.

Comparative study of middle managers in the UK and Japan is an interesting application of some of the ideas of what we have labelled GLPT. The work of Hassard et al. contains an underlying assumption that global capitalism is intimately connected to the intensification of the labour process, manifested as increased workloads and the introduction of neo-Taylorist techniques such as the close surveillance of individual performance and the installing of individualistic reward systems. This process touches not only the rich industrial countries but also the less developed economies: although the empirical studies mainly focus on developed industrial nations, a similar type of approach could be applied for researching the effects of the new ideologies on the working conditions and experiences of the employees in developed countries. The hypothesis of globally intensifying labour process is then explored through case studies of different organisations across a variety of national-institutional contexts. While there are national-institutional variations in the way in which the labour process is transformed, the overall trend is towards intensified control and exploitation of the worker input, including also middle managers.

Postcolonial Discourse Analysis

Postcolonial Discourse Analysis (PCDA) is an interpretative form of critical inquiry. It has its roots in the pioneering work of Saïd. Saïd's study on Orientalism (Saïd, 1978) opened new avenues for analysing the relations between West and non-West, which has led to an emergence of postcolonial analysis as a theory in its own right (Bhabha, 1994; Spivak, 1987; Young, 2001). According to Saïd, 'Orient', or, more generally, non-West, is a Western construction. Analysing the discursive production of West and non-West is influenced by the ideas of critical theory where ideological beliefs about various social groups are seen as manifestations of dominance and hegemony. In addition, Saïd's approach has been inspired by the work of Foucault, especially in regards to how the non-West, or the Other, is constructed in various linguistic and institutional practices. Foucault's (1977, 1978) ideas have helped postcolonial theory to study both non-West and West as mutually sustaining subject positions that are ideologically imposed but at the same time empower those who adapt them as bases of identity and agency. This hybrid theoretical background has given rise to a vivid research programme, also applied to organisation and management studies (e.g. Prasad, 1997, 2003; Westwood, 2001, 2004, 2006; Westwood & Jack, 2006, 2007).

While there are numerous potential objects of inquiry, perhaps the most interesting stream of research has focused on the way in which differences between West and non-West are constructed in the theory and practice of international management. Following Saïd and other postcolonial writers, organisational studies have concentrated on the production and consumption of ideas about cultural identity in discursive and institutional practices. The main questions have been 'How are West and non-West represented and constructed in discourses of comparative management?' and 'What are the implications of colonial identities to the structuring of power in West non-West relations?' The research programme is epistemologically constructionist or relativist, meaning that it is mainly interested in the linguistic and textual articulations of identities and social relations, acknowledging that its own truth claims are also rhetorical accomplishments that have no external reference point outside of the discussion into which they participate. Constructionist epistemology is complemented with a relational ontology that assumes that the social world is composed of emerging and evolving relations of actors and identities. In terms of methodology, PDA leans on discourse analytical approaches, which implies a close reading of selected disciplinary, institutional and media texts in order to reveal the tacit privileges and hierarchies inscribed to the meaning constructions of literary and oral representations of cultural difference.

Postcolonial discourse analysis looks at the discursive processes of producing identities and relations between West and non-West. Essentially, PDA aims to reveal the implicit Western perspective in the allegedly 'neutral' descriptions and representations of non-West, West and the relations between them. As such, its empirical scope is somewhat broader than that of GLPT, encompassing a wealth of scientific, disciplinary and institutional (e.g. media) texts engaging with international relations and business management.

This has led scholars to inquire about the underlying assumptions of authoritative texts such as the academic writings on cross cultural management (Kwek, 2003) and stereotypical notions that are reproduced in textbooks on international management (Tipton, 2008). Westwood (2001, 2006) has provided particularly insightful analyses that criticise the very conceptions that characterise comparative international management. The point is that the Other (non-West) is always represented as underdeveloped, dangerous, exotic or mystical while the West is seen as developed, modern, rational, and normal. Although these analyses have not only focused on IHRM practices, the conclusion is clear: both the problems (HRM and other management issues) and the solutions (specific HRM practices) that are usually considered in this field echo this colonial mindset. Thus, postcolonial analysis can bring another critical perspective to comparative IHRM by deepening our understanding of the fundamental reasons of what is seen as normal and natural and what is not – as well as the implications of such assumptions.

Another important aspect of postcolonial analysis is its linkage to neocolonialism (Banerjee & Linstead, 2001, 2004). In this view, neocolonial means a new form of colonialism linked with contemporary globalisation. Corporate-driven globalisation tends to imply homogenisation and American cultural imperialism. While this is a relevant point for most areas of international management research, IHRM is a case in point here. As illustrated by the recent writings in comparative HRM (Brewster, 2007), the American dominance is evident in the assumptions that the specific practices originating from US corporations would be universal, normal, or transferrable to all places on the globe. This kind of neo-colonialism is not, however, normal or natural, and such assumptions bring with them cultural insensitivity, stereotypical thinking and prejudice – in the worst cases, something that comes close to xenophobia. Furthermore, such thinking is ideological in the sense of reproducing neoliberal ideals and Anglo-American hegemony.

Although postcolonial analysis is often thought to apply mainly to classic cases of colonial (Western) powers and colonised ones (non-West), constructions of postcolonial relationships can be found elsewhere, too. A revealing example is provided by Vaara et al. (2005), who have studied mergers and acquisitions in the Nordic financial services sector. Among other things, they analysed the language policy in a Finnish–Swedish merger, which led to the choice of Swedish as the official language. Their analysis showed how language skills can be seen as empowering or disempowering resources in organisational communication, how language skills became associated with professional competence, and how this led to the creation of new social networks that favoured Swedish-speakers. The case also illustrated how language can be regarded as an essential element in the construction of international confrontation, how this policy led to a construction of superiority (Swedes) and inferiority (Finns), and also reproduced post-colonial identities in the merging bank (Swedes as the colonial power). Finally, they also pointed out how such policies ultimately led to the reification of post-colonial and neo-colonial structures of domination in this setting. However, despite the interesting dynamics inside Europe, it is appropriate to note that the main interest of postcolonial theory lies in the contested power relations between the advanced West and the developing countries of the East and South.

Transnational Feminism

Feminism provides an array of critical perspectives that can be useful in comparative HRM. This, however, requires a broad conception of HRM and the key issues at play. One of key points of feminist organisation and management studies has been to extend organisation analysis to issues such as civil rights, well-being, equal opportunities, work–life balance, family and sexuality. These issues are not usually seen as the immediate concerns of management in general or (I)HRM in particular; however, the feminist argument is that they should be. In fact, in addition to bringing up marginalised or silenced issues, or giving voice to those who are under-represented or in a less privileged position, feminism emphasises societal and corporate responsibility for such issues.

Feminism has a great deal to offer to contemporary analyses of globalisation from the point of view of linking the global division of labour to social relations between women and men and gendered social practices in and around organisations. For example, Calás and Smircich (1993) showed how a discourse that emphasises women's specific qualities in management is appropriated by management writers. Calás and Smircich demonstrated how this discourse serves to legitimate the gendered status quo where men occupy the central positions in the international arena while women 'keep the home fires burning'. Such observations have clear linkages to IHRM – especially in terms of explaining why inequality still prevails at top echelons in global corporations.

There is, however, not one form of feminism, but many. For example, Calás and Smircich (2006) distinguish liberal, radical, psychoanalytic, socialist, poststructuralist/postmodern and transnational/(post)colonial feminism. We will here focus attention on transnational feminism because of its potential for opening up new avenues for critical analysis in comparative HRM. The key characteristic of transnational feminism is that while it continues to probe into central questions of inequality from a feminist angle, it also problematises key assumptions of Western feminism. This is the case especially with how dominant Western feminist discourses tend to construct the women in the Third World. In this sense, transnational feminism is linked with postcolonial analysis. For instance, Mohanty (1997, 2004) has made the point that Western discourses of Third World women construct them as oppressed, underdeveloped and lacking essential qualities that they 'should have'. This picture is problematic precisely in the sense that again Western models and ideologies are naturalised, and the multiple and different cultural issues and values that are relevant are disregarded. As a result, the constructions of 'normal' or preferred careers, responsibilities at work and at home, equal opportunities and related HRM practices remain one-sided and ideologically laden. Moreover, even the well-intended feminist analyses easily portray Third World women as victims and passive recipients of knowledge and aid, thus reducing their agency and subjectivity.

Some forms of transnational feminism also question the usefulness of 'gender' as a sufficient category to be applied across cultures. It is less clear what the alternative is, but the implication is that future analyses of (I)HRM would do well to map out various complex linkages between gender, race, religion, nationality, education, career and sexuality without assuming that the solutions that appear the most natural or progressive from the Western point of view would be that for other cultures, religious settings, forms of family and so forth.

Mohanty (1997) provides an analysis that advances such understanding. Her critical starting point is that exploitation in its various kinds is linked with the political economy of globalisation in its material and discursive forms. She has chosen to speak of 'One-Third/Two-Thirds' worlds instead of the common notion of the 'Third World'. Through such discursive choices, she has focused attention on commonly held and naturalised conceptions that deal with the legitimacy of Western consumerism and its ideals set for women – as well as men – in different parts of the world. As a way to improve the state of affairs, she has called for transnational solidarity building and struggle against harmful forms of globalisation (Mohanty, 2004).

Such reflections may at first appear remote for comparative HRM, but we maintain that they are not, if we wish to pursue broad understanding of the issues that HRM can or should be dealing with, and a critical attitude toward the universalist 'best practices' and other solutions provided. The fact remains, however, that to date we lack studies that would spell out the full-fledged implications of transnational feminism on IHRM and comparative HRM. This is a major challenge for future research.

CONCLUSION

The starting point for this chapter has been a need to spell out specific ways in which we could advance critical analysis in comparative HRM. We think that comparative HRM – more than other approaches or emergent sub-fields in HRM – can precisely lead to better understanding of broader social and societal issues in and around globalising organisations. For this purpose, we have argued that comparative HRM should be linked with critical management studies; at least in the sense that comparative HRM could make use of specific theoretical and methodological approaches that have already proven useful in other areas and have particular potential in view of the issues that IHRM can and should deal with. Hence, we have proposed global labour process theory, postcolonial analysis, and transnational feminism as examples of perspectives that can further advance the comparative approach to HRM. As our discussion has illustrated, there are seminal studies that at least implicitly already deal with key issues of HRM in globalising organisations and economy. However, it is equally clear that a great deal can and should be done to further our understanding in these important and fascinating areas. It is also important to note that our discussion of the three critical perspectives is in no way meant as an exhaustive presentation of the available critical perspectives on comparative human resource management. Rather, we would like to invite a multitude of different theoretical programs to enrich and challenge the current state-of-the-art in this developing area of management studies scholarship.

REFERENCES

Alvesson, M. & Deetz, S. 2006. Critical theory and postmodernism approaches to organizational studies. In S. Clegg, C. Hardy, B. Lawrence & W. R. Nord (eds), *The Sage Handbook of Organization Studies*. London: Sage Publications.

Alvesson, M. & Willmott, H. 1996. *Making Sense of Management*. London: Sage Publications.

Alvesson, M. & Willmott, H. 2003. *Studying Management Critically*. London: Sage Publications.

Banerjee, S. B. & Linstead, S. 2001. Globalization, multiculturalism and other fictions: colonialism for the new millennium? *Organization*, **8**(4): 683–722.

Banerjee, S. B. & Linstead, S. 2004. Masking subversion: neocolonial embeddedness in anthropological accounts of indigenous management. *Human Relations*, **57**(2): 221–247.

Barley, S. & Kunda, G. 1992. Design and devotion: surges of rational and normative ideologies of control in managerial discourse. *Administrative Science Quarterly*, **47**: 363–399.

Barratt, E. 2003. Foucault, HRM and the ethos of the critical management scholar. *Journal of Management Studies*, **40**(5): 1069–1087.

Bauman, Z. 2000. *Liquid Modernity*. Cambridge, UK: Polity.

Bhabha, H. 1994. *The Location of Culture*. London: Routledge.

Braverman, H. 1974. *Labour and Monopoly Capital: The Degradation of Work in The Twentieth Century*. New York: Monthly Review Press.

Brewster, C. 1999. Strategic human resource management: the value of different paradigms. In R. S. Schuler & S. Jackson (eds), *Strategic Human Resource Management: A Reader*. Oxford: Blackwell.

Brewster, C. 2007. Comparative HRM: European views and perspectives. *International Journal of Human Resource Management*, **18**(5): 769–787.

Brewster, C., & Hegewisch, A. 1994. Policy and Practice in European Human Resource Management: The Price Waterhouse Cranfield Survey. London: Routledge.

Brewster, C., Mayrhofer, W. & Morley, M. (eds) 2004. *Human Resource Management in Europe. Evidence of Convergence?* Oxford: Elsevier/Butterworth-Heinemann.

Burrell, G. & Morgan, G. 1979. *Sociological Paradigms and Organizational Analysis*. Oxford: Elsevier/Butterworth-Heinemann.

Calás, M. B. & Smircich, L. 1993. Dangerous liaisons: the 'feminine in management' meets 'globalization'. *Business Horizons*, **36**(2): 73–83.

Calas, M. B. & Smircich, L. 2006. From the 'woman's point of view' ten years later: towards a feminist organization studies. In S. Clegg, C. Hardy & W. R. Nord (eds), *The Sage Handbook of Organization Studies*, 2nd edn, London: Sage Publications, pp. 284-346.

Clark, T. & Pugh, D. 2000. Similarities and differences in European conceptions of human resource management. *International Studies in Management and Organization*, **29**(4): 84–100.

Dickmann, M., Brewster, C. & Sparrow, P. R. 2008. *International Human Resource Management: A European Perspective*. London: Routledge.

Dore, R. 2000. *Stock Market Capitalism: Welfare Capitalism: Japan and Germany Versus the Anglo-Saxons*. Oxford: Oxford University Press.

Drori, G., Meyer, J. W. & Hwang, H. 2006. *Globalization and Organization: World Society and Organizational Change*. Oxford: Oxford University Press.

Foucault, M. 1977. *Discipline and Punish*. London: Penguin.

Foucault, M. 1978. *History of Sexuality*. New York: Pantheon Books.

Ghoshal, S. 2005. Bad management theories are destroying good management practices. *Academy of Management Learning & Education*, **14**(1): 75–91.

Giddens, A. 1979. *Central Problems in Social Theory*. London: Macmillan.

Giddens, A. 1984. *The Constitution of Society*. Cambridge: Polity.

Granovetter, M. 1985. Economic action and social structure: the problem of embeddedness. *American Sociological Review*, **91**(3): 481–510.

Habermas, J. 1972. *Knowledge and Human Interests.* Oxford: Elsevier/ Butterworth-Heinemann.

Habermas, J. 1984. *The Theory of Communicative Action. Vol 1. Reason and the Rationalization of Society.* Oxford: Elsevier/Butterworth-Heinemann.

Hall, P. & Soskice, D. 2001. *Varieties of Capitalism: the Institutional Foundations of Comparative Advantage.* New York: Oxford University Press.

Hassard, J., McCann, L. & Morris, J. 2007. At the sharp end of new organizational ideologies: ethnography and the study of multinationals. *Ethnography*, **8**(3): 324–344.

Jackson, T. 2004. HRM in developing countries. In A.-W. Harzing & J. V. Ruysseveldt (eds), *International Human Resource Management.* London: Sage Publications.

Keating, M. & Thompson, K. 2004. International human resource management: overcoming disciplinary sectarianism. *Employee Relations*, **26**(6): 595–612.

Knights, D. & Willmott, H. 1989. Power and subjectivity at work: from degradation to subjugation in social relations. *Sociology*, **23**(4): 535–558.

Kunda, G. & Ailon-Suday, G. 2005. Managers, markets and ideologies: design and devotion revisited. In S. Ackroyd, R. Batt, P. Thompson & P. S. Tolbert (eds), *The Oxford Handbook of Work and Organization.* Oxford: Oxford University Press.

Kwek, D. 2003. Decolonizing and re-presenting culture's consequences: a postcolonial critique of cross-cultural studies in management. In A. Prasad (ed.), *Postcolonial Theory and Organizational Analysis: A Critical Engagement.* New York: Palgrave Macmillan.

Legge, K. 1989. Human resource management: a critical analysis. In J. Storey (ed.), *New Perspectives on Human Resource Management.* London: Routledge, pp. 19–40.

Lilja, K. 1998. Finland. In A. Ferner & R. Hyman (eds), *Changing Industrial Relations in Europe.* Oxford: Blackwell.

Lindeberg, T., Manson, B. & Vanhala, S. 2004. Sweden and Finland: small countries with large companies. In C. Brewster, W. Mayrhofer & M. Morley (eds), *Human Resource Management in Europe: Evidence of Convergence?* Oxford: Elsevier/ Butterworth-Heinemann.

Maurice, M. & Sorge, A. 2000. *Embedding Organizations: Societal Analysis of Actors, Organizations and Socio-Economic Context.* Amsterdam: John Benjamins.

McCann, L., Hassard, J. & Morris, J. 2004. Middle managers, the new organizational ideology and corporate restructuring: comparing Japanese and Anglo-American management systems. *Competition and Change*, **8**(1): 27–44.

McCann, L., Morris, J. & Hassard, J. 2008. Normalized intensity: the new labour process of middle management. *The Journal of Management Studies*, **45**(2): 343.

McKinlay, A. & Starkey, K. P. 1998. *Foucault, Management and Organization Theory: From Panopticon to Technologies of Self.* London: Sage Publications.

Mintzberg, H. 2004. *Managers not MBAs.* San Francisco: Barrett-Koehler.

Mohanty, C. T. 1997. Women workers and capitalist scripts: ideologies of domination, common interests, and the politics of solidarity. In J. Alexander & C. T. Mohanty (eds), *Feminist Genealogies, Colonial Legacies, Democratic Futures.* New York: Routledge, pp. 3–29.

Mohanty, C. T. 2004. *Feminism Without Borders.* Durham & London: Duke University Press.

Morgan, G., Kristensen, P. H. & Whitley, R. 2001. *The Multinational Firm: Organizing Across Institutional and National Divides.* Oxford: Oxford University Press.

Morgan, G., & Smircich, L. 1980. The case for qualitative research. *Academy of Management Review*, **5**(4): 491–500.

Morris, J., Hassard, J. & McCann, L. 2006. New organizational forms, human resource management and structural convergence: a study of Japanese organizations. *Organization Studies*, **27**(10): 1485–1511.

Pfeffer, J. & Fong, C. 2005. The business school 'business': some lessons from the US experience. *Journal of Management Studies*, **41**(8): 1501–1520.

Prasad, A. 1997. The colonizing consciousness and representations of the other. In P. Prasad (ed.), *Managing the Organizational Melting Pot.* London: Sage Publications.

Prasad, A. 2003. *Postcolonial Theory and Organizational Analysis*. London: Palgrave.

Quack, S., Morgan, G. & Whitley, R. 2000. *National Capitalisms, Global Competition and Economic Performance*. Amsterdam: John Benjamins Publishing.

Saïd, E. 1978. *Orientalism*. New York: Vintage Books.

Scott, R. 2001. *Institutions and Organizations*, 2nd edn. London: Sage Publications.

Sennett, R. 1998. *The Corrosion of Character: The Personal Consequences of Work in the New Capitalism*. London: W. W. Norton.

Sennett, R. 2006. *The Culture of the New Capitalism*. New Haven, CT: Yale University Press.

Spivak, G. 1987. *In Other Worlds: Essays in Cultural Politics*. New York: Methuen.

Tainio, R. & Lilja, K. 2002. The Finnish business system in transition: outcomes, actors, and their influence. In B. Czaniawska & G. Sevon (eds), *The Northern Lights: Organization Theory in Scandinavia*. Malmö: Liber.

Tipton, F. B. 2008. Thumbs-up is a rude gesture in Australia: the presentation of culture in international business textbooks. *Critical Perspectives on International Business*, **4**: 7–24.

Townley, B. 1993. Foucault, power/knowledge, and its relevance for human resource management. *Academy of Management Review*, **18**(3): 519–545.

Vaara, E., Tienari, J., Piekkari, R. & Säntti, R. 2005. Language and the circuits of power in a merging multinational corporation. *Journal of Management Studies*, **42**(3): 595–623.

Westwood, R. 2001. Appropriating the other in discourses of comparative management. In R. Westwood & S. Linstead (eds), *The Language of Organization*. London: Sage Publications.

Westwood, R. 2004. Towards a postcolonial research paradigm in international business and comparative management. In R. Marschan-Piekkari & C. Welch (eds), *Handbook of Qualitative Research Methods in International Business*. Cheltenham, UK: Edward Elgar.

Westwood, R. 2006. International business and management studies as an orientalist discourse: a postcolonial critique. *Critical Perspectives on International Business*, **2**(2): 91–113.

Westwood, R. & Jack, G. 2006. Postcolonialism and the politics of qualitative research in international business. *Management International Review*, **46**(4): 481–501.

Westwood, R. & Jack, G. 2007. Manifesto for a post-colonial international business and management studies: a provocation. *Critical Perspectives on International Business*, **3**(3): 246.

Whitley, R. & Kristensen, P. H. 1996. *The Changing European Firm*. London: Routledge.

Whitley, R. 2002. *Competing Capitalism: Institutions and Economies*. Volumes 1 and 2. Cheltenham, UK: Edward Elgar.

Wikipedia. 2009. Global financial crisis of 2008–2009. Available at: http://en.wikipedia.org/w/index.php?title=Global_financial_crisis_of_2008%E2%80%932009&oldid=279166396.

Young, R. 2001. *Postcolonialism: An Historical Introduction*. Oxford: Blackwell.

5 Empirical research issues in comparative HRM

Ingo Weller and Barry Gerhart

Human resource management (HRM) is about the policies, practices and systems that influence organisational effectiveness by affecting employees' behaviour, attitudes, and performance. HRM shapes and influences the human capital of the organisation (Noe et al., 2006). Its ultimate goal is to provide business value through the management of people (Barney & Wright, 1998; Becker & Gerhart, 1996). Successful strategy execution depends on the HRM system effectively developing and motivating its human capital and making sure that structures and processes permit it to be put to productive use. In this chapter we discuss methodological challenges in doing empirical research on HRM and effectiveness in the field of comparative HRM. Some methodological issues we discuss here will be specific to comparative HRM research, while others apply to HRM research in both single-nation and comparative contexts.

It is widely recognised that cross-country differences are important for the management of people in organisations. As highlighted by new institutionalists (Wood et al., this volume), countries differ in regulations, institutions, and culture (Brewster, 1999; Brewster et al., 2004; Dowling et al., 2008; Evans et al., 2002; Hofstede, 1980, 2001; Kostova, 1999). While new institutionalism covers a range of fairly heterogeneous approaches, the basic premise is that advances in technology and communications lead to less diversification globally (Wood et al., in this volume), a process called isomorphism (Kostova & Roth, 2002). Thus, the institutionalist approach stresses the tendency of organisations to respond to their environment in ways that signal conformity and enhance legitimacy (DiMaggio & Powell, 1983; Meyer & Rowan, 1977). To the degree that 'final convergence' (Mayrhofer & Brewster, 2005; Tregaskis & Brewster, 2006) is limited by national regulations, institutions and culture, institutionalists would expect that the managerial discretion of multinational firms is constrained by the respective national settings they are operating in. Following this line of thought, some of the key questions of comparative HRM research are: (1) How much do countries differ in their use of particular HRM practices and systems? (2) What specific country characteristics account for country effects? (3) To what degree do certain HRM practices and systems fit certain countries and show misfit in others, as evidenced by effectiveness outcomes? and (4) To what degree are differences in either use or effectiveness of HRM practices/systems stable versus changing over time?

A common explanation for country differences/effects is national culture (Kirkman et al., 2006). In thinking about the four key questions raised above, it is clear that one theme is an interest in understanding the degree to which organisations are constrained by country differences such as national culture in choosing which HRM practices/systems to use. To the degree organisations are constrained, it suggests the need for them to localise HRM to fit different country contexts, rather than standardise across countries towards a global version of HRM (Dowling et al., 2008). In the case of national culture, the constraint argument has been made frequently (e.g. Adler, 2002; Early & Erez, 1997; Hofstede, 1983, 1993, 2001; House et al., 2004; Laurent, 1983; Trompenaars & Hampden-Turner, 2000). In other words, the answer from this perspective to the four questions above would be that HRM practices differ significantly between countries, have differential effectiveness across countries, and remain stable over time. National culture would be seen as the key reason for these country effects. The implication for organisations then is that they need to localise (rather than standardise) HRM to a considerable degree to fit different national cultures.

However, the empirical support for these conclusions, upon close examination of the empirical evidence is less compelling than might be expected (Gerhart, 2008a; Gerhart & Fang, 2005; Kirkman et al., 2006). For example, Gerhart and Fang (2005) re-examined Hofstede's results and found that about 4 per cent of the variance in individual cultural values was explained by country membership (as measured by the ICC(1)). Given that Hofstede's study was conducted with a single firm (IBM), one can easily conclude that the results are indicative of strong self-selection tendencies of individuals into certain organisations, and that organisations have quite some discretion in 'exporting' their organisational cultures. In addition, there is more evidence that organisations do show varying degrees of consistency across countries in HRM and other organisation practices. In another example, Beck, Kabst and Walgenbach (2009) – analysing a sample of 14 European countries from the Cranet project (Brewster et al., 2004) – found headquarters influence on subsidiary management practices, when headquarters and subsidiaries operated in different countries and systems of vocational education and training. In the light of their findings, they suggested considerable potential for managerial agency above and beyond local cultural influences. Other research has also documented headquarters effects on HRM (e.g. Ferner & Quintanilla, 1998; Quintanilla & Ferner, 2003) and/or organisation practices (Kostova & Roth, 2002), again suggesting that organisations have some discretion and do not necessarily find the need to localise all aspects of HRM fully.

Certainly, there are both constraints and room for discretion (Brewster, 1999; Dowling et al., 2008; Gerhart, 2008a). Our objective here is not to provide a comprehensive review of the literature in an attempt to conclusively say what their relative importance is. Instead, we wish to caution against focusing only on constraints and to map out in this chapter some ideas and methods that should be useful in understanding the relative role of constraints and discretion. For interesting substantive work on the constraints versus discretion debate, in addition to that discussed above, we also refer the reader to work by Brewster et al. (2004); Pudelko et al. (2006); and Pudelko and Harzing (2007).

Our discussion of quantitative methods in comparative HRM-effectiveness research focuses on two major conceptual and technical challenges that comparative HRM researchers (and also single-country HRM researchers) must deal with: level of analysis and inferring causality in studying the HRM-effectiveness link. Comparative HRM research is necessarily a multilevel endeavour. For example, country effects (e.g. national cultures, institutions and legal regulations, industrial and competitive forces, etc.) may vary in the degree to which they constrain versus enable managerial agency in managing HRM (Gerhart, 2008a, b; Gerhart & Fang, 2005). Staffing practices may differ across countries (e.g. because of country legislation) and organisations (e.g. because of firm histories; Dierickx & Cool, 1989), and attract workers with specific knowledge stocks, skills and abilities that they anticipate will fit the organisation (Bloom & Milkovich, 1999; Ployhart, 2006; Schneider, 1987). As such, there are three basic levels to consider: individuals, firms and countries. In comparative HRM research, we need to determine at which level of analysis the main source of variation (and explanatory power) resides.

The ultimate goal of the HRM function is to create business value, which is important for multiple stakeholders, including, of course, shareholders and employees. To understand whether and to what degree HRM influences effectiveness, it is desirable to use designs (e.g. longitudinal) that permit stronger causal inferences, and to be aware of specification challenges that may arise, as well as the statistical methods available that can potentially deal with these challenges. It is also important to be as specific as possible regarding the magnitude of HRM effects (i.e. report relevant effect size estimates). These considerations are important in both single-country and comparative HRM research. To give policy advice, we need to be as confident as possible of what HRM's effects really are.

This chapter is organised as follows: in the next section we provide a short outline of the multilevel structure of comparative HRM research with a focus on culture research; we explain the potential pitfalls in the analysis of multilevel data, and provide recommendations on how to analyse such data. More specifically, we introduce HLM techniques (hierarchical linear modelling) to solve some of the problems frequently encountered in comparative HRM research. The section after that deals with the HRM-performance link and, in particular, highlights specification errors in management-performance regression models. Among others, we explain the endogeneity problem and its potential consequences, and outline a few potential solutions.

MULTIPLE LEVELS OF ANALYSIS IN COMPARATIVE HRM RESEARCH

A fundamental issue in addressing the four central comparative HRM questions is how to most effectively deal with the multilevel nature of conceptual models and the multilevel data needed to test it. We illustrate how hierarchical linear modelling (HLM, e.g. Raudenbush & Bryk, 2002) can be used to address these questions. However, given the central role of concepts such as national culture and HRM practices in such comparative research, we begin with a brief treatment of issues in defining and measuring these constructs before addressing the four substantive comparative HRM questions.

National Culture

Hofstede has defined national culture as the 'collective programming of the mind'. His focus was on cultural values, which he defined as a 'broad tendency to prefer certain states of affairs over others' (1980: 19). Hofstede saw cultural values as 'an attribute of individuals as well as of collectivities' though he stated that 'culture presupposes a collectivity'. Thus, Hofstede's definition of national culture also includes the shared aspect and, likewise, implies that within-country variance (where values are shared) should be considerably less (given 'broad tendency' differences) than between-country variance (Gerhart, 2008b). National culture means are more likely to be effective in explaining country effects to the degree that individual cultural values vary greatly between countries and vary little within countries, consistent with Hofstede's definition. We can use HLM to address this question. Consider a hypothetical example where we have data on 1000 respondents in 10 countries.[1] We use a two-level HLM model. In HLM analysis (Raudenbush & Bryk, 2002; Hox, 2002; Snijders & Bosker, 1999), one typically begins with a 'null model' (i.e., with no independent variables other than intercepts), which is called a 'random intercepts' model. At level 1, the model is:

$$ICV_{ij} = \beta_{0j} + r_{ij}$$

with ICV as the individual cultural values of individual i in country j, β_{0j} as a country specific intercept, and r_{ij} is the idiosyncratic error term. Specific level 1 predictors of ICV (e.g. demographics) could also be added to this model. The country specific intercept is then specified on 'level 2', the macro level, as

$$\beta_{0j} = \gamma_{00} + u_{0j}$$

where γ_{00} is the 'grand mean', and u_{0j} is a country specific error term (a so-called 'random-effect'). Again, this is a random intercepts model, to which could be added specific level 2 explanatory variables. As illustrated in Figure 5.1, the 10 country intercepts (i.e., the β_{0j} terms) will have a certain distribution around the grand mean γ_{00} (note that the grand mean equals the mean of country intercepts only if all of the subgroups have the same size). Around the country means, individual observations will also follow a certain (within-country) distribution. The closer the individual observations are centred around the country intercept (i.e. the smaller the within-country variance), the more reliable is the country intercept. The closer the country means are centred around the grand mean, the less variance in individual cultural values that is explained by country variance relative to individual variance. This relation is easily expressed by the ICC(1), which is defined as the level 2 (between) variance divided by total variance, that is

$$ICC(1) = \tau_{00} / (\tau_{00} + \sigma^2)$$

where τ_{00} is the level 2 variance, $\tau_{00} = Var(u_{0j})$, and σ^2 is the level 1 variance, $\sigma^2 = Var(r_{ij})$.[2] ICC(1) (Bliese, 2000), also known as ICC(1,1) (Shrout & Fleiss, 1979), tells us how much of the variance in individual responses (cultural values) can be predicted by country membership. If all of the individual variance is attributable to country, ICC(1) = 1, all individual responses equal the country means, and σ^2 is zero. If individual variance is completely idiosyncratic, ICC(1) = 0, the country means coincide with the grand mean, and τ_{00} is zero. In most cases, of course, the estimate falls somewhere in between. As we saw in the case of Hofstede's

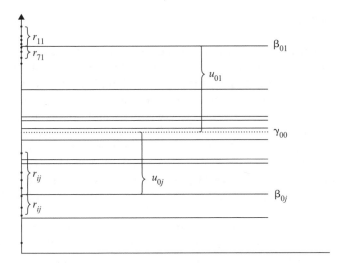

Figure 5.1   Macro and micro variance in individual cultural values

(1980, 2001) data, however, Gerhart and Fang (2005) found an ICC(1) of less than 0.05.

ICC(1) ranges between 0 and 1, and values above 0.10 and 0.25 have been described as medium and large, respectively (Cohen, 1988). In addition to examining the magnitude of the ICC(1) estimate, the statistical significance of the variances should be interpreted. On a different but related note, we can also use HLM strategies to estimate average group-mean reliability. Inferences drawn from small, few, or unevenly sized subsamples may be unreliable. For example, in Figure 5.1 β_{0j} appears less reliable as an intercept estimate than the mean for country 1, β_{01}. An ICC-based coefficient of group-mean reliability is the ICC(2) (Bliese, 2000) or ICC(1,k) (Shrout & Fleiss, 1979).[3]

As a recommendation, researchers should estimate both effect sizes and significance levels to determine the impact of macro level variables (e.g. country) on individual level attributes such as cultural values. Moreover, researchers should report means and standard deviations of the variables of interest for the total sample and for each country (or macro unit) separately. They should realise that low group-mean reliability (low ICC(2) values) may limit the potential to interpret results. However, as noted above, a high ICC(2) does not necessarily imply high predictive power. Reliability, of course, is a necessary, but not sufficient condition for this. In a similar vein, a considerable degree of within-country variation relative to between-country variation (low ICC(1) values) indicates significant potential for managerial agency.

HRM Practices

There are many issues regarding what concepts are most central to HRM and how to measure such concepts. A model that has received increasing attention is the AMO model, which suggests that HRM practices increase organisational effectiveness to the degree that they increase employees' ability to contribute, motivation to contribute, and opportunity to contribute (Appelbaum et al., 2000; Boxall & Purcell, 2003; Gerhart, 2007). Our focus here, however, is on a level of analysis issue that arises in some research intended to examine the effect of HRM. Specifically, one often sees studies that measure HRM practices and assess their impact at the individual level of analysis. Yet, the source of true variance in HRM practices is almost always not individual level, idiosyncratic differences in perceptions of HRM practices, but rather the variance in perceptions of HRM practices that is shared by multiple respondents. We would argue that any study of 'HRM practices' must be conducted at the level of analysis where true variance in HRM practices takes place. In a design with one employee per organisation or unit, it is not possible to compute an ICC. That is a strong indicator that the design is not adequate for studying HRM practices.[4] In other cases, a researcher may have multiple employee respondents from each organisation or unit. There are, in fact, three different options in analysing such data (Raudenbush & Bryk, 2002):

1. Individual level: N = # employees.
2. Aggregate level: N = # employing units (units within a single organisation, units across multiple organisations, or organisations).
3. HLM.

Option 1, the individual level analysis, may not make sense conceptually and may not be supported by the ICC(1). Think of a single organisation study with employees from multiple units. If there is institutional evidence (e.g. a stated policy) that HRM practices are permitted to vary within the organisation, the ICC(1) is likely to be nontrivial, and the individual level design is not likely to be adequate. That is because observations nested within a unit or organisation are dependent to a degree (as indicated by a nonzero ICC(1)), thus violating a key assumption of ordinary least squares.[5] The consequence would be standard errors that are too small, thus increasing the probability of Type I error (i.e. rejecting the null hypothesis when it is true).

Option 2, the aggregate level, averages employee responses (by unit or organisation). The drawback here is that degrees of freedom are lost, compromising statistical power (relative to the HLM option), making Type II errors (failure to reject the null hypothesis when false) more likely.

Option 3, HLM, avoids inflating Type I errors (as in Option 1, individual level analysis) and also has more statistical power than Option 2, the aggregate level analysis. As we have seen, HLM also is useful for understanding at which levels variance is smaller or larger.

KEY COMPARATIVE HRM QUESTIONS AND HLM ANALYSIS

Question 1: How much do countries differ in their use of particular HRM practices and systems?

We begin by specifying a level 1 random intercepts model, but this time at the organisational level, i. The dependent variable could be organisation culture or it could be use of one or more HRM practices, the example we use.

$$\text{HRM}_{ij} = \beta_{0j} + r_{ij}$$

The model could be expanded to include explanatory variables such as size, industry, employee characteristics and other factors thought to influence HRM practices within countries. Next, we specify a level 2 random intercepts only model that specifies the intercepts from the level 1 model as a function of country, j:

$$\beta_{0j} = \gamma_{00} + u_{0j}$$

As before, we can compute the ICC(1) to estimate the overall effect of the level 2 variable, in this case, country.

Question 2: What specific country characteristics (e.g. national culture) account for country effects?

Researchers often mistakenly equate country effects to national culture effects. For example, Bhagat and McQuaid observed that 'culture has often served simply as a synonym for nation. . .[and] national differences found in the characteristics of organisations or their members have been interpreted as cultural differences' (1982: 653–685). In a more recent review article, Yeganeh and Su (2006) similarly state that 'most researchers, especially during the last decade, adhere to a culture-bound perspective' and that this has led to 'overemphasising the importance of culture to the detriment of other social, economic, or contextual variables' and that 'many cross cultural researchers simply [compare] some aspects of organisational behaviour and then, in the absence of other explanations for these differences, attribute them to culture' (2006: 364; see also Schaeffer & Riordan, 2003; Sawang et al., 2006).

Clearly, there is a need to distinguish between country and national culture effects. As the comparative HRM literature recognises, national culture effects are just one of a multitude of contextual effects which may influence HRM use and effectiveness across countries. Employment laws and regulations, industry structure and competition, and other institutional factors (e.g. labour unions) all play some role as well. Thus, researchers need to specify carefully their conceptual model and then take care to ensure that their measures correspond to the theoretical constructs accordingly. Once that is done, HLM is well-suited to decomposing the overall country effect into specific country characteristics, including culture.

To estimate the culture effect, we add national culture means scores (and/or other explanatory variables that may explain country effects) to the level 2 random intercepts model specified above:

$$\beta_{0j} = \gamma_{00} + \gamma_{01} NC_j + u_{0j}$$

where NC_j is the national culture mean score. The ICC(1) estimate obtained from this last model is called a 'conditional ICC' (Raudenbush & Bryk, 2002), which will be the same size (maximum) or smaller than the ICC(1) from the intercepts only model. To estimate the percentage of the overall country effect explained specifically by national culture (i.e. the proportion of variance explained in β_{0j} by national culture), we need to compute the variance of the intercepts (τ_{00}) with and without national culture in the model and use the following equation:

$$[\tau_{00} \text{ (intercepts only)} - \tau_{00} \text{ (national culture)}] / \tau_{00} \text{ (intercepts only)}$$

For example, if τ_{00} (intercepts only) = 100 and τ_{00} (national culture) = 80, then we would have (100 − 80)/100 = 0.20, or 20 per cent of the country effect on HRM explained by national culture.

Question 3: To what degree do certain HRM practices and systems fit certain countries and show misfit in others, as evidenced by effectiveness outcomes?

We again use a two-level HLM model, here with effectiveness as the dependent variable and HRM as the independent variable. We then introduce cross-level interactions (estimated using slopes-as-intercepts models) to determine whether HRM effects vary by country:

$$\text{Effectiveness}_{ij} = \beta_{0j} + \beta_{1j}\,\text{HRM}_{ij} + r_{ij}$$
$$\beta_{0j} = \gamma_{00} + u_{0j}$$
$$\beta_{1j} = \gamma_{10} + u_{1j}$$

In the model, the country effect is accounted for with a random effect, and the interaction with HRM becomes more obvious when we plug the level 2 equations into the level 1 equation:[6]

$$\text{Effectiveness}_{ij} = [\gamma_{00} + u_{0j}] + [\gamma_{10}\,\text{HRM}_{ij} + u_{1j}\,\text{HRM}_{ij}] + r_{ij}$$

We can further expand the model and check if the effectiveness of HRM practices differs by country and also national cultures:

$$\text{Effectiveness}_{ij} = \beta_{0j} + \beta_{1j}\,\text{HRM}_{ij} + r_{ij}$$
$$\beta_{0j} = \gamma_{00} + \gamma_{01}\,\text{NC}_j + u_{0j}$$
$$\beta_{1j} = \gamma_{10} + \gamma_{11}\,\text{NC}_j + u_{1j}$$

In general, when testing for interaction, all lower order effects must also be included in the model. In HLM analysis, it is thus necessary to expand the level 2 equations. Most statistical packages will provide significance tests for the random components of the models. If statistically significant random variation remains after macro-level variables are controlled for (i.e. u_{0j} and/or u_{1j} remain significant in the culture model), this tells us that there is unobserved heterogeneity at the country level which is not sufficiently described by national culture. HLM analysis may thus provide an exploratory basis for further theorising on the determinants of HRM practice effectiveness across countries.

Question 4: To what degree are differences in either use or effectiveness of HRM practices/systems stable versus changing over time?
To address this question, one would use the same models as above, but those two-level models would need to become three-level models because year would need to be added as a level 3 variable. Thus, organisations are at level 1, countries are at level 2, and years are at level 3. One would address the preceding three comparative HRM questions in the same way as above, except now there would be tests of whether findings regarding country effects on HRM practices and differential effectiveness of HRM

practices are stable over years. Likewise, it would be possible to compare the ability of national culture to explain any such country effects at different points in time, using the same general approach as described earlier.

So far we have focused on the advantages of HLM analysis for comparative HRM research. A positive issue is that ICC analysis is readily incorporated in HLM. Further, HLM can be used to determine the amount of variance at different levels of analysis. However, HLM analysis is best-suited to datasets that contain a sufficiently large number of higher-level units (e.g. organisations). The reason is that the reliability of the grand mean estimate (Figure 5.1) increases with the number of groups, and likewise the Bayesian HLM estimators increase in precision. Since HLM analysis has large-sample or asymptotic properties (i.e. it uses Bayesian estimators and full or restricted maximum likelihood algorithms; Hox, 2002), OLS regression may be superior if there are only a few higher-level units.[7]

In addition, it is important to note that HLM is not the only means for obtaining correct standard error estimates with multi-level data. OLS regression with robust and clustered (or cluster-adjusted) standard errors also provides correct standard errors when observations are nested within some otherwise not controlled for higher-level units (Steenbergen & Jones, 2002). Clustered standard errors are available for various regression models and econometric packages such as STATA (for STATA, cf. Stata, 2005) (Lin & Wei, 1989; Rogers, 1993). However, single-level regression does not account for ICC analysis and fit between conceptual and empirical models is hard to determine and may be hard to achieve.

HRM-PERFORMANCE LINKS AND MODEL ENDOGENEITY

Now we turn to the causal link between HRM practices and firm performance. The analysis of the management–performance link is frequently subject to concerns of model misspecification. Take a study that finds a positive effect of the use of contingent reward systems (e.g. merit pay) on firm performance.[8] One may argue that successful firms can afford contingent reward systems, and thus the use of contingent reward systems is not exogenous, but rather endogenous to firm performance. In somewhat more technical terms, endogeneity can be defined more broadly to include any situation where the independent variable in a regression model is correlated with the error term, $\text{cov}(x_i, r_i) \neq 0$. If endogeneity exists, the expected value of the residual is no longer zero, $\text{E}(r_i \mid x_{1i}, x_{2i}, \ldots, x_{ki}) \neq 0$, and OLS estimates are biased and inconsistent (Wooldridge, 2006). We note that the term 'endogeneity' can be used in one of two ways. It can be used to refer specifically to simultaneity bias (as in the brief example above) or it can be used to refer more broadly, as just stated, to any situation where the error term is not independent of one or more so-called exogenous or independent variables.

Using the broad definition of endogeneity means that a number of different specification errors can be subsumed under that general heading (Hamilton & Nickerson, 2003; Shaver, 1998; Wooldridge, 2006). Specification errors that cause endogeneity comprise omitted variables (unobserved heterogeneity), measurement error, and simultaneity (i.e. reciprocal or non-recursive causation). While these problems have distinct features and precursors, they have in common that they result in nonzero covariance between the exogenous variables and the residual, and thus change in the variable of interest originates partly within the model under study (this change is endogenous rather than exogenous).

Omitted Variables Bias

Omitted variables bias occurs if some unmeasured causes ('unobserved heterogeneity') are correlated with the exogenous variables of the model. In the above example, prior performance is likely to be correlated with the use of contingent reward systems. Prior performance is unmeasured, however, and thus captured by the error term. As a consequence the error term is correlated with the reward system measure. More generally, the HRM-performance link may be estimated with a fully (i.e. 'correctly') specified regression model (compare Kmenta, 1971: 392–393):

$$\text{Perf}_i = \delta_0 + \delta_1 \, \text{HRM}_i + \delta_2 \, \text{Control}_i + e_i$$

where Perf is firm performance of firm i, HRM is the practice (e.g. a contingent reward system), and Control is a control variable of interest. If we omit the control we estimate instead:

$$\text{Perf}_i = \beta_0 + \beta_1 \, \text{HRM}_i + r_i$$

The control variable effect is now contained in the error term $(r_i = \delta_2 \, \text{Control}_i + e_i)$ which is thus correlated with HRM if the control variable was correlated with HRM.[9] There may be many reasons why a control variable is omitted, e.g., theory is incomplete, or data are unavailable. In any case, β_1 will be different from δ_1:

$$\beta_1 = \delta_1 + \delta_2 \, \pi_1$$

where π_1 is the coefficient from an auxiliary regression of the control on HRM:

$$\text{Control}_i = \pi_0 + \pi_1 \, \text{HRM}_i + u_i$$

The bias in the reduced HRM model on performance (without the control) grows more severe as δ_2 and π_1 deviate more from zero. Beck et al. (2008) provide compelling evidence that omitted variable bias can be substantial in organisational research (see also Huselid & Becker, 2000). Several approaches exist to lessen concerns about endogeneity from omitted variables. One is the randomised experiment (Cook & Campbell, 1979). Under random assignment, $\text{cov}(\text{HRM}_i, r_i)$ is zero by definition. Of course, random assignment in studying HRM-effectiveness relationships is not a practical option. Two alternative approaches, which may have greater practical application are propensity scores or selection models, and fixed-effects methodologies.

Propensity scores (Rosenbaum & Rubin, 1983; Heckman et al., 1999) are a more sophisticated case of the better-known matching procedures. For example, Fulmer, Gerhart, and Scott (2003) used a matching approach to compare the '100 Best Companies to Work For' with a set of companies matched on industry, size and previous financial performance. Matching can become unwieldy, though, as the number of boundary conditions (i.e. relevant controls like industry, firm size, age, etc.) increases. In terms of experimental research, a propensity score is the probability of receiving a treatment, conditional on a set of observables. The score can be derived by regressing participation in the treatment (e.g. by using a binary logit or probit model) on a set of covariates, and can then be used as a covariate in the final model. The idea lies in the so-called counterfactual approach to causality (also called Rubin's model). That is, to infer how a company reacts (e.g. in terms of performance) to a certain treatment (e.g. implementation of the reward system), we need to know how it would have reacted in the absence of the treatment. While facts are never counterfactual, we can compare two sets of companies that are identical except for the treatment. It can be shown then that, in large samples, 'if treatment and control groups have the same distribution of propensity scores, they have the same distribution of all observed covariates, just like in a randomised experiment' (Rubin, 2001: 171).

While the propensity score approach has many positive features, it comes at some costs (see Gerhart, 2007, for a discussion): propensity scores are estimated with known and observable variables, and the estimation may also be subject to omitted variables; non-response is assumed to be random; assignment to the treatment needs to be exogenous to the outcome variable; and responses in one treatment group must not be affected by the treatment received by another group (i.e. SUTVA – stable unit treatment value assumption; Rosenbaum & Rubin, 1983). The latter case occurs, for example, when groups compete for resources. In comparative HRM research this may be the rule, though, and no exception: companies that implement a contingent rewards practice are likely to attract a certain workforce, and this workforce is thus unavailable to other companies with similar practices. Another problem is that propensity score groups (treatment/no treatment) can more easily be established if relatively few companies in the sample receive the treatment. In sum, propensity score methods are currently receiving a great deal of attention in the methodological literature; because the method requires some strict assumptions to be met, however, there appear to be few (or virtually no) applications in the management and in the international HRM literature as of yet.

Sampling issues are also important to consider. In comparative HRM research, one rarely, if ever, encounters the use of random samples of the respective country populations. Failure to generate random samples is a widespread phenomenon in applied research. Short, Ketchen and Palmer, for example, found that less than 20 per cent of the studies in strategic management research on performance used a random sample, and that the 'size and direction of the association [among strategy and performance] is partly a function of sampling procedures' (2002: 379). They also noted that 'past sampling practices have rarely been in accordance with established methodological guidelines' and that an 'improvement in future sampling practices will help the field . . . to achieve its objective of explaining the determinants of performance' (2002: 382). Given that most samples in comparative HRM research are not random either, alternative methods should be used if possible.

Closely related to the propensity score methodology and developed in the context of concerns about sampling are selection models. Sample selection bias occurs if the outcome variable is restricted in range, i.e. observations above or below a certain threshold remain unobserved. For example, firms with less effective HRM practices may be less successful and thus less likely to survive than those with more effective strategies (Gerhart et al.,1996). The issue is, in essence, an omitted variable problem: firms have an inherent and unmeasured probability to survive, and thus different probabilities to be sampled (Beck et al., 2008). The consequence of observing survivors only (i.e. the more successful firms) is a downward bias in the estimate of the HRM-performance relation. The Heckman two-step correction procedure (Heckman, 1979) estimates a selection equation and a substantive equation. From the selection equation the inverse Mills ratio is calculated and then added as an additional variable to the substantive equation. The success of this 'correction' depends, however, on the specific characteristics of the data (Stolzenberg & Relies, 1997). Thus, whenever a Heckman correction is used, the full selection equation (variables, coefficients, and fit) must be reported.

Finally, a different approach to omitted variables and endogeneity is the panel (or cross-sectional time-series) fixed-effects methodology. As a requirement for the fixed-effects model (FE-model), one needs multiple measurements of the same variables (i.e. panel data), and sufficient variation in between the measurements. Basically, in panel models the residual term is split into two components: a time-constant term and a time-varying term. Corresponding to our earlier example, and using the error components model, firm performance can be modelled as:

$$\text{Perf}_{it} = \beta_0 + \beta_1 \text{HRM}_{it} + v_i + r_{it}$$

where Perf is performance of firm i at time t, HRM is the practice of firm i at t, v_i is the time-constant error component ('unit-fixed-effect'), and r_{it} is the time-varying idiosyncratic error. Essentially, the fixed-effects model predicts changes in the dependent variable from changes in the independent variable (within-estimation), and thus it differences away all time-constant residual variation across panel waves:

$$\text{Perf}_{it} = (\beta_0 + \delta_0) + \beta_1 \text{HRM}_{it} + v_i + r_{it}$$

$$\text{Perf}_{it\text{-}1} = \beta_0 + \beta_1 \text{HRM}_{it\text{-}1} + v_i + r_{it\text{-}1}$$

with δ_0 as a time dummy (Wooldridge, 2006). The fixed-effects model then specifies

$$(\text{Perf}_{it} - \text{Perf}_{it\text{-}1}) = \delta_0 + \beta_1 (\text{HRM}_{it} - \text{HRM}_{it\text{-}1}) + (r_{it} - r_{it\text{-}1})$$

In this last equation the time-constant error has disappeared.[10] As a consequence, the fixed-effects model controls for all unobserved heterogeneity which is time-invariant (or at least quasi-constant over time). Typical examples include industry, competition, and country membership. As such, unmeasured national culture components which are stable over time can be controlled for by fixed-effects models. The FE-estimator has many favourable properties (Wooldridge, 2002; Beck et al., 2008), but costs as well: measurement error may be exacerbated by using difference scores (as the FE-estimator does) (Cronbach & Furby, 1970); time-invariant variables fall out of the model; and degrees of freedom are lost from the denominator which decreases efficiency.

In general, panel models are suspect for non-spherical error terms, i.e. the disturbances are supposed to be heteroskedastic (errors have unstable variances conditional on the values of the exogenous variables), autocorrelated (errors of the same unit are correlated over time), or contemporaneously correlated (errors of different units are correlated at one point of time). All these problems are serious issues in comparative HRM research. For example, the same type of measurement error might appear across all panel waves in each unit (e.g. organisation) if the same single respondent is the source of information. Many advanced econometric programs such as STATA allow the estimation of heteroskedasticity robust standard errors for fixed-effects models, and have special procedures for AR(1) regressions which control for autocorrelation.[11]

A related question is whether fixed-effects models are to be preferred over random-effects. While the fixed-effects model is similar to a dummy approach, in the random-effects model v_i is drawn from a random population (Wooldridge, 2006). Whether to use fixed- or random-effects depends in part on the question whether the exogenous variables are correlated with v_i or not. The random-effects model assumes that $\text{cov}(X_i, v_i) = 0$; the fixed-effects model allows the correlation. In comparative HRM research the fixed-effects model will be adequate in most instances. First, we seldom have a real random sample, which would argue in favour of the random-effects model.[12] Second, HRM practices are likely to be correlated with the governance mechanisms with which the practices are implemented and enforced (e.g. control systems, labour relations, etc.). Such governance mechanisms are usually fairly stable over time (in between panel waves), and in most cases remain unobserved; random-effects estimates will be biased then.

In many cases, multilevel issues are neglected with panel data. If there are only a few higher-level units in the data, cross-level interactions between the level 2 constructs (e.g. country dummies, national culture scores) and the level 1 explanatory variables can be introduced to the FE-panel model. With many countries and substantial intra-country correlations (i.e. a nontrivial ICC(1)) the dummy approach becomes unwieldy. Generalised estimating equations (GEE) may then be used to model both the longitudinal data structure and intra-cluster correlations introduced by country membership (Ballinger, 2004; Ghisletta & Spini, 2004).

From the above discussion it appears that the choice of the 'best' model is difficult for many reasons. The first step should always be to develop strong theory, and then to evaluate how assumptions and predictions can be modelled statistically. One might think, for example, that including more control variables will reduce omitted variable bias. However, arbitrarily adding control variables will primarily reduce efficiency, and the

F-statistic or an equivalent indicator (like the deviance statistic) will show the loss in statistical power. In a similar vein, Gerhart (2007) employs an example where a mediator is incorrectly modelled as a simple control:

$$\text{Perf}_i = \beta_0 + \beta_1 \text{HRM}_i + \beta_2 \text{AMO}_i + r_i$$

where AMO is a composite of human capital ability, motivation, and opportunity to contribute. Using a hypothetical but realistic correlation matrix of the variables, Gerhart (2007) demonstrates that the effect of HRM on performance differs by a factor of 4, depending on whether AMO is considered as a control or as a mediator of the HRM-performance relation (i.e., in the mediator case the indirect effect contributes to the total effect also).[13] In other words, it is primarily a theoretical question which model is adequate for the question of interest.

Measurement Error and Construct Validity

Measurement error may be introduced through various sources. In comparative HRM research studies are frequently conducted at the firm level (as, for example, in the Cranet project). In the standard design of such studies, HRM practices are measured as the percentage of employees covered by the practice. Also rating scales are sometimes applied to measure the strength, importance, or use of the practices. Depending on whether the scores of the HRM practices are modelled as reflective measures (as compared to formative measures; see Diamantopoulos & Winklhofer, 2001; Edwards & Bagozzi, 2000), internal consistency is the typical standard of reliability (estimated with a coefficient such as Cronbach's alpha, or with more sophisticated methodologies such as LISREL; Jöreskog & Sörbom, 1999). Recent evidence suggests, however, that measurement error due to the sampling of raters may be much more substantial. Gerhart, Wright and colleagues (Gerhart et al., 2000a, b; Wright et al., 2001) reported in their first study that inter-rater reliability in studies at the firm level was 0.30 at best, and probably as low as 0.20. Basically, this means that the obtained scores reflect the idiosyncratic perceptions of informants rather than valid reflections of the practices in the firms. As such, in research on HRM and performance where multiple sources of measurement error exist (in both items and raters), estimation of a generalisability coefficient is recommended (Cronbach et al., 1972; Gerhart et al., 2000a).

Another and also a very promising approach is to use multiple respondents from different perspectives. For example, Fulmer et al. (2003) used the employees' views in organisations to construct their index of employee relations, which they hypothesised to predict performance. In the same vein, Ostroff, Kinicki and Clark (2002) created organisational level variables from individual responses, and used different subsamples in each organisation to create the different variables, thus eliminating within-person correlations between measures. The multiple respondent approach, while undoubtedly more demanding than the standard single respondent approach, is also useful to eliminate common method bias (Doty & Glick, 1998; Podsakoff et al., 2003), which occurs if the independent and dependent variables are all reported by the same source (e.g. a single informant). Strategies to control for common methods bias include the multitrait–multimethod matrix (Campbell & Fiske, 1959), which is particularly promising if assessed with confirmatory methods (Widaman, 1985).[14] Another suggestion is the use of a marker variable (Lindell & Whitney, 2001). The fixed-effects approach presented earlier can also be used to eliminate time-invariant measurement error (e.g. bias from a single respondent with consistently positive or negative response errors across scales and time).

Simultaneity (Reciprocal Causality)

In a recursive model, causation runs in one direction. In a non-recursive model causation is reciprocal, i.e. there is simultaneity (Duncan, 1975). The following example was adapted from Duncan (1975), Chapter 5 (see also Gerhart, 2007). Take a simple model of performance and HRM, where both variables predict each other (i.e. both are exogenous and endogenous):

$$\text{Perf}_i = \beta_0 + \beta_1 X_{1i} + \beta_2 \text{HRM}_i + u_i$$

$$\text{HRM}_i = \delta_0 + \delta_1 X_{1i} + \delta_2 \text{Perf}_i + e_i$$

In the joint model, HRM practices predict performance, and performance predicts HRM. OLS estimates will be biased because the right hand side variables are correlated with the errors. For example, if performance predicts HRM, then u_i, the error in the performance equation, will be correlated with HRM. Duncan (1975) demonstrates that (as applied here) the OLS estimate of β_2 will be biased and equal instead:

$$\beta_2^{\text{OLS}} = \beta_2 + r(\text{HRM}_i, u_i) / [1 - r^2(\text{HRM}_i, X_1)]$$

The second part of the equation is usually referred to as simultaneity bias. To correct for endogeneity from simultaneity several solutions have been suggested. We will briefly refer to IV (instrumental variables) methods, and simultaneous equation modelling such as LISREL.

First, to establish a causal relation of HRM practices and perform-ance, time precedence of cause and effect is a necessary condition (Cook & Campbell, 1979; Mitchell & James, 2001). As such, longitudinal data are required for causal analysis. However, as Blossfeld and Rohwer (2002) illustrate we need three measurements of the same variables to satisfy a strict definition of causality: at t_1 we record the values of the independent and dependent variables, HRM and performance. Later, we observe changes in both variables at t_3. Panel estimators such as the FE-estimator will predict the change in performance from the change in HRM. However, to establish causality in the hypothesised direction we need a third point of measurement in between t_1 and t_3, that is, we need to observe the change in HRM (t_2) and then decide whether it precedes the change in performance or not. The question of time and temporally informed theory is probably the most urgent question in organisational research (see, e.g. the contributions to the Special Issue on 'Time in Organisations' of the *Academy of Management Review*, Vol. **26**, No. 4; Goodman et al., 2001). In particular, we need stronger theory about (1) when a cause is likely to occur in the time frame of the study window, (2) how much time elapses before the cause shows an effect, and (3) about when and how the relation among cause and effect changes over the time of the study. Event history methods with time-varying covariates are among the most promising approaches for the analysis of such theory, but they are also demanding in terms of data collection (Blossfeld & Rohwer, 2002). Interestingly, a recent review finds that the condition of time precedence is only seldom met in the HRM-performance literature; even worse, HRM practices are often measured after performance (Wright et al., 2005).

If only cross-sectional data are available (this is the more common case in comparative HRM research), IV methods may help to reduce endog-eneity concerns.[15] In principle, in IV estimation the endogenous explana-tory variable is replaced by an estimate of that variable which is not correlated with the error term. Think again of an HRM practice which we suspect to be endogenous in the prediction of firm performance (because of a non-recursive relationship):

$$\text{Perf}_i = \beta_0 + \beta_1 X_{1i} + \beta_2 \text{HRM}_i + u_i$$

A special case of IV methods is the so-called two-stage least squares (2SLS) estimator. In 2SLS, the first stage is to estimate the HRM practice from the full set of exogenous variables from the performance model, plus at least one additional exogenous variable Z (we use two Zs in the example below):

$$\text{HRM}_i = \pi_0 + \pi_1 X_{1i} + \pi_2 Z_{1i} + \pi_3 Z_{2i} + e_i$$

Based on some econometric assumptions (cf. Wooldridge, 2006, Chapter 15) we know that the best 'instrumental variable' for HRM (i.e. a predictor of performance that is not correlated with u_i) is:

$$\text{HRM}_i^* = \pi_0 + \pi_1 X_{1i} + \pi_2 Z_{1i} + \pi_3 Z_{2i}$$

For HRM* not to be a perfect linear combination of X_1, a necessary condition is that either π_2 or π_3 are different from zero (identification assumption): if the effects of Z_1 and Z_2 are not jointly significant in the HRM equation 'we are wasting our time with IV estimation' (Wooldridge, 2006: 526). In the second stage of 2SLS we can then use the predicted values of HRM (as empirical counterparts to the population model HRM*) in the estimation of performance. The reason is that HRM consists of two components: HRM* which is not correlated with u_i, and e_i which is potentially correlated with u_i. Thus, 2SLS first 'purges [HRM] of its correlation with u_i before doing the OLS [performance] regression' (Wooldridge, 2006: 526).

The IV and 2SLS estimators may differ substantially from OLS estimates. Moreover, they are consistent rather than unbiased (i.e. they have favourable large sample properties but may be unreliable in smaller samples). Most statistical packages such as STATA have commands for 2SLS or IV estimation. While the two stages can be separately performed by OLS, one should avoid doing the second stage manually because the standard errors and test statistics are not valid. The reason is that if we plug HRM = HRM* + e_i into the performance equation, the error term ($u_i + \beta_2 e_i$) includes e_i, but the standard errors are based on u_i only (Wooldridge, 2006). Finally, the success of IV or 2SLS estimation is based on the credibility of the assumptions that a) the instruments are exogenous to performance, $\text{cov}(Z_i, u_i) = 0$, and b) that the partial R^2 between the Zs and the endogenous explanatory variable is sufficiently large. Given these restrictions, researchers need to provide a convincing rationale for the instruments. Second, statistical tests such as the Hausman (1978) test should be used to evaluate the potential for endogeneity in the given data. Third, the full results of the equation used to obtain the predicted variable values must be reported (Bound, Jaeger, & Baker, 1995; Staiger & Stock, 1997). While simultaneity is clearly an issue, there are only a few examples of IV or 2SLS in the HRM-performance literature. Gerhart (2007) summarises the existing evidence and gives some further recommendations.

A structural equations modelling (SEM) approach such as LISREL can also be used to estimate parameters from a non-recursive model. LISREL is most useful when there are (1) measurement error issues, (2) simultaneity issues, or (3) where a full-information estimator (e.g. maximum-likelihood) is useful to either increase efficiency or to provide for a goodness of fit test for a system of equations. If none of these conditions hold, then LISREL may be unnecessary and more parsimonious methods should be preferred. In addition, econometricians have long relied more heavily on limited information estimators such as 2SLS as compared to full-information estimators such as maximum-likelihood because the latter (1) assume multivariate normality, (2) while having superior large-sample properties, may not perform as well in finite samples, which empirical research uses, and (3) allow a specification error in one equation (e.g. an incorrectly specified zero path) to bias parameter estimates for other equations (Bollen, 1996; Curran et al., 1996; Kennedy, 1992).

SUMMARY

Our goal was to give a review of primarily quantitative methodological issues in the comparative HRM literature, and to provide some recommendations and solutions for these issues. To sum up:

1. Stronger and more substantive theory is needed. Such theory needs to specify cause-and-effect relations, when causes are supposed to influence the outcome, how long the reaction will take, and how and when relations will change over time. Measurement error can be reduced and construct validity enhanced if theory explicitly states the boundary conditions of effects and the domains of the constructs of interest.
2. Sampling issues are salient problems in comparative HRM research. To enhance comparability across nations (or organisations) we need more studies of random samples from different countries and organisations. The analysis of pooled cross-sectional data from random samples can enhance our understanding of HRM policy effects (Wooldridge, 2006). Better, however, are panel data from random samples that allow for advanced causal modelling strategies that have the potential to bring the field forward.
3. HLM methods (including ICC analysis) should be used to estimate the within and between portions of variance in multilevel data, and to determine the influence of macro level constructs (e.g. national cultures) on micro level units (e.g., individuals, or organisations). ICC analysis should also be used to determine country (or group) mean reliability, and to decide how much macro variance is attributable to specific macro level constructs such as culture, institutions, regulations and competition.

4. The analysis of the HRM-performance link is often limited by endogeneity concerns. Omitted variables, measurement error, and simultaneity, are major issues in this respect. Strong theory and the collection of longitudinal data are the best advice to overcome such limitations. In the absence of panel data, propensity score techniques, selection models, and IV estimation may help reduce endogeneity concerns. With panel data the fixed-effects approach is useful. Combinations of panel and HLM methodologies are particularly promising.

5. There is no universal or general 'best modelling strategy'. Rather, the question of interest, the theory used, and the data collected determine which model is the most adequate. If doubts remain, Blossfeld and Rohwer (2002) are probably right: 'In summary, specification bias is pervasive in empirical social research. What can be recommended in such a situation. . .? First, . . . try to find better data that allow for representation of the important factors in the model' (2002: 277), and 'the most sensible strategy is to estimate and compare a variety of different models and to find out to what degree the estimation results are robust (i.e. do not depend on the selected model)' (2002: 276).

NOTES

1. $K = 10$ level 2 (country) observations is not considered a sufficient sample size. We use $K = 10$ here to simplify the pictorial representation in Figure 5.1.
2. This regression-based equation for ICC(1) refers to the HLM-case. Here the formula for ICC(1) equals eta-squared (η^2): ICC(1) = η^2 = $SS_{between}$ / SS_{total}, i.e. between variance divided by total variance. If estimated from a one-way random-effects ANOVA model, the ICC(1) is defined as ICC(1) = $(MSB - MSW)$ / $[MSB + (k - 1) MSW]$, where MSB is the mean square between, MSW is the mean square within, and k is group size (Shrout & Fleiss, 1979). In the ANOVA case, η^2 asymptotically approaches ICC(1) as group size increases. When group sizes are small (or only few groups exist, or gross outliers dominate the distribution), η^2 values are likely to be inflated and need to be corrected. Bliese and Halverson (1998) provide solutions and recommendations for applied organizational research.
3. The ICC(2) can be constructed from a one-way random-effects ANOVA model, and is then defined as ICC(2) = $(MSB - MSW)$ / MSB, with MSB as the between-country mean square, and MSW as the within-country mean square. ICC(2) is thus a function of group size and the ICC(1) via the Spearman-Brown correction formula (compare Bliese, 2000). As an estimate of reliability, ICC(2) values > 0.70 indicate acceptable stability of the group means. Note that both ICC(1) and ICC(2) are omnibus tests. In particular, ICC(2) does not inform us if some of the groups are unreliable; rather, it gives us an overall estimate.
4. The issue here is somewhat different than that debated in *Personnel Psychology* (Gerhart et al. 2000a, b; Huselid & Becker, 2000). That debate concerned the reliability and validity of responses from one HRM manager/executive per organisation. However, there was no debate over level of analysis. These respondents are in a better position than the typical employee respondent to describe HRM practices at the organisation level.
5. Typically, one would use dummy variables to control for the higher level units then.

      In fact, the dummy approach equals a 'fixed-effects' multilevel strategy, where each dummy represents a fixed-unit effect. However, the approach is easily complicated and sometimes unwieldy when many higher-level units need to be controlled for. HLM provides random-effects methodologies to account for the complexity.

6. From the single equation it becomes obvious that the HLM approach explicitly models potential heteroskedasticity with a random term,

7. The dummy variable approach becomes unwieldy with many groups, in particular if we expect the slopes of some explaining variables to vary across groups. In this instance, we need to add cross-level interactions with the explaining variables and all of the categories of the higher-level variable that are supposed to influence the lower-level effect.

8. For the following discussion it is of no regard whether the HRM-performance relationship is subject to cross-country differences. The HLM-view makes the relationship more complex in terms of a cross-level interaction; the focal question (HRM-performance linkage) remains the same, however.

9. As Gerhart (2007) points out, it is the partial correlation of the independent and the omitted variable (corrected for third variable influences) that determines whether omitted variables bias is serious or negligible. As such, the correlation between the independent and the omitted variable may be high and still produce little bias in the OLS estimates.

10. More specifically, we have presented the first-difference estimator here (Wooldridge, 2006). The first difference estimator equals the fixed-effects estimator only if there are exactly two panel waves to be differenced. With more than two panel waves the first difference estimator will yield different results. The fixed-effects estimator works very similarly, though, since it time-demeans the data instead of differencing them. See Wooldridge (2006) for an easy to read introduction.

11. As Certo and Semadeni (2006) report, contemporaneous correlation has not received as much attention, and causes problems for fixed-effects, random-effects, and GLS estimators alike (in particular if the errors are also heteroskedastic). The problem is decidedly lessened when time dummies are used. As a recommendation, one should always use time dummies with panel regression models of any kind. Specific panel models such as PCSE (panel corrected standard errors) which control for heteroskedasticity, autocorrelation, and contemporaneous correlation (Beck & Katz, 1995), are not recommended in the context of typical HRM data which are cross-sectionally dominated (i.e. the number of units is substantially larger than the number of repeated measurements: $N > T$). The same applies for GLS estimators (Certo & Semadeni, 2006).

12. Wooldridge (2006) suggests to use the fixed-effects estimator if all members of a population are sampled (e.g. 100 Best Companies to Work For), or if few members with distinctive (i.e. fixed) features are observed; to the contrary, the random-effects estimator should be used if a random sample is drawn from the population (e.g. a random sample of 50 firms from the 100 Best Companies to Work For).

13. Testing for mediation may be intricate. In Gerhart's (2007) example, the indirect effect of HRM on performance equals the difference in the HRM coefficients from a full and a reduced model (i.e., with and without AMO in the model). Another approach is to estimate the HRM–AMO relation, and the AMO–performance relation, and then take the product of the coefficients as the indirect effect of HRM on performance (Alwin & Hauser, 1975). To assess mediation, the Baron and Kenny (1986) approach has been very influential in psychological research. However, this approach does not offer a coherent significance test for the indirect path. Sobel (1982) derived a simple estimator for the confidence interval of the indirect effect, which has become very popular over the years. However, as Shrout and Bolger (2002) criticize, Sobel's (1982) 'products of coefficients' approach assumes that the product of the estimates is normally distributed, and that this assumption 'does not hold when the null hypothesis that $a \times b = 0$ is false, that is, when mediation is present' (p. 426). Based on extensive simulations, MacKinnon et al. (2002) recommended 'difference in coefficients' methods as powerful and reliable tests of mediation.

14. We should note, however, that the assessment of MTMM-matrices with confirmatory methods such as LISREL is sometimes problematic. In Widaman's (1985) much cited suggestion, nested models are formulated which allow for the evaluation of overall fit across models (i.e. the evaluation of how many traits and methods are represented in the data). Such nested models are often hard to estimate, and in particular, local under-identification frequently causes problems. Marsh (1989) and Eid (2000) have developed Widaman's (1985) strategy further and suggested some solutions.
15. Note, however, that reducing endogeneity (through a technical procedure such as IV estimation) does not remedy the substantial problem (time precedence needed to establish a causal relation).

REFERENCES

Adler, N. J. 2002. *International Dimensions of Organizational Behavior*, 4th edn. Cincinnati, OH: South-Western.
Alwin, D. F. & Hauser, R. M. 1975. The decomposition of effects in path analysis. *American Sociological Review*, **40**: 37–47.
Appelbaum, E., Bailey, T., Berg, P. & Kalleberg, A. 2000. *Manufacturing Advantage: Why High Performance Work Systems Pay Off*. Ithaca, NY: Cornell University Press.
Ballinger, G. A. 2004. Using generalized estimation equations for longitudinal data analysis. *Organizational Research Methods*, **7**: 127–150.
Barney, J. B. & Wright, P. 1998. On becoming a strategic partner. The role of human resources in gaining competitive advantage. *Human Resource Management*, **37**: 31–46.
Baron, R. M. & Kenny, D. A. 1986. The moderator–mediator variable distinction in social psychological research: conceptual, strategic, and statistical considerations. *Journal of Personality and Social Psychology*, **51**: 1173–1182.
Beck, N., Brüderl, J. & Woywode, M. 2008. Momentum or deceleration? Theoretical and methodological reflections on the analysis of organizational change. *Academy of Management Journal*, **51**: 413–435.
Beck, N., Kabst, R. & Walgenbach, P. 2009. The cultural dependence of vocational training. *Journal of International Business Studies*, **40**(3): 1374-1395.
Beck, N. & Katz, J. N. 1995. What to do (and not to do) with time-series cross-section data. *American Political Science Review*, **89**: 634–647.
Becker, B. & Gerhart, B. 1996. The impact of human resource management on organizational performance: progress and prospects. *Academy of Management Journal*, **39**(1): 779–801.
Bhagat, R. S. & McQuaid, S. L. 1982. Role of subjective culture in organizations: a review and directions for future research. *Journal of Applied Psychology*, **67**: 653-685.
Bliese, P. D. 2000. Within-group agreement, non-independence, and reliability: implications for data aggregation and analysis. In K. J. Klein & S. W. J. Kozlowski (eds), *Multilevel Theory, Research, and Methods in Organizations*. San Francisco, CA: Jossey-Bass, pp. 349–381.
Bliese, P. D. & Halverson, R. R. 1998. Group size and measures of group-level properties: an examination of eta-squared and ICC values. *Journal of Management*, **24**(2): 157–172.
Bloom, M. & Milkovich, G. T. 1999. A SHRM perspective on international compensation and rewards. In P. Wright, L. Dyer, J. W. Boudreau & G. T. Milkovich (eds), *Research in Personnel and Human Resources Management* Vol. 4. Stamford, CT: JAI Press, pp. 283–303.
Blossfeld, H. P. & Rohwer, G. 2002. *Techniques of Event History Modeling. New Approaches to Causal Analysis*, 2 edn. Mahwah, NJ: Lawrence Erlbaum Associates.
Bollen, K. A. 1996. An alternative Two Stage Least Squares (2SLS) estimator for latent variable equations. *Psychometrika*, **61**: 109-121.
Bound, J., Jaeger, D. & Baker, R. 1995. Problems with instrumental variables estimation

when the correlation between the instruments and the endogenous explanatory variables is weak. *Journal of the American Statistical Association*, **90**: 443–450.

Boxall, P. & Purcell, J. 2003. *Strategy and Human Resource Management*. Hampshire, UK: Palgrave Macmillan.

Brewster, C. 1999. Different paradigms in strategic HRM: questions raised by comparative research. In P. Wright, L. Dyer, J. W. Boudreau & G. T. Milkovich (eds), *Research in Personnel and Human Resources Management*. Stamford, CT: JAI Press, pp. 213–238.

Brewster, C., Mayrhofer, W. & Morley, M. 2004. *Human Resource Management in Europe: Evidence of convergence?* London: Butterworth-Heinemann.

Campbell, D. T. & Fiske, D. W. 1959. Convergent and discriminant validation by the multitrait-multimethod matrix. *Psychological Bulletin*, **56**: 81–105.

Certo, S. T. & Semadeni, M. 2006. Strategy research and panel data: evidence and implications. *Journal of Management*, **32**: 449–471.

Cohen, J. 1988. *Statistical Power Analysis for the Behavioral Sciences*, 2nd edn. Hillsdale, NJ: Lawrence Erlbaum Associates.

Cook, T. D. & Campbell, D. T. 1979. *Quasi-experimentation*. Chicago: Rand-McNally.

Cronbach, L. J., & Furby, L. 1970. How we should measure change – or should we? *Psychological Bulletin*, **74**(1): 68–80.

Cronbach, L. J., Gleser, G. C., Nanda, H. & Rajaratnam, N. 1972. *The Dependability of Behavioral Measurements: Theory of Generalizability of Scores and Profiles*. New York: John Wiley.

Curran, P. J., West, S. G. & Finch, J. F. 1996. The robustness of test statistics to nonnormality and specification error in confirmatory factor analysis. *Psychological Methods*, **1**(1): 16–29.

Diamantopoulos, A. & Winklhofer, H. M. 2001. Index construction with formative indicators: an alternative to scale development. *Journal of Marketing Research*, **38**(2): 269–277.

Dierickx, I., & Cool, K. 1989. Asset stock accumulation and sustainability of competitive advantage. *Management Science*, **35**: 1504–1511.

DiMaggio, P. J. & Powell, W. W. 1983. The iron cage revisited: institutional isomorphism and collective rationality in organizational fields. *American Sociological Review*, **48**(2): 147–160.

Doty, D. H. & Glick, W. H. 1998. Common methods bias: does common methods variance really bias results? *Organizational Research Methods*, **1**: 374–406.

Dowling, P. J., Festing, M. & Engle, A. D. S. 2008. *International Human Resource Management*, 5th edn. London: Thomson Learning.

Duncan, O. D. 1975. *Introduction to Structural Equation Models*. New York: Academic Press.

Early, P. C. & Erez, M. 1997. *The Transplanted Executive: Why You Need to Understand How Workers in Other Countries See the World Differently*. New York: Oxford University Press.

Edwards, J. R. & Bagozzi, R. P. 2000. On the nature and direction of relationships between constructs and measures. *Psychological Methods*, **5**(2): 155–174.

Eid, M. 2000. A multitrait-multimethod model with minimal assumptions. *Psychometrika*, **65**: 241–261.

Evans, P., Pucik, V. & Barsoux, J. L. 2002. *The Global Challenge: Frameworks for International Human Resource Management*. New York: McGraw-Hill/Irwin.

Ferner, A. & Quintanilla, J. 1998. Multinationals, national business systems and HRM: the enduring influence of national identity or a process of 'Anglo-Saxonization'. *International Journal of Human Resource Management*, **9**(4): 710–731.

Fulmer, I. S., Gerhart, B. & Scott, K. S. 2003. Are the 100 Best better? An empirical investigation of the relationship between being a 'Great Place to Work' and firm performance. *Personnel Psychology*, **56**(4): 965–993.

Gerhart, B. 2007. Modeling HRM and performance linkages. In P. Boxall, J. Purcell & P. Wright (eds), *The Oxford Handbook of Human Resource Management*. Oxford, New York: Oxford University Press, pp. 552–580.

Gerhart, B. 2008a. Cross-cultural management research: assumptions, evidence, and suggested directions. *International Journal of Cross Cultural Management*, **8**(3): 259–274.

Gerhart, B. 2008b. How much does national culture constrain organizational culture? *Management and Organization Review*, **5**: 241–259.

Gerhart, B. & Fang, M. 2005. National culture and human resource management: assumptions and evidence. *International Journal of Human Resource Management*, **16**(6): 971–986.

Gerhart, B., Trevor, C. O. & Graham, M. 1996. New directions in employee compensation research. In G. R. Ferris (ed.), *Research in Personnel and Human Resources Management*, **14**: 143–203.

Gerhart, B., Wright, P. M. & McMahan, G. C. 2000a. Measurement error in research on the human resources and firm performance relationship: further evidence and analysis. *Personnel Psychology*, **53**: 855–872.

Gerhart, B., Wright, P. M., McMahan, G. C. & Snell, S. A. 2000b. Measurement error in the research on human resource and firm performance: how much error is there and how does it influence effect size estimates? *Personnel Psychology*, **53**(4): 803–834.

Ghisletta, P. & Spini, D. 2004. An introduction to generalized estimation equations and an application to assess selectivity effects in a longitudinal study on very old individuals. *Journal of Educational and Behavioral Statistics*, **29**: 421–437.

Goodman, P. S., Lawrence, B. S., Ancona, D. G. & Tushman, M. L. 2001. Introduction. *Academy of Management Review*, **26**(4): 507–511.

Hamilton, B. H. & Nickerson, J. A. 2003. Correcting for endogeneity in strategic management research. *Strategic Organization*, **1**(1): 51–78.

Hausman, J. A. 1978. Specification tests in econometrics. *Econometrica*, **46**(6): 1251–1271.

Heckman, J. J. 1979. Sample selection bias as a specification error. *Econometrica*, **47**: 153–161.

Heckman, J. J., LaLonde, R. J. & Smith, J. A. 1999. The economics and econometrics of active labor market programs. In O. Ashenfelter & D. Card (eds), *Handbook of Labor Economics*, Vol. 3a. Amsterdam: Elsevier, pp. 1865–2097.

Hofstede, G. 1980. *Culture's Consequences: International Differences in Work-related Values*. Beverly Hills: Sage Publications.

Hofstede, G. 1983. The cultural relativity of organizational practices and theories. *Journal of International Business Studies*, **14**(2): 75–89.

Hofstede, G. 1993. Cultural constraints in management theories. *Academy of Management Executive*, **7**(1): 81–94.

Hofstede, G. 2001. *Culture's Consequences: Comparing Values, Behaviors, Institutions, and Organizations Across Nations*, 2nd edn. Thousand Oaks, CA: Sage Publications.

House, R. J., Hanges, P. J., Javidan, M., Dorfman, P. W. & Gupta, V. 2004. *Culture, Leadership, and Organizations: The GLOBE Study of 62 Societies*. Thousand Oaks: Sage Publications.

Hox, J. 2002. *Multilevel Analysis. Techniques and Applications*. London: Lawrence Erlbaum Associates.

Huselid, M. A. & Becker, B. E. 2000. Comment. *Personnel Psychology*, **53**(4): 835–854.

Jöreskog, K. G. & Sörbom, D. 1999. *LISREL 8: Structural Equation Modeling with the SIMPLIS Command Language*. Lincolnwood, IL: Scientific Software International.

Kennedy, P. 1992. *A Guide to Econometrics*, 3rd edn. Cambridge, MA: MIT Press.

Kirkman, B. L., Lowe, K. B. & Gibson, C. B. 2006. A quarter century of *Culture's Consequences*: a review of empirical research incorporating Hofstede's cultural values framework. *Journal of International Business Studies*, **37**: 285–320.

Kmenta, J. 1971. *Elements of Econometrics*. New York: Macmillan.

Kostova, T. 1999. Transnational transfer of strategic organizational practices: a contextual perspective. *Academy of Management Review*, **24**(2): 308–324.

Kostova, T. & Roth, K. 2002. Adoption of an organizational practice by subsidiaries of multinational corporations: institutional and relational effects. *Academy of Management Journal*, **45**(1): 215–233.

Laurent, A. 1983. The cultural diversity of western conceptions of management. *International Studies of Management & Organization*, **13**(1/2): 75–96.

Lin, D. Y. & Wei, L. J. 1989. The robust inference for the Cox proportional hazards model. *Journal of the American Statistical Association*, **84**: 1074–1078.

Lindell, M. K. & Whitney, D. J. 2001. Accounting for common method variance in cross-sectional research designs. *Journal of Applied Psychology*, **86**(1): 114–121.

MacKinnon, D. P., Lockwood, C. M., Hoffman, J. M., West, S. G. & Sheets, V. 2002. A comparison of methods to test mediation and other intervening variable effects. *Psychological Methods*, **7**(1): 83–104.

Marsh, H. W. 1989. Confirmatory factor analyses of multitrait-multimethod data: many problems and a few solutions. *Applied Psychological Measurement*, **13**: 335–361.

Mayrhofer, W. & Brewster, C. 2005. European human resource management: researching developments over time. *Management Revue*, **16**(1): 36.

Meyer, J. W. & Rowan, B. 1977. Institutional organizations: formal structure as myth and ceremony. *American Journal of Sociology*, **83**(2): 340–363.

Mitchell, T. R. & James, L. R. 2001. Building better theory: time and the specification when things happen. *Academy of Management Review*, **26**(4): 530–547.

Noe, R. A., Hollenbeck, J. R., Gerhart, B. & Wright, P. 2006. *Human Resource Management. Gaining a Competitive Advantage*, 5th edn. Boston: McGraw-Hill/Irvin.

Ostroff, C., Kinicki, A. J. & Clark, M. A. 2002. Substantive and operational issues of response bias across levels of analysis: an example of climate-satisfaction relationships. *Journal of Applied Psychology*, **87**(2): 355–368.

Ployhart, R. E. 2006. Staffing in the 21st century: new challenges and strategic opportunities. *Journal of Management*, **32**(6): 868–897.

Podsakoff, P. M., MacKenzie, S. B., Jeong-Yeon, L. & Podsakoff, N. P. 2003. Common method biases in behavioral research: a critical review of the literature and recommended remedies. *Journal of Applied Psychology*, **88**(5): 879.

Pudelko, M., Fink, G., Carr, C. & Wentges, P. 2006. The convergence concept in cross cultural management research. *International Journal of Cross Cultural Management*, **6**: 15–18.

Pudelko, M. & Harzing, A.-W. 2007. Country-of-origin, localization, or dominance effect? An empirical investigation of HRM practices in foreign subsidiaries. *Human Resource Management*, **46**(4): 535–559.

Quintanilla, J. & Ferner, A. 2003. Multinationals and human resource management: between global convergence and national identity. *International Journal of Human Resource Management*, **14**(3): 363–368.

Raudenbush, S. W. & Bryk, A. S. 2002. *Hierarchical Linear Models: Applications and Data Analysis Methods*, 2nd edn. London: Sage Publications.

Rogers, W. H. 1993. Regression standard errors in clustered samples. *Stata Technical Bulletin*, **13**: 19–23.

Rosenbaum, P. R. & Rubin, D. B. 1983. The central role of the propensity score in observational studies for causal effects. *Biometrika*, **70**: 41–55.

Rubin, D. B. 2001. Using propensity scores to help design observational studies: application to the tobacco litigation. *Health Services & Outcomes Research Methodology*, **2**(3–4): 169.

Sawang, S., Oei, T. P. S. & Goh, Y. W. 2006. Are country and culture values interchangeable? *International Journal of Cross Cultural Management*, **6**(2): 205–219.

Schaeffer, B. S. & Riordan, C. M. 2003. A review of cross-cultural methodologies for organizational research: a best-practices approach. *Organizational Research Methods*, **6**: 169–215.

Schneider, B. 1987. The people make the place. *Personnel Psychology*, **40**(3): 437–453.

Shaver, J. M. 1998. Accounting for endogeneity when assessing strategy performance: does entry mode choice affect FDI survival? *Management Science*, **44**(4): 571–585.

Short, J. C., Ketchen, J. D. J. & Palmer, T. B. 2002. The role of sampling in strategic management research on performance: a two-study analysis. *Journal of Management*, **28**(3): 363–385.

Shrout, P. E. & Fleiss, J. L. 1979. Intraclass correlations: uses in assessing rater reliability. *Psychological Bulletin*, **86**(2): 420–428.

Snijders, T. A. B. & Bosker, R. J. 1999. *Multilevel Analysis. An Introduction to Basic and Advanced Multilevel Modeling.* London: Sage Publications.

Sobel, M. E. 1982. Asymptotic confidence intervals for indirect effects in structural equation models. *Sociological Methodology*, **14**: 290–312.

Staiger, D. & Stock, J. H. 1997. Instrumental variables regression with weak instruments. *Econometrica*, **65**(3): 557–586.

Stata, C. 2005. *Stata User's Guide. Release 9*. College Station, TX: Stata Corp.

Steenbergen, M. R. & Jones, B. S. 2002. Modeling multilevel data structures. *American Journal of Political Science*, **46**(1): 218.

Stolzenberg, R. M. & Relies, D. A. 1997. Tools from intuition about sample selection bias and its correction. *American Sociological Review*, **62**(3): 494–507.

Tregaskis, O. & Brewster, C. 2006. Converging or diverging? A comparative analysis of trends in contingent employment practice in Europe over a decade. *Journal of International Business Studies*, **37**(1): 111–126.

Trompenaars, F. & Hampden-Turner, C. 2000. *Riding the Waves of Culture: Understanding Cultural Diversity in Business*, 2nd edn. London: Nicholas Brealey.

Widaman, K. F. 1985. Hierarchically nested covariance structure models for multitrait-multimethod-data. *Applied Psychological Measurement*, **9**: 1–26.

Wooldridge, J. M. 2002. *Econometric Analysis of Cross Section and Panel Data*. Princeton, NJ: Princeton University Press.

Wooldridge, J. M. 2006. *Introductory Econometrics. A Modern Approach*, 3rd edn. Mason, OH: Thomson-South Western.

Wright, P. M., Gardner, T. M., Moynihan, L. M. & Allen, M. R. 2005. The relationship between HR practices and firm performance: examining causal order. *Personnel Psychology*, **52**(2): 409–446.

Wright, P. M., Gardner, T. M., Moynihan, L. M., Park, H. J., Gerhart, B. & Delery, J. E. 2001. Measurement error in research on human resources and firm performance: additional data and suggestions for future research. *Personnel Psychology*, **54**(4): 875–901.

Yeganeh, H. & Su, Z. 2006. Conceptual foundations of cultural management research. *International Journal of Cross Cultural Management*, **6**: 361–376.

PART II

HRM TASKS AND THEMES

6 Recruitment and selection in context
Irene Nikandrou and Leda Panayotopoulou

The process of recruitment and selection is a crucial one, as ensuring the right people to join the workforce helps the organisation meet its short- and long-term objectives. Indeed, both HRM and line managers around the world agree that selecting the right person to fill a job vacancy is an important factor contributing to organisational effectiveness. For the organisation, recruitment and selection imply long-term commitment to a decision that may have a considerable impact on its operations.

The context in which organisations operate is changing and the role of the recruitment and selection process is becoming increasingly important. Demographic changes and growing globalisation have led to changes in the labour markets, characterised by a diversified workforce. This raises issues of fairness and equal opportunities in the selection process (Beaumont, 1993). Moreover, the demand for a more flexible, multi-skilled labour force and the emphasis on teamwork has led to the adoption of a 'social process' or 'exchange' model which emphasises the fit of the person with 'the team or organization' (Newell, 2005).

Recruitment and selection is a two-way decision-making process. The organisation seeks, assesses and decides to make an offer of employment to the candidate, while at the same time, the candidate decides whether to apply and enter into an employment relationship with the organisation. Thus, the whole process involves issues of power, politics, ethics, diversity and equal opportunity, as well as knowledge (Iles, 2007).

In this chapter, we will review the existing literature on recruitment and selection practices, emphasising the contextual factors that contribute to its distinctive form. We examine the nature and form of the factors affecting the relevant processes. We need to examine how recruitment and selection relates, interacts and is influenced by its context. Intense competition, changing demands, speed, flexibility, adaptability and low cost are forces that demand a deep understanding from Human Resource Management (HRM), in order to define and implement adequate HRM strategies and practices. In addition to these institutional factors, Aycan (2005) supports the notion that cultural contingencies affect both the why and the way recruitment and selection is conducted. Towards the end of the chapter we focus in on the national context and the differences in recruitment and selection found at that level.

RECRUITMENT AND SELECTION METHODS AND CRITERIA

With increasing emphasis on people as an important source of competitive advantage, organisations need to develop a systematic approach to recruitment and selection. Organisations need, first, to determine the vacancy, and then to decide the kind of person they want. This is the stage where selection criteria are identified. Then, they must decide what mechanisms will attract the most appropriately qualified people, using the most apt recruitment method or methods, followed by the communication of the recruitment message. The third step is to see how they can identify and assess the candidates, by choosing a mix of selection techniques. Finally, there comes the decision of who is to be involved in the process and the level of centralisation of decision making.

Recruitment Methods

A number of recruitment methods are available to organisations. Some of the most common methods used for recruitment include informal personal contacts, advertisements, electronic recruitment, formal personal contacts, such as careers fairs and open days, and external assistance, such as employment agencies and 'head hunters'. Recruitment methods can be distinguished along two dimensions: (1) level of formality, formal versus informal ('word of mouth') recruitment method, and (2) orientation, that is, internal versus external recruitment. Several studies have shown that recruitment methods are related to turnover and employee morale (Kirnan et al., 1989; Terpstra, 1996). Informal recruitment through existing employees reduces both voluntary and involuntary turnover due to the fact that they have more realistic information about the job and the organisation. Moreover, even though organisations may use a variety of recruitment methods for different managerial levels, it seems that internal recruitment may be preferred, as it is cost effective and contributes to the improvement of the quality of the internal labour market (Heraty & Morley, 1998). Increased career opportunities, skills updating and recognition through promotion create a positive organisational climate and improved morale with motivated employees.

Selection Methods

Usually, a selection process involves a combination of several methods. A number of factors affect which methods are to be used. The available time to fill the position, cost, custom and practice, accuracy, acceptability and appropriateness of the methods, the abilities that HRM and the line managers involved bring to the process, selection criteria for the position to be filled, level of vacancy are all factors which affect the choice of the methods to be used.

The question to be answered here is whether there are some selection practices more commonly used in some nations than in others.

Interviewing is the most popular selection method in nearly all countries. Application forms, references, work sampling and graphology are less commonly used methods of selection. A distinction can be made between 'subjective' and 'objective' methods. Objective methods such as the use of testing as a selection tool are growing, especially for managerial employees (Torrington et al., 2002). Assessment centres are used mainly for managers in large private sector organisations. In the universalistic or 'best practice' approach (Brewster, 1999) the emphasis is on psychometrics, to identify and match the 'right' people to the 'right' jobs. Assessment of candidates through tests, assessment centres and/or other methods stress the importance of 'person-job' fit through objective measures.

Selection Criteria

Hiring criteria should be closely aligned with job requirements, while being consistent with long-term organisational goals and strategies of the firm (Olian & Rynes, 1984). The question is whether there are some universally desirable selection criteria that can be used for recruiting new employees in any organisational setting. A first distinction can be made between 'hard' and 'soft' criteria (Aycan, 2005; Tung, 1998). 'Hard criteria' include such aspects as technical competence, job-related knowledge, cognitive skills and so forth. According to Huo et al. (2002), the evaluation of technical skills has two aspects: ability and potential. In other words, are job candidates able to do the job, or do they have the potential to meet the technical requirements? This question reflects, in part, the difference between 'jobs' and 'careers'. The former assumes that jobs can be clearly defined and that specific skills exist to fit them, while the later points at the unpredictability of the nature of the job in the future (Schneider, 1988). 'Soft criteria' are human relational, social and interpersonal skills. Huo et al (2002) make a further distinction of the job candidate's social calibre on the basis of interpersonal or inter-organisational skills. The former is assessed by the person's ability to get along with other organisational members and their level of fit with the company's values and culture. The latter refers to the candidate's connections to internal or external constituencies.

Another distinction, relevant to the nature of the skills acquired by the national educational system, is that between 'specialists' and 'generalists'

(Segalla et al., 2001). Specialists are individuals with highly technical, narrowly focused skills that make functional mobility more difficult, while generalists may have degrees in psychology or human relations and are considered to have a broader perspective (Olian & Rynes, 1984; Schneider, 1988).

Moreover, there is the distinction between 'doing' and 'being', or 'active' versus 'passive' (Schneider, 1988). This means that selection can be based either on achievement and concrete results, or on who the person is or knows – aspects such as socio-economic background, ascribed status, family ties, school and birthplace (Aycan, 2005).

Next, we will examine the various contextual factors that influence the recruitment and selection practices.

THE CONTEXT

Interest in the impact of context on human resource management (HRM) practices is not new. Both the classical HRM models of Beer et al. (1984) and Fombrun et al. (1984) recognise contextual factors in terms of economic, political and cultural forces. However, recent work seems to give less explicit attention to context, even though all research incorporates contextual factors. The contextualist paradigm, common in Europe, has been based on the assumption that contextual factors contribute to a distinctive form of HRM in Europe in comparison to the rest of the world (Brewster & Larsen, 2000). The focus is on understanding what is different between and within the various HRM systems in various contexts. The contextual factors are seen as aspects of the subject/cluster rather than external factors to it. Brewster (1995) proposed a 'European model of HRM' which places HRM practices at the intersection of international, national and organisational levels. Ignjatovic and Svetlik (2003) and Sparrow and Hiltrop (1997) suggest that cultural factors, institutional factors such as trade unions, labour legislation, business structure and the degree of state ownership and the role and competence of HRM experts have an impact on HRM and its distinctive forms in Europe. Thus, to understand HRM in Europe one has to analyse HRM endogenous and exogenous factors as shaping HRM practices.

In this framework, the concept of 'fit' is helpful. This would encompass both cultural factors and societal values, and institutional factors, such as education systems, labour markets, legal environments, industries or sectors and stakeholder interests such as unions, professional bodies, work councils and so forth. There are four levels of analysis in relation to 'fit' and the study of HRM. First, within the system of HRM practices one has to examine how the various practices complement each other (Wright & McMahan, 1992), or how they promote the same outcomes (Wright, 1998), or possibly, how they counteract each other. This fit among a set of related HRM practices is referred to as horizontal fit or 'internal alignment' (Becker & Gerhart, 1996). Second, for HRM to be effective, it must add value to the organisation's key resource, that is, the human factor, by aligning employee perceptions and behaviours to business strategy. The alignment of HRM practices to business strategy is called vertical or strategic fit. Third, at the organisational level of analysis we give emphasis to how HRM practices support other systems (operations, finance, marketing, etc.) within the organisation. This has been referred to as 'organizational fit' (Wood, 1999). Finally, Wood (1999) mentions one more type of fit, that is, 'environmental fit', which refers to the fit between HRM and the organisation's environment.

Horizontal Fit

By examining the internal fit among the HRM practices one can understand the logic of the HRM system. The unique bundles of HRM practices that an organisation possesses contribute to the creation of a sustainable competitive advantage (Wright & McMahan, 1992). The selection of the right people to join the organisation, the accumulation and the development of the human resources can be a basis for creating a largely inimitable competitive advantage (Raghuram & Arvey, 1994).

A well-known distinction in HRM philosophy concerns the 'buy' or 'make' orientation (Miles & Snow, 1978) that incorporates the notion of HRM bundles, pointing to the need for consistency between all HRM practices. Organisations adopting the 'buy' orientation turn to the external labour market as a source of employees, generally compensate them on a performance basis, and provide minimum attention or commitment to training and career development. Wages, benefits and labour fluctuation are determined by market pressures. On the other hand, the ideal-type 'make' orientation uses external recruitment only at the entry level, emphasises training and career development, and assesses and rewards performance based on internal rather than market criteria. Behaviour and process are important and employees are expected to show loyalty and remain with the organisation for a long time. These are, of course, ideal types and most organisations will in practice use different orientations for different groups within their employment.

Sonnenfeld et al. (1988) propose a typology of career systems based on human resourcing and assignment flow. They argue that organisations may focus either on the internal or the external market to identify the right people. Those organisations that rely on the internal market view people as assets with long term development value. On the other hand, organisations may allocate new tasks based either on the individual contribution to performance or on group contribution. Organisations that reward individual contribution expect individuals to add value on a continuous basis, whereas those that emphasise group contribution view employees as having extrinsic value. More recently, Scholarios et al. (2003) examine the effects of recruitment and selection experiences on career expectations and orientation. They argue that sophisticated selection procedures such as psychometric testing, work samples and assessment centres may enhance career clarity.

A typical example of horizontal fit is lifetime employment, a distinct feature of the Japanese HRM system. Lifetime employment is not a contract, but a particular way of thinking that makes employees devote to the organization and stay there until their retirement. On the other hand, the firm does not terminate the employment lightly. It provides a long socialisation process, continuous training, skills updating in cases of restructuring, internal career paths, seniority-based promotions, and skill-grade pay assisted by broadly designed job classifications that encourage long-term learning (Koen, 2005). Therefore, an important selection criterion used by Japanese firms is 'trainability', the ability to learn, rather than the ability to execute duties (Huo et al., 2002).

In European organisations recruitment and training are closely linked and used as a mechanism to retain employees. The only exception is Germany, where retraining is less used as an option, as employees are unwilling to do a job that does not match their skills (Dietz et al., 2004).

Vertical Fit

In the current literature, HRM is considered a source of organisational competence and competitive advantage (Budhwar, 2000). In order to achieve this, human resources must be fully integrated into the strategic planning process (Guest, 1987). Budhwar and Sparrow (1997) argue that internal organisational policies related to recruitment act as significant determinants of the levels of integration of HRM into the corporate strategy. Brewster and Larsen (1992) define integration as 'the degree to which the HRM issues are considered as part of the formulation of the business strategy'. The rationale for the linkage between strategy and HRM practices was developed by Schuler and Jackson (1987). They argued that, in order to perform a specific task, employees need certain technical knowledge, skills and abilities, but also certain role behaviours stemming from the social environment in which they work. There are likely to be major differences in these needed role behaviours across different strategies, as they require different necessary organisational conditions for their implementation. Beyond that, staffing practices should also consider what skills, aptitudes and behavioural styles are most compatible with future organisational objectives and directions (Olian & Rynes, 1984).

Therefore, Schuler and Jackson (1987) have developed six HRM practice 'menus' that concern different aspects of HRM and together define how HRM practices link with strategy. Each of the choices runs along a continuum and different choices stimulate and reinforce different role behaviours. The recruitment and selection – or staffing choice, as they name it – involves choices between internal or external recruitment sources, narrow or broad paths, single or multiple ladders, explicit or implicit criteria, limited or extensive socialisation and closed or open procedures. Similarly, Olian and Rynes (1984) indicate five stages of the staffing process that require different strategic decisions according to the type of strategy implemented by the organisation. These stages involve decisions concerning the choice of selection criteria, the selection of the recruitment method, the marketing strategy development, the choice of selection techniques and the final decision.

Raghuram and Arvey (1994) examine links between business strategy and staffing and training practices. Based on the Miles and Snow (1978) typology, they examine two strategic types, that is, defenders and prospectors. Defenders compete on the basis of low price and high quality, they operate in a relatively stable environment and, therefore, they have a rather narrow focus. They emphasise efficiency and internal stability, which imply 'building' skills internally through extensive training and internal staffing (1978: 59). On the other hand, prospectors compete on the basis of new products and markets and they operate in a highly unstable environment. Rapid growth, innovation and skill flexibility demand a more external focus from the organisation, or the relevant part of the organisation. Thus, buying already developed skills through external staffing, requiring low amounts of training, are the main characteristics of the prospectors. In practice, whilst the results of this study supported the association of prospect strategy with the practice of 'buying' skills, there was no evidence of a significant relationship of staffing and training with the defence dimension. Similarly, Peck (1994) examined the relationship between the 'buy' and 'make' HRM orientations and the two strategy typologies of Miles and Snow (1978) and Schuler and Jackson (1987). She argued that staffing and development are positively associated with organisational strategy, providing empirical support for the Schuler and Jackson (1987) typology. A more recent cross-country study (Bowen et al., 2002) revealed slight geographical differences in vertical fit between

10 countries. More specifically, the authors studied three types of organisational strategy and their links to various HRM practices, including hiring criteria. They found HRM practices to be strongly linked to 'cost leadership strategy' in Korea and China, to 'differentiation strategy' in China, Japan and Indonesia, and to 'organizational capability' in the Anglo countries (Australia, Canada, United States). These results imply a cultural effect on the issue of vertical fit.

Organisational Fit

At the organisational level of analysis we give emphasis to how HRM practices support other systems within the organisation, which has been referred to as 'organizational fit' (Wood, 1999).

Recruitment and selection policies and practices vary according to the life cycle stage of the organisation. Thus, when organisations first start operating they need to attract the best technical and professional workforce, whilst when they are mature they need to give less emphasis to recruitment (Legge, 1995).

Size also matters, as the larger the organisation is, the more complex its management, and the greater the need for rules and formalised procedures (Sisson & Marginson, 1995). Large organisations may have organised HRM departments that emphasise formal and objective recruitment and selection methods. In small organisations, personnel functions may not exist and reliance on informal and more subjective channels and methods of recruitment and selection may be used. Moreover, the financial position and constraints of an organisation will influence both the number and quality of recruitment and selection methods available for use (Beardwell et al., 2004: 201). In countries with a high percentage of SMEs, like Greece and Cyprus, there is a major impact of the founder/owner of the firm in recruitment and selection decision making, leading recruitment to rely to a large extent on family, friends and personal referrals (Stavrou-Costea & Manson, 2006). Also, Segalla et al. (2001) report that Spanish managers indicate that having the qualities to handle small and medium size firms is the second most important criterion when hiring international managers.

Trade unions may not affect the way firms recruit and select employees directly, but they can affect choices about staffing practices and the extent of use of specific recruitment and selection methods. There are very few studies examining the impact of unionism on staffing and hiring practices. Barron and Bishop (1985) reinforce the point that unionism reduces staffing costs in some areas by reducing hours spent per application, the number of applicants interviewed per offer, and the number of offers per hire. However, the use of selection tests is negatively associated with unionisation (Cohen & Pfeffer, 1986). According to Freeman and Medoff (1983) it is the economic effects of unionism that affect organisational recruitment and selection practices through wage effects, and voice effects. They argue that as unions push for higher wages, higher-quality applicants are attracted. This, in turn, pushes companies to identify superior workers to offset the effect of higher wages through productivity gains. Moreover, unions provide employees with a voice mechanism to express their dissatisfaction and concerns while, at the same time, demanding more job security and better working conditions from companies, which leads to reduced turnover and increased tenure (Freeman, 1980; Koch & Hundley, 1997). In addition, unionism requires management to 'share' authority with non-management employees. Thus, the union voice effect affects hiring practices by making dismissal more costly. At the same time, HRM specialists need to adopt more sophisticated selection methods to identify superior applicants, as it is more difficult and expensive to dismiss less satisfactory employees once they are hired. In a study conducted in United States, Koch and Hundley (1997) found that there is strong evidence that unionisation is associated with decreased use of recruitment sources. As unionism contributes to higher wages, jobs become more attractive, thus increasing the supply of applicants and reducing the need for costly recruitment methods.

Of course, when we examine the effect of unionism on recruitment and selection practices, for comparative purposes, we need to examine the structure and the nature of employee relations in each country and how they affect wages and working conditions.

Environmental Fit

National culture
National culture is the set of collective beliefs and values that distinguish people of one nationality from those of another (Hofstede, 1991) and it is considered an important cause of the differentiation of HRM across countries. In the literature one can find comparative HRM studies that conclude that national culture is a decisive factor in shaping HRM (see, e.g. Heijltjes et al., 1996). In a study of MNCs in 12 countries, Sparrow et al. (1994) found differences in the HRM practices that are perceived to be a source of competitive advantage across the countries. National culture is incorporated in various HRM models as a major factor affecting the formation of HRM practices (Aycan, 2003; Jackson & Schuler, 1995; Milliman et al., 1991; Schuler et al.,1993). Some authors argue that national culture affects some aspects of organisational practices more than others; for example, those aspects of management practices that involve

human interactions with one another (Tayeb, 1998). Tayeb (1995) also suggests that while the 'what' question in HRM might be universal, the 'how' question is culture-specific. For instance, as a practice, employee training and development might be universal, but the degree of reliance on e-learning versus more traditional training methods is very likely to be affected by national culture.

In the literature there is evidence that national culture influences multiple aspects of the recruitment and selection processes (e.g. Aycan, 2005; Huo et al., 2002). First, it affects the criteria used for selecting employees. Interpersonal criteria are more important in collectivistic cultures, low on performance orientation and high on femininity, while 'hard criteria' like knowledge, skills and abilities are more common in cultures that are high on performance orientation or universalism (Aycan, 2005). For example, the selection criteria most commonly used in the United States, very high on performance orientation, are a person's ability to perform the technical requirements of a job and proven work experience in a similar job (Huo et al., 2002). In Japan and Taiwan, highly collectivistic societies, getting along with others is extremely important (Huo et al., 2002). Budhwar and Khatri (2001) suggest that collectivistic and high power distance countries, like India, tend to place greater importance on criteria such as ascribed status and socio-political connections. When it comes to 'generalists' and 'specialists', the match between a specialised position and the capacities of a specialised person is valued in the United States and Germany (Koen, 2005), the Italians, the English and the French tend to choose candidates with a generalist educational background (Segalla et al., 2001), while the Dutch assess a mix of generalist and specialist factors (Koen, 2005).

Second, national culture affects the choice of methods used for both recruitment and selection. Internal recruitment is preferred in cultures with high uncertainty avoidance, as they tend to maintain the status quo (Aycan, 2005). Also, in collectivistic cultures, the limited use of external recruitment sources is due to the fact that it is difficult for externally recruited candidates to get into strong social networks and cope with the resistance following their appointment, especially in cases where an internal candidate is supported (Björkman & Lu, 1999). Also, in highly collectivistic organisations, employees are highly committed to their organisation, ready to make personal sacrifices to fulfil their obligations, while organisations take responsibility for employee welfare (Gelfand et al., 2004). Thus, internal recruitment methods are more likely to be employed. Past studies have shown positive relationships between in-group collectivism and word-of-mouth (Lee, 1999), especially since this method of recruitment is believed to increase commitment and loyalty (Bian & Ang, 1997).

Budhwar and Khatri (2001) argue that internal recruitment promotes loyalty to the organisation. Moreover, in highly human-oriented societies the need for belonging and affiliation motivates people, which may promote internal recruitment (Kabasakal & Bodur, 2004).

Cultures that are collectivistic, avoid uncertainty and are oriented toward ascribed status tend to adopt informal and network-based recruitment channels and methods, as opposed to cultures high on universalism or performance orientation, where recruitment is more formal, structured and widespread (Aycan, 2005). Thus, in low performance-oriented cultures where societal and family relationships are valued, it is more common for organisations to adopt informal recruitment methods (Javidan, 2004). Moreover, Wasti (2000) argues that recruitment through personal contacts promotes loyalty and commitment to the organisation. Societies that are high on uncertainty avoidance tend to rely on formalised policies and procedures and thus adopt more formal recruitment methods (Javidan, 2004). Denmark is an example of a country high in uncertainty avoidance, with one of the highest percentages in Europe of recruitment through newspapers for all the managerial levels (Papalexandris & Panayotopoulou, 2004). In South Korea, employee referral is a commonly used recruiting method for blue-collar employees (Koch et al., 1995).

Regarding selection methods, different methods are used to varying degrees across countries, and this can be partly attributed to differences in national culture. For example, there is a higher use of interview panels in cultures that are high on future orientation, performance orientation or uncertainty avoidance, like Switzerland where the use of interview panels is over 54 per cent (Papalexandris & Panayotopoulou, 2004). Moreover, in Korea the participation of several executives in the interview process is a means of assessing the applicant's potential for working in harmony and becoming part of a team (Lee, 1999). Aycan (2005) mentions that leaderless group discussion is less effective in high power distance cultures. Psychometric testing is avoided in some cultures, like the French, as it can be considered offensive in violating the candidate's privacy (Steiner & Gilliland, 1996). France also has the particularity of using graphology as a selection tool to a larger extent than any other European country (Buyens et al., 2004). The validity of assessment centres as a selection technique has varying cross-cultural validity and utility, because cultural context determines what constitutes good performance (Briscoe, 1997). So, while it is very popular in North America (Briscoe, 1997), its use is almost non-existent in Denmark, Finland, Norway and Sweden (Lindeberg & Vanhala, 2004; Rogaczewska et al., 2004). In general, according to Aycan (2005), in cultures that are high on performance orientation or universalism, selection methods are standardised and job-specific, whereas they are not standardised, are broad-ranging and rely on face-to-face interactions in cultures high on particularism or femininity.

Institutional factors

When organisations decide to turn to the external labour market for recruitment they need to know the profile of the skills, competencies, age and sex distribution existing in the market. A high proportion of women in the labour market may be an indicator of a need for more flexible or 'family friendly' working arrangements. Unemployment rates influence the availability of skills and competences, increase the number of potential recruits and influence the recruitment and selection process. Recruitment and selection may also be seen as a means to fight unemployment and poverty. In former socialist countries, the system provided for full employment. This created problems of unemployment when, in competitive market conditions, organisations in these countries proved to have too many people for their needs. Thus, recruitment and selection can also be seen as a mechanism for meeting societal as well as economic needs. Svetlik and Alas (2006) report that new EU countries, such as Bulgaria, Cyprus, the Czech Republic and Estonia use more informal channels for recruiting their managers than old EU countries. They offer three possible reasons to explain this deviation. First, the organisational culture in the majority of new EU countries favours informality; second, the labour market mechanisms are less developed in these countries; and, finally, the relatively small size of these countries allows informal networks to have a greater role in shaping the labour market.

The level of dynamism in the environment influences the degree of formalisation of selection standards, with organisations operating in a stable environment often clearly articulating the types and levels of qualifications required of job applicants, as opposed to firms operating in a more dynamic environment (Olian & Rynes, 1984). Moreover, innovation, dynamism and the need for multi-experiences may force organisations to emphasise external recruitment to fill their vacancies (Heraty & Morley, 1998). The majority of UK and Irish organisations use internal sources for managerial recruitment, even though there is a trend towards the use of external sources in both countries (Atterbury et al., 2004). According to Atterbury et al. (2004) this trend may reflect the growing pressures for innovation which push organisations to attract 'new' people from other organisations.

Another aspect of external context likely to influence the level of formality is market growth. Several authors have used market growth as an indicator of industry attractiveness. Market growth increases competitive intensity, which forces organisations to give greater emphasis to creating sustained competitive advantage (Lado & Wilson, 1994). Market growth is related to the degree to which organisations define higher levels of formalisation and systematisation of corporate strategies (Cunha et al., 2003). It is expected that organisations that operate in growing markets emphasise the systematic analysis of market and formalization of recruitment methods. Koubek and Vatchkova (2004) mention that organisations in the Czech Republic and Bulgaria do not use modern selection methods, due to inadequate competence and professional capacity in recruitment and selection.

The availability of required skills is also influenced by the education system. Ashton et al. (2000) suggest that to understand the process of skill formation one has to study the underlying relationships between the state, in the form of the political elite and the apparatus of state, the education and training systems which deliver skills, capital in the form of employers through which the demand for skills arise, and workers in the form of employees and their organisations which influence the supply of skills. The educational system influences the choice of recruitment methods. For example, in France the educational elite system of the 'grandes écoles' provides the organisations with a prestigious source of new managerial blood, thus limiting the use of internal recruitment for junior managers (Buyens et al., 2004). The educational system also influences the selection criteria used. In some contexts it is more important to evaluate the candidates' potential to do a good job rather than their technical skills. In Japan the state focuses on the provision of academic education, leading organisations to recruit talented generalists and to invest in training them for a wide array of responsibilities (Huo et al., 2002). Likewise, the German system of initial vocational training is standardised, rendering less important for organizations to test the technical knowledge of employees holding such qualifications (Koen, 2005).

The internet and advances in technology are affecting the type of labour demanded, while at the same time provide a new channel for recruitment and selection. Huo et al. (2002) argue that the spread of the internet has contributed to an accelerated convergence in recruiting practices.

Legislation plays a significant role in the recruitment and selection process by creating boundaries within which organisations must operate, even though they are free to choose the people they want to recruit. Thus, in some countries legislation provides the framework for protecting employees against discrimination on grounds of gender, race or disability. These rules vary between countries, so that, for example, the rules governing non-discrimination in the United States in relation to affirmative action might be illegal in Europe, which requires that each selection decision must be non-discriminatory in its own right.

CONCLUSION

The analysis presented here has important implications for both practitioners and academics. Even though we have identified the factors affecting recruitment and selection, we must mention that differences exist among organisations in the same cultures, sectors, and of similar size, thus reinforcing the importance of managerial choice and the impact of organisational fit decisions. HR managers should be context sensitive when designing and implementing a recruitment and selection system. In particular, differences between organisations in recruitment and selection practice could reflect a strong preference for a particular method, or custom and practice, and the roles and the power position of the recruiters, whether they are in-house or external consultants; or they could be part of different strategic choices. Also, when MNCs are involved, hiring practices may resemble those of the parent company (standardisation), or be adapted to the local needs and culture (localisation). For example, Pudelko and Harzing (2007) found that US subsidiaries are localising their HRM practices in Japan and Germany, although this localisation seems set to decrease in the future; subsidiaries of Japanese MNCs tend to abandon traditional Japanese HRM practices and move toward US practices; German subsidiaries tend to adopt US practices, while they are unwilling to adapt to the Japanese host practices. Furthermore, differences can be found in HRM practices within the same organisation for employees at different levels, or between core and peripheral workforce members. All the above require increased knowledge, flexibility, adaptability and holistic thinking on the part of HRM practitioners.

Further than studying the differences and/or similarities found within and between organisations in terms of recruitment and selection, researchers in this area should take into account all four levels of fit to better understand the recruitment and selection process. Since there is a lack of studies incorporating multilevel variables, future research could benefit from such an approach.

REFERENCES

Ashton, D., Sung, J. & Turbin, J. 2000. Towards a framework for the comparative analysis of national systems of skill formation. *International Journal of Training and Development*, 4(1): 8-25.
Atterbury, S., Brewster, C., Communal, C., Cross, C., Gunnigle, P. & Morley, M. 2004. The UK and Ireland: traditions and transitions in HRM. In C. Brewster, W. Mayrhofer & M. Moorley (eds), *Human Resource Management in Europe: Evidence of Convergence?* Oxford: Elsevier Butterworth-Heinemann, pp. 29–72.

Aycan, Z. 2003. Human resource management in cultural context. Paper presented at the 7th International Human Resource Management conference, Limerick, Ireland.

Aycan, Z. 2005. The interplay between cultural and institutional/structural contingencies in human resource management practices. *International Journal of Human Resource Management*, **16**(7): 1083–1119.

Barron, J. M. & Bishop, J. 1985. Extensive search, intensive search, and hiring costs: new evidence on employer hiring activity. *Economic Inquiry*, **23**(July): 363–382.

Beardwell, I., Holden, L. & Claydon, T. 2004. *Human Resource Management: A Contemporary Approach*, 4th edn. Prentice Hall: Harlow.

Beaumont, P. B. 1993. *Human Resource Management: Key Concepts and Skills*. London: Sage Publications.

Becker, B. & Gerhart, B. 1996. The impact of human resource management on organizational performance: progress and prospects. *Academy of Management Journal*, **39**(4): 779–801.

Beer, M., Spector, B., Lawrence, P. R., Quinn Mills, D. & Walton, R. E. 1984. *Human Resource Management*. New York: Free Press.

Bian, Y. & Ang, S. 1997. Guanxi networks and job mobility in China and Singapore. *Social Forces*, **75**(3): 981–1005.

Björkman, I. & Lu, Y. 1999. The management of human resources in Chinese–Western joint ventures. *Journal of World Business*, **34**(3): 306–325.

Bowen, D., Galang, C. & Pillai, R. 2002. The role of human resource management: an exploratory study of cross-country variance. *Asia Pacific Journal of Human Resources*, **40**(1): 123–145.

Brewster, C. 1995. Towards a European model of human resource management. *Journal of International Business*, **26**(1): 1–22.

Brewster, C. 1999. Different paradigms in strategic HRM: questions raised by comparative research. In P. Wright, L. Dyer, J. Boudreau & G. Milkovich (eds), *Research in Personnel and HRM*, Greenwich, CT: JAI Press Inc., pp. 213–238.

Brewster, C. & Larsen, H. H. 1992. HRM in Europe: evidence from ten countries. *International Journal of Human Resource Management*, **3**(3): 409–433.

Brewster, C. & Larsen, H. H. 2000. *Human Resource Management in Northern Europe*. Oxford: Blackwell.

Briscoe, D. 1997. Assessment centers: cross-cultural and cross-national issues. *Journal of Social Behavior and Personality*, **12**(5): 261–266.

Budhwar, P. 2000. Strategic integration and devolvement of human resource management in the UK manufacturing sector. *British Journal of Management*, **11**(4): 285–302.

Budhwar, P. S. & Khatri, N. 2001. A comparative study of HR practices in Britain and India. *International Journal of Human Resource Management*, **12**(5): 800–826.

Budhwar, P. S. & Sparrow, P. 1997. Evaluating levels of strategic integration and devolvement of human resource management in India. *International Journal of Human Resource Management*, **8**: 476–494.

Buyens, D., Dany, F., Dewettinck, K. & Quinodon, B. 2004. France and Belgium: language, culture and differences in human resource practices. In C. Brewster, W. Mayrhofer & M. Moorley (eds), *Human Resource Management in Europe: Evidence of Convergence*. Oxford: Elsevier Butterworth-Heinemann, pp. 123–159.

Cohen, Y. & Pfeffer, J. 1986. Organizational hiring standards. *Administrative Science Quarterly*, **31**(March): 1–24.

Cunha, R., Cunha, M., Morgado, A. & Brewster, C. 2003. Market forces, strategic management, HRM practices and organizational performance, a model based in a European sample. *Management Research*, **1**(1): 79–91.

Dietz, B., Hoogendoorn, J., Kabst, R. & Schmelter, A. 2004. The Netherlands and Germany: flexibility or rigidity? In C. Brewster, W. Mayrhofer & M. Moorley (eds), *Human Resource Management in Europe: Evidence of Convergence?* Oxford: Elsevier Butterworth-Heinemann, pp. 73–94.

Fombrun, C. J., Tichy, N. M. & Devanna, M. A. 1984. *Strategic Human Resource Management*. New York: Wiley.

Freeman, R. B. 1980. The exit-voice tradeoff in the labor market: unionism, job tenure, quits, and separation. *Quarterly Journal of Economics*, **94** (June): 643–673.

Freeman, R. B. & Medoff, J. L. 1983. The impact of collective bargaining: can the new facts be explained by monopoly unionism? In J. D. Reid (ed.), Supplement 2 of *Research in Labor Economics*. Greenwich, CT: JAI Press, pp. 3-26.

Gelfand, M. J., Bhawuk, D. P. S., Nishii, L. H. & Bechtold, D. J. 2004. Individualism and collectivism. In House et al. (eds), *Culture, Leadership and Organizations: the GLOBE Study of 62 Societies*. Thousand Oaks, CA: Sage Publications, pp. 437–512.

Guest, D. 1987. HRM and industrial relations. *Journal of Management Studies*, **24**(5): 503–521.

Heijltjes, M., Van Witteloostuijn, A. & Sorge, A. 1996. HRM in relation to generic strategies: a comparison of chemical and food and drink companies in the Netherlands and Great Britain. *International Journal of Human Resource Management*, **7**(2): 383–412.

Heraty, N. & Morley, M. 1998. In search of good fit: policy and practice in recruitment and selection in Ireland. *Journal of Management Development*, **17**(9): 662–685.

Hofstede, G. 1991. *Cultures and Organizations*. London: Harper Collins Business.

Huo, P. Y., Huang, H. J. & Napier, N. 2002. Divergence or convergence: a cross-national comparison of personnel selection practices. *Human Resource Management*, **41**(1): 31–44.

Ignjatovic, M. & Svetlik, I. 2003. European HRM clusters. *EBS Review*, **17**(Fall): 25–39.

Iles, P. 2007. Employee resourcing and talent management. In J. Storey (ed.), *Human Resource Management: A Critical Text*, 3rd edn. London: Thomson, pp. 97–114.

Jackson, S. & Schuler, R. 1995. Understanding HRM in the context of organizations and their environments. *Annual Review of Psychology*, **46**: 237–264.

Javidan, M. 2004. Performance orientation. In House et al. (ed.), *Culture, Leadership and Organizations: The GLOBE Study of 62 Societies*. Thousand Oaks: Sage Publications, pp. 239–281.

Kabasakal, H. & Bodur, M. 2004. Humane orientation in societies, organizations, and leader attributes. In House et al. (ed.), *Culture, Leadership and Organizations: The GLOBE Study of 62 Societies*. Thousand Oaks, CA: Sage, pp. 564–601.

Kirnan, J. P., Farley, J. & Geisinger, K. 1989. The relationship between recruiting sources, applicant quality and hire performance: an analysis by sex, ethnicity and age. *Personnel Psychology*, **42**(2): 293–308.

Koch, M. J. & Hundley, G. 1997. The effects of unionism on recruitment and selection methods. *Industrial Relations*, **36**(3): 349–370.

Koch, M. J., Nam, S. H. & Steers, R. M. 1995. Human resource management in South Korea. In L. F. Moore & P. D. Jennings (eds), *Human Resource Management on the Pacific Rim*. Berlin: Walter de Gruyter, pp. 217–242.

Koen, C. 2005. *Comparative International Management*. London: McGraw-Hill.

Koubek, J. & Vatchkova, E. 2004. Bulgaria and Czech Republic: countries in transition. In C. Brewster, W. Mayrhofer & M. Moorley (eds), *Human Resource Management in Europe: Evidence of Convergence?* Oxford: Elsevier Butterworth-Heinemann, pp. 313-351.

Lado, A. A. & Wilson, M. C. 1994. Human resource systems and sustained competitive advantage: a competency-based perspective. *Academy of Management Review*, **19**(4): 699–727.

Lee, H. C. 1999. Transformation of employment practices in Korean businesses. *International Studies of Management and Organization*, **28**(4): 26–39.

Legge, K. 1995. *Human Resource Management: Rhetorics and Reality*. Basingstoke, UK: Macmillan Business.

Lindeberg, T. & Vanhala, S. 2004. Sweden and Finland: small countries with large companies. In C. Brewster, W. Mayrhofer & M. Moorley (eds), *Human Resource Management in Europe: Evidence of Convergence?* Oxford: Elsevier Butterworth-Heinemann, pp. 279–312.

Miles, R. E. & Snow, S. S. 1978. *Organizational Strategy, Structure, and Process*. New York: McGraw-Hill.

Milliman, J., Von Glinow, M. A. & Nathan, M. 1991. Organizational life cycles and strategic international HRM in multinational companies: implications for congruence theory. *Academy of Management Review*, **16**(2): 318–339.

Newell, S. 2005. Recruitment and selection. In S. Bach (ed.), *Managing Human Resources*, 4th edn. Oxford: Blackwell.

Olian, J. & Rynes, S. 1984. Organizational staffing: integrating practice with strategy. *Industrial Relations*, **23**(2): 170-183.

Papalexandris, N. & Panayotopoulou, L. 2004. Exploring the mutual interaction of societal culture and human resource management practices: evidence from 19 countries. *Employee Relations*, **26**(5): 495–509.

Peck, S. 1994. Exploring the link between organizational strategy and the employment relationship: the role of human resources policies. *Journal of Management Studies*, **31**(5): 715–730.

Pudelko, M. & Harzing, A. W. 2007. Country-of-origin, localization, or dominance effect? An empirical investigation of HRM practices in foreign subsidiaries. *Human Resource Management*, **46**(4): 535–559.

Raghuram, S. & Arvey, R. D. 1994. Business strategy links with staffing and training practices. *Human Resource Planning*, **17**(3): 55–73.

Rogaczewska, A. P., Holt Larsen, H., Nordhaug, O., Doving, E. & Gjelsvik, M. 2004. Denmark and Norway: siblings or cousins? In C. Brewster, W. Mayrhofer & M. Moorley (eds), *Human Resource Management in Europe: Evidence of Convergence?* Oxford: Elsevier Butterworth-Heinemann. pp. 231–277.

Schneider, S. C. 1988. National versus corporate culture: implications for human resource management. *Human Resource Management*, **27**(2): 231–246.

Scholarios, D., Lockyer, C. & Johnson, H. 2003. Anticipatory socialisation: the effect of recruitment and selection experiences on career expectations. *Career Development International*, **8**(4): 182–197.

Schuler, R., Dowling, P. & De Cieri, H. 1993. An integrative framework of strategic international human resource management. *International Journal of Human Resource Management*, **4**(4): 717–764.

Schuler, R. & Jackson, S. 1987. Linking competitive strategies with HRM practices. *Academy of Management Executive*, **1**(3): 207–219.

Segalla, M., Sauquet, A. & Turati, C. 2001. Symbolic versus functional recruitment: cultural influences on employee recruitment policy. *European Management Journal*, **19**(1): 32–43.

Sisson, K., & Marginson, P. 1995. Management: systems, structures and strategy. In P. Edwards (ed.), *Industrial Relations: Theory and Practice*. Oxford: Blackwell, pp. 157–188.

Sonnenfeld, J. A. & Peiperl, M. A. 1988. Staffing policy as a strategic response: a typology of career systems. *Academy of Management Review*, **13**(4): 588–600.

Sparrow, P. R. & Hiltrop, J. M. 1997. Redefining the field of European human resource management: a battle between national mindsets and forces of business transition? *Human Resource Management*, **36**(2): 201–219.

Sparrow, P., Schuler, R. & Jackson, S. 1994. Convergence or divergence: human resource practices and policies for competitive advantage worldwide. *International Journal of Human Resource Management*, **5**(2): 267–299.

Stavrou-Costea, E. & Manson, B. 2006. HRM in small and medium enterprises: typical, but typically ignored. In H. H. Larsen & W. Mayrhofer (eds), *Managing Human Resources in Europe*. London: Routledge, pp. 107–130.

Steiner, D. & Gilliland, S. 1996. Fairness reactions to personnel selection techniques in France and United States. *Journal of Applied Psychology*, **81**(2): 134–142.

Svetlik, I. & Alas, R. 2006. The European Union and HRM: impact on present and future members. In H. H. Larsen & W. Mayrhofer (eds), *Managing Human Resources in Europe* 21-43. London: Routledge, pp. 21–43.

Tayeb, M. 1995. The competitive advantage of nations: the role of HRM and its socio-cultural context. *International Journal of Human Resource Management*, **6**(3): 588–605.

Tayeb, M. 1998. Transfer of HRM practices across cultures: an American company in Scotland. *International Journal of Human Resource Management*, **9**(2): 332–358.

Terpstra, D. 1996. The search for effective methods (employee recruitment and selection. *HR Focus*, **17**(5): 16–18.

Torrington, D., Hall, L. & Taylor, S. 2002. *Human Resource Management*, 5th edn. Harlow, UK: Prentice Hall.

Tung, R. L. 1998. American expatriates abroad: from neophytes to cosmopolitans. *Journal of World Business*, **33**: 125–144.

Wasti, S. A. 2000. A cultural analysis of organizational commitment and turnover intentions in a collectivist society. Working Paper: University of Illinois.

Wood, S. 1999. Human resource management and performance. *International Journal of Management Reviews*, **1**(4): 367–413.

Wright, P. M. 1998. HR fit: does it really matter? *Human Resource Planning*, **21**(4): 56–57.

Wright, P. M. & McMahan, G. C. 1992. Theoretical perspectives for strategic human resource management. *Journal of Management*, **18**(2): 295–320.

7   HRM activities: pay and rewards
Marion Festing, Allen D. Engle Sr.,
Peter J. Dowling and Ihar Sahakiants

Compensation is crucial for both employers and employees. It is an important source of motivation and an instrument for attracting and retaining employees (Milkovich and Newman, 2008). At the same time, it represents a significant part of the production costs of the firm, especially in developed industries. Most of the research in the field of international reward systems focuses on monetary elements of pay, which makes the analysis incomplete. Therefore, this chapter takes a broader perspective by focusing on the total compensation concept. This includes, in addition to the monetary elements, the non-monetary contributions of the employer. It has increasingly been used in recent work to provide the international comparability of national compensation data.

Despite the importance of the field of compensation and rewards, the topic of international or comparative rewards is still an underdeveloped area. It is part of comparative management research, the major objective of which is to 'identify aspects of organizations which are similar and aspects which are different in cultures around the world' (Adler, 1984: 32). The academic work in this field either takes a macro-economic approach focusing on indicators for labour costs and productivity or follows a Human Resource Management perspective. In the latter case, latent variables such as the impact of the institutional or cultural environments on the choice of pay elements and attitudes are at the centre of consideration. The complexity involved in considering the variety of influence factors on international compensation explains the research deficit in this field and the limited amount of suggested practical implications for designing international pay systems (Milkovich and Newman, 2008).

However, there has been a growing interest in the topic of comparative compensation over the last decades, which can be explained in the first place by the growing internationalisation of national economies, or to use Perlmutter's (1969) terminology, by the shift from an ethnocentric to a geocentric mentality in many cases. At the same time the research interests have shifted from a focus on expatriate compensation (e.g. Reynolds, 1986) to a more encompassing view of international compensation, ranging from cross-national compensation studies (Lowe et al., 2002), transnational remuneration practices (Festing et al., 2007), to emerging global compensation structures (Baranski, 1999; Dwyer, 1999; Festing and Perkins, 2008; Gross and Wingerup, 1999; Milkovich and Bloom, 1998; White, 2005).

The objective of this contribution is to build on this knowledge and to draw a holistic picture of comparative rewards considering the various practices, the prevalent theoretical explanations and methodological approaches as well as the limited empirical evidence. Main research questions include: what are the differences in approaches to compensation in international contexts; how can these differences be explained and what are the limits for international best practices in certain national contexts; and what are the possibilities for global standardisation of compensation practices? For a descriptive analysis illustrating our results we will use selected data generously provided by Hewitt Associates.

In the next section, the authors will introduce the total rewards concept. A literature review on international compensation and comparative studies of pay systems will also be presented. We provide empirical data on comparative rewards and discuss this in the context of possible influence factors accounting for international differences. The conclusion draws implications for the possibilities and limits of convergence or divergence of compensation practices across the globe and discusses whether there is a possibility for standardisation of compensation practices in multinational enterprises. Finally, the implications of this approach for future research are discussed.

UNDERSTANDING TOTAL REWARDS

Recently, there has been increased attention on the total compensation approach to international compensation in both the academic (Milkovich and Bloom, 1998; Milkovich and Newman, 2008) and the practitioner literature (Hewitt Associates, 1991; Milkovich and Newman, 2008; White, 2005). Manas and Graham (2003) define total compensation as a part of total rewards, which includes extrinsic and quantifiable elements of total rewards such as fixed and variable pay, benefits and perquisites (see Figure 7.1).

The importance of non-monetary compensation elements in national and international contexts can be presented by their relative weight in the total remuneration package. For example, according to a recent assessment of a German management institute (Institut der deutschen Wirtschaft, 2008), the compensation for hours worked in Germany (including variable pay) accounts for about 76 per cent of the total cash

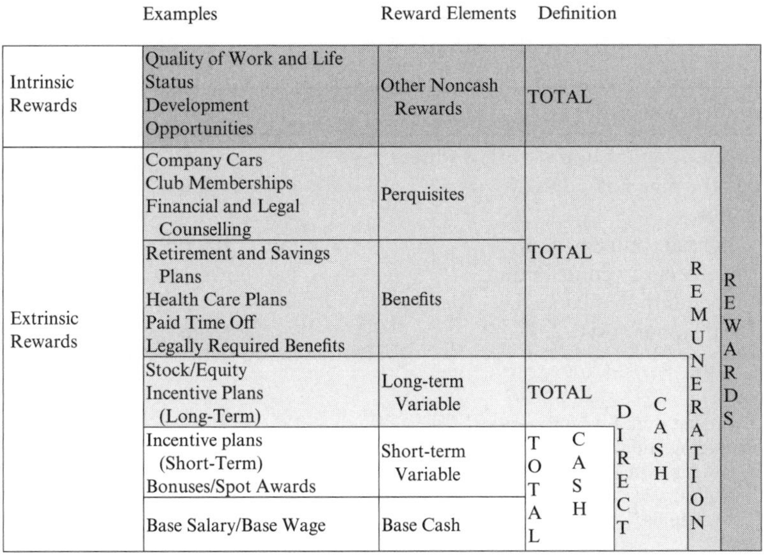

Examples   Reward Elements   Definition

Examples	Reward Elements	Definition				
Intrinsic Rewards — Quality of Work and Life, Status, Development Opportunities	Other Noncash Rewards	TOTAL				R E M U N E R A T I O N
Extrinsic Rewards — Company Cars, Club Memberships, Financial and Legal Counselling	Perquisites					R E W A R D S
Retirement and Savings Plans, Health Care Plans, Paid Time Off, Legally Required Benefits	Benefits	TOTAL				
Stock/Equity Incentive Plans (Long-Term)	Long-term Variable	TOTAL	D I R E C T	C A S H		
Incentive plans (Short-Term), Bonuses/Spot Awards	Short-term Variable	T O T A L	R E M U N E R A T I O N	C A S H	C O M P E N S A T I O N	T O T A L R E W A R D S
Base Salary/Base Wage	Base Cash					

Source: Adapted from Manas and Graham (2003: 2).

Figure 7.1   Components of a total rewards approach

compensation package, excluding employers' social security contributions and training costs. Table 7.1 shows that compensation for time not worked accounts for nearly 17 per cent of total pay. Performance neutral bonuses (for example the Christmas bonus or the '13th salary') are often a part of the employment contract and account for about 7% of total pay.

A strong argument in favour of using the total compensation approach for international comparisons of the pay structures is the substitutive effect between the monetary (wages/salaries and incentives) and non-monetary (benefits and perquisites) elements of pay, which may vary significantly between different countries and cultures. A study by Zhou and Martocchio (2001) focusing on compensation award decisions and mainly looking at the determination of bonus amounts and non-monetary recognition by Chinese and American managers underlines the importance of looking at these dimensions simultaneously. The results of this study showed that, compared with their American counterparts, Chinese managers (1) put less emphasis on work performance when making bonus decisions; (2) put more emphasis on relationships with co-workers when making non-monetary decisions; (3) put more emphasis on relationships with managers when making non-monetary award decisions; and (4) put more emphasis on personal needs when making bonus decisions (Zhou

Table 7.1   Labour costs in Germany: manufacturing industry, in per cent to gross wages and salaries[a]

Remuneration elements	2004	2007
Compensation for hours worked (direct pay)[b,c]	75.8	76.1
+ Pay for time not worked[d]	16.6	16.6
+ Bonuses	7.6	7.3
= total cash compensation	100.0	100.0
+ Social security contributions	26.1	25.7
+ Other additional personnel expenses[e]	4.5	4.3
= Total labour costs	130.6	130.0

Notes:
a.   Compensation for hours worked.
b.   Including additional payments for performance.
c.   Calendar adjusted.
d.   Including vacation, paid sick leave, paid days off.
e.   Less refunds.

Source: Adapted from Schröder (2008: 4, 11)

and Martocchio, 2001: 115). Thus, this broader conceptualization of total compensation ensures more objective comparisons of compensation packages. For example, in multinational enterprises (MNEs) it can be used as an important instrument to benchmark pay systems around the globe, either to install external competitiveness or to promote internal consistency. Furthermore, the total compensation approach can be instrumental in ensuring the strategic flexibility necessary to operate in multiple institutional environments (Gross and Wingerup, 1999; Milkovich and Bloom, 1998; White, 2005).

THE NATIONAL CONTEXT AS A MAJOR DETERMINANT OF PAY PRACTICES

Research on the determinants of pay practices is rich and varied. Milkovich and Newman (2008) have identified four groups of factors explaining the variations in compensation designs: institutional, economic, organisational and employee pressures (see also Gerhart, 2008). These four groups of factors can be summarised in three levels of analysis featuring individual (employee), organisational and environmental (economic and institutional) factors. Table 7.2 presents examples of the parameters included in each level. While we will briefly discuss how individual and organisational

Table 7.2   Factors influencing compensation decisions

Levels of analysis	Factors
Individual	Age
	Job tenure
	Marital status
	Family size
	Education
	(Churchill et al., 1979; Huddleston et al., 2002)
Organisational	Stage in the product life cycle
	Size of the firm
	Industry traits
	Ownership structure
	Organisational culture
	Profitability
	(Balkin and Gomez-Mejia, 1987)
Environmental	Employer federations
	Trade unions
	Social contract
	Culture/politics
	Competitive dynamics/markets
	Taxes
	(Milkovich and Newman, 2008)

factors influence compensation decisions the focus clearly is on the impact of the environmental factors as these matter the most in comparative rewards. However, taking this simplifying approach, we do not deny the interrelationships between the mediation of national effects for example through organisational practices and thus multi-level effects (Bowen and Ostroff, 2004; Brewster et al., 2007; Ostroff and Bowen, 2000).

The first level of analysis deals with individual preferences and expectations of employees that influence compensation decisions. According to Dittrich and Carrell (1976), negative perceptions of pay-related organisational fairness result in absence and turnover of employees. This points to the relative nature of the justice perception of pay (Milkovich and Newman, 2008). The pay levels and structures are compared to those of the social referents chosen by an individual. For instance, Kulik and Ambrose (1992) have identified a variety of personal characteristics that determine the process of referent selection: gender, race, age, position and professionalism. This means that any international comparison and measurement of specific national attitudes and values should control for these variables to achieve valid results. Furthermore, situational factors such as job facet comparison, changes in allocation procedures and physical proximity (Kulik and Ambrose, 1992) may deliver additional insights about the perception of justice in the international context.

In a globalised economy supported by sophisticated information and communication devices individuals can theoretically compare their pay conditions with anyone around the globe with the same demographic features and holding comparable positions, but in most cases the limits of physical proximity seem to hamper selection of referents outside of national borders. Moreover, individual differences not only have an impact on the selection of referents but also on pay preferences themselves, including elements of monetary and non-monetary rewards. A study by Churchill et al. (1979) suggested that in the United States older workers expressed higher preference for extrinsic rewards than their younger counterparts, while Frey (1997) presents empirical studies from Europe and the United States supporting his contention that explicit rewards 'crowd out' intrinsic rewards across a wide range of employee groups. Milkovich and Newman (2008) report preferences amongst American employees for pension plans among older workers and preferences for health insurance among employees with dependents.

The second level of analysis presented in Table 7.2 concerns the impact of organisational features on compensation decisions. Here, an important influence factor is the corporate strategy (Boudreau and Ramstad, 2007). In the case of remuneration this was confirmed by an early empirical study by Balkin and Gomez-Mejia (1987). However, especially in large international and diversified corporations other contingencies such as the functional area matter as well. For instance, in their analysis of factors influencing compensation strategies in foreign subsidiaries in Finland, Björkman and Furu (2000) noted a higher incidence of pay-for-performance (PfP) schemes in sales companies than in production and R&D units. Similar results were found by Hannon et al. (1990). They found that organisations adopting research and development intensive strategies differ in the pattern of their pay practices from other firms. The impact of ownership structures on both CEO compensation and the pay of all employees (Werner et al., 2005) is another example of the influence of contingencies. In international comparisons these factors become crucial due to significant variations in ownership and control schemes around the globe (Whitley, 1999).

The third level of analysis deals with the external contextual factors, which according to Hofer (1975) include economic conditions, demographic trends, socio-cultural trends, political, legal and other environmental factors. The explicit consideration of environmental factors in the study of comparative human resource management reflects a contextual rather than a universalistic paradigm (Brewster, 2007). This points to two major explanations in the variation of HRM practices including compensation: the institutional approach (DiMaggio and Powell, 1983; Whitley, 1992) and the cultural perspective (Sánchez Marín, 2008a, 2008b; Sparrow, 2009). The institutional approach highlights the importance of exogenous factors and recognises that contextual institutional pressures may be powerful influences on pay strategy (De Cieri and Dowling, 1999; Sánchez Marín, 2008a, 2008b; Wächter et al., 2003). Whitley (1992) has noted that differences in business practices and organisational structures around the globe are important features of distinctive business systems which are linked to the institutional environments in which they develop and emphasise the contextual nature of firms as economic agents (1992: 7). These environmental factors become of primary importance especially for MNEs that operate in multiple institutional contexts and are confronted with the need to promote internal consistency and at the same time face local isomorphic pressures (Festing et al., 2007; Festing and Sahakiants, 2010a, 2010b; Rosenzweig and Nohria, 1994). Empirical studies have confirmed the impact of institutional factors on compensation design (see, for example, Wächter et al., 2003). Trade unions, which are part of the national institutional environment play an important role in the collective determination of wages and salaries in many countries (Parboteeah and Cullen, 2003; Traxler et al., 2008) and may oppose the diffusion of compensation practices (Kurdelbusch, 2002). However, according to Brewster et al. (2007), the empirically tested correlation between union density and the incidence of PfP practices is far from obvious. The key focus of both trade unions and legislators often seems to concern working hours. For example, the latest OECD Economic Policy Reforms Report (2008a) indicates that high union density accounts for lower hours actually worked by men and higher hours actually worked by women. However, no other elements of rewards seem to be as much effected by national institutions as benefits – largely due to the influence of taxation laws. As Brewster et al. (2007: 122) point out 'in China, but also in Japan and Korea, employees value benefits increases and bonuses above basic pay increases, partly because tax is levied on basic pay'. The same is true in the United States, while in Europe benefits are less common.

Contextual paradigm researchers have also extensively explored the impact of cultural variables on national compensation design (Gomez-Mejia and Welbourne, 1991; Newman and Nollen, 1996; Schuler and Rogovsky, 1998; Tosi and Greckhamer, 2004; Townsend et al., 1990) either by applying Hofstede's dimensions (Hofstede, 1980) directly or using such similar cultural factors as 'individualism/collectivism' as reference points (Lowe et al., 2002). Following the national culture approach means that 'national culture can play a significant part in the evolution of pay systems and the effectiveness of compensation strategies' (Gomez-Mejia and Welbourne, 1991: 39). Since Hofstede's research many other scholars have recognised the importance of culture and its impacts on human resource and compensation issues (Gerhart, 2008; Rogovsky et al., 2000; Sparrow, 2004). Tosi and Greckhamer (2004) present evidence that cultural dimensions may influence CEO pay practices more powerfully, as compared to overall firm practices, due to the 'symbolic' attention socially ascribed to more public and visible executive pay practices.

Some researchers have pointed out deficiencies of cultural typologies and their application to the comparative studies of remuneration designs (Milkovich and Bloom, 1998; Milkovich and Newman, 2008). Vernon states: 'Assertions about the nature of a particular nation's culture are sometimes ill-based and simplistic, evidence of a particular pay system is sketchy, and the claim that there is some link between the two is left unsubstantiated by any contrast with the situation in other nations' (2006: 225). To conclude the discussion on the influence of national contexts on compensation decisions, it should be mentioned that even though the arguments based on the institutional point of view seem to be much more robust, the importance of research based on the cultural perspective should not be underestimated. Thus, some researchers call for a richer theoretical framework which allows for the explicit inclusion and further development of cultural and institutional arguments (see, for example, Brewster, 2004; Sánchez Marín, 2008a, 2008b; Sorge, 2004).

It should be borne in mind that due to the large number of contingency factors effecting compensation strategy (Balkin and Gomez-Mejia, 1987) and the large choice of benefit programmes that could potentially be offered to employees, even a nationwide comparison of total compensation can be problematic. An international comparison of total compensation is even more complex in the view of different regulatory environments with respect to taxation, social security systems and work time regulations. However, a number of features that may characterise each country or region could be identified with respect to the elements and structure of pay and are analysed in the next section.

EMPIRICAL EVIDENCE FOR NATION-BASED DIFFERENCES IN TOTAL COMPENSATION: ANALYSING ELEMENTS OF TOTAL REWARDS

There are considerable pay level and pay mix variations across nations (Dowling et al., 2005). First of all, compensation levels differ due to varying economic conditions in low and high pay countries. This is confirmed by macroeconomic indicators such as gross domestic product (GDP) per capita levels calculated by purchasing power parity (UNDP, 2007). These variations have been extensively studied by a number of national and international organisations that carry out regular surveys on international pay (e.g., the Organisation for Economic Co-operation and Development and the European Foundation for the Improvement of Living and Working Conditions). The information provided by these agencies along with the data from the national or supranational organisations, like the Bureau of Labour Statistics of the US Department of Labor or International Labour Organization, are rich but sometimes limited in their comparability due to aggregation problems. Besides evidence on pay level, evidence on pay mix is collected by most of the leading international HR consulting firms.

Evidence on Working Hours and Paid Leave

Working hours and paid leave provide important additional information when analysing pay level in a comparative way because these two elements provide data on how the institutional context influences total compensation packages. There are different sources of information on working hours and paid leave such as the International Labour Organization database on working time around the world (International Labour Organization, 2009). However, while the comparison of statutory minimum vacation can provide an accurate picture of the differences in some regulatory environments around the globe, there are substantial differences in some countries between the mandatory minimum and customary length of the paid time off. For instance, the statutory minimum vacation in Germany is 24 days (further information can be retrieved from Germany Trade and Invest, 2009; or International Labour Organization, 2009) which is less than the common vacation period of 30 days. In Germany, this is the result of the influence of trade unions that stipulate in collective agreements the duration of the paid time off, which normally exceeds the statutory minimum. Even though nearly 62 per cent of German enterprises were not bound by any collective agreement in 2006, a significant number of these companies (26 per cent) used collective agreements as a guide to arrange employment conditions (Institut der deutschen Wirtschaft, 2008; see International Labour Organization, 2009). A second way to compare working time internationally is to measure the hours worked per year in different countries. However, the evidence delivered by this approach, used for example by the OECD (2008a), is also limited because the statistics include both full-time and part-time positions.

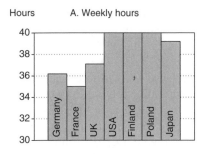
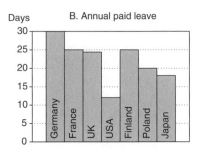
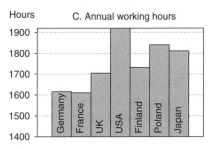

Source: BDA (2005), Institut der deutschen Wirtschaft (2008).

*Figure 7.2   Collectively agreed annual working time of workers in
manufacturing, 2004*

Differences in working arrangement can be shown by comparing collectively agreed working hours and paid days off. Figure 7.2 presents graphs of data for workers in manufacturing with regard to (A) Weekly hours, (B) Annual paid leave, and (C) Annual working hours. For example, a customary vacation of 30 days in Germany may account for about 17 per cent of total cash compensation, whereas the share of vacation in the United States may constitute only 9 per cent of total cash rewards. Thus, a focus on the base pay rate alone does not make compensation at different locations comparable. International comparative data on vacations is an underrated but important issue for MNEs. For example, agreements on vacation time for international transferees have become an indispensable part of transfer planning (Poe, 2001). Employees on international assignments often have a choice between a longer vacation or the monetary equivalent. For instance, according to Oechsler et al. (2008), BASF, one of the world's largest MNEs in the chemical industry, offers its transferees a choice between taking a vacation according to German home country regulations or an additional allowance to compensate for the shorter annual leave in the host country.

Total Cash Compensation

The data presented in this section of the chapter (provided courtesy of Hewitt Associates, one of the leading HR management consulting firms) allows us to go into further detail with respect to specific positions that provides greater comparability than publicly available aggregated data. These results are based on the total compensation survey data for 2007 from 15 countries, which covered 784 companies for the position of General Manager, 820 companies for the position of Head of HRM and 284 companies for the position of Junior HRM Specialist. The data in Figure 7.3 is based on median values for all companies ranked by sales volumes and positions and shows total cash compensation levels which includes base pay and short-term variable compensation. The comparison of total cash compensation levels for these positions shows the following patterns:

● Levels of executive total cash compensation in the USA significantly exceed the levels in other countries, which has been confirmed by recent studies on global executive compensation (e.g. Berrone and Otten, 2008).

● The United States, Western European countries and Mexico lead with respect to pay levels for General Manager and Head of HRM positions.

Share of Target Variable Pay

An analysis of the share of variable pay in Figure 7.4 allows us to observe further differences between the countries surveyed with respect to the pay structure:

● Figure 7.4 shows comparable shares of variable compensation for executives in all countries presented with the exception of the United States, where companies traditionally strongly promote PfP schemes for senior manager positions.

● The data clearly indicate that for lower management positions the spread of PfP schemes does not vary a great deal, with the exception of India where there is a relatively high level of variable pay because of the widespread practice of cash allowances paid on top of the base salary, including lunch, house, travel, medical and other allowances.

With respect to the ratio of variable pay to total pay, Tosi and Greckhamer (2004) reported in their study on the cultural influences on

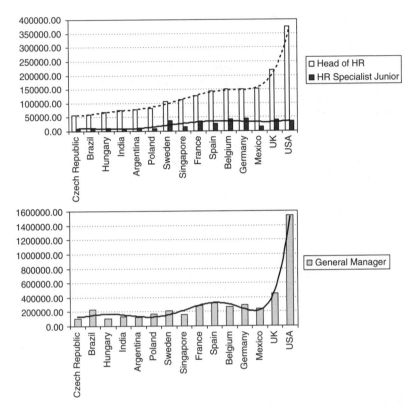

Note: The data for the positions of Head of HR and General Manager in the USA stem from a report for 2008 (Hewitt Associates, 2008)

Source: Hewitt Associates (2007a, 2007b, 2008).

Figure 7.3   International comparison of total cash compensation levels in euros, 2007

CEO compensation that this ratio is influenced by cultural concepts such as Hofstede's individualism dimension. At least for the United States the data presented here could be interpreted to support this conclusion. On the other hand, Balkin (2008) notes that in addition to 'cultural norms that emphasize individualism', high US CEO pay compared to CEO compensation levels in enterprises of comparable size in other leading industrial economies could be explained by institutional factors such as: (1) the system of corporate governance (e.g. in the United States it is quite common for the roles of Chairman of the Board of Directors and CEO to be held by the same individual but this is much less common in countries

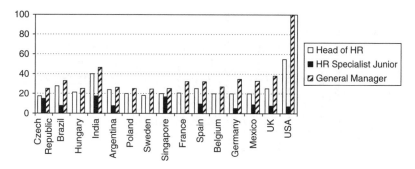

Note: Refer to note to Figure 7.3.

Source: Hewitt Associates (2007a, 2007b, 2008).

Figure 7.4   *Share of target variable pay as percentage of base salary, 2007*

such as Britain); (2) regulations that require CEO pay disclosure; (3) regulations that facilitate the early adoption of stock options; (4) decentralised rules of incorporation; and (5) mega-stock option grants diffused as a CEO pay practice (2008: 202–203). The data in Figure 7.4 may in fact show the complex interaction between a pattern of cultural values and assumptions interacting with historically derived, yet dynamic institutional and contextual artefacts codified into laws and operating on a national level. The difficulty is that all national pay systems probably result from a complex web of cultural–historical–institutional and regulatory elements (Balkin, 2008: 202–203; Berrone et al., 2008; Greene, 2008). Recent institutional concerns over the dysfunctional consequences of executive pay programmes may yet result in even more explicit and transparent systems in North America (Makri and Gomez-Mejia, 2007; Thompson, 2006). The extent to which culture interacts with other contextual variables to influence reward preferences clearly warrants future research (Chiang, 2005).

Increased applications of more formalised performance management systems as a 'best practice' across cultures may provide a more standardised, explicit platform for justifying PfP practices for a range of employee groups (DeNisi et al., 2008: 254–258). At the same time, an adequate conceptualisation of a performance management system that 'travels well' across cultures continues to elude practitioner and researcher alike (Brody et al., 2006; Engle et al., 2008). In the absence of a compelling, flexible performance management system, it is highly likely that local and regional compensation traditions will continue to operate. It is also the case that the exact nature of the targets and systems operationalised as triggers to performance based payouts vary significantly amongst firms that

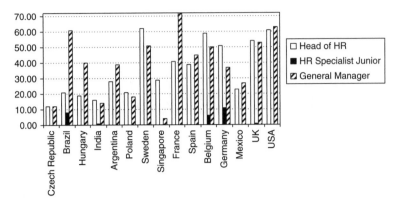

Notes:
Refer to note to Figure 7.3.
a   For the United States the data on nonqualified stock options only is available. In UK,
    there are statistics on both approved and non-approved stock options (the prevalence
    of both types is nearly the same for all the companies surveyed). In order to maintain
    comparability of the data with the prevalence of nonqualified stock options in the
    United States, the statistics for the UK include the incidence of non-approved stock
    options only.

Source: Hewitt Associates (2007a, 2007b, 2008).

Figure 7.5   Prevalence of stock option schemes, 2007[a]

emphasise variable pay (Hope and Fraser, 2003). Wide variations in some combination of internal and external measures of performance, combined with latitude in weights placed on these measures and the timing of these combinations of triggers provide ample opportunity for 'gamesmanship' by the actors of these PfP systems (Ellig, 2008).

Benefits and Other Elements of Total Compensation

An international comparison of other elements of total compensation is far more difficult. Varying local social security and taxation laws as well as the specifics of local financial markets makes national comparisons of long-term incentives, benefits and perquisites a very problematic area. A comparison of the prevalence of certain compensation elements can give an idea of differences with respect to total pay structures across the globe. As an example of this approach, Figure 7.5 shows the prevalence of stock option plans across a number of countries. There is considerable variation in Figure 7.5 with a high degree of use of stock option plans in the USA and a number of other countries such as the UK, France, Sweden and Brazil and relatively few countries reporting stock option plans for junior

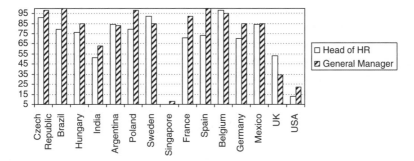

Notes: Refer to note to Figure 7.3.

Source: Hewitt Associates (2007a, 2007b, 2008).

Figure 7.6   Percentage prevalence of company cars, 2007

managers. This data on the prevalence of stock options plans is consistent with data related to management positions provided by the Cranet survey (Brewster et al., 2007).

Pendleton et al. (2002) examined the extent of financial participation in the European Union and reported that the incidence of profit sharing and share ownership differed considerably among Member States and was greatly influenced by the degree of national legislative and fiscal support for these practices. Festing et al. (1999) reported similar results and note that legal complexity and a formalised German workplace industrial relations system are the main reasons that financial participation schemes are not common in Germany. In summary, country level factors strongly influence the incidence of financial participation in Europe and their impact exceeds the importance of many internal influencing factors in global pay systems.

Figure 7.6 shows the prevalence of provision of company cars as a benefit across a range of countries. With the clear exception of the United States and Singapore, the prevalence of company cars for executives is common in most of the countries surveyed – especially in Europe. Just as reported nearly two decades ago (Hewitt Associates, 1991), company owned cars are provided by nearly all companies in Belgium, mainly due to taxation issues. It is interesting to note that while company-owned cars are relatively rare in the United States, the Hewitt survey found that 40 per cent of the US companies surveyed provided access to a company aircraft for their CEO. While the comparative data on the prevalence of company cars delivers important information with respect to job benchmarking and differences among the countries, it is impossible to compare the monetary values of this perquisite consistent with the total remuneration approach. There are numerous schemes to obtain cars ranging from direct purchase to leasing and employees are often required to pay contributions for the private use of company owned cars from their net income. This however does not diminish the primary impact of national tax environments on decisions with respect to perquisites in general and corporate cars in particular. A similar conclusion can be drawn with regard to comparison of total cash compensation levels across countries – there are significant differences in taxation and social security regulations among countries as well as significant variations in cost-of-living that account for differences with respect to real compensation levels.

CONCLUSION

Convergence and Divergence in International Pay Systems

Recently, Fay (2008) reviewed the theoretical arguments for and against convergence of compensation practices. He pointed out the limits of such convergence at the international level, because of considerable variation in compensation levels and practices within and across nations. While there is multiple evidence of convergence of pay structures across the globe (Abe, 2007; Milkovich and Bloom, 1998; White, 2005) there is evidence from the emerging economies that wage systems are under considerable pressure relative to the developed economies. Table 7.3 shows that the average inflation-adjusted pay increases within the period from 2002 to 2007 in a number of new EU member states, India and China exceeded pay increases in developed industrial economies. While the forces for integration of the world economy are high, it is less clear that in emerging economies legislators and trade unionists will be motivated to make the relevant concessions necessary for higher integration. A recent OECD study (2008c), notes that while national governments support measures to improve the efficiency of national economies, regional and state governments often appear to make less effort to alter labour market regulations.

Implications for MNEs: Space for Global Standardisation of Compensation Practices

Morgan et al. (2003) underscore the fact that unlike 'the nationally based firm, the multinational does not exist in a unified institutional context that reinforces and reproduces particular practices' (2003: 389). MNEs react to this situation by trying to install a 'transnational social space . . . [by

Table 7.3   Average annual pay increases in selected countries, 2002–2007

Country	Actual average pay increase[a]	Average pay increases over inflation[b]
Europe		
Spain	4.07%	0.93%
Belgium	3.50%	1.55%
Germany	3.18%	1.59%
Switzerland	2.45%	1.61%
Netherlands	3.48%	1.63%
United Kingdom	3.83%	2.06%
Poland	5.12%	3.14%
Czech Republic	5.28%	3.26%
North America		
United States	3.55%	0.88%
BRIC States		
Brazil	8.75%	1.34%
China	7.93%	5.88%
India	13.03%	8.32%

Notes:
a. Based on internal analyses for 2002-2007 by Hewitt Associates.
b. Based on OECD statistics on consumer price indexes (CPI) growth rates for 2002–2007 (OECD, 2009).

means of] creation of common policies and procedures and the application of formal means of monitoring and accounting for performance' (2003: 389). Lowe et al. note that 'the traditional factors of production (capital, technology, raw materials and information) are increasingly fungible, with employee quality the only sustainable source of competitive advantage to developed country multinationals' (2002: 46). A way to maintain this competitive advantage is to promote internal consistency by means of standardised HRM practices, including rewards. The topic of international standardisation of compensation practices has been increasingly discussed both in the academic (Festing et al., 2007; Festing and Perkins, 2008) and practitioner literature (Baranski, 1999; Dwyer, 1999; Gross and Wingerup, 1999; Milkovich and Bloom, 1998; White, 2005).

Dowling et al. (2008) identified three groups of factors driving the globalisation of pay practices:

1. global competition for talent due to the increased international mobility ('organisational flexibility')

2. growing transparency and manageability of international pay systems owing to the development of the information and computer technology ('effective knowledge management') and
3. the need to promote 'a strong global culture' as a key to the organisational success.

Due to significant variations of economic conditions among countries, such standardisation of pay practices could be implemented by introducing global compensation elements, including non-monetary rewards and salary level determination systems (Abosch et al., 2008). For example, employees at a specified job grade could be eligible for a base salary on a certain market level (e.g. 25th or 75th percentile), a specified percentage of variable pay based on individual, organisational unit or global performance, stock options and perquisites (e.g. company car).

However, as noted above, such standardisation strategies can be significantly hampered by national social, political and legal institutions, especially employment regulations in the form of statutory minimums with respect to pay or benefits. While there is evidence that the wages and salaries offered to the employees of MNEs as a rule exceed the average country levels (OECD, 2008b), regulations or collectively agreed practices such as compulsory vacations considerably hinder the implementation of a universal strategy. Local institutions can also significantly influence the transfer of PfP schemes. For example, all companies in France with over 50 employees must implement a statutory profit-sharing (participation) plan. Fakhfakh and Perotin (2000) have noted the positive impact of voluntary profit-sharing schemes on factor productivity in French companies, but Hewitt Associates report that legally required participation is not regarded by employees as part of their compensation but rather seen as an 'acquired right' which has little or motivational effect, even though it may be worth as much as two months' salary per year in a highly profitable organization' (Hewitt Associates, 1991: 289).

Trends and Directions for Future Research

The research literature on international compensation has increasingly concentrated on the incidence of pay elements, notably PfP schemes, including short-term and long-term incentives (Antoni et al., 2005; Kurdelbusch, 2002; Pendleton et al., 2001). However, there is dearth of comparative research on such non-monetary rewards as paid time off, pension plans or medical insurance. There is also insufficient research on the impact of universal healthcare provided by the national governments of many developed economies (e.g. in the European Union, Canada,

Australia and New Zealand) compared to the United States where employers have traditionally funded much of the cost of health insurance for both employees and retirees – a situation dramatically illustrated by the current difficulties of the major US auto manufacturers that are carrying very large pension and health insurance liabilities for their retirees. A comprehensive measurement of value of benefits for employees in different countries would support international total compensation comparisons.

Additional areas where further research is needed include:

- The future direction of hierarchical pay patterns in executive compensation (particularly in the United States and the UK) in the light of the 2008 financial crisis and an apparent disconnect between executive pay and long-term firm performance.
- The need to expand the scope of research on cross-national pay and practice. Current empirical research and publication has a clear North American bias in terms of the number of articles published and the subject matter and firms surveyed. Much of the data we have is from US-based researchers, consulting firms or samples. Recent activities by the academic Cranet consortium and more globally focused consulting firms have partially alleviated this problem but significant concerns remain in terms of the over-weighted North American samples in cross-national reward research. There is a clear paucity of research in Latin America and the emerging economies outside of China and India.
- A comprehensive analysis of total compensation practices in international enterprises with respect to the comparable contingency factors among employees with comparable demographic features to allow further insights into a number of topics, including comparative analysis of preferences for and motivational effect of the elements of pay; variations of distributive and procedural justice perceptions across the nations; convergence of pay practices.

In an initial step toward building a vocabulary with which to more effectively pursue cross-cultural reward studies, we present a series of models. Milkovich and Bloom (1998) outline a three-part model of global compensation strategy from the firm perspective. In the first element, core pay practices are standardised across all the regions and cultures in which the firm operates; next, a crafted set of pay practices are customised to local and regional contexts and markets; finally, individual employees are given a choice of pay practices, along the lines of flexible benefits. It is this combination of these three elements that provides the global firm with a combination of systematic logic and responsiveness to local and individual interests.

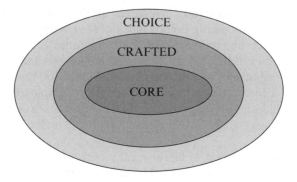

Source: Adapted from Milkovich and Bloom (1998: 22)

Figure 7.7 Elements of global pay

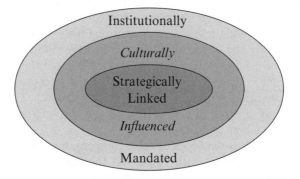

Figure 7.8 Institutional, cultural and strategic discretion in pay

We present a proposed approach to comparative or cross-cultural management based on a similar composite model. In the outer oval we present externally influenced, institutionally mandated pay elements, required by legislation as well as industrial regulation. In the intermediate (mid-grey) oval we present culturally influenced norms and values, practices influenced by historical context, local and regional supply and demand and the need for competitive responsiveness. Finally, the centre oval represents strategically linked practices, dependent on more internally based decisions of business intent and executive practice (for more on the theoretical origins supporting internal as opposed to external foci for pay systems see Dowling et al., 2005).

Given this framework, researchers can distinguish between 'demanding contexts' characterised by prescribed legislation and/or strongly held values and preferences effecting major reward system decisions, and more 'permissive contexts' characterised by limited legislative or institutional frameworks and/or more indifferent social norms or values related to employment exchange and rewards. More demanding social or institutional contexts are associated with pay systems that emphasise local customisation and an external focus to the rewards system. More permissive contexts are thought to be associated with global (or firm level) standardisation and an internal focus to the reward system. How these two roughly outlined contexts relate to specific pay practices (e.g. base cash, short-term variable, long-term variable, benefits, perquisites and other noncash rewards, as shown in Figure 7.1) is a starting point for a more systematic approach to a very complex topic area. Distinguishing between when a given pay practice is an independent variable, varying over a wide range; an independent variable, ranging over a narrower or prescribed range; or is a constant, prescribed and given, is a critical first step in this challenging and complex subject area.

REFERENCES

Abe, M. 2007. Why companies in Japan are introducing performance-based treatment and reward systems: the background, merits, and demerits. *Japan Labor Review*, **14**(2): 7–36.

Abosch, K., Schermerhorn, J. and Wisper, L. 2008. Broad-based variable pay goes global. *Workspan*, **5**(8): 56–62.

Adler, N. J. 1984. Understanding the ways of understanding: cross-cultural management methodology reviewed. In R. N. Farmer (ed.), *Advances in International Comparative Management,* vol. 1. Greenwich, CT: JAI Press, pp. 37-67.

Antoni, C. H., Berger, A., Baeten, X., Verbruggen, A., Emans, B., Hulkko, K., Vartiainen, M., Kessler, J. and Neu, E. 2005. *Wages and working conditions in the European Union.* Dublin: European Foundation for the Improvement of Living and Working Conditions.

Balkin, D. B. 2008. Explaining high US CEO Pay in a global context. In L. Gomez-Mejia and S. Werner (eds), *Global Compensation. Foundations and Perspectives.* London and New York: Routledge, pp. 192–205.

Balkin, D. B. and Gomez-Mejia, L. R. 1987. Toward a contingency theory of compensation strategy. *Strategic Management Journal*, **8**(2): 169–182.

Baranski, M. 1999. Think globally, pay locally: finding the right mix. *Compensation & Benefits Review*, **31**(4): 15–24.

BDA. 2005. Internationaler Vergleich der tariflichen Jahressollarbeitszeit für Arbeiter im verarbeitenden Gewerbe zum 01.11.2004. Retrieved January 10, 2012, from http://www.einzelhandel.de/pb/site/hde/get/params_Dattachment/53460/Internationaler%20Arbeitszeitvergleich%202004.pdf.

Berrone, P., Makri, M. and Gomez-Mejia, L. 2008. Executive compensation in North American high-technology firms: a contextual approach. *The International Journal of Human Resource Management*, **19**(8): 1534–1552.

Berrone, P. and Otten, J. 2008. A global perspective on executive compensation. In L. Gomez-Mejia and S. Werner (eds), *Global Compensation. Foundations and Perspectives.* London and New York: Routledge, pp. 206–218.

Björkman, I. and Furu, P. 2000. Determinants of variable pay for top managers of foreign subsidiaries in Finland. *International Journal of Human Resource Management*, **11**(4): 698–713.

Boudreau, J. and Ramstad, P. 2007. *Beyond HR: The New Science of Human Capital.* Boston, MA: Harvard Business School Press.

Bowen, D. E. and Ostroff, C. 2004. Understanding HRM-firm performance linkages: the role of the 'strength' of the HRM system. *Academy of Management Review*, **29**(2): 203–221.

Brewster, C. 2004. European perspectives on human resource management. *Human Resource Management Review*, **14**(4): 365–403

Brewster, C. 2007. Comparative HRM: European views and perspectives. *International Journal of Human Resource Management*, **18**(5): 769–787.

Brewster, C., Sparrow, P. and Vernon, G. 2007. Comparative HRM: reward. In C. Brewster, P. Sparrow and G. Vernon (eds), *International Human Resource Management*, 2nd edn. London: Chartered Institute of Personnel and Development, pp. 121–147.

Brody, R. G., Lin, S. and Salter, S. B. 2006. Merit pay, responsibility, and national values: A US–Taiwan Comparison. *Journal of International Accounting Research*, **5**(2): 63–79.

Chiang, F. 2005. A critical examination of Hofstede's thesis and its application to international reward management. *International Journal of Human Resource Management*, **16**(9): 1545–1563.

Churchill Jr, G. A., Ford, N. M. and Walker Jr, O. C. 1979. Personal characteristics of salespeople and the attractiveness of alternative rewards. *Journal of Business Research*, **7**(1): 25–50.

De Cieri, H. and Dowling, P. 1999. Strategic human resource management in multinational enterprises: theoretical and empirical developments. In P. Wright, L. Dyer, J. Boudreau and G. Milkovich (eds), *Research in Personnel and Human Resource Management*, Supplement 4. Stamford, CT. and London: JAI Press, pp. 305–327.

DeNisi, A. S., Varma, A. and Budhwar, P. S. 2008. Performance management around the globe: what have we learned? In A. DeNisi, A. Varma and P. Budhwar (eds), *Performance Management System: A Global Perspective*. London/New York: Routledge, pp. 254–261.

DiMaggio, P. J. and Powell, W. W. 1983. The iron cage revisited: institutional isomorphism and collective rationality in organizational fields. *American Sociological Review*, **48**(2): 147–160.

Dittrich, J. E. and Carrell, M. R. 1976. Dimensions of organizational fairness as predictors of job satisfaction, absence, and turnover. *Academy of Management Proceedings*, **76**: 79–83.

Dowling, P., Engle, A., Festing, M. and Müller, B. 2005. Complexity in global pay: a meta-framework. Paper presented at the 8th Conference on International Human Resource Management, Cairns, Australia.

Dowling, P., Festing, M. and Engle, A. 2008. *International Human Resource Management*, 5th edn. London: Thomson Learning.

Dwyer, T. D. 1999. Trends in global compensation. *Compensation & Benefits Review*, **31**(4): 48–53.

Ellig, B. 2008. What pay for performance should measure. *World at Work Journal*, **17**(2): 64–75.

Engle, A., Dowling, P. and Festing, M. 2008. State of origin: research in global performance management, a proposed research domain and emerging implications. *European Journal of International Management*, **2**(2): 153–169.

Fakhfakh, F. and Perotin, V. 2000. The effects of profit-sharing schemes on enterprise performance in France. *Economic Analysis: A Journal of Enterprise & Participation*, **3**(2): 93–111.

Fay, C. H. 2008. The global convergence of compensation practices. In L. Gomez-Mejia and S. Werner (eds), *Global Compensation*. London/New York: Routledge, pp. 131–141.

Festing, M., Eidems, J. and Royer, S. 2007. Strategic issues and local constraints in transnational compensation strategies: an analysis of cultural, institutional and political influences. *European Management Journal*, **25**(2): 118–131.

Festing, M., Groening, Y., Kabst, R. and Weber, W. 1999. Financial participation in Europe–determinants and outcomes. *Economic & Industrial Democracy*, **20**(2): 295.

Festing, M. and Perkins, S. 2008. Rewards for internationally mobile employees. In P. Sparrow, M. Dickmann and C. Brewster (eds), *International HRM: A European Perspective*, 2nd edn. London and New York: Routledge, pp. 150–173.

Festing, M. and Sahakiants, I. 2010a. Compensation practices in Central and Eastern European EU member states – an analytical framework based on institutional perspectives, path dependencies and efficiency considerations. *Thunderbird International Business Review*, **52**(3): 203-216.

Festing, M. and Sahakiants, I. 2010b. Compensation practices in Central and Eastern Europe: a case study of multinational corporation subsidiaries in the Czech Republic, Poland and Hungary. Paper presented at the 11th International Human Resource Management Conference, Birmingham, UK.

Frey, B. 1997. *Not Just for the Money: An Economic Theory of Personal Motivation.* Cheltenham, UK: Edward Elgar Publishing.

Gerhart, B. 2008. Compensation and national culture. In L. Gomez-Mejia and S. Werner (eds), *Global Compensation, Foundations and Perspectives.* London and New York: Routledge, pp. 142–157.

Germany Trade and Invest. 2009. Investment guide to Germany. Retrieved January 10, 2012, from http://www.gtai.de/GTAI/Content/DE/Trade/Fachdaten/PUB/2009/06/pub 200906088004_13669.pdf.

Gomez-Mejia, L. R. and Welbourne, T. 1991. Compensation strategies in a global context. *Human Resource Planning*, **14**(1): 29–41.

Greene, R. J. 2008. Reward management in multinational enterprises: global principles; local strategies. *World at Work Journal*, **17**(3): 45–54.

Gross, S. E. and Wingerup, P. L. 1999. Global pay? Maybe not yet! *Compensation & Benefits Review*, **31**(4): 25–43.

Hannon, J., Milkovich, G., Gerhart, B. and Friedrich, T. 1990. The effects of research and development intensity on managerial compensation in large organizations. Paper presented at the Academy of Management; Proceedings.

Hewitt Associates. 1991. *Total Compensation Management. Reward Management Strategies for the 1990s.* Oxford: Basil Blackwell.

Hewitt Associates. 2007a. TCM^{TM} cash and prevalence reports. Retrieved August 29, 2008, from Global Total Compensation Management (TCM^{TM}) database.

Hewitt Associates. 2007b. TCM^{TM} general industry/financial services/retail total compensation by industry: management & professional, Vol. I. Retrieved August 29, 2008, from Global Total Compensation Management (TCM^{TM}) database.

Hewitt Associates. 2008. TCM^{TM} general industry/retail total compensation by industry: executive, Vol. I. Retrieved August 29, 2008, from Global Total Compensation Management (TCM^{TM}) database.

Hofer, C. W. 1975. Toward a contingency theory of business strategy. *Academy of Management Journal*, **18**(4): 784–810.

Hofstede, G. 1980. *Culture's Consequences: International Differences In Work-related Values.* Beverly Hills/London: Sage Publications.

Hope, J. and Fraser, R. 2003. New ways of setting rewards: the beyond budgeting model. *California Management Review*, **45**(4): 104–119.

Huddleston, P., Good, L. and Frazier, B. 2002. The influence of firm characteristics and demographic variables on Russian retail workers' work motivation and job attitudes. *International Review of Retail, Distribution & Consumer Research*, **12**(4): 395–421.

Institut der deutschen Wirtschaft. 2008. *Deutschland in Zahlen 2008.* Köln: Deutscher Instituts-Verlag GmbH.

International Labour Organization. 2009. Working Time Database [Data file]. Retrieved January 28, 2009, from http://www.ilo.org/travaildatabase/servlet/workingtime.

Kulik, C. T. and Ambrose, M. L. 1992. Personal and situational determinants of referent choice. *Academy of Management Review*, **17**(2): 212–237.

Kurdelbusch, A. 2002. Multinationals and the rise of variable pay in Germany. *European Journal of Industrial Relations*, **8**(3): 325–349.

Lowe, K. B., Milliman, J., De Cieri, H. and Dowling, P. J. 2002. International compensation practices: a ten-country comparative analysis. *Human Resource Management*, **41**(1): 45–66.

Makri, M. and Gomez-Mejia, L. 2007. Executive compensation: something old, something new. In S. Werner (ed.), *Managing Human Resources in North America*. London/New York: Routledge, pp. 158–171.

Manas, T. M. and Graham, M. D. 2003. *Creating a Total Rewards Strategy: A Toolkit for Designing Business-based Plans*. New York: AMACOM.

Milkovich, G. T. and Bloom, M. 1998. Rethinking international compensation. *Compensation & Benefits Review*, **30**(1): 15–23.

Milkovich, G. T. and Newman, J. M. 2008. *Compensation*, 9th International edn. Boston/Burr Ridge, IL: McGraw-Hill.

Morgan, G., Kelly, B., Sharpe, D. and Whitley, R. 2003. Global managers and Japanese multinationals: internationalization and management in Japanese financial institutions. *International Journal of Human Resource Management*, **14**(3): 389–407.

Newman, K. L. and Nollen, S. D. 1996. Culture and congruence: the fit between management practices and national culture. *Journal of International Business Studies*, **27**(4): 753–779.

OECD. 2008a. *Economic Policy Reforms: Going for Growth*. Paris: OECD Publishing.

OECD. 2008b. *Employment Outlook*. Paris: OECD Publishing.

OECD. 2008c. Economic reform: a mixed scorecard. *OECD Observer*, **266**: 25–26.

OECD. 2009. StatExtracts: prices and purchasing power parities: consumer price indices (MEI) [Data file]. Retrieved January 28, 2009, from http://webnet.oecd.org/wbos/index.aspx.

Oechsler, W. A., Trautwein, G. and Schwab, M. 2008. Internationales personalmanagement: transfer von mitarbeiterinnen und mitarbeitern. In J. Zentes and B. Swoboda (eds), *Fallstudien zum Internationalen Management: Grundlagen – Praxiserfahrungen – Perspektiven*, 3rd edn. Wiesbaden: Gabler, pp. 605–622.

Ostroff, C. and Bowen, D. E. 2000. Moving HR to a higher level: HR practices and organizational effectiveness. In K. Klein and S. Kozlowski (eds), *Multilevel Theory, Research, and Methods in Organizations: Foundations, Extensions, and New Directions*. San Francisco: Jossey Bass, pp. 211–266.

Parboteeah, K. P. and Cullen, J. B. 2003. Social institutions and work centrality: explorations beyond national culture. *Organization Science*, **14**(2): 137–148.

Pendleton, A., Poutsma, E., Brewster, C. and van Ommeren, J. 2002. Employee share ownership and profit sharing in the European union: incidence, company characteristics and union representation. *Transfer*, **8**(1): 47–62.

Pendleton, A., Poutsma, E., van Ommeren, J. and Brewster, C. 2001. *Employee Share Ownership and Profit-Sharing in the European Union*. Luxembourg: Office for Official Publications of the European Communities.

Perlmutter, H. V. 1969. The tortuous evolution of the multinational corporation. *Columbia Journal of World Business*, **4**(1): 9–18.

Poe, A. C. 2001. When in Rome. . . determining vacation time for international transferees. Retrieved September 2, 2008, from http://www.shrm.org/.

Reynolds, C. 1986. Compensation of overseas personnel. In J. Famularo (ed.), *Handbook of Human Resource Administration*. New York: McGraw-Hill, pp. 47–61.

Rogovsky, N., Schuler, R. S. and Reynolds, C. 2000. How can national culture affect compensation practices of MNCs? *Global Focus*, **12**(4): 35–42.

Rosenzweig, P. M. and Nohria, N. 1994. Influences on human resource management practices in multinational corporations. *Journal of International Business Studies*, **25**(2): 229–251.

Sánchez Marín, G. 2008a. The influence of institutional and cultural factors on compensation practices around the world. In L. Gomez-Mejia and S. Werner (eds), *Global Compensation. Foundations and Perspectives*. London and New York: Routledge, pp. 3–17.

Sánchez Marín, G. 2008b. National differences in compensation: the influence of the institutional and cultural context. In L. Gomez-Mejia and S. Werner, (eds), *Global Compensation. Foundations and Perspectives*. London and New York: Routledge, pp. 18–28.

Schröder, C. 2008. Die struktur der arbeitskosten in der deutschen wirtschaft. *IW-Trends,* **35**(2): 1-16.

Schuler, R. S. and Rogovsky, N. 1998. Understanding compensation practice variations across firms: the impact of national culture. *Journal of International Business Studies,* **29**(1): 159–177.

Sorge, A. 2004. Cross-national differences in human resource management and organization. In A. W. Harzing and J. van Ruysseveldt (eds), *International Human Resource Management*, 2nd edn. London et al.: Sage Publications, pp. 117–140.

Sparrow, P. 2004. International rewards systems: to converge or not to converge? In C. Brewster and H. Harris (eds), *International HRM: Contemporary Issues in Europe*. London/New York: Routledge, pp. 102–119.

Sparrow, P. 2009. International reward management. In G. White and J. Drucker (eds.), *Reward Management: A Critical Text,* 2nd edn. London/New York: Routledge, pp. 233-257.

Thompson, M. A. 2006. Investors call for better disclosure of executive compensation in Canada. *Focus: Workspan*, **2**(6): 5–6.

Tosi, H. L. and Greckhamer, T. 2004. Culture and CEO compensation. *Organization Science*, **15**(6): 657–670.

Townsend, A. M., Scott, K. D. and Markham, S. E. 1990. An examination of country and culture-based differences in compensation practices. *Journal of International Business Studies,* **21**(4): 667–678.

Traxler, F., Arrowsmith, J., Nergaard, K. and López-Rodó, J. M. M. 2008. Variable pay and collective bargaining: a cross-national comparison of the banking sector. *Economic & Industrial Democracy*, **29**(3): 406–431.

UNDP. 2007. *Human Development Report 2007/2008*. New York, Palgrave Macmillan.

Vernon, G. 2006. International pay and reward. In T. Edwards and C. Rees (eds), *International Human Resource Management*. London: FT/Prentice Hall, pp. 217–241.

Wächter, H., Peters, R., Tempel, A. and Müller-Camen, M. 2003. *The 'Country-of-Origin Effect' in the Cross-National Management of Human Resources*. Munich and Mering: Rainer Hampp Verlag.

Werner, S., Tosi, H. L. and Gomez-Mejia, L. 2005. Organizational governance and employee pay: how ownership structure affects the firm's compensation strategy. *Strategic Management Journal*, **26**(4): 377–384.

White, R. 2005. A strategic approach to building a consistent global rewards program. *Compensation & Benefits Review*, **37**(4): 23–40.

Whitley, R. 1992. Societies, firms and markets: the social structuring of business systems. In R. Whitley (ed.), *European Business Systems: Firms and Markets in Their National Contexts*. London et al.: Sage Publications, pp. 5–45.

Whitley, R. 1999. *Divergent Capitalisms: The Social Structuring and Change of Business Systems*. New York: Oxford University Press.

Zhou, J. and Martocchio, J. J. 2001. Chinese and American managers' compensation award decisions: a comparative policy-capturing study. *Personnel Psychology*, **54**(1): 115–145.

8 Human resource development: national embeddedness

Olga Tregaskis and Noreen Heraty

In a commentary on *Education across Europe*, the OECD, acknowledged human capital as a major factor driving economic growth, both in the world's most advanced economies and in those experiencing rapid development. This reflects a widely accepted recognition that an organisation's ability to create and share knowledge is a critical determinant of competitive functioning and organisational capabilities around the world today. Ulrich (1997: 10) describes organisational capabilities as the DNA of competitiveness and notes that an organisation is effective not because of its structure, but rather as a result of the set of capabilities that are embedded in the firm. The chapter explores some of the dimensions of human resource development (HRD) as the vehicle for initiating and sustaining organisational capabilities. We begin with a brief examination of the organisational logic underpinning investment in human resource knowledge and skills and use this as the foundation for exploring variation in national or geographic approaches to skills development. Beyond the organisational level, we review wider national systems as the fulcrum upon which variation in HRD systems and practices might be understood. Drawing upon the European institutional tradition where institutions are defined as the 'building blocks for social order, both to govern and to legitimize behaviour' (Bosch et al., 2007: 253; Streeck & Thelen, 2005), we review both the national business systems literature and the more specialised literature on national innovations systems to demonstrate their influence on the nature of firm level skills and learning. The chapter concludes with an examination of globalisation pressures and what these mean for the significance of national institutions in shaping firm level behaviour.

HUMAN RESOURCE DEVELOPMENT AND FIRM LOGIC

The development of national competitive capability is strongly predicated upon an appropriate organisational base that places developed organisational learning processes as the vehicle for organisational knowledge and skill development. Kang et al. (2007) highlight knowledge as the most distinctive and imitable resource available to firms that enables them to employ, manipulate, and transform various organisational resources effectively. This notion of employees as representing the source of prime sustainable competitive advantage is largely attributable to the early work of Barney (1991) and Prahalad and Hamel (1990) on both the resource-based view of the firm and the development of core competencies, and, for the purposes of this chapter, has spawned a growing literature on, among others, organisational learning (Nonaka, 1991; Pedler et al., 1994; Prahalad et al., 1990; Senge, 1990; Watkins & Marsick, 1996) and human capital accumulation (Antonacopoulou & Fitzgerald, 1996; Carmeli & Schaubroeck, 2005; Hitt et al., 2001; Huselid, 1995). Here, competitive-based human capital is conceptualised as the levels and types of education, knowledge, skills, ideas and experience available to the organisation, and is, according to Luthans and Youssef (2004), accumulated only through time, tenure and organisational-specific developmental efforts. An organisation's absorptive capacity (Cohen & Levinthal, 1990), which reflects the stock of knowledge accumulated within the firm that is embodied in skilled human resources and accrued through in-house learning efforts, is seen as a critical enabler of competitive functioning and, as organisations struggle with competitiveness issues, we have witnessed renewed interest in exploring the value and nature of work based learning and HRD.

Garavan and McCarthy (2008) note that organisational learning is generally defined as a process enhancing the actions of organisations through better knowledge and understanding (Korth, 2000; Lundberg, 1995), and is conceptualised as an iterative process that involves action and reflection, change and the creation of new knowledge and insight (Gond & Herrbach, 2006). It is also recognised as having a strong collective identity (Adler & Cole, 1993; Cook & Yanow, 1993, Huber, 1991). Kogut & Zander (1992: 385) underscore this presumption that organisational knowledge be understood as socially constructed and point to the importance of the manner in which human resources are organised as a means of developing new knowledge. Drucker (1992) similarly depicts organisations as knowledge communities where knowledge is created, shared and stored, thus compelling organisations to build continuous learning into their operating systems, a point that is echoed by both Adler et al. (1999), who suggest that the main task of management involves the creation of an environment of knowledge interaction between individuals and the organisation, and Ulrich et al. (1993), who call for learning to become part of the organisation's normal functioning. Indeed, Appelbaum and Reichart (1998) caution that how well or badly the organisation learns will depend on the policies, structures and processes that characterise the organisation.

However, notwithstanding the broad acceptance of the value and utility of well-developed and appropriate HRD effort, here we echo Garrick (1999) in cautioning that any true understanding of HRD in organisations must necessarily be predicated by an awareness of the range of influences that affect it: including personal, political, and institutional features. This embedded nature of HRD is taken up in the following sections of this chapter and we argue that the nature of an organisation's HRD effort is inexorably shaped and moulded by the national institutional and regulatory systems within which it operates. Learning embeddedness, as originally depicted by Polanyi (1962), acknowledges that all forms of exchange are inherently rooted in social relationships – here we argue that an organisation's HRD efforts are embedded in the social and institutional environment within which it is situated.

NATIONAL INSTITUTIONS AND HUMAN RESOURCE DEVELOPMENT

While a range of institutional perspectives exist, the one we focus on here is the varieties of capitalism perspective offered by Hall and Soskice (2001), which has been extensively applied to the consideration of human resource development in organisations (e.g. Estevez-Abe et al., 2001; Lam, 2003; Tregaskis et al., 2010). This varieties of capitalism perspective explores the country-specific institutions that are seen to explain the competitiveness of nations and isolate two divergent economic trajectories. The first one is the liberal market economies (LME) where activity is said to be managed primarily through hierarchies and the market. The second type, co-ordinated market economies (CME), uses non-market relations between actors as key organising mechanisms giving rise to longer time horizons for activity and variety of action. While greater detail is provided in Chapter 2, for our purposes here it is sufficient to note that these two market trajectories signpost different perspectives on training and development. In LMEs, for example, employment conditions can become a critical bargaining tool for organisations who often engage in poaching to attract and retain scarce and valuable skill and knowledge resources. Here, employees are encouraged to invest in transferrable skills and to use their investment in skills as a route to employability while, in turn, firm strategy is adaptive and reinforces the skills available in the labour market. CMEs, by contrast, support career trajectories which evolve around firm-specific skills to a greater degree. Moreover, education and training systems tend to be tailored to the needs of flexible labour markets, in that they provide certification and qualification of general skills as opposed to specialised skills. In this way, labour market skills are more transferrable and therefore the mobility of the labour market is protected. General education is provided by educational institutions through a combination of state and individual funding. Firms therefore focus on specific skills but these are generally not sufficiently in-depth to lead to certification or qualification. In contrast, CMEs tend to emphasise specialisation in skill development, some of which is conducted through strong academic–industry partnerships. For example, apprenticeships can play an important role in the development of organisational or industry-specific skills. Such divergent approaches arguably lead to labour markets in LME which are rich in general transferrable skills and thus promote greater labour mobility, while in CMEs, there is likely to be a stronger reliance on specialised internal labour markets that result from the close tying of skills development to the needs of the firm or industry. Given the considerable employer costs associated with the development of specialised skills and developed internal labour markets, human resource management strategies are likely then to be heavily geared toward retaining and maximising the benefits of this internal labour market. Beyond the level of the individual firm, an educational system that promotes in-depth industry or firm-specific skills also facilitates the development of a common knowledge base, thus making inter-firm collaboration and knowledge transfer feasible.

In sum, the national business systems (NBS) analysis suggests that institutional complementarities support differentiating skill development and utilisation within organisations. Hall and Soskice (2001) go on to argue that these institutional variations are a source of comparative advantage and are aligned with cross-national differences in organisational strategies. They specifically explore comparative advantage in relation to innovation and contrast organisational strategies of incremental innovation with those of radical innovation. They would argue that radical innovation reflects a significant change in the production process or the development of new technology or product/service. Incremental innovation reflects small improvement changes in a process or product/service. Radical innovations are required in industries such as biotechnology or telecommunications where technology development is rapid and research is a strong underpinning force in achieving innovation. Incremental innovation is demanded in industries dependent on capital goods such as the production of machine engines or specialised equipment. Incremental innovation here provides competitive advantage by improving upon an established product, increasing efficiencies associated with its production, quality control and maintaining the customer base.

From the varieties of capitalism argument it would therefore follow that the national institutions associated with CMEs are supportive of industry and organisational strategies reliant on incremental innovation. This is because of the supply of high-skilled labour at the shop-floor level within industry or firm-specific skills that are able to meet this strategic demand; the industrial relations context where internal labour markets are valued and workers have the autonomy and involvement to participate in the innovation process; and the collaborative inter-firm relations where customers are likely to value incremental innovation. LMEs are arguably supportive of radical innovation strategies given the financial arrangements which emphasise shareholder value and which encourages risk taking through development of new products/services which may yield significant financial gains; employment legislation that allows labour costs to be cut if new products/service are subsequently unsuccessful; a mobile labour market where new skills can be brought in on a needs basis to support the development of new projects; and inter-firm relations where new knowledge and skills can be acquired quickly through acquisition, poaching or product licensing.

Estevez-Abe et al. (2001) examine in more detail how different national approaches to skill formation shape organisational radical or incremental innovation strategies by examining the role of employment and unemployment protection. Comparing 18 OECD countries they found the countries clustered as follows:

- Weak employment and unemployment protection and a focus on the development of general skills represented by the Anglo-Saxon countries including the United States, UK, Australia, New Zealand, Canada and Ireland.
- Strong employment or/and unemployment protection and firm/industry/occupational specific skills. This includes the continental European countries along with Japan. Within this, there were countries such as Japan and Italy that had a particularly strong focus on firm-specific skills and employment protection; while Denmark, Switzerland and the Netherlands focused on industry-specific skills and unemployment protection.

Estevez-Abe et al. suggest that the linkages between social protection and the emphasis on general or specialised skill formation puts certain countries in a stronger position to pursue business strategies more or less reliant on radical or incremental innovation. Economies where labour flexibility at the lowest cost to employers coupled with transferrable general skills, exemplified in the Anglo-Saxon countries, allows organisations to be responsive and to change direction to pursue new business opportunities. However, where firm or industry-specific skills are dominant it makes it more difficult for organisations to change business direction rapidly. This coupled with high costs associated with labour skills makes them more vulnerable to the risks associated with failed exploration into new areas. In contrast, these countries can maximise the returns on current products via their on-going improvement and development due to the in-depth skills profile of their internal labour markets.

Using an index of scientific citation rates and low-wage employment these researchers found empirical support for the proposed relationship between skills and social protection on the one hand and incremental or innovation strategy on the other. Specifically, the Anglo-Saxon countries were found to have much higher scientific citation rates, which were taken as a proxy for radical innovation, compared to continental European countries and Japan. Firms that have high skills and stronger social protection were much less likely to penetrate markets that relied on low-tech product markets.

This work emphasised the nature of the interaction between the social protection system, skills trajectories and firm level strategy. However (as indicated in Chapter 2), the NBS literature has a number of weaknesses and in particular has faced criticism for its lack of attention to the dynamic nature of the interplay between institutions and organisation so some have argued that their contribution lies in their heuristic value (Bosch et al., 2007). Future work needs to unpick the nature of the interaction between actors within the institutional systems as a means of understanding how both organisations and institutions are changing in response to competitive demands for learning and innovation.

NATIONAL INNOVATION SYSTEMS AND HRD

While the NBS literature focused on understanding how institutions affect business organisation, the innovations literature focuses on understanding how institutions and organisations interact and, in so doing, impact innovation performance and competence development. The work from the national innovations systems (NIS) literature looks at the institutional arrangements associated with technical innovation (Doremus et al., 1999; Patel & Pavitt, 1991, 1997; Pavitt, 1999) and, arguably, it brings the organisation and sector into greater focus (Guerreri & Tylecote, 1997; Lundvall, 2007) in that it provides a useful analytical tool for examining human resource development in a comparative context. The national innovations systems literature is diverse, but for the purposes of this chapter we draw on two particular strands: first, evidence looking narrowly at innovation in terms of scientific and technology related activity (e.g. Doremus et al.,

1999); and second, a perspective which uses the term innovation in a much broader sense in order to capture institutions that shape firm innovation in a whole range of 'competence building in socio-economic activities' (Lundvall et al., 2002: 216). This latter approach is particularly concerned with institution and organisation systemic feedback that contributes to interactive learning processes.

The work on innovation from the science and technology tradition suggests that institutional arrangements shape national approaches to the development and diffusion of innovation, thus giving rise to national technological specialisation. For example, arrangements with respect to focus and funding of science and technology policy; the funding and location of R&D activity; and the technical orientation of corporate activity all contribute to the type of technology developed and how it is developed (Doremus et al., 1999). We argue that this has important consequences for how human resources are organised in terms of training, skill development and learning to support innovation. According to Doremus et al. (1999), it is possible to explain the divergent approaches to innovation adopted by countries in terms of their national innovation institutional arrangements. For example, the science and technology policy of government can be diffused through rules and regulations affecting intellectual property or tax incentives. But it is also transmitted in the way education is organised, the nature and manner of skills that are developed, the types of communication infrastructures that are supported, and the closeness of relationships between government, universities and industry. Thus different technological advances require different human capital investments for their efficient absorption, and this requires the appropriate institutional structures and environments to be in place to facilitate their development. Here more than anywhere else we can see the intersection between the macro business system that creates the appropriate institutional framework to deliver innovation and the local organisational structure and systems that promote the development of appropriate knowledge, skills and competencies. We turn now to consider these issues and how they may impact on human resource development in firms.

The United States, UK and France in the 1990s directed most of government R&D expenditure to defence. The United States has also concentrated on R&D in health and is still by far the greatest investor in health-related R&D, accounting for three-quarters of that of the OECD countries (OECD, 2007). In proportionate terms, health related R&D was just over 0.22 per cent of GDP in the United States in 2006, the UK was the second largest investor at 0.11 per cent, France invested 0.06 per cent, which compares with 0.03 per cent for both Japan and Germany. In contrast, Japan focused more on energy R&D and Germany on industrial

Table 8.1   *Share of business R&D in the manufacturing sector by technology intensity*

	High-technology	Medium-high technology	Medium-low- and low-technology
Finland	66.4	19.5	14.0
Canada	64.3	16.3	19.4
United States (2003)	63.6	26.3	10.1
Ireland	62.7	22.3	15.0
United Kingdom	62.5	28.2	9.2
Korea	60.2	29.6	10.1
Sweden (2003)	58.5	34.1	7.4
Denmark	57.9	26.5	15.5
OECD (2003)	53.0	35.4	11.7
France (2003)	51.8	34.8	13.5
Netherlands	50.9	36.9	12.2
Belgium	49.5	29.9	20.5
EU (2003)	46.7	42.2	11.2
Italy	46.5	41.0	12.5
Japan (2003)	42.8	43.8	13.4
Spain	35.9	39.1	25.0
Germany	33.5	58.6	7.8
Norway	31.6	32.5	36.0
Poland	30.5	48.2	21.3
Australia (2003)	26.5	39.2	34.2
Czech Republic	18.8	66.6	14.6

Source: OECD 2007

R&D. Thus, the United States, UK and France have tended to adopt radical innovation strategies which are science-intensive and where the primary motivation for effort and funding is linked to finding the next new technology or scientific breakthrough. The types of industries that R&D activity and investment focused on in the United States, UK and France, tend to be what are referred to as technology intensive, i.e. aerospace, instruments, pharmaceuticals, office machinery and computers, electrical machinery, electronic equipment and components. Recent data from the OECD Science, Technology and Industry Scoreboard suggest that these divisions in country preferences for R&D activity in high, medium and low technology intensive manufacturing remain (see Table 8.1).

In terms of skill development it could be argued that this strategy has reinforced, and been reinforced by, the use of university programmes to supply highly specialised science and technology graduates and PhDs.

Close relationships between universities and private industry in the United States are argued as central to the innovation capability of the United States enabling organisational flexibility (Doremus et al., 1999). US universities are also the main destination for students overseas to study for graduate and PhD programmes (OECD, 2007). US universities are viewed as undertaking a significant proportion of world-class research that, since it is funded by industry, is therefore easily accessible to industry. External labour markets and employee mobility provide the means through which skills and knowledge are shared (Lam, 2003). Professional networks across science communities or communities of practice (Brown & Duguid, 1991) are also arguably significant in this context as a means through which employees can update their skills and knowledge base. As competition is high among R&D intensive industries, collaboration is minimal. This places a high price on specific skills, which makes individual knowledge and skills a valuable commodity. In this way, providing demand for these skills remains, there is an incentive for individuals to invest in their own skill development and for the employer in return to provide high financial rewards or the opportunity for skill enhancement.

By contrast, the German innovation system is seen as supportive of incremental innovation, whereby technological change is aided by adaptation and its primary focus is the diffusion of innovation as opposed to the pursuit of a specific mission. Thus most of the financial resources have been devoted to technology diffusion (Doremus et al., 1999). German R&D activity also focuses on supporting medium technology intensive industries such as industrial chemicals and motor vehicles (see Table 8.1). The dual-system of vocational education is often seen as one of the primary institutional structures reinforcing this innovation system. An apprenticeship system which combines quality academic study and practical experience has yielded a skilled labour force, and for skills to be updated through the process of work and how work is organised. In addition, R&D activity is co-ordinated across firms, whereby SMEs have the opportunity to tap into technology resources they are unable to support themselves and industrial standards institutes take responsibility for diffusing best practice across the industrial base (Doremus et al., 1999). The implication for human resource development in firms within this type of innovation system is quite different. For example, the dual-system places considerable emphasis on the firm to support skill creation and its ongoing development. Skills and knowledge are of less value as an individual commodity and more value to the firm. This is because more of the labour market share similar skill sets and wage protection for skilled employees prevents employers using financial incentives to poach skilled staff. In addition, the value of skills to the employer comes into play when skilled employees, who require less supervision than their counterparts in the UK or United States, are able to problem solve and innovate to improve performance as an integral dimension of work organisation. This capability is obviously critical to sustaining an innovation strategy based on incremental adaption, as opposed to radical innovation.

Japan has been identified as characterising yet another approach to innovation, which Doremus et al. (1999) refer to as producer-orientated. Here is it argued that Japan combines elements of both a mission-orientated and diffusion-orientated approach to innovation. Business R&D concentrates on medium technology intensive industries and low technology industries (e.g. basic metals, stone, glass sectors) and scale-intensive industries. For example, Table 8.1 shows that 57 per cent of Japan's industrial R&D investment is in the medium and low technology intensive industries. Because Japan's technological base began at such a low point in comparison with other major industrial players, it adopted a strategy of attempting to innovate rapidly and share those innovations widely. As a result there has been significant government support for R&D activities by firms and through making government R&D resources available to commercial firms. In addition, there has been a strong pursuit by Japanese companies to gain new technology through acquisition. The pursuit of standardisation in technology has also enabled its widespread diffusion through the economy. Again, in terms of human resources development, this strategy has encouraged the close alignment of educational programmes to commercial needs. Standardisation has made it easier to supply skilled workers to meet firm needs and to integrate the technology with skills provision. Thus, like Germany, the inward labour market is a critical competitive resource.

This analysis suggests that variation in national innovations systems reinforce technological specialisation as opposed to convergence (Doremus et al., 1999). Thus from a human resource development perspective there are strong institutional forces at play that support the pursuit of specific firm level skill responses and are in turn reinforced by these. This line of analysis also argues that institutions and the organisation of production within sectors may be a more significant consideration than national context alone. As firms globalise and markets become more international in scope the importance of sector across national contexts comes to the fore. This is an issue we return to in the concluding section of the chapter.

LEARNING AND INSTITUTIONAL PERSPECTIVES

The second stream of work within the NIS tradition is that by Lundvall (1985), Freeman (1987), and Edquist (2005). Lundvall et al. (2002) note that the NIS as a concept was originally applied to many of the richer countries in Europe such as the UK, France and Scandinavia, and also the United States. However, more recently it is being applied to developing countries as a means of understanding institutional change and the development of organisational capabilities. One of the key strands of this literature is that success in innovation is linked with long-term relationships and close inter-organisational interactions e.g. between customers and suppliers, between creators of knowledge and end users. Lundvall (1985) identified the key institutional drivers affecting what he refers to as interactive learning, i.e. learning through relationships and social interaction. The first is time, in that the long-term or short-term horizon for performance characterised by the governance structures of Japan or Germany can make investment in certain technologies and activities more viable than others. The second is trust, in that the development of trust among key actors involved in the social exchange of knowledge or its co-creation is critical. The third is the dominance of either an instrumental or a communicative rationality in the exchanges of knowledge-based goods. The former is more likely to restrict interactive learning while the latter is more conducive to interactive learning and thus an enabler of innovation. The argument of Lundvall and colleagues would thus suggest that these institutional drivers support to a greater or lesser degree interactive learning, which in turn impacts on and is impacted by the nature of innovation in firms. They are not advocating the allocation of countries into typologies but, instead, suggesting that firms in countries will adopt a range of ways of organising for innovation, yielding different types of innovation. Interactive learning is one way in which firms might organise within a country and the propensity to organise in this way will be affected by broader institutional factors associated with how learning is developed and organised in national labour markets.

Developing this line of analysis further we would argue that the organisational work on social capital development has a bearing here in terms of how firms may organise their human resource development activity to support interactive learning. Taylor (2006) argued that there is a significant role for the human resource function to develop the architecture to support the development of social capital within firms and across inter-organisational boundaries. Social capital is seen as an important precursor to organisational learning (Nahapiet & Ghoshal, 1998). Social capital can be defined as 'an asset embedded in relationships – of individual, communities, networks or societies (Leana & Van Buren Iii, 1999: 539; cf. Coleman, 1990; Nahapiet & Ghoshal, 1998). Like other organisational assets it is considered to be something that needs to be managed in order to yield organisational benefits. Achieving this in practice requires attention to structural, cognitive and relational issues. For example, the structural dimensions of social capital capture the extent to which relationships with members internal or external to the organisation are strong or weak. There is contradictory evidence with regard to the impact of these on learning; strong ties facilitate the easy diffusion of knowledge and co-development of new knowledge because of familiarity among knowledge holders; equally too much familiarity can stifle creativity or innovation. The cognitive dimension refers to a shared understanding or common language among actors, which enables tacit knowledge to be exchanged more easily and to be combined in novel ways (Gulati et al., 2000). The relational dimension refers to the nature of the personal relationship among actors and one of the fundamental characteristics facilitating effective relations is trust. High-trust relations are more likely to foster the sharing of critical skills and knowledge resources that will enable organisations to achieve innovations relating to their core competences (Wood & Brewster, 2005).

As we have seen from earlier discussions, the relationships between firms, and between firms and government agents or universities, in the development of human resource capabilities is quite distinct across national contexts and industrial sectors. Therefore we might conclude that the way in which social capital or interactive learning processes are developed will vary across countries and the extent to which they are evidenced in countries will vary. Evidence from Lam (2003) for example showed that Japanese R&D firms were less likely than United States or UK firms to adopt intra-organisational learning mechanisms. She explained this as a function of the Japanese national business system, which reinforced the legitimacy of home country technologies, in contrast with US or UK business systems, which have a strong tradition of looking to overseas employees as knowledge contributors. Equally, work by Tregaskis et al. (2010) found national differences in the adoption of socially based learning structures which were explained in terms of the legitimacy of these as transnational learning media in different country contexts. In sum, this work suggests that we might anticipate a continued divergence in the routes adopted by firms to develop their human resources. However, this divergence should not be interpreted as the superiority of sets of practices over another, but rather considered in the light of different routes to learning and innovation which are consistent with the legitimacy they are afforded in different countries, sectors and the national innovation strategies pursued.

The link between how firms organise for learning and development and differences in national innovation strategies is pursued further by Arundel and colleagues, (Arundel et al., 2006) where, using data from the Third European Survey of Working Conditions, they identified different modes of work organisation. One work organisation mode they differentiated was what they referred to as discretionary learning. This was reflected by employee discretion in how work tasks were performed, opportunity to learn new things as part of the work process, and responsibility for problem solving. This was contrasted with other modes of work organisation, such as lean production, where in addition to the characteristics of discretionary learning the work rate of employees was tightly constrained by managers, peers or production goals. They found that when the inevitable effects of establishment size, sector and occupation were taken into account, country effects remained. Specifically, the discretionary mode of learning was widely adopted in the Netherlands and Denmark, and to a lesser extent in Belgium, Luxembourg, Finland and Germany. It was found least in Greece, Italy, Spain, France, Ireland, Portugal and the UK. In contrast, the lean innovation mode was dominant in the UK, Ireland and Spain, and adopted to a much lower degree in countries such as Sweden, Austria, Denmark and Germany where discretionary learning was more widespread. They go on to argue that the discretionary learning mode is linked to in-house innovation capability, while lean organisation is linked to technology adoption capability. Thus while both modes of work organisation are reliant on employee capabilities to learn and problem-solve in the job, the way in which these skills are used for strategic purposes can vary. Thus the embeddedness of the firm in the national innovation context is an important explanation of this relationship.

The work from the national innovation systems literature complements the national business systems literature and provides insights into the specific national institutions that shape firm embeddedness and, we have argued, associated human resources development structures and activities. Institutions in the form of science and technology policy and funding shape the types of organisational activities and strategies that find support; the content and emphasis of educational programmes shape the mix of labour market skills; the social capital inherent in the learning and development networks, whether these be university–industry, government–industry or producer–supplier, shape how new skills are acquired and applied for competitive purposes. These have different emphases in different countries that combine to create divergent organisational responses. But importantly the systemic view also considers that these institutions are influenced by organisational action and thus will evolve as technology and competitive pressures evolve. In the final section of the chapter we look at some of the recent debates regarding institutional embeddedness with regard to globalisation. We consider how globalisation might impact on conceptual models of embeddedness and the implications for how we understand human resource development in firms.

GLOBALISATION AND THE EMBEDDEDNESS OF HRD

Globalisation on many levels, including the internationalisation of businesses, financial markets, consumer markets and technology, has had a significant impact on the interconnectedness of economic activity across countries and regions of the world. Here we consider the globalising effect of multinationals, supra-national institutions and sub-national institutions, and the potential consequences for human resource development approaches.

First, the multinational is seen as one of the lead drivers of globalisation (e.g. Held et al., 1999 for an overview) or global dominance effects. As multinationals expand their global reach it is argued they attempt to increase their control of overseas operations to minimise costs and maximise efficiencies. This has the effect of promoting greater standardisation across the supply chain of firms captured within the MNC network as pressures to integration across activities on multiple levels such as cross-border investment, production and intra-organisational trade enhance. In contrast, the network models of MNC organisation suggest that the strength of the multinational lies in its ability to leverage the local competitive advantage which is embedded within the local communities and combine this with knowledge from other local sites to create global innovation (e.g. Ghoshal & Bartlett, 1990; Hedlund, 1999). In this way, national comparative advantage remains important to the MNC as actions that undermine this could have knock-on effects for the global capabilities of the firm. The evidence, perhaps not surprisingly, demonstrates that the globalising impact of the MNC is mixed and full of contradiction (see, for example, Kristensen & Zeitlin, 2006). While the evidence is well debated in Chapter 2, it is worth reiterating here that different priorities with respect to global learning, coupled with strategic cost management models that can result in the loss of recently developed skill sets, do have appreciable effects on the globalisation of the HRD effort.

In an examination of the influence of MNC country of origin on the diffusion of human resource practices across national borders, Ferner and Varul (2000) argue that firms may assimilate practices from other countries into their own models of operating, such that 'a distinctive national business system may learn to adapt to the demands of internationalized operation while retaining and even consolidating its distinctiveness'. Indeed, recent survey data on foreign and home owned MNCs operating in the UK (Edwards et al., 2007), and in Ireland (Lavelle et al., 2009) attest to the continuing significance of country of origin in explaining the diversity of MNC practice. One stream of analysis from this work examined the presence of intra-organisational learning structures (e.g. expatriate assignment, international project groups) in the UK operations of home- and foreign-owned firms. These structures were argued to be key elements supporting global learning in multinationals in that they allowed, for example, new knowledge to be created through identifying synergies, or for best practices to be diffused. The results suggested that the extent to which such global learning structures were adopted was dependent, in part, on the country of origin of the parent. Specifically, it was argued that the way in which skills and knowledge were created differs in Japanese firms compared to US, German and other European firms because of their embeddedness in institutions affecting career progression, international mobility, internal labour utilisation and the strategic business function of subsidiaries (Tregaskis et al., 2010). Similarly, Lam (2003) argued that the distinctive national institutions in Japan towards firm-specific skill development meant Japanese firms were less able to create systems to support the development of knowledge and skills in international learning spaces when compared with US MNCs. In sum, the evidence suggests that while MNCs may be seen as sources of innovation on global practices this has not necessarily led to standardisation across MNCs or a weakening of the impact of national business systems. Instead firms appear to be more or less able to absorb elements of global practice and assimilate them within their norms of practice creating an adjustment but not necessarily a fundamental shift in the assumption of organisation.

Second, globalisation is argued to have brought into play the importance of supranational institutions and their role in shaping organisational behaviour and skill acquisition at the national and firm level. As discussed in Chapter 2, while globalisation has initiated institutional changes at the supra-national level that have affected a wide variety of organisational behaviours, there is less evidence that national models are becoming obsolete. Indeed, it may we be the case that we are likely to see greater variation across countries. For example, Bosch et al. (2007: 262) argued that while the institutional structures around skill acquisition may have prevented UK manufacturing moving from a low-skills base dependent on mass production, in parallel there has been the growth of its 'specialization in tradable as well as more domestically-orientated services'. As a consequence, the low-skills base in manufacturing may be of less salience than in the past because the nature of productive activity is changing. They also showed that the supra-national governance structures which have led to de-regulation of product-markets (e.g. move toward privatisation of transport, energy and telecommunications) has led to greater variety in national employment models, not greater homogeneity. This is largely explained by the extent to which product-markets and employment market regulation are intertwined. In Scandinavian countries, such as Sweden and Denmark, labour standards are statutory and collectively agreed. Therefore multinationals attempting to provide services in industries protected by these agreements must conform to national pay levels and agreements. In Germany, however, the privatisation of telecommunications and establishment of call centres by foreign firms who were not bound by collective agreements has led to a fragmentation of collective bargaining and low wages. This has implications for the scope of maintaining a high investment skills models in labour-intensive industries embedded within a high protection employment model.

Finally, institutions at the sub-national regional level are becoming recognised as potentially powerful players in interpreting local responses to globalisation pressure (Cantwell & Piscitello, 2002; Ferner et al., 2006). Here the evidence suggests that regions within countries have organised as competitive clusters whereby businesses are attracted to certain regions because of the availability of specific skills and knowledge resources. The types of actors that are important here include, for example, trade unions, economic development agencies, those involved in skill provision, research bodies or employers groups. Sub-national governance structures have been identified as particularly pertinent in debates on the supply and demand for high and low skills (Fuller et al., 2002; Keep et al., 2004). Also, where local supply chains and clustering of businesses in related areas are found, it raises the importance of sub-national actors in sustaining the cluster (Maskell & Malmberg, 1999; Porter, 1998). This is an issue that comes to the fore when you consider for example countries where institutional arrangements at the sub-national level vary significantly as in the case of eastern and western Germany, or Spain where autonomous regional governments exist or Canada and the United States which are organised as federal states. Crouch (2005) argues that the role of sub-national actors is important to consider as they can potentially work to create specific local advantages that are aimed at encouraging business to a local region, remain there and which can shape the nature of labour market skills in those local areas. He refers to this as 'institutional entrepreneurship' and makes the important point that such action may be contradictory to the national business model. However, the role of these sub-national players and how they interact with local or global business and supra-national institutions and their impact on learning and skills is largely under-researched.

CONCLUSION

In this chapter we have considered the strategic logic underpinning management models of human resource development in firms. While these models allude to the embeddedness of the organisation in local and international environments, there is scant evidence of conceptualisation of how this embeddedness operates and the effects on how practices are incorporated into firms' management regimes. Therefore we have drawn on the institutional literature to consider the nature of institutions that shape labour market skills acquisition and firm behaviour. The NBS literature demonstrated the importance of the interaction between national approaches to skill development focused on general or specific skills and the mobility of these skills on the one hand and on the other firm strategies with regard to incremental or radical innovation. The NIS literature focused more narrowly on technical innovation in firms. This work highlighted some of the sectoral nuances associated with innovation strategies and skills accumulation. It demonstrated the close interaction between what firms do and need in terms of knowledge and skills and how they resource this depending on the tradition of the national institutions. One of the issues emerging from this literature base is that it suggests that multinational corporations from specific countries may develop specialised capabilities in innovation, which they attempt to export to their operations overseas. Therefore, in certain industries, such as pharmaceuticals or electronics, sector may be the more significant organising regime. However, the evidence also suggests that certain sectors are more dominant in certain countries than others. For example, US companies are dominant in pharmaceutical and biotechnology due to the embeddedness in supportive science based institutions. When looking at globalisation debates and the influence of multinationals on national models of employment and skills acquisition, the interaction between sector and MNC country of origin requires closer scrutiny.

The role of national institutions was also considered in relation to learning and innovation in firms. As evidenced in the introduction to this chapter, organisational learning processes are widely propagated in the management literature as fundamental to the renewal of organisational knowledge and the development of competitive capabilities. However, the evidence from Lundvall and colleagues, Lam, and Tregaskis and colleagues suggests that organisational learning practices as strategic capabilities are inextricably tied to national institutional structures for skill development and innovation. Thus Japanese organisations adopt organisational learning practices that are distinctly Japanese in orientation and different to those adopted by US firms or European firms. We would argue that it is not merely the case that certain organisational learning practices act as substitutes but rather that when practices such as expatriate assignments or international project teams are adopted by a firm they are interpreted within the context of the management model already in existence at the national level. As such international project teams in US firms may be used to promote social capital in firms and the co-collaboration of knowledge given the embeddedness of institutions in structures that support the use of international labour markets as knowledge resources and international mobility of staff. In contrast Japanese companies may be more likely to use international project teams for the diffusion of process innovation associated with technology. Both mechanisms support organisational learning imperatives, but the learning inputs and outcomes differ. The nature of the interaction between organisational learning mechanisms and institutional embeddedness of firms raises many questions that warrant further investigation.

In conclusion, we looked at the relevance of embeddedness debates on learning in firms in the face of globalisation pressures. We would argue that globalisation has not negated the significance of the national embeddedness of firms and national institutions on firm behaviour. Rather the debates highlight the relevance of multi-level actors in the process of organisational and institutional change. Globalisation, it could be argued, had spawned greater intra-model variation whereby within countries regional variations exist, sectoral variations transcend national borders and variations between multinationals of the same country of origin exist. This variety requires comparative research that can explore the complexity of these interactions through multivariate models in order to more effectively tease out the commonality and variation in firm level human resource development, and the extent to which these are explained by organisational contingencies and the institutions in which these are embedded.

REFERENCES

Adler, P. S. & Cole, R. E. 1993. Designed for learning: a tale of two auto plants. *Sloan Management Review*, **34**(3): 85–94.

Adler, P. S., Goldoftas, B. & Levine, D. I. 1999. Flexibility versus efficiency? A case study of model changeovers in the Toyota production system. *Organization Science*, **10**(1): 43–68.

Antonacopoulou, E. D. & Fitzgerald, L. 1996. Reframing competency in management education. *Human Resource Management Journal*, **6**(1): 27–49.

Appelbaum, S. H. & Reichart, W. 1998. How to measure an organization's learning ability: the facilitating factors. *Journal of Workplace Learning*, **10**(1): 15–28.

Arundel, A., Lorenz, E., Lundvall, B.-A. & Valeyre, A. 2006. The organisation of work and innovative performance: a comparison of the EU-15, 22nd EGOS Colloquium. Bergen.

Barney, J. 1991. Firm resources and sustained competitive advantage. *Journal of Management*, **17**(1): 99–120.

Bosch, G., Rubery, J. & Lehndorff, S. 2007. European employment models under pressure to change. *International Labour Review*, **146**(3/4): 253–277.

Brown, J. S. & Duguid, P. 1991. Organizational learning and communities of practice: toward a unified view of working, learning, and innovation. *Organization Science*, **2**(1): 40–57.

Cantwell, J. & Piscitello, L. 2002. The location of technological activities of MNCs in European regions: the role of spillovers and local competencies. *Journal of International Management*, **8**(1): 69–96.

Carmeli, A. & Schaubroeck, J. 2005. How leveraging human resource capital with its competitive distinctiveness enhances the performance of commercial and public organizations *Human Resource Management*, **44**(4): 391–412.

Cohen, W. M. & Levinthal, D. A. 1990. Absorptive capacity: a new perspective on learning and innovation. *Administrative Science Quarterly*, **35**(1): 128–153.

Coleman, J. S. 1990. *Foundations of Social Theory*. Cambridge, MA: Belknap Press for Harvard University Press.

Cook, S. D. & Yanow, D. 1993. Culture and Organizational Learning. *Journal of Management Enquiry*, **2**(4): 373–390.

Crouch, C. 2005. *Capitalist Diversity and Change*. Oxford: Oxford University Press.

Doremus, P. N., Keller, W. W., Pauly, L. W. & Reich, S. 1999. *The Myth of the Global Corporation*. Princeton, NJ: Princeton University Press.

Drucker, P. 1992. *Managing for the Future*. Oxford: Butterworth-Heinemann.

Edquist, C. 2005. Systems of innovation: perspectives and challenges. In J. Fagerberg, D. Mowery & R. R. Nelson (eds), *The Oxford Handbook of Innovation*. Oxford: Oxford University Press.

Edwards, T., Tregaskis, O., Edwards, P., Ferner, A., Marginson, P., Adam, D., Arrowsmith, J., Budjanovcanin, A. & Meyer, M. 2007. Charting the contours of MNCs in Britain: methodological challenges in survey research. Jointly published by DMU's Occasional Paper Series and Warwick Business School's Papers in Industrial Relations.

Estevez-Abe, M., Iversen, T. & Soskice, D. 2001. Social protection and the formation of skills: a reinterpretation of the welfare state. In P. Hall & D. Soskice (eds), *Varieties of Capitalism. The Institutional Foundations of Comparative Advantage*. Oxford: Oxford University Press, pp. 145–183.

Ferner, A., Quintanilla, J. & Sánchez-Runde, C. 2006. *Multinationals, Institutions and the Construction of Transnational Practices. Convergence and Diversity in the Global Economy*. Basingstoke, UK: Palgrave.

Ferner, A. & Varul, M. 2000. 'Vanguard' subsidiaries and the diffusion of new practices. *British Journal of Industrial Relations*, **38**(1): 115–140.

Freeman, C. 1987. *Technology Policy and Economic Performance: Lessons from Japan*. London: Pinter.

Fuller, C., Bennett, R. & Ramsden, M. 2002. The economic development role of English RDAs: the need for greater discretionary power. *Regional Studies*, **36**(4): 421–428.

Garavan, T. N. & McCarthy, A. 2008. Collective learning processes and human resource develoment. *Advances in Developing Human Resources*, **10**(4): 451–471.

Garrick, J. 1999. *Understanding Learning at Work*. London: Routledge.

Ghoshal, S. & Bartlett, C. A. 1990. The multinational corporation as an interorganizational network. *Academy of Management Review*, **15**(4): 603–625.

Gond, J. & Herrbach, O. 2006. Social reporting as an organizational learning tool: a theoretical framework. *Journal of Business Ethics*, **65**(4): 359–371.

Guerreri, P. & Tylecote, A. 1997. Interindustry differences in technical change and national patterns of technological accumulation. In C. Edquist (ed.), *Systems of Innovation: Technologies, Institutions and Organisations*. London: Pinter, pp. 107–129.

Gulati, R., Nohria, N. & Zaheer, A. 2000. Strategic networks. *Strategic Management Journal*, **21**(3): 203–215.

Hall, P. & Soskice, D. 2001. *Varieties of Capitalism*. Oxford: Oxford University Press.

Hedlund, G. 1999. The intensity and extensity of knowledge and the multinational corporation as a nearly recompensable system (NRS). *Management International Review*, 1(1): 1–22.

Held, D., McGrew, A., Goldblatt, D. & Perraton, J. 1999. *Global Transformations: Politics, Economics and Culture*. Stanford, CA: Stanford University Press.

Hitt, M. A., Biermant, L., Shimizu, K. & Kochhar, R. 2001. Direct and moderating effects of human capital on strategy and performance in professional service firms: a resource-based perspective. *Academy of Management Journal*, 44(1): 13–28.

Huber, G. P. 1991. Organizational learning: the contributing processes and the literatures. *Organizational Science*, 2(1): 88–115.

Huselid, M. 1995. The impact of human resource management practices on turnover, productivity and corporate financial performance. *Academy of Management Journal*, 38(3): 635–672.

Kang, S., Morris, S. & Snell, S. 2007. Relational archetypes, organizational learning, and value creation: extending the human resource architecture. *Academy of Management Review*, 32(1): 236–256.

Keep, E., Mayhew, K. & Payne, J. 2004. From skills revolution to productivity miracle – not as easy as it sounds? *Oxford Review of Economic Policy*, 22(4): 539–559.

Kogut, B. & Zander, U. 1992. Knowledge of the firm, combinative capabilities and the replication of technology. *Organization Science*, 3(3): 383–397.

Korth, S. 2000. Single and double-loop learning: exploring potential influence of cognitive style. *Organization Development Journal*, 18(3): 87–98.

Kristensen, P. H. & Zeitlin, J. 2006. *Local Players in Global Games*. Oxford: Oxford University Press.

Lam, A. 2003. Organizational learning in multinationals: R&D networks of Japanese and US MNEs in the UK. *Journal of Management Studies*, 40(3): 673–703.

Lavelle, J., McDonnell, A. & Gunnigle, P. 2009. *Human Resource Practices in Multinational Companies in Ireland: A Contemporary Analysis*. Dublin: The Stationery Office.

Leana, C. R. & Van Buren, H. J. 1999. Organizational social capital and employment practices. *Academy of Management Review*, 24(3): 538–555.

Lundberg, C. C. 1995. Learning in and by organizations: three conceptual issues. *International Journal of Organizational Analysis*, 3(1): 353–360.

Lundvall, B.-A. 1985 *Product Innovation and User–Producer Interaction*. Aalborg, Denmark: Aalborg University Press.

Lundvall, B.-A., Johnson, B., Andersen, E., S. & Dalum, B. 2002. National systems of production, innovation and competence building. *Research Policy*, 31(2): 213–231.

Lundvall, B. 2007. National innovation systems: analytical concept and development tool. *Industry & Innovation*, 14(1): 95–119.

Luthans, F. & Youssef, C. M. 2004. Human, social and now positive psychological capital management: investing in people for competitive advantage. *Organizational Dynamics*, 33(2): 143–160.

Maskell, P. & Malmberg, A. 1999. The competitiveness of firms and regions: 'ubiquitification' and the importance of localized learning. *European Urban and Regional Studies*, 6(1): 9–25.

Nahapiet, J. & Ghoshal, S. 1998. Social capital, intellectual capital, and the organizational advantage. *Academy of Management Review*, 23(2): 242–266.

Nonaka, I. 1991. The knowledge creating company. *Harvard Business Review*, 69: 96–104.

OECD. 2007. *Science, Technology and Industry Scoreboard*. Paris: OECD Publishing.

Patel, P. & Pavitt, K. 1991. Large firms in the production of the world's technology: an important case of 'non-globalisation'. *Journal of International Business Studies*, 22(1): 1–21.

Patel, P. & Pavitt, K. 1997. Technological competencies in the world's largest firms: complex and path-dependent, but not too much variety. *Research Policy*, 26(2): 533–546.

Pavitt, K. 1999. *Technology, Management and Systems of Innovation*. Cheltenham, UK: Edward Elgar.

Pedler, M., Boydell, T. & Burgoyne, J. 1994. *A Manager's Guide to Self-development.* London: McGraw-Hill.

Polanyi, M. 1962. *Personal Knowledge.* Chicago: University of Chicago Press.

Porter, M. 1998. Cluster and the new economics of competition. *Harvard Business Review,* **76**(6): 77–91.

Prahalad, C. & Hamel, G. 1990. The competence of the corporation. *Harvard Business Review,* **68**(3): 79–93.

Senge, P. 1990. *The Fifth Discipline.* New York: Doubleday.

Streeck, W. & Thelen, K. 2005. *Beyond Continuity. Institutional Change in Advanced Political Economies.* Oxford: Oxford University Press.

Taylor, S. 2006. Emerging motivations for global HRM integration. In A. Ferner, J. Quintanilla, & C. Sanchez-Runde (eds), *Multinationals and the Construction of Transnational Practices: Convergence and Diversity in the Global Economy.* London: Palgrave.

Tregaskis, O., Edwards, T., Edwards, P., Ferner, A. & Marginson, P. 2010. Transnational learning structures in multinational firms: organisational context and national embeddedness. *Human Relations,* **63**(4): 471–499.

Ulrich, D. 1997. *Human Resource Champions: the Next Agenda for Adding Value and Delivering Results.* Boston, MA: Harvard Business School Press.

Ulrich, D., Von Gilnow, M. A. & Jick, T. 1993. High-impact learning: building and diffusing learning capability. *Organization Dynamics,* **22**(2): 52–67.

Watkins, K. E. & Marsick, V. J. 1996. *In Action: Creating the Learning Organization.* Alexandria, VA: American Society for Training and Development.

Wood, G. & Brewster, C. 2005. Trust, intrafirm, and supplier relations. *Business & Society Review,* **110**(4): 459–483.

9 Comparing national approaches to management development
Christopher Mabey and Matias Ramirez

The strategic training and development of managers is widely regarded as one of four progressive HRM policies (Becker & Huselid, 1998). It might also be asserted that management development is central to an organisation's approach to HRM and a telling signal of the value it places upon its staff. Furthermore, at a macro level, there is a persistent belief that national productivity is closely connected to a country's collective management and leadership capability. Although the logic and plausibility of this skills–performance link has been questioned (e.g. Grugulis & Stoyanova, 2006), this does little to diminish the preoccupation of governments, both national and international, with the calibre of their managers and leaders. In this chapter, we set out to do three things. First, in section one, we assemble what is currently known about the way organisations in different countries develop their managers, looking primarily at studies in Europe and S.E. Asia. Then in section two, we seek to explain why differences in policy and practice occur, looking first at macro-institutional variables and then at micro, firm-level factors like ownership.

In the third and final section, we take stock of current knowledge in the field of comparative management development. Here we argue that, to understand the richness and variability of management development interventions as part of wider HRM strategies, we require a more theoretically informed and sophisticated analysis than has been hitherto undertaken. In particular, we make a case for meso-level analyses in order to understand the role that local and international networks can play in developing managerial skills. Linked to this we recommend drawing upon knowledge exchange theories, and particularly the notion of social capital, to alert us to some of the more subtle and potentially damaging dimensions of management development in an international context.

COMPARATIVE ANALYSES OF MANAGEMENT DEVELOPMENT[1]

Despite its importance as a central human resource strategy, especially in international firms, surprisingly little comparative research has been published on the way organisations train and develop their managers. Here we review a number of studies that begin to illuminate country difference.

Differing Assumptions Governing Management Development

Given the very different cultural conceptions of what a manager is and does in the first place (as illustrated by the final column of Table 9.1 below), it should come as no surprise that nationally distinctive approaches to management development exist. For example, in a paper which seeks to penetrate the national psyche with regard to managers and their development, Lawrence (1993) notes that: 'Management development is less salient in France because in that country management is regarded more as a state of being than as the result of fashioned development processes within the company. It is or connotes an identity, more than an activity or set of capabilities' (1993: 17). This contrasts with the conception of management in Britain where it is seen as essentially an interpersonal task, focused on getting things done (Sparrow, 1996). In this context, personal experience is prized and management development is pre-occupied with 'soft' skills, especially the ability to motivate, lead and get the best from teams, and elitism codified in national culture is eschewed. However, this perception that management is generalisable from one function and industrial sector to another is quite different again from the German conviction that specialist knowledge (especially technical) and experience is all important. Lawrence (1993) notes that this prevalent view, together with a variety of historical factors militate against a flourishing management development activity in Germany, with the result that it is less widespread, salient and more restrained by the personnel function.

By contrast, it has been argued that the practice of management development is seen as a science by many Asian governments and thus that it can be taught and applied like any systematic operation. This is reflected in how managers learn in countries like China, Hong Kong and Singapore (Borgonjon & Vanhonacker, 1992; Warner, 1992). In countries like China, the result can be that when personnel managers work on a problem in their business, they invariably seek a 'systematic' approach to training (Branine, 1996). In turn, Asian managers typically appreciate lectures and more of a structured type of learning delivered by 'experts'. Furthermore, while they may look to Western management to provide the science there is caution among Chinese officials and administrators concerning the full adoption of Western principles. In efforts to reinforce traditional values that include preserving the doctrine of present leadership while introducing Western management values to suit the needs of society, the result can be an interesting collage of desired leadership attributes (Fu & Tsui, 2003). Within this, the underlying cultural traits remain resistant to change: 'The main features of uniquely adapted Chinese models of management development and training are teacher-centred, culturally bound and politically oriented, making it fundamentally different from the learner-centred approach of western countries' (Branine, 2005: 468).

Having established that countries differ in their overall stance towards management development, we now draw upon comparative research to consider how this translates into strategy.

Strategic Approaches to Management Development

Conceptual studies

Attempts have been made to predict how firms in different national cultures might approach training and development, in terms of initial investment and the way needs assessment might be conducted. For example, Aycan (2005) makes these observations about training generally, which can also be applied to management development. She notes that in cultures where there is a heavy emphasis on performance excellence and quality, there is a large budgetary allocation to the widespread application of training and development activities. Examples include China (Tsang, 2001) and the United Arab Emirates (Wilkins, 2001). The importance of training and development, however, is undermined in fatalistic cultures where managers assume that employees, by nature, have limited capacity that cannot be improved (Aycan et al., 2000). In performance-oriented cultural contexts, training and development are primarily geared towards improving individual or team performance. However, in collectivistic cultures, such activities serve an additional purpose and that is to increase loyalty and commitment to the organisation. Wong et al. (2001) reported that by providing training Chinese organisations instilled the perception that the organisation treated employees well. This perception, in turn, stimulated the need to reciprocate the favour (the indigenous concept of 'pao' – paying back those who treat you well) by working hard and staying committed to the firm. In such contexts, training and development is used as a tool to motivate employees and reward loyalty and commitment, a phenomenon observed in India (Sinha, 1997) and China (Tsang, 2001).

Training needs are determined on the basis of performance outcomes especially in performance-oriented or universalistic cultures. In low performance-oriented and high power distance contexts, decisions on who will participate in training are based on criteria other than job performance. Employees who maintain good relations with higher management are selected for attractive training programmes (i.e. training overseas or in resorts) as a reward for their loyalty (Sinha, 1997). There is also in-group favouritism based on kinship or tribal ties in collectivist cultures (Wilkins, 2001). In low power distance cultures, training needs are usually determined jointly by the employee and his/her superior. In collectivistic and high-power distance cultures, training needs of the work group are determined by the paternalistic manager in an authoritarian or consultative way (Wilkins, 2001). However, this may not be resented, because superiors are assumed to know what is best for the employees.

This conceptual analysis leads Aycan (2005) to offer two propositions. First, that cultural fatalism or a low performance orientation will correlate negatively with the level of investment in training and development activities. Second, that in low-power distance, high performance-oriented or universalistic cultures, training and development needs will be determined based on performance evaluation outcomes, and the needs assessment will be conducted participatively. In high-power distance, collectivistic or paternalistic cultures, selection for training will not be based primarily on performance, but on group membership (i.e. in-group favouritism); and needs assessment will not be conducted in a participatory manner.

Empirical studies

Empirical work which measures comparative grass-roots management development activity is still sparse. One major European study is that conducted by a team of researchers including the authors of this chapter (Mabey & Gooderham, 2005; Mabey & Ramirez, 2004; Ramirez, 2004). This was based on telephone interviews with the HR manager and a line manager in each of 600 private sector organisations in six European countries; these firms were all domestically owned (across manufacturing, transport/distribution and service sectors) and ranged from SMEs to firms with more than a thousand employees. The majority of European organisations claim to have a specific budget for staff training generally, the exceptions being Denmark where this is true for only half the companies and Spain where the figure is only 25 per cent. The HRD managers in less than half of the organisations in the sample claim to have a management development policy statement, although the proportion increases to two-thirds for those located in Norway. These percentages have not changed markedly (by more than 9 per cent) since 1993, except in the UK where there has been an increased adoption of policy statements from 24 to 43 per cent and in France where the use of policies has dropped from 52 to 42 per cent (Brewster & Hegewisch, 1994).

When it comes to the systems and practices in place to facilitate management development (such as appraisals, career planning, fast-tracking and evaluation), Spain is the poor relation, with significantly less in the way of development practices than all other countries, except France. Over half (56 per cent) of all companies use fast-track management development for selected managers. This approach is particularly favoured in France (77 per cent), Norway (71 per cent) and Germany (67 per cent). Appraisals are widely used for managers in Europe (62 per cent), and of these, 59 per cent claim that development needs are discussed at appraisals. The figures for France and the UK are far above the average. Line managers claim career planning takes place in 55 per cent of organisations (compared with HR managers who claim 60 per cent), but there is a wide variation for two countries: Denmark (88 per cent) and the UK (31 per cent). With some notable exceptions, management development – certainly at a procedural level – is relatively healthy in European organisations. The question remains: how does this translate into practice?

We have briefly assessed two types of study: those that have taken cultural attributes and predicted difference in policy and practice based on these; and those that have set out to analyse management development practice at organisation level empirically. Both point to national and/or regional groupings in the way managers are typically developed. In a study contrasting leadership styles in the United States, Japan and Taiwan, Von Glinow et al. (1999) conclude that, in comparison with many other political and economic factors, culture is probably the most stable factor that drives management thinking. In particular, they find that the more a given culture assumes human potential to be uneven across organisational members (as against 'talent' being uniformly distributed), the more likely it is that leader training will emphasise specialised expertise rather than general management skills. An important caveat made by these authors – and one which applies to this whole discussion – is that national boundaries may not always coincide with cultural boundaries. In their research, Von Glinow and her team found cultural heterogeneity (internal dissimilarities) to be highest in the United States and lowest in Japan. However, despite being an important explanatory factor, culture alone does not account for all the differences in management development in different country settings. In the next sections we explore a number of other potential determinants.

HOW CAN DIFFERENCES IN MANAGEMENT DEVELOPMENT BE EXPLAINED?

Theorists in the field of international human resource management have, for some time, been seeking to identify the factors, external and internal to the firm, which shape HRM policies and practices (De Cieri & Dowling, 1999; Harzing & Ruysseveldt, 1995; Schuler et al., 2002). In order to understand the differing management development pathways then, we need to take account of macro factors like institutional context in the country of operation (with its attendant laws and regulations, politics, labour markets and industry characteristics). Alongside this, we should also consider salient micro-level factors relating to the firm, in particular the nature of ownership (Jackson & Schuler, 1995). In this section we briefly assess these explanatory variables in turn.

Macro-level Institutional Effects[2]

Comparing national approaches to management development through an institutional lens relies on the notion that the training practices adopted by firms in different countries represent more than deviations along a 'best practice' trajectory, but instead reflect the existence of different industrial infrastructures and sets of interlocking institutions that shape the paths firms take toward skill formation (see Chapter 2 and Hall & Soskice, 2001; Boyer, 1990). Hence, although, as is often the case, the formal content and label of management skills development between countries may appear similar, the process and definitions behind common terms can diverge significantly (Lane, 1989) as illustrated in Table 9.1.

An initial task therefore is to think about how institutional differences in management tasks can be conceptualised. One approach emphasises the level of coordination of decision making. Whitley's (1992) institutional framework of business systems encompasses issues such as the separation of technical knowledge of line managers from production, the distance between managers and subordinates and how the authority of the former is conceived. The argument can be further elaborated to suggest that the sorts of skills firms want their managers to develop, the discretion managers have to use these skills subsequently and how managers themselves view their training can all be strongly influenced by the societal system in which managers live and work. Thus, for example, in Germany, the rigorous training means that in manufacturing sectors in particular, managers gain their authority as so-called players (Lam, 1994), in contrast to France, where formal hierarchies within organisations traditionally played an important role for attainment of authority.

Table 9.1 European management development systems

	Skills type	Career paths	Who pays for training?	Agents driving training and status of training institutions	Distinguishing national characteristics of managers
UK	Managers can maintain skills when moving jobs (Buechtemann & Verdier, 1998)	Less emphasis on firm level career development (Bournois, 1994).	Growing general business education financed by employee (Bennett, 1997).	High status of chartered institutions. Low status of vocational training (Iversen et al., 2001).	High premium on the 'gifted amateur' (Bennett, 1997). Managers are 'specialist co-ordinators' (Lam, 1994).
Germany	VET for managers and employees technical/ scientific skills prior to becoming managers (Streeck 1995). Formal management education emphasizes scientific. Theoretical principles.	Strong emphasis on succession planning (Bournois et al., 1994). Low mobility between firms (Lane, 1989).	Hands-on managerial training funded by firms (Lane, 1989).	High status of VET for managers (Streeck, 1995). Formal management training roots lies in the *Diplom Kaufman* and BWL in the university system (Shenton, 1986). High level CEOs would have PhDs.	Managers are subject to intense monitoring (Prouise, 1994). Managers are "players" (Lam, 1994). High consensus between managers and workers.

Table 9.1 (continued)

	Skills type	Career paths	Who pays for training?	Agents driving training and status of training institutions	Distinguishing national characteristics of managers
France	*Grandes Ecoles* vocational origins and proximity to business world (Shenton, 1996).	More likely to lose skill status when moving jobs (Eyraud et al., 1999). Job hierarchies and seniority. Internal labour markets (Maurice 1986). Promotion into *cadre* status is rare (Tregaskis, 1997).	Law requires firms to spend at least 1.5% of wage bill on training (Thomson et al., 2001).	*Grandes Ecoles* technocratic elite (Shenton 1996). 75% of senior execs in large firms have *Grandes Ecoles* qualification (Bennett, 1997).	Managers are 'coordinators' (Lam 1994). Comparatively weak retention and short term training plans.
Spain	Traditional focus on internal training (Baruel, 1996).	Foreign assignments play an important role in career (Bournois, 1994). Careers paths offered to high proportion of managers.	Training and development concentrated within large firms (Paralleda et al., 2002).	Successful MBAs because of traditional weakness of other management education. (Shenton, 1996).	Few apprenticeships (Paralleda et al., 2002). Weak retention and comparatively short term training plans.

Norway	Emphasis on company and VET training.	Strong long-term commitment, though increasing mobility.	Norwegian private sector finances their management development programme	Large firms recruit from elite engineering or business schools.	Managerial autonomy, functional responsibilities and task variation enshrined in legislation
Denmark	Combination of experiential firm-specific learning with formal education and VET.	Strong promotion and internal labour market opportunities.	State offers affordable post-graduate managerial training.	Combines VET and formal MBA education (Brewster, 1992). High degree of social capital. Cooperative and consensual system between State, employers, trade unions and individual managers.	Managers willing and encouraged to take risks is supported by safety net (Hofstede, 1985).

Source: Adapted from Mabey and Finch-Lees (2008: 182–183).

A second highly influential approach that differentiates country specific institutions on training and development emerges from the varieties of capitalism literature (Hall & Soskice, 2001). This literature has emphasised skills type differences as one of the principle institutional differentiators between coordinated and liberal market economies (Estevez-Abe et al., 2001). Building on Becker's (1964) original distinction between general and firm-specific skills, the argument is made that firm-specific skills would be of benefit only in the organisation in which skill development takes place. General training, on the other hand, can be of benefit to all firms because the skill is not firm-specific. However, unless there exists an institutional mechanism, such as government regulation or inter-firm agreements to prevent poaching, firms will generally be reluctant to invest in generalist skills. On the other hand, unless there is a degree of employment security, employees will be reluctant to limit themselves to firm specific skills, for they forfeit employability if they lose their jobs. The following section applies this institutional analysis to three country groupings in Europe.

Denmark, Germany and Norway
Denmark, Germany and Norway have traditionally been viewed as co-ordinated market economies with high levels of interaction and communication between businesses, the state, financial institutions and trade unions. Nevertheless, it is apparent that some important distinctions can be drawn in relation to management development. Germany has traditionally been considered an archetypal example of a highly integrated autonomous national system of interlocking institutions. Shenton (1996) suggested that management training and education in Germany has evolved following quite distinct German traditions and studies have found that, above all the European countries, the German system of management development emphasises in-house training, a relatively long horizon for developing in-house skills and long tenure for managers (Ramirez & Mabey, 2005). As has been mentioned, many high-level German managers undertake vocational education comprising administrative and technical skills. There has recently been an expansion of formal managerial educational training although, as with the rest of the university system, it steers away from direct contact with the business community, preferring to leave hands-on management to firm-specific on-the-job training. Hence, although some important qualitative changes may be appearing, the training system still appears to be consistent with its traditional institutions.

Norway, by contrast, has been strongly influenced by the different traditions of the larger countries and its neighbours. During the inter-war period this included North American ideologies of management emanating from the era of mass production that emphasises a clear distinction between managers and subordinates. However, in contrast to the UK, which after World War II incorporated much of the ideology of Taylorism into managerial methods, it was the egalitarian management system that predominated. Significantly, the emphasis on consensual and transparent forms of communication, where different parties within the labour market define together what is good management and good quality of working life, has become institutionalised in Norwegian legislation. Indeed, Norwegian law today goes relatively far in demanding that employers satisfy the psychological needs of employees for autonomy, functional responsibilities, and task variation. Despite this, the Norwegian system has been open and flexible, allowing different ideologies to live side-by-side and different modes of thinking to be considered (Ramirez 2004).

The case of Denmark is interesting for, as Ramirez and Mabey (2005) suggest, the country appears to have been able to combine a combination of high manager retention, strong career structures but also strength in generalist, vocational, and internal firm-specific training for managers, which is quite unique. Traditionally, the Danish institutional system has been considered egalitarian with high levels of integration between different parts of the economy. The state also recently altered its policy toward business, moving away from providing economic support through tax breaks, toward encouraging Danish businesses to develop their social capital, expressed in strong inter-organisational linkages. Thus, the ability to successfully combine the strengths of public and private sector practices suggests a highly cohesive, consensual but at the same time flexible system of institutions and actors that are conducive to long-term investment in training and development.

Spain and France
The distinguishing feature of the French business system that arose after World War II emphasised the role of state in a whole series of spheres that go beyond purely education. For example, the hierarchical and formal organisation of French firms is closely tied to tiers of so-called cadres, a conceptualisation of management unique to France. The occupation of management in France is a highly respected rank that demands high educational achievement (Tregaskis, 1997). Managers are furthermore divided into a series of formal titles that have legally defined spans of autonomy for decision making and working time, and spans of responsibility. With respect to training, a tax is levied on all companies employing more than 10 people at a rate of 1.2 per cent of wages (Thomson et al., 2001). Tregaskis (1997) suggested that one of the effects of the training levy is that this considerably limits the discretion organisations have over levels of training and expenditure, in contrast to the UK, for example, where HR managers have continually to justify their training expenditure

based on the impact it has on company performance. In France, there has also traditionally existed little inter-firm managerial mobility, particularly at the lower level, and strong internal labour markets have defined managerial careers through promotion. High-level management education is formally embedded, not in the university system, but in the vocational chamber of commerce, which after World War II was assimilated into the Grandes Écoles system that attracted the brightest students.

Ramirez and Mabey (2005) suggest that in the early part of the 2000s, French line managers revealed a pessimistic view of managerial retention and long-term development in France. One reason for this may be that during the 1990s, the French state consciously retreated from its interventionist role and offered management of large firms the autonomy to restructure (Hancke, 2002). This led to a dismantling of large conglomerates, greater foreign ownership of French firms, and strategies based on acquisition and selling off of subsidiaries. As discussed earlier, this suggests a certain discord between official institutions and changes in the strategies of firms that are restructuring in the short term, following some of the practices of Anglo-Saxon firms.

Although its integration into the European market during the 1980s and 1990s has transformed large parts of the economy, a great deal of HRM literature about Spain still focuses on the slowness of the transition away from the rigid bureaucratic structures of the Franco era. Indeed, it is often judged that the modern sectors of the economy with more advanced management systems are restricted to large firms linked to overseas networks. Nevertheless, important economy-wide changes, including the deregulation of labour markets and the rise of temporary contracts appear to have had widespread effects in the economy (Paralleda et al., 2002). The idea of a combination of different, not entirely coherent, elements of the Spanish management training appears in the evidence from recent European research (Mabey & Ramirez, 2004). This suggests that formal hierarchical managerial structures with internal labour markets are still widespread in Spanish companies. These would formalise issues such as job grading and pay structures. Nevertheless, as with France, a comparatively pessimistic view of managerial retention and long-term development is found (Ramirez & Mabey, 2005). This view is reinforced by Shenton (1996), who suggested that the popularity of MBAs in Spain derives from the weakness of firm-led management development.

United Kingdom

The case of the UK is significant in the changing attitude in favour of management education that has occurred over the past two decades and the means by which this is being provided. During the 1980s and 1990s in particular, various government reports consistently attributed the UK's low productivity performance, in part at least, to the poor skill level of UK managers. The aversion to formal management training has strong roots in the UK's education and business culture. The latter restricted management training to on-the-job or within the professions, and corporate recruiters did not expect managers to have knowledge of business or economics, a stark difference with Germany (Shenton, 1996). The result has been that traditionally the number of UK managers with secondary and higher level qualifications have been well below that of its European neighbours and the United States. Furthermore, the fragmented nature of UK institutions and the traditional laissez-faire attitude in relation to regulation meant a lack of continuity in organisational training structures and policies and exhortatory rather than proactive policies (Thomson et al., 2001). Nevertheless, during the 1990s, it is clear that important changes occurred in the direction of formalising a more professional managerial class. Many of these have come from radical improvements in the provision of formal managerial education, as universities across the board, including those with highest prestige, have become involved in teaching management. Second, the status of postgraduate MBA and master's level qualifications has improved (Thomson et al., 2001).

The shift toward formal management development education can, in part, be explained by the growing status of management qualifications. However, as discussed in section one, above, UK firms tend to rely on external training as a means to develop managers to a greater degree than five of its major European partners, as against vocational and firm-specific training. This may also be associated with the fact that relatively weak career structures and job security emphasises the need for managers to avoid getting locked in to narrow firm-specific skills. Hence, managers may be prepared to invest in generalist training on their own time and from their own resources to maintain their skills in the labour market.

While cultural and institutional factors are likely to shape the way firms in different countries build their pool of management capability, other cross-cutting factors at the level of the firm may also be influential. Here we focus on ownership, namely whether the organisation is domestic and a multi-national (MNC).

Micro-level Effects: The Effects of Ownership[3]

International HRM research has been dominated by examination of the link between the strategy–structure configuration in an internationalising firm and the competing demands for globalisation on the one hand (e.g. Evans et al., 2002) and the need for local responsiveness on the other (e.g. Rosenzweig

& Nohria, 1994; Whitley, 1992). From this we can begin to discern the likely implications of such strategies upon management development policies and practices. For instance, we know that the potential influence of multinational parent companies over host country management practices is likely to be powerful. This is especially the case in the arena of management development because it is typically seen as a way of exerting control and/or inculcating cultural expectations and building internationally skilled high-potential managers (Scullion & Starkey, 2000). Second, it has been established that there is a tendency for MNC subsidiaries to adopt parent or 'best practice' norms particularly in more macro-HRD practices like training needs analysis, management development delivery and evaluation procedures, while allowing their subsidiaries considerably greater autonomy in the local implementation of training (Noble, 1997; Tregaskis, Heraty, & Morley, 2001). Third, it is well known that the economies of scale associated with MNCs permit access to a richer vein of resources for management development than is possible for many domestic companies. Indeed there is empirical evidence that US-based MNCs diverge from their host country counterparts by attempting to apply their parent company HRM practices to their subsidiaries in western Europe (Gooderham et al., 2004).

The influence of parent MNCs upon the organisational and managerial practices of local subsidiaries has long been debated (e.g. Gooderham et al., 1999; Kostova & Roth, 2002; Rosenzweig & Nohria, 1994), and valuable attempts have been proposed to help us understand how HRM strategies/policies arise from the interplay of endogenous and exogenous factors in a given country (De Cieri & Dowling, 1999; Schuler et al., 2002). However, such research has tended to focus on the diffusion of parent MNC practices upon foreign subsidiaries (Schuler et al., 2002) and has neglected HRM policies and practices within the parent company's country. Also, with isolated exceptions (Buck et al., 2003: Griffith, 2004), such studies have taken little account of the impact of HRM policies and practices upon performance outcomes. Furthermore, despite being emblematic of so-called progressive HRM (Becker & Huselid, 1998), the distinctive contribution of management development in an international context has been somewhat subsumed within studies of overseas assignments and repatriation in MNCs (Harzing, 1999; Scullion & Collings, 2006).

Skill capability, career aspirations and the motivation of employees are all closely connected to the educational and professional systems and institutional norms of a given country, as are differing cultural definitions of effective performance (Neelankavil, 2000). For all this, it is clear that a firm's chosen international strategy will directly affect its patterns of management development. In particular, it is likely that domestic organisations (those located in a single country with limited international relations) will seek to create their management capability in distinctively different ways to their multi-national counterparts.

Most studies of HRM in multi-nationals have exclusively focused on parent–subsidiary relations. In order to identify any distinctions in the way MNCs and domestic companies undertake their management development policies and practices, we need to control for country. If significant differences are found in the way domestic organisations and MNC parents develop their managers, despite sharing a common economic, institutional and cultural context, we can reasonably attribute this to their international strategy. This was attempted in a study of management development in Norway, Germany, UK and Spain (Mabey, 2008). Support was found for the impact of country on the amount of management development undertaken, as well as the ethos and systems governing such activities. It was also established that taking an international strategic stance leads to greater investment in management development systems and the amount/ diversity of activities undertaken than it does in their domestic counterparts. The study compared MNCs and domestic companies (working in similar private sectors) co-located in the same countries, so culturally, economically, politically and institutionally these firms were therefore embedded in common settings; the one key difference was that the domestic companies were focused exclusively upon the local marketplace with no international strategies, whereas the MNCs patently did. Therefore, it was likely that significant differences were explained by the existence of an international strategy and not by that of a foreign parent.

So, being part of an MNC definitely augments the resource available for, and the volume of activity devoted to, management development. However more research comparing domestic and their MNC counterparts is needed to determine the relative effects of company and country of operation. Furthermore the degree to which any of these factors moderate the relationship between investment in managers and firm performance remains an open question. For instance, Kay (2003) and Cassis (1997) have argued that while the basic determinants of business performance lie within the firm and are unique to each successful company, national environments do matter; Cassis notes that: 'striking the right balance between the nation and the firm is not simple' (1997: 237).

MANAGEMENT DEVELOPMENT: AVENUES FOR FUTURE RESEARCH

There is evidence that management development is being taken ever more seriously by firms in the US (Michaels et al., 2000), in Western Europe

(Scullion & Starkey, 2000; Brewster et al., 2004), in Central Europe (Gudic, 2001) and in S.E. Asia (Osman-Gani & Tan, 2000) and China (Wang & Wang, 2006). However, two aspects remain underdeveloped in the current literature. In conducting comparative analysis there is need for a more cogent explanation for why firms located in different countries vary in their preferred approaches to developing their management cadres. In this chapter we have begun to assemble some potential variables, but these tend to be either exclusively macro or micro in nature. Our recommendation is that future studies adopt a deliberately meso-level approach, which accounts for, and explores the connecting mechanisms between, these two sets of factors. Second, given the twin opportunities of operating in an increasingly global and knowledge-based economy, we identify theories associated with knowledge transfer and social capital in particular as having potential for informing research in the arena of international management development.

The Need for Meso-level Analysis

The analysis so far has taken a macro and micro approach to understanding the evolution of management development across nations. However, in recent years, social science researchers have increasingly been urged to adopt a method of thinking which integrates different levels of analysis incorporating both individual and contextual factors (Rousseau & House, 1994). The limits of relying exclusively on micro and macro level analysis of training has been made more evident by growing interest in new patterns of learning based on new inter-firm collaborative projects, such as the development of the Linux open source software systems, that relied on the development of skills and training through communities of practice that span across organisational boundaries. These processes suggest further emphasis on so-called meso-level analysis is required, that focuses on training in relation to different levels of decision making, including formal and informal international and regional networks. In this sense, a key feature of the meso-level approach is its focus on relational configurations. Not only does this shift the attention towards process and relations (as opposed to actors and formal structures), but it is also well suited to understand the different types of networks individuals rely on to develop knowledge, skills and careers. Hence it helps to produce a more varied picture of management development.

The following sub-section begins to demonstrate what a meso-level approach might look like and what it can reveal. We draw upon in-depth interviews undertaken with human resource development managers in Germany, UK and Spain to explore three themes that emerge through meso-level thinking in management development (Mayrhofer et al., 2005): the struggle to create intermediary institutions to complement micro level processes of change in Germany, the importance of informal networks as a support to management training in the UK and how meso-level networks can counter stereotypical approaches to management in Spain.

The role of intermediary institutions in Germany

An important challenge to Germany's training system appears to lie in finding effective meso-level institutions to allow a transition from over-whelmingly firm-centred management training practices to a more open system of training. Line manager accounts from the four organisations studied in the research suggest that, in Germany, employers have managed very well for a long time by taking on vocationally and technically proficient recruits and grooming them via internal and idiosyncratic socialisation. However, the post-war system of governance of training appears to be changing rapidly. On the one hand, trade unions and works councils no longer have a strong influence on the promotion of training and development for lower level managers, which has led to less pressure for good quality training for junior management. On the other hand, important changes in economic pressures are now challenging the in-house approach, forcing organisations to consider external provision. In a parallel process, a wide range of private suppliers have emerged to offer management development. These include specialised training companies, freelance trainers and consultants as well as professional associations (Avery et al., 1999).

Despite these twin institutional initiatives and singular professional associations such as Deutsche Gesellschaft für Personalführung (DGfP), it is very difficult to distinguish between good and bad service providers, due mainly to an absence of market regulation or widely accepted and transparent accreditation requirements. Thus, while the effectiveness of training and development in the past may have been well measured and understood by reliance on the cultural context of the firm, the crucial task of establishing effective formal quality meso-level measures has been more problematic. Hence, while each of the interviewed companies emphasised the importance of management development for overall corporate performance, human resource managers interviewed confirmed their concern about their respective company's ability to effectively and reasonably measure the impact of management development on corporate performance

The role of networks in the UK

In the UK, by contrast, meso-level coordinating mechanisms have been the traditional reference points for managers and firms. Indeed a central theme emerging from the UK case studies is how the motivation for management training, the diffusion of new management practices and the relevance of different forms of training for individual managers are strongly influenced by the networks and relationships that both firms and individual managers form through the training. Thus, although line manager perceptions of the effectiveness of management development courses in enterprises were generally ambivalent, one durable legacy for the interviewed managers had been the contacts and networking opportunities that had emerged amongst the course participants. Those managers that had been on the courses formed new coalitions and problem-solving techniques and engaged in reciprocal 'favours' which cut across divisional boundaries. Two aspects of these informal networks are notable. The first is at a personal level. As individuals moved on to different jobs they kept in touch and shared information on where new job opportunities were emerging and others were closing. Therefore, management development was interpreted by managers in ways that were useful both to the firm and to them individually – an aspect noted by Kamoche (2000) in his ethnographic account of an international management development programme for senior managers working for a multi-national enterprise. A second feature of the informal networks that emerged was the establishment of communities of practice. These informal non-hierarchical problem solving networks have recently aroused much interest as an important source of innovation (Wenger, 1998). In one large construction contractor enterprise, an offshoot of a management training programme was that engineers from different parts of the business came together to share knowledge on a specific engineering problem. Critically, the appeal in this network appeared to be that it was not driven by the hierarchy, but by common interest and this in turn led to innovation.

A further development of the network concept can be seen in an interview with a construction contractor. Here, a crucial motivator for management development was the need to close the skills gap with the firm's customers. In short, management development was heavily mediated by a network of customers, competitors and suppliers within which the firm was embedded. Similarly, interviews with a large car manufacturer firm revealed a number of parallels. Most managers in the firm had joined with little formal management qualification or experience. Nevertheless, its recent incorporation into a large international company had led to very different development expectations, with numerous opportunities for movement within the firm and internal courses of diverse nature widely available. The discussion of the UK emphasises the importance of managerial networks (within the firm and beyond it) for mediating, or indeed instigating, learning outcomes. Firms and individuals that are not part of a network will be isolated and are likely to reduce their capability for learning and knowledge capture/diffusion.

Counter-cultural approaches in Spain
The limited literature on training and development with Spanish organisations has suggested that the primary factors influencing training and development in Spanish organisations are both structural and cultural: provision is more likely in larger organisations and those associated with firms located in non-manufacturing and chemical industries. Furthermore, cultural assumptions regarding team learning in three Spanish organisations have noted the traditional low mobility of the Spanish labour market favours long-lasting employment and allows for lengthy socialisation (Sauquet & Bonet, 2003). However, the interviews suggested that the extent to which these institutional factors shape management development in Spanish organisations is neither straightforward nor inevitable.

In contrast to the national overview given above, training in a large manufacture of motor vehicles was found to be far from reactive. The human resources policy of the company established a specific management development programme (provided in approximately equal proportions by internal, external and tutor-supervised training on the job) aimed at improving management performance and enabling the company to become more competitive in the currently changing situation. Two key factors 'push back' against the rather instrumental national training context described above. The first is being part of an international enterprise with all the stimulus, facilities and opportunities for development that this connotes. The second is the consistent use of external consultants and so-called 'eminent personalities'. These individuals are engaged by the company precisely because they are part of their own professional networks. As externally esteemed experts or 'gurus', their input serves the purpose of questioning and challenging more traditional managerial mind-sets which are seen by senior managers to obstruct progress (Clark & Salaman, 1997).

These three country cameos suggest a far richer picture of the factors that influence practices of management training. For example, they reveal the importance of networks not only materially for providing learning and development and stimulating more progressive management development, but also as important reference point for managers. Meso analysis also provides indications that while cultural preferences dictate a certain style of management, these values can be countered when companies are exposed to international networks that expose the organisation to different approaches to training. Also, membership of a salient network can act as a signpost to confer status, identity and, in some cases, authority.

Evans (2002) also makes the point that actors in close-knit networks are more likely to be dynamic rather than inert. This suggests that managers from regions or sectors where management networks are weak and ineffective are less likely to be innovative. For organisations, it also points to the value of promoting informal communities of practice, action learning and external networking as intrinsic design features within their management development programmes. In short, we find that neither institutional determinism on the one hand, nor organisational agency on the other, tell the whole story. Government policy makers, training agencies and HRM departments would do well to appreciate the complexity of macro and micro factors that combine to shape the design, delivery and ultimate effectiveness of management development investment.

The Shifting Landscape of Management Development Research

The simultaneous pursuit of global co-ordination and multinational responsiveness creates a natural learning agenda for many organisations. This involves the sharing of information and the joint implementation of strategy through an integrated network where resources, products, information and people flow freely between units. International productive capabilities may be assigned to different national subsidiaries according to their strengths. This requires senior managers who are not only internationally mobile but who are mentally versatile and culturally sensitive (Mabey & Finch-Lees, 2008).

From a research perspective, MNCs undoubtedly play a major role in the dissemination of HRM practices, with parent companies often using management development as 'corporate glue' (Gratton, 1996). However, theory is running a little behind practice. One potentially fruitful field of theory is that arising from work on knowledge transfer and social capital. The possibility of intra-corporate knowledge exchange is one of the guiding hallmarks of the so-called 'transnational' firm. But the successful diffusion of knowledge in such a firm is by no means automatic and requires concerted effort and significant internal coordination. This is especially the case for tacit knowledge, which is, by definition, non-procedural, experiential, subjective, like the local 'know-how' relating to marketing and distribution, management systems and product design. It is here that a firm's intangible assets lie, rather than in more explicit, declarative types of knowledge such as the reporting of monthly financial data (Gupta & Govindarajan, 2000).

Nahapiet and Ghoshal (1998) refer to three dimensions of social capital. There is a growing evidence to suggest that HRM generally, and management development in particular, can help create all three forms of social capital and effective knowledge transfer (Gooderham, 2006). For example, mechanisms to build structural capital might include: intranet communities as sources of knowledge sharing where high degrees of reciprocity and identity can be established despite the absence of face to face contact (Teigland, 2000); inter-unit taskforces and global forums set up to solicit a wide-range of ideas and deliberately counter business ethno-centric solutions and international assignments for individual and organisational development. Indeed, case studies of Singapore owned subsidiaries in China indicate the importance of Chinese managers spending time not only at corporate headquarters but also in other parts of the MNC (Tsang, 2001). To create cognitive capital self-development is required, especially that which raises awareness of one's cultural assumptions and how they interact with host-country values and behaviour. Management development methods will include cross-cultural sensitivity workshops, diversity training with multi-cultural teams, field trips aided by tools for ethnographic orientation, action learning with a multicultural set, job rotation involving international assignments; and multicultural team-building exercises might be used.

Finally, the strategy of holding training in different countries alongside international action learning programmes, to facilitate both formal and informal interaction, offer a means to build relational capital. In effect, such networks can facilitate the transfer of knowledge. However, this needs to be qualified in two ways. First, the socio-institutional heritage of different countries will exert a strong influence on the way such networks operate, as illustrated in the case of Western companies operating in China (Walder, 1989; Shenkar et al., 1998). Second, inclusion in, or exclusion from, networks and participation in management development initiatives can 'cut both ways'. It has been found that women in UK organisations are disproportionately less likely to benefit from personal and professional development afforded by overseas assignments due to gender bias arising from the predominant use of 'closed, informal selection processes' (Harris, 2002). This is despite evidence that European women are more effective than men as leaders in regions like Asia because they frequently utilise intuitive and empathetic skills that are highly valued in such host cultures (van der Boon, 2003). Many international management development activities are designed to foster heterogeneity, where individuals can 'retain their dimensions of diversity while at the same time avoiding such damaging processes as dysfunctional interpersonal conflict, miscommunication, higher levels of stress, slower decision-making and problems with group cohesiveness' (Kyriakidou, 2005: 112). Yet, there is always a danger that international management development programmes, far from legitimising, celebrating and benefiting from the diversity, which is inherent to effective knowledge diffusion, can have the opposite effect of reinforcing inequality, homogenising corporate behaviour and perpetuating cultural conformity (Kamoche, 2000; Frenkel & Shenhav, 2006). Building on these insights we advocate the mining of knowledge transfer theory to inform management development research in an international context. This will help orientate future research on some of the more subtle processes at work around management development activities like the need for trust-building and cultural respect and the dangers of colonialism, issues of inclusion and exclusion, and potential discrimination.

NOTES

1. This section draws upon Chapter 8 from Mabey and Finch-Lees (2008).
2. This section draws extensively on the discussion and research results published in Ramirez (2004) and Ramirez and Mabey (2005).
3. This section draws upon a paper by Mabey (2008) in *Journal of Internal Business Studies*, **39**(8): 1327–1342.

REFERENCES

Avery, G., Donnenberg, O., Gick, W. & Hilb, M. 1999. Challenges for management development in the German-speaking nations for the twenty-first century. *The Journal of Management Development,* **18**(1): 18.
Aycan, Z. 2005. The interplay between cultural and institutional/structural contingencies in human resource management practices. *International Journal of Human Resource Management,* **16**(7): 1083–1119.
Aycan, Z., Kanungo, R. N., Mendonca, M., Yu, K., Deller, J. & Stahl, G. 2000. Impact of culture of human resource management practices: a 10-country comparison. *Applied Psychology,* **49**(1): 192–221.
Baruel, J. 1996. Spain in the contest of European human resource management. In T. Clarke (ed.), *European Human Resource Management.* Oxford: Blackwell, pp. 93–117.
Becker, B. 1964. *Human Capital: A Theoretical and Empirical Analysis, with Special Reference to Education.* New York: Columbia University Press.
Becker, B. & Huselid, M. 1998. High performance work systems and firm performance: a synthesis of research and managerial implications. *Research in Personnel and Human Resource Management,* **16**: 53–101.
Bennett, R. 1997. *European Business.* London: Pitman.
Borgonjon, J. & Vanhonacker, W. R. 1992. Modernizing China's managers. *China Business Review,* **19**(5): 12.
Bournois, F., Chauchat, J.-C. & Rousillon, S. 1994. Training and management development in Europe. In C. Brewster & A. Hegewisch (eds), *Policy and Practice in European HRM.* London: Routledge, pp. 122–138.
Boyer, R. 1990. *The Regulation School: A Critical Introduction.* New York: Columbia University Press.
Branine, M. 1996. Observations on training and management development in the People's Republic of China. *Personnel Review,* **25**(1): 25.
Branine, M. 2005. Cross-cultural training of managers: an evaluation of a management

development programme for Chinese managers. *The Journal of Management Development,* **24**(5/6): 459.

Brewster, C. & Hegewisch, A. 1994. *Policy and Practice in European Human Resource Management: The Price Waterhouse Cranfield Survey.* London: Routledge.

Brewster, C. and Larsen, H.H. 1992. Human resource management in Europe: evidence from ten countries. *International Journal of Human Resource Management,* **3**(3): 409–434.

Brewster, C., Mayrhofer, W. & Morley, M. 2004. *Human Resource Management in Europe: Evidence of Convergence?* Oxford: Butterworth-Heinemann.

Buck, T., Filatotchev, I., Demina, N. & Wright, M. 2003. Insider ownership, human resource strategies and performance in a transition economy. *Journal of International Business Studies,* **34**(6): 530–549.

Buechtemann, C. F. & Verdier, E. 1998. Education and training regimes: macro-institutional evidence. *Revue d'Economie Politique,* **108**(3): 291–320.

Cassis, Y. 1997. *Big Business: The European Experience in the Twentieth Century.* Oxford: Oxford University Press.

Clark, T. & Salaman, G. 1997. The management guru as organizational witchdoctor. *Organization,* **31**(1): 85–107.

De Cieri, H. & Dowling, P. J. 1999. Strategic HRM in multinational enterprises: theoretical and empirical developments. Greenwich, CT: JAI Press Inc.

Estevez-Abe, M., Iversen, T. & Soskice, D. 2001. Social protection and the formation of skills: a reinterpretation of the welfare state. In P. Hall & D. Soskice (eds), *Varieties of Capitalism: The Institutional Foundations of Comparative Advantage.* Oxford: Oxford University Press, pp. 145–183.

Evans, P., Pucik, V. & Barsoux, J. L. 2002. *The Global Challenge: Frameworks for International Human Resource Management.* New York: McGraw-Hill/Irwin.

Eyraud, F., Marsden, D. & Silvestre, J. 1990. Internal and occupational labour markets in Britain and France. *International Labour Review,* **129**(4): 501–517.

Frenkel, M. & Shenhav, Y. 2006. From binarism back to hybridity: a postcolonial reading of management and organization studies. *Organization Studies,* **27**(6): 855–876.

Fu, P. & Tsui, A. 2003. Utilizing printed media to understand desired leadership attributes in the People's Republic of China. *Asia Pacific Journal of Management,* **20**(4): 423.

Gooderham, P. 2006. Knowledge-transfer in multi-national corporations. In R. Lines, I. Stensasker & A. Langley (eds), *New Perspectives on Organizational Change and Learning.* Bergen: Fagbokforlat, pp. 35–53.

Gooderham, P., Morley, M., Mayrhofer, W. & Brewster, C. 2004. HRM: a universal concept. In C. Brewster, W. Mayrhofer & M. Morley (eds), *European HRM: Convergence or Divergence?* London: Butterworth-Heinemann, pp. 1–26.

Gooderham, P. N., Nordhaug, O. & Ringdal, K. 1999. Institutional and rational determinants of organizational practices: human resource management in European firms. *Administrative Science Quarterly,* **44**(3): 507–531.

Gratton, L. 1996. Implementing a strategic vision: key factors for success. *Long Range Planning,* **29**(3): 290–303.

Griffith, R. 2004. Foreign ownership and productivity: new evidence from the service sector and the R&D lab. *Oxford Review of Economic Policy,* **20**(3): 440.

Grugulis, I. & Stoyanova, D. 2006. Skills and performance. Economic and Social Research Council, Vol. SKOPE Issue Paper 9. Swindon.

Gudic, M. 2001. *Assessing Management Training Needs in Central and Eastern Europe: A Cross-country Survey.* Turin: European Training Foundation/CEEMAN.

Gupta, A. & Govindarajan, V. 2000. Knowledge flows within multinational corporations. *Strategic Management Journal,* **21**(4): 473.

Hall, P. & Soskice, D. 2001. *Varieties of Capitalism: the Institutional Foundations of Comparative Advantage.* New York: Oxford University Press.

Hancke, B. 2002. *Large Firms and Institutional Change: Industrial Renewal and Economic Restructuring in France.* Oxford: Oxford University Press.

Harris, H. 2002. Think international manager, think male: why are women not selected for international management assignments? *Thunderbird International Business Review*, **44**(2): 175.

Harzing, A.-W. 1999. *Managing the Multinational*. Cheltenham, UK: Edward Elgar.

Harzing, A.-W. & Ruysseveldt, J. v. 1995. *International Human Resource Management*. London: Sage Publications.

Hofstede, G. 1985. The interaction between national and organizational value systems. *Journal of Management Studies*. **22**(4): 347–357.

Iversen, T., Estevez-Abe, M. and Soskice, D. 2001. Social protection and the formation of skills: a reinterpretation of the welfare state. *American Political Science Association*, **95**: 875–893.

Jackson, S. E. & Schuler, R. S. 1995. Understanding human resource management in the context of organizations and their environments. *Annual Review of Psychology*, **46**: 237–264.

Kamoche, K. 2000. Developing managers: the functional, the symbolic, the sacred and the profane. *Organization Studies* (Walter de Gruyter GmbH & Co. KG.), **21**(4): 747.

Kay, J. 2003. *The Truth about Markets*. London: Allen Lane.

Kostova, T. & Roth, K. 2002. Adoption of an organizational practice by subsidiaries of multinational corporations: institutional and relational effects. *Academy of Management Journal*, **45**(1): 215–233.

Kyriakidou, O. 2005. Operational aspects of international human resource management. In M. Özbilgin (ed.), *International Human Resource Management: Theory and Practice*. Basingstoke, UK: Palgrave Macmillan.

Lam, A. 1994. The utilisation of human resources: a comparative study of British and Japanese engineers in electronics industries. *Human Resource Management Journal*, **4**(3): 22–40.

Lane, C. 1989. *Management and Labour in Europe*. Cheltenham, UK: Edward Elgar.

Lawrence, P. 1993. Management development in Europe: a study in cultural contrast. *Human Resource Management Journal*, **3**(1): 11–23.

Mabey, C. 2008. Management development and firm performance in Germany, Norway, Spain and the UK. *Journal of International Business Studies*, **39**(8): 1327–1342.

Mabey, C. & Finch-Lees, T. 2008. *Management and Leadership Development*. London: Sage Publications.

Mabey, C. & Gooderham, P. 2005. The impact of management development on perceptions of organizational performance in European firms. *European Management Review*, **2**(2): 131.

Mabey, C. & Ramirez, M. 2004. *Developing Managers: A European Perspective*. London: Chartered Management Institute.

Maurice, M., Sellier, F. & Sivestre, J.-J. 1986. *The Social Foundations of Industrial Power*. Cambridge: Cambridge University Press.

Mayrhofer, W., Mabey, C., & Ramirez, M. 2005. Developing managers in Europe: a meso-level analysis of regional patterns. International Human Resource Management Conference. Cairns.

Michaels, E., Handfield-Jones, H. & Axelrod, B. 2000. *The War for Talent*. Boston, MA: Harvard Business School Press.

Nahapiet, J. & Ghoshal, S. 1998. Social capital, intellectual capital, and the organizational advantage. *Academy of Management Review*, **23**(2): 242–266.

Neelankavil, J. P. 2000. Determinants of managerial performance: a cross-cultural comparison of the perceptions of middle-level managers in four countries. *Journal of International Business Studies*, **31**(1): 121–140.

Noble, C. 1997. The management of training in multinational corporations: comparative case studies. *Journal of European Industrial Training*, **21**(3): 102.

Osman-Gani, A. A. M., & Tan, W.-L. 2000. International briefing 7: training and development in Singapore. *International Journal of Training & Development*, **4**(4): 305.

Paralleda, M., Saez, F., Sanroma, E. & Torres, C. 2002. *La Formacion Continua en las Empresas Espanolas y el Papel de las Univeridades*. Madrid: Civitas.

Ramirez, M. 2004. Comparing European approaches to management education, training, and development. *Advances in Developing Human Resources*, 6(4): 428.

Ramirez, M. & Mabey, C. 2005. A labour market perspective on management training and development in Europe. *International Journal of Human Resource Management*, 16(3): 291–310.

Rosenzweig, P. M. & Nohria, N. 1994. Influences on human resource management practices in multinational corporations. *Journal of International Business Studies*, 25(2): 229–251.

Rousseau, D. M. & House, R. J. 1994. Meso organizational behaviour: avoiding three fundamental biases. In C. L. Cooper, & D. M. Rousseau (eds), *Trends in Organizational Behaviour*, Vol. 1. New York: Wiley, pp. 13–30.

Sauquet, A. & Bonet, E. 2003. Implications of national cultural impacts for conflict resolution and team learning in Spain: observations from a comparative case study. *Advances in Developing Human Resources*, 5(1): 41–63.

Schuler, R. S., Budhwar, P. S. & Florkowski, G. W. 2002. International human resource management: review and critique. *International Journal of Management Reviews*, 4(1): 41.

Scullion, H. & Collings, D. G. 2006. *Global Staffing*. London: Routledge.

Scullion, H. & Starkey, K. 2000. In search of the changing role of the corporate human resource function in the international firm. *International Journal of Human Resource Management*, 11(6): 1061–1081.

Shenkar, O., Ronen, S., Shefy, E. & Chow, I. 1998. The role structure of Chinese managers. *Human Relations*, 51(1): 51.

Shenton, G. 1996. Management education model in Europe: diversity and integration. In M. Lee, H. Letiche & R. Crawshaw (eds), *Management Education in the New Europe*. London: International Thomson Publishing Inc., pp. 32–47.

Sinha, J. B. P. 1997. A cultural perspective on organizational behaviour in India. In P. C. Early & M. Erez (eds), *New Perspectives on International Industrial/Organizational Psychology*. San Francisco: The New Lexington Press, pp. 53–75.

Sparrow, P. R. 1996. Careers and the psychological contract: understanding the European context. *European Journal of Work and Organizational Psychology*, 5(4): 479–500.

Streeck, W. (1995), German capitalism: does it exist, can it survive? In *Modern Capitalism or Modern Capitalisms*, C. Crouch and W. Streeck (eds). Paris: La Découverte.

Teigland, R. 2000. Communities of practice. In J. Birkinshaw & P. Hagström (eds), *The Flexible Firm*. Oxford: Oxford University Press.

Thomson, A., Mabey, C., Storey, J., Gray, C. & Iles, P. 2001. *Changing Patterns of Management Development*. Oxford: Blackwell Publishers Ltd.

Tregaskis, O. 1997. The role of national context and HR strategy in shaping training and development in French and UK organizations. *Organization Studies* (Walter de Gruyter GmbH & Co. KG.), 18(5): 839.

Tregaskis, O., Heraty, N. & Morley, M. 2001. HRD in multinationals: the global/local mix. *Human Resource Management Journal*, 11(2): 34–56.

Tsang, E. 2001. Managerial learning in foreign-invested enterprises of China. *Management International Review*, 41(1): 29.

van der Boon, M. 2003. Women in international management: an international perspective on women's ways of leadership. *Women in Management Review*, 18(3/4): 132.

Von Glinow, M. A., Huo, Y. P. & Lowe, K. 1999. Leadership across the Pacific Ocean: a tri-national comparison. *International Business Review*, 8(1): 1–15.

Walder, A. 1989. Factory and manager in an era of reform. *The China Quarterly*, 118: 242–264.

Wang, J. & Wang, G. 2006. Exploring national human resource development: a case of China management development in a transitioning context. *Human Resource Development Review*, 5(2): 176.

Warner, M. 1992. *How Chinese Managers Learn*. London: Macmillan.

Wenger, E. 1998. *Communities of Practice: Learning, Meaning and Identity*. New York: Cambridge University Press.

Whitley, R. 1992. *European Business Systems: Firms and Markets in their National Contexts.* London: Sage Publications.
Wilkins, S. 2001. International briefing 9: training and development in the United Arab Emirates. *International Journal of Human Resource Management*, **5**(2): 153–165.
Wong, C.-s., Wong, Y.-t., Hul, C. & Law, K. S. 2001. The significant role of Chinese employees' organizational commitment: implications for managing employees in Chinese societies. *Journal of World Business*, **36**(3): 326.

10 Comparative employment relations: definitional, disciplinary and development issues

Werner Nienhüser and Chris Warhurst

In the United States, the hotel industry is regarded as a 'classic low wage' industry (Bernhardt et al., 2003). Concerned about the perilous low level of wages in the US industry, a multinational team of US-led researchers turned their attention to Europe, anticipating that similar jobs in the European hotel industry would be better. 'In fact', the researchers discovered, 'things don't seem that much better on the other side of the Atlantic' (Vanselow et al., 2010: 270). Jobs in the European countries' hotels were also low skilled and work intensification was likewise common. As in the United States, low pay was endemic but, strikingly, the relative level of that low pay varied amongst the countries. Moreover, some aspects of hotel jobs in Germany were becoming to resemble those in the United States. The initial expectations of an enlightened European hotel industry were thus confounded: there were as many differences amongst the countries of Europe as there were between those countries and the United States, and even then, jobs in Europe were changing. These findings were replicated across a number of other service and manufacturing industries included in the study, 'there is no simple one-dimensional US versus Europe story. There is variation within Europe too', Solow and Wanner (2010: xx) noted. Whilst this research was overtly concerned with job quality, as Solow and Warner note, defining job quality is difficult, even pointless they say; in practice, the focus was employment relations within each country, how those employment relations are constructed and how they are developing or might be developed.

This example neatly captures how the term 'employment relations' envelops both practice and a field of study – both a set of material practices and a way of looking at those practices. It also highlights how employment relations are dynamic; that the practices and the ways of looking at them develop. In this respect, a key debate in an era of putative 'globalisation' centres on not just what shapes employment relations but also the extent to which employment relations in different countries are converging or remain different.

This chapter maps out and engages with these debates and

developments. The chapter has two main objectives, firstly, to outline how employment relations are understood and, secondly, to highlight how employment relations are said to be changing. Given our opening comments, the starting point to understanding comparative employment relations has to be an explication of those relations; more precisely what characterises and shapes employment relations as practice. This explication is the focus on the next section of this chapter. The chapter then outlines the differing disciplinary lenses through which employment relations are typically studied and explained. These two discussions are used in the chapter's third section to frame an exposition of what is happening to employment relations – or rather the claims that are being made about what is happening to employment relations, with an illustration from a key recent debate about Japanisation. The end of the chapter offers some suggestions about the future agenda for employment relations in terms of practice and field of study.

CHARACTERISING EMPLOYMENT RELATIONS: SIMILAR TERM – DIFFERENT MEANINGS / SAME MEANING – DIFFERENT TERMS

It would be useful to be able to start with a clear definition of 'employment relations'. Unfortunately, providing this definition is no easy task. There are competing proprietorial claims to employment relations both as practice and field of study, and which also reflect the development of both over the last half century. The two key claimants are 'industrial relations' and, more recently, 'human resource management'. Whilst historically sequential and nominally different, the two terms are useful analytical springboards for they indicate a common concern through which employment relations can start to be characterised and its features identified.

For historical reasons, the starting point is industrial relations. It is within industrial relations that what is now termed employment relations were framed for most of the second half of the twentieth century. According to Bamber et al. (2004: 1) industrial relations focuses 'on the institutions involved with collective bargaining, arbitration and other forms of joint regulations' within frameworks of national law. This focus belies a primary concern with trade unions and management's negotiations with those unions over pay, the terms and conditions of employment, and employee voice, for example – sometimes with the state acting as third party convenor or mediator, sometimes with the state aligning with one side in those negotiations. Indeed, the key actors shaping industrial relations are employers, trade unions and the state. Bi- and tri-lateral arrangements between these actors are sometimes referred to as 'corporatism', which itself has a number of forms in different countries (Panitch, 1981). As such, the individual country – or, less often, a sector within a country – is the primary level of analysis for industrial relations. It is interesting to note that texts claiming to offer 'comparative' industrial or employment relations are often little more than a collection of national country studies – albeit sometimes very good collections (e.g. Bamber et al., 2004; Ferner and Hyman, 1998). It is also unfortunately true that industrial relations has become synonymous not just with collective action but also, in attempting to deal with the putative 'labour problem', with conflict, and so associated with confrontation, strikes and disruption (Bray et al., 2009; Kochan, 1998). Some interests in some countries, for example employer associations such as the Business Council of Australia and the Howard Governments in Australia over the turn of the twenty-first century, have used these 'unhelpful connotations' to attack and undermine trade unions (Bray et al., 2009: 5). Whilst the attack upon trade unions in Australia was overt, similar outcomes have occurred in other countries with trade union density, coverage and power having declined in most of the advanced economies over the last decades of the twentieth century. As a consequence, the capacity and willingness of employers (and the state) to countenance trade unions has also declined (Kelly, 1994).

In this respect, 'human resource management' (HRM) is sometimes claimed to have superseded industrial relations, and has now become the main claimant on employment relations. Concerned with 'all those activities associated with the management of the employment relationship' (Boxall and Purcell, 2003: 1), within this approach, staff in organisations dealing with personnel issues no longer sit down around a table with trade union officials to hammer out collectively applied terms and conditions of employment but instead are tasked with aligning the organisations' human resource needs (read labour power) with the needs of individual employees and so are more concerned with planning and development issues (Schein 1988) and, in its harder US version, the 'auditing' of human resources to better match organisational supply and demand (Legge, 1995). However, although supposedly shifting away from the 'labour problem', the (now recast) management of performance is still 'the dominant research issue' according to Guest (1997: 263). Indeed generating 'high performance work systems' has become the Holy Grail of human resource management. Of course, delivery remains illusive. As a consequence, as it faces a crisis of legitimacy, human resource management has attempted to become more 'strategic' (Kochan, 2007). The attempt by human resource professionals to better manage the relationship with individual employees has become distilled into 'employee relations'. With its 'milder tone' (McKenna and Beech, 2002: 255), employee relations is an HRM approach that seeks direct communication with employees at the level of the individual employee. Now though, human resource professionals themselves need to possess the right 'skills and competencies' to elicit 'performance benefits' from employees (CIPD 2009). Again however, the 'roots' of employee relations are to be found in the organisational provision of social welfare as a means of social control to address the 'labour question' (Blyton and Turnbull, 1998).

What the shift from industrial relations to human resource management, with its variant employee relations, over the last 50 years reveals is that whilst terminology and (some) practices change, the concerns remain the same. Whether cast as the 'labour problem', 'performance management' or 'labour question', the need to elicit efficacious labour from employees is the key issue. It is not surprising therefore that, despite the different terminology, it is often difficult to disentangle industrial relations and human resource management in terms of purpose – and the same is true of the turn to 'employment relations'.

The attempt to align employer and employee interests again features in the broad definition of employment relations offered by Rollinson and Dundon (2007: 5); they state that, as a field of study, it 'embraces the potentially wide range of interactions and processes by which parties to the relationship adjust to the needs, wants and expectations of each other in the employment situation'. This bland definition masks a number of complex issues and also the crux of the 'relationship'. As Edwards (1995: 47) makes clear,

> the subject of employment relations has developed a focus on the organization and control of the employment relationship: the processes through which employers and employees – who are tied together in relations of mutual dependence underlain by exploitation – negotiate the performance of work tasks, together with the laws, rules, agreements and customs that shape these processes.

As with HRM, the decision to use the term employment relations rather than industrial relations is often simply a matter of choice, framed by the shift from collectivism to individualism in the workplace (e.g. Rose, 2004) and, with this shift, the need for practitioners (and some academics) to maintain their utility (see Blyton and Turnbull, 1998; also Edwards, 2003). It is as if employment relations is for researchers of industrial relations who dare not speak its name given its bad press through association with (declining) trade unions and who feel uncomfortable with the more managerialist human resource management. Occasionally the mask slips to reveal the overlaps, as McKenna and Beech illustrate: 'Prior to the advent of HRM, employee relations was often called industrial relations' (2002: 255; see also CIPD, 2009). Of course, the approach to dealing with the labour/performance problem/question often but not always differs (Blyton and Turnbull, 1998; Legge, 1995) but, at its most base, employment relations, as with industrial relations, human resource management and employee relations, is concerned with the employment relationship and what is a reward–effort (or wage–effort) bargain. At the centre of this bargain is a labour contract: a legal artefact in which one party (the employer) agrees to exchange money (pay) for what becomes the employee's labour (effort and time usually) (Kaufman, 2004a).

The employment relationship has a number of complexities. Firstly, although it is contract based, what is being exchanged in that contract – labour – is not like other commodities in that it is intangible; what is bought by employers is potential, not actual, labour. It only becomes actual labour in its execution. This complexity is often called the indeterminacy of labour. Through the employment relationship employers seek to overcome this indeterminacy not just by signing a contract but, in the workplace, having the right to direct, monitor, evaluate and even discipline employee performance – within reasonable limits (Kaufman, 2004b). As a consequence, the employment relationship is continuous, not a one-off exchange (Blyton and Turnbull, 1998) and is often a contested because what is exchanged can at times be scarce or abundant and employer profits can be high or low (Edwards, 1979; Rollinson and Dundon, 2007).

The second complexity arises from the various – and usually said to be differing – interests and objectives brought to the employment relationship by the key actors concerned with it – employers, employees and the state. In the workplace the interests of employers (and their proxies managers) and employees can be conflictual, co-operative or harmonious as Fox (1974) long ago noted in what remains an important exposition of the ideologies informing industrial relations. The interests of employers and employees are in general conflictual regarding the appropriation and distribution of surplus value arising from expended labour. At the same time, employers and employees have a mutually common interest – to maintain the organisation, and its profitability if in the private sector (Cressey and MacInnes, 1980). As a consequence, some form of compromise, or at least acquiesce, is usually achieved. If acquiesce occurs it is because an asymmetry of power exists within the employment relationship usually in favour of employers – which is why collective action through trade unions often provides more power for employees.

A third complexity arises out of the embeddedness of the employment relationship within countries and, as a consequence, how these interests and objectives can be mediated by the laws, rules, regulations and norms of each country. These country differences are sometimes referred to as 'business systems' (Whitley, 1992) or 'production regimes' (Gallie, 2007). The legal context of countries is particularly important here because it defines the content of the labour contract, for example regulations for ending the contract, and the basic rights and obligations of the exchange parties. Other important influences are the industrial structure and labour market of each country – both of which can be dynamic; each country has sunset and sunrise industries, and rising and falling levels of unemployment, both of which affect the bargaining power of the parties. Union density too within countries influences the voice or exit options for employees within the employment relationship (Hirschman, 1970).

Referring to both a field of study and material practices, the analytical core of employment relations is thus the employment relationship and the exchange between employer and employee centred on the reward-effort bargain. This relationship is complex, contextual and dynamic. This characterisation provides some clarity though belies a number of underpinning theoretical considerations that usefully signal the importance of recognising the range of disciplines that seek to explain employment relations, and to which we now turn.

THE DIFFERENT DISCIPLINARY LENSES ON EMPLOYMENT RELATIONS

It should be noted that employment relations is not a discipline but a field of study upon which different disciplinary lenses focus, as Table 10.1 illustrates. The key disciplines concerned with employment relations are economics, sociology, political science and social psychology. Within each discipline there are core assumptions (e.g. efficiency and cost minimising, power and conflict, need satisficing) about employment relations drawn first from particular theoretical approaches (transaction cost theory, labour process theory, institutional theory and the psychological contract) and, second, pitched at particular levels of analysis (individual, firm or national level). We now briefly review these different approaches, showing how they conceptually capture and present employment relations. It should be noted that theories can be used cross-disciplinarily, becoming decoupled from their disciplinary origin. Transaction cost theory, for instance, has become influential in sociology and the political sciences; likewise, the varieties of capitalism approach has crossed over from political economy/sciences into sociology.

Within economics, transaction cost theory seeks to explain what type of employment relations occurs under which circumstances (Williamson,

Table 10.1   Different approaches to employment relations

Discipline	Typical theories	Core assumption on mechanism explaining differences in ER	Employment relations are mainly seen as. . .	Typical level of analysis
Economics	Transaction cost theory	Cost-minimising behaviour (of the employer)	Cost-minimising institutions regarding the effort–reward bargain	Firm
Sociology	Labour process theory	Power-maximising behaviour (of the employer)	Means of power and exploitation	Country, historical analysis
Political Economy/ Political Sciences	Institutional theory (Varieties of capitalism)	Adaption to the institutional context	Institutional context securing the supply of a adequately skilled and motivated workforce at reasonable wages	Country
Social Psychology	Psychological contract	Need (of the employee) for a balanced, equitable psychological contract	(Implicit) contract between employer and employee	Individual (firm)

1984, 1985). The theory assumes that transactions in general and the effort–reward bargain in particular are characterised by incomplete information and the possibility of opportunistic behaviour. Because of these uncertainties, individuals and firms safeguard against negative consequences by means of specific institutional arrangements. The institutionalisation and operation of the employment relationship and the resulting nature of employment relations are understood as institutional arrangements that reduce the uncertainties in the exchange between employee and employer (Williamson, 1984; Williamson et al., 1975). The employer attempts to secure income from investments in human capital and to ensure control of productivity. In contrast to classical and neo-classical economics, transaction costs as well as production costs (wages) are important. Transaction costs include the costs of procuring information about the employee, the costs of the possible *ex-post*-negotiation performance of the employee and other conflicts between the employer and employee (Williamson, 1984).

The central hypothesis of transaction cost theory regarding employment relations and its core, the employment relationship, can be summarised as follows: the harder the monitoring[1] of the productivity of an employee and the more the employer needs firm-specific qualifications, the more a long-term employment relationship is effective and the less effective is a market-oriented, short-term relationship (spot market). Long-term employment helps prevent the migration of specific human capital. Examples of jobs for which such an exchange system would be efficient could include consulting activities by bank employees when granting loans or in the real estate business. An example of jobs for which employees can be hired and fired without incurring costs would be migrant workers in (Californian) agriculture (Williamson 1984).[2] Transaction cost theory thus attempts to answer the question why there are differences in firm strategies: different forms of employment relations are seen as institutional arrangements for regulating the transactions within the employment relationship; and differences in employment relations depend on the need for firm-specific human capital and the extent of control problems. A key assumption of transaction cost theory is that the claims of employers and employees cannot be completely specified and claims must therefore be enforced within the work process – within the exchange itself – and cannot be adequately addressed externally. Hence, the typical level of analysis of transaction cost theory is the firm.

A sociologically based theory, labour process theory, also takes the indeterminacy of labour (i.e. that the employer purchases potential not actual labour) as its explicit starting point but, unlike transaction cost theory, posits that an asymmetry of power exists in the employer's favour in the exchange with the employee (Marginson, 1993). Nevertheless, a transformation problem exists for the employer – the transformation of potential labour power into actual labour through work (Müller-Jentsch, 2004). Following Marx, Braverman (1974) argued that labour organisations and the type of employment relations provide capitalists with a solution to their problems. Braverman assumes that employers not only have to solve the problem of surplus value production but also have to deal with the problem of surplus value appropriation. In order to solve both problems employers have to exert control – practically, have to manage workers (Nienhüser, 2004; Warhurst, 1997). For Braverman, scientific management or Taylorism was the means of control and with it came a specific form of employment relations. Scientific management involved the creation of managers as agents of capitalist owners who have conceptual responsibility for organising work, leaving workers only the execution of managerial defined tasks, which were sub-divided, standardised and simplified. The result is a loss of control over work by employees and work that is deskilled, with employees to be incentivised by piece-rate payments (Taylor, 2006[1911]).

Braverman's deskilling thesis has been criticised as too simplistic. More diverse typologies of control take into account that employees can resist managerial imposition and that excessive Taylorism can have effects on employees (alienation, demotivation, learned helplessness) that can also be negative for management. Other types of control give employment relations (starting at the firm level) other forms. Simple control is based on personal supervision and sanctioning of employees by their immediate superiors. Technical control is exercised through a technical arrangement of the labour process, for instance in the form of assembly-line work. With bureaucratic control, behaviour is governed by (mostly written) rules and regulations. With responsible autonomy, management transfers some task responsibility to employees and increases loyalty to the organisation through benefits (Edwards, 1979; Friedman, 1977). For labour process theorists this last type represents a 'sophisticated' solution to the problem of transformation and appropriation (for further elaboration, see Thompson and Smith, 2010).

From this perspective, the employment relationship and employment relations are means of solving or reducing the problem of control for the employer. The transformation problem results from the indeterminacy of the employment contract. Over time, as markets, technology and workers' political organisation changes, so too must the means of control. Thus whilst the form of employment relations changes on the surface, the deeper structural issue remains: with the exchange, a transformation problem characterised by capitalist exploitation and managerial control.

Political economy – an amalgamation of political science and economics and which understands the economy as mediated by politics – brings another disciplinary lens to the study of employment relations. Formerly a critique of neo-classical economics, institutional theory, posits that economic activity is a political rather than utilitarian outcome. Through institutional theory, the central impact of country-specific institutions, rules, norms and values become important because it is recognises that each nation-state has a distinct legal framework, financial and banking regulations, training and education policies, industrial relations systems and familial arrangements for example. Organisations are embedded within configurations of these institutions, which are external and are superior to the firm (Zucker, 1987). Economic actors within firms adopt organisational forms that are legitimate within the normative order of the institutional configurations within which they are embedded.

The latest, and very influential, development from within the political economy perspective, sometimes called the 'new institutionalists' (Kelly and Frege, 2004: 182; and see Chapter 2), is the 'varieties of capitalism' approach of Hall and Soskice (2001). This approach examines how firms and other actors, such as government and producer groups, solve coordination problems through either market or non-market institutions. The 'spheres' over which the co-ordination problems ranges include on the one hand industrial relations and bargaining over wages and working conditions and relations with employees such as information sharing and work-effort incentives and, on the other hand, the adequate supply of financial resources, raw material and so forth as well as a stable demand for products and services (Kenworthy, 2009). The first category of problems refers to employment relations. Not surprisingly the approach has quickly gained purchase amongst researchers of employment relations, even spawning 'Varieties of Unionism' (Frege and Kelly 2004).

The review of the varieties of capitalism approaches in Chapter 2 discusses the distinction Hall and Soskice (2001) make between liberal market economies (LMEs) and co-ordinated market economies (CMEs). Such different arrangements also cover employment relations. The political economy of a country can be understood as offering opportunities for, and constraints on, how firms structure work and the wage–effort bargain, resulting in different forms of employment relationships and employment relations. It is implied that firms in LMEs and CMEs respond differently to similar changes in their environment, for example to globalisation, with its increasing wage competition. In LMEs, for instance, there is an expectation of stronger and faster wage reductions; in CMEs there is more decentralised bargaining and a stronger trend toward reduced union influence (Thelen, 2001).

Although the varieties of capitalism literature provides a currently popular approach to studying comparative employment relations – and it at least delivers comparative analysis – the approach is not without its critics (see Chapter 2). They have argued that national ideal types may not be applicable to all sectors within a country; that the approach implicitly seeks to defend the German model; or that it simply elucidates category difference and, in reality, a dualist opposition (Allen, 2004; Crouch, 2009; Kenworthy, 2009). What is clear, as Crouch (2009: 79) suggests, is that varieties of capitalism has become 'the emblematic citation for all studies of diversity in capitalist economies'.

Psychology research on employment relations often draws on the idea of a 'psychological contract' between employer and employee (Rousseau, 1995; Coyle-Shapiro et al., 2004) and it is a theory that is gaining traction in HRM as a field of study. In stark contrast to theories within the political economy approach, its level of analysis is the individual. The core of employment relations is conceptualised as an informal psychological contract between employer and employee. The construct of the psychological contract as used currently was provided by Rousseau (1995) but it has a long history going back to the work of Argyris (1960) and Blau (1964). Also Fox's (1974) seminal work on industrial relations included a very similar concept drawing on Gouldner's construct of a 'norm of reciprocity' (Gouldner, 1960; Guest, 2004: 545). The psychological contract seeks to achieve both high performance and high employee satisfaction (Guest, 2007), drawing as it does on psychological theories about needs, cognitions and values (cf. different contributions in Coyle-Shapiro et al., 2004). Guest rightly argues that the psychological contract now provides an 'analytical framework for the analysis of employment relations' (2004: 545).

The contract centres on promises and obligations, for example over pay for performance, working hours and employers' accommodation of employees' domestic responsibilities (Guest, 2007). These contracts can be transactional and so explicit and formal or relational and so implicit and informal but trust and fairness are important: 'whether the promises and obligations have been met, whether they are fair and their implications for trust' (Guest, 2004: 549) – in short, whether or not employees and employers each deliver their side of the 'deal'. Two issues then arise: what are the determinants and consequences of the psychological contract. Guest suggests a kind of causal chain: the state of the contract is influenced by human resource policies and practices, which are in turn determined by contextual factors such as sector, firm size, ownership, business strategy and union recognition (2004: 550). The consequences centre on attitudinal outcomes such as commitment, work satisfaction, motivation or stress and also behavioural outcomes such as work attendance, intention to quit, job performance and 'organisational citizenship behaviour'. An important debate in this approach is over whether or not the nature of the psychological contract has changed, with Herriot and Pemberton (1995) framing the change in terms of 'old' and 'new' deals. In the old deal, secure, long-term, upwardly mobile careers within tall organisational hierarchies were offered by employers in exchange for employee loyalty and commitment. Now, with flatter organisations, employers can no longer offer such careers and workers face employment insecurity, must provide for their own 'employability' (Bridges, 1995) and accept 'boundaryless careers' (Arthur and Rousseau, 1995). As Guest (2007) notes, this change creates problems for employers: contract violation can be frequent, workers' expectations difficult to discern and thereby meet, and contracts more bespoke than generic.

Although analyses of the consequences of the breaking the psychological contract include employee satisfaction, it is employee performance that is again the driving concern. With the individual as the level of analysis, most empirical studies concentrate on the consequences of the subjectively perceived failure of the employer to meet the psychological contract. As such Guest (2004: 545f.) explicitly criticises the psychological contract for having 'typically been studied from the individual worker's perspective' and points out that there is too little research on the perceptions of the employer within the contract. Nevertheless outcomes for workers are still studied in relation to an employer perspective, with issues in the interests of employers at the heart of analyses. Moreover, because of the level of analysis, institutions other than the firm and the psychological contract's connectedness to – and embeddedness within – the societal level are too often ignored.

Although the different disciplines offer a number of theories with varying core assumptions and are pitched at different levels of analysis, the key concern throughout is still with employee performance, no matter how that performance is framed. It is noteworthy, however, that different disciplinary approaches dominate the study of employment relations in different countries. For example, economic theories tend to dominant in the United States, and sociological and psychological theories in the UK, whilst in Germany sociological theories still prevail but economic theories seem to be gaining ground (see also Frege, 2005; Keller, 2005). Thus, there remains a conceptual coherence to the study of employment relations but also a need for different disciplinary inputs (with expertise often centred in different countries) if a rounded understanding is to be generated about employment relations.

THE DEVELOPMENT OF EMPLOYMENT RELATIONS

Some of these theories underpin attempts to explain what is happening to employment relations, to which this section of the chapter now turns. Basically, there are two camps in the debate about the future of employment relations. Echoing wider debates about globalisation (for an overview see Warhurst and Nickson, 2001), these two camps argue polemically for, on the one hand, convergence or, on the other, continued diversity in employment relations. Both camps have an inherent interest in comparative analysis, for comparative analysis allows for the identification of developmental trajectories. For example, and to return to the hotel industry example at the start of this chapter, one interesting possibility to emerge from the research findings about employment relations in German hotels is that they are becoming more like those in the Anglo-Saxon countries such as the United States or the UK (cf. Bernhardt et al., 2003; Dutton et al., 2008; Vanselow, 2008). However, as this example once again illustrates, the issue is not just one of difference but, implicitly and sometimes explicitly, also perceived superiority and the transfer, through adoption or adaption, of types of employment relations.

Discerning this possibility requires points of analysis – descriptively the past and current characterisation of each country's employment relations – and also sometimes, based on the dynamic between these two points, prescriptive articulation of a third point, the future point of arrival for these countries' employment relations. At the start of the latter half of the twentieth century there was a common assumption that a 'one best way', usually the putative American model, was the future of employment relations and all other industrialised countries would adopt this model, including, as it did, scientific management (Thompson, 1989; Warhurst and Nickson, 2001). As Lawrence (1988) has noted, that differences might exist in employment was only really appreciated in the late 1970s and early 1980s when studies began to emerge that highlighted 'national–cultural' based industrial organisation, and, as a consequence, attention turned to comparative analysis – in Lawrence's case of management styles in a range of different countries (e.g. Lawrence, 1980). It is an approach that remains popular, as the best-selling edited collections on industrial relations (more recently retitled employment relations) by Bamber and his colleagues (1987; 2004) and also Morley et al. (2006) illustrate. If researchers in management, industrial and employment relations discovered the importance of comparative analysis from the late 1970s onwards, it was a key feature of organisational sociology from the 1950s, prompted by the seminal work on bureaucracy by Stinchcombe (1959). Comparative analysis is a field of research rather than a discipline though it does draw upon the disciplines that we identified earlier: sociology, economics and psychology for example (Hofstede 1995). Its purpose is to classify types and then discern and explain the identified similarities and differences between these types. Of course what to compare and how to compare then become salient issues.

In this respect, one of the key problems in comparative analysis is the 'incommensurability of concepts' (Sztompka, 1990: 47). At its most basic, there can be different terms for the same instruments: for example in Britain the 'collective agreement', in the United States the 'labor contract' and in Australia the 'industrial award'. Language, Hofstede (1995) has noted, is the most clearly recognisable part of a culture and so affects the study of employment relations – as Crompton and Lynette (2006) discovered in their research of Portugal and the UK. Portugal has strong labour market protection and the deregulation of employment has been resisted by employees because of the benefits that accrue with job tenure. By contrast, the UK labour market is lightly regulated and employment relations are increasing individualistic. When the researchers asked respondents in a survey about the importance of 'moving up the job ladder at work', the Portuguese answers were puzzling. It turned out that the translation by the Portuguese team of the English wording was correct but that the meaning of the phrase varied between employees of the two countries: 'In Portugal, "moving up the job ladder" means progression through an ordered hierarchy, whereas in Britain, "moving up the job ladder" has come to mean "putting oneself forward for individual enhancement"' (Crompton and Lynette, 2006: 408). Contextualisation is therefore important in comparative analysis. Unfortunately, too often, that contextualisation is too readily ignored. The outcome is poor research, even if it produces headline-grabbing claims, as we will see in our example of Japanisation below.

The convergence thesis too emerged out of an academic headline grabbing futuristic account by economist Clark Kerr and his colleagues (1960) of the consequences of industrialism as it spread throughout the world in the latter half of the twentieth century. They argued that the logic of industrialism dictated that countries industrialising required and adopted certain characteristics: the use of particular technologies; an ideological consensus centred on pluralism, urbanisation and big government; an increasingly higher skilled and more educated workforce; and a rule-bound industrial relations system. 'Industrial systems,' the authors argued, 'tend to become more alike . . . The process of convergence moves sometimes faster sometimes slower . . . but it is a long-run development' (1960: 296). Some critics argued that Kerr and his colleagues were masking US values and imperialism, and decried the American ethnocentrism of the logic being asserted. Others questioned the deterministic assumptions underpinning the logic and whether industrialism did generate convergence. They pointed out different countries exhibited different solutions to the same industrial relations problems or that some but not all aspects of employment converged such that national regulatory regimes mediated industrialism (for a short overview, see Bamber et al., 2004).

These criticisms did not stop more radical sociologists countering with their own logic. Braverman's (1974) kick-starting analysis of labour process through deskilling was a challenge to optimistic accounts, such as those of Kerr and his colleagues, that workers were now being employed in more skilled jobs. Braverman stated that Taylorism represented 'nothing less than the explicit verbalisation of the capitalist mode of production' (1974: 86). Braverman however also had his critics, even from those broadly sympathetic to his 'It's capitalism, stupid!' position, for his tendency to substitute one universal claim with another: job amelioration with the degradation of work; and one form of determinism – technology – with another – mode of production. The pervasiveness of Taylorism, assumed by Braverman was challenged by comparative analyses that show a variety of forms of control and the uneven application and extent of Taylorism where it was introduced (Lane, 1987). Friedman (1977) and Littler (1982) demonstrated the differences between Japanese and British labour processes resulting from different national political and cultural trajectories. Different forms of employee resistance too exist and develop historically (Edwards, 1979). The second wave of labour process analysis post-Braverman therefore concluded that labour process analysis 'must be supplemented by reference to "cultural" factors resting on distinctive national and historical traditions' (Thompson, 1989: 216). As such, the possibility of continued divergence needed to be recognised and a conceptual framework provided for its study. Unfortunately, as Nichols (1994) pointed out, labour process theory accepted the first point but failed to deliver the conceptual framework of the second.

In a still influential article, Lane (1987) had already taken up this challenge of providing a conceptual framework and sought to show how labour process analysis needed to be supplemented by analyses that are sensitive to culture, comprising national institutional histories and social vales and attitudes (see also Smith and Meiksins, 1995; Warhurst, 1997). Unfortunately, at the time, her approach was over-shadowed by work that became paradigm-setting in the study of cross-national management and organisation – Hofstede's (1980) *Culture's Consequences* (see Chapter 3). Hofstede argued that cultural dimensions exemplified the 'collective mental programming' (1995: 142) by which individual countries' workplace practices were shaped. Britain, for example, was characterised as low on power distance and uncertainty avoidance and high on individualism and somewhat high on masculinity. As a consequence, the British workplace is like 'a village market; no decisive hierarchy, flexible rules, and a resolution of problems by negotiating' (p. 155). Moreover, the diffusion of management practices is limited, he insisted, constrained by this programming: countries could only successfully adopt other countries' management models, theories and practices if those nations were culturally close; even then 'convergence . . . will never come' he claimed (p. 157). Hofstede's dimensions, or variants of them, are still very influential in research of cross-cultural management, as Trompenaars and Turner

(1997) exemplify. Brewster (1995) gave lukewarm support for Hofstede's culturalist approach: 'it is the best we have' he stated, and at least 'makes us aware of cultural differences and the challenges that exist' (1995: 215). Others (Baskerville, 2003; and see Chapter 7) made more detailed and explicit challenges

What was required was a more systematic approach to discerning national differences and this approach seemed to be provided with sociologist Marc Maurice and his colleagues' (1979, 1980) identification of 'societal effects' to explain differences in the organisation of manufacturing in France, Germany and, later, Britain. Intending to avoid 'vaguely specified cultural variables' and utilising 'closely matched-pair comparisons', the research sought to examine 'the interaction of people at work, work characteristics of jobs, systems of recruitment, education, training, remuneration and industrial relations' (1980: 61). In the first study comparing France and Germany, the researchers found that the span of control between supervisors and employees was greater in France than in Germany; that in France the dispersion of salary levels was also longer; and that qualification levels were highest amongst German employees, both blue and white-collar. These findings seemed to be explicable only by reference to factors external to the firm – the 'societal effects' and the historical interconnectedness of manufacturing, industrial relations, education and training for example. The upshot, according to Rose (1985: 74), is that 'employment relationships are . . . societally specific'. Unfortunately Rose, in his critical overview of the research of the 'Aix group' as it became known, claims that the research falls short of its aim, failing to make the bridge between the particular cases and general theorisation. The 'text never settles down into a sustained exposition of the concepts and procedures of the societal approach . . . nowhere are the numerous explanatory asides, passing comments, and definite claims for it threaded together to show with clarity and precision what it does involve,' he says (1985: 76).

It did pave the way though for the mainstreaming of economics-based institutional theory into comparative analysis. For these theorists organisational forms are symbolic rather than technically superior, and organisational isomorphism occurs so that firms come to resemble each other with common structures, practices and strategies that facilitate their aggregate distinctiveness. Embeddedness does not mean that reproduction is mechanically determined but rather, and echoing Maurice et al., the rational actions of management are informed by the institutions of business education for example (Fores et al., 1992). The past therefore shapes the present. The approach has been criticised for being too static: good at identifying the process of reproduction but unable to explain innovation, and so how structures, practices and strategies change. Indeed, 'path dependency' has emerged as a sub-field within this approach (Liebowitz and Margolis, 1995). Neo-institutionalism attempts to deal with this problem by recognising that a plurality of organisational forms is possible shaped not only by embeddedness but also, and now foregrounding choice and not just constraint, the conscious enactment of that embeddedness by economic actors (Di Maggio, 1990; Granovetter, 1985; Whitley, 1992). However, difference rather than commonality remain the key focus and forces that might create pressures for commonality are downplayed. As Smith and Meiksins (1995) observe, 'systems effects', not only societal effects, exist that reflect the political economy of modes of production and comprise distinct social relations and which also affect the social organisation of economic activity regardless of within which national state that activity occurs. Thus the institutional arrangements of states within capitalism are more similar to each other than they are to those within the former state socialist countries because as different modes of production they have different political economies (for a short discussion see Warhurst, 1998). It should be noted that most of the 'new institutionalists' (Kelly and Frege's phrase, 2004: 182) who have taken up the 'varieties of capitalism' approach of Hall and Soskice (2001) bodyswerve this criticism by only focusing on capitalist countries.

Such debates, whether arguing for convergence or diversity, have at their heart three concerns: difference, superiority and transfer – the later involving either adoption or adaption. Focusing on employment relations specifically, these concerns coalesced and are starkly highlighted in research on Japanisation. Long before the twenty-first century was being described as China's 'red dawn' (Harris, 2010), the new century was being hailed as Japan's century. In the 1980s and into the 1990s there was a welter of books and articles proclaiming Japan as the new superpower from which other countries had to learn (e.g. Horsley and Buckley, 1990). In particular, a social and physical technology, 'lean production', was feted; as prominent MIT-based eulogists Womack et al. (1990: 12) proclaimed, 'lean production . . . will change everything in almost every industry – choices for consumers, the nature of work, the fortune of companies, the fate of nations'. Of course, Japan's economy nosed-dived in the 1990s and interest shifted elsewhere. By then, however, there had been a raft of studies that examined Japanese employment relations drawing upon some of the approaches outlined above and which produced widely differing findings, as Table 10.2 illustrates.

Table 10.2 does not depict the debate chronologically, rather its claims and approaches; and is not a comprehensive review of the Japanisation debate. Instead it identifies some of the key positions in that debate. The starting point was Womack et al.'s (1990) claim that classic lean

Table 10.2   Understanding the Japanese model of employment relations

Claim	Approach	Example
Superior and can be universalised through transfer and adoption; provides convergence	Technologically determinist, within a broad definition of technology[a]	Womack et al. (1990)
Rooted in and specific to country-of-origin/ host country adoption problems; questions transferability and convergence	Variations in national institutional arrangements matter, variously influenced by culturalism, societal effects and labour process theory	Wilkinson and Oliver (1990)
No comprehensive form but disaggregated by production chain and country	Focus on business strategy, influenced by labour process theory	Dedoussis and Littler (1994)
Not superior but is different; lack of understanding of residual country-specific differences	Critical accounting, echoing institutional theory	Williams et al. (1994)

Note: a.   See Friedman (1990).

production was to be found at auto manufacturer Toyota, but there was general consensus about the Japanese model of employment relations inherent to this technology: quality orientated and 'just-in-time' work, seniority-based wages, lifetime employment, company welfarism, enterprise unionism. Using 'half the human effort' (p. 13) and yet being 'twice as productive' (p. 81), Womack et al. argued that lean production was superior and would become 'the standard global production system' (p. 278) supplanting Fordist mass production and any residual craft production. Indeed, through Japanisation these practices were transferred into Europe, the United States and elsewhere through the inward investment of Japanese firms or through their adoption by European and US firms in their home territories (Elger and Smith, 1994a; Kirkland, 1990; Thompson and McHugh, 1990; Womack et al., 1990). The Japanese model was therefore different but its transfer not only possible but an imperative.

And yet some practices did not travel; lifetime employment and seniority-based wages for example (Thompson and McHugh, 1995). Indeed, it was argued that there were obstacles to Japanisation. These obstacles arose because of differences between country of origin and host countries. This argument had two dimensions: firstly, that the Japanese model was a product of a particular, historical institutional arrangements between capital, the state and labour in Japan and, secondly, that different institutional environments and cultures existed in host countries such as the UK – as the infamous banner, 'We're Brits not Nips', held up by striking British Ford workers protesting about the Japanisation of the company hammered home (Thompson, 1988; see also Morris and Wilkinson, 1995; Wilkinson and Oliver, 1990). Further research revealed this limited transfer to be an outcome not just of 'cultural constraint' but also of firm strategy. Japanese firms investing overseas tended to target geographical locales with low wage costs and acquiescent labour (Elger and Smith, 1994b). Examining the management practices of Japanese firms in Australia, and working within the labour process tradition, Dedoussis and Littler (1994) argued that a 'peripheral model of Japanese management' had been established whereby the parent companies sought cost-minimisation with overseas workforces, 'hiving off labour intensive activities to subsidiaries and subcontracting firms' (p. 176). 'Human resource management practices . . . in overseas Japanese firms differ significantly compared with human resource management practices . . . in parent companies,' Dedoussis and Littler (p. 177) conclude. Even more damning, far from heralding a new form of production, Japanese transplants continued 'conventional Taylorised mass production techniques' according to Danford (1998: 41) in his empirical research of Japanese firms in Wales. In other words, transfer was neither desired nor intended by the Japanese parent firms. Instead these firms relied upon and exploited national differences in order to maximise profitability. Finally, Williams and his colleagues (1994) challenged not the feasibility and desirably of transferred Japanisation but its very claim to be superior. Revisiting the calculations used by Womack et al. (1990) as the basis for the claim of higher Japanese performance, Williams et al. (1994) discovered serious flaws in the measurements. Productivity studies, they state, tend to focus only on the bottom line and not how that bottom line is calculated. Applying a consistent form of calculation across Japanese, US and European auto manufacturers reveals Toyota to be no more productive, even less productive, than many of its competitors. Indeed the reputation of US manufacturers is 'rehabilitated', with Ford 'captur[ing] the title of most productive assembler from Toyota' (p. 257). Too many researchers in Europe and the United States failed to identify and appreciate that productivity and performance measurement is done differently in Japan. Whilst productivity and performance measurement may seem technical and boring, Williams et al. comment, if done properly it raises important political issues which, in the case of Japanisation, were being used to destabilise existing capital, state and labour settlements in the United States, Europe and elsewhere.

What the research on Japanisation highlights more generally are the competing claims about the development of employment relations and the factors that influence that development. Different approaches don't just claim different futures; they also foreground different issues. No single approach has a monopoly on understanding. As with globalisation (Warhurst and Nickson, 2001), any perceived developmental trajectory in employment relations – whether convergent or divergent – can continue or be checked – or simply be contested. The future is a matter of empirical investigation and, as the Japanisation debate indicates, research of employment relations past, present and future benefits greatly from comparative research.

CONCLUDING REMARKS ON THE FUTURE OF EMPLOYMENT RELATIONS

This chapter has sought to outline how employment relations are understood and how they are changing, doing so by distinguishing between employment relations as practice and field of study. At the heart of employment relations, as we demonstrated, are common concerns that centre on what is variously cast as the 'labour problem', 'labour question' or, more recently, 'performance management'. These differing terms though do not emerge from a vacuum but align with competing proprietarial claims over employment relations as practice and field of study: what was once industrial relations is now human resource management, most obviously. Often the use of the terms industrial relations, human resource management and employment relations is simply a matter of choice reflecting the shift from collectivism to individualism in the workplace (e.g. Rose, 2004) and, with this shift, the need for practitioners (and some academics) to maintain their utility (see Blyton and Turnbull, 1998).

The key actors shaping employment relations as practice are employers, trade unions and the state, and their interests. The balance of power between these three actors is dynamic temporally, and varied spatially, most obviously by country. If employment relations is centred on the labour problem, understanding that labour problem requires more than just the study of work, it requires appreciation and analysis of the contextual factors that influence how that work, and the transformational problem, is shaped, for example embeddedness within the political economy narrowly defined as the nation-state and more widely conceived as related to mode of production (Warhurst, 1997).[3] In this respect, the differing disciplinary lenses that we noted do not simply mark out the interests of researchers in different countries (e.g. Frege, 2005) but highlight the range of issues that need to be taken into account in the study of employment relations.

Any discussion of the future of employment relations needs to encompass developments in the practice and the field of study. The question as to what model of employment relations practice will dominate in the future is of course not easy to answer. In the 1990s it was quite usual to map out the future as one of competing practice between Japanese, German and Anglo-Saxon models (e.g. Kelly, 1994). What is included within the scope of discussion is, as we noted, linked to notions of perceived superiority. In this respect, whilst the latter two models are still benchmarks – as the job quality research cited at the start of this chapter highlights – the Japanese model has vanished from debate, to be replaced recently by concern with China, with its state-led marketisation of its economy and its economic dynamism and growing political influence. Moreover, as with Japan before it, there is now significant investment by Chinese firms in European countries and firms, including the purchase of European auto manufacturers (*Guardian Weekly*, 2010). If Japan was once cited as the model for the future, Halper (2010) raises the possibility of China now being that model. However, as with Japan before it, such prescriptions have often fallen at the hurdle of evidence – or simply unforeseen economic problems. Whether, on the basis of economic superiority, China provides that model remains to be seen. What is clear is that employment relations remain dynamic both as practice and field of study.

It is more usual in the advanced economies to centre debate on the battle of practice between the German and Anglo-Saxon models. The German model with its long-term employment, highly qualified employees with general skills, strong co-determination and trade unions, multi-employer bargaining and an extensive welfare system is often held up as best practice, with advocates amongst UK economic commentators such as Hutton (1995) arguing for its adoption in the Anglo-Saxon countries. Even US business professors such as Pfeffer (1998) advocate this model because it aligns well with the workplace Holy Grail of HRM – the illusive High Performance Work System – and offers positive economic performance and social benefits. Nevertheless, the German model's adoption by other countries is not evident, and indeed, is itself regularly claimed to be under threat (Lane, 1987; Grahl and Teague, 2004) as the research into employment relations in German hotels indicates (Vanselow, 2008). The model has also come under fire from advocates of the Anglo-Saxon model that is characterised by the individualisation of employee interests and representation, and flexible forms of employment (Bosch et al., 2009). Some argue that a US or Anglo-Saxon model of employment relations will become more widespread so that if a new convergence is to emergence, it will be one driven by the Anglo-Saxon variety of capitalism (e.g. Stanford, 2008). This potential development needs to be understood recognising that models of employment relations are also normative and some forms of employment relations can have an advantage in 'system competition'. Thus, a model (in the sense of an ideal type) has a 'competitive advantage' if it accords with the productive forces. The Anglo-Saxon model fits better with the current and dominant neo-liberalism, and advantage accrues for those models of employment relations that align with that neo-liberalism. And yet, as we noted above, claims about trends disappear as often as they appear; what seems likely today, sometimes seems laughable tomorrow. What actually happens has to be the subject of empirical investigation informed by appropriate theoretical frameworks.

The question as to how the future of the study of employment relations will develop is more difficult to answer. Certainly, as HRM struggles to assert its legitimacy it is possible that it too will wither as a way of framing analysis of and practice within the employment relationship. Thus as industrial relations was displaced, so too might HRM. It is instructive to note that the use of the term 'employment relations' is becoming more in vogue (e.g. Bamber et al., 2004; Bray et al., 2009; Rose, 2004) and it is possible that those academic departments once called 'industrial relations' but which by the 1990s had been renamed 'human resource management' might soon undergo another name change. Certainly employment relations appears less loaded normatively than HRM and so is potentially more palatable to researchers who look fondly on industrial relations.

Given our comments in this chapter, it is easier to say what kind of research is desirable: longitudinal, international, multi-level research that has at its analytical core the employment relationship. Being comparative, such research would be able to establish essentiality, difference and developments, (cf. Stinchcombe, 1959). It should be remembered however that the analytical tools used in this research will develop as much as the practice that they examine. There is an emerging trend to draw more on theoretical perspectives from the economics and psychology disciplines such as transaction costs and the psychological contract. Rightly focusing on the exchange relationship between employer and employee these approaches have advantages but also shortcomings in ignoring the embeddedness of the employment relationship beyond that of the individual or at best firm level. Such approaches run the risk of being blind to social and economic inequalities, power differences and domination structures.

These disciplinary approaches, however, are also subject to the very influences that bear upon employment relations as practice, with research on employment relations also varying between countries. Drawing on an analysis of 1300 articles in industrial relations journals, Frege (2005) found distinctive US, UK and German 'research patterns'.[4] In the United States, where researchers primarily are trained as economists, the analysis of labour markets and pay is more prevalent than in the UK or Germany; research is mainly also quantitative and draws more on large-scale datasets and level of analysis tends to be the micro (individual) level. In contrast to the US literature, research in the UK is dominated by sociologists, with research focusing much more on trade unions; using more on small-scale samples, most obviously case studies, and is pitched at the firm level more than the individual level. In Germany, sociologists in particular undertake less empirical research, offering 'think pieces' and 'essays' focused on the firm level. Frege concludes that even if (industrial) employment relations in the advanced economies converge and international communication between research communities increases, there is still a 'distinctive national research pattern' (p. 203) that shows no sign of convergence. Context clearly still matters: how employment relations is studied still differs in the three countries and is an outcome of 'long-standing intellectual traditions' (p. 204; also Keller, 2005). These findings underpin our argument that not only must explanations of differences in employment relations take context into account, but we also need to be aware that the theories used to explain these differences can also be context-influenced. Of course, name changes and disciplinary demarcations cannot be allowed to mask the common concern: the labour problem. This concern will remain so long as paid employment exists. Understanding how the field of study and practice of employment relations develop temporally and spatially is the reason why comparative analysis is so important.

NOTES

1. Williamson (1984) speaks of 'metering'; we use the term 'monitoring' instead.
2. Williamson 1984 differentiates two other forms of employment relations, analytically located between the mentioned two extreme constellations spot market and relational teams.
3. There are yet other influences such as gender regimes that we have not discussed in this chapter but which are no less important (for a discussion see Rubery 2009).
4. The findings refer to industrial relations, but can – with caution – be applied to the study of employment relations.

REFERENCES

Allen, M. 2004. The varieties of capitalism paradigm: not enough variety? *Socio-Economic Review*, **2**: 87–108.

Argyris, C. 1960. *Understanding Organisational Behaviour.* Homewood, IL: Dorsey Press.
Arthur, M. & Rousseau, D. 1995. *The Boundaryless Career.* Oxford: Oxford University Press.
Bamber, G. & Lansbury, R. 1987. *International and Comparative Industrial Relations.* London: Sage Publications.
Bamber, G., Lansbury, R. D. & Wailes, N. 2004. Introduction. In G. J. Bamber, R. D. Lansbury and N. Wailes (eds), *International and Comparative Employment Relations.* London: Sage Publications, pp. 1–35.
Baskerville, R. F. 2003. Hofstede never studied culture. *Accounting, Organizations and Society,* **28**: 1–14.
Bernhardt, A., Dresser, L. & Hatton, E. 2003. The Coffee Pot Wars: unions and firm restructuring in the hotel industry. In E. Appelbaum, A. Bernhardt and R. J. Murnane (eds), *Low Wage America.* New York: Russel Sage Foundation, pp. 33–76.
Blau, P. M. 1964. *Exchange and Power in Social Life.* New York: John Wiley and Sons.
Blyton, P. & Turnbull, P. 1998. *The Dynamics of Employment Relations.* London: Macmillan.
Bosch, G., Lehndorff, S. & Rubery, J. 2009. *European Employment Models in Flux: A Comparison of Institutional Change in Nine European Countries.* Basingstoke, UK: Palgrave Macmillan.
Boxall, P. & Purcell, J. 2003. *Strategy and Human Resource Management.* London: Palgrave.
Braverman, H. 1974. *Labor and Monopoly Capital.* New York: Monthly Review Press.
Bray, M., Waring, P. & Cooper, R. 2009. *Employment Relations: Theory and Practice.* Sydney: McGraw-Hill.
Brewster, C. 1995. National cultures and international management. In S. Tyson (ed.), *Strategic Prospects for HRM.* London: Institute of Personnel and Development, pp. 206–228.
Bridges, W. 1995. *Job Shift.* London: Nicholas Brealey.
Clark, T. & Pugh, D. 1999. Similarities and Differences in European Conceptions of Human Resource Management. *International Studies of Management & Organization,* **29**(4): 84–100.
Chartered Institute of Personnel and Development (CIPD). 2009. Employee relations: an overview. Available at: http://www.cipd.co.uk/subjects/empreltns/general/emprelsovr.htm.
Coyle-Shapiro, J. A. M. & Conway, N. 2004. The employment relationship through the lens of social exchange. In J. A. M. Coyle-Shapiro, L. M. Shore, M. S. Taylor and L. E. Tetrick (eds), *The Employment Relationship. Examining Psychological and Contextual Perspectives.* Oxford: Oxford University Press, pp. 5–28.
Cressey, P. & MacInnes, J. 1980. Voting for Ford: industrial democracy and the control of labour. *Capital and Class,* **11**: 5–33.
Crompton, R. & Lynette, C. 2006. Some issues in the cross national comparative research methods: a comparison of attitudes to promotion and woman's employment in Britain and Portugal. *Work, Employment and Society,* **20**(2): 403–440.
Crouch, C. 2009. Typologies of capitalism. In B. Hanké (ed.), *Debating Varieties of Capitalism.* Oxford: Oxford University Press, pp. 75–94.
Danford, A. 1998. Work organisation inside Japanese firms in South Wales: a break from Taylorism?' in P. Thompson and C. Warhurst (eds), *Workplaces of the Future.* London: Macmillan, pp. 40–64.
Dedoussis, V. & Littler, C. R. 1994. Understanding the transfer of Japanese management practices: the Australian case. In T. Elger and C. Smith (eds), *Global Japanisation?* London: Routledge, pp. 175–194.
DiMaggio, P. J. 1990. Cultural aspects of economic action and organisation. In R. Friedland and A. F. Robertson (eds), *Beyond the Marketplace.* New York: Aldine de Gruyter, pp. 113–136.
Dutton, E., Warhurst, C., Lloyd, C., James, S., Commander, J. & Nickson, D. 2008. Just like the elves in Harry Potter: room attendants in UK hotels. In G. Lloyd, G. Mason and

K. Mayhew (eds), *Low Wage Work in the UK*. New York: Russell Sage Foundation, pp. 96–130.

Edwards, P. 1995. From industrial relations to the employment relationship. *Relations Industrielles*, **50**: 39–65.

Edwards, P. 2003. The employment relationship and the field of industrial relations. In P. Edwards (ed.), *Industrial Relations: Theory and Practice*, 2nd edn. Malden, MA: Blackwell, pp. 1–35.

Edwards, R. C. 1979. *Contested Terrain: The Transformation of the Workplace in the Twentieth Century*. New York: Basic Books.

Elger, T. & Smith, C. 1994b. Global Japanisation? Convergence and competition in the organisation of the labour processes. In T. Elger and C. Smith (eds), *Global Japanisation?* London: Routledge, pp. 31–59.

Ferner, A. & Hyman, R. 1998. *Changing Industrial Relations in Europe*. Oxford: Blackwell.

Fores, M., Glover, I. and Lawrence, P. 1992. Management thought, the American identity and the future of European labour processes. Aston/UMIST Conference on the Labour Process, Aston University.

Fox, A. 1974. *Beyond Contract: Work, Power and Trust Relations*. London: Faber and Faber.

Frege, C. 2005. Varieties of industrial relations research: take-over, convergence or divergence? *British Journal of Industrial Relations*, **43**(2): 179–207.

Frege, C. M. & Kelly, J. (eds) 2004. *Varieties of Unionism*. Oxford: Oxford University Press.

Friedman, A. 1977. *Industry and Labour*. London: Macmillan.

Gallie, D. 2007. Production regimes and the quality of employment in Europe. *Annual Review of Sociology*, **33**: 85–104.

Gouldner A. W. 1960. The norm of reciprocity: a preliminary statement. *American Sociological Review*, **25**: 161–178.

Grahl, J. G. & Teague, P. 2004. The German model in danger. *Industrial Relations Journal*, **35**(6): 557–573.

Granovetter, M. 1985. Economic action and social structure: the problem of embeddedness. *American Journal of Sociology*, **91**: 481–510.

Guardian Weekly. 2010. Beijing goes on a buying spree. *Guardian Weekly*, 2 July 2010: 17.

Guest, D. E. 1997. Human resource management and performance: a review and research agenda. *International Journal of Human Resource Management*, **8**(3): 263–276.

Guest, D. E. 2004. The psychology of the employment relationship: an analysis based on the psychological contract. *Applied Psychology*, **53**(4): 541–555.

Guest, D. E. 2007. HRM: towards a new psychological contract. In P. Boxall, J. Purcell & P. M. Wright (eds), *The Oxford Handbook of Human Resource Management*. Oxford: Oxford University Press, pp. 128–146.

Hall, P. A. & Soskice, D. 2001. An introduction to varieties of capitalism. In P. A. Hall & D. Soskice (eds), *Varieties of Capitalism: The Institutional Foundations of Comparative Advantage*. Oxford: Oxford University Press, pp. 1–68.

Hall, P. A. & Soskice, D. (eds) 2001. *Varieties of Capitalism: The Institutional Foundations of Comparative Advantage*. Oxford: Oxford University Press.

Halper, S. 2010. *The Beijing Consensus*. London: Basic Books.

Harris, P. 2010. Hollywood Finds a New Enemy to Fight – China. *Observer*: 12.

Herriot, P. & Pemberton, C. 1995. *New Deals*. Chichester, NY: Wiley.

Hirschman, A. O. 1970. *Exit, Voice, and Loyalty*. Cambridge, MA: Harvard University Press.

Hofstede, G. 1980. *Culture's Consequences*. London: Sage Publications.

Hofstede, G. 1995. The cultural relativity of organisational practices and theories. In J. Drew (ed.), *Readings in International Enterprise*. London: Routledge, pp. 141–158.

Horsley, W. & Buckley, R. 1990. *Nippon: New Superpower*. London: BBC Books.

Hutton, W. 1995. *The State We're In*. London: Cape.

Kaufman, B. E. 2004a. Employment relations and the employment relations system: a guide to theorizing. In B. E. Kaufman (ed.), *Theoretical Perspectives on Work and the*

Employment Relationship. Champaign, IL: Industrial Relations Research Association, pp. 41–75

Kaufman, B. E. 2004b. Towards an integrative theory of human resource management. In B. E. Kaufman (ed.), *Theoretical Perspectives on Work and the Employment Relationship*. Champaign, IL: Industrial Relations Research Association, pp. 321–366.

Keller, B. 2005. The industrial relations field in Germany: an empirical and comparative analysis. *Advances in Industrial and Labor Relations*, **14**: 239–277.

Kelly, J. 1994. *Does the Field of Industrial Relations Have a Future?* Oxford: British Universities Industrial Relations Association.

Kelly, J. & Frege, C. 2004. Conclusions: varieties of unionism. In C. M. Frege and J. Kelly (eds), *Varieties of Unionism*. Oxford: Oxford University Press, pp. 181–196.

Kenworthy, L. 2009. Institutional coherence and macroeconomic performance. In B. Hanké (ed.), *Debating Varieties of Capitalism*. Oxford: Oxford University Press, pp. 180–199.

Kerr, C., Dunlop, J. T., Harbison, F. H. & Meyers, C. A. 1960. *Industrialism and Industrial Man*. Cambridge, MA: Harvard University Press.

Kirkland, R. I. 1990. The big Japanese push into Europe. *Fortune*, (2 July): 26–32.

Kochan, T. A. 1998. What is distinctive about industrial relations research. In K. Whitfield and G. Strauss (eds), *Researching the World of Work*. Ithaca, NY: Cornell University Press, pp. 31–50.

Kochan, T. A. 2007. Social legitimacy of the human resource management profession: a US perspective. In P. Boxall, J. Purcell & P. M. Wright (eds), *The Oxford Handbook of Human Resource Management*. Oxford: Oxford University Press, pp. 599–619.

Lane, C. 1987. Capitalism or culture? A comparative analysis of the position in the labour process of lower white-collar workers in the financial services of Britain and the FDR. *Work Employment and Society*, **1**: 57–83.

Lawrence, P. 1980. *Managers and Management in Germany*. London: Croom Helm.

Lawrence, P. 1988. In another country. In A. Bryman (ed.), *Research Methods and Organisation Studies*. London: Unwin Hyman, pp. 96–107.

Legge, K. 1995. *Human Resource Management: Rhetorics and Realities*. Houndmills: Macmillan.

Liebowitz, S. J. and Margolis, S. E. 1995. Path dependence, lock-in, and history. *Journal of Law, Economics and Organization*, **11**(1): 205–226.

Litter, C. 1982. *The Development of the Labour Process in Capitalist Societies*. London: Heinemann.

Marginson, P. 1993. Power and efficiency in the firm: understanding the employment relation. In C. Pitelis (ed.), *Transaction Costs, Markets and Hierarchies*. Oxford: Oxford University Press, pp. 133–165.

Maurice, M. 1979. For a study of the social effect: universalism and specificity in organisation research. In C. J. Lammers and D. J. Hickson (eds), *Organisations Alike and Unlike: International and Inter-institutional Studies in the Sociology of Organizations*. London: Routledge and Kegan Paul, pp. 42–58.

Maurice, M. & Sellier, F. 1979. A societal analysis of industrial relations: a comparison between France and West Germany. *British Journal of Industrial Relations*, **17**: 322–336.

Maurice, M., Sorge, A. & Warner, M. 1980. Societal differences in organizing manufacturing units: a comparison of France, West Germany, and Great Britain. *Organization Studies*, **1**: 59–86.

McKenna, E. & Beech, N. 2002. *Human Resource Management*. London: FT Prentice Hall.

Morley, M., Heraty, N. & Collings, D. (eds) 2006. *International Human Resource Management and International Assignments*. London: Palgrave Macmillan.

Morris, J. & Wilkinson, B. 1995. The transfer of Japanese management to alien institutional environments. *Journal of Management Studies*, **32**(6): 719–730.

Müller-Jentsch, W. 2004. Theoretical approaches to industrial relations. In B. E. Kaufman (ed.), *Theoretical Perspectives on Work and the Employment Relationship*, pp. 1–40. Champaign, IL: Industrial Relations Research Association, pp. 1–40.

Nichols, T. 1994. Theoretical perspectives in industrial sociology and the labour process debate. Work, Organisation and Social Structure Conference.

Nienhüser, W. 2004. Political (personnel) economy: a political economy perspective to explain different forms of human resource management. *Management Revue*, **15**(2): 228–248.

Panitch, L. 1981. Trade unions and the capitalist state. *New Left Review*, **125**: 21–43.

Pfeffer, J. 1998. *Human Equation: Building Profits by Putting People First*. Boston, MA: Harvard Business School Press.

Rollinson, D. & Dundon, T. 2007. *Understanding Employment Relations*. London: McGraw-Hill Higher Education.

Rose, E. 2004. *Employment Relations*. London: Prentice Hall/Financial Times.

Rose, M. 1985. Universalism, culturalism and the Aix Group: promise and problems of a societal approach to economic institutions. *European Sociological Review*, **1**: 65–83.

Rousseau, D. M. 1995. *Psychological Contracts in Organizations: Understanding Written and Unwritten Agreements*. Thousand Oaks: Sage Publications.

Rubery, J. 2009. How gendering the varieties of capitalism requires a wider lens. *Social Politics*, **16**(2): 192–203.

Schein, E. H. 1988. *Organizational Psychology*. Upper Saddle River, NJ: Pearson Education Limited.

Smith, C. & Meiksins, P. 1995. System, society and dominance effects in cross-national organisational analysis. *Work, Employment and Society*, **9**: 241–267.

Solow, B. & Wanner, E. 2010. Foreword. In J. Gautié and J. Schmitt (eds), *Low-Wage Work in the Wealthy World*. New York: Russel Sage Foundation, pp. xv–xx.

Stanford, J. 2008. *Economics for Everyone: A Short Guide to the Economics of Capitalism*. London: Pluto Press.

Stinchcombe, A. L. 1959. Bureaucratic and craft administration of production: a comparative study. *Administrative Science Quarterly*, **4**: 168–187.

Sztompka, P. 1990. Conceptual frameworks in comparative enquiry divergence or convergent. In M. Albrow & E. King (eds), *Globalisation, Knowledge and Society*. London: Sage Publications, pp. 47–61.

Taylor, F. W. 2006 [1911]. *The Principles of Scientific Management*. New York: Cosimo.

Thelen, K. 2001. Varieties of labor politics in the developed democracies. In P. A. Hall & D. Soskice (eds), *Varieties of Capitalism: The Institutional Foundations of Comparative Advantage*. Oxford: Oxford University Press, pp. 71–104.

Thompson, P. 1988. Japanisation? Threat or myth? *International Labour Reports*, **27–28**: 7–8.

Thompson, P. 1989. *The Nature of Work*. Houndmills: Macmillan.

Thompson, P. & McHugh, D. 1995. *Work Organisations*. Houndmills: Macmillan.

Thompson, P. & Smith, C. 1992. Socialism and the labour process in theory and practice. In C. Smith & P. Thomson (eds), *Labour in Transition*. London: Routledge, pp. 3–33.

Thompson, P. & Smith, C. 2010. *Working Life*. London: Palgrave.

Trompenaars, F. & Turner, C. H. 1997. *Riding the Waves of Culture: Understanding Cultural Diversity in Business*. New York: McGraw-Hill.

Vanselow, A. 2008. Still lost and forgotten? The work of hotel room attendants in Germany. In G. Bosch and C. Weinkopf (eds), *Low-wage Work in Germany*. New York: Russel Sage Foundation, pp. 214–252.

Vanselow, A., Warhurst, C., Bernhardt, A. & Dresser, L. 2010. Working at the wage floor: hotel room attendants and labor market institutions in Europe and the US. In J. Gautié & J. Schmitt (eds), *Low-wage Work in the Wealthy World*. New York: Russel Sage Foundation, pp. 269–318.

Warhurst, C. 1997. Political economy and the social organisation of economic activity: a synthesis of neo-institutional and labour process analyses. *Competition and Change*, **2**(2): 213–246.

Warhurst, C. 1998. Recognising the possible: the organisation and control of a socialist labour process. *Administrative Science Quarterly*, **43**(2): 470–497.

Warhurst, C. & Nickson, D. 2001. From globalisation to internationalisation to

Americanisation: The example of 'Little Americas' in the hotel sector. In M. B. Taggart and M. McDermott (eds), *Multinationals in a New Era: International Strategy and Management*. London: Palgrave, pp. 207–225.

Whitley, R. 1992. The social construction of organisations and markets: the comparative analysis of business recipes. In M. Reed & M. Hughes (eds), *Rethinking Organisation*. London: Sage Publications, pp. 120–143.

Wilkinson, B. & Oliver, N. 1990. Obstacles to Japanisation: the case of Ford UK. *Employee Relations*, **12**: 17–21.

Williams, K., Haslam, C., Williams, J. & Johal, S. 1994. Deconstructing car assembler productivity. *International Journal of Production Economics*, **34**: 253–265.

Williamson, O. E. 1984. Efficient labour organization. In F. H. Stephen (ed.), *Firms, Organization and Labour*. London: Macmillan, pp. 87–118.

Williamson, O. E. 1985. *The Economic Institutions of Capitalism*. Simon and Schuster: New York.

Williamson, O. E., Wachter, M. L. & Harris, J. 1975. Understanding the employment relation: the analysis of idiosyncratic exchange. *The Bell Journal of Economics*, **6**: 250–278.

Womack, J. P., Jones, D. T. & Roos, D. 1990. *The Machine that Changed the World*. New York: Macmillan.

Zucker, L. G. 1987. Institutional theories of organisation. *American Review of Sociology*, **13**: 443–464.

11 Organising HRM: the HRM department and line management roles in a comparative perspective[1]

Julia Brandl, Ina Ehnert and Anna Bos-Nehles

A core characteristic of human resource management (HRM) work is that it cannot be fully allocated to one particular actor or unit within the organisation (Tsui & Milkovich, 1987). Instead, HRM work involves HRM specialists, line and top management. Organising HRM work addresses the task of assigning HRM tasks and authority to different units within an organisation and enabling these units to coordinate their work with each other. The varying roles of HRM specialists, the debate of devolving operational HRM tasks from HR specialists to line managers (e.g. Bos-Nehles, 2010; Perry & Kulik, 2008) and the longstanding question of whether HRM is a specialist or a generalist task (Baron & Kreps, 1999: 503) indicate that organising HRM work is not straightforward. But what are the possible alternative ways to organise HRM work? And why do organisations employ a particular form of organising HRM?

In this chapter, we outline three options for organising HRM work and review how HRM scholars have explained differences and similarities in the prevalence of these alternatives in a cross-national perspective. Our subsequent focus on the national context builds on the premise that organisations are open systems that need to relate their structural elements to their environments in order to survive. While contextual factors relevant for organising HRM work can be found at various levels (e.g. industry, sector, organisational), the national context is a particularly promising perspective: first, government activities such as labour legislation and structuring of labour markets have contributed to the rise of the HRM function in organisations (Baron et al., 1986; Jacoby, 2003). Second, the HRM function operates within the specific societal context that sets limits or encourages development towards decentralisation and devolution (Andolšek & Štebe, 2005: 327).

We review four theoretical perspectives that seek to explain why there are differences and similarities in organising HRM work across countries: contingency theory, cultural theories, institutional theory and paradox/duality theory. We examine what factors these perspectives see as relevant and review how far HRM scholars have applied these perspectives in cross-national comparative studies. After reading the chapter, one should have an overview of major alternatives to organising the HRM function, acknowledge the key arguments of major theoretical perspectives and understand the usefulness and potential of these perspectives for explaining cross-national differences and similarities in organising HRM work.

We begin by outlining three options for organising HRM work that we contrast along several dimensions. Building on this framework, we review how major theoretical perspectives explain differences and similarities and for each theoretical perspective we examine the core arguments and how they have informed empirical research on organising HRM work. Finally, we discuss research gaps and present prospects for future research.

OPTIONS FOR ORGANISING HRM WORK

We differentiate three major forms for organising HRM work that we see as generic alternatives. Following Whitley's (1999) concept of work systems, we see options for organising HRM work as internally consistent alternatives of organising HRM that can be differentiated along six characteristics covering how work processes are organised and controlled, how workplace relations among actors are shaped and what employment policies apply. Depending on the particular configuration of these characteristics, we talk about classic, neo-classic and modern ways of organising HRM work (see Table 11.1).

Classic HRM Organisation

The classic HRM organisation has its roots in ideals of Scientific Management and Max Weber's bureaucracy model. HRM tasks are precisely defined so that responsibilities for them can be assigned to different entities that assume distinct roles in managing people. This often means centralisation of HRM tasks (e.g. formulating and implementing HRM strategy, administrative tasks) in the HRM department (Kreps & Baron, 1999: 507). In contrast, the roles of line managers are limited to the application of HRM rules. The HRM department's major role is to administer HRM processes. Core components of this role involve providing instructions to line management, checking line managers' compliance with rules and implementing HRM strategy. A further characteristic of the classic form of organising HRM work is high control over HRM tasks by the centralised units (Whitley, 1999: 90), which prescribe to other units, usually line managers, what HRM tasks need to be accomplished and how to execute them (see Harris et al., 2002). The separation of responsibilities

Table 11.1   Alternatives for organising HRM work

Work systems characteristics	Classic	HRM work type Neo-classic	Modern
Task fragmentation (specialisation)	High	Low	Low
HRM strategy integration and devolvement	Low	High	Limited to high
Control of HRM work	High	Some	Some
Separation of HRM specialists from line managers	High	Low	Low to high
Employer commitment to in-house HRM practice	Low	Considerable	Limited
Rewards for engaging with HRM activities tied to. . .	Standardised jobs/roles	Skills, individual performance	Skills, personal evaluation and individual performance

Source: Own elaboration, adapted and extended from Whitley, 1999.

between HRM department experts and line management 'laymen' is associated with a segmentation of knowledge, i.e. the prevalence of distinct skills in each unit. Typically, HRM department positions are staffed with highly specialised employees who are technically skilled in administering HRM processes. In contrast, line managers require no special HRM skills. Since needs for mutual consultation between HRM department and line managers are limited, specialist HRM tasks can be centralised and electronic media be used for facilitating communication (see Martin et al., 2008). Replacement of individual HRM specialists is fairly easy, as is externalisation of HRM tasks. The latter can range from specialised in-house units, such as 'centres of expertise', through 'business within the business' solutions to external consultancy (Adams, 1991; Sparrow & Braun, 2008; Ulrich et al., 2008). In extreme cases, the organisation outsources all HRM tasks to external service providers. Expected role behaviour is achieved through rewards that are tied to specific roles and job-descriptions. Meeting the demands of roles defined in job descriptions is the base for assessing performance. The technical and specialised nature of HRM jobs suggests the relevance of operational performance measures (e.g. costs for administering pay-rolls).

Empirical studies suggest that the classic HRM organisation is common in practice. In the UK, organisations tend to keep most HRM responsibilities centralised in the HRM department (Budhwar, 2000; Farndale, 2005; Larsen & Brewster, 2003). For the Netherlands, Nehles et al. (2006) find that many line managers lack information on HRM policies and procedures and support from HR professionals. The focus on administrative tasks is very common in organisations in Spain (Cascon-Pereira et al., 2006) as well as in Portugal (Cabral-Cardoso, 2004). It is also widely spread in Slovenia, where two out of every three HRM directors are not positioned as members of top management (Zupan & Kaše, 2005). The focus on administrative tasks is also frequent in Africa, however, with a more pragmatic approach that is often difficult for Western managers to understand (see Chapter 23). Instead of centralising tasks to HRM departments, there is a belief that a good generalist should be able to apply skills across a range of subject areas, resulting in a general administrator role of HRM (Taylor, 1992).

Neo-classical HRM Organisation

The neo-classical HRM organisation has its roots in behavioural perspectives of the firm which emphasise that factors such as bounded rationality, psychological contracts, group processes and associated concepts characterise organisational settings and propose a higher task complexity and mutual dependence between organisational entities (Whitley, 1999: 92). Assuming that employees desire to be recognised as individuals, HRM tasks are both complex and holistic and require different organisational units to share responsibility for conducting HRM work. Devolving HRM tasks to line managers is crucial to success as direct supervisors understand employee needs and have considerable influence on how HRM tasks are executed. This creates a mutually dependent relationship between the HRM department and line managers: HRM specialists support line managers with solutions for accomplishing HRM tasks and revise these solutions based on line managers' success with implementing them. Similarly, HRM specialists rely on exchange with top management for developing workable solutions. The possibilities for controlling the execution of HRM work in a mechanistic way are rather limited because it is hard to disentangle the exact responsibility of HRM specialists and non-specialist managers for HRM tasks. Given the need for intensive co-operation, skill requirements for HRM specialists become similar to those of top or line managers and vice versa. This is indicated by the need for HRM departments to develop business competencies (Ulrich, 1997) and line managers to elaborate HRM competencies (Whittaker & Marchington, 2003). If the accomplishment of

HRM tasks requires a broad range of professional skills, including technical and social competencies as well as solid business knowledge, it becomes rather difficult for companies to outsource HRM tasks or replace individual actors. Since professional skills are crucial to success in the neo-classical HRM organisation, organisational members are rewarded for investments in the development of skills and individual performance.

The neo-classic HRM model is frequently found in organisations in Northern European countries, as these are characterised by high levels of devolution of HRM responsibilities to line managers and strategic integration of HRM (Mayrhofer et al., 2004). In Denmark, for example, the devolvement of HRM tasks to line managers is very common. The neo-classical model is also reported in the Philippines, where Audea et al. (2005) suggest there are high levels of adoption of HRM practices and the HRM department takes a strategic role.

Research on the transition from classic to neo-classical models of organising HRM work points to mixed success. For instance, public sector organisations in Australia try to make the move from the classic model to more devolution and strategic integration, but realise that taking this step is difficult in practice. While involvement of line managers has increased in Australian organisations (Kulik & Bainbridge, 2006), Teo and Rodwell (2007) find that line managers are not willing to accept the responsibilities associated with operational HRM tasks. As a result, HRM specialists get a dual role of administrative experts and strategic partners to line managers. Josserand et al. (2006) explore reasons for the failed transition and suggest that HRM specialists perceived difficulties in taking on the new role, and at the same time line managers drove them back to their administrative role because of their lack of business understanding.

Modern HRM Organisation

The modern[2] HRM organisation assumes the ongoing contestation of HRM purposes by highly complex and dynamic environments with uncontrollable developments. Its theoretical roots are systems development and evolutionary approaches. HRM structures are decentralised, flexible, informal, fluid, non-linear and in a process of continuous change. The constant changeability of organising HRM work is reflected in 'flexible specialisation' (Whitley, 1999). HRM tasks are varied and wide-ranging. HRM work becomes a task of all managers and even of all organisation members. However, it might be that the organisational form does not have line managers in the hierarchical sense (see McConville & Holden, 1999). Integration of HRM topics in strategic business planning is important, but not restricted to input by HRM specialists. The holistic view of HRM work goes along with a need for strong discretion of organisational entities managing HRM work. For example, HRM specialists should act as 'navigators' who steer between opposing forces like short-term success and long-term legitimacy (Evans et al., 2002). The challenge for organisation members is to cope with the inconsistencies and contradictory requirements arising from the dynamic environments. Control over managing HRM work is accomplished through cultural integration. Organisation members should be equipped with excellent self-management, networking and often also with cross-cultural skills in addition to their technical qualifications. Knowledge of HRM work is continuous within the company, i.e. HRM specialists and line managers share experience and have similar skills and backgrounds. Networks and flat hierarchies characterise managing HRM tasks, lowering boundaries between actors. In these settings, commitment to structures and responsibilities is rather limited. Replacement of existing solutions is encouraged by, for example, high mobility of HRM staff but also by a limited commitment of line managers to share long-term HRM risks (e.g. investment in integration of new organisation members). Needed role behaviour is achieved by rewarding individual capabilities and networks.

Evidence for the existence of modern forms of organising HRM work comes from project-based organisations in Sweden. Söderlund and Bredin (2006) argue that in project-based organisations employees need special attention from HRM managers to meet their broader responsibilities. They identify four challenges that are of importance for developing HRM to meet the requirements of project operations: the competence issue, the trust issue, the change issue and the people issue. Bredin and Söderlund (2007) suggest a split of line management responsibilities into two separate roles: the line manager focuses on the technical supervising tasks and the line competence coach focuses on the people management tasks. Multinational companies (MNCs) are another setting where HRM roles and corresponding tasks are wide-ranging and a broad range of skills is needed for managing HRM. In addition, it is argued that the transition of dependencies between headquarters and subsidiaries makes their HRM structures dynamic (Farndale et al., 2010).

Having outlined the three alternatives for organising HRM work, we next look at what fosters or hinders the prevalence of a particular form of organising HRM work in a cross-national perspective. To this end, we review some theoretical perspectives and related empirical studies. The key arguments of these perspectives and relevant studies are summarised in Table 11.2.

Table 11.2 Theoretical perspectives used in cross-national research on organising HRM work and associated empirical studies

Theoretical perspective	Core arguments	Exemplary variables	Exemplary empirical studies	Main ideas
Contingency	Organisations are structured so that they fit with their external environment Match between structure and environmental factors ('best fit') makes the organisational structure efficient Particular HR work organisations should be chosen to resemble relevant contingent factors	Business strategy, HR strategy, organisational size, life-stage/ age, industry and sector, internation- alisation strategy, complexity and stability of national organisational contexts	Bowen et al. (2002) Budhwar and Sparrow, (1997); Budhwar (2000)	Linkages between business strategies and strategic role of the HR department vary across national settings Strategic HR role is linked to organisational capability strategy in Australia, Canada, United States, Latin America and China; it is linked to differentiation strategy in Australia, China and Korea and to cost leadership strategy in Australia, United States, China and Korea Cross-national differences in the prevalence of a neo-classic HR work organisation may not be fully explained with a contingency perspective Organisational size and life-stage may be relevant to the prevalence of neo-classic HR organisation types in the UK and India Classic HR organisation in India corresponds to predominance of small and young organisations in this setting Partial realisation of neo-classic HR organisation in UK corresponds to operation of large and old firms in this setting

Table 11.2 (continued)

Theoretical perspective	Core arguments	Exemplary variables	Exemplary empirical studies	Main ideas
				Suggest that growth of organisations in India promotes transition from classic to neo-classic HR organisation
			Farndale et al. (2010)	Corporate HR roles depend on the extent of mutual intra-organisational reliance in the relationships between headquarter and subsidiaries
				Corporate HR role is limited to influence HRM indirectly ('guardian of culture') if subsidiaries are independent from other subsidiaries and headquarter
				With increasing dependency, the corporate HR role is getting stronger, focussing on HR processes and managing knowledge
Cultural	Organisational members' carry (implicit) theories about useful forms of organising HR work	Attitudes to and beliefs about power differences, uncertainty tolerance, national background	Laurent (1986)	Views of organisational processes and the nature of organising work differ across managers' national backgrounds
	These theories are acquired through socialisation in a specific (national) setting			German managers' view resembles the classic or neo-classic HR organisation; British managers' assumptions come closer to the modern HR organisation

Institutional	National settings are characterised by distinctive institutions/social arrangements	Industrial relations system (unionisation, legislation), business systems characteristics, labour market relations, supra-national organisations, professional associations, national policy		
			Budhwar and Sparrow (2002)	Theories guide decisions about HR work types
				Perceptions of conditions and consequences of neo-classic HR work differ cross-nationally
				Indian managers have more favourable perceptions of neo-classic HR work than UK managers
			Brandl et al. (2009)	Perceptions of Danish line managers of the importance of HR work differ across gender and public or private organisations
				Danish HRM context resembles the neo-classic HR organisation
			Osland and Osland (2009)	In the Central American context family-run local enterprises are organised in a classic way and Sophisticated local enterprises and MNCs are organised in a neo-classic or modern way
	These institutions shape the structure of organisations		Barnett et al. (1996)	Neo-classic HR organisation is fostered by the industrial relations system
				Local HR tradition and credibility can hinder transition from classic to neo-classic form
	HR work type reflects the country's particular institutional arrangement		Brewster et al. (2006)	Business system characteristics influence whether HR work is transactional or strategic
				Large HR department size represents transactional, routine work (classic) whereas small size stands for strategic work (neo-classic)
			Wächter et al. (2006)	HR role dynamics (e.g. functional specialisation, HR-staff ratio and status) in MNC subsidiaries are only little affected by national business systems, except for Germany

Table 11.2 (continued)

Theoretical perspective	Core arguments	Exemplary variables	Exemplary empirical studies	Main ideas
			Tung and Havlovic (1996)	Involvement of HR departments in planning and task focus is shaped by the national political-economic environment
				Trustful environment and unionisation foster neo-classic HR organisation
			Jacoby (2004), Jacoby et al. (2005)	Corporate governance structure is associated with HR department size, devolvement, strategic integration
				Historically evolved variants within national settings of neo-classic models do not converge
			Jennings et al. (1995)	External and internal labour market relations foster the centralisation of HR work (bureaucratisation) and strategic integration (professionalism)
				Multiple factors need to be considered to explain the emergence of the particular forms of organising HR work
			Brandl et al. (2008)	Social policy is associated with the organisation of women-led HRM departments
				Maternity leave programs and public childcare foster the strategic role of female HR directors (neo-classic HRM work organisation)

			Baron et al. (1986); Dobbin and Sutton (1998)	HRM work organisation is influenced by national state activities
				National state promotes bureaucratic control and internal labour markets that encourage centralisation of HRM tasks within organisations (classic HRM work organisation)
				Organisations respond to employee rights initiatives by expanding the tasks of the HRM department and increasing its status (neo-classic HRM work organisation)
Duality/paradox	Organisational success or failure depends on how organisations cope with (unavoidable) contradictory forces	Change versus stability, centralisation versus de-centralisation, specialism versus generality, strategic roles versus administrative HR roles, employees versus employer	Stiles and Trevor (2006)	Major tensions in organising HR work in MNCs are strategic versus other roles, creating the balance between centralisation and de-centralisation and aligning interests of different stakeholders
	Organisations should reconcile and dynamically balance contradictions			Country of origin may account for how MNCs deal with tensions in organising HR work in their subsidiaries
	Co-existence of multiple forms of organising HR work (e.g. through hybrids) as a mechanism for taking into account contradictory requirements			Specifically, Japanese MNCs lack tight coordination between corporate HR and HR in Chinese business units; European MNCs show strong coordination efforts

CONTINGENCY APPROACHES

Core Concepts

Breaking with the universalistic idea that 'one solution fits all', the core assumption of contingency approaches is that organisations are structured so that they fit with their external environment (see Chapter 1). Thus, a particular HRM work organisation should be chosen to reflect relevant contingent factors: internal factors, such as strategy, size, age, and external factors, such as industry and sector (for an overview see Donaldson, 2001).

Cross-national comparisons using the contingency perspective (e.g. Hickson et al., 1974) hold that linkages between contingencies and structural elements are stable across countries. They address the complexity and stability of national organisational contexts to account for differences and similarities in organisational structures. Hence, explanations of differences and similarities of organising across countries should take into account how diverse and how dynamic national settings are. Contingency approaches suggest that the classic HRM work model is more appropriate in national settings where organisations find conditions of low complexity and high stability. Following the argument that organisations seek to deal with their environment effectively, this type is most common. The neo-classic HRM organisation develops as a reaction to increasing complexity and dynamics occurring in national environments. Organisations may find it useful to manage strategic changes; strategic involvement of HRM specialists helps them to anticipate changes and develop strategic plans. Finally, the modern HRM organisation is a consequence of highly complex contexts with very diverse demands as we find them typically in MNCs.

Empirical Research in the Contingency Tradition

Empirical research that builds on contingency assumptions has paid particular attention to the linkage between an organisation's HRM strategy and the organisation of HRM work. Bowen et al. (2002) examine whether the strategic role of the HRM department is consistent with three HRM strategies – organisational capability, differentiation and cost leadership proposed by Schuler and Jackson (1987) – in a sample of organisations in Anglo, Asian and Latin countries. Their study examined whether such contingencies apply beyond the US context. They find that high HRM status in organisations in Australia, Canada, United States, Latin America and China is linked with the organisational capability strategy of the HRM department; in Australia, China and Korea with a differentiation strategy; and with leadership strategy in Australia, United States, China and Korea. In sum, the study provides limited support for a one-to-one linkage between HRM strategy and HRM organisation. Their study reveals that linkages between business strategies and types of HRM organisation do vary across national settings. However, the fact that the neo-classical HRM organisation is found in all strategy types in Canada and China suggests that a particular business strategy does not entirely determine a particular HRM work organisation; the absence of a business strategy-HRM work linkage in other countries may indicate a limited importance of business strategy for organising HRM work. Overall, the study of Bowen et al. (2002) indicates that cross-national differences in the prevalence of a neo-classic HRM organisation cannot be fully explained with a contingency perspective that focuses on HRM strategy.

Studies of HRM organisation in the UK and Indian manufacturing sector (Budhwar, 2000; Budhwar & Sparrow, 1997) also draw on the contingency perspective, but argue that a broader set of contingency factors may be relevant to understand the prevalence of specific HRM organisation types within a national setting. Beyond organisational policies, they refer to organisational size and life-stage as well as to the interplay of these factors with other factors (e.g. national culture, national business system; see below). Although Budhwar (2000) does not compare companies cross-nationally, his findings are consistent with factors that are highlighted by the contingency perspective. In the Indian context, where small and young organisations predominate, low strategic integration of HRM departments and low devolvement of HRM work to line managers are often found, pointing to the predominance of the classic HRM work organisation. In the UK, where large and old firms operate, devolvement is often low too; however, more organisations tend to integrate their HRM department strategically. The fact that the neo-classic model has not fully arrived yet in the UK is nevertheless consistent with contingency assumptions that stress the importance of industry characteristics for the nature of organisational structure, given that in the manufacturing sector line manager involvement in HRM does not create competitive advantage.

Arguing that internationalisation strategy is a critical factor in how HRM work is organised, Farndale et al. (2010) examine, in an exploratory analysis of 16 MNCs with headquarters in different countries, how corporate HRM roles vary based on how MNCs design the relationships between headquarter and subsidiaries. In line with their reasoning that corporate HRM roles depend on the extent of mutual intra-organisational reliance in these relationships, the study provides evidence that in the case of independent subsidiaries the corporate HRM role has limited influence. This is reflected in the predominance of the 'guardian of culture' role

(Brewster et al., 2005). With increasing dependence, the corporate HRM role also increases, focussing on HRM processes and managing knowledge. We think that this work is particularly interesting for comparative research on organising HRM work because it is one of the few studies that takes into account corporate internationalisation strategies. The findings suggest that internationalisation strategy is indeed an important contingency for organising HRM work (see also Stiles & Trevor, 2006; below). Although the study focuses on the role of corporate HRM, findings suggest that independent and interdependent relationships promote modern forms of organising HRM work ,whereas dependent relationships foster neo-classic forms of organising HRM work. Given the different countries of origin of the MNCs investigated in the study, it would be interesting to examine whether the fit between internationalisation strategy and HRM organisation applies for all MNCs regardless from which national settings they originate.

CULTURAL APPROACHES

Core Concepts

Cultural approaches to cross-national comparative research on HRM work are based on the assumption that similarities and differences in organising HRM work between countries prevail due to values and assumptions of individuals who operate in these settings (see Chapter 3). Managers carry implicit theories about organising in their 'heads' (Laurent, 1986), comprising, for example, ideas about whether or not HRM work is part of line managerial work. These theories will also include attitudes towards the distribution of power differences and uncertainty. Managers select HRM work models that match their implicit theories of adequate organisational forms.

Other than contingency theory, cultural approaches emphasise that HRM work models are applied regardless of their efficiency. This is based on the assumption that individuals do not constantly evaluate alternatives for organising HRM work. Instead, they are satisfied with solutions as long as these are perceived as working sufficiently (March & Simon, 1958). Also, when organisation members examine possibilities for improving HRM work, their existing knowledge allows them to consider only a limited number of alternatives. These alternatives are influenced by the specific social context in which they are socialised.

Scholars employing cultural approaches to examine cross-national patterns in organising often refer to Hofstede's (1980) work. He identifies cultural dimensions that could be related with the selection of particular organisational models. The power distance dimension, for example, reflects to what extent one accepts the uneven distribution of power between supervisors and subordinates. In settings where power distance is high, subordinates expect that they will be told what to do. This encourages and stabilises a hierarchical distribution of HRM work as represented in the classic and neo-classic models. With his uncertainty avoidance dimension, Hofstede (1980) examines how comfortable one is with unfamiliar situations. If uncertainty avoidance is high, organisation members expect a clear chain of command in their organisation and defined areas for their own responsibility, also encouraging the stabilisation of classic and neo-classical models.

The focus of cultural approaches is not limited to explaining the cross-national variability of organisational forms. Assuming that culture shapes the meaning that organisational members attribute to models of organising, cultural approaches can also shed light on the meaning organisational members attach to forms of organising HRM work (Inzerilli & Laurent, 1983). Hence, 'even if the structure of different organizations may appear the same on some objective dimensions the meaning of structure to the organization members may be quite different, and this difference may be important in influencing their behavior' (Inzerilli & Laure, 1983: 98). Budhwar and Sparrow (2002) build on this perspective when comparing British and Indian managers' understandings of the neo-classical model.

Empirical Research in the Cultural Tradition

Empirical research on HRM work using culture approaches has been rather limited to date. Those that there are cover different aspects, but point to considerable cross-national differences in managers' belief structures. Frequently cited is the study by Laurent (1986), who compares assumptions of managers from 10 Western European countries about their understanding of organisational processes. Exploring cross-national differences in managers' agreement to statements about managing organisations, he explains that the German managers' view of organisations is 'a coordinated network of individuals who make appropriate decisions based on their professional competence and knowledge' (Laurent, 1986: 96), which corresponds to the classic or neo-classic HRM organisation. In contrast, the British managers tend to see organisations as 'a network of relationships between people who get things done by influencing each other by communicating and negotiating' (Laurent, 1986: 96), a view which comes closer to the modern HRM organisation.

Budhwar and Sparrow (2002) analysed a matched sample of 48 Indian and British firms in the manufacturing sector to compare HRM managers' understanding of two core elements of the neo-classic model for organising HRM work: strategic integration and devolvement of HRM work to line management. They employ a multi-mapping methodology for assessing companies' HRM specialists' understanding of these elements and of the influence of national culture on them. The study reveals considerable cross-national differences in how HRM specialists interpret the conditions for and consequences of the neo-classical model. Indian HRM specialists conceptualise integration as a result of recent economic reforms and associate it primarily with MNCs. Devolvement of HRM work to line managers is seen as a necessity of the economic liberalisation process (Budhwar & Sparrow, 2002: 618). British HRM specialists, in contrast, emphasise a larger variety of issues associated with devolvement, also including dysfunctional outcomes. Given that cultural approaches see such theories as crucial for decision making, the study suggests cross-national differences in the use of the neo-classical model: the narrowly defined scope of strategic integration in India suggests that HRM specialists will employ this concept less widely than their British counterparts. On the other hand, they have fewer concerns with devolving HRM tasks to line managers and, therefore, may more deliberately delegate responsibility for operational HRM work than British HRM specialists.

Brandl et al. (2009) studied how much attention line managers in Denmark pay to HRM tasks, assuming that perceived importance is critical for successful devolvement of HRM responsibilities to the line. Their nationwide survey of 1500 Danish managers finds that line managers show considerable interest in HRM tasks in relation to other managerial duties, which facilitates the implementation of the neo-classical HRM organisation that is very common in Denmark. Their findings also reveal that managers' importance ratings differ considerably across HRM tasks: while interest in 'motivating others' and 'staff well-being' is high, 'team building', 'handling conflicts' and 'coaching' are seen as less important.

For the Central American context, Osland and Osland (2005) based on an expert panel and their personal work experience in the region, suggest that HRM in Central America varies widely (see also Chapter 22). Cultural features that characterise the Central American context are strong personal relationships, loyalty and collectivism. Family-run local enterprises are characterised by the classic HRM organisation ('paternalism'), whereas neo-classic and modern HRM organisation models dominate in sophisticated local enterprises and MNCs operating in the region. Osland and Osland (2005) suggest that the neo-classic and modern HRM models are increasingly 'imported' by MNCs and by talents starting their career in MNCs who return to their family-owned business at a later point in time.

INSTITUTIONAL APPROACHES

Core Concepts

Institutional explanations for comparing HRM work assume that organisations adopt particular forms of organising HRM because social arrangements pressure them to do so (see Chapter 2). National settings are characterised by institutions such as laws, agreements and standards that make up the distinct social arrangement. Organisations recognise these institutions and develop structures that allow them to operate within these arrangements. The HRM organisation therefore reflects the particular institutional arrangement. The institutional tradition is a collection of approaches under headings such as 'varieties of capitalism' (Hall & Soskice, 2001), 'business systems approach' (Whitley, 1999) and 'world polity approach' (Meyer et al., 1997).[3]

The first two approaches share the key argument that existing variations between different systems of economic organisation remain and are reproduced through different social arrangements at national level. For example, Whitley (1999: 19) asserts that 'nation states constitute the prevalent arena in which social and political competition is decided in industrial capitalist societies', implying that organising HRM work is shaped by the existence of national interest groups and rules that govern their interaction and control over resources. For example, the classic HRM model is unlikely where managers share experiences or skills with the workforce or where labour organisations (e.g. unions) are incorporated into state mechanisms for regulating conflicts between interest groups (Guillén, 1994). The neo-classical model is less likely where managers and workers have distinct backgrounds, or where they are mobile between firms or industries, where owners reject long term risks with specific firms; the neo-classical model is likely where strong industrial and craft unions have limited control over work organisations. Finally, the modern HRM model is encouraged by a strong public training system and where trust and authority are highly personal and less provided by employer and employee trust.

The world polity approach postulates the de-legitimation of national organisational forms as universalistic standards and Western principles of rationality such as autonomy or formalisation diffuse globally (Meyer et al., 1997). The worldwide expansion of autonomy of organisations and individuals brings about extension of strategic activities in organisations and involvement of organisation members in strategy-making processes. World cultural models of managing employees promoted by globally acting organisations, best practice and social movements (e.g. HRM professional associations) encourage organisations to reorganise their

HRM work so that they meet universalistic standards. The world polity approach suggests the worldwide diffusion of neo-classic and modern HRM models in the long run and the replacement of classic HRM models. Differences between countries are explained through different exposure of countries to global models of organising.

Empirical Research in the Institutional Tradition

A considerable number of scholars have drawn on institutional perspectives to study variations between forms of organising HRM work cross-nationally. Barnett et al. (1996) combine institutional arguments with a negotiated order approach to compare the development of HRM department roles in response to the public sector reform in Australia and UK. Using an exploratory research design based on interviews with senior managers, they examine how three Australian hospitals and a UK NHS Trust develop their HRM function. While the Australian organisations have established administrative HRM roles, in the UK setting the HRM manager was appointed to the board of directors and was responsible for a broader spectrum of HRM activities (corresponding to the neo-classical model). Barnett et al. (1996) explain the more constrained roles of HRM specialists in Australia by the role of the National Health Commission and the industrial relations system as well as with the lack of an HRM tradition in the investigated organisations.

Emphasising the relevance of political-economic and socio-cultural environmental factors for the shape of the HRM department, Tung and Havlovic (1996) suggested that specialised HRM departments have a narrower task range in the Czech Republic than in Poland because of their association with spying activities on employees' lives during the post-World War II communist era. Consistent with this reasoning, they show that Czech companies involve their HRM departments less in training activities but more in recruitment and payroll activities compared to companies in Poland and that unionisation in the Czech context increased the likelihood of the HRM department's involvement. This study is a rare attempt to highlight the role of political legacy for the organising of HRM work.

Using Cranet data from 18 European countries and Japan, Brewster et al. (2006) analyse how the resources allocated to HRM departments are associated with national business systems characteristics. The authors argue that in Rhineland economies and Japan, which represent large firm models, the transactional nature of HRM work requires larger HRM departments, whereas in countries with compartmentalised, transitional or peripheral business system models, the emphasis on strategic HRM work suggests small HRM department. Brewster et al. (2006) find that HRM departments are smaller in the former communist countries of central Europe as well as in southern Europe. In Japan, HRM departments are larger, but not in Germany. While the study affirms the relevance of the national regulatory context for HRM departmental size, the lack of direct correlations for the remaining countries suggests that other factors play a considerable role for HRM department size. Another explanation for missing correlations might be that small HRM departments are found in modern as well as in neo-classical organisational forms. Interpreting the study in the light of our framework is not straightforward because our classic, neo-classic and modern organisation models are not directly associated with HRM departmental size.

Building also on the business systems perspective, Wächter et al. (2006) examine the operation and roles of HRM departments of US MNC subsidiaries in Spain, UK, Ireland and Germany. Assuming that typical features of US HRM departments are internal functional specialisation (employment management, compensation, training and employee relations), relatively small size and low hierarchical level, the authors explore whether and how these three characteristics vary and how such variations may be associated with national institutional conditions. Wächter et al. (2006) find that national institutional factors play a minor role in determining HRM department roles, which they suggest to be largely determined by efficiency pressures and the differentiation between transactional and strategic HRM tasks. Germany is an exception to this rule because the institutional context requires relations between HRM departments and works councils. HRM departments have addressed these pressures by devolving transactional tasks to line managers and by trying to increase their strategic involvement. The study is notable because the detailed case analyses reveal how roles are dynamically negotiated between subsidiary managers and headquarters.

Jacoby et al. (2005) analyse the role of HRM executives in the United States and Japan from a varieties of capitalism perspective to examine whether coordinated (Japan) and liberal market (United States) economies converge. Building on a survey of 229 Japanese and 149 US firms they trace changes in organising HRM work over the last five years. They find that in both countries companies have reduced HRM department staff, however, in Japan reduction is realised by buying services from outsourced in-house units (see Adams, 1991) and in the United States external service-providers are used. Responsibility devolvement to line management has increased in Japan in a limited number of companies while devolvement has been widespread in the United States. The study shows that the number of HRM executives who are involved strategically has increased in the United States, whereas involvement in Japan is still higher. This study is remarkable because of its comprehensive analysis of recent developments in organising HRM work showing that while organisations respond to global pressures to deregulation, their responses vary depending on national institutional traditions.

Within a neo-institutional framework, Jennings et al. (1995) analyse how the relationship between external and internal labour markets accounts for the emergence of bureaucratised and professionalised HRM departments in the Pacific Rim area. Jennings et al. (1995) suggest that in countries where external labour allocation is managed by external agencies (e.g. public education and labour management) bureaucratisation inside the organisation is low. Synthesising findings from their previous research, they explain that bureaucratisation is more likely in Australia, Canada and the United States, where organisations are responsible for controlling HR practices. Professionalisation, i.e. the acknowledgement of specialised disciplinary knowledge, resembles strategic integration in the neo-classical HRM organisation. Jennings et al. (1995) specify seven factors that foster professionalisation: the existence of professional associations, prevalence of bureaucratic HRM models, prevalence of large firms and cultural support for specialisation, unionisation, state involvement and an educated workforce. An interesting aspect of Jennings et al.'s (1995) study is that the establishment of the classic HRM model (bureaucratisation) can go hand in hand with the rise of the neo-classical model.

Recognising that HRM specialist positions are increasingly staffed with female professionals who have traditionally been associated with a classic HRM work organisation, Brandl et al. (2008) look at the influence of national social policy and culture on the organisation of women-led HRM departments. In a study of 984 companies with female HR directors in 16 countries they find that enabling social policy programmes (e.g. public childcare, maternity leave programmes) are associated with a more strategic role of women-led HRM departments. This suggests that the inclusion of female HRM professionals in senior positions does not hinder the emergence of a neo-classical HRM work organisation when the state intervenes to reduce productivity differences between men and women. Brandl et al.'s (2008) study notes that institutional factors are more relevant for shaping roles in organisations than cultural attitudes.

The importance of the nation state for the HRM work organisation is also the topic of Baron et al.'s (1986) study of the transformation of the employment relationship and evolution of personnel administration in the United States between the Depression and World War II. They argue that the state played a considerable role in the spread of the classic HRM work organisation, as it promoted bureaucratic control and internal labour markets. Building on the relevance of legislation for the role of HRM departments, Dobbin and Sutton (1998) analyse US managers' responses to the federal employment rights revolution of the early 1970s in a survey of 279 organisations. They suggest that the room for interpretation in the legislation allowed organisations to respond to initiatives in the areas of equal employment opportunity, health and safety, and benefits by founding new departments dedicated to these issues. This fuelled an increase in the importance of HRM departments and their transformation from the classic to the neo-classical HRM work organisation.

DUALITY/PARADOX THEORY

Core Concepts

About 20 years ago, paradoxes, dualities or dilemmas became a major concern for scholars of organisation (e.g. Cameron & Quinn, 1988) and HRM (e.g. Evans, 1999; Evans & Doz, 1989). Research on these phenomena has formed the emerging body of work that is referred to as paradox/duality theory.[4] Assuming that contradictory forces or 'poles' operate in organisations, paradox/duality theory asserts that organisational success or failure depends on how organisations cope with such forces. In contrast to contingency perspectives that suggest organisations need to adjust their structure so that it is aligned with one particular context, duality/paradox theory postulates that organisations should accept the coexistence of contradictions and should reconcile and dynamically balance them (Evans, 1999: 369). The rationale for this 'Janusian thinking' (Rothenburg, 1979) is that maximising consistency in one direction, however beneficial it seems, can be dysfunctional for organisations. For example, delivering HRM services through virtual processes with responsive and temporary networks requires new skills like self-management and collaboration that make contractual relationships less permanent and more outcome-focused with a strong role for the team or contract managers (Evans et al., 2002: 464). These changes challenge the integrative role of HRM work. In order to avoid potentially destructive results that may lead to an alternative extreme (e.g. a highly centralised HRM department) and ongoing cycles of crisis and alternation between extremes, organisations should constantly pay 'a minimal level of attention' (Evans et al., 2002: 82) to alternative options.

Since tensions in organising work such as 'change versus continuity', 'centralisation versus de-centralisation' and 'generality versus specialisation' cannot be avoided (Evans, 1999, 1991), organisations need to manage them actively. A particular concern for organisational design is then to find out when tensions are constructive, fostering organisational development by enhancing creativity, and when they are destructive, leading to stagnation and other problematic outcomes for the organisation.

Duality/paradox theory so far has informed cross-national comparative research on HRM work mainly by highlighting typical dilemmas faced by organisations that operate in different national settings. For example, a common tension for organising HRM work in MNCs lies in the opposing forces for local responsiveness and global integration that occurs as business internationalises (Scullion & Starkey, 2000: 1063). The paradox to be managed here is 'how can we provide an appropriate degree of integration to affiliates that need their local autonomy?' (Evans, 1991: 113). Holding that 'either/or' solutions are likely to be ineffective, duality/paradox theory suggests the co-existence of multiple forms of organising HRM work (e.g. through hybrids) as a mechanism for taking into account contradictory requirements.

Empirical Research in the Duality/Paradox Tradition

The small, but growing body of work on organising HRM work in MNCs (e.g. Farndale et al., 2010; Scullion & Starkey, 2000; Stiles & Trevor, 2006) underlines the validity of duality/paradox theory. In MNCs, the question of how HRM work should be organised is less straightforward as different countries, business divisions and organisational levels are involved. Stiles and Trevor (2006: 62) assert that 'the theoretical position that embraces the notion of tensions or paradoxes or dilemmas seems to be the most accurate reflection of the lived experience of HR professionals'. Based on a comparative case study of a Dutch and a Japanese MNC in China, Stiles and Trevor (2006: 50) assess how the HRM departments of these two companies balance three types of tensions that they see as important in the multinational context: strategic versus other HRM roles (Ulrich, 1997), opposing interests between management and employees and centralising versus de-centralising HRM activities.

The comparison of a Dutch and a Japanese MNC in China illustrates how the approaches to reconcile these tensions vary cross-nationally. The tension between strategic and operational HRM roles is managed in both companies by subdividing the HRM function into corporate, line and internal consultancy units (Stiles & Trevor, 2006: 58). This indicates a coexistence of classic and neo-classical HRM work models. Apart from these similarities in structure, however, substantial differences prevail in managing the global integration of HRM activities. In the case of Philips operating in China, Stiles and Trevor (2006: 60) find considerable efforts to manage coordination tightly between locally operating HRM units. This is realised for example through sharing resources for administrative HRM between the locally operating shared service centres, exchanging best practices between the division-specific HRM units responsible for consulting and executing business-specific HRM policies and programmes in the specific business divisions and by promoting consistency between the shared service centres and HRM in the business units through a functional HRM unit.

By contrast, in the Japanese MNC in China, although HRM work is also devolved to HRM units in the business divisions, some HRM activities (e.g. performance management) remain centralised in corporate HRM that also holds wide-ranging responsibilities for implementing HRM solutions. Within this structure of minimal coordination through corporate HRM, the HRM units in the Chinese divisions operate under a highly fragmented regional structure with 'no transfer of knowledge or best practice' (Stiles & Trevor, 2006: 59). The lack of coordination of HRM work between the business divisions in China is reflected in the inconsistency of HRM practices (e.g. different work conditions for same jobs). The finding that employment is considered as 'an element of the production process' (Stiles & Trevor, 2006: 59) indicates that the local Chinese HRM units predominantly follow the classic HRM organisation.

Since the two firms operate in the same business and are similar in other contingency factors like expansion strategy, Stiles and Trevor (2006: 62) see the different solutions for organising HRM work within the Chinese subsidiaries, one being integrated and the other one fragmented, as an indicator for the relevance of country of origin for how MNCs deal with tensions in organising HRM work. This illuminates that duality/paradox theory and institutional approaches are not mutually exclusive but complement each other. Duality/paradox theory highlights potentially interesting foci for comparisons of organising HRM work, whereas institutional approaches may explain how MNCs from particular national contexts address these foci (e.g. Ferner & Varul, 2000). Therefore, we think it is worth combining the two approaches in future studies to understand how MNCs organise their HRM work across different countries more fully.

KEY ISSUES AND FUTURE DIRECTIONS

Although the research reviewed in this chapter indicates substantial activity in the field of cross-national comparative research on organising HRM work, we would also like to suggest areas that deserve more attention. We highlight in this section three issues that we believe have interesting potential to elaborate previous work. Research on some of these issues is already underway, and with the issues discussed below we intend to underline the importance of further moving in these directions.

The first issue concerns the elaboration of frameworks for studying the ways in which HRM work is organised in practice. There are multiple ways how HRM work can be allocated and coordinated within organisations. Emerging organisational forms like the Shared Service Centre (SSC) emphasise the interaction between HRM departments and line management and the devolvement of responsibility for implementing HRM from centralised HRM specialists to line managers. At the same time, they stress standardisation and self-services (Farndale et al., 2009; Reilly, 2000). The co-existence of multiple ways for delivering HRM tasks in practical models means that HRM scholars are confronted with a high complexity when they want to compare the variety of forms of organising HRM empirically. We see the current challenge for HRM scholars particularly in expanding their research to more recent organisational forms. Several authors have started to structure alternative forms for organising HRM work. They have identified such forms empirically (e.g.; Ulrich et al., 2008; Valverde et al., 2006) and they have developed frameworks for particular types of organisations such as MNCs (e.g. Farndale et al., 2010; Scullion & Starkey, 2000; Stiles & Trevor, 2006). The scheme that we have introduced in this chapter is applicable to any organisational setting and we are convinced that it offers a useful device for conducting future research in this field, in particular for developing a theory-guided way for structuring the multiple HRM organisational forms in practice.

The second basic issue concerns the shift from descriptive research to explanatory research designs. Although descriptive research has provided rich data on cross-national differences and similarities, explanations are still very much in their infancy. While our overview also indicates that theoretical perspectives have received considerable attention, we still lack an understanding of what drives the variety of HRM work forms. This may be for several reasons: (1) Conceptual perspectives and empirical analyses are sometimes loosely coupled, i.e. theoretical approaches are discussed but it remains relatively vague how they exactly relate to the area under study. To address such problems, future research should be devoted to developing testable, theoretically grounded frameworks that can serve as guides to new empirical research. (2) The range of theoretical frameworks for comparative research is not fully explored. While contingency and institutional perspectives have received a fair amount of attention, paradox/duality and cultural approaches are still underused. (3) We believe that a combination of different theoretical perspectives is fruitful for improving our understanding of HRM work forms. This goes together with the need to examine relationships between drivers of organisational forms. Jennings et al. (1995: 354) explain that: 'while no one factor seems to provide a unique rationale for bureaucratization in corporate HRM systems, several factors seem necessary for its development'. The combination of national and organisational factors is a useful step in this direction.

The third basic issue of need concerns the constructs for cross-national comparative research. As we observe a focus on survey-based research in our review, two areas deserve attention to tackle this issue. (1) The direct assessment of explanatory factors: often, HRM scholars have used countries as proxies for constructs instead of assessing these factors directly. When different theoretical perspectives classify country in a similar manner, the difficulty is that findings cannot be uniquely attributed to one theoretical perspective. This hinders the theoretical development of the field. Additionally, national contexts may provide too broad categories that do not adequately represent the explanatory factors themselves. Supporting this concern, Jennings et al. (1995) argue that the United States, although nominally a liberal market capitalism, has elements of a stakeholder approach (i.e. responsibilities to customers, communities and employees). (2) We examine the issue of 'comparing like with the like' (Wächter et al., 2006: 249). For example, when HRM departments consume plenty of resources, this can either signify large administrative tasks or indicate involvement in additional strategic activities. To tackle such differences in meanings, we suggest that a combination of quantitative and qualitative research methods will be beneficial for interpreting data.

CONCLUSION

Managing people requires organisations to make decisions about how different units contribute to this work and coordinate their activities with each other. Recognising the growing interest in the impact of national contexts on organising HRM work and given the purpose of this handbook, this chapter has provided an overview of comparative research on organising HRM work in a cross-national perspective. We have outlined three alternatives that companies may employ for organising HRM work – classic, neo-classical and modern – and sketched out four theoretical perspectives that provide answers about which factors drive cross-national differences and similarities in organising HRM work – contingency theory, cultural, institutional approaches and paradox/duality theory. Our review of empirical work has shed light on core differences and similarities between national settings, has assessed the extent to which particular theoretical perspectives have been used so far and what major findings they have produced. The literature reviewed in this chapter has strengthened our impression that the national setting exerts considerable influence on how companies organise HRM work. We reasoned that future research comparing HRM work in a cross-national perspective should focus more on the following aspects: (1) to expand the focus of research on modern HRM models needed for increasing numbers of flexible, network and project organisations, (2) employ theoretical frameworks that help in understanding cross-national developments, and (3) to develop robust constructs for empirical research.

NOTES

1. Acknowledgements: We would like to thank Hartmut Wächter for his constructive and detailed comments on an earlier draft of this chapter. Also thanks to Freddy Hällsten for his helpful feedback on issues discussed in the chapter.
2. The meaning of 'modern' is not 'more recent' or 'better' but it is used as an alternative to imply a systems development perspective.
3. While these approaches acknowledge that institutions 'matter' for organising HRM work, they differ considerably in their explanations as to *why* organisations conform (see Scott, R. W. 2001. *Institutions and Organizations.* 2nd edn. Thousand Oaks, CA: Sage Publications.
4. Despite subtle differences between the concepts paradox, duality and dilemma, the conceptual and empirical work can be perceived as one school of thought (Ehnert, I. 2009. *Sustainable Human Resource Management: a Conceptual and Exploratory Analysis from a Paradox Perspective.* Heidelberg: Physica-Verlag).

REFERENCES

Adams, K. 1991. Externalization vs. specialization: what is happening to personnel? *Human Resource Management Journal*, 1(4): 40–54.
Andolšek, D., & Štebe, J. 2005. Devolution or (de)centralization of the HRM function in European organizations. *International Journal of Human Resource Management*, 16(3): 311–329.
Audea, T., Teo, S. T. & Crawford, J. 2005. HRM professionals and their perceptions of HRM and firm performance in the Philippines. *The International Journal of Human Resource Management*, 16(4): 532–552.
Barnett, S., Patrickson, M. & Maddern, J. 1996. Negotiating the evolution of the HR function: practical advice from the health care sector. *Human Resource Management Journal*, 6(4): 18–37.
Baron, J. N., Dobbin, F. R. & Jennings, P. D. 1986. War and peace: the evolution of modern personnel administration in the US industry. *American Journal of Sociology*, 92(2): 350–386.
Baron, J. N. & Kreps, D. M. 1999. *Strategic Human Resources: Frameworks for General Managers.* New York: Wiley.
Bos-Nehles, A. C. 2010. The line makes the difference: line managers as effective HR partners. Zutphen: CPI Wöhrmann Print Service.
Bowen, D. E., Galang, C. & Pillai, R. 2002. The role of human resource management:

an exploratory study of cross-country variance. *Human Resource Management*, **41**(1): 103–122.

Brandl, J., Madsen, M. & Madsen, H. 2009. The perceived importance of HR duties to Danish line managers. *Human Resource Management Journal*, **19**(2): 194–210.

Brandl, J., Mayrhofer, W. & Reichel, A. 2008. The influence of social policy practices and gender egalitarianism on strategic integration of female HR directors. *International Journal of Human Resource Management*, **19**(11): 2113–2131.

Bredin, K. & Söderlund, J. 2007. Reconceptualising line management in project-based organisations: the case of competence coaches at Tetra Pak. *Personnel Review*, **36**(5): 815–833.

Brewster, C., Sparrow, P. R. & Harris, H. 2005. Towards a new model of globalising HRM. *The International Journal of Human Resource Management*, **16**(6): 949–970.

Brewster, C., Wood, G., Brookes, M. & van Ommeren, J. V. 2006. What determines the size of the HR function? A cross-national analysis. *Human Resource Management*, **45** (1): 3–21.

Budhwar, P. 2000. Evaluating levels of strategic integration and devolvement of human resource management in the UK. *Personnel Review*, **29**(2): 141–161.

Budhwar, P. & Sparrow, P. 1997. Evaluating levels of strategic integration and devolvement of human resource management in India. *The International Journal of Human Resource Management*, **8**(4): 476–494.

Budhwar, P. & Sparrow, P. 2002. Strategic HRM through the cultural looking glass: mapping cognitions of British and Indian HRM managers. *Organization Studies*, **23**(4): 599–638.

Cabral-Cardoso, C. 2004. The evolving Portuguese model of HRM. *The International Journal of Human Resource Management*, **15**(6): 959–977.

Cameron, K. S. & Quinn, R. E. 1988. *Organizational Paradox and Transformation*. Cambridge: Ballinger.

Cascon-Pereira, R., Valverde, M. & Ryan, G. 2006. Mapping out devolution: an exploration of the realities of devolution. *Journal of European Industrial Training*, **30**(2): 129–151.

Dobbin, F. & Sutton, J. R. 1998. The strength of a weak state: the rights revolution and the rise of human resources management divisions. *American Journal of Sociology*, **104**(2): 441–476.

Donaldson, L. 2001. *The Contingency Theory of Organizations*. Thousand Oaks, CA: Sage Publications.

Ehnert, I. 2009. *Sustainable Human Resource Management: a Conceptual and Exploratory Analysis from a Paradox Perspective*. Heidelberg: Physica-Verlag.

Evans, P. 1991. Duality theory: new directions for human resource and organizational management. In B. Staffelbach & P. Benz (eds), *Die Personalfunktion der Unternehmung im Spannungsfeld von Humanität und wirtschaftlicher Rationalität*. Heidelberg: Physica-Verlag, pp. 97–125.

Evans, P. 1999. HRM on the edge: a duality perspective. *Organization*, **6**(2): 325–338.

Evans, P. & Doz, Y. 1989. *The Dualistic Organization*. Houndmills, UK: Macmillan Press.

Evans, P., Pucik, V. & Barsoux, J.-L. 2002. *Global Challenge: International Human Resource Management*. New York: McGraw-Hill.

Farndale, E. 2005. HR Department professionalism: a comparison between the UK and other European countries. *The International Journal of Human Resource Management*, **16**(5): 660–675.

Farndale, E., Paauwe, J. & Hoeksema, L. 2009. In-sourcing HR: shared service centres in the Netherlands. *The International Journal of Human Resource Management*, **20**(3): 544–561.

Farndale, E., Paauwe, J., Morris, S. S., Stahl, G. K., Stiles, P., Trevor, J. & Wright, P. 2010. Context-bound configurations of corporate HR functions in multinational corporations. *Human Resource Management*, **49**(1): 45–66.

Ferner, A. & Varul, M. Z. 2000. Internationalisation and the personnel function in German multinationals. *Human Resource Management Journal*, **10**(3): 79–96.

Guillén, M. F. 1994. *Models of Management: Work, Authority, and Organization in a Comparative Perspective*. Chicago: University of Chicago Press.

Hall, P. A. & Soskice, D. 2001. *Varieties of Capitalism: the Institutional Foundation for Comparative Advantage.* Oxford: Oxford University Press.

Harris, L., Doughty, D. & Kirk, S. 2002. The devolution of HR responsibilities – perspectives from the UK's public sector. *Journal of European Industrial Training*, **26**(5): 218-229.

Hickson, D. J., Hinings, C. R., McMillan, C. J. & Schwitter, J. P. 1974. The culture-free context of organization structure: a tri-national comparison. *Sociology*, **8**: 59–80.

Hofstede, G. 1980. *Culture's Consequences: International Differences in Work-Related Values.* Beverly Hills, CA: Sage Publications.

Inzerilli, G. & Laurent, A. 1983. Managerial views of organization structure in France and the USA. *International Studies of Management and Organization*, **13**(1–2): 97–118.

Jacoby, S. M. 2003. A century of human resource management. In B. E. Kaufman, R. A. Beaumont & R. B. Helfgott (eds), *Industrial Relations to Human Resources and Beyond.* Armonk: Sharpe, pp. 147–171.

Jacoby, S. M., Nason, E. M. & Saguchi, K. 2005. The role of the senior HR executive in Japan and the United States: employment relations, corporate governance, and values. *Industrial Relations*, **44**(2): 207–241.

Jennings, P. D., Cyr, D. & Moore, L. F. 1995. Human resource management on the Pacific Rim: an integration. In L. F. Moore & P. D. Jennings (eds), *Human Resource Management on the Pacific Rim.* Berlin: de Gruyter, pp. 351–379.

Josserand, E., Teo, S. & Clegg, S. 2006. From bureaucratic to post-bureaucratic: the difficulties of transition. *Journal of Organizational Change Management*, **19**(1): 54-64.

Kreps, D. & Baron, J. 1999. *Strategic Human Resources: Frameworks for General Managers.* Hoboken: Wiley.

Kulik, C. T. & Bainbridge, H. T. 2006. HR and the line: the distribution of HR activities in Australian organisations. *Asia Pacific Journal of Human Resources*, **44**(2): 240–256.

Larsen, H. H. & Brewster, C. 2003. Line management responsibility for HRM: what is happening in Europe? *Employee Relations*, **25**(3): 228–244.

Laurent, A. 1986. The cross-cultural puzzle of international human resource management. *Human Resource Management*, **25**(1): 91–102.

March, J. G. & Simon, H. 1958. *Organizations.* New York: John Wiley & Sons.

Martin, G., Reddington, M. & Alexander, H. 2008. *Technology, Outsourcing and Transforming HR.* Oxford: Butterworth-Heinemann.

Mayrhofer, W., Morley, M. & Brewster, C. 2004. Convergence, stasis, or divergence? In C. Brewster, W. Mayrhofer & M. Morley (eds), *Human Resource Management in Europe. Evidence of Convergence?* Oxford: Elsevier.

McConville, T. & Holden, L. 1999. The filling in the sandwich: HRM and middle managers in the health sector. *Personnel Review*, **28**(5/6): 406–424.

Meyer, J., Boli, J., Thomas, G. & Ramirez, F. 1997. World society and the nation-state. *American Journal of Sociology*, **103**(1): 144–181.

Nehles, A. C., van Riemsdijk, M. J., Kok, I. & Looise, J. C. 2006. Implementing human resource management successfully: the role of first-line managers. *Management Revue*, **17**(3): 256–273.

Osland, A. & Osland, J. 2005. Contextualization and strategic international human resource management approaches: the case of Central America and Panama. *International Journal of Human Resource Management*, **16**(2): 2218–2236.

Perry, E. L. & Kulik, C. T. 2008. The devolution of HR to the line: implications for perceptions of people management effectiveness. *The International Journal of Human Resource Management*, **19**(2): 262–273.

Reilly, P. 2000. HR shared services and the realignment of HR, Report 368. Brighton, UK: Institute for Employment Studies.

Rothenburg, A. 1979. *The Emerging Goddess.* Chicago: University of Chicago Press.

Schuler, R. S. & Jackson, S. E. 1987. Linking competitive strategies with human resource management practices. *The Academy of Management Executive*, **1**(3): 207–219.

Scott, R. W. 2001. *Institutions and Organizations*, 2nd edn. Thousand Oaks, CA: Sage Publications.

Scullion, H. & Starkey, K. 2000. In search of the changing role of the corporate human resource function in the international firm. *International Journal of Human Resource Management*, **11**(6): 1061–1081.

Söderlund, J. & Bredin, K. 2006. HRM in project-intensive firms: changes and challenges. *Human Resource Management*, **45**(2): 249–265.

Sparrow, P. & Braun, W. 2008. HR sourcing and shoring: strategies, drivers, success factors and implications for HR. In C. Brewster, M. Dickmann & P. Sparrow (eds), *International HRM: Contemporary Issues in Europe*. London: Routledge, pp. 39–66.

Stiles, P. & Trevor, J. 2006. The human resource department: roles, coordination and influence. In G. A. B. Stahl (ed.), *Handbook of Research in International Human Resource Management*. Cheltenham, UK: Edward Elgar Publishing Limited, pp. 49–67.

Taylor, H. 1992. Public sector personnel management in three African countries: current problems and possibilities. *Public Administration and Development*, **12**(2): 193–207.

Teo, S. & Rodwell, J. J. 2007. To be strategic in the new public sector, HR must remember its operational activities. *Human Resource Management*, **46**(2): 265–284.

Tsui, A. S. & Milkovich, G. T. 1987. Personnel department activities: constituency perspectives and preferences. *Personnel Psychology*, **40**(3): 519–537.

Tung, R. L. & Havlovic, S. J. 1996. Human resource management in transitional economies: the case of Poland and the Czech Republic. *International Journal of Human Resource Management*, **7**(1): 1–19.

Ulrich, D. 1997. *Human Resource Champions: the Next Agenda for Adding Value and Delivering Results*. Boston, MA: Harvard Business School Press.

Ulrich, D., Younger, J. & Brockbank, W. 2008. The twenty-first-century HR organization. *Human Resource Management*, **47** (4): 829–850.

Valverde, M., Ryan, G. & Soler, C. 2006. Distributing HRM responsibilities: a classification of organisations. *Personnel Review*, **35**(6): 618–636.

Wächter, H., Peters, R., Ferner, A., Gunnigle, P. & Quintanilla, J. 2006. The role of the international personnel function in US MNCs. In P. Almond & A. Ferner (eds), *American Multinationals in Europe: Managing Employment Relations across National Borders*. Oxford: University of Oxford Press, pp. 248–269.

Whitley, R. 1999. *Divergent Capitalisms: The Social Structuring and Change of Business Systems*. Oxford: Oxford University Press.

Whittaker, S. & Marchington, M. 2003. Devolving HR responsibility to the line: threat, opportunity or partnership? *Employee Relations*, **25**(3): 245–261.

Zupan, N. & Kaše, R. 2005. Strategic human resource management in European transition economies: building a conceptual model on the case of Slovenia. *International Journal of Human Resource Management*, **16**(6): 882–906.

12 Comparative analysis of employment contracts
Paul Sparrow

This chapter looks at the nature of employment contracts through a comparative lens. The study of employment contracts is for Tsui and Wang (2002) one of five lenses that have been used to examine the employment relationship. Employment contracts were seen in terms of discussion of the labour contract and the compensation or incentive contract, i.e. a primarily economic and legalistic orientation. The broader topic of the employment relationship, which study of employment contracts provides some insight into, has also been studied from psychological, administrative employer–employee exchanges, workforce governance and human resource management perspectives. Here we are concerned with comparative insight into the nature of the employment contract – a construct to be defined in the next section.

First, however, it is worth briefly reminding ourselves of the journey that such comparative research has been on. The earliest comparative human resource management (HRM) researchers, such as Pieper (1990), were aware that attention needed to be given to national differences in the scope of employment legislation in terms of its potential impact on factors as diverse as recruitment and dismissal, formalisation of educational certification, pay, health and safety, the working environment, hours of work, forms of employment contract, consultation and co-determination rights. Whitley (1992) drew attention to the need to understand how the role of the state, financial sectors, national systems of education and training, and labour relations systems combined to create unique 'logics of action' in each country.

As the field of comparative HRM developed, Sparrow and Hiltrop (1997: 204) noted that the range of contextual factors that impacted any interpretation of comparative data, had to be understood as an 'institutional web' or 'force field framework' that surrounded any labour legislation (with the employment contract being one example of such legislation). This web sent signals about, and also created, important employee and employer behaviours, with regard to the:

- levels of organisational autonomy, and the rights of managers to manage as opposed to the rights of employees for participation,

- level of antagonism towards unions,
- relative burden of social security payments,
- nature and expectations of state intervention in either the external or internal labour markets of organisations, and
- employment philosophies, levels of corporate and social responsibility.

Moreover, it was argued that any comparative analysis had to understand the different biases created by these institutional webs (the philosophies and legislative focus) along two important dimensions:

1. whether legislation was primarily designed to protect the interests of the employee or the employer; and
2. how recently new demands on the employment relationship had been codified.

Early discussion of the employment contract therefore tended to make somewhat broad-brush statements about the national setting. For example, it would stress that labour laws in Japan are considered to be geared towards protecting the employees, thereby making large-scale redundancies difficult for firms to implement, noting that firms must agree on redundancies with the Ministry of Health, Labour and Welfare before taking action. Sparrow and Hiltrop (1997) made similar distinctions within the European Union (EU) with observations that Portuguese legislation incorporates a high employee bias whilst in the UK the bias is strongly towards employers. In countries such as Italy, Ireland and Spain attention was drawn to a proliferation of generally protectionist labour legislation, high levels of state ownership and a reliance on internal regulation of labour markets. In Greece, attention was drawn to the fact that historically hostile employer–employee industrial relationships have long impacted custom and practice within the employment relationship. How recently employment legislation has been enacted is also an important factor. Following the initial creation of a Single European Market, in countries such as Greece the complex labour legislation and how recently it had been codified meant that HRM functions actually spent considerable time simply ensuring compliance with legal requirements, whereas, in contrast, Denmark, with its highly structured welfare system, had for a long time already exceeded the minimum standards of social and employment legislation that were set by the EU. The recent effect of labour codification has been important too in shaping the conduct of the employment relationship during the subsequent integration of Eastern European states into the EU.

Since these early generalisations, as this chapter demonstrates, the complexity of insight has developed at a rapid pace. I first ask, what exactly is the phenomenon that we wish to gain comparative insight into? Attention is given to what an employment contract actually is, the nature of its terms, and how the rights and obligations – codified or implied – of the contract are in turn embedded in highly nationalistic legal systems and frameworks. Beyond the explicit legal formalities of the employment contract there are important implied terms that relate to underlying presumptions as to what constitutes faithful service, obedience, care and respect. I then give attention to some of the typical and notable cross-national differences in the terms of the employment contract, using the examples of termination and use of fixed-term contracts. The chapter explores how comparative researchers have attempted to understand the institutional and cultural web that surrounds the employment contract and the codification of the employment relationship within employment contracts. The legal origins hypothesis is discussed, and attention drawn to the comparative processes through which legal rules are formulated and how regulatory cultures and legal styles operate. I argue that study of employment contracts can also contribute to comparative analyses of working time, and help researchers draw high-level policy distinctions between issues such as healthy, family-friendly, or productive working time. I use some recent work on the relative productivity of the United States versus Europe to exemplify this latter type of research. Finally, I argue that explanation of international differences in the employment relationship – and the contract within it – tends to rely on one of two paradigms – either cultural or institutional. In practice, however, there tend to be different communities of researchers from each tradition, and therefore different literatures. Using debates about reforms in relation to the rewards elements of employment contracts, as triggered by the Kostenkrise debate in Germany and the Risutora process in Japan, I argue that separation of these two perspectives is in practice unrealistic. I conclude that comparative study of employment contracts is best conducted by examining the inter-dependency of external institutional and cultural factors, and by understanding in a comparative sense the effect of both these webs on employee and the employer logics of action. Such study can only be best achieved when we research comparative attempts to change contracts.

DEFINING THE EMPLOYMENT CONTRACT

What is the phenomenon that the chapter attempts to provide comparative insight into? What is an employment contract? The first challenge for any comparative analysis is to decide upon the common boundaries to be drawn around the topic under study. The employment contract is a contract of service (or apprenticeship) between an employer and an employee, rather than a contract for services. Under law the contract may be expressed or implied and, if it is expressed, it may still have standing whether it is oral or in writing. As an agreement between an employer and an employee, it sets out an individual's employment rights, responsibilities and duties. These are called the 'terms' of the contract.

In most instances a contract is considered to exist the moment an individual accepts a job offer: once an individual starts work, then they have accepted the terms offered by an employer. There is then always a contract between an employee and employer.

Contracts give both the employee and the employer certain rights and obligations – the contract terms. The rights an employee has under their contract of employment (contract terms) are in addition to the rights they have under (national and pan-national) law. Contract terms can come from a number of different sources. They may be verbally agreed, in a written contract or similar document, in an employee handbook, on a company notice board, in the job advert, in an offer letter from the employer, required by law, in a collective agreement (agreements with a trade union, industry body or staff association, which typically provide for issues such as co-operation between the parties to the collective agreement, as well as provisions relating to the terms of employment such as working hours, holidays and salaries), or considered as implied terms (not written down anywhere, but understood to exist, and deemed relevant because they are necessary to make the contract work, assumed to be obvious in that they are general terms which are implied into most contracts of employment, or have become custom and practice specific to a kind of work).

THE PSYCHOLOGICAL CONTRACT IN COMPARATIVE CONTEXT

Before exploring the issues associated with understanding the formal contract from a comparative perspective, I highlight the research task that is associated with comparative understanding of the implicit, or psychological, contract. The psychological contract captures the set of expectations held by an individual employee that specifies what the individual and the organisation expect to give and receive in the working relationship (Rousseau, 1990). Rousseau (1995) went on to identify four levels of analysis:

- individual-level psychological contracts;
- contracts implied by third parties;
- normative contracts shared across groups at unit, work or organisational level; and
- shared social contracts that reflect the broad beliefs about obligations associated with a society's culture.

Study of the psychological contract explores the open-ended agreements concerning the social and emotional aspects of exchange between employer and employee – the unwritten and reciprocal expectations that act as deep drivers of employee behaviour (and indirectly shape the extent to which the formal contract even needs to be codified).

Sparrow (1996), in asking whether the literature on psychological contracting was transferable across countries, identified a series of cross-cultural and psychological dynamics that must be considered when we attempt to understand contractual behaviour in a comparative context. He later argued that (Sparrow, 1998):

- Evidence from the field of comparative HRM made it abundantly clear that distinctive patterns of HRM policy and practice could be seen to send very different structural signals about the nature of the psychological contract.
- The work of organisational sociologists and political economists showed that national business systems were subject to distinctive policy trajectories, creating unique institutional contexts within which the formal-informal contract trade off takes place.
- Evidence from cross-cultural research highlights several mechanisms through which national culture impacts upon the internal motivational schema that employees have and the external social cues (in formal contracts) that they will respond to.
- Evidence from social psychologists and sociologists highlights a number of ways in which societal and institutional processes feed directly into the trade-off between the formal and informal aspects of the contract.

There are then good reasons to assume that many of the mechanisms of the psychological contract should operate differently across cultures and countries. These mechanisms have been examined from a theoretical perspective by Rousseau and Schalk (2000), Sparrow (1998), and Thomas et al. (2003). The latter note that national culture influences the psychological contract through the zone of negotiability that is deemed acceptable:

'every society . . . sets a zone of negotiability through its own set of constraints and guarantees . . . between societies the zone of negotiability is shaped by societal tolerance for unequal outcomes and . . . societal regulation of employment' (Thomas et al., 2003: 286).

Researchers therefore need to interpret two things:

- the contractual and behavioural signals that are sent by the general nature of HRM in that setting, and
- the mechanisms through which cross-cultural differences in the psychological contracting process are created.

There are a number of improvements in our research understanding, however, that must first occur before we can better understand the cross-cultural dynamics of psychological contracts, not least of which is the need for a clearer specification of generic human functioning and linkage between key psychological variables that are involved in the psychological contracting process (Sparrow, 2006). This understanding of generic (universal) functioning is needed for a number of reasons:

1. The assertion that national culture influences work attitudes and behaviours mainly (but indirectly) through organisational practices (Fisher et al., 2005; Ostroff & Bowen, 2000) suggests that we need to understand better the processes through which organisational culture and organisational practices mediate national culture effects, and in turn through this mediation impact upon subsequent psychological dynamics.
2. Bandura's (2002) arguments about the need to incorporate cross-culturally generalisable human functions, such as the role of agency in the employment relationship, suggests that we need to develop a more complete functional model that elicits the constructs involved in the chain of national culture – organisation culture – HRM practice – psychological outcome.
3. Erez and Gati (2004) observe that there are dynamic and two-way (i.e. top-down and bottom-up) processes involved in psychological contracting, and suggest that generic function modeling needs to allow for an understanding of not just how national culture exerts an influence on work attitudes through its influence on organisational culture and organisational practices (for which we can insert principally human resource management practices), but also of how national culture as enacted within firms and within individuals also creates a bottom-up influence on the adoption, customisation and redirection of those practices.

Therefore, before we can make sense of the different impacts that national culture has on the psychological contract, we need to clarify how these elements generally relate to and influence each other. It is beyond the scope of this chapter to review this evidence, but Figure 12.1 shows the complex set of linkages into which cross-cultural insight is needed for the psychological contract to become a powerful analytical tool across cultures (Sparrow, 2006).

Given the combination of top-down and bottom-up cultural influences on the psychological contract, as globalisation deepens it is inevitable that comparative researchers will also be required to adopt more innovative research methods and frames of analysis. In addition to the traditional cultural and institutional perspectives outlined throughout this chapter, a range of important contextual and temporal factors that become important during periods of change now need to also be considered as they impact employment relationship behaviour across cultures.

Tipton (2009) has drawn attention to the overlap between the study of national culture, and that of national identities, with the latter perspective being more accepting that the strength of effect of culture – the content and salience of culture – forms part of a wider constellation of factors. Static conceptualisations of culture, and indeed of the psychological contract within cultures, are inappropriate. Taking an identity perspective, the impact of national culture on behaviour (employment contract-related behaviour, for example) will emerge more or less at specific points of time and under specific circumstances.

This view can be allied with that of the multiple cultures argument alluded to above (Erez et al., 2004; Sackmann & Phillips, 2004). Recent conceptions of organisations operating in a multi-cultural context consider that culture must be a collective, socially constructed phenomenon and that organisations are home to and carriers of several cultures at the levels that include function, organisation and business unit, profession and occupational group, ethnic group, project-based network, regional institution, geographical and economic region, ideology and religion. Sackmann and Phillips (2004: 378) point out that 'individuals may identify with and hold simultaneous membership in several cultural groups'. Given that members of national communities hold multiple identities, and the habits developed within these more micro-level communities shape the interactions these group members have with institutions: 'the ongoing history of the relationship between individual and national culture suggests that . . . they will reflect the contemporary need to accommodate changes in the relationship' (Tipton, 2009: 160).

This brings us to change in the psychological contract both over time and across different cultures. Where change in this employment relationship is

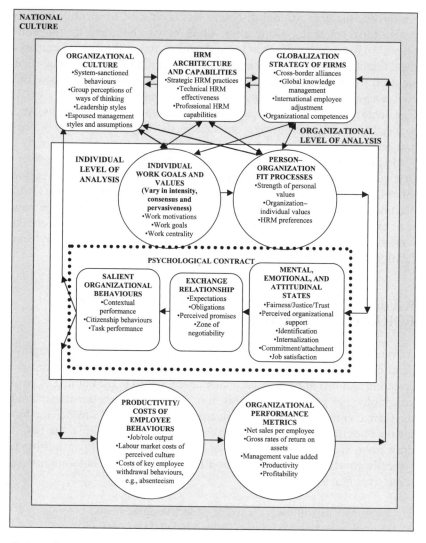

Source: Sparrow, P.R. (2006) International management: some key challenges for industrial and organizational psychology, *International Review of Industrial and Organizational Psychology. Volume 21*, London: John Wiley, pp. 189–266.

Figure 12.1   An organisational functioning model: cause–effect linkages within an embedded cultural context

concerned, the generational discourse has been used to identify various generational segments – Generation X and Y, baby boomers, the millennials and so forth, as a metaphor both of culture and of the implied employment relationship. A more sociological view of cultural change argues that we need to understand phenomena such as change in the psychological contract and employment contract through the impact of the more partial, fragmentary and episodic attachments as experienced by generations. And we need to avoid generalising from a distinctly Anglo-Saxon view of generational characteristics (Egri & Ralston, 2004).

Much of the popular HRM discourse talks about the 3Gs of diversity: gender, geography and generation. As globalisation progresses, the interplay between the last two of these – geography and generation – will become an area of potentially fruitful investigation. A key challenge now is to extend our insights into generational culture into a more informed cross-national understanding of such generational effects on employment relationship behaviour.

RIGHTS AND OBLIGATIONS AS IMPLIED IN FORMAL CONTRACTS

An understanding of the implicit context that surrounds the employment contract – the psychological contract – is then key to comparative research, and this understanding must be embedded in the context of both geography and generation. But so, too, is the need to better understand the formal employment contract in comparative terms. Consider the following situation with regard to employment contracts within the UK. I draw upon Snape's (1999) analysis of how the employment relationship is typically governed under a Common Law system by the combination of three sets of factors:

1. a complex mix of individual and collective agreements,
2. the rights and obligations enshrined in legal statutes, and
3. the implicit and explicit understandings of such rights and obligations.

These rights and obligations – codified or implied – are in turn embedded in highly nationalistic legal systems and frameworks. Without understanding the workings of the surrounding legal system, any examination of even codified rights becomes almost meaningless. Moreover, as the following example shows, the employment contract is not only embedded in complex legal histories, but also in presumptions of service that have deep cultural meaning and interpretation. Without insight into the cultural embeddedness of these terms, interpretation of the codified artefacts of the employment contract can be very misleading.

In the UK, the contract of employment and the implied and express terms within it, are determined by both Contract Law (statutes) and by Common Law (the latter is established by judges' decisions and not by statute). I pick up international differences in the nature of such law later in the chapter. However, returning to a UK context, both sources of law are used to establish three things: whether a person is regarded as an employee in first place; if so, is the employer entitled to exercise control over what the employee does and how he or she does it; is the employee integrated into the structure of the organisation; and is there a mutual obligation to supply and accept work? If the answers to the preceding questions are yes, then that individual may be considered as an employee and so may claim certain entitlements. Beyond the legal formalities of the employment contract, there are terms that can be implied on behalf of the parties and that are deemed to apply in the absence of some express provision to the contrary, whether the employer or employee appreciates their existence. These terms relate to presumptions as to what constitutes 'faithful service, obedience and care (respect)'.

1. *Faithful service*: What is deemed to be faithful service in turn is variously described as a duty of trust and confidence. This is seen as a series of fidelity obligations which failure to perform constitutes a breach of contract with resulting possible disciplinary action, or dismissal in relation to gross breach. This incorporates the obligation not to commit theft, defraud an employer, to cooperate with an employer and not to frustrate the common venture. Part of an employee's unwritten duties is the presumption that they must further the employer's objectives at all times. Faithful service also covers norms and practices in terms of issues such as work to rule, fighting at work, drinking at work, swearing, lateness or absenteeism, accepting secret bribes and profits, misusing confidential information and working in competition where employer has confidential information to impart.
2. *Obedience*: The principle of obedience conveys the implicit assumptions that are deemed to be implied by employment contracts that, in the absence of any express provision, may be considered to limit the liability of the employee. The principle is that at all times employees should obey lawful and reasonable orders incidental to employment (but they need not obey unlawful orders).
3. *Duty of care and respect*: The duty of care and principle of respect are the most important of the implied terms of the employment contract in the UK. They are developed and interpreted through a maze of case

law, and might relate to issues such as a failure to provide adequate support for the employee, the undermining of authority when found to be unable to cope with a role an employee is promoted into, falsely accusing an employee of incompetence in front of fellow employees, or of theft, a failure to listen to grievances, failure to provide an adequate working environment or to look at health and safety requirements, arbitrary treatment of employee less favourably than colleagues, and even the playing practical jokes on the employee! Reasonable care also applies to the setting up a reasonably safe system of work including matters such as training, instruction, protective equipment and clothing, safety procedures, safe access and exits, and fire drills.

In addition to these three obligations, there are also implied terms with regard to the provision of work and payment of wages (if an employer is prepared to pay an employee, the latter cannot complain that no work is provided, except where the employee is commission based, or highly-skilled, where they must be provided with work in order to maintain or enhance their skills).

Why is the surface codification of terms in the contract potentially misleading? The fidelity of the three obligations of faithful service, obedience and respect have then created a series of 'implied terms' that are considered to be general to all UK employment contracts. Typically, these implied terms have evolved by the courts at a time before governments ever became involved in the employment relationship (indeed, even today, most of the terms in UK employment contracts are the creation of the judiciary, many stemming back to the nineteenth century).

Clearly comparative researchers do need to develop considerable component knowledge to understand how employment contracts operate in practice. Moreover, they need to be able to compare like with like, where possible. Is it possible to categorise employment contracts in meaningful and comparable ways across countries?

CATEGORISING EMPLOYMENT CONTRACTS

There has been a considerable history of attempts at designing a mutually exclusive and exhaustive set of categories that capture all types of employment contracts, and to capture the necessary rules of application across countries. By way of example, the International Labour Organization (ILO) considers that whilst there are a number of different bases of comparative data capture, the most appropriate is to use the job as the unit of analysis. The International Classification of Status in Employment

(ICSE), used by the ILO, considers that employment contracts are best categorised in terms both of the:

- type of economic risk carried by an employee and
- authority that is involved in the job – defined as the set of task and duties that are designed to be performed by one person.

Using economic risk and authority levels as a basis of comparison, it becomes possible to differentiate for example between various forms of employment contracts that may be considered to be associated with self-employment. Self-employment contracts have to be further distinguished according to the type of authority they have over the productive unit – they may either represent this productive unit or may work for it. Applying such economic risk and authority level logics, employment contracts are coded into five categories.

1. Employees, where there is a basic remuneration not directly dependent on the revenue of the employer. Using an analysis of ILO data for 2009, it can be seen that in the United States of America 93 per cent of all contracts relate to those for employees. Comparable figures are 92.7 per cent in Russia, 88.4 per cent in Germany (a fraction more in Japan), 86.7 per cent in the UK, 74.5 per cent in Italy and Malaysia, 64.9 per cent in Greece, down to 32.6 per cent in Indonesia. Such data across countries of course typically also needs to be able to distinguish different types of paid employment jobs, according to the duration of contract and the type of security against its termination. Employees with stable contracts are distinguished from other 'employees' as a function of the extent to which they, on a continuous basis, have a contract, or a series of contracts, with the same 'employer'. Within this categorisation a further distinction is made between regular employees as opposed to employees with stable contracts, on the basis of the extent to which these contracts oblige the 'employer' to pay regular social security contributions and/or the extent to which the jobs are subject to national labour legislation.

2. Self-employed, but where they are an employer – their job is one in which the remuneration depends directly on the expectation of profits derived from the goods and services produced but, to effect this, the job holder must engage one or more people to work for them as 'employees', on a continuous basis. The proportion of employees with all types of self-employed contracts varies from 6.9 per cent in the United States, 11.6 per cent in Germany, 12.9 per cent in the UK, 32.9 per cent in Poland, to 56 per cent in Morocco.

3. Own-account workers, who hold self-employment jobs that have the

same authority over the economic unit as the 'employers' category, but who do not engage 'employees' on a continuous basis. Again, figures range from 47.5 per cent of contracts in Indonesia, 34.2 per cent in Pakistan, 20.9 per cent in Greece, to 7.0 per cent in Japan and 5.3 per cent in France.

4. Members of producers' cooperatives. The contract relates to people who hold self-employment jobs in a co-operative producing goods and services. Members however take part on an equal footing in making major decisions concerning the cooperative. Contract proportions can be 0.01 per cent in France, 0.15 per cent in Italy, to 1.6 per cent in Morocco.

5. Contributing family workers. Here self-employment jobs are held in an establishment operated by a related person, but the job has too limited a degree of involvement in its operation for the job holder to be considered a partner in the operation of the productive unit, typically because their degree of commitment to the operation of the unit, in terms of working time or other factors, is not at a level comparable to that of the head of the enterprise. Contract proportions vary from 28.9 per cent in Pakistan, down through 4.6 per cent in Malaysia, 4.1 per cent in Poland and 3.5 per cent in Japan, to 0.4 per cent in the UK, and 0.08 per cent in the United States.

Matters get more complicated when special and ambiguous sub-categories become important in particular countries, either because they sit between paid employment and self-employment, or have to be further separated out from these categories. From a contract perspective these sub-categories can include owner–managers of incorporated enterprises who are 'employees' but from an authority perspective can be seen as 'employers'. Then there are contractors, outworkers (homeworkers) and franchisees who, again from a contract perspective, may be 'self-employed' yet from an authority perspective may frequently be seen in a similar situation to 'employees' – such as casual workers and seasonal workers.

Official data, then, where they exist in such standard form, can allow for some limited but crude comparative analysis of the type of economic risk carried by an employee and the authority levels that are involved in jobs.

CROSS-NATIONAL DIFFERENCES IN THE TERMS OF THE EMPLOYMENT CONTRACT

Given the theme of economic risk and authority levels, one of the obvious ways in which countries are compared is in terms of the level of organisational autonomy in relation to specific terms of the employment contract. There are notable cross-national differences in such terms. Using a European Employment Law digest provided by Wragge & Co.,[1] I provide some example stipulations with regard to rights of termination and the use of fixed-term (non-permanent) contracts.

For example, with regard to termination, in the UK employees with one month to two year's service have a statutory notice period of one week. If they have more than two years service there is an additional one week's notice for each year of service up to a maximum of 12 weeks. The majority of employment contracts in practice stipulate more favourable notice provisions. In France there is no statutory minimum notice period for an employee who has less than six months of service; one month's notice period is required for an employee with six months to two years of service and two month's for an employee with at least two years of service. In Belgium the law does not state what constitutes adequate notice, except for white-collar employees whose gross annual salary does not exceed €28 580 (2008 value). If salaries are less than this then the employer must give at least three month's notice for each commenced five-year period of employment. If salaries are higher, then the notice period may not be less than the statutory minimum of three months for each commenced five-year period of employment. If no agreement exists on the length of the notice period, the matter is referred to the competent labour court, which usually takes into account the employee's age, seniority, function and remuneration. All salary and perks normally paid to the employee in return for the work performed may be considered, such as a 13th month, double vacation allowance, bonuses, private use of a company car, group insurance premiums and so forth. This leaves ample room for discretion and makes it almost impossible to calculate the length of the notice period with any real certainty.

With regard to the use of fixed-term contracts, in the UK since the introduction of legalisation in 2004, less favourable treatment on grounds of fixed-term status has been rendered unlawful and employees employed on successive fixed-term contracts for a period of four years or more become permanent employees. In Germany the 'normal' contract is not fixed. Special provisions allow fixed term contracts for a maximum of two years. Fixed term contracts are allowed only for objective reasons, such as for completion of a defined project, to fill the absence of another employee or if the type of service justifies the fixed term. In France, fixed-term employment contracts (*contrat à durée déterminée*) may only be used in a limited number of circumstances (for example to replace a temporarily absent employee, whose position is to be eliminated, who is working part-time on a temporary basis, about to join the company, meet a temporary increase in business and so forth). An employer may not enter into a fixed-term employment contract on a long-term basis to perform duties falling within the normal business operations of the company, and the law prohibits the use of fixed-term contracts to: replace an employee on strike; perform dangerous activities; fill a vacancy created by a temporary increase in business in a company where an employee was made redundant on economic grounds within the last six months (although there are rare exceptions to this prohibition); or fill a position previously occupied by a temporary employee or by an employee under a fixed-term contract. In Spain, as a consequence of the 'stability in employment principle', the general rule is that employees are hired through permanent employment contracts – nevertheless, Spain has one of the highest frequencies in Europe of short-term employment. Under Italian Labour Law, employment agreements represent an open-term contract. Fixed-term agreements can be entered into if justified by technical, organisational or production related reasons, or by the need to replace employees temporarily absent from work who are entitled to keep their job position.

As such examples begin to demonstrate, in order to understand how regulatory frameworks operate – and to provide research insight into the management of changes in the nature of employment contracts and the role of labour laws – we must position employment law, and the nature of employment contracts within this, in the broader setting of social law (i.e. how it is connected to social security law, human rights law and the law and practice as it relates to employment policy).

Employment law is just one of the means through which states or legal systems direct the operation of labour markets. Both the ILO's Employment Relationship Recommendation 2006 (No. 198) and the European Union's (2006) Green paper of the time on Modernising Labour Law to meet the challenges of the 21st Century argued that we need to move towards a complex and experimental regulatory framework to determine the personal scope of legislation.

In analysing the components that needed to be given comparative consideration, Freedland (2007: 4) developed a framework to compare and understand how the contractual aspects of individual work and employment relations across Europe can be seen from a legal perspective. He argued that in any one country there is a 'family of personal work contracts' (a different set of relations as established for standard employees, public officials, liberal professions, entrepreneurial workers, marginal workers and labour market entrants). Within this family, the standard employment contract numerically occurred most frequently but, by looking at the whole family of work contracts and in going beyond what might be inferred from legal systems and labour market administration arrangements, it becomes clear that the employment contract is not necessarily 'the supremely dominant paradigm' within any one country.

DISENTANGLING THE COMPONENT FACTORS WITHIN THE EMPLOYMENT CONTRACT

Comparative researchers, then, have to understand the institutional and cultural web that surrounds the employment relationship and its codification within employment contracts. However, they must also understand:

- the web of components within the contract and
- how these components also combine to create logics of action.

This is bringing new inter-disciplinary understandings into comparative analysis. Consider how the debate over the role of employment contracts and how they create labour market flexibility has led, indirectly, to a more sophisticated set of understandings about the comparative analysis of employment contracts. Interestingly for comparative HRM researchers, these insights are coming from comparative legal scholarship and from comparative economics (see also Chapter 2).

Botero et al. (2004) developed the 'legal origins' hypothesis with regard to employment law. Attention is given to the previously understated processes through which legal rules are formulated and the implicit operation of a regulatory culture and legal style. These represent 'institutional technologies for the social control of business' (p. 1345). The hypothesis argues that national regulatory systems are the product of the original legal family systems (English common law or the civil law in its French, German or Nordic variants) which, through means of colonialisation, military conquest or other form of legal transplantation, have come to dominate the majority of legal systems across the globe. Common law is associated with a system based on greater contractual autonomy and a system of self-regulation of contracts, and civil law with a system that limits the doctrine of judicial precedent through the application of more rigorous deductive logic and is based on more centralised state management of the economy.

This understanding has come to influence the analyses of the like of the World Bank, the OECD, the European Commission and the ILO. With regard to change in regulation, this hypothesis argues that systems based in common law are more likely to change and produce efficient rules for governance because they have an in-built 'adaptability channel' (the creation of new interpretations and incremental adjustments to the needs of the economy over time through case law that affords superior protection to shareholder and creditor rights) and a 'political channel' (whereby there are fewer opportunities for vested interests to extract rents via legal system, for example by denying entry into product markets or by requiring more formalised dispute-resolution procedures).

However, there are dangers in attempting to over-theorise these developments. Deakin et al. (2007) point out that the same effect might be created in one system through the rule of law and in another through the use of self-regulatory instruments or 'soft' law, and mandatory rules may not be applied in certain industries or regions, especially within developing countries. There may be 'functional equivalents' in both systems that lead to more similarity than at first meets the eye. Deakin et al. (2007: 134) created a longitudinal data set to track changes in labour law and related business law in France, Germany, the United States, the United Kingdom and India over the period 1970–2006, and on this basis point out that these two channels represent a somewhat 'over-stylised account' of how underlying principles of 'good faith' and 'capacity' are put into practice.

The analysis lends some qualified support to the legal origins hypothesis with regard to employment law (convergence in corporate governance has led to a rising protection of shareholder rights regardless of legal origin across all countries, and although creditor rights remain idiosyncratic they are not linked to common law or civil law systems).

In relation to labour law, there is clear divergence between the three common law systems (UK, United States and India) and between the two civil law variants (France and Germany). Germany, the United States and India have witnessed very little regulatory change (some small incremental change in Germany) but both in France and the UK, despite having contrasting civil and common law systems, change has been both marked and in different directions. The UK has moved from a system of substantial protection of labour interests in 1970 (although still below the aggregate level of France, Germany and India) through a rapid decline in the intensity of regulation in the 1980s and 1990s, with a moderate rise in regulation again as it incorporated EU legislation from the late 1990s onwards. In France, the Auroux laws in 1982 saw some increases in employee protection, with subsequent changes reversing this shift slightly, but not to pre-1982 levels.

Significant differences also exist across common law systems. In the United States, there is still weak regulation of labour laws, especially with regard to working time, where laws date back to federal legislation enacted in the 1930s. There is a rigid and unreformed system of industrial relations that provides for neither compulsory worker representation, as with European co-determination, nor a meaningful right to strike. The employment-at-will principle in individual employment law preserves an untouched managerial power to discipline, and even the common law principles of fairness based on the concept of mutual trust and confidence seen in the UK does not operate in the United States. Deakin et al. (2007: 153) conclude that whilst 'the legal origins hypothesis has important implications for policy in the area of labour law and industrial relations . . . not least because of the high standing it currently enjoys in certain official circles [they refer to the World Bank] . . . the debate is only just beginning. . . the explanations given for the empirical findings are not particularly secure'.

Better analysis, they argue, can only be based on institutional analysis over time. Given such variation, it is not surprising, then, that the ILO finds it difficult to formulate any normative basis on which to judge the success of any worker-protective employment legislation. They use the notion of a 'disguised' or 'ambiguous' employment relationship – disguised by the impact of legislation outside employment legislation or ambiguous with regard to whether atypical categories of work fall within the remit of the employment contract – to explain how contiguous social developments over time can lead to the failure or distortion of anticipated effects.

HOURS OF WORK AND INTERNATIONAL STANDARDS ACROSS EMPLOYMENT CONTRACTS

Picking up on the notion of disguised and ambiguous employment contracts, much attention has been given to aspects of the employment contract that are associated with issues of national and cross-national policy interest. I use the issue of work hours as an example. The ILO has always considered this aspect of employment contracts of vital importance in standard setting for contracts. So too has the Organisation for Economic Co-operation and Development (OECD) and the World Bank. The EU has also issued several directives relating to working hours.

The ILO (2005) studied existing limits on normal daily and weekly hours of work in 177 countries throughout the world, as well as the changes to these limits over the last 20 years. They noted that comparative analysis has to make sense of the growing diversification, decentralisation and individualisation of the hours that people work. New forms of employment, such as part-time working, have gained ground. The ILO notes that in some countries working time has been reduced in order to create jobs, while in others it has been extended. Working time is no longer automatically organised on a weekly or annual basis, with a more flexible approach being adopted. For an increasing number of employees, the length of the working day and week is becoming a variable or flexible feature of employment, influenced primarily by the pattern of demand confronting the firms in which they work. Therefore the notion that there is a 'standard' working week is giving way to schemes of hours averaged over longer intervals of time.

The process of globalisation and the resulting intensification of competition, the associated development in information and communications technologies, and new patterns of consumer demand for goods and services in the '24-hour economy' have had a large impact on production methods and work organisation. The following quote shows how analysis of developments within employment contracts with regard to working time have to be understood in their broader context (International Labour Organization, 2005: 8–9):

> Enterprise strategies [have evolved] such as new methods of flexible production (just-in-time, lean production, etc.) and a much more flexible organisation of work, including working time. . . From the perspective of workers, there have been profound demographic changes, particularly the increasing entry of women into the paid labour market and the resulting increased feminisation of the labour force; the related shift from the single 'male breadwinner' household to dual-earner households; and a growing concern over the quality of working life, particularly in the industrialized world. . . reflected in a variety of working time arrangements which vary from conventional full-time, permanent, weekday work in terms of either their duration and/or timing: part-time work, flexitime and 'time banking' accounts in which workers can credit or debit their hours just like money in a bank, working 'on call' (as and when needed), and the averaging of working time over periods of up to a year.

Cross-national comparison of employment contracts, then, with regard even to one issue such as working time, has to take into account a number of different factors:

1. Different meaning that may be given to 'hours of work' and the work components that constitute this. There may be contrasting interpretations given to 'normal hours of work' (those stipulated in laws or regulations, collective agreements or arbitral awards, or establishments' rules or customs) as being expected to be spent on work activities during a reference period such as one day or one week.
2. Similarly there are differences of interpretation given to the 'hours actually worked' (the hours that workers actually spend on work activities during a specified reference period). For example, in relation to part-time work, the phrase in the ILO Convention 'whose normal hours of work are less than those of comparable full-time

workers' is interpreted differently according to national laws. In France a person working up to four-fifths of normal hours of work is considered part time. In Spain a part-time worker is one who works up to two-thirds of the hours specified by collective agreement or of the hours normally worked in the enterprise. In Ireland and the UK a person is considered to work part time if they work less than 30 hours a week. To understand differences in working hours, attention has to be given to a range of components including productive time, time spent on ancillary activities, unproductive time, and resting time.

3. The difference between statutory limits with respect to normal working hours in a given country and the extent to which these reflect the hours actually worked. With regard to hours of work, ILO data for 2008 show that the average hours worked across all employees per week range from 30.4 hours in Canada (measures hours paid for), 34.4 hours in Norway (measures hours actually worked), 34.5 hours in Australia, 34.6 hours in Italy, 34.7 hours in Spain, 35 hours in France, 36.1 hours in Ireland and Sweden, 36.3 hours in Finland, 39.8 Hours in Poland, 40.1 hours in Greece, 40.6 hours in Chile, 40.7 hours in Japan, 44.5 in Mexico, 46.3 in Singapore (hours paid for), 46.9 in Costa Rica, 48 in Paraguay, 49.7 hours in Turkey and 53.1 in Peru (hours paid for).

4. Variations of hours worked within a country across sectors and occupations. In Austria around the average hours worked of 34.3 hours, figures vary from 29 hours in education, to 33.1 hours in wholesale and retail trade (which includes repair of motor vehicles, motorcycles and personal and household goods), to 35.3 hours in manufacturing. In France average hours are 37.5, but in manufacturing they are 37.4 hours and in hotels 40.3 hours. In Germany there is relatively little variation across sectors, with manufacturing hours having a typical 38.4 hours. In the United States labour-related establishment surveys show that hours actually worked average 33.6, but these vary massively from 25.4 hours in hotels and restaurants to 45.3 in mining and quarrying. Gender variations are also marked, with female average hours being 34.4 hours in Japan, 29.2 hours in Australia, 29.4 hours in Austria, 29.8 hours in Italy, 31.3 hours in Finland, 33 hours in Sweden, 34.3 hours in Finland, 36.4 hours in France, 36.7 hours in Greece, 37.2 hours in Poland, generally, of course, in inverse correlation with the proportion of female part-time work.

5. Arrangements for the variable distribution of working hours, where methods of organising working time can allow for its adjustment in accordance with variations in the volume of an undertaking's activities over a certain period.

6. The concept and types of 'exceptions' that employers can make to adjust work hours.
7. Policies concerning hours of work, such as measures for the progressive reduction of hours of work, and whether it is used to achieve the goal of either creating additional workplaces; or achieving a balance between the work and family lives of employees.
8. Working-time arrangements as they differ from the standard full-time working week, such as for part-time work, compressed work-weeks, staggered working-time arrangements, variable daily shift lengths, annualised working hours, flexitime, on-call work, the ability of workers to influence the length and arrangement of their working hours.
9. Measures of enforcement, such as notification of hours of work and rest, inspections and penalties.
10. Consultation processes of employers' and workers' organisations.

All of this makes comparisons of employment contracts extremely difficult. In practice, working time laws and policies have a limited influence on actual working hours, especially in developing economies, and their legislation with regard to maximum weekly hours, overtime payments, exceptions and exemptions, and informal employment. In these economies the influence of wages on working hours is particularly strong. Wages undermine statutory hours limits, with long working hours and overtime work often used to compensate workers for low wages.

USING THE DETAIL OF EMPLOYMENT CONTRACTS TO MAKE COMPARATIVE EMPLOYMENT POLICY DISTINCTIONS

Of more value, perhaps, are attempts to use comparative analyses of working time to draw high-level policy distinctions. Again, using the work of the ILO as an example, consideration has been given to issues such as:

- healthy working time (the absence of undermining factors that reinforce long work hours, such as wages);
- family-friendly working time (preserving sufficient time to combine paid work with family and domestic obligations, such as childcare and elder care);
- gender equality (work–family reconciliation measures to ensure gender equality and the avoidance of disproportionate responsibility for caring and domestic obligations);

- productive working time (the extent to which employment contracts provide incentives for firms to modernise their working time arrangements, and to invest in improving their technology and enhancing the skills of their workers); and
- levels of choice and influence over working time (the extent to which contracts advance the influence that workers have on their work schedules and the degree of choice they have over how they divide their time).

I use recent work on the relative productivity of the United States versus Europe to exemplify this type of research. Causa (2008) recently engaged with the 'are Europeans lazy or Americans crazy?' debate in which economists, noting that gaps in income per capita between the two are largely accounted for by differences in levels of labour utilisation measured by hours worked per person, look at the outcome of the employment relationship through its impact on labour utilisation either in terms of employment participation (the extensive margin) and hours worked by individuals (the intensive margin). Much previous work, in focusing on the hours worked per capita (the average per individual), conflates these two separate margins. Previously, the primary determinants of hours worked per capita have been found to be marginal taxation policies, and to some extent both levels of union density (via their support for work-sharing arrangements in declining industries) and levels of within-skill wage inequalities where the returns on working hours becomes greater the longer the hours. In practice 'it is difficult to disentangle the separate influences on incentives, institutions and policy, and to separate these factors from cultural and other fixed factors' (Causa, 2008: 8). Moreover, 'the literature on the impact of working-time regulations has focused on the consequences, within countries, of domestic reforms in the relevant legislation. One important finding is that the effect of regulations on employees' working time schedules are extremely mixed' (Skuterud, 2007). Causa (2008: 37) notes that these findings are 'heterogeneous – and even opposite – across genders, occupations, firm sizes, and sectors'. Moreover, 'the impact of working-time regulations governing weekly normal hours decreases with education levels, suggesting that limitations are not binding for workers at the high end of the earnings/education distribution (for example, managers and academics), but are important for low and medium-educated employees' (Causa, 2008, p. 39).

Causa (2008) carried out an investigation for the OECD to determine how policy determinants (including taxation, working time regulation and other labour and product market policies) explained cross-country differences in the hours worked. Policies and institutions were found to have different impacts on working hours for men and for women. Working time regulations had a significant impact on the hours actually worked by men (depending on level of education). High marginal taxes created a disincentive to work longer hours for women, but this had no impact on the hours worked by men. Other labour market policies, such as stringent employment protection of workers on regular employment contracts, and attempts to restrain competition in product markets, had a negative impact on the hours worked by men over and above their impact also on employment levels. However, it is important to note that 'an important proportion of the cross-country variation remains country specific, time invariant, and unexplained' (Causa, 2008: 52), again signaling the need for more comprehensive frameworks that capture the outcomes of employment relationship.

THE TWO DOMINANT PARADIGMS: CULTURAL AND INSTITUTIONAL EXPLANATIONS OF THE FACTORS THAT SURROUND THE EMPLOYMENT CONTRACT

What, then, can be said about comparative analysis of employment contracts? Since the earliest attempts to create comparative frameworks to understand the employment contract, there have been a series of increasingly complex and inclusive examinations of the factors involved. Explanation of international differences in the employment relationship – and the contract within it – tends to rely on one of two paradigms (Buck & Shahrim, 2005; Festing et al., 2007; Parboteeah & Cullen, 2003):

1. Cultural explanations (see Chapter 3), which highlight the role of historically determined notions that are accepted by groups of individuals who share some common historical experience about what is good, right and desirable.
2. Institutional explanations (see chapter 2), which highlight the role of social structures (laws that provide enforcement, educational and training systems that shape socialisation, and economic systems that shape incentives) that help individuals make sense of, and in turn make decisions about, work that will be deemed legitimate, reasonable and appropriate.

Increasingly, analyses draw upon complex combinations of these two sets of factors. Separation of the two (in practice there tend to be different communities of researchers coming from each tradition, and different literatures) is in practice unrealistic. To exemplify this, Sparrow (2009) explored the narratives around institutional reforms in relation to the rewards elements of employments contracts as triggered by the Kostenkrise debate in Germany and the Risutora process in Japan.

In Germany the debate about national competitiveness focused on subsequent adjustments to the tarifverträge (the conventional contracts that covered wage rates, bonuses and sick pay, training, part-time work, work hours and levels of job security). These regulated German pay and compensation negotiations and were traditionally negotiated across employers within an industrial sector. Labour market reforms throughout the late 1990s until the mid 2000s led to growth in 'mini-jobs' (part-time posts paying no more than €400 a month regardless of work hours), a rise in the proportion of German workers earning 'low pay', agreements to exceptions from industry-wide wage deals and more acceptance of pay for performance, and more idiosyncratic patterns of wage negotiation.

In Japan the Risutora process focused attention on five HRM issues: the introduction of performance based career and compensation standards; open feedback systems regarding performance evaluation; more differentiated employment tracks between core, specialist and flexible employment groups; externalisation of much corporate welfare; and non-discriminatory hiring practices. This has been associated with more active involvement in wage system management by individual firms, reducing the level of overtime payments, changes in internal labour markets with more employee transfers between companies, reforms to arrangements for employee and role grading systems, job and performance evaluation, and changes in labour laws to enable consideration of performance-based pay systems.

The problem for researchers was that the two narratives showed that comparative analysis of employment contracts – as they related to the rewards system – was not possible without understanding the wage system within its broader social contract. A broad range of factors were in fact involved in these reform processes, and without insight into the interplay between these factors and the contractual detail, the impact of changes in the contract could be misjudged. Bearing in mind that the analysis focused on just one element of contracts (as they related to rewards) it was still necessary to explain the surrounding institutional web in terms of the regulatory arrangements for cross-firm and within-firm wage negotiations, the density and tightness of such arrangements, their scope across flexibility elements (of function, reward, time, security), their inclusion of monetary and non-monetary elements, and the quality of regulatory enforcement.

It was also evident that different, but functionally equivalent, institutional solutions could be used to produce the same behavioural consequences from contractual changes. However, this required insight into the power that employees had in the employment relationship and also the impacts of the benefits system and corporate taxation policies on incentives. There were a number of factors internal to the firm that mitigated the contractual changes, such as the level of differentiation in skills levels across the hierarchy, the performance incentives that were inherent in the career and compensation systems, whether there was a reliance on stock or flow pay progression systems, and the role of job versus personal factors in determining pay progression and employee value. The institutional processes that flowed from legal reform were in turn blunted or sharpened by competences internal to organisations (the competences needed to manage change in rewards processes) such as job analysis and job evaluation, line management performance management skills, risk avoidance behaviour, and the channels for and quality of performance feedback.

Finally, behaviour was influenced through the social contract, as evidenced through the trade-offs individuals made between security and commitment, income inequalities over their careers and their preferred lifetime earnings patterns, and differences in social access to different qualities of employment experience.

The inter-dependence of external institutional and cultural factors, the effect of both these webs, and how they impact employee and employer logics of action, is then often only really understood when you attempt to change the perceived logic of action.

CONCLUSION: HOW BROAD SHOULD OUR ANALYTICAL FRAMEWORKS BE?

So, what should we conclude from this analysis? The underlying message is that, to borrow a distinction used in the field of organisational learning and HRM strategy (Henderson & Clark, 1990), comparative researchers need both component knowledge (knowledge of the parts rather than the whole) and architectural knowledge (the shared understanding of the interconnection of all components, or how things fit together). This chapter started by conveying increasingly detailed component knowledge (in relation to the legal underpinnings of the employment contract and differences in its regulation) and has moved to increasingly broad and integrative examples of understanding comparative issues in their examination.

Commentators coming from a national employment model perspective exemplify an architectural perspective. For them, any analysis of the employment contract and 'even the individualised decisions made by actors pursuing their own interests are embedded in and shaped by the institutional and social environment' (Bosch et al., 2007: 253). These institutions embody social values and the historical compromises made by different actors in relation to employment conditions. 'An employment contract is necessarily incomplete, since the actual performance required and the rewards offered are constantly subject to new decisions after the contract has been concluded' (Bosch et al., 2007: 254). There is always debate as to how broad a set of institutional arrangements one must consider for it still to be of path relevance to the phenomenon under study – in this instance the nature of employment contracts.

The national employment model school perhaps takes the broadest view, arguing that any one component (such as the employment contract) can only be seen and understood as it operates in relation to all of the societal institutions that produce, and reproduce, labour. This means not only elements of the industrial relations and production systems, but also 'the multiplicity of institutions influencing labour supply, utilisation and demand in a given country' (Bosch et al., 2007: 254), i.e. the family, educational, training and social security systems as well. Under what became known as the varieties of capitalism approach, a number of typologies have been created as analytical tools that highlight major institutional similarities or points of difference, based on the use of a series of high-profile reference countries.

Bosch et al. (2007), reviewing the institutional theories examined in Chapter 2, argue that what is needed now is the development of further hybrid typologies that will facilitate a 'more subtle understanding of the different employment and social outcomes of various combinations of production, employment and welfare regimes, in particular different employment levels and structures' (p. 260). I would place employment contracts within employment structures.

Because of the many internal pressures to reform welfare and employment regimes (largely as a result of demographic pressures such as the ageing and feminisation of the economically active population), and external pressures (through globalisation, developments in technologies of service and production, new forms of governance, and the hard and soft policies of supra-national organisations such as the EU, the OECD, World Trade Organization and the World Bank) we need to develop more insightful analytical frameworks. For Bosch et al. (2007) the primary need is to better understand and differentiate:

- the potential for creative adaptation to a changing environment;
- how competing systems have the capacity to withstand (or not) external pressures or to mobilise resources for efficient change;

- how country-specific political, economic and social factors may be used to explain the success or otherwise of such changes;
- how (sadly seen only very rarely) preventive strategies and models of employment relationship may be used, as opposed to changes dictated by periodic crises in employment models, as is being experienced in the world today; and
- how in an age of globalisation nations may prosper by building on their institutional differences rather than by just becoming more similar.

The question is, how deep and cross-disciplinary must our component knowledge be, and how broad and integrative must our architectural knowledge be, in order to ensure balanced and insightful analysis? It has been argued that although broad-brush in nature, early commentary on country differences did had some value, notably by alerting researchers to differences in terms of the:

- levels of organisational autonomy, voluntarism, and state abstention from the employment relationship (the range of employee-organisation interactions that have the force of law),
- scope of activity that is considered to represent a basic 'floor of rights' (the rights of an individual in matters as varied as unfair dismissal, redundancy, equal opportunities, maternity leave, employment rights for the disabled, confidentiality of computerised data, and health and safety at work),
- level of structural support that exists for collective bargaining (the legal mechanisms serving to legitimise principles of collectivism and pluralism, the regulation and scrutiny placed over internal trades unions, the circumscription of organisational rights, union membership agreements, the ability of unions to obtain funds, the conduct of union-member relations), and
- restrictions or boundaries placed around what is deemed to be lawful action within the employment relationship (such as with respect to the calling of industrial conflict, the direction of actions, rights to picket, etc.).

Since these early stipulations, as this chapter demonstrates, the complexity of insight has developed at a rapid pace.

A series of cross-cultural and psychological dynamics are now being considered as researchers attempt to understand behaviour surrounding the implicit, or psychological, contract in a comparative context. This work shows that there are good reasons to assume that many of the mechanisms of the psychological contract operate differently across cultures and countries. Moreover, as static conceptualisations of culture and indeed of the psychological contract within cultures become increasingly inappropriate, comparative researchers will be required to adopt more innovative research methods and frames of analysis. In addition to the traditional cultural and institutional perspectives outlined throughout the chapter, important contextual and temporal factors will become important during the forthcoming period of globalisation and change. The overlap between the study of national culture, and that of national and generational identities, as they both impact behaviour within the employment contract, needs to be investigated. We shall see more examination of the interplay between geography and generation, and an extension of study of generational culture into a more informed cross-national understanding of generational effects on employment relationship behaviour.

In examining research on the formal employment contract, too, the thrust of the analysis has been to show that there are immense difficulties both in interpreting official statistics, and more importantly in understanding the meaning of the resultant variations in employment contract and classification of employees. Without a comparative understanding of the workings of the surrounding legal system, examination of even codified rights becomes almost meaningless. Given the variations that exist, it is difficult to formulate any normative basis on which to judge the success of any employment legislation across countries. In practice, within countries the employment relationship is disguised and ambiguous – disguised by the impact of multiple forms of legislation and legislation outside employment legislation and ambiguous with regard to how categories of work fall within the remit of the employment contract. Therefore we must understand how regulatory frameworks operate and – in order to provide research insight into the management of changes in the nature of employment contracts and the role of labour laws in relation to this – we must position employment law and the nature of employment contracts within the broader setting of social law. Finally, comparative research into employment contracts must understand how these components combine to create logics of action. This requires new inter-disciplinary understandings, but also comparative analysis based on institutional analysis over time. Only then can we explain, in a comparative context, how contiguous social developments over time lead to successful change in, or the failure or distortion of, changes in employment contracts and planned or anticipated effects on the employment relationship.

NOTE

1. See: http://www.wragge.com/eelc_3500.asp.

REFERENCES

Bandura, A. 2002. Social cognitive theory in cultural context. *Applied Psychology: An International Review*, **51**(2): 269–290.
Bosch, G., Rubery, J. & Lehndorff, S. 2007. European employment models under pressure to change. *International Labor Review*, **146**(3–4): 253–277.
Botero, J. C., Djankov, S., La Porta, R., Lopez-de-Salanes, F. & Shleifer, A. 2004. The regulation of labor. *Quarterly Journal of Economics*, **119**(4): 1339–1382.
Buck, T. & Shahrim, A. 2005. The translation of corporate governance changes across national cultures: the case of Germany. *Journal of International Business Studies*, **36**(1): 42–61.
Causa, O. 2008. Explaining differences in hours worked among OECD Countries: an empirical analysis. OECD Economics Department Working Papers, No. 596. Paris: OECD.
Deakin, S., Lele, P. & Siems, M. 2007. The evolution of labour law: calibrating and comparing regulatory regimes. *International Labor Review*, **146**(3–4): 133–162.
Egri, C. P. & Ralston, D. A. 2004. Generation cohorts and personal values: a comparison of China and the US. *Organization Science*, **15**(2): 210–220.
Erez, M. & Gati, E. 2004. A dynamic, multi-level model of culture: from the micro level of the individual to the macro level of a global culture. *Applied Psychology: An International Review*, **53**(4): 583–598.
Festing, M., Eidems, J. & Royer, S. 2007. Strategic issues and local constraints in transnational compensation strategies: an analysis of cultural, institutional and political influences. *European Management Journal*, **25**(2): 118–131.
Fisher, R., Ferreira, M. C., Assmar, M. L., Redford, P. & Harb, C. 2005. Organizational behaviour across cultures: theoretical and methodological issues for developing multi-level frameworks involving culture. *International Journal of Cross Cultural Management*, **5**(1): 27–48.
Freedland, M. 2007. Application of labour and employment law beyond the contract of employment. *International Labor Review*, **146**(1–2): 3–20.
Henderson, R. M. & Clark, K. B. 1990. Architectural innovation: the reconfiguration of existing product technologies and the failure of established firms. *Administrative Science Quarterly*, **35**: 9–30.
International Labour Organization (ILO). 2005. Report III (Part 1B) General survey of the reports concerning the Hours of Work (Industry) Convention, 1919 (No. 1), and the Hours of Work (Commerce and Offices) Convention, 1930 (No. 30). Geneva: ILO.
Ostroff, C. & Bowen, D. E. 2000. Moving HR to a higher level. HR practices and organizational effectiveness. In K. J. Klein & S. W. J. Kozlowski (eds), *Multilevel Theory, Research and Methods in Organizational Psychology*. San Francisco: Jossey-Bass, pp. 211–266.
Parboteeah, K. P. & Cullen, J. B. 2003. Social institutions and work centrality: explorations beyond national culture. *Organization Science*, **14**(2): 137–148.
Pieper, R. 1990. *Human Resource Management: An International Comparison*. Berlin: Walter de Gruyter.
Rousseau, D. M. 1990. New hire perceptions of their own and their employer's obligations: a study of psychological contracts. *Journal of Organizational Behavior*, **11**(5): 389–400.
Rousseau, D. M. 1995. *Psychological Contracts in Organizations: Understanding Written and Unwritten Agreements*. London: Sage Publications.
Rousseau, D. M. & Schalk, R. 2000. *Psychological Contracts in Employment: Cross-national Perspectives*. Thousand Oaks, CA: Sage Publications.

Sackmann, S. A. & Phillips, M. E. 2004. Contextual influences on culture research: shifting assumptions for new workplace realities. *International Journal of Cross Cultural Management*, **4**(3): 370–390.

Skuterud, M. 2007. Identifying the potential of work sharing as a job creation strategy. *Journal of Labor Economics*, **25**(2): 265–287.

Snape, R. 1999. Legal regulation of employment. In G. Hollinshead, P. Nicholls & S. Tailby (eds), *Employee Relations*. London: Financial Times/Pitman.

Sparrow, P. R. 1996. Careers and the psychological contract: understanding the European context. *The European Journal of Work and Organizational Psychology*, **5**(4): 479–500.

Sparrow, P. R. 1998. Re-appraising psychological contracting: lessons for employee development from cross-cultural and occupational psychology research. *International Studies of Management and Organisation*, **28**(1): 30–63.

Sparrow, P. R. 2006. International management: some key challenges for industrial and organizational psychology. *International Review of Industrial and Organizational Psychology*, **21**: 189–266.

Sparrow, P. R. 2009. International reward management. In G. White & J. Drucker (eds), *Reward Management: A Critical Text*. London: Routledge, pp. 233–257.

Sparrow, P. R. & Hiltrop, J. M. 1997. Redefining the field of European human resource management: a battle between national mindsets and forces of business transition. *Human Resource Management*, **36**(2): 201–219.

Thomas, D. C., Au, K. & Ravlin, E. C. 2003. Cultural variation and the psychological contract. *Journal of Organizational Behavior*, **24**(5): 451–462.

Tipton, F. B. 2009. Modeling national identities and cultural change: the Western European, Japanese and United States experiences compared. *International Journal of Cross Cultural Management*, **9**(2): 145–168.

Tsui, A. & Wang, D. 2002. Employment relationships from the employer's perspective: current research and future directions. *International Review of Industrial and Organizational Psychology*, **17**: 77-114.

Whitley, R. D. 1992. *European Business Systems: Firms and Markets In Their National Contexts*. London: Sage Publications.

13 Careers: a country-comparative view
Mila Lazarova, Françoise Dany and Wolfgang Mayrhofer

In this chapter, we describe the state of comparative research on individual careers and organisational career management activities. This is an under-developed but growing area of inquiry. There is an increasing number of studies that are still exploring basic issues such as the application and relevance of career-related constructs across various national, institutional or cultural contexts but we are not yet at a stage where a coherent body of comparative research has taken shape. Given the rather 'disjointed' state of our knowledge at this point, our objective is not a review of all that has been published to date but rather a critical analysis of the field. Due to space limitations, we include only a few relevant examples to illustrate our points.

The chapter is organised as follows. We first clarify the key concepts in two related areas of research, i.e. careers from an individual standpoint and career management from the organisational standpoint. We then provide an overview of studies that explicitly address individual careers and career management activities across national/cultural contexts. In a final step, we present insights from two large-scale comparative projects with direct relevance to career studies, one looking at careers from an individual perspective and one investigating, among others, career management-related HRM practices.

DEFINITIONS AND BACKGROUND

Careers: The Individual Perspective

Much of the current research on careers is strongly influenced by the US view that focuses on the subjective dimension of careers. In that perspective, career is defined as the evolving sequence of a person's work experience over time (Arthur et al., 1989: 8). Following the steps of the Chicago School (Hughes, 1958), numerous scholars refuse to reduce careers to the paths of those benefiting from hierarchical advancements within organisations. Putting to the fore that a career mainly refers to the meanings individuals attribute to their situations, they claim that career should not been equated to a series of 'objective' promotions. Rather, in addition to vertical, it can involve horizontal or even radial movements (Schein, 1971). A career move does not need to be a positive experience nor should it involve change in occupation. Plateauing should not be considered to represent experiencing a glass ceiling; for instance, many professionals grow within their occupation without experiencing any job changes. Researchers have also suggested considering as career moves even the experiences of parents shifting from one job to another in order to make a living, while their main concern is to raise their children.

In a context where careers are less linear and less predictable, helping everyone to achieve professional goals and/or find a balance between professional and personal life becomes a key priority. The consequence is a growing number of scholars standing against every ideological approach that overlooks the differences regarding individual expectations and constraints towards careers. The very fact that individuals have personal career orientations, or anchors (Derr, 1986; Schein, 1990), explains the fact that careers have been increasingly viewed as belonging to individuals. Besides noting that individuals are likely to hold different career orientations due to differences in competencies and personality as well as differences in cycles of their biological life and their careers, the individually driven view of careers also builds on the assumption that in the current environment individuals have more opportunities to act as sculptors rather than as sculptures (Alvarez, 2000; Bell & Staw, 1989), even if they are not aware of such opportunities.

Both the literature dedicated to the boundaryless career (Arthur & Rousseau, 1996a) and research on the shift from a relational to a transactional employment relationship (Rousseau & Schalk, 2000) suggest that there is a need to break away from the tendency to restrict a career to 'a succession of related jobs, arranged in a hierarchy of prestige, through which persons move in an ordered more or less predictable sequence' (Wilensky, 1961: 523). Because of the claim that employers themselves admit that it is no longer possible for them to promise anyone an organisational career, the boundaryless career is now assumed to be prototypical rather than atypical (Arthur, 1994). From that perspective, individuals are no longer supposed to develop specific relationships with their employers. Instead, according to the metaphors introduced by the new careers literature, they should act as 'career capitalists' (Inkson & Arthur, 2001) and develop 'intelligent careers' (Arthur et al., 1995). Careers are viewed as the result of individual decisions and organisations are no longer described as being in charge of career management. They are just settings that offer specific experiences on which individuals must build to enhance their career capital.

We should note here that while now established, the boundaryless career perspective has been under increased criticism, even within the United States where it originated. Criticism has been directed at the individualistic bias inherent in the perspective, which talks about what individual actors gain but rarely discusses dangers and drawbacks for the individual, group, organisation or larger community. Its broad relevance has also been questioned, as it applies primarily to professional workers in select industries, and so has its overly optimistic stance. The literature tends to highlight and celebrate those that benefit from boundaryless careers but largely ignores those whose job security diminishes as a result to a shift to boundaryless careers (Cadin et al., 2000; Dany, 2003; Dany et al., 2003; Guest, 2004; Mallon, 1998; Pringle & Mallon, 2003; Zeitz et al., 2009).

Career Management: The Organisational Perspective

Even if one takes for granted the claims about the dominance of the individual drivers of career and subjective definitions of career success, we should recognise that individuals are not the only party that holds expectations regarding careers. Employers, too, are interested in some forms of 'steering' (if not exactly 'managing') the careers of their employees over time. Even though individuals may feel obliged to take care of their careers by themselves, research has shown that at least some of them still appreciate having career management programmes offered by their employers (Dany, 2003). In other words, the arguments in favour of an individually driven view of career do not imply the end of career management. Both individual and organisational decisions still shape careers. Yet, this mutual interaction can operate in very different ways depending on a multitude of circumstances.

Career management is one of the core elements of HRM and usually linked to training and development as one of the major functions of the HRM department (see, e.g. Devanna et al., 1984). At the individual level it comprises initiatives such as personal career development, support during career transitions or career coaching and at the organisational level it refers to issues such as organisational career trajectories, promotion criteria or the existence of support programmes for specific employee groups such as high potentials or minorities.

Several main goals continue to justify employers' commitment to career management (Greenhaus et al., 2010: 382ff.). The most important rationale involves employee development. Transferring employees across jobs or locations enhances their understanding of how their company operates, helps them build important professional skills and develops their capability to navigate new situations. From an individual standpoint, such transfers (and the resulting idiosyncratic career paths) are important vis à vis both internal and external employability. From an organisational standpoint, they offer greater flexibility. Career management programmes are not only a tool in the 'war for talent' (in particular, through the development of high flyers), but also make organisational exits easier or help organisations avoid redundancies altogether. A related objective of career management is succession planning (Rothwell et al., 2005), which has retained its salience even in circumstances that make it difficult for organisations to make any firm promises regarding long-term careers. Besides contributing to achieving fit between companies' needs and their human resources, career management can also be used to influence employee attitudes and behaviour. For example, career management programmes can be used to sustain employee motivation and commitment and decrease turnover by promoting employees to higher status positions or by assigning them to projects that increase their employability, highlight new interesting aspects of their jobs or that allow them to lead more balanced lives. By matching employees' interests and capabilities with organisational opportunities, career management programmes can help an organisation achieve a balance between individual career needs and the company's workforce needs.

Careers and Career Management Across Countries and Cultures

As in much of management research, the majority of published studies on careers and career development originate in the United States and closely reflect elements of specific cultural values and institutional arrangements common to the industrialised Western democracies (Peiperl & Gunz, 2007). This is hardly surprising. Careers do not develop in a vacuum but are bound by a larger context. The concepts of career and core career attributes are influenced by the social, economic, cultural and institutional environment (Byars-Winston & Fouad, 2006; Inkson et al., 2007; Khapova & Korotov, 2007; Mayrhofer et al., 2007).

In terms of institutional influences, some key factors that determine what career patterns are possible – and which of those are more or less common – across different countries include educational systems, regulation of labour markets, prevalent organisational structures ('traditional' bureaucratic and hierarchical organisations or 'new' flat and project-based organisations), levels of economic and technological development, unemployment levels, importance of social class, division of labour, gender egalitarianism, protection of employees' rights and broader regulation of industrial relations (Byars-Winston & Fouad, 2006; Inkson et al., 2007; Khapova & Korotov, 2007; Mayrhofer et al., 2007). With regards to culture values, career research often assumes individualistic values, autonomous personal achievement orientation, independent construal of the self, rational and linear problem-solving approaches (Byars-Winston & Fouad, 2006; Fouad & Arbona, 1994; Hartung, 2002; Thomas & Inkson, 2007). However, both role salience and role values differ across cultures (Hartung, 2002). Furthermore, variations in cultural values have long been recognised (e.g. Hofstede, 2001; Schwartz, 2006; Triandis et al., 1988; Trompenaars & Hampden-Turner, 2004). Taking Hofstede's framework as a starting point, Thomas and Inkson (2007) stipulate that individualism/collectivism influences the degree to which people feel they are responsible for their actions, the extent to which they strive for independence and individual rewards, feel loyalty to and are ready to subject their personal interests to those of their extended family and community. Individualism and collectivism also influence the perceptions of psychological contracts perceived by managers (see also Sparrow, 1996). Power distance influences the beliefs of whether it is appropriate for everyone to strive to reach the top of the organisational hierarchy. Uncertainty avoidance impacts the acceptance of formal procedures and roles and preferences for stability. Masculinity/femininity is closely related to accepted definitions of success – advancement or maintaining harmonious relationships with others. Beyond accounting for the impact of national culture values, researchers have noted that there is sufficient diversity within many nations that requires that differences across ethnic groups be acknowledged and studied purposefully (Byars-Winston & Fouad, 2006; Fouad, 1993; Fouad & Arbona, 1994).

While the importance of context and the value of investigating similarities and differences in careers and career management across national borders was recognised decades ago (e.g. Schein, 1984), research on such issues is still in its infancy. A recent review of the field concluded that career research has been characterised by parochial theoretical development and a fragmented and incoherent research framework (see Tams & Arthur, 2007; Thomas & Inkson, 2007; Dany et al., 2011). While we generally agree with this assessment, it must be pointed out that the number of 'international' career studies has been on the rise in the last decade. Several streams of research can be identified (Tams & Arthur, 2007; Thomas & Inkson, 2007).

Oldest and most numerous (yet least relevant to comparative HRM) are the studies on managing the career paths of *expatriate employees* across postings in different countries. Second, recently research has begun investigating *the impact of globalisation* on careers (e.g. careers of migrant workers, global interdependencies affecting careers). The third group, most relevant to comparative research, includes studies of *careers across cultures.* The literature contains examples of both emic and etic approaches. Some researchers take the path of indigenous research and explore how careers develop and change in specific cultural and institutional settings (e.g. Kato & Suzuki, 2006, on careers in Japan). Others take an established framework (typically one that originates in the United States) and apply it to a new environment, discussing similarities and differences found along the way (for example, see the study on careers and changing career patterns in Russia, Khapova & Korotov, 2007). There are also comparative studies that collect data on careers from matched samples across different countries. One recent example is Malach-Pines & Kaspi-Baruch's (2008) study on whether career-related attitudes differ across seven countries. Finally, Thomas and Inkson (2007) identify a related stream, what they call *intercultural research* – research that 'seeks to understand the interactions between culturally different actors and considers the culture of all parties in the interaction, as well as contextual explanations for observed similarities and differences' (p. 459). They suggest that this is an important direction for careers research but so far no study can be clearly defined as truly intercultural.

A review of published research suggests that the larger part of international studies focus on comparing experiences of individuals rather than on comparing organisational approaches to career management. This is likely to be a reflection of the emphasis on conceptualising careers at an individual level rather than as an organisational construct. This is very much in line with recent trends in (US) research on careers as 'owned' by individuals (e.g. boundaryless careers, renewed interest in protean careers). These trends have dominated the field at a time when international research on careers has been gaining traction and have undoubtedly influenced the issues being studied. The international transferability of the boundaryless careers concept has been successfully questioned based on arguments that environmental conditions and institutional arrangements in many countries do not reflect flexible economies with permeable boundaries and dynamic organisational structures such as the one in the United States where the construct originated (e.g. Dany, 2003; Kelly et al., 2003; Pringle & Mallon, 2003; Thomas & Inkson, 2007).

Research has provided strong evidence that there are differences in both how individuals think about their careers and in how organisations approach career management across national borders. For example, Malach-Pines and Kaspi-Baruch (2008) examined how several career attitudes (e.g. factors and individuals that influence career choice, expectations from an MBA degree, work values, and traditional and protean career attitudes) and found differences across samples of male and female students from Cyprus, Hungary, India, Israel, Turkey, the United

Kingdom and the United States. The study found strong and consistent evidence for cross-national differences and only limited evidence for gender differences. In another example, Gerpott et al. (1988) found differences in management career orientation in Germany, the UK and the United States and attributed them to differences in R&D and educational systems across countries and to different attitudes towards the concept of professionalism. Similarly, in a more recent study Hansen and Willcox (1997) commented on how career norms in Germany differ from those in the United States due to the different emphasis on technical and subject matter specialisation versus general specialisation and social skills.

Research has also investigated whether career concepts translate across cultures and has found that such translations are imperfect, at best. Thus, Khapova and Korotov (2007) examined the applicability of nine key career constructs (career definition, objective career, subjective career, objective career success, subjective career success, knowing-why, knowing-whom, knowing-how and mobility) to careers in Russia. They concluded that Western career concepts can be used in a non-Western environment but only carefully so, as they may have different meanings in the new context. As one example, Russians experience boundaryless careers but for different reasons than employees in the Anglo-Saxon world. Further, in a fast changing environment like Russia the meaning of each career attribute is continuously changing to reflect the dynamism that characterises the social, political and economic landscape of the country. In another study, Song and Verbel (2007) compared the use of social networks in job searches of US and Chinese students. Both groups were found to make extensive use of their social networks, but there were important differences in how people used their relationships and what the related outcomes of having used a relationship were. The authors attributed the differences to the different nature of social relationships in the two countries – weak ties in the United States against *guanxi*, implying many more obligations, in China. Social networks may successfully help identify employment opportunities in both countries, but may constrain career choices in China as career decisions may become less independent as a result of using *guanxi*. Accordingly, Song and Verbel (2007) suggested that there is only limited generalisability of career practices across contexts.

As noted earlier, there are fewer comparative studies on company career management practices to date and a number of them come from related areas such as management or HR development. While a coherent picture has not yet emerged, they too appear to highlight differences across countries. In an early study, Lawrence (1992) described management development across several European countries and concluded that each country had a different definition of what constitutes good management and what the characteristics of a good manager are. These differences were reflected in their management development approaches. A review paper by Hansen and Brooks (1994) identified a number of differences across countries (for example, management training in the United States emphasises speed and instant solutions, whereas in China it focuses on ascribed status and loyalty; American careers develop within occupations but across organisations while the opposite is true in Japan where job rotation and the development of generalists is the norm) and concluded that career development studies revealed much variation in comparative organisational approaches. A more recent study by Kelly at al. (2003) looked at the prevalence of 'new careers' in Ireland, China, Hong Kong and Singapore. They found support for their research proposition that different levels of environmental turbulence will result in different levels of prevalence of traditional versus 'new' career types. Thus Hong Kong organisations were most likely to support traditional career paths (e.g. 50 per cent of respondents said that their companies support fast trackers, 37 per cent took sole responsibility for employee training, many had within-function career paths only and supported primarily vertical promotions). This can be contrasted with the case of Ireland, where significantly less support for traditional career paths was reported and new careers seem more accepted (e.g. 27 per cent of organisations supported fast track programmes, 22 per cent took sole responsibility for training, organisations had multiple career paths, with a mixture of within- and cross-function paths, Irish organisations provided training from a wider variety of sources than their Asian counterparts). A major European study on management development and its links to organisational performance by Mabey and his colleagues (Mabey & Gooderham, 2005; Mabey & Ramirez, 2005) showed that in addition to contextual factors such as sales turnover, size and country, variables capturing the way management development is conceived and implemented also influence perceived company performance. Causal path analysis shows that a favourable strategic fit and organisational fit significantly predicts line manager perceptions of the importance given to management development, which in turn distinguishes high- from low-performing companies. In another example, Dany and colleagues (2006; 2007) investigated the differences between career management HRM practices across six countries. They did not find support for the existence of a dominant model of career management across the countries and concluded that careers still appear to be strongly marked by specific traditional orientations reflecting larger HRM differences across nations.

It must be noted that the literature has also provided evidence for similarities across countries. Thus Claes and Quintanilla (1994) suggested that there were more similarities than differences in career patterns and career and work meanings among young people across seven countries of the European Union. In line with such findings, there have been recent discussions of whether we are witnessing convergence towards Western-like career patterns and practices. To that end, Tams and Arthur (2007) comment that while there is evidence that globalisation enhances the ability to work across nations and leads to cultural change and some convergence, it is still premature and simplistic to confirm the inevitable arrival of widespread convergence towards Western capitalism (see also Inkson et al., 2007). These are issues that should be explored by future research, along with questions regarding whether such convergence is desirable, effective and beneficial to all employees (Tams & Arthur, 2007).

While all these studies represent significant advances in comparative research, above and beyond simplistic application of Anglo-Saxon models to other contexts, a great majority of them compare only a small number of countries. In the following sections, we highlight two recent studies from large-scale projects that take careers research even further. They include a broad range of countries and utilise research on culture clusters to study career related issues.

Individual Careers

Culture clusters and careers
As noted previously, the literature agrees that context does matter for careers (Mayrhofer et al., 2007). This is also true for career transitions occurring at the intersection of individual perceptions and institutional contexts (Ng et al., 2007). There is an agreement among scholars that in order to reflect the true diversity in careers and to learn more about differences in perceptions and conceptualisations, career theory should pay more attention to the cultural context (Schein, 1984; Tams & Arthur, 2007). While culture differences affect career transitions (Laurent, 1986), and career management (Derr & Laurent, 1989, Segalla et al., 2001), the literature has also recognised that there are commonalities across distinct contexts and cultures. They point towards generic qualities of careers or universalistic perceptions moulded by widely shared beliefs or myths that are just as important to consider in career theory and practice. In other words, knowing more about new careers requires fine-grained analyses examine both the differences and the common tendencies in careers all over the world.

Surprisingly little is known about the specifics of career concepts (Arthur et al., 1989) and career success (Gunz & Heslin, 2005) in different countries and cultures (Tams & Arthur, 2007), age groups and professional groups. This has been exacerbated by an increasing variety of careers, discussed under labels such as boundaryless (Arthur & Rousseau, 1996b) or protean (Hall, 1996) careers, and significant changes in the relationship between organisations and individuals such as changing psychological contracts (Rousseau, 1995). These developments potentially affect individuals' conceptualisations of careers and career success since the influencing factors on careers and careers themselves become more complex (Arthur et al., 2005; Sturges, 1999). There is considerable work on the meaning of careers and career success within the evolving new careers (see, e.g. Arthur et al., 1999; Collin & Young, 2000). However, research on individual conceptualisations of careers and career success, both of which are closely linked with individual values, from a culture-comparative angle and focusing on specific national contexts has been widely neglected (Brown, 2002; Heslin, 2005; Spokane et al., 2003) although it has been shown that work-related values are influenced by national cultural differences (Hofstede, 1996; Triandis, 1994).

To that end, a number of different approaches have been suggested to differentiate the world into coherent clusters. For example, based on his framework of 'cultural values' (Schwartz, 1994) that uses seven cultural dimensions (i.e. autonomy (intellectual), autonomy (affective), embeddedness, mastery, harmony, egalitarianism and hierarchy to identify major world regions), Schwartz differentiates between eight major cultural regions: English speaking, Western Europe, East Europe (Orthodox), East-Central and Baltic Europe (Protestant, Catholic), Confucian Asia, South and South-East Asia, and Muslim Middle-East and sub-Saharan Africa (Schwartz, 2008).

Career concepts, career success and career transitions
Based on Schwarz' clustering, the 5C-project (Collaboration for the Cross-Cultural Study of Contemporary Careers) focuses on views of career concepts, career success and career transitions of business school graduates, nurses and blue-collar workers from two different age cohorts in 11 countries (Austria, China, Costa Rica, Israel, Japan, Malaysia, Mexico, South Africa, the United States, Spain, Serbia and Montenegro). Data gathering has been conducted through fully transcribed semi-structured face-to-face interviews in the respective local language(s) with an average length of 45 minutes. Using a variant of qualitative content analysis (Mayring 2003), an open coding process following the suggested paraphrasing ⇨ generalisation ⇨ categorisation procedure was applied to the available texts.

Overall, 5C data analyses suggest a number of major results. First, both for views on career success and on career transitions and their triggers and outcomes, contextual factors matter greatly. This includes cultural as well as institutional aspects, for example, cultural values, economic stability, political situation and historical development of the country in the array of nations. Second, the development status of economies and historical background where careers are embedded also influences the perceptions of professional identities. In countries with a more stable economic background professional identities seem to be more strongly distinguished from each other and lead to a more occupational specific picture of categories, for example, in Austria and Spain. A greater variety of categories common to all professional groups are mentioned in countries that go through transition, for example, Serbia and China. It seems that the developmental stages of the economy as well as the education system influence the construction of professional identities.

Against this backdrop, Chudzikowski et al. (2009) investigate how individuals conceptualise causes of career transitions, focusing on the three European countries of Austria, Serbia and Spain in comparison to the United States and China. They show that perceptions of internal (to the person) drivers of career transitions as activating forces are evident in all five countries and that contemporary notions of occupational careers are highly individualised, a characterisation strongly emphasised in the current career literature. In the European culture clusters, causes of career transitions are attributed both internally and externally. China, representing the Confucian cultural region, stresses external causes for career transitions. By contrast, in the United States only internal attributions of causes are reported.

Also using 5C data, Demel et al. (2009) analyse different aspects of career success at a global level. Achievement, satisfaction and job-task characteristics emerge as the top three main categories of meaning of career success at an aggregated level in all 11 countries. In addition, the data show that both objective and subjective career success are emphasised in most countries, except in Japan where the top three frequently mentioned categories all belong to the objective dimension. Regarding major influencing factors on career success, they stem from the person, one's social and work context. Factors concerning the person comprise one's personal history, e.g. life experiences, family background; learning and development, traits, skills, for example, task-related, socio-emotional and learning skills; motives; and career management. Social context refers to one's family and friends as well as non-work network. Work context includes one's work network both inside and outside the company, above all peers, superiors, the company and broader work-related network. Besides influencing factors closely connected to the individual's self and immediate environment, they also show the importance of external, less controllable factors. This includes the context of society and culture, for example, governmental policies, availability of education, learning and developmental support/barriers, discrimination as well as the global context, for example, globalisation and competition. Furthermore, luck and contingencies are widely mentioned.

Organisational Career Management

Clusters of HRM
Echoing research on cultural values and clusters of countries with similar values, research in the broader area of HRM has also put forward the idea that clustering of countries can be observed based on how national organisations tend to manage their human resources. Given that career management practices represent a core aspect of HRM, we briefly review the most salient propositions of this literature, as this can contribute to our understanding of how careers are managed across the world.

Arguably the most elaborate debate in comparative HRM is about differences between the US version of HRM and its basic assumptions – organisations' objectives and their strategies are 'good' either for the organisation or for society; a great degree of managerial freedom; largely unrestricted handling of human resources – and the situation in Europe (see Brewster, 1993, 1995; Gooderham et al., 2004; Guest, 1990). Consequently, the notion of 'European HRM' was developed (see, e.g., Brewster, 1993, 1994; Larsen & Mayrhofer, 2006; Sparrow & Hiltrop, 1994). Further to that, several ways of distinguishing between regional clusters have been proposed. Thus, Hall and Soskice (2001) and Gooderham et al. (1999) contrast Anglo-Saxon-style free-market capitalism with capitalism varieties where there is greater state intervention. Garten (1993) shares this view, though also noting the existence of government-induced market systems such as Japan. Hollingsworth and Boyer (1997) focus on the presence or absence of communitarian infrastructures and find the Anglo cultures distinct from the rest of Europe. Others emphasise the importance of the role of the state and differ between countries such as the UK, Ireland and the Nordic countries in which the state has a limited role in industrial relations and the Roman-Germanic countries such as France, Spain, Germany, Italy, Belgium, Greece and the Netherlands where the opposite is true (Due et al., 1991: 90). Arguments have also been made for a 'northern European' approach to HRM based around those countries where English is widely spoken and trade unions are stronger (Brewster & Larsen, 2000b). One analysis of HRM practices found 'three clusters: a Latin cluster [which includes Spain, Italy, France]; a central European cluster . . . and a Nordic cluster' (Filella, 1991: 14). While comparative research in HRM struggles to find conclusive results, it remains clear that within Europe clusters of countries with different patterns of HR activities exist. More recently, HRM approaches in various parts of Asia, especially in China, India and Japan have also received more attention (see, e.g., Budhwar, 2004; the special issue of Management Revue 4/2007 on HRM in Asia Pacific, guest-edited by Chris Rowley and Malcolm Warner; Sparrow & Budhwar, 1996).

Career management

There are few sources that can be used for a comprehensive and integrated international comparison of core aspects of HRM. Arguably, Cranet, an international research network dedicated to analysing HRM developments in public and private sector organisations with more than 200 employees at the national and country-comparative level in a trend-study since 1989, is a primary source (for an overview see Brewster et al., 2004). Currently, more than 40 countries are part of the network. Each country is represented by a national university which is responsible for creating a representative sample of the respective company population. For the purposes of this chapter, we examined the 2004–2005 Cranet database to provide some illustrative examples of how career management related HR practices differ across countries. Building on previous research (e.g., Filella, 1991; Brewster & Larsen, 2000b; Brewster et al., 1997), we differentiate between five clusters: Anglo (including the UK, United States, Canada, Australia and New Zealand), Nordic (Scandinavian countries), Southern Latin (including France, Greece, Spain and Portugal), Germanic (including Austria, Benelux-countries, Germany and Switzerland), and Eastern Europe (including all the former communist countries). We take a more comprehensive view of career management and expand our discussion beyond practices directed directly to career development. Instead, we consider a multitude of HR practices related to careers (e.g. recruitment, appraisal, and training and development) as well as the interface between the organisation and its environment in terms of employees leaving the organisation. In this way we to get a sense of whether organisations in each cluster lean towards a relational or a transactional employment model and the related career paths that may emerge from their overall stance.

Recruitment and selection

Regarding recruitment and selection for different employment groups, we observe the following (see Table 13.1).

Looking across all employee categories, organisations in the Southern/ Latin and the East European cluster tend to use internal recruitment more. This is especially true for management and professional/technical positions. For example, more than half of the East European organisations

Table 13.1   Internal recruitment: different employee groups

Internal Recruitment	Anglo	Germanic	Nordic	South/Latin European	East European
Management positions	35.1%	35.2%	27.9%	38.5%	52.9%
Professional/ Technical positions	12.7%	12.7%	12.4%	27.9%	27.2%
Clerical positions	22.7%	22.1%	19.4%	27.2%	24.8%
Manual positions	13.1%	18.1%	15.9%	17.3%	13.1%

Table 13.2   Use of selection method in one or more employee categories

	Anglo	Germanic	Nordic	South/Latin European	East European
Interview panels	79.6%	70%	75.8%	30.8%	63.9%
One-to-one interviews	73.5%	83%	69.6%	95.3%	89.9%
References	80.5%	61.1%	74.4%	56%	61.1%
Psychometric tests	42.8%	32.9%	58.4%	39.2%	32.6%
Assessment centres	24.7%	46.4%	8.8%	22.2%	15.5%

(52.9 per cent) use this recruitment channel, compared to only one in four (27.9 per cent) in the Nordic cluster.

In terms of selection methods used in one or more employee categories, a number of differences occur between the five clusters (Table 13.2).

While assessment centres are quite popular in the Germanic cluster where roughly every other organisation uses them for selection (46.4 per cent), only about one in ten relies on assessment centres in the Nordic cluster (8.8 per cent). Compared to all other clusters, the Southern/Latin European cluster relies more heavily on one-to-one interviews (95.3 per cent; least used in the Anglo cluster, 73.5 per cent) but less so on interview panels (30.8 per cent; mostly used in the Anglo cluster, 79.6 per cent). References are most popular in the Anglo (80.5 per cent) and in the Nordic cluster (74.4 per cent).

Table 13.3   Career-relevant use of performance appraisal data

	Anglo	Germanic	Nordic	South/Latin European	East European
HR planning	48.5%	34.3%	29.0%	47.2%	45.9%
Analysing T&D needs	85.2%	69.6%	47.8%	74.1%	59.1%
Career planning	68.8%	67.6%	36.8%	67.1%	46.0%
Pay determination	54.4%	56.8%	40.1%	64.5%	65.6%

Performance appraisal

In all clusters at least 80 per cent of the organisations use formal performance appraisal. In essence, this means that, by and large, nearly all organisations formally evaluate their employees. It is no surprise that these numbers are highest in management and lowest in manual employees.

Typically, performance appraisal results are used for a variety of reasons. Major uses include HR planning, training and development needs, career planning and determination of monetary compensation (Table 13.3).

Overall, the Nordic cluster stands out as making least use of performance appraisal data for career-relevant issues. There is also a considerable split between the Anglo cluster and the rest with regard to using performance appraisal data for analysing training and development needs. While nearly nine out of ten organisations in the Anglo cluster (85.2 per cent) use it for this purpose, this is true for only one out of two in the Nordic cluster.

Training and development

HRM activities in the area of training and development are closely connected to various aspects of organisational career management. To start with, it is essential to know how much time and money organisations invest into training and development and how many employees are affected (Table 13.4).

From a comparative angle, two facets are remarkable. First, organisations in the Germanic cluster invest the least, both in terms of money spent and days per employee used for training and development. By and large, the same is true for the percentage of employees affected by formal training measures. Second, the Anglo and the Nordic cluster put a strong focus on internal training for their employees, with more than half of them (59.1 per cent and 53.6 per cent, respectively) receiving internal training.

More specifically, organisations use a great array of career development activities for their employees (Table 13.5).

Table 13.4 Investment into training and development

	Anglo	Germanic	Nordic	South/Latin European	East European
% of payroll spent on training	3.6%	2.8%	3.3%	3.3%	3.1%
Average number of days of training across employee categories	4.9	3.5	4.8	5.0	4.7
% of employees receiving internal training	59.1%	37.5%	53.6%	41.7%	42.0%
% of employees receiving external training	24.5%	20.6%	25.1%	20.8%	21.3%
% receiving internal and external training	37.8%	34.7%	39.4%	37.4%	29.0%

Looking at managerial development measures, the data indicate that the East European cluster is least active in terms of the activities listed above. In nearly all cases, organisations in this cluster use these activities least. Furthermore, the analyses suggest that organisations in the Nordic cluster are less inclined to use instruments that emphasise formal career and succession procedures. This is in line with a more decentralised approach to HRM which is typical of a Nordic approach to HRM (Brewster & Larsen, 2000a).

When looking at the career development activities for non-management employees, the basic pattern is similar (Table 13.6).

Organisations in the Nordic cluster emphasise a great variety of methods (on average 4.2 methods used, compared to 3.1 in the South/Latin European cluster) and, in particular, networking and experience schemes, which tend to be more organic and unstructured. Again, organisations in the East European cluster tend to use the activities analysed more sparingly.

Turnover and decrease in workforce
Looking at organisational career management also requires an analysis of staff turnover and various forms of leaving the organisations and decrease in the workforce (Table 13.7).

Table 13.5   Career development activities for management (%
organisations reporting use)

	Anglo	Germanic	Nordic	South/Latin European	East European
Special tasks/projects to stimulate learning	81%	77.4%	68.7%	68.1%	63.1%
Cross-organis- ational/ disciplinary/ functional tasks	81.8%	80.2%	75.5%	79.8%	65.7%
Project team work	87.6%	86.4%	80.6%	81.7%	77.5%
Networking	73.4%	67.5%	70.2%	47.7%	53.4%
Formal career plans	56.3%	52.0%	47.2%	48.9%	46.6%
Assessment centers	22.7%	43.3%	19.9%	29.9%	21.8%
Succession plans	56.9%	63.7%	39.6%	51.9%	43.6%
Planned job rotations	35.1%	43.2%	40.2%	59.0%	41.4%
'High flyer' schemes	26.1%	44.5%	32.8%	46.1%	40.9%
Secondments to other organisations	33.2%	36.2%	29.6%	34.8%	37.7%
Average number of methods used	5.80	6.20	5.60	5.80	5.20

The data show that in terms of annual staff turnover, organisations in the Anglo cluster have the highest figure (14.6 per cent), nearly double as much as in the Germanic cluster (7.6 per cent). Against the backdrop of different market regimes – liberal versus coordinated market economies – including a varying density of legal regulations, this does not come as a surprise. Organisations in the Germanic cluster make heavy use of early retirement schemes, which again is supported by legal regulations partly encouraging organisations and individuals to take this option.

Configurations of career management practices
Going beyond descriptives, Dany et al. (2007) recently investigated more formally the clustering of different configurations of career management practices across Anglo-Saxon countries (United States, Canada, and New Zealand), France and two Germanic countries (Germany and Austria). Based on the premise that careers are strongly marked by the contexts in which they unfold, the main proposition of their study is that the US way of managing careers has not spread as much as many commentators are

*Table 13.6   Career development activities for non-management (%
companies reporting use)*

	Anglo	Germanic	Nordic	South/Latin European	East European
Non-managerial career development					
Special tasks/project to stimulate learning	79.3%	76.3%	73.8%	69.2%	57.5%
Cross-organisational/ disciplinary/ functional tasks	77.5%	84.0%	77.3%	61.0%	61.0%
Project team work	83.3%	96.7%	81.9%	74.6%	73.0%
Networking	48.6%	50.0%	62.1%	35.0%	43.5%
Experience schemes	35.0%	54.8%	68.3%	40.3%	64.9%
Average number of methods used	3.4	3.6	4.2	3.1	3.2

Table 13.7   Annual staff turnover and decrease in workforce

	Anglo	Germanic	Nordic	South/Latin European	East European
Annual staff turnover	14.6%	7.6%	8.6%	11.5%	9.4%
Compulsory redundancies	22.1%	22.9%	25.8%	13.8%	25.1%
Outsourcing	9.7%	15.2%	13.2%	11.9%	15.1%
Voluntary redundancies	17.3%	24.5%	23.2%	21.2%	13.3%
Early retirement	12.2%	25.4%	19.2%	17%	15.6%
Internal transfers	19.6%	24.8%	28%	17.5%	24.7%

suggesting. From a theoretical standpoint, they contrast the transactional approach to career management, which is likely to characterise the Anglo-Saxon model, and the relational approach, likely to be more prevalent in countries with stronger labour regulations. They also examine the extent to which the boundaryless career model is reflected in HRM practices in organisations that exist in different contexts. The focus of the study is a comparison between Anglo Saxon countries (representing the 'at will' employment environment), France (representing a context dominated by rigid regulations regarding the employment relationship and a fairly

Dendrogram using Average Linkage (Between Groups)

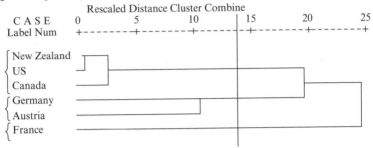

Source: Dany et al. 2007.

Figure 13.1   Clusters analysis

unique approach to career management) and two Germanic countries (representing an 'intermediate model' where labour regulations permit certain amount of flexibility).

A cluster analysis of the relevant country data from the Cranet dataset did indeed confirm that distinct clusters existed, with Anglo Saxon countries and Germanic countries grouped in two respective clusters and France exhibiting a unique profile of career management practices (Figure 13.1).

The authors then performed more detailed analyses of patterns of differences and similarities of specific career management related HRM practices (e.g. the use of internal or external recruitment, narrower or larger use of selection methods, prevalence of people-oriented or others-oriented selection methods, the use of performance appraisals to determine training and career planning, whether pay was related to individual or collective performance, the proportion of payroll costs invested in training, the number of training and career development programmes offered to managerial and non-managerial staff and the number of training days per employee category, turnover rates and ways in which companies manage downsizing). While not all specific hypotheses of the study were supported, the results clearly demonstrated differences across the three clusters: career management related practices exhibited a more relational approach in the French model and a more transactional approach in the Anglo model with Germanic organisations holding an intermediate position. This leads Dany et al. (2007) to conclude that career management still appears to be strongly marked by traditional orientations characterising HRM practices around the world, in contrast to the view that countries are converging to a dominant (US-based) career management approach. Further, the results suggested that the emphasis put on the critical role of individuals in managing their career risks underestimating the critical necessity of employers' commitment to employee development, even in a new career context. In line with warnings that the employability rhetoric is ahead of the practices (Gratton, 1999), the Cranet data indicates that firms' disengagement from people development is less dramatic than frequently assumed.

CONCLUDING REMARKS

Despite the success of the US rhetoric and the individual perspective, careers are still marked by contexts. Differences according to cultural and institutional factors still exist in the way companies manage career. Likewise, individuals all over the world may have different expectations toward their careers. From this perspective, we believe that more research is needed to better understand these differences and the factors that contribute to them. We contend, in particular, that an interesting avenue for research would be to know more about the pros and the cons of various ways of managing individual careers and establishing organisational management practices. While the literature does not show any conclusive evidence regarding career clusters, we believe that comparative research on career would help draw attention on commonalities and differences which have been overlooked so far but that can be very useful to push forward our understanding of career.

REFERENCES

Alvarez, J. L. 2000. Theories of managerial action and their impact on the conceptualization of executive careers. In M. Peiperl, M. Arthur, R. Goffee & T. Morris (eds), *Career Frontiers*. Oxford, UK: Oxford University Press, pp. 127–137.

Arthur, M. B. 1994. The boundaryless career: a new perspective for organizational inquiry. *Journal of Organizational Behavior*, **15**(4): 295–306.

Arthur, M. B., Claman, P. H. & DeFillippi, R. J. 1995. Intelligent enterprise, intelligent careers. *Academy of Management Executive*, **9**(4): 7–22.

Arthur, M. B., Hall, D. T. & Lawrence, B. S. 1989. Generating new directions in career theory: the case for a transdisciplinary approach. In M. B. Arthur, D. T. Hall, & B. S. Lawrence (eds), *Handbook of Career Theory*. Cambridge: Cambridge University Press, pp. 7–25.

Arthur, M. B., Inkson, K. & Pringle, J. K. 1999. *The New Careers: Individual Action and Economic Change*. London: Sage Publications.

Arthur, M. B., Khapova, S. N. & Wilderom, C. P. M. 2005. Career success in a boundaryless career world. *Journal of Organizational Behavior*, **26**(2): 177–202.

Arthur, M. B. & Rousseau, D. B. (eds) 1996a. *The Boundaryless Career. A New Employment Principle for a New Organizational Era*. New York: Oxford University Press.

Arthur, M. B. & Rousseau, D. M. (Eds.). 1996b. *The boundaryless career. A new employment principle for a new organizational era.* New York: Oxford University Press.

Bell, N. E. & Staw, B. M. 1989. People as sculptors versus sculpture: the role of personality and personal control. In M. B. Arthur, D. T. Hall & B. S. Lawrence (eds), *Handbook of Career Theory.* Cambridge: Cambridge University Press, pp. 232–251.

Brewster, C. 1993. Developing a 'European' model of human resource management. *International Journal of Human Resource Management,* **4**(4): 765–784.

Brewster, C. 1994. European HRM: reflection of, or challenge to, the American concept? In P. S. Kirkbride (ed.), *Human Resource Management in Europe.* London: Routledge, pp. 56–89.

Brewster, C. 1995. Towards a 'European' model of human resource management. *Journal of International Business Studies,* **26**(1): 22.

Brewster, C. & Larsen, H. H. (eds) 2000a. *Human Resource Management in Northern Europe.* Oxford: Blackwell.

Brewster, C. & Larsen, H. H. 2000b. The Northern European dimension. a distinctive environment for HRM. In C. Brewster & H. H. Larsen (eds), *Human Resource Management in Northern Europe.* Oxford: Blackwell, pp. 24–38.

Brewster, C., Larsen, H. H. & Mayrhofer, W. 1997. Integration and assignment: a paradox in human resource management. *Journal of International Management,* **3**(1): 1–23.

Brewster, C., Mayrhofer, W. & Morley, M. (eds) 2004. *Human Resource Management in Europe. Evidence of Convergence?* Oxford: Elsevier/Butterworth-Heinemann.

Brown, D. 2002. The role of work and cultural values in occupational choice, satisfaction, and success: a theoretical statement. *Journal of Counseling & Development,* 80(Winter 2002): 48–56.

Budhwar, P. S. (ed.) 2004. *Managing Human Resources in Asia-Pacific.* London: Routledge.

Byars-Winston, A. M. & Fouad, N. A. 2006. Metacognition and multicultural competence: extending the culturally appropriate career counseling model. *Career Development Quarterly,* **54**: 187–201.

Cadin, L., Bailly-Bender, A.-F. & de Saint Giniez, V. 2000. Exploring boundaryless careers in the French context. In M. A. Peiperl, M. B. Arthur, R. Goffee & T. Morris (eds), *Career Frontiers: New Conceptions of Working Lives.* Oxford: Oxford University Press, pp. 228–255.

Chudzikowski, K., Demel, B., Mayrhofer, W., Briscoe, J. P., Unite, J., Bogicevic Milikic, B., Hall, D. T., Heras, M. L., Shen, Y. & Zikic, J. 2009. Career transitions and their causes: a country-comparative perspective. *Journal of Occupational and Organizational Psychology,* **82**: 825–849.

Claes, R. & Quintanilla, A. R. S. 1994. Initial career and work meanings in seven European countries. *Career Development Quarterly,* **42**(4): 337–352.

Collin, A. & Young, R. A. (eds). 2000. *The Future of Careers.* Cambridge: Cambridge University Press.

Dany, F. 2003. 'Free Actors' and organizations: critical remarks about the new career literature, based on French insights. *International Journal of Human Resource Management,* **14**(5): 821–838.

Dany, F., Guedri, Z., Hatt, F., Lazarova, M. & Mayrhofer, W. 2006. Careers around the world: what can be drawn from a comparison of HR practices in different national context? Paper presented at the 22nd EGOS Colloquium, July 2006, Bergen, Norway.

Dany, F., Hatt, F., Lazarova, M. & Mayrhofer, W. 2007. One world, one flow? HR practices to manage organizational careers: a comparative study. Paper presented at the 67th Academy of Management Annual Meeting, August 2007, Philadelphia, PA.

Dany, F., Louvel, S. & Valette, A. 2011. Academic careers: the limits of the 'boundaryless approach' and the power of promotion scripts. *Human Relations,* **64** (7): 971–996.

Dany, F., Mallon, M. & Arthur, M. 2003. The odyssey of career and the opportunity for international comparison. *International Journal of Human Resource Management,* **14**(5): 705–712.

Demel, B., Yan, S., Hall, D. T., Mayrhofer, W., Chudzikowski, K., Unite, J., Briscoe, J.,

Abdul Ghani, R., Bogicevic Milikic, B., Colorado, O., Fei, Z., Las Heras, M., Ogliastri, E., Pazy, A., Poon, J., Shefer, D., Taniguchi, M. & Zikic, J. 2009. Cracking the fortune cookies: influencing factors in career success across 11 countries. Paper presented at Academy of Management Meeting. Chicago, IL, USA, 9–11 August.

Derr, C. B. 1986. Five definitions of career success: implications for relationships. *Review of Applied Psychology*, **35**: 415–435.

Derr, C. B. & Laurent, A. 1989. The internal and external career: a theoretical and cross-cultural perspective. In D. T. H. M. B. Arthur & B. S. Lawrence (eds), *Handbook of Career Theory*. New York: Cambridge University Press, pp. 454–476.

Devanna, M. A., Fombrun, C. J. & Tichy, N. 1984. A framework for strategic human resource management. In C. J. Fombrun, N. Tichy & M. A. Devanna (eds), *Strategic Human Resource Management*. New York: Wiley, pp. 11–17.

Due, J., Madsen, J. S. & Jensen, C. S. 1991. The social dimension: convergence or diversification of IR in the Single European Market? *Industrial Relations Journal*, **22**(2): 85–102.

Filella, J. 1991. Is there a Latin model in the management of human resources? *Personnel Review*, **20**(6): 14–23.

Fouad, N. A. 1993. Cross-cultural vocational assessment. *Career Development Quarterly*, **42**(1): 4–13.

Fouad, N. A. & Arbona, C. 1994. Careers in a cultural context. *Career Development Quarterly*, **43**(1): 96–104.

Garten, J. E. 1993. *A Cold Peace: America, Japan and Germany and the Struggle for Supremacy*. New York: Times Books.

Gerpott, T. J., Domsch, M. & Keller, R. T. 1988. Career orientatations in different countries and companies: an empirical investigation of West German, British and US industrial R&D professionals. *Journal of Management Studies*, **25**(5): 439–462.

Gooderham, P., Morley, M., Mayrhofer, W. & Brewster, C. 2004. Human resource management: a universal concept? In C. Brewster, W. Mayrhofer & M. Morley (eds), *European Human Resource Management: Convergence or Divergence?* London: Butterworth-Heinemann, pp. 1–26.

Gooderham, P. N., Nordhaug, O. & Ringdal, K. 1999. Institutional and rational determinants of organizational practices: human resource management in European firms. *Administrative Sciences Quarterly*, **44**(3): 507–531.

Greenhaus, J. H., Callanan, G. A. & Godshalk, V. M. 2010 *Career Management*, 4th edn. Los Angeles, CA: Sage Publications.

Guest, D. E. 1990. Human resource management and the American dream. *Journal of Management Studies*, **27**(4): 377–397.

Guest, D. E. 2004. Flexible employment contracts, the psychological contract and employee outcomes: an analysis and review of the evidence. *International Journal of Management Reviews*, **5/6**(1): 1–19.

Gunz, H. P. & Heslin, P. A. 2005. Reconceptualizing career success. *Journal of Organizational Behavior*, **26**(2): 105.

Hall, D. T. 1996. Protean careers of the 21st century. *Academy of Management Executive*, **10**(4): 8–16.

Hall, P. A. & Soskice, D. 2001. An introduction to the varieties of capitalism. In P. A. Hall & D. Soskice (eds), *Varieties of Capitalism. The Institutional Foundations of Comparative Advantage*. Oxford: Oxford University Press.

Hansen, C. D. & Brooks, A. K. 1994. A review of cross-cultural research on human resource development. *Human Resource Development Quarterly*, **5**(1): 55–74.

Hansen, C. D. & Willcox, M. K. 1997. Cultural assumptions in career management: practice implications from Germany. *Career Development International*, **2**(4): 195–202.

Hartung, P. J. 2002. Cultural context in career theory and practice: role salience and values. *Career Development Quarterly*, **51**: 12–25.

Heslin, P. A. 2005. Conceptualizing and evaluating career success. *Journal of Organizational Behavior*, **26**(2): 113.

Hofstede, G. 1996. *Culture's Consequences: International Differences in Work-Related Values.* Newbury Park, CA: Sage Publications.

Hofstede, G. 2001. *Culture's Consequences,* 2nd edn. Thousand Oaks, CA: Sage Publications.

Hollingsworth, J. R. & Boyer, R. (eds). 1997. *Contemporary Capitalism.* Cambridge: Cambridge University Press.

Hughes, E. C. 1958. *Men and Their Work.* Glencoe, IL: Free Press.

Inkson, K., Khapova, S. N. & Parker, P. 2007. Careers in cross-cultural perspective. *Career Development International,* **12**(1): 5–8.

Kato, I. & Suzuki, R. 2006. Career 'mist,' 'hope,' and 'drift': conceptual framework for understanding career development in Japan. *Career Development International,* **11**(3): 265–276.

Kelly, A., Brannick, T., Hulpke, J., Levine, J. & To, M. 2003. Linking organisational training and development practices with new forms of career structure: a cross-national exploration. *Journal of European Industrial Training,* **27**(2/3/4): 160–168.

Khapova, S. N., & Korotov, K. 2007. Dynamics of western career attributes in the Russian context. *Career Development International,* **12**(1): 68–85.

Larsen, H. H. & Mayrhofer, W. (eds). 2006. *Managing Human Resources in Europe. A Thematic Approach.* London: Routledge.

Laurent, A. 1986. The cross-cultural puzzle of international human resource management. *Human Resource Management,* **25**(1): 91–102.

Lawrence, P. 1992. Management development in Europe: a study of cultural contrast. *Human Resource Management Journal,* **3**(1): 11–23.

Mabey, C. & Gooderham, P. 2005. The impact of management development on the organizational performance of european firms. *European Management Review,* **2**(2): 131–142.

Mabey, C. & Ramirez, M. 2005. Does management development improve organizational productivity? A six-country analysis of European firms. *International Journal of Human Resource Management,* **16**(7): 1067–1082.

Malach-Pines, A. & Kaspi-Baruch, O. 2008. The role of culture and gender in the choice of career in management. *Career Development International,* **13**(4): 306–319.

Mallon, M. 1998. The portfolio career: pushed in or pulled to it? *Personnel Review,* **27**(5): 361–377.

Mayrhofer, W., Meyer, M. & Steyrer, J. 2007. Contextual issues in the study of careers. In H. P. Gunz & M. Peiperl (eds), *Handbook of Career Studies.* London: Sage Publications, pp. 215–240.

Ng, T. W. H., Sorensen, K. L., Eby, L. T. & Feldman, D. C. 2007. Determinants of job mobility: a theoretical integration and extension. *Journal of Occupational & Organizational Psychology,* **80**(3): 363–386.

Peiperl, M. & Gunz, H. P. 2007. Taxonomy of career studies. In H. P. Gunz & M. Peiperl (eds), *Handbook of Career Studies.* London: Sage Publications, pp. 39–54.

Pringle, J. K. & Mallon, M. 2003. Challenges for the boundaryless career odyssey. *International Journal of Human Resource Management,* **14**(5): 839–853.

Rothwell, W. J., Jackson, R. D., Knight, S. C. & Lindholm, J. E. 2005. *Career Planning and Succession Management: Developing Your Organization's Talent – for Today and Tomorrow.* Westport, CT: Praeger.

Rousseau, D. B. & Schalk, R. 2000. *Psychological Contracts in Employment: Cross-national Perspectives.* Thousand Oaks, CA: Sage Publications.

Rousseau, D. M. 1995. *Psychological Contracts in Organizations: Understanding Written and Unwritten Agreements.* Thousand Oaks, CA: Sage Publications.

Schein, E. 1990. *Career Anchors: Discovering Your Real Values.* San Diego, CA: Pfeiffer & Company.

Schein, E. H. 1971. The individual, the organization, and the career: a conceptual scheme. *Journal of Applied Behavioral Science,* **7**: 401–426.

Schein, E. H. 1984. Culture as an environmental context for careers. *Journal of Occupational Behaviour,* **5**: 71–81.

Schwartz, S. H. 1994. Beyond individualism/collectivism: new dimensions of values. In

U. Kim, H. C. Triandis, C. Kagitçibasi, S. C. Choi & G. Yoon (eds), *Individualism and Collectivism: Theory Application and Methods*. Newbury Park, CA: Sage Publications.

Schwartz, S. H. 2006. A theory of cultural value orientations. *Comparative Sociology*, **5**(2–3): 137–182.

Schwartz, S. H. 2008. Introduction. In S. H. Schwartz (ed.), *Cultural Value Orientations: Nature and Implications of National Differences*. Moscow: Publ. House of SU HSE.

Segalla, M., Sauquet, A. & Turatic, C. 2001. Symbolic versus functional recruitment: cultural influences on employee recruitment policy. *European Management Journal*, **19**(1): 32–43.

Song, L. J. & Werbel, J. D. 2007. Guanxi as impetus? Career exploration in China and the United States. *Career Development International*, **12**(1): 51–67.

Sparrow, P. & Hiltrop, J. M. 1994. *European Human Resource Management in Transition*. Hempel Hempstead: Prentice Hall.

Sparrow, P. R. 1996. Transitions in the psychological contract: Some evidence from the banking sector. *Human Resource Management Journal*, **6**(4): 75–92.

Sparrow, P. R. & Budhwar, P. S. 1996. HRM in the new economic environment: an empirical study of India. *Management Research News*, **19**(4/5): 30–35.

Spokane, A. R., Fouad, N. A. & Swanson, J. L. 2003. Culture-centered career intervention. *Journal of Vocational Behavior*, **62**(3): 453–458.

Sturges, J. 1999. What it means to succeed: personal conceptions of career success held by male and female managers at different ages. *British Journal of Management*, **10**(3): 239–252.

Tams, S. & Arthur, M. 2007. Studying careers across cultures: distinguishing international, cross-cultural and globalization perspectives. *Career Development International*, **12**(1): 86–98.

Thomas, D. C. & Inkson, K. 2007. Careers across cultures. In H. P. Gunz & M. A. Peiperl (eds), *Handbook of Career Studies*. Thousand Oaks, CA: Sage Publications, pp. 451–471.

Triandis, H. C. 1994. Cross-cultural industrial and organizational psychology. In H. C. Triandis, M. D. Dunnette & L. M. Hough (eds), *Handbook of Industrial and Organizational Psychology*, Vol. 4, 2nd edn. Palo Alto, CA: Consulting Psychologists Press, pp.103–172.

Triandis, H. C., Bontempo, R., Villareal, M. J., Asai, M. & Lucca, N. 1988. Individualism and collectivism: cross-cultural perspectives on self-ingroup relationships. *Journal of Personality and Social Psychology*, **54**(2): 323–338.

Trompenaars, F. & Hampden-Turner, C. 2004. *Managing People Across Cultures*. Chichester, UK: Capstone Publishing Ltd.

Wilensky, H. L. 1961. Orderly careers and social participation: the impact of work history on social integration in the middle mass. *American Sociological Review*, **26**: 521–539.

Zeitz, G., Blau, G. & Fertig, J. 2009. Boundaryless careers and institutional resources. *International Journal of Human Resource Management*, **20**(2): 372–398.

14 Flexible work practices
Maria C. Gonzalez and Phil Almond

In all reference books the term 'flexibility' has been defined more or less as follows: 'a relatively ambiguous term which did not begin to have an impact until after the second half of the 1970s. It nearly always refers to labour, but may also have various shades of meaning (for example, flexibility of the labour force, flexibility of the wage earners, flexibility of wage structures, flexibility of labour markets). The one common element is that there is never enough flexibility. (Bruno, 1989: 33, quoted in Prieto, 1993: 615)

The search for 'flexibility' is perhaps the most perennial of leitmotifs within HRM. As the 23-year-old quotation above reflects, its vagueness of meaning allows it to be interpreted with radically different meanings by people with different interests. It can also refer to policy and practice at the workplace/firm level, or to the regulation of national labour markets.

Although authors have approached the flexibility debate from a huge variety of perspectives, the overarching narrative behind the need of employers to attain more flexible working practices – at least in developed countries where the majority of jobs are of a certain quality and are embedded in the wider framework of a welfare state – is relatively uncontested. It starts, whether explicitly or otherwise, with the crisis of the Fordist production regime, with its narrowly defined, Taylorist jobs and inflexible labour markets. Increased international competitive pressures from the 1970s onwards, along with technological progress, led to interest in new work organisation mechanisms and HRM practices which would enhance firms' responsiveness to consumer demands. More specifically, speed, adaptability and/or innovation, and therefore performance, could be fostered by increasing organisational flexibility. This could happen through various kinds of flexibility of work and employment (see below) with the overall aim of generating broader repertoires of behaviour and/or skills among workers. This broad narrative has been shared, among others, by Marxian researchers whose aim is to understand the dynamics of contemporary capitalism (Boyer, 1986; Boltanski & Chiapello, 1999), by proponents of the flexible specialisation thesis (Piore & Sabel, 1984), and by liberal researchers whose – sometimes implicit – aim is to encourage firms to move towards forms of work organisation based on increased responsibility, autonomy and involvement for at least core workers (e.g. Appelbaum et al., 2000; Delaney & Huselid, 1996; MacDuffie, 1995; Osterman, 1994; Walton, 1985).

Within this overall search for flexibility, much attention has been paid to the dichotomy between functional and numerical (Atkinson, 1984), or internal and external (Capelli & Neumark, 2004), flexibility. A significant preoccupation has been whether these relatively distinct forms of flexibility apply mainly to separate groups of workers (functional for the 'core', numerical for the 'periphery'), or whether this distinction is too simplistic, with both forms of flexibility being sought from all types of workers (Kalleberg, 2001).

Flexibility research has, in a sense, been founded on implicit international comparisons from the outset: much talk of the need to move towards more flexible working systems was built on an understanding of the differences between Western and Japanese models of management, as the latter were seen as increasingly dominant in the 1980s, the period when much of this research originated. Equally, as we will see below, much early research contrasted work organisation in 'low trust' industrial relations contexts such as the UK, United States or France, with 'high trust' systems such as Germany or Sweden.

Despite this, flexibility has not proved an easy subject for HRM academics to research comparatively. This is partly because it requires us to understand organisational policies and practices that are beyond the remit of human resource managers, and particular HRM policies are often poor proxies for the elusive 'flexibility'. It is also because of confusion in terminology; as flexibility means so many things to different people, it can be hard to make sensible comparisons between different pieces of research.

This chapter, therefore, begins by defining what is meant by flexibility, and delimiting the scope of our review. We then move on to an analysis of the predominant themes of comparative analysis, and how these have changed over recent years; this is followed by a brief review of some recent qualitative research. It then analyses quantitative research, drawing on surveys of managers and employees, with a critical focus on the methodologies that have been used in such research. The concluding section reviews explanations for cross-national differences in the extent and types of flexibility in different countries, and offers some suggestions as to the potential future course of research.

DEFINITIONS

The phrase 'flexible work practices' is interpreted here to mean internal flexibility, and thus to exclude external flexibility practices (flexibility of contract – see Chapter 12; for an analysis of converging and diverging trends in Europe in this area, see Tregaskis & Brewster, 2006). We also concentrate on flexibility *of* employees, rather than flexibility for employees (Kelliher & Anderson, 2008: 420), which is aimed at making paid work and private life more compatible.

Internal flexibility may concern working time (practices such as flexible timetables, Brewster et al, 1994), annualisation of hours (EIRO, 2003), etc.) often referred to as *temporal flexibility* (Blyton, 1992; Tüselmann, 1996). It would also include flexibility of working space (including telework; see Haddon & Brynin, 2005), and workers' geographical mobility, whether domestic or international (Carnicer et al., 2004), generally referred to as *spatial flexibility* (Shockley & Allen, 2007). Finally, it has to do with the reform of work organisation (issues of job design and the effort–reward bargain) towards more efficient and adaptable organisations. This chapter, for reasons of space, focuses on flexibility of work organisation and related HRM practices.

Flexibility of work organisation or job design, encompasses the flexibilisation of the contents of work itself (*functional flexibility*), and of the employment relationship (*contractual flexibility*) (Oeij & Wiezer, 2002); we concentrate here on the former, although the latter may be an important independent variable in many cases (see below).

We see the contents of work itself as comprising: *task content* (characteristics of the tasks in terms of difficulty and/or responsibility), *task variety* (how similar are the tasks comprised in a job in terms of content) and *task discretion* (how the work is done), and time discretion (control over the pace of work, and when to do what). Work enrichment may refer to the widening of any or various elements of this list. Together, task discretion and time discretion constitute job discretion, or *job autonomy*, a frequent focus of research into functional flexibility, as we will see.

Our focus, then, is on functional flexibility, and our definition follows quite closely that of Prieto (1993: 617), who sees it as:

> a widening of skills – from the standpoint of both ability and responsibility – of wage earners so that they might carry out various tasks resulting in internal mobility. This is the most complicated form of flexibility because it frequently implies a change in the organizational structure. If it is to be implemented successfully wage earners must be given a certain level of autonomous decision making in carrying out their task and functions. It also requires a reduction in hierarchical levels and greatly improved communications.

This 'skills–mobility–autonomy–decentralisation–participation' theoretical approach to flexibility is archetypical of the HRM literature (e.g. Guest, 1987). Further, flexible work practices are the traditional core of the still dominant HRM-performance approach. For instance, Ichniowski et al.'s (1996: 322) analysis of the American literature concluded that if innovative human resource management practices improved productivity, it was primarily through the use of systems of related work practices designed to enhance worker participation and flexibility in the design of work and decentralisation of managerial tasks and responsibilities.

APPROACHES TO RESEARCHING FLEXIBLE WORKING PRACTICES

Since the 1980s, the literature on flexibility of work has gone through two broad distinctive phases. Early research, most of which was conceived before the notion of flexibility achieved its later prominence, emphasised comparative statics: certain countries' employment systems seemed to allow a greater degree of flexibility of work than others. Typically, Germany, Scandinavian countries and sometimes Japan, were seen as having more adaptable forms of work organisation than either the UK or the United States (Lane, 1989; Maurice et al., 1980) or France (Maurice et al., 1986). This was related to a wide range of societal factors, but within the industrial relations literature the main emphasis was on the dichotomy between high and low trust workplace industrial relations, and the greater degree of vocational training, and hence skills, of (particularly German) workers.

In terms of methodology, much of this research was inspired by the LEST school (Maurice et al., 1986), which compared 'matched plants' across different societies. For our purposes, the important thing to bear in mind about this research was that its measurements of organisational phenomena had their roots in older, contingency school research into organisations and bureaucracy (at the same time as being critical of them, cf. the contributions to Lammers & Hickson, 1979). Typical objects of investigation would include cross-national differences in wage gaps between different groups of workers, the nature and shape of hierarchies, the span of control of supervisors, job characteristics, the conditions of access to jobs, and skill characteristics. The focus was therefore on relatively generic organisational phenomena, rather than on specific human resource management initiatives.

This research typically led to a cross-national perspective on work and job organisation similar to the distinction reported by an OECD publication in the mid 1990s (Vickery & Wurzburg, 1996; see also Kern & Schumann, 1987; Lorenz, 1992; Streeck, 1987): the UK and United States had a market-driven approach, where short-termism led to the predominance of numerical and external flexibility; Japan adopted a 'relations-based' company-centred approach, with a focus (at least for core workers) on functional flexibility and internal development; while some European economies – particularly the Nordic countries and to a lesser extent Germany – had, through 'decision-making by consensus', also adopted a model based on functional flexibility and internal development. This 'European' model did not however extend to countries such as France, which, despite having high levels of employment security, had failed to establish high-trust industrial relations systems in work systems that followed Taylorist ideas quite closely.

In summary, the post-war workplace compromises in Germany, Scandinavia or Japan relied less on either a strict Taylorist/Fordist division of labour (France, United States), or on unions being reliant on protecting sectional interests through job demarcations (the UK), and thus allowed a greater degree of flexibility *avant la lettre*. Such findings featured heavily in Boyer's (1986) influential comparative study of how different new national flexibility compromises might offer routes out of the crisis of the Fordist system. These distinctions are still sometimes rehearsed in comparative institutionalism (Hall & Soskice, 2001; Marsden, 1999), and retain a degree of validity where reference is to the 'typical' national enterprise in manufacturing. Beyond this, the quantitative findings below show the continued importance of national effects. Certainly, if nothing else, it is important to bear in mind that how 'flexible' the organisation of work is cannot be read off from closeness of fit to popular models of high performance work systems, as different national systems have different resources for, and constraints on, flexibility.

More recently, though, it has become clear that national approaches to flexibility cannot be captured very accurately by an external/internal flexibility dichotomy. The various competitive pressures resulting from contemporary patterns of globalisation – alongside related trends such as the declining strength of organised labour, the deregulatory impulses of states and the increased influence of multinationals – have meant that employers in all countries have sought to use several adjustment strategies in parallel. They seek both internal and external flexibility – albeit from different starting positions and with varying degrees of success – rather than simply choosing between one and the other.

This has led, in broad terms, to the second phase of research on work flexibility. Following worldwide dominance effects which have led to the predominant 'best practice' HRM and work organisation models following a mixture of Japanese work organisation practice – or rather, a Western interpretation of it (Womack et al., 1990) – and neo-liberal American human resource management ideas, research has entered a 'post lean production' phase. Formal structures of job organisation based on HPWS/lean production policies have diffused internationally, first through the export of work organisation and HRM methods by American and Japanese multinationals, then through imitation in other firms. As a result, there has been a wave of quantitative, survey-based research, which typically aims to investigate either the extension, or performance, of 'high performance' systems, albeit normally on a national rather than cross-national basis.

This raised the question of cross-country functional equivalents among some HRM scholars (e.g. Godard, 2004). The best-known example is Appelbaum and Batt's (1994) identification of different competitive clusters of flexible practices such as Swedish socio-technical systems, Japanese lean production, American lean production, and American team production, the main difference between them being their granting different degrees of autonomy to workers. Given that the most typically studied flexible work practices (team work, job rotation, employee involvement and cross-training) have been found to be the core of HRM in the UK (de Menezes & Wood, 2006) while being also typical of lean production (Pil & MacDuffie, 1996), the innovative character of these practices may have become relative, at least in the UK and a sector like automobiles. Whether job autonomy or work enrichment more generally becomes the next flexibility aspiration in these contexts remains to be seen.

RECENT COMPARATIVE CASE STUDIES

In recent qualitative research, the main focus has been on plant-level comparisons of the introduction and operation of various aspects of 'new' work organisation, with a particular – disproportionate – emphasis on team working. In many ways, this research has its origins in the 'Japanisation' literature (Addullah & Keenoy, 1995; Oliver & Wilkinson, 1992; Turnbull, 1986). This tended to find, at most, only explicit features of the Japanese system reaching countries such as the UK (Saka, 2002), rather than its full modus operandi. It has tended to concentrate on manufacturing industry, and within this, on the auto industry. The comparison is most frequently between either the UK or United States and one of the 'coordinated market economies' of Europe, usually Germany or Sweden. Plant-level comparisons are often between the same multinational in different countries and usually with a focus on team working. These patterns of concentration of research potentially offer useful data on how predominant 'global' practices have affected those workplaces, in both liberal and co-ordinated market economies, where they are most likely to be found. It should be recognised, though, that the collective bias inherent in concentrating comparative research on certain practices in certain types of workplace means that this research is much less useful if the goal is to compare 'typical' practices across countries.

With the partial exception of Mueller (1992), who from a study of nine European engine plants saw convergence on functional flexibility and job enrichment overcoming societal effects, the findings of such research typically reflect the problematic encounter between 'old' and 'new' forms of qualitative flexibility, that is, between nationally inherited resources and constraints for flexibility, and new management practices. The discussion on teams, for example, typically starts from an ideal–typical dichotomy between two types of team structure (cf., for example, Greenwood & Randle, 2007):

1. Socio-technical team organisation. This is associated with the regulatory frameworks and production cultures of Nordic economies. It features job autonomy, long job cycles, functional flexibility and reduced worker hierarchy (Appelbaum et al., 2000; Bacon & Blyton, 2003); improving working conditions is a significant goal here.
2. Lean teams. Originating in Japanese production systems but seen as characteristic of Anglo-Saxon economies (Benders & van Hootegem, 1999; Payne & Keep, 2005). These feature work intensification, task enlargement, strong management control and constrained job autonomy (Garrahan & Stewart, 1992); the goal is rationalisation.

Thus, were this dichotomy to be fully realised empirically, firms in both sorts of economy would have team working and other functional flexibility practices, but those in the Nordic countries would see a much greater degree of flexibility of work organisation in practice. Early research in this area largely reflected such institutional differences between Japan, Europe and North America (see, for example, Appelbaum & Batt, 1994; Berggren, 1992; Clarke, 1992; Smith et al., 1995).

More recently, the international effects of lean production, both in terms of work organisation and downsizing, mean that evidence is somewhat more mixed, while still pointing to some national differences. Rather than attempt to be comprehensive, we offer here certain 'representative' findings from some of the better comparative studies.

Greenwood and Randle's (2007) comparison of steel plants in the UK and Sweden showed that UK teams had only moderate levels of autonomy and were quite closely supervised, that their ability to define and organise their skill and training needs was limited, and that they had no input into job design or work flow. But in one (of two) Swedish cases, downsizing had also led to reduced autonomy, less frequent job rotation, and less worker choice over tasks; in the other Swedish case, while work intensification was reported, this did not seem to have reduced the degree of autonomy. Job intensification had reduced the time spent in learning activities in both UK cases and one Swedish case. The main national difference was in the nature of training; in the UK this was more addressed at immediate production needs through job enlargement rather than skill enhancement, which remained more characteristic of the Swedish plants.

Wergin's Anglo-German comparison in the auto industry (2003) showed the most innovative, autonomous form of team working occurring in a German plant, while the most 'structurally conservative' form, with teams having the least functional flexibility, was in a Japan-owned UK plant. The main conclusion here, though, was that national effects were moderated by local factors, especially local union relations (the importance of local social climate is reflected in an array of cases, see Bélanger et al., 2003; Danford, 1998; Kahancová, 2007; Saka, 2002).

Despite, interestingly, finding little difference in worker perceptions, Froebel and Marchington's (2005) Anglo-German comparison in pharmaceuticals showed, within a general climate of job intensification, greater (team) autonomy in Germany, more job enlargement due to more skilled employees, and a greater participation of individuals in team decision making. In the UK case, decision making was largely left to the team leader (this is a relatively common finding, see Saka, 2002). Relatedly, Delmestri and Walgenbach (2005), through a UK–German–Italian comparison of middle managers, showed their greater involvement in technical problem-solving in Germany and Italy than in the UK, where lines of differentiation in the hierarchy remained pronounced (see also Ackroyd, 1996 for the UK).

Ortiz's (1999) work, again on team working in auto plants, in the UK and Spain, reports mainly on differences in union reactions to its introduction, and the effects of negotiation. Its chief finding is that worker representatives in Spain were less negative to new forms of work organisation than their British counterparts, as the former saw this as a chance to extend their influence into the territory of work organisation, while the latter perceived it as more of a threat to their roles. He concludes that functional flexibility practices fit better into industrial relations systems such as that in Germany and Sweden, than the adversarial UK system, with Spain taking an intermediate position.

Köhler and Woodard's (1997) somewhat neglected study of work systems in the machine-building sector in Germany and Spain, with secondary data from France and Japan, is interesting in containing elements of both the phases of research which we highlight, as well as in expanding research beyond the Anglo-German/Swedish dichotomies. While, as expected, they found much higher task differentiation between jobs in the more 'Taylorist' France and Spain than Germany, they somewhat surprisingly found that this was not replicated for Spain in 'functional differentiation', their term for the reality of informal organisation. In the Spanish case, the explanation put forward for the finding was the prevalence of an informal craft-based structure due to incomplete Taylorist rationalisation, and thus higher, if perhaps unplanned, levels of worker autonomy. For Japan, they also suggested that low formal differentiation was accompanied by levels of informal differentiation that were higher than the European countries, except France. This research is important in that it shows that the dynamics of modernised work organisation may have different effects on different elements of jobs and tasks in different places. It is also useful methodologically in developing measures for the important concept of the division of labour, measures which venture beyond the purely formal.

Such qualitative research focusing more on generic indicators of work organisation and flexibility than specific change programmes, such as team working, has become less fashionable, and largely confined to bodies such as the European Foundation. Unfortunately, it has also suffered from some puzzling methodological decisions, such as failures to match firms according to sectors/product markets (Goudswaard & de Nanteuil, 2000), or decisions to choose 'success stories' (Asplund & Oksanen, 2003), which is not particularly useful for comparative analysis.

More qualitative research is needed on internal flexibility, particularly founded on an analysis of job content and boundaries rather than only on specific innovations such as teams. As Kalleberg (2001: 497) reflects, case studies are often chosen because they are sites in which innovations are expected, rather than because of being 'typical'. This is not necessarily problematic in its own terms, but does make generalisation beyond a vanguard of cases within each nation difficult. Also, more qualitative research is needed on issues related to job classification; it is simply not possible that the reduction in grade structures in processes such as broadbanding or competence-based structures, very often introduced at the point of significant changes in work organisation (Almond & Gonzalez, 2006), does not have radically different implications in different employment systems (Marsden, 1999), but this is rarely touched on except in a small number of non-comparative cases (cf. Adler, 1992).

QUANTITATIVE RESEARCH

Cross-country quantitative research in flexible work practices is more rare than country-focused studies and, thus, comparative research in this area is dominated by the comparison of results of national cases using national or sectoral data from employers (overwhelmingly focused on manufacturing), most often with those obtained for the United States. In Europe, there is also a wealth of studies based on employee data obtained through the European Working Conditions Survey. Given limits of space we will focus on analysing the approach and results of cross-country studies only.

The key reference in cross-national research in this area is the longitudinal study by Pil and MacDuffie (1996) of the world automobile industry. They established that (1) prior performance was not a predictor of adoption of flexible work practices; (2) implementation of flexible automation was independent of an earlier use of flexible forms of work such as teams and job rotation and that they were substitutes in many plants in the world; (3) that earlier adoption of complementary HRM practices made more likely the adoption of flexible practices in a second stage, while early adoption of flexible work practices did not predict later adoption of HRM practices. Also, they observed qualitatively some common traits of the quickest adopters of flexible working practices, among which fostering learning across functional and divisional boundaries may be noted.

However, this sort of analysis of determinants of adoption of flexible work practices with a *contingency approach* by which they may be specific to particular industries, types of firms or institutional frameworks has not led to a consensus on the contingencies that matter, or to a general contingency model that could be tested across industries (Capelli & Neumark, 2001) or countries. This could be partly because some cross-country studies with a universalist approach have not attempted to explain the differences found (e.g. Ahmad & Schroeder, 2003). Connectedly, Kalleberg (2003: 171–172) criticises the lack of attention to supra-organisational institutions in shaping firms' practices, as well as the focus on the establishment, given that functional flexibility can be obtained from workers of other firms in supply chains (see also Prieto, 1993).

In terms of *explanatory variables* for the extension of flexible work practices in comparative cross-national approaches, from descriptive data for several countries, Arnal et al. (2001) have posited a positive relationship of flexible practices with information and communications technology expenditure as a share of GDP. Conversely, Godard (2004) has argued that in social market economies such as Germany or Sweden many of the participatory practices are redundant because of institutionalised systems of participation. How new work organisation practices are adopted will, therefore, be different in terms of impact on workers and team involvement is more likely in such economies.

Yet, the limit of both these approaches has been shown by Gallie (2007) through the case of Germany. He points out the limited adoption of multi-functional and/or autonomous teams in Germany because of the reluctance of specialised skilled workers, managers and works councils. He also observes that task discretion and workers' influence over work organisation are higher in the UK (liberal market economy) than in Germany and even higher in the Nordic countries. Also, though Germany shares a strong emphasis on initial vocational training with the Nordic countries, they differ strongly in terms of continuing training. With regard to the latter, Germany is well below the Nordic countries and even below the UK according to several indicators. He also suggests that these differences may have effects for gender equality, in that continuous training may compensate for the disadvantages for women created by the emphasis on initial training being focused on specific skills. Consequently, he questions whether Germany and the Nordic countries should be grouped together at all. He finds that the influence in government of social-democratic parties and the strength of organised labour translating into prominent policy concerns regarding the quality of work – and we could add equal opportunities – are much better explanatory variables of patterns of work organisation with high levels of workers' autonomy, influence and teamwork.

From an economics perspective, Blasi and Kruse (2006: 572), using US data, offer other explanatory variables for cross-national research by positing that innovative work practices may be affected by the export orientation of the companies of a country or by the particular stage of the globalisation process. More mixed is the approach of Arundel et al. (2006) that linked the extension of different work systems in European countries to three variables: employers' expenditure on training, unemployment social protection and generalised trust in a society (see below).

Regarding the determinants of *job discretion*, Poutsma et al. (2003) looked at individual and group-based decision-making autonomy in ten European countries in 1996 and they found qualification levels, technical innovation and intensity of competition made high levels of decision-making autonomy more likely, whereas firm size made it less likely. By countries, taking Portugal as country of reference, the Netherlands, Ireland and the UK were significantly more likely to have a high degree of workers' decision-making autonomy, whereas Italy and Spain were significantly less likely. Between 1996 and 2001, however, workers' job control was found to decline significantly in seven out of the EU-15 countries (Belgium, France, Great Britain, Italy, the Netherlands, Spain and Sweden) and to increase significantly only in Denmark (Gallie, 2005: 361).

Conversely, Saloniemi and Zeytinoglu (2007), finding no significant differences in the proportion of workers that feel they have control over their method of work between fixed-term and permanent jobs in Finland

and Canada, back the convergence hypothesis of a global trend in terms of flexibility.

By looking at the impact of flattening of management structures, job rotation, employee involvement and teamwork on numerical flexibility in ten European countries, the OECD (1999) gives us indirect indicators of the impact of these practices on workers. All the practices were positively associated with working time flexibility, outsourcing and a rise in the proportion working part-time. All but job rotations were associated with downsizing. Job rotation was also positively associated with working time reduction and increasing use of temporary contracts. Flattening of management structures was also positively associated with a rise in subcontracting and in the proportion of temporary contracts.

Turning now to the comparison of European countries on the basis of employee data, Bauer (2004) analysed the impact on job satisfaction of flexible work practices through the European Working Conditions Survey (EWCS) 2000 data. He found that being involved in flexible work systems (with autonomy in decision making, communication, teamwork and job rotation) has a positive significant association with job satisfaction in most EU-15 countries, the exceptions being Belgium, Greece, Ireland and Portugal. However, as to the individual components of the flexible work system, teamwork or job rotation do not contribute significantly to such effects, and the positive association of autonomy with job satisfaction is significant for only eight of the 15 countries. Communication, however, increases the job satisfaction of workers significantly in all countries except in Greece.

More recently, on the basis of the EWCS 2005, Smith et al. (2008) have studied the EU-27 impact of country on several job characteristics (see Table 14.1) that can be considered proxies for work organisation. Viewing these results, Spain, followed by the UK, are the national contexts that may have introduced the least flexible working practices; the Netherlands and Sweden may be at the other end of the spectrum.

Tangian (2007) defined functional flexibility as the changeability of tasks, of teams, and of the content of work, and built an index of functional flexibility on the basis of the data of the following questions from EWCS 2005: frequency of interrupting a task and switching to unforeseen tasks; solving unforeseen problems by oneself; learning new things; rotation of tasks between colleagues; necessity of different skills in rotating tasks; agent deciding on rotation of tasks; and necessity of further training. On the basis of this index the country with the highest level of functional flexibility was Denmark (66 per cent), followed by Slovenia (64 per cent), Norway and the Netherlands (62 per cent). The least functional flexibility was found in Spain (46 per cent), followed by Lithuania

Table 14.1   EU-27 countries that significantly explain the likelihood of job characteristics (country of reference: France), EWCS 2005 data.

Decreases likelihood of a. . .	Increases likelihood of a. . .
. . .job involving monotonous not complex tasks	
Working in Austria, Germany or the Netherlands	Working in Cyprus, Greece, Spain or the UK
. . .job involving complex non-monotonous tasks	
Working in Estonia, Ireland, Spain or the UK	Working in Austria, Germany, the Netherlands, Romania, Slovakia or Sweden
. . .job with a high level of autonomy	
Working in Austria, Bulgaria, the Czech Republic, Germany, Italy, Slovenia or Spain	Working in Latvia
. . .job that involves problem-solving and learning	
Working in Bulgaria, Cyprus, Germany, Greece, Hungary, Italy, Latvia, Lithuania, Romania, Spain or the UK	Working in Denmark, the Netherlands or Sweden

Source: Elaborated from Burchell et al. (2007: 26–28)

and Hungary (47 per cent), Portugal (50 per cent) and Italy (51 per cent) (Tangian, 2007: 24).

Another proxy for flexible work practices that can be obtained from the EWCS 2005 is the number of employees working in autonomous teams that can decide on the division of tasks, as a percentage of the number of employees working in all teams. Parent-Thirion et al. (2007: 52–53) looked at flexible forms of work organisation in European countries by assessing the combined pattern resulting from job rotation and teamwork. The basic indicators were qualified by whether the job rotation involved different skills and by whether the team was autonomous. A combination of these 'advanced' flexible forms of work was most extended among Nordic countries and least in southern and eastern European countries. The sector where this advanced combination was most extended was in health, and it was the least extended in the transport and communications sector. As for occupations, professionals, managers and skilled workers were the most exposed to such work practices, and unskilled workers, machine operators and clerical workers the least.

A study that included all the aforementioned variables sees different patterns of work organisation prevailing in different European countries (Eurofound, 2008).

- *Lean-production* (26 per cent of the employees). Defined by a higher level of teamwork and job rotation, high levels of constraints on the pace of work and self-assessment of quality of work and quality norms; is more apparent in the UK and Ireland along with many of the Eastern European countries and Finland, Luxembourg, Malta and Portugal. It is also more present in manufacturing than in services and more present in jobs occupied by men.
- *Taylorism* (20 per cent of the employees). Defined by low autonomy at work, few learning dynamics, little complexity and an overrepresentation of the variables measuring constraints on the pace of work, repetitiveness and monotony of tasks; is more extended in Southern Europe and many eastern countries. It is more present in manufacturing than in services and more present among younger employees.
- *Discretionary-learning forms* (38 per cent of the employees). Defined by high levels of autonomy at work, learning and problem-solving, task complexity, self-assessment of quality of work and quality norms and, to a lesser extent, teamwork; are more extended in Denmark, Sweden and the Netherlands. They are also more present in services than in manufacturing, and more likely among senior managers, professionals and technicians and among older employees.
- *Traditional or simple structures* (16 per cent of the employees). Characterised by all variables of work organisation being underrepresented and methods being largely informal and non-codified; are most apparent in southern and certain eastern European countries. Also more present among service and sales workers, unskilled workers and jobs occupied by women.

According to this study discretionary-learning forms of work organisation and lean production are associated with greater use of indefinite contracts and incentives, higher levels of training provided by the employer and higher involvement of employees. In this, it seems that the American 'high-performance work organisation' has two expressions in Europe – one close to American lean production, and another with less emphasis on teamwork and job rotation and more on worker autonomy than the American team production. In terms of impact on workers there are two important differences between European lean production and discretionary learning work: working conditions are better and employee satisfaction

Table 14.2   *National differences in forms of work organisation (per cent of employees by country in each organisational class), EWCS 2005 data*

	Discretionary learning	Lean production	Taylorist organisation	Traditional organisation	Total
Belgium	43.3	24.6	16.3	15.8	100.0
Denmark	55.2	27.1	8.5	9.2	100.0
Germany	44.3	19.9	18.4	17.4	100.0
Greece	24.0	29.1	22.6	24.3	100.0
Italy	36.8	24.1	24.6	14.6	100.0
Spain	20.6	24.6	27.5	27.3	100.0
France	47.7	23.8	17.5	11.0	100.0
Ireland	39.0	29.2	11.3	20.5	100.0
Luxembourg	42.7	29.6	13.9	13.8	100.0
Netherlands	51.6	24.3	11.4	12.7	100.0
Portugal	24.9	30.3	32.5	12.3	100.0
United Kingdom	31.7	32.4	17.7	18.2	100.0
Finland	44.9	29.9	12.6	12.7	100.0
Sweden	67.5	16.0	6.9	9.6	100.0
Austria	47.3	22.4	18.3	12.0	100.0
Bulgaria	20.6	27.2	32.7	19.5	100.0
Czech Republic	28.0	26.7	22.5	22.9	100.0
Estonia	40.7	33.4	11.2	14.7	100.0
Hungary	38.3	18.2	23.4	20.1	100.0
Lithuania	23.5	31.1	22.0	23.4	100.0
Latvia	33.4	34.5	17.1	15.0	100.0
Poland	33.3	32.6	18.9	15.2	100.0
Romania	24.0	33.4	27.6	14.9	100.0
Slovenia	34.9	32.1	16.7	16.3	100.0
Slovakia	27.2	21.0	33.8	18.1	100.0
Cyprus	26.4	27.0	21.2	25.4	100.0
Malta	45.6	34.2	12.1	8.2	100.0
EU-27	38.4	25.7	19.5	16.4	100.0

Source: Valeyre et al. (2009: 22)

is higher among employees working under discretionary-learning forms of work organisation (Eurofound, 2008).

These results are consistent with those obtained on the basis of the EWCS 2000 for the EU-15 (Arundel et al., 2006: 13), and the EWCS 2005 for the EU-27 (Valeyre et al., 2009: 22). In Table 14.2 below the differences for EU-27 countries can be seen.

Arundel et al. (2006) find a strong correlation between the frequency of discretionary learning and the percentage of enterprises providing training to employees that also points to a north–south divide in Europe. Discretionary learning is linked to two further variables: generalised trust in a nation and the system of unemployment protection (measured by the proportion of in-work income maintained by someone that becomes unemployed). High levels of trust are argued to support the high levels of autonomy needed in discretionary learning work forms. For these authors, unemployment protection buffers workers from the limited tenures that can be offered by organisations competing on knowledge. With these variables they explain the predominance of lean production in the UK, despite the high expenditure on training, by low trust and intermediate protection (Arundel et al., 2006: 28).

In an earlier paper, some of the authors (Lorenz & Valeyre, 2004: 15) had found that the relative likelihood of the continuous learning model (taking as reference country Germany and as reference work system Taylorism) was significantly positive in the Netherlands, Denmark and Sweden, significantly negative in Greece, Ireland, Portugal, Spain, Italy and the UK, and non-significant in Belgium, Finland, France, Luxemburg and Austria. Regarding the control variables used, the learning model is more likely in smaller establishments and for occupational groups other than operators and unskilled workers; it is also more likely to be found in services than in manufacturing with the exception of hotels and restaurants in services and of electrical machinery and electronics in manufacturing, when using the vehicle sector as reference category. Regarding the relative likelihood of the lean model, it was significantly positive in the UK, Denmark, the Netherlands, Sweden, France and Spain, and non-significant in other countries.

In the period 1995–2005 in the EU-15 levels of autonomy fell and work intensity increased for all groups of workers except for those over 55 (Villosio et al., 2008: 40–41). Being older also made people less likely to have a job that involves problem-solving and learning but more likely to have a job with a high level of autonomy (Burchell et al., 2007: 28–29). It would be of interest to explore further the reasons for the positive link between discretionary-learning forms and age. It is possible, for instance, that the access to jobs of greater quality in terms of working conditions is connected to internal labour markets of firms. A further issue for research is that occupational structures across Europe are likely to exhibit differences that are not captured by the EWCS occupational variables. The links of different work organisation forms with occupation and skills could be better examined comparatively by ranking occupations in each country according to the average educational level attained by occupants – as recently proposed by Garrido and Gutierrez (2009) for labour market segmentation analysis.

DISCUSSION

Functional flexibility is an elusive concept that is not easy to measure. This is particularly the case on a cross-national basis, especially if, as Godard suggests, certain institutionalised practices in more coordinated economies are a functional equivalent for some of the firm-level flexibility policies that management research tends to concentrate on. For this reason, it may be more useful, in a comparative sense, to use measures derived from more generic features of jobs than to measure fit with an Anglo-American concept of what represent high flexibility practices.

In this sense, some of the work done with European Working Conditions Surveys is interesting. The various treatments of this data reported above seem to provide some continued support for the idea of substantial national differences, notwithstanding the various forces for convergence. Some of these differences are not hugely different from what might have been predicted by older institutionalist research; the highest levels of many of the proxies for functional flexibility seem to be found in some of the more 'coordinated' employment systems, such as the Scandinavian countries and the Netherlands, and the lowest where there are greater problems with coordination (Spain, the new EU states), while the UK and Ireland have perhaps seen a limited form of diffusion of functional flexibility based around lean production.

However, these results do not offer support to a simplistic 'varieties of capitalism' division, and it is worth emphasising the questions that they raise. First, there appears to be a difference between one of the emblematic coordinated economies, Germany, and its Scandinavian/Dutch counterparts; from Burchell et al. (2007), German jobs appear to be relatively complex, but to have low degrees of autonomy and problem-solving. This apparently contradictory finding obviously warrants further research, but may indicate an organisation of work predominantly based on high initial levels of skill rather than on flexibility, with problem-solving primarily in the hands of first-level managers, who are likely to have relatively high levels of technical competence (Gallie, 2007).

From Arundel et al. (2006), there is a broad north–south split in the continued use of Taylorist or traditional forms of work organisation. There also appears to be a second split between whether the prevalent 'new' model of work organisation is closer to the discretionary learning or lean production model, which broadly corresponds to the varieties of capitalism dichotomy. Clearly such results, as national averages, do not mean that individual enterprises cannot follow policies that are distinctive (or have different work organisation for different groups of workers), while qualitative results reflect the challenges even in higher trust countries such as Sweden. Equally, survey or case-study questions posed to employees to an extent give subjective answers. These may be based on cultural assumptions about what are appropriate levels of autonomy, etc., as much as objective differences. Nevertheless, from the various pieces of research reported here, a number of variables seem, both at micro and macro levels, to affect functional flexibility (cf. Köhler & Woodard, 1997).

First, there is the issue of skills; advanced forms of flexibility plainly depend on workers available on the labour market being sufficiently qualified, whether in initial or continuous training or preferably both (Gallie, 2007). Training is more likely to lead to flexibility when it is broad-based rather than focusing narrowly on jobs as defined at a specific moment by employers (Marsden, 1999). As the flexicurity debate (Tangian, 2007) reflects, attention needs to be paid to how qualitative flexibility is shaped by national levels of employment protection (Almond et al., 2006). To this we need to add the issue of incentives for training through internal or occupational labour markets; far more attention needs to be paid to firm- or sector-level job classification systems and possibilities for career progression through upskilling, and to national differences in skills by occupational level, as possible explanatory variables. In the UK and United States employers have frequently sought to remove old 'rigidities' in job classification through processes of 'broadbanding'; while this may increase flexibility in the short term, it runs the risk of provoking skill shortages and a lack of incentives and hence problems of employee commitment in the longer term (Grimshaw et al., 2002). Meanwhile the efforts of employers in sectoral industrial relations systems to deal with the emergence of new kinds of jobs by adjusting classification systems, while hardly a new trend (Donnadieu & Denimal, 1993), remains woefully under-researched in terms of its impact on job content.

Second, as reflected above, issues of power between social actors retain their importance (Gallie, 2007). Weak employee representation is likely to lead to the limited forms of flexibility brought about by intensification, as has occurred in many workplaces in the UK or United States, but also to poorly represented workers in segmented labour markets such as Spain (Gonzalez & Almond, 2006). Strong representation in low trust systems (now a rarity) is likely to limit flexibility, while strong protection of employee interest in higher trust systems seems to be most conducive to discretionary learning models of flexibility. The fragmentation caused by the decentralisation of collective bargaining in countries such as Germany may cause problems of coordination in this respect (cf. Martinez Lucio et al., 2007).

Third, Köhler and Woodard see enterprise culture and cultural traditions as independent variables. As Payne and Keep (2005) reflect, the willingness to experiment with work organisation in the Nordic countries is likely to be related to a general culture of civic participation. National models of management (Guillén, 1994) are logically likely to be to some extent dependent on such wider cultural norms. Research that investigates workplace culture on a comparative basis, going beyond the dated practice of following the measurements developed by Hofstede (1980), would be useful in expanding on this point.

We should not neglect variance in the *demand* for advanced forms of flexibility. UK commentators on skills (cf. Payne & Keep, 2005) increasingly argue that a policy concentration on problems of labour supply has neglected the problem that many employers do not actually demand high skills, and are content to compete through neo-Fordist, low discretion forms of work. This orientation, they argue, has been encouraged by state concentration on attracting investment through 'labour market flexibility'. Although comparative research here is lacking, this serves as a useful reminder that we should not assume that employers want the same levels of functional flexibility in all countries.

Future comparative HRM research in flexible working practices, whether quantitative or qualitative, needs to concentrate much more on job content and skills, defined in generic terms which minimise the culturally bounded nature of the dependent variable, and less on specific management initiatives such as team working whose relationship to functional flexibility is to a large extent contingent. More research is required in smaller, indigenous companies, particularly outside manufacturing. It also needs to go beyond the coordinated/liberal economy dichotomy by placing greater emphasis on those economies which do not fit comfortably in either group, if only as basic triangulation.

Finally, limitations of data, particularly on the quantitative side, have meant that much of the material here has concentrated on EU countries. It is worth re-iterating that in the poorer countries which account for an increasing proportion of industrial production, managerial methods that owe more to Taylorist methods (or sometimes even pre-Taylorist coercion) remain readily available. In such scenarios, the more positive features of work flexibility, in terms of worker autonomy and involvement, are rarely even considered, except perhaps in a small number of global firms in advanced manufacturing where the functional need for cross-national learning on work organisation is high. Elsewhere, the Japanese production system as exemplified by Toyota (Smith, 1997) clearly fits into the lean production model – and indeed is the inspiration for it – while other industrialised Asian countries such as Korea seem to represent a confusion between lean production, traditional collectivist forms of management, and elements of 'Anglo-Saxon' HRM (Bae & Rowley, 2001).

Overall, it is unlikely to be a coincidence that moves towards discretionary learning models at a wider societal level have tended to be more widespread where workers possess countervailing resources, not least in the form of welfare states, flexible systems of learning and a degree of trade union power.

REFERENCES

Ackroyd, S. 1996. Organization contra organizations: professions and organizational change in the United Kingdom. *Organization Studies*, **17**(4): 599–621.
Addullah, S. & Keenoy, T. 1995. Japanese managerial practices in the Malaysian Electronics Industry: two case studies. *Journal of Management Studies*, **32**(6): 747–766.
Adler, P. 1992. *Technology and the Future of Work*. Oxford: Oxford University Press.
Ahmad, S. & Schroeder, R. G. 2003. The impact of human resource management practices on organizational performance: recognizing country and industry differences. *Journal of Operations Management*, **21**(1): 19–43
Almond, P. & Gonzalez, M. 2006. Varieties of capitalism: the importance of political and social choices. *Transfer*, **12**(3): 407–425.
Almond, P., Muller-Camen, M., Collings, D. & Quintanilla, J. 2006. Pay and performance. In P. Almond & A. Ferner (eds), *American Multinationals in Europe*. Oxford: Oxford University Press, pp. 119–146.
Appelbaum, E., Bailey, T., Berg, P., & Kalleberg, A. 2000. *Manufacturing Advantage: Why High-Performance Work Systems Pay Off*. Ithaca, NY: Cornell University Press.
Appelbaum, E. & Batt, R. 1994. *The New American Workplace*. Cornell: ILR Press.
Arnal, E., Ok, W. & Torres, R. 2001. Knowledge, work organisation and economic growth. OECD Labour Market and Social Policy Occasional Papers, No. 50: OECD Publishing.
Arundel, A., Lorenz, E., Lundvall, B. & Valeyre, A. 2006. The organization of work and innovative performance: a comparison of the EU-15. Druid Working Paper, No. 06-14.
Asplund, R. & Oksanen, J. 2003. Functional flexibility strategies: evidence from companies in five small European economies. Research Institute of the Finnish Economy Discussion Papers, No 874.
Atkinson, J. 1984. *Flexibility, Uncertainty and Manpower Management*. Brighton: Institute of Manpower Studies.
Bacon, N. & Blyton, P. 2003. The impact of teamwork on skills: employee perceptions of who gains and who loses. *Human Resource Management Journal*, **13**(2): 13–29.
Bae, J. & Rowley, C. 2001. The impact of globalization on HRM: the case of South Korea. *Journal of World Business*, **36**(4): 402–428.
Bauer, T. K. 2004. High performance workplace practices and job satisfaction: evidence from Europe. IZA Discussion Papers, No 1265.
Bélanger, J., Edwards, P. & Wright, M. 2003. Commitment at work and independence from management. *Work and Occupations*, **30**(2): 234–252.
Benders, J. & van Hootegem, G. 1999. Teams and their context: moving the team discussion beyond existing dichotomies. *Journal of Management Studies*, **36**(5): 609–628.
Berggren, C. 1992. *Alternatives to Lean Production*. Ithaca: ILR Press.
Blasi, J. & Kruse, D. 2006. US high-performance work practices at century's end. *Industrial Relations*, **45**(4): 547–578.
Blyton, P. 1992. Flexible times? Recent developments in temporal flexibility. *Industrial Relations Journal*, **23**(1): 26–36.
Boltanski, L. & Chiapello, E. 1999. *Le Nouvel Esprit du Capitalisme*. Paris: Gallimard.
Boyer, R. 1986. *La Flexibilité du Travail en Europe*. Paris: La Découverte.
Brewster, C., Hegewisch, A. & Mayne, L. 1994. Flexible working practices. In C. Brewster

& A. Hegewisch (eds), *Policy and Practice in European Human Resource Management.* London: Routledge.

Bruno, S. 1989. La flexibility: un concept contingent. In M. Maruani, E. Reynaud & C. Romani (eds), *La Flexibilité en Italie.* Paris: Syros, pp. 33–49.

Burchell, B., Fagan, C., O'Brien, C. & Smith, M. 2007. Working conditions in the European Union: the gender perspective. Luxembourg: Office for Official Publications of the European Communities.

Capelli, P. & Neumann, D. 2001. Do 'high performance' work practices improve establishment-level outcomes? *Industrial and Labor Relations Review,* **54**(4): 737–775.

Capelli, P. & Neumark, D. 2004. External churning and internal flexibility: evidence on the functional flexibility and core-periphery hypotheses. *Industrial Relations,* **43**(1): 148–182.

Carnicer, M., Sanchez, A., Perez, M. & Jimenez, M. 2004. Analysis of internal and external labour mobility: a model of job-related and nonrelated factors. *Personnel Review,* **33**(2): 222–240.

Clarke, O. 1992. Employment adjustment: an international perspective. In K. Koshiro (ed.), *Employment Security and Labor Market Flexibility: An International Perspective.* Detroit: Wayne State University Press, pp. 218–244.

Danford, A. 1998. Teamworking and labour regulation in the autocomponents industry. *Work, Employment and Society,* **12**(3): 409–431.

de Menezes, L. M. & Wood, S. 2006. The reality of flexible work systems in Britain. *International Journal of Human Resource Management,* **17**(1): 106–138.

Delaney, J. & Huselid, M. 1996. The impact of human resource management practices on perceptions of organizational performance. *Academy of Management Journal,* **39**(4): 949–969.

Delmestri, G. & Walgenbach, P. 2005. Mastering techniques or brokering knowledge? Middle managers in Germany, Great Britain and Italy. *Organization Studies,* **26**(2): 197–220.

Donnadieu, G. & Denimal, P. 1993. *Classification–Qualification, de l'Evaluation des Emplois à la Gestion des Compétences.* Paris: Editions Liaisons.

EIRO. 2003. *Annualised Hours in Europe.* Dublin: European Foundation for the Improvement of Living and Working Conditions.

Eurofound, E. F. f. t. I. o. L. a. W. C. 2008. Working conditions in the European Union: Work organisation: Executive summary, (EF/08/68/EN).

Froebel, P. & Marchington, M. 2005. Teamworking structures and worker perceptions: a cross-national study in pharmaceuticals. *International Journal of Human Resource Management,* **16**(2): 256–276.

Gallie, D. 2005. Work pressure in Europe 1996–2001: trends and determinants. *British Journal of Industrial Relations,* **43**(3): 351–375.

Gallie, D. 2007. Production regimes and the quality of employment in Europe. *Annual Review of Sociology,* **33**: 85–104.

Garrahan, P. & Stewart, P. 1992. *The Nissan Enigma: Flexibility at Work in the Local Economy.* London: Mansell.

Garrido, L. & Gutierrez, R. 2009. More quantity and better quality. Occupational change in 21st century Spain. Paper presented at The Dualisation of European Societies? Conference held at Green Templeton College, University of Oxford, 24–25 April.

Godard, J. 2004. A critical assessment of the high-performance paradigm. *British Journal of Industrial Relations,* **42**(2): 349–378.

Gonzalez, M. & Almond, P. 2006. Varieties of capitalism and employer opportunism, Paper presented at World Congress of the International Industrial Relations Association, Lima.

Goudswaard, A. & de Nanteuil, M. 2000. *Flexibility and Working Conditions: A Qualitative and Comparative Study in Seven EU Member States.* Dublin: European Foundation for the Improvement of Living and Working Conditions

Greenwood, I. & Randle, H. 2007. Team-working, restructuring and skills in UK and Sweden. *European Journal of Industrial Relations,* **13**(3): 361–378.

Grimshaw, D., Beynon, H., Rubery, J. & Ward, K. 2002. The restructuring of career paths in large service sector organizations: 'delayering', upskilling and polarisation. *Sociological Review*, **50**(1): 89–116.

Guest, D. E. 1987. Human resource management and industrial relations. *Journal of Management Studies*, **24**(5): 503–521.

Guillén, M. 1994. *Models of Management: Work, Authority, and Organization in a Comparative Perspective*. Chicago: University of Chicago Press.

Haddon, L. & Brynin, M. 2005. The character of telework and the characteristics of teleworkers. *New Technology, Work and Employment*, **20**(1): 34–46.

Hall, P. & Soskice, D. 2001. *Varieties of Capitalism*. Oxford: Oxford University Press.

Hofstede, G. 1980. *Culture's Consequences*. Beverly Hills, CA: Sage Publications.

Ichniowski, C., Kochan, T., Levine, D., Olson, C. & Strauss, G. 1996. What works at work: overview and assessment. *Industrial Relations*, **35**(3): 299–333.

Kahancová, M. 2007. One company, four factories: coordinating employment flexibility practices with local trade unions. *European Journal of Industrial Relations*, **13**(1): 67–88.

Kalleberg, A. 2001. Organizing flexibility: the flexible firm in a new century. *British Journal of Industrial Relations*, **39**(4): 479–504.

Kalleberg, A. L. 2003. Flexible firms and labour market segmentation: effects of workplace restructuring on jobs and workers. *Work and Occupations*, **30**(2): 154–175.

Kelliher, C. & Anderson, D. 2008. For better or for worse? An analysis of how flexible working practices influence employees' perceptions of job quality. *International Journal of Human Resource Management*, **19**(3): 419–431.

Kern, H. & Schumann, M. 1987. Hacia una reprofesionalizacion del trabajo industrial. *Sociología del Trabajo*, **1**:11–21.

Köhler, C. & Woodard, J. 1997. Systems of work and socio-economic structures: a comparison of Germany, Spain, France and Japan. *European Journal of Industrial Relations*, **3**(1): 59–82.

Lammers, C. & Hickson, D. 1979. *Organizations Alike and Unlike*. London: Routledge.

Lane, C. 1989. *Management and Labour in Europe*. Aldershot, UK: Edward Elgar.

Lorenz, E. 1992. Trust and the flexible firm: international comparisons. *Industrial Relations*, **31**(3): 455–472.

Lorenz, E. & Valeyre, A. 2004. Organisational change in Europe: national models or the diffusion of a new 'one best way'. Druid Working Paper, No 04-04.

MacDuffie, J. 1995. Human resource bundles and manufacturing performance: flexible production systems in the world auto industry. *Industrial & Labor Relations Review*, **48**(2): 197–221.

Marsden, D. 1999. *A Theory of Employment Systems*. Oxford: Oxford University Press.

Martinez Lucio, M., Skule, S., Kruse, W. & Trappmann, V. 2007. Regulating skill formation in Europe: German, Norwegian and Spanish policies on transferable skills. *European Journal of Industrial Relations*, **13**(3): 323–340.

Maurice, M., Sellier, F. & Sylvestre, J.-J. 1986. *The Social Foundations of Industrial Power*. Cambridge, MA: MIT Press.

Maurice, M., Sorge, A. & Warner, M. 1980. Societal differences in organizing manufacturing units. *Organization Studies*, **1**(1): 59–86.

Mueller, F. 1992. Societal effects, organizational effects and globalisation. *Organization Studies*, **15**(3): 407–428.

OECD. 1999. New enterprise work practices and their labour market implications. *Employment Outlook 1999*, June, OECD Publishing, Chapter 4, pp. 179-221.

Oeij, P. & Wiezer, N. 2002. *New Work Organisation, Working Conditions and Quality of Work: Towards the Flexible Firm?* Dublin: European Foundation for the Improvement of Living and Working Conditions.

Oliver, N. & Wilkinson, B. 1992. *The Japanization of British Industry*, 2nd edn. Oxford: Blackwell.

Ortiz, L. 1999. Unions' responses to teamwork: differences at national and workplace levels. *European Journal of Industrial Relations*, **5**(1): 49–69.

Osterman, P. 1994. How common is workplace transformation and who adopts it? *Industrial and Labor Relations Review*, **47**(2): 173–188.

Parent-Thirion, A., Fernández Macías, E., Hurley, J. & Vermeylen, G. 2007. *Fourth European Working Conditions Survey*. Luxembourg: Office for Official Publications of the European Communities .

Payne, J. & Keep, E. 2005. Re-visiting the Nordic approaches to work re-organisation and job redesign: lessons for UK skills policy. *Policy Studies*, **24**(4): 204–225.

Pil, F. T. & MacDuffie, J. P. 1996. The adoption of high-involvement work practices. *Industrial Relations*, **35**(3): 423–455.

Piore, M. & Sabel., C. 1984. *The Second Industrial Divide*. New York: Basic Books.

Poutsma, E., Hendrixx, J. & Huijgen, F. 2003. Employee participation in Europe: in search of the participative workplace. *Economic and Industrial Democracy*, **24**(1): 45–76.

Prieto, C. 1993. The management of the work-force: a sociological criticism of prevailing fashions. *International Journal of Human Resource Management*, **4**(3): 611–634.

Saka, A. 2002. Institutional limits to the internalization of work systems: a comparative study of three Japanese multinational companies in the UK. *European Journal of Industrial Relations*, **8**(3): 251–275.

Saloniemi, A. & Zeytinoglu, I. U. 2007. Achieving flexibility through insecurity: a comparison of work environments in fixed-term and permanent jobs in Finland and Canada. *European Journal of Industrial Relations*, **13**(1): 109–128.

Shockley, K. & Allen, T. 2007. When flexibility helps: Another look at the availability of flexible work arrangements and work-family conflict. *Journal of Vocational Behavior*, **71**(3): 479–493.

Smith, M., Burchell, B., Fagan, C. & O'Brien, C. 2008. Job quality in Europe. *Industrial Relations Journal*, **39**(6): 586–603.

Smith, M., Masi, A., van den Berg, A. & Smucker, J. 1995. External flexibility in Sweden and Canada: a three industry comparison. *Work, Employment and Society*, **9**(4): 689–718.

Smith, V. 1997. New forms of work organization. *Annual Review of Sociology*, **23**: 315–339.

Streeck, W. 1987. The uncertainties of management in the management of uncertainty: employers, labor relations and industrial adjustment in the 1980s. *Work Employment and Society*, **1**(3): 281–308.

Tangian, A. S. 2007. Is flexible work precarious? A study based on the 4th European Survey of Working Conditions 2005, WSI-Diskussionspapier, No 153, June.

Tregaskis, O. & Brewster, C. 2006. Converging or diverging? A comparative analysis of trends in contingent employment practice in Europe over a decade. *Journal of International Business Studies*, **37**(1): 111–126.

Turnbull, P. 1986. The 'Japanisation' of production and industrial relations at Lucas Electrical. *Industrial Relations Journal*, **17**(3): 193–206.

Tüselmann, H. 1996. Progress towards greater labour flexibility in Germany: the impact of recent reforms. *Employee Relations*, **18**(1): 50–67.

Valeyre, A., Lorenz, E., Cartron, D., Czismadia, P., Gollac, M., Illéssy, M. & Makó, C. 2009. *Working Conditions in the European Union: Work Organisation*. Dublin: European Foundation for the Improvement of Living and Working Conditions.

Vickery, G. & Wurzburg, G. 1996. Flexible firms, skills and employment. OECD Observer, No. 202.

Villosio, C., Di Pierro, D., Giordanengo, A., Pasqua, P. & Richiardi, M. 2008. *Working Conditions of an Ageing Workforce*. Luxembourg: Office for Official Publications of the European Communities.

Walton, R. 1985. From control to commitment in the workplace. *Harvard Business Review*, March–April: 77–84.

Wergin, N.-E. 2003. Teamwork in the automobile industry: an Anglo-German comparison. *European Political Economy Review*, **1/2**: 152–190.

Womack, J., Roos, D. & Jones, D. 1990. *The Machine That Changed The World*. London: Macmillan.

15 Financial participation
Andrew Pendleton and Erik Poutsma

In recent decades many countries have witnessed an increase in the use of employee share ownership plans and profit sharing ('financial participation'). Indeed, by the end of the twentieth century employee financial participation had come to be a widespread feature of human resource management and employment practices in large firms in some countries. In the UK, for instance, nearly all firms in the FTSE 100 (the 100 largest listed firms) had at least one all-employee share ownership plan. Nevertheless, pronounced differences remain between countries in the extent and significance of financial participation. In some countries, there is extensive statutory and fiscal support for financial participation; in others there is little or none. It has become clear from several surveys and comparisons (Lowitzsch, 2006; Poutsma, 2001; Uvalic, 1991; Vaughan Whitehead, 1995) that the availability of fiscal benefits to companies and employees are an extremely important, probably the most important, influence on the use of financial participation schemes. Appeals to promote financial participation have therefore typically called on governments to introduce or improve legislation and fiscal provisions. But a deeper question is why legislation has been more prevalent in some countries than others?

This question has not been fully addressed in the literature on financial participation though many accounts touch on a broad set of reasons for national differences. Some years ago, Poole (1989) proposed that 'favourable conjunctures' could explain the popularity or growth of financial participation in given countries. This might be a combination of economic and political circumstances. For instance, the UK position can partly be explained by a shift of economic power from workers to firms and a political emphasis on undermining trade unionism and promoting employer–employee co-operation in the early 1980s; these formed a backdrop to legislation to promote employee share ownership. More recently, notions of 'national business systems' and 'varieties of capitalism' provide a more comprehensive and theoretically-grounded way of looking at the use of financial participation. They may help to explain why various forms of financial participation are more appealing in some national contexts than others. However, the financial participation literature has only just begun to draw on these ideas (Croucher et al., 2010).

In this chapter, we outline the main forms of financial participation and present some country profiles of financial participation. We then present some recent survey evidence on the incidence of financial participation in Europe and elsewhere, before reflecting on reasons for differences between countries in the character and incidence of financial participation.

FINANCIAL PARTICIPATION: DIVERSITY IN FORMS AND MEANING

Financial participation or 'economic democracy' is the participation of employees in enterprise profits and outcomes. In the European Union (EU) financial participation is often referred to as PEPPER – Promotion of Employee Participation in Profits and Enterprise Results – and a number of major inquiries have been referred to as PEPPER reports (Lowitzsch, 2006; Poutsma, 2001; Uvalic, 1991). It is often considered alongside employee participation in enterprise decision making, usually referred to as direct participation (where individual employees participate) and indirect participation (where representatives participate on employees' behalf). These other forms are also sometimes referred to as 'industrial democracy'.

There is a wide diversity in the characteristics of financial participation schemes around the world but policy makers and scholars usually identify two main forms: profit sharing and employee share ownership (see Poutsma, 2001). However, the picture is usually complicated by the presence of hybrid arrangements: particular financial participation plans may have elements of both profit sharing and share ownership. Each of these two main forms has a number of sub-types, which once again may be combined with others. To complicate matters further, either type of financial participation may also be combined with employee savings schemes or pension arrangements. As pension arrangements become more diverse in many countries, the relationship with financial participation has become more complex.

Profit sharing is the sharing of profits by giving employees, in addition to a fixed wage, a variable income component linked directly to profits or some other measure of enterprise results. Contrary to traditional bonuses linked to individual performance (such as piece rates), profit sharing is a collective scheme applied to all or to a large group of employees. Some definitions of profit sharing emphasise that it should be based on a formula that is used from year to year, to distinguish it from one-off or irregular bonuses awarded when the company is doing well. In practice, profit sharing can take various forms. At the enterprise level, it can provide employees with immediate or deferred benefits; it can be paid in cash, enterprise shares or other securities; or it can be allocated to specific funds invested for the benefit of employees. At higher levels, profit sharing takes the form of economy-wide, sectoral or regional wage-earners' funds.

The simplest form of profit sharing is *cash-based profit sharing* (CPS) – in this instance, employees receive cash payments based on profits more or less at the time that the profits are determined. This form of profit sharing typically does not attract any fiscal concessions because it can be difficult to differentiate the profit shares from base wages, thereby raising tax compliance issues.

Deferred profit sharing (DPS) is a form of deferred compensation under which the allocated profit share is held by the employer for a while, most commonly in trust, and is not immediately available to the employee. A typical scheme would release the payment to employees after about three years. A DPS scheme might allocate a percentage of profits to enterprise funds, which are then invested (either in the company, other companies or other investment vehicles) in the name of the employee. Alternatively, the amount can be allocated to the employee's account, with a certain minimum retention period before the amount is made available. Generally, in most countries with any statutory policy on financial participation, a DPS plan must be approved by tax authorities, particularly where tax concessions to employer or employee are involved. In fact, most countries regulate plan features, such as eligibility, contribution rates, vesting, investments and distribution.

Share-based profit sharing consists of granting employees shares in the company based on profits or some other measure of performance. These shares are usually frozen in a fund for a certain period before employees are allowed to sell them. When shares are subject to a minimum retention period, the term 'deferred share-based profit sharing' is preferred.

There is often a close relationship between profit sharing and asset accumulation/savings plans. The employee's profit shares may be paid into an enterprise-based savings plan for the employee. In some instances, employee contributions into these plans from profit sharing are matched by further employer contributions. In some countries, governments give bonuses on employee contributions. There may be further tax benefits on the interest accruing from these savings. Whilst the link between profit sharing and these savings plans has often taken a medium-term character, changes in pensions regimes have recently encouraged more long-term linkages between profit sharing and employee savings. With the decline in state-provided and employer-provided pensions in many countries, there has been increasing attention paid to personal pensions. In some instances, profit shares can be used for contributions to pension plans.

A variant of profit sharing is gain-sharing. Here employees share in the gains obtained from efficiency programmes and reductions in costs.

These plans are seen as especially suitable for non-profit and public sector organisations,. They rarely attract tax benefits because it can be difficult to demonstrate a separation between the base wage and the gain-sharing payment for tax compliance purposes.

Employee share ownership provides for employee participation in enterprise results via either dividends or the appreciation of employee-owned capital, or a combination of the two. Where appreciation in the market value of shares is the primary benefit, financial participation is indirectly linked to company profits.

There are several types of employee share ownership plan. The first is the award of free shares to employees. Here there is an obvious overlap with profit sharing schemes in so far as the distribution of shares might be financed out of profits. Alternatively, share ownership plans may provide for employees to purchase shares in the company, possibly on advantageous terms (e.g. at a discount on market price). In some plans employers may match the purchases made by employees. Once again, there may be a link with pensions in that the share purchases may be part of larger and wider portfolios of investments made by the employee in conjunction with their employer (as in 401(k) plans in the United States). Another form of share acquisition is the stock option plan. Employees may be granted the right to acquire shares at some point in the future, typically between three and ten years ahead. Although this does not necessarily lead to ownership, because the employee may simultaneously exercise the option and sell the shares, in most all-employee plans of this sort some employees will exercise and hold. There is another potential link with savings plans in that there may be arrangements for employees to save from their salary so as to accumulate the capital necessary to exercise the option.

There is a wide diversity of taxation arrangements for employee share-ownership plans depending on the kind of gains that employees make from them. Where shares are distributed freely or at a discount, employees gain an employment benefit on the value of the shares (or the discount) and hence would normally expect to pay income tax on this. Tax advantageous schemes may waive this income tax liability (and associated social insurance charges). The growth in value of shares may be taxed at capital gains tax rates rather than income tax rates, and these are often more advantageous to the employee because of either lower marginal rates or additional tax exempt allowances.

There is wide diversity between countries in the point at which tax becomes liable in employee share plans, especially those based on granting of options. Some tax at grant, some at exercise, some at sale of the shares and some on a combination of these.

Employee share ownership can be both individual and collective. In some cases shares are held collectively for employees, and are not distributed to individual employees. In this instance, the dividends received by the trust are then distributed to employees as a profit-share. Alternatively, shares may initially be held collectively but then distributed to individual employees over time. This is typically what occurs in ESOPs (Employee Share Ownership Plans). In this form of share ownership, shares are initially passed to an employee benefits trust, financed either by loans, profits, or a gift from the company owner. ESOPs have acquired a specific meaning in the United States, where they have grown tremendously over the last 30 years, largely as a result of favourable tax considerations for companies that establish them. The chief difference between ESOPs and other share ownership plans is that ESOPs typically enable a higher proportion of the firm to be owned by employees. From the point of view of the employee participant, he or she could experience little difference between an ESOP and a deferred profit-sharing plan, at least to the extent that the profit-sharing trust invests in shares of the sponsoring employer, since it is possible that in neither case does the participant receive any shares (or cash) until distribution at some future time. Employers may also establish ESOPs in the hope of realising many of the same indirect advantages as those listed above for deferred profit-sharing plans, including the establishment of an ownership culture.

By and large, employee share-ownership plans should be differentiated from workers' co-operatives and worker-managed firms. Co-operatives are usually required to abide by a set of principles including 100 per cent worker ownership and equal distribution of ownership by employee-owners, though it is not necessarily the case that all those employed by co-operatives are owners. The most well-known workers' co-operatives are those grouped in the Mondragon region of northern Spain. For a variety of reasons, co-operatives are often small in size and are often concentrated in certain areas of economic activity, such as those that are labour-intensive (Bonin et al., 1993). Firms with share ownership plans are often keen to distinguish themselves from co-operatives: they emphasise their 'conventional' management structures compared with what they see as worker 'interference' in management in co-operatives. This criticism of co-operatives is often unfair but it is undoubtedly the case that the small size of many co-operatives does facilitate more collective forms of management. There has been a great deal of discussion about the long-term viability of worker's co-operatives in the literature (Estrin & Jones, 1992). There appears to have been a decline recently in the number of co-operatives in some economies (the United States and UK, for instance) but they are more entrenched in some European economies such as France and Italy.

THE INCIDENCE OF FINANCIAL PARTICIPATION AROUND THE WORLD

There are pronounced differences in the incidence and character of financial participation between countries. Unfortunately, it is difficult to make systematic comparisons because the information available on financial participation differs between countries. Generally speaking, where financial participation is more prevalent there is a greater level of information about it. Relevant statistical information is not collected in many countries with low levels of financial participation because the schemes in use do not have a clear legal identity.

There are therefore not many comparative data sources that have information on the incidence and development of financial participation. There are almost no data available on African and Latin America countries, and limited data are available from Asia. The only comprehensive sources of comparative data are the Cranet HRM Surveys with organisation level data and European Working Conditions Surveys with employee level data. The Cranet survey is carried out on a global scale, involving a network of more than 40 top business schools and universities, collecting factual, representative and comparative data. The data are collected using a postal survey of senior HRM Directors from organisations in all sectors of the economy with more than 100 employees. The survey is conducted periodically and therefore also provides longitudinal information about human resource management policies and practices.

Figure 15.1 provides an overview of the use of employee share ownership in most EU countries based on the Cranet network data of 2004. These are data of private sector organisations with more than 200 employees. Pendleton et al., (2003) used an earlier dataset of Cranet that showed that in general the use of schemes is higher for management and professional staff than for clerical staff and manual workers. However, it is important to bear in mind that this does not necessarily mean that schemes are more common for management staff in a given workplace. The figures refer to the proportion of workplaces with a scheme for the particular occupational group, so the distribution of schemes between occupations in a country is obviously affected by the occupational composition of workplaces. To counter this problem the figure distinguishes between narrow-based plans, available only for management and selected groups, and broad-based plans, where all occupational groups are eligible to participate. In interpreting these results it should be borne in mind that 'broad-based' does not necessarily mean a high participation rate. We know from other sources that participation rates in share schemes are typically lower than in profit sharing schemes.

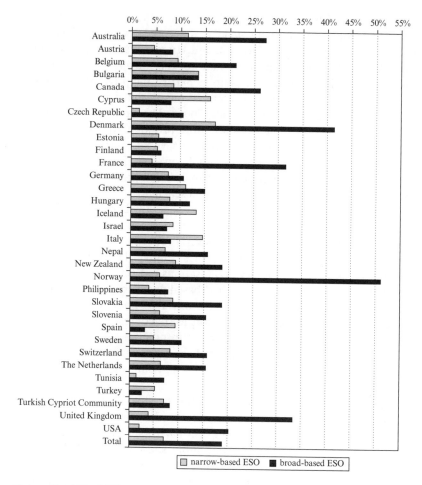

Notes: Total *N* = 3656.

Source: Cranet, 2004.

Figure 15.1 *Incidence rates of employee share schemes for private sector companies (200+) per country, 2004*

Figure 15.1 presents the incidence of narrow-based and broad-based share schemes. In general, the proportion of companies with schemes is low; on average 19 per cent for broad-based schemes and 7 per cent for narrow-based schemes. Broad-based share ownership plans are most common in Norway, Denmark, France, the UK and Australia followed by Canada and the United States. Mediterranean countries, such as Spain,

Italy, Tunisia, Turkey and Cyprus, and some other European countries, such as Estonia and Finland, tend to have the lowest incidence. The incidence rates in Slovakia, Slovenia and Hungary take an average position. Although some new member states of the European Union initially promoted employee share ownership as part of the privatisation process at transition, employee share ownership has declined in most of these countries subsequently (Hashi et al., 2006). The table also shows that the differences between countries are more pronounced for broad-based than for narrow-based schemes. This is very similar to the results of the previous Cranet survey in 1999 (see Pendleton et al., 2001, 2003), where it was found that narrow-based schemes are less determined by country and institutional differences than broad-based schemes.

The incidence rates of profit sharing are generally higher than for share schemes: 31 per cent for broad-based and 10 per cent for narrow-based schemes (see Figure 15.2). As can be seen, France has substantially more broad-based profit sharing than any other country. This is because profit sharing is compulsory for larger organisations in France. Other countries with relatively high incidence of broad-based profit sharing are Germany, Finland, Austria, Netherlands and Switzerland. Some countries where share ownership is relatively widespread have relatively little profit sharing: the UK and Denmark are cases in point. Again, narrow-based profit sharing is more evenly distributed among countries, suggesting that certain arrangements in specific countries may influence the existence of broad-based schemes.

Figure 15.3 presents the incidence rate for stock option plans. Here again, on average only a minority of companies offer these plans: 9 per cent broad-based and almost 15 per cent narrow-based plans. The striking difference with share schemes and profit sharing is that the incidence rate of narrow-based schemes is higher than broad-based schemes in most countries (with exceptions for the United States, Iceland, Bulgaria, Cyprus and Greece). Stock options may be a typical part of remuneration policy for management and less for all employees. Again, we experience large differences in incidence rates between countries, suggesting diversity in arrangements and country specific determinants of the existence of schemes.

The Cranet data provide organisation-level information. One of the few sources for employee-level data is the European Working Conditions Survey (Welz & Fernández-Macías, 2007). This is a face-to-face employee-level survey conducted periodically in all EU and other European countries by the European Foundation for the Improvement of Living and Working Conditions. In most countries the survey aims to sample 1000 employees and self-employed: response rates range from around 30 to 70 per cent.

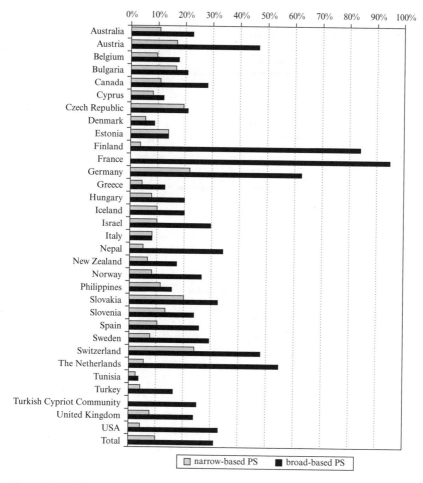

Notes: Total $N = 3656$.

Source: Cranet, 2004.

Figure 15.2 *Incidence rates of profit sharing schemes for private sector companies (200+) per country, 2004*

The survey is primarily concerned with working and employment conditions rather than pay, so is not an ideal means for examining financial participation. Nevertheless, the survey contains useful questions on income received from profit sharing and share ownership, and provides a welcome employee-level source of data on the incidence of financial participation. As pointed out by Welz and Fernández-Macías (2007), this survey gives a

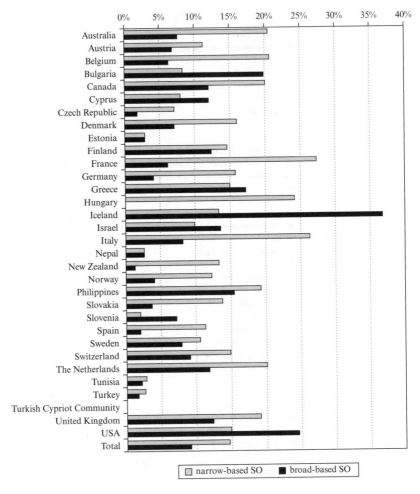

Notes: Total *N* = 3656.

Source: Cranet, 2004.

Figure 15.3 *Incidence rates of stock option schemes for private sector companies (200+) per country, 2004*

rather different picture to that provided by Cranet. The contrast between their findings and those from previous (company-based) surveys is considerable. They found that the use of financial participation is very low in most countries, and much lower than regularly estimated using company-based surveys: only around 12 per cent of European employees receive income from some form of profit-sharing scheme, and only 2.3 per cent from shares in the companies they work for. Only in six countries (Slovakia, Slovenia, Sweden, the Netherlands, Finland and France) does profit sharing affect more than one fifth of employees, and in only four (Ireland, France, Luxembourg and Belgium) do more than five per cent receive income from shares in their companies. Welz and Fernández-Macías (2007: 17) compared data from the surveys in 2000/2001 and 2005 and concluded that in almost all cases there is an increase in the proportion of employees receiving profits and shares as part of their remuneration. Although the levels are low, in the last five years they have been consistently increasing in all the 15 EU states that were members in both surveys except for the UK. They have not been increasing in most new member states.

Their analysis also reveals that financial participation is very unevenly distributed among different types of companies, jobs and individuals. Employees in managerial positions are more than four times more likely to participate in these schemes than manual workers, even after controlling for variables such as sector, establishment size or education. Financial participation is also distributed unevenly between men and women, and between permanent and temporary workers. They conclude that the low incidence of financial participation at the level of the individual employee, and the high unevenness of its distribution, puts a question mark against it from a policy perspective. The findings we have discussed suggest that some of the concerns regarding the distributional effects of financial participation schemes (which would reinforce pre-existing inequalities in pay and earnings) seem well-founded (Welz & Fernández-Macías, 2008: 495).

One limitation of the survey is that, whilst it probably reliably identifies profit sharing, its reference to incomes received from shares is likely to understate employee participation in share ownership plans. As the discussion of share ownership plans earlier indicated, employees may participate in share plans for some time before they receive any direct benefits from it.

FINANCIAL PARTICIPATION IN ACTION: SELECTED COUNTRIES

The previous section has provided a broad indication of the prevalence of financial participation around the world. However, to fully understand the operation of financial participation it is necessary to consider it within its national institutional context. To this end we provide short sketches of financial participation in selected countries in Europe and beyond. As will become clear, profit sharing, share ownership, and employee savings plans can be closely intertwined. This reflects differences between countries in the history of financial participation. These country profiles show that there are substantial national differences in the embeddedness of the phenomenon.

France

Profit sharing is deeply entrenched in France, and is inter-connected with employee savings plans and increasingly employee share ownership. The profit-share system was introduced by General de Gaulle in the 1960s with the intention of bridging the gap between capital and labour and promoting national unity. There are two main forms of profit sharing in operation. First, deferred profit sharing (*Participation*) is compulsory in firms with more than 50 employees. Profits are shared according to a mandatory pre-set formula or one agreed by collective bargaining. The profit share is paid into a fund and attracts tax advantages if it is held there for at least three years. Second, there is a voluntary cash profit sharing scheme (*Interessement*). Tax benefits may be secured if the profit share is paid into a company savings scheme (*Plan d' épargne d' entreprise (PEE)*). PEE contributions can be supplemented by bonus payments from the company and voluntary employee contributions (up to a quarter of annual salary) (see Degeorge et al., 2004; Poutsma, 2001). Most of the funds in savings plans are invested in *Fonds Communs de Placement d' Entreprise (FCPE)*, which in turn either invest in a diversified fund or in the shares of the employer. This is the most common means of promoting employee share ownership in the French system. Recent evidence indicates that nearly half of PEEs are used as a means for employee share acquisition and approximately one-quarter of employee savings are invested in company shares. Employee contributions to the PEE, including any derived from bonus payments, are exempt from taxes, whilst employer contributions can be offset against corporation tax. Social security charges are not levied on the contributions. In 2001 the Fabius Law enabled small and medium-sized enterprises (SMEs) to collaborate to provide a joint PEE. In 2003, a new savings plan – *Plan d'Epargne Retraite Colectif (PERCO)* – was launched in which savings are frozen until retirement: these funds are not permitted to invest more than five per cent of their assets in company shares. Since 2005 it has been possible for firms to offer free shares to employees with a vesting period of two years followed by a holding period of two years (or a vesting period of four years), and these can be paid to the FCPE.

An important feature of *Interessement* is that it can only be introduced either through a collective agreement with trade unions, with the involvement of trade union representatives at enterprise level, with the works council, or with the agreement of a two-thirds majority of the employees. Recent French legislation also gives employees a right to representation on the company's board when they hold three per cent or more of the company's shares.

United Kingdom

The UK has extensive arrangements for financial participation. There are currently two main all-employee plans in widespread use in the UK: the Save As You Earn (SAYE) share option/saving plan introduced in 1984 and the Share Incentive Plan introduced in 2000. In SAYE (widely referred to as 'Sharesave') employees can take out options to be exercised in three, five, or seven years time, at up to 20 per cent discount on market value at the time of grant. There is no income tax payable on the eventual sale of shares: there is a capital gains tax (CGT) liability instead, with marginal CGT rates usually being lower than the corresponding marginal income tax rate for most employees. The employee accrues the funds to exercise the options by participating in a Save As You Earn savings plan. The Share Incentive Plan is a 'modular' plan with provision for grants of free shares, share purchases by employees, awards of matching shares to supplement employee purchases, and share awards based on the dividends accruing to employee share owners. The UK also has the Enterprise Management Incentives plan, a set of arrangements for employees to be awarded options, and Company Share Options. Although both are aimed primarily at managers, they can be used for all-employee plans.

Employee share ownership is firmly entrenched in the UK. Most FTSE 100 firms have at least one all-employee plan, and they are also widespread amongst other listed firms. In recent years governments have been keen to encourage the use of share plans in unlisted companies, and the Share Incentive Plan and Enterprise Management Incentives were explicitly designed with this aim. The Workplace Employment Relations Survey indicates that just under 30 per cent of workplaces with five or more employees have a share ownership plan (see Pendleton, 2007). The rationale for share ownership plans in the UK focuses very much on their favourable effects for companies, and the broader economy. It has been argued that share plans have the potential to enhance company productivity by aligning employee interests with those of the firm. During the Thatcher years in the 1980s, broader objectives included promotion of an 'enterprise culture' and weakening trade unions. There has been little attention in the UK to the potential for share ownership plans to redistribute wealth and to promote long-term savings.

The UK was notable in the late 1980s and 1990s for having a

profit-sharing plan explicitly based on the views of Martin Weitzman – Profit-Related Pay (PRP). Here the intention was to combat 'wage stickiness' and stimulate employment creation by providing tax benefits for wage flexibility. In PRP schemes part of employees' pay was explicitly linked to profits and hence could vary over time. To induce employees to bear this risk the profit-related element was granted income tax concessions. This scheme was very popular indeed with several thousand companies using it at its height. However, much of its popularity seems to have been based on the potential to operate 'cosmetic' profit sharing, with pay flexibility being more apparent than real. Thus, tax concessions were granted in effect for pay that was fixed rather than flexible. For this reason, this scheme was abolished in 1997. There is currently no tax-approved cash profit-sharing scheme in the UK. The closest to profit sharing is the Free Shares element of the Share Incentive Plan (which replaced the earlier share-based Approved Profit Sharing Plan).

Unlike France there is no requirement in the UK that financial participation has to be introduced with the agreement of employee representatives or employees themselves (though individual employee consent is necessary for joining a plan). However, research has shown that many of those companies operating a share plan do have union representation: but these representatives have little involvement in the design, implementation, or operation of the plan (Pendleton, 2005).

Germany[1]

In Germany, financial participation has been viewed primarily as a form of employee participation in productive capital and as a means to achieve a modest redistribution of wealth. The role of financial participation as a means to promote social consensus at work has received less emphasis, probably because there are alternative and well-developed institutions to achieve social dialogue and partnership such as Works Councils and employee board representation. However, with the recent spread of 'liberal market economy' philosophies amongst top listed companies, the role of financial participation (employee share ownership, in particular) as a tool to encourage employee commitment has achieved greater prominence.

Financial participation has been supported in Germany by the combination of three pieces of legislation: the Fifth Capital Formation Law, the Third Capital Participation Law and the Income Tax Law. These provide the conditions under which employees may make regular savings and receive bonuses on these savings from the state and their employer (a profit share may be used for this). These savings may be invested in various vehicles, such as building societies, and in the employer. In the case of the latter, savings may be used to acquire employer shares, to make a loan to the employer, or to enter into a 'silent partnership' arrangement with the employer. In the latter, the participating employee receives a profit share on their invested savings but does not acquire the control rights typically held by full shareholders. This type of arrangement is typically found in private limited companies (*GmbH*) without a readily tradable share capital, and has been a common form of financial participation (see Carstensen et al., 1995). The Capital Formation and Capital Participation laws have restricted the eligibility of these arrangements to lower income groups and have set out the maximum amounts that may be contributed by employers and the state. The Income Tax law has provided for tax and social security concessions though these have been fairly modest.

It is perhaps not surprising that the incidence of financial participation, share ownership plans especially, has not been high in Germany. The IAB Establishment Panel (a nationally representative survey conducted regularly by the Institute for Employment Research) found that profit sharing was used in 9 per cent of establishments in 2005. Employee share ownership was found in just 2 per cent of establishments. With both forms, the likelihood of its use tends to grow with establishment size. Although the incidence of share ownership plans is low, participation rates are relatively high, with around half of employees on average participating. Employee loans and silent partnerships are more common than share ownership plans but, as they are predominantly used in the SME sector, their employee coverage is considerably smaller.

In the last five years there has been an extensive public debate on financial participation with all of the major political parties developing proposals to extend it. The Christian Democrats (CDU) proposed that financial participation should focus on enterprise level and that tax concessions should be made more favourable. Meanwhile, the Social Democrats (SPD) favoured the creation of a 'German Fund', which would acquire shares in a range of companies, thereby spreading risk for participating employees. The outcome was a compromise between the two sets of proposals. Tax concessions on acquiring employer shares have been increased, as have the size of the bonuses on savings arrangements. Eligibility to receive these benefits has also been widened somewhat. Nevertheless, the size of the concessions remains relatively small compared with other major European countries. More innovative has been the introduction of 'special employee participation funds' (*Mitarbeiterbeteiligungs-Sondervemogen*). Employees can acquire shares in these funds, which then invest in the employing enterprise and other companies in the same sector or region. Most of the employee subscriptions have to be invested in participating companies, and there are restrictions on how much may be invested in any single company. The benefit for employees, compared with single company financial participation, is that risk is diversified and the shares are readily tradable. In principle, this makes share-based financial participation attractive for employees of non-listed companies. At the time of writing, the take-up by companies is not thought to be high.

Australia

In Australia financial participation has predominantly focused on employee share ownership rather than profit sharing. Employee share ownership has enjoyed bipartisan support in Australia since the mid-1970s though concrete initiatives from government have been less in evidence. Over the years, the rationale for employee share ownership in Australia has focused on promoting an identity of interests between employees and employer and on encouraging long-term savings by employees. Until the introduction of compulsory occupational superannuation funds in the 1990s, there was considerable concern about low savings rates amongst Australian workers. Against this, there has been a persistent anxiety in Australian politics that employee share ownership is prone to 'rorting' (i.e. tax evasion and excessive extraction of benefits from companies, especially by top managers). This tension colours the nature and extent of legislative support for share ownership in Australia, and was exemplified by recent legislative reforms by the Rudd Labour Government.

In the 1990s and early 2000s, the Coalition Government believed that share ownership could fit with its policy of decentralisation of wage bargaining and the promotion of individualism in Australian industrial relations (Waring & Burgess, 2006). The apparent capacity of share ownership to weaken worker attachment to trade unions appears to have been a significant factor in this government's interest in employee share ownership. In 2000 the Nelson Committee of the House of Representatives conducted a major review of employee share ownership ('*Shared Endeavours*'). In both the Majority and Minority Reports a series of recommendations were advanced to promote employee share ownership, most of which were not implemented by the Coalition Government. Nevertheless, this government announced a policy objective of doubling the number of employees able to benefit from share ownership plans in five years, and from 2006 started to amend tax law to encourage share plans.

The incoming Labour Government in 2007 claimed it wanted to promote employee share ownership during the election campaign. However, in its 2009 budget it restricted the two main tax concessions by which employees in Australia had acquired shares so as to focus government support for share ownership on low and middle income workers. This concern both to promote share ownership and restrict the tax benefits associated with it reflects the ambivalence that has characterised Australian policy towards employee share ownership over many years. In the furore that followed, and the withdrawal by some companies of their share plans, the Government revised its approach. New legislation was passed in autumn 2009 which built upon traditional approaches to promoting share ownership via tax concessions but also provided a more explicit legal recognition of share plans.

There are two main ways in which employee share ownership is promoted. The first (called the 'reduction concession') enables employees on taxable incomes of up to AU$180000 to receive up to AU$1000 of benefit in employer shares each financial year free of income and fringe benefits tax at the time of grant. Any subsequent increase or decrease in the value of the shares is treated as a taxable capital gain/loss in the financial year the shares are sold. Shares must be held for three years while still employed by the organisation and there can be no forfeiture clause. The second (the 'deferral concession') enables employees to defer income tax on share-based remuneration benefits for up to seven years. This concession is available for salary sacrifice share schemes involving share benefits up to $5000 per annum or where there is the potential for forfeiture. This concession also applies to option-based plans. The employee becomes entitled to exercise these options after satisfying performance hurdles. Income tax on the benefit of the option can be deferred if there is a real risk of forfeiture. For tax benefits to be available at least 75 per cent of permanent employees of three years standing must have a right to participate.

Recent research has found that 57 per cent of listed companies have a broad-based share ownership plan and that most of these had adopted the plan since 2000. Most plans are structured to take advantage of tax exemptions, and require employees to subscribe to shares or options (or both) (see Landau et al., 2009). In the economy more widely, 4 per cent of businesses with more than ten employees had a broad-based share plan in the mid-2000s (Department of Employment and Workplace Relations, 2004). The proportion of employees receiving shares was 5.9 per cent (Australian Bureau of Statistics, 2005: see also Landau et al., 2010).

United States[2]

The United States has a long history of support for employee share ownership, with substantial ownership of employer shares and active public discussions of the topic dating back to the 1920s and before. The notion that ordinary workers may own their firm, or part of it, harks back to Jeffersonian ideas about broad-based ownership of property and wealth articulated by many of the other founders of the country across the political spectrum at the time (Blasi & Kruse, 2006). In the 1950s and 1960s American investment expert Louis Kelso devised what came to be known as the ESOP (Employee Stock Ownership Plan) as a means of widening the ownership of productive assets and overcoming the fundamental divide between capital and labour. Kelso attracted the support of Senator Russell Long, who was instrumental in drafting the landmark Employment Retirement Income Security Act (ERISA) passed in 1974. This introduced a set of tax benefits for ESOPs. In a leveraged ESOP, a corporation can borrow funds to purchase company stock and pay for the stock out of its profits while deducting the principal and interest on the loan from its corporate income for tax purposes. In a non-leveraged ESOP (similar to a stock bonus plan) a corporation contributes cash or stock to a worker trust. In both cases, workers gain stock without buying it with their savings or pledging any personal assets for the loans or contributions by the company. With these methods, Kelso overcame the barrier to regular working people buying parts of their companies. The ESOP then holds employee allocations of shares in a trust. Profit sharing has an even longer pedigree in American history and was common from the mid-1800s and throughout the 20th century. Sometimes cash or deferred profit sharing were used to buy company stock. This form of employee ownership grew dramatically in the wake of ERISA but has stabilised more recently. ESOPs are mainly found in privately owned, rather than listed, companies. Very few ESOPs involve wage concessions or purchases of failing firms by workers despite the fact that a small number of such cases have received extensive attention in the media. Most are medium size firms that were profitable under family ownership and were sold to the employees and professional managers.

The other main forms of share scheme in the United States are broad-based stock option plans, 401(k) plans, and employee stock purchase plans (so-called '423 plans' as they meet the rules of Internal Revenue Code Section 423). Stock options are widespread in listed companies in the United States and recent estimates suggest there are approximately 3000 broad-based plans. The 401(k) plans are a self-directed defined contribution retirement plan whereby employees allocate funds to a variety of investment funds and assets. These may include employer stock. In some cases employers match employee contributions with awards of their stock. The result has been that many employees hold a substantial component of their 401(k) investments in employer shares. While the employer match in stock is not based on worker savings, the fact that much of 401(k) employee ownership is bought with worker savings makes it substantially more risky than ESOPs (Mitchell & Utkus, 2003). Finally, employee stock purchase plans, whereby employees use their wages to acquire company shares on favourable terms, are also widespread.

The General Social Survey of 2006 showed that about 18 per cent of employees reported owning some company stock; about 5 per cent of employees participate in ESOPs; about 20 per cent of workers are eligible for a defined contribution plan that holds employer stock in a 401(k). In 2006, 9 per cent of employees held stock options. In addition, in 2006, 38 per cent of employees were covered by profit sharing (Kruse, et al., 2010). Financial participation is therefore relatively widespread in the United States.

The development of share ownership in the United States has taken two alternative directions in recent years. One has seen share ownership plans substituting for wages. Blasi and Kruse (2006) draw attention to the decline of collective bargaining in the United States and of the notion of a constantly increasing 'fixed wage' adjusted for inflation.. They suggest that some share ownership plans have increasingly substituted for part of core wages rather than supplementing them and spreading wealth. The 401(k) form of employee ownership funded by employee savings is an example of this type. In so far as they form part of a shift to defined contribution pension systems they form part of a system that is characterised by increasing insecurity and risk for the worker. The second direction has seen employee stock ownership contributing to genuine enhancements of employee wealth. Some plans, most notably those taking the ESOP form, do spread wealth, do not substitute for fixed wages, and allow many workers to accumulate meaningful capital incomes on top of fair wages (Kruse et al., 2008).

NATIONAL DIFFERENCES IN FINANCIAL PARTICIPATION

The preceding discussion shows that there are clear differences between countries in the incidence and character of financial participation. A key question is why these differences are present. There appear to be two levels at which analysis needs to take place. One concerns the presence of legislation and fiscal concessions for financial participation in a country: the more developed these are the greater the capacity and opportunity for firms to operate financial participation schemes. The other concerns the propensity of firms to use financial participation where such arrangements are present. Clearly, the presence of legislation and tax concessions may influence firm behaviour but there are also other possible influences on corporate behaviour. Specifically, these may include ownership structures, trade unions and industrial relations arrangements, along with prevailing ideologies. In other words, the institutional environment in which firms operate is likely to structure and influence the decisions (or 'non-decisions') that they make on financial participation. But equally, the nature of the business system is likely to have an influence on the propensity of governments to take action in this area. At the same time, government influences the nature of the business system. There is thus a highly complex set of inter-relationships between actors and institutions.

The evidence to date shows that legislative and fiscal frameworks have a critical influence on the incidence and character of financial participation in a country. They provide an opportunity for firms to use financial participation, and incentives to do so. The role of government action is well expressed in the EU proposal for a Council Recommendation by the European Commission in 1992 (repeated in a Commission communication in 2002: Commission of the European Communities, 2002):

> the development of financial participation schemes is strongly influenced by government action. Governments are primarily responsible for the creation of a legal and fiscal framework that may flavour such schemes but may also impede their introduction. This is illustrated by the finding of the PEPPER Report that in those countries where a particular type of financial participation scheme has been encouraged by government, the schemes most commonly introduced by enterprises are indeed the ones promoted through official government measures. In particular the availability of tax incentives makes a big difference. (Commission of the European Communities, 2002: 19)

Within a European context, the prevalence of financial participation in countries such as France and the United Kingdom is testament to long-standing legislation. The recent growth in financial participation in several European countries, such as Belgium and Germany, reflects recent government initiatives to promote financial participation. Government action operates in two ways. First, it can remove obstacles to the use of share plans or profit sharing by firms. For instance, in the absence of specific government action employee share ownership plans may be inhibited by a requirement to tax employees twice – once at the point of grant (if there is a discount) and once at the point of sale. A further impediment (mainly removed in Europe by the Prospectus Directive) is the typical requirement in securities law for a prospectus to be issued by companies whenever they offer shares for sale. Second, fiscal and social security concessions can provide an incentive for firms to implement financial participation plans.

A deeper question is why some governments have been more (or less) likely to promote financial participation through legislation. One influence is likely to be the objectives, policies, and strength of the 'social partners': trade unions and employers' associations (see Pendleton & Poutsma, 2004). Left-wing union movements have tended to oppose employee share ownership on the grounds that it blurs a fundamental conflict between capital and labour. As for employers' associations, there is a tension between desires to promote co-operation and an anxiety that employee share ownership might weaken managerial control. Some employer bodies are more supportive of financial participation than others. Besides the role of specific groups, governmental action is influenced by the broader institutional environment or business system in which governments' operate. For instance, in economies where there are well-developed and liquid stock markets and dispersed ownership, governments are more likely to see stock-based instruments as a viable form of employee reward. Black et al., (2007) find that the prevalence of share ownership plans in countries is associated with the extent of ownership dispersion in the listed company sector.

At a broader level still, it is noticeable that share ownership plans receive most support from governments and are most prevalent in those countries that are viewed as 'liberal market economies' in the 'varieties of capitalism' literature. In these countries it is said that exchanges between key factors, such as labour and firms, are predominantly market or transactional in character whereas in 'coordinated market economies' there is greater emphasis on relationships. Thus, in the latter, employee commitment might be secured through well-developed systems for employee involvement and representation whereas in LMEs there is a greater reliance on market-based rewards such as company stock plans (see Blair, 1995).

At firm level, institutional isomorphism (homogenisation) in the use of employee financial participation is likely. Firms may mimic their rivals in the use of practices, they may react to coercive pressures to conform to legislation and informal rules, or they may uphold and follow certain employment practices and norms found in the business system. The existing 'order', however, may be disrupted by outsiders. For instance, the spread of financial participation in countries that have not been noted for extensive financial participation has been stimulated by the presence of US multinationals transferring practices common in the United States to their overseas subsidiaries (Poutsma et al., 2005).

Over the last decade or so there have been major changes in institutions, especially in systems of collective bargaining and other elements of employment relations. In many of the more regulated and centralised national systems of collective bargaining, like Germany and the Scandinavian countries, there has been substantial decentralisation of collective bargaining. Alongside these changes in the processes of collective bargaining, pay systems themselves have become more individualistic (cf. Traxler et al., 2008). Financial participation is often seen as being a key component of these trends: it is viewed as contributing to high performance and flexibility (Kaarsemaker & Poutsma, 2006; Poutsma & Nijs, 2003). This suggests gradual growth of the phenomenon in the near future. Despite this possible trend the differences in adoption between firms located in different national settings will probably persist, reflecting directional convergence, developments in the same direction, but not final convergence to one universal model.

CONCLUSIONS

In this chapter we showed the large differences in use of financial participation practices by companies located in different countries. The country profiles show that corporate behaviour is influenced by a complex set of actors and institutions. Legislation and tax concessions are important as are institutions such as trade unions and industrial relations. From a comparative HRM perspective, financial participation is embedded in distinct settings. The concept of 'national business system' is useful in understanding the ways that the contexts in which firms operate continue to differ, and in this chapter we have highlighted the interaction between institutions in shaping the form and adoption of financial participation. The persistence of contrasting national business systems means that the contexts in which firms manage their workforces differ markedly. One implication of the way that firms are embedded in distinct national contexts is that HRM practices are not universally applied. It means that multinational companies will probably need to amend any practices that they might want to transfer across their subsidiaries: even where they can operate the same practices in different settings, the operation, meaning and results of those practices might be quite different in different contexts.

ACKNOWLEDGEMENTS

We thank the partners of the Cranet Network for providing the data, and the School of Management at Cranfield University for coordinating the network.

NOTES

1. We are grateful to Peter Wilke and Stefan Stracke for assistance with the information on Germany
2. We are grateful to Joseph Blasi for his assistance in preparing this section.

REFERENCES

Australian Bureau of Statistics. 2005. *Spotlight: Employee Share Schemes.* Canberra: Australian Labour Market Statistics.

Black, B., Gospel, H. & Pendleton, A. 2007. Finance, corporate governance, and the employment relationship. *Industrial Relations*, **46**(3): 643–650.

Blair, M. 1995. *Ownership and Control: Rethinking Corporate Governance for the Twenty-first Century.* Washington, DC: Brookings Institution.

Blasi, J. & Kruse, D. 2006. The political economy of employee ownership in the United States: from economic democracy to industrial democracy. *International Review of Sociology*, **16**(1): 127–147.

Bonin, J., Jones, D. & Putterman, L. 1993. Theoretical and empirical studies of workers' cooperatives: will the twain ever meet? *Journal of Economic Literature*, **31**(3): 1290–1320.

Carstensen, V., Gerlach, K. & Hubler, O. 1995. Profit sharing in German firms. In F. Buttler, W. Franz, R. Schettkat & D. Soskice (eds), *Institutional Frameworks and Labor Market Performance: Comparative Views of the US and German Economies.* London: Routledge.

Commission of the European Communities 1992. Council Recommendation n° 92/443/EEC of 27 July 1992 concerning the promotion of participation by employed persons in profits and enterprise results (including equity participation). Official Journal L245(26/08/1992): 0053–0055.

Commission of the European Communities. 2002. Communication from the Commission to the Council, the European Parliament, the Economic and Social Committee and the Committee of the Regions: on a Framework for the Promotion of Employee Financial participation. C. o. t. E. Communities, COM (2002) 364 final. Brussels.

Croucher, R., Brookes, M., Wood, G. & Brewster, C. 2010. Context, strategy and financial participation: a comparative analysis. *Human Relations*, **63**(6): 835–855.

Degeorge, F., Jenter, D., Moel, A. & Tufano, P. 2004. Selling company shares to reluctant employees: France Telecom's experience. *Journal of Financial Economics*, **71**(1): 169–202.

Department of Employment and Workplace Relations. 2004. Employee share ownership in Australia: aligning interests. Executive Summary. Canberra

Estrin, S. & Jones, D. 1992. The viability of employee-owned firms: evidence from France. *Industrial and Labor Relations Review*, **45**(2): 323–338.

Hashi, I., Lowitzsch, J., Uvalic, M. & Vaughan Whitehead, D. 2006. PEPPER III: an overview of employee financial participation. In J. Lowitzsch (ed.), The PEPPER II Report: Promotion of Employee Participation in Profits and Enterprise Results in the new Member and Candidate Countries of the European Union. Berlin: Free University, Inter-University Centre at the Institute for Eastern European Studies.

Kaarsemaker, E. & Poutsma, E. 2006. The fit of employee ownership with other human resource management practices: theoretical and empirical suggestions regarding the existence of an ownership high-performance work system, or theory O. *Economic & Industrial Democracy*, **27**(2): 669–685.

Kruse, D., Freeman, R. & Blasi, J. 2008. Do workers gain by sharing? Employee outcomes under employee ownership, profit sharing, and broadbased sock options, NBER working paper series, 14233.

Kruse, D. L., Blasi, J. R. & Park, R. 2010. Shared capitalism in the US economy: prevalence, characteristics, and employee views of financial participation in enterprises. In

D. L. Kruse, R. B. Freeman & J. R. Blasi (eds), *Shared Capitalism at Work: Employee Ownership, Profit and Gain Sharing, and Broad-based Stock Options*. Chicago: University of Chicago Press, pp. 41–75.

Landau, I., Mitchell, R., O'Connell, A., Ramsay, I. & Marshall, S. 2009. Broad-based employee share ownership in Australian listed companies: survey report, Research Report. Melbourne: University of Melbourne Law School.

Landau, I., O'Connell, A. & Ramsay, I. 2010. *Employee Share Schemes: Regulation and Policy*. Melbourne: Melbourne University Law School.

Lowitzsch, J. 2006. The PEPPER III Report: promotion of employee participation in profits and enterprise results in the new member and candidate countries of the European Union Berlin: Free University, Inter-University Centre at the Institute for Eastern European Studies.

Mitchell, O. & Utkus, S. 2003. The role of company stock in defined contribution plans. In O. Mitchell & K. Smetters (eds), *The Pension Challenge: Risk Transfers and Retirement Income Security*. Philadelphia: University of Pennsylvania Press.

Pendleton, A. 2005. Employee share ownership, employment relationships, and corporate governance. In B. Harley, J. Hyman & P. Thompson (eds), *Participation and Democracy at Work: Essays in Honour of Harvie Ramsay*. London: Palgrave.

Pendleton, A. 2007. The study of employee share ownership using WERS: an evaluation and analysis of the 2004 survey. In K. Whitfield, & K. Huxley (eds), *Innovations in the 2004 Workplace Employment Relations Survey*. Cardiff: Cardiff University.

Pendleton, A., Poutsma, E., Brewster, C. & Van Ommeren, J. 2001. *Employee Share Ownership and Profit Sharing in the European Union*. Dublin: European Foundation for the Improvement of Living and Working Conditions.

Pendleton, A., Poutsma, E., Van Ommeren, J. & Brewster, C. 2003. The incidence and determinants of employee share ownership and profit sharing in Europe. In T. Kato & J. Pliskin (eds), *The Determinants of the Incidence and the Effects of Participatory Organizations*. Amsterdam: JAI Press.

Pendleton, A. D. & Poutsma, F. 2004. *The Policies and Views of Peak Organisations towards Financial Participation (Synthesis Report)*. Dublin: European Foundation.

Poole, M. 1989. *The Origins of Economic Democracy: Profit-sharing and Employee-shareholding Schemes*. London: Routledge.

Poutsma, E. 2001. *Recent Trends in Employee Financial Participation in the European Union*. Luxembourg: Office for Official Publications of the European Communities.

Poutsma, E., Ligthart, P. & Schouten, R. 2005. Employee share ownership in Europe. The influence of US multinationals. *Management Revue*, **16**(1): 99–122.

Poutsma, F. & Nijs, W. F. 2003. Broad-based employee financial participation in the European Union. *International Journal of Human Resource Management*, **14**(6): 863–893.

Traxler, F., Brandl, B. & Glassner, V. 2008. Pattern bargaining: an investigation into its agency, context and evidence. *British Journal of Industrial Relations*, **46**(1): 33.

Uvalic, M. 1991. The promotion of employee participation in profits and enterprise results. C. o. t. E. Communities. Social Europe, Supplement 3/91. Luxembourg: Office for Official Publications of the European Communities.

Vaughan Whitehead, D. 1995. *Workers' Financial Participation: East-West Experiences*. Geneva: International Labour Office.

Waring, P. & Burgess, J. 2006. Work choices: the privileging of individualism in Australian industrial relations. *International Journal of Employment Studies*, **14**(1): 61–80.

Welz, C. & Fernández-Macías, E. 2007. *Financial Participation of Employees in the European Union: Much Ado about Nothing?* Dublin: European Foundation for the Improvement of Living and Working Conditions.

Welz, C. & Fernández-Macías, E. 2008. Financial participation of employees in the European Union: much ado about nothing? *European Journal of Industrial Relations*, **14**(4): 479–496.

16 Performance management
Paul Boselie, Elaine Farndale and Jaap Paauwe

Performance management (PM) is one of the key HRM issues facing contemporary organisations. The process of measuring and subsequently actively managing organisation and employee performance in order to improve effectiveness is critical to organisation development and survival (Den Hartog et al., 2004). Performance management today encompasses a whole range of HRM activities beyond what we might traditionally assume to have been limited to annual performance appraisals, such as goal setting, feedback, consequences for training and development and remuneration.

The growing importance of performance management in both theory and practice is clear for all to see. A recent special issue of the *European Journal of International Management* (2008) emphasises this further. The discussions presented suggest the latest trends in performance management include:

- a global tendency towards performance management through culture management;
- aligning corporate goals with individual employee goals;
- using PM for talent management and leadership development;
- using PM as a mechanism for distinguishing good performers from bad performers;
- linking PM and 360-degree feedback systems;
- integrating PM and information technology systems;
- emphasising self-appraisal and appraisals by peers; and
- PM as a tool for general employee development purposes.

Performance management is seen as the key to maximising the return on investment in human capital and hence creating corporate competitive advantage. These are some of the findings of the Global Human Resource Research Alliance (GHRRA) – collaboration between the universities of Cambridge, Cornell, INSEAD and Erasmus/Tilburg – based on extensive case study research within leading multinational corporations (MNCs) including Shell, Unilever, IKEA, Siemens, Procter & Gamble and IBM. Another particularly informative piece of research which explores international developments in HRM practices is the Cranet survey. This quantitative data is a rich source of information on how the use of different performance management systems in different countries has changed (or remained the same) over the last decade. We will return to these studies shortly, as they provide us with a unique opportunity to study contemporary performance management in different organisations and in different countries around the world.

The aim of this chapter is to define performance management, giving an overview of the most important developments over time, and comparing performance management in different contexts using both case study data from large multinationals and country survey data. As you can see above, it is already becoming clear that there are many dimensions to the performance management tools being used in organisations today. We therefore start here by exploring what performance management means, especially in an international context.

Definitions of Performance Management

Firstly, performance management can be seen as a broad range of activities which creates a bridge between managing employee performance and enhancing overall firm performance. Performance management thus 'deals with the challenge organisations face in defining, measuring, and stimulating employee performance with the ultimate goal of improving organisational performance' (Den Hartog et al., 2004: 556). This view is upheld by DeNisi (2000), who maintains that performance management refers to the range of activities engaged in by an organisation to enhance the performance of a target person or group, with the ultimate purpose of improving organisational effectiveness.

Baron and Armstrong (1998: 38) emphasise the strategic and integrated nature of performance management, which in their view focuses on 'increasing the effectiveness of organisations by improving the performance of the people who work in them and by developing the capabilities of teams and individual contributors'. However, they go further and start to describe more about the process and characteristics of performance management. They see it as a continuous process involving performance reviews focusing on the future rather than the past. In their empirical research among British practitioners they find that the *key characteristics of performance management* (those identified by more than half of the respondents) are: goal setting and evaluation (85 per cent of respondents); annual appraisal (83 per cent of respondents); and personal development programmes (68 per cent of respondents). Less frequently mentioned items include self-evaluation (45 per cent of respondents); pay for performance (43 per cent of respondents); coaching and mentorship (39 per cent of respondents); career management (32 per cent of respondents); competence management (24 per cent of respondents); and 180-degree feedback systems (20 per cent of respondents). In summary, goal setting, employee monitoring and modification through employee development are the central characteristics according to Baron & Armstrong's (1998) analysis. However, these data are more than ten years old and changes might have taken place in the performance management arena. The empirical results of more recent studies (GHRRA and Cranet) will shed light on performance management characteristics in contemporary settings.

One core part of the performance management process is undoubtedly the (annual) appraisal meeting. This is: 'the system whereby an organization assigns some 'score' to indicate the level of performance of a target person or group' (DeNisi, 2000: 121). This may or may not then be linked to an employee's rewards. A second core feature is the focus on competence development (through training, coaching and feedback) and individual career planning (Fletcher, 2001; Roberts, 2001). Thirdly, there is the important task of goal setting: the setting of corporate, departmental, team, and individual objectives (sometimes labelled 'policy deployment', the cascading down of strategic objectives to a meaningful set of targets for every individual involved) (Roberts, 2001). Thus, performance management involves the day-to-day management, as well as the support and development of people.

Alongside the variation in content of a PM system, according to Baron & Kreps (1999), performance management can also have different purposes including:

- an extensive evaluation to improve job matching,
- communication of corporate values and objectives,
- providing information for self-improvement, training and development, and career development,
- linking pay to individual and/or team performance,
- collecting information for hiring strategies,
- validating HR practices including appraisal and rewards, retention and reductions in workforce,
- and input for legal defences (for example when an organisation is trying to fire an employee because of poor job performance).

However, how does an organisation know what elements to include in a PM system in order to achieve the desired outcomes? Baron & Kreps (1999) summarise the *important and relevant aspects* of different performance evaluation systems that need to be taken into account when designing a performance management system.

1. Who or what is to be evaluated? One can look at an individual's attitudes, behaviours or cognitive abilities, but one can also look at team performance or subunit outcomes.
2. Who performs the evaluation? Traditionally the direct supervisor plays an important role in being the evaluator. However, more recently we have seen developments towards including self-evaluations, evaluations by peers and even including evaluations by customers.
3. What is the time frame? Traditionally appraisals took place on an annual basis. Nowadays we can see illustrations in practice of employee monitoring on a monthly, weekly and even daily basis.
4. Should we be using objective or subjective evaluations? Objective evaluations include hard data, for example productivity and service quality outcomes, while subjective data are mainly collected using questionnaires ranking the candidate on the basis of multiple criteria, for example, with respect to the candidate's individual job performance, employee development and general attitude towards the job and colleagues.
5. Do we apply relative or absolute performance indicators? Relative performance indicators represent an individual's score in comparison to another person or the general average score. Absolute performance indicators focus on the real score.
6. Should we use a forced distribution? In a forced distribution approach, individual employees are ranked and the evaluator is forced to classify the candidates into different groups ranging from poor performers to high performers. Forced distribution is often introduced to create variance in scores otherwise the organisation runs the risk of ending up with 80 per cent relatively good performers, 10 per cent excellent performers and only 10 per cent poor performers.
7. How many performance indicators should be used? The evaluation might include multiple outcome variables rather than a single one. However, using multiple performance indicators raises questions about the weights of the indicators and the technique for calculating the overall score.

There is thus a considerable range of considerations regarding the design and implementation of performance management systems, especially when in addition to the points raised above; we start to add the complexity of multiple country contexts. First, however, we start our comparative assessment by considering how performance management has developed over time.

Performance Management Developments over Time

Performance management has it roots in the early 1900s with special attention for this practice in the US and British military for evaluating officers (Den Hartog et al., 2004). Furthermore, Peter Drucker's (1954) concept of 'management by objectives' being part of a new school of thought (business administration and management) has played an important role in linking appraisal to goal setting and people management. Bach (2000: 241) argues that 'assessment of performance has become a pervasive feature of modern life', identifying three main reasons for the growing popularity of performance management in the 1980s:

1. Globalisation resulted in increased competition and therefore a growing performance focus and more attention for achieving organisational goals by good people management.
2. Everybody including HR professionals, line managers and employees were dissatisfied with the administrative nature of the classic performance appraisals, mainly perceived as annual administrative obligations.
3. The HR professionals saw in PM an instrument for showing the added value of human resource management (HRM) in an organisation.

Guest & Conway (1998) argue that performance management before 1990 was focussed primarily on the content and the system, with an emphasis on the direct supervisor as the evaluator. They also point out that performance management before 1990 was typically top-down, being the property of the HR department and with a strong link to performance-related pay. After 1990, performance management changed fundamentally to include more attention to the underlying process, a joint evaluation (employee and supervisor), 360-degree feedback instead of top-down evaluation, performance management being the property of line management, and finally a strong focus on employee development instead of performance-related pay (Guest & Conway, 1998) (see Figure 16.1).

In summary, in recent times there has been quite a marked shift in performance management from content to process, from supervisor evaluation to joint evaluation, from top-down to 360-degree, from performance-related-pay to development, and from performance management being the property of the HR department to it being owned by line management (see Figure 16.2). As performance management has been expanding in these new directions, what does this mean for its linkage with other aspects of the HRM system?

Performance management

Old	New
• Focus on content and system	• More focus on process
• Direct supervisor as evaluator	• Joint evaluation (employee and supervisor)
• Top-down approach	• 360 degree feedback
• HR-department as owner	• Line management as owner
• Linked to merit- or performance related pay	• Linked to employee development, human capital

Source: Adapted from Guest & Conway, 1998

Figure 16.1   Performance management shifts

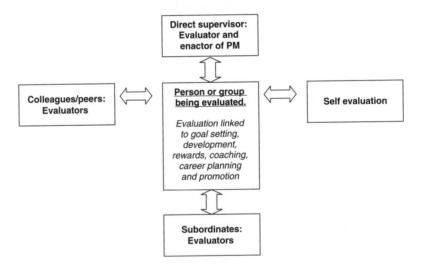

Figure 16.2   Performance management

PERFORMANCE MANAGEMENT AND HRM

Performance management is often seen as a microcosm of HRM, transferring the broader debate around the added value of human resource management to the performance management arena (Bach, 2000; Den Hartog et al., 2004; Dewettinck, 2008). Special attention in both areas (HRM and performance management) is paid to the alignment with the overall business strategy (strategic fit), the alignment of practices towards a high performance work system (horizontal or internal fit), line management involvement in the enactment of the practices, soft versus hard approaches (stressing the employee developmental side versus the individual perform- ance side), and the special attention to the search for interventions to increase firm performance. An ideal performance management system of practices is actually a sort of mini-high performance work system focused on goal setting, monitoring, appraising, developing and reward- ing employees in order to increase employee performance and to achieve organisational goals.

However, this performance management system can take many guises. Several authors emphasise the relevance of different contextual factors that affect the ideal system for an organisation (Den Hartog et al., 2004; Dewettinck, 2008). These contextual factors may include industry charac- teristics, firm size, degree of unionisation and the history of the organisa- tion. Most importantly here, they may also include potential country and cultural differences affecting performance management in an organisation in a specific geographical location.

Claus & Briscoe (2008) present an overview of 64 articles published between 1985 and 2005 on employee performance management from an international perspective. The authors conclude that the academic litera- ture on cross-border performance management is relatively atheoretical and exploratory in nature. They also conclude that the design and the sub- stance of the empirical studies are weak. Claus & Briscoe (2008) noted that 26 performance management articles focused on culture (e.g. Björkman & Lu, 1999), of which 16 articles stem from non-Western countries includ- ing China and India (e.g. Shen, 2004), 7 articles explicitly focused on the transferability of Western performance management (e.g. Galang, 2004), and 3 articles on the issue of convergence/divergence (e.g. Ployhart et al., 2003). The majority of the empirical articles identified are focused upon or based upon performance management in multinational companies (e.g. Lam et al., 2002). Furthermore, there is a significant number of perform- ance management articles devoted to expatriate performance management (e.g. Caligiuri, 2000). By far the majority of empirical performance man- agement articles identified by the authors used survey data (e.g. Shadur et al., 1995), while only 3 articles applied a case study method (e.g. Lunnan et al., 2005).

Overall, Claus and Briscoe (2008) summarise the following major themes and findings from their literature review:

- Performance ratings of expatriates are influenced by the national- ity of raters and ratees, the type of rater (self-evaluation, front line manager or peer), personality characteristics of the raters and ratees, and by contextual factors including company size, international nature of the company, organisational structure, position and task of the expatriate and geographical location.

- Context is important in performance management. Contextual factors that affect performance management include cultural factors affecting leadership styles and communication.
- The international literature focuses almost exclusively on the performance appraisal process rather than on the broader issue of the performance management system.
- The convergence/divergence of performance management practices debate is mainly focused on the transferability of Western performance management practices to Asian countries, in particular China. Most empirical studies indicated a trend towards convergence. The convergence in this context refers to the tendency of applying universalistic performance management practices or best practices, such as 360-degree feedback mechanisms, irrespective of the country.

Building on this work by Claus and Briscoe (2008), we now have the unique opportunity to study performance management in an international comparative setting using two distinct datasets:

1. Comparative interview data from large, high-performing multinational companies (Global HR Research Alliance);
2. Comparative survey data from a range of organisation in different countries (Cranet).

The following sections describe how this data was gathered and the findings which emerged.

METHODS

Global HR Research Alliance

This study was designed to explore what MNCs themselves described as HR excellence, and was carried out as part of a collaborative project together with Cambridge University (UK), Cornell University (United States), Insead (Singapore) and Erasmus University Rotterdam/Tilburg University (The Netherlands). Companies were selected for inclusion based on superior business performance and reputation as an employer based on 2004 Fortune and similar listings. Results from 16 companies (ABB, BAe Systems, BT, EDF, IBM, IKEA, Infosys, Matsushita, Oracle, Procter & Gamble, Rolls Royce, Samsung Electronics, Shell, Siemens, TCL, Unilever) are discussed here.

In 2004/5, interviews were held with 248 interviewees (153 HR professionals and 95 representatives of senior management, line managers and employee representatives) in the 16 multinationals based in 19 countries (Belgium, Brazil, China, Dubai, France, Germany, India, Italy, Japan, Korea, Malaysia, Netherlands, Norway, Singapore, Spain, Switzerland, Sweden, UK, United States). These interviews were carried out at corporate headquarters, regional or country level offices, or at division or site level within a specific business. The questions asked covered the whole range of HRM practices in these MNCs to try to uncover what they considered to be examples of best practice.

Case studies of each company describing their best practices in HRM were then drawn up and are analysed further here. The first step in the analysis was to group the companies at a regional level to try to observe patterns in performance management activities. This resulted in seven Anglo-American MNCs, six continental European MNCs; and five Asian MNCs.

Cranet Survey

The Cranet network is a global network of over 30 prestigious business schools and universities, one in each participating country, that collaborate to conduct joint research in the field of HRM in Europe. The data is collected through a standardised questionnaire that is sent to HR directors at organisational level. It covers the major areas of human resource management. The survey gathers figures or requests yes/no answers to factual questions rather than asking for opinions. It is addressed to the most senior HR/Personnel specialist within the organisation and on average around 70 per cent of respondents fit this description. Only organisations with at least 200 employees are included in the study presented here. Data is used here from survey rounds in 1995, 1999/2000 and 2004 to show how HRM practice use has changed over time. Eight countries were selected from the full data set for discussion (see Table 16.1), based on the range of data available in each on performance management practices. Japan was included in particular to show a non-Western perspective; however, there is only data from 1999/2000 available for this country.

There are three key questions included in the survey which relate to performance management which are analysed further here:

Table 16.1   Number of responses per country per survey round

	1995	1999	2004
Denmark	443	292	303
France	403	327	–
Japan	–	593	–
Spain	250	261	–
Sweden	344	315	370
Switzerland	187	130	189
The Netherlands	217	167	272
UK	1178	897	847

- Who is appraised (management, professional, clerical, manual staff)?
- Who contributes to the appraisal (next level manager, the employee, subordinate)?
- What are the outcomes of the appraisal system (training, promotion, career development, performance-related pay)?

RESULTS

Comparative Analysis I: Performance Management in High-performing Multinationals (GHRRA Study)

The first stage of the analysis was to look at what was common across this group of high-performing MNCs in terms of performance management. The findings can be divided into multiple dimensions, such as content, aims, and design criteria as described above. However, more nuanced thinking behind the performance management systems also emerged.

Firstly, these MNCs were talking about the *strategic aims of performance management*. More specifically, the emphasis was on creating alignment within the company, for example, to create a high performance culture, and performance management was seen as a tool to achieve this. In addition to alignment, another strategic goal was the development of individuals for the future, linked to talent management and succession planning processes. Thus, performance management is being used as a tool to support forward thinking and planning in these firms.

Secondly, interviewees talked about the performance management process in terms of the *actual outcomes*. Three key foci emerged here:

1. career planning: facilitating succession planning, identifying high
   potentials and promotion opportunities;
2. development: creating personal development plans;
3. reward: determining performance-related pay, employee benefits and
   bonuses.

The third issue that interviewees raised was the *criteria used in performance
evaluation*. Here there was a clear dichotomy between a desire to assess
current performance at an individual or team level. The focus on technical
skills and behavioural aspects was another issue raised by the interviewees. Firms were also using performance management as a means to assess
potential performance (future performance). For this, they were taking
capability or competency approaches, considering a person's current skill
set against desired competency models of different job profiles.

The actual *performance management tools and processes* themselves can
be divided into two categories. Those designed to provide feedback, such as
twice annual appraisal meetings, two-way feedback, 360 degree appraisals
and benchmarking. The second set of tools were designed more as supporting frameworks: defining competency frameworks for specific roles in the
organisation, producing scorecards to enable discussion about performance, applying forced ranking/distribution systems, and clear goal setting.

One striking finding from the case studies is the extent to which information technologies (IT) are playing a leading role in these performance
management developments. IT enables standardisation of systems; this
means it is easier to have a single performance management system for
all employees across the globe, and to benchmark internally on employee
performance. The IT systems also enable online support and resources,
creating a broader toolkit for managers undertaking the performance
evaluation and recording process.

Having reached these broad conclusions about what these high-
performing MNCs from across the world have in common regarding
performance management, the case study data was then – as a next step
– explored for any differences between MNCs in Anglo-American contexts (United States and UK), continental European contexts (Sweden,
Switzerland, France, Germany and the Netherlands) and Asian contexts
(China and Singapore). This part of the analysis, perhaps surprisingly,
raised very few results. Perhaps the nature of these globally operating
firms means that they are benchmarking against each other, and hence are
adopting very similar practices. Indeed, true patterns of difference in the
data hardly emerged; however, some underlying trends were discernable.
For example, there appeared to be the strongest talk of linking performance management to corporate level activity (goal setting and culture)

Table 16.2   Percentage of firms with an appraisal system in operation for the following staff grades

	1995				1999			
	Mgt	Prof	Clerical	Manual	Mgt	Prof	Clerical	Manual
Denmark	42	41	39	23	56	48	47	32
France	85	77	61	53	86	84	75	67
Japan	–	–	–	–	83	82	79	77
Spain	63	77	64	56	59	66	46	40
Sweden	87	83	83	63	89	84	95	80
Switzerland	89	94	89	87	93	95	92	91
Netherlands	79	82	79	78	84	82	82	82
UK	90	87	76	51	92	90	85	68

Notes: Mgt = Management.   – = no data available.

within the Anglo-American firms. In the Asian firms, there appeared to be slightly more focus on measuring current performance rather than potential performance (which perhaps is surprising given the traditionally longer-term approach to the employment relationship within such firms). The Continental Europe sample could be said to be paying the most attention to employee development issues emerging from the performance management process, with a clear separation (for example, in the Netherlands) between assessment for the purpose of determining reward, and assessment for development purposes.

The survey data in the following analysis may shed further light on potential differences at country level.

Comparative Analysis II: Comparing Performance Management in Different Countries Using Cranet Data

Because this data is collected from a range of different types of organisation (with a dominance of domestic organisations rather than the purely MNC sample presented above), we can gain a clearer picture at country level of performance management practices. The following three tables show how the different aspects of performance management have changed over time in multiple countries.

Table 16.2 shows a very clear increase in the use of appraisal systems for all grades of staff (particularly clerical and manual staff who were starting from the lowest level) between the mid and late-1990s in all countries. The only figure which did not increase during this period was the

Table 16.3   *Percentage of firms where the following people contribute formally to the appraisal process*

	1995			1999			2004		
	Next level man-ager	Self	Subor-dinate	Next level man-ager	Self	Subor-dinate	Next level man-ager	Self	Subor-dinate
Denmark	21	34	5	31	73	18	59	98	22
France	47	67	5	39	73	5	–	–	–
Japan	–	–	–	82	10	2	–	–	–
Spain	44	22	8	47	61	7	–	–	–
Sweden	–	–	–	23	90	16	68	88	35
Switzerland	44	76	23	46	85	19	68	88	26
Netherlands	63	75	6	67	88	11	63	83	16
UK	65	86	7	61	94	12	80	99	23

use of appraisal systems for professional staff in the Netherlands, which remained stable at 82 per cent of firms having such a system in operation. This is true in all countries surveyed.[1] In most countries, the more senior you are, the more likely you are to be appraised.

Table 16.3 considers who is involved in evaluating employees. Here again we can see many increases particularly in employees themselves being given the opportunity to contribute to the appraisal process. For example, in Denmark this figure has jumped from 34 per cent of firms in 1995, to 73 per cent in 1999, and to 98 per cent in 2004. The 360-degree approach of asking subordinates also to contribute has seen a considerable increase too. This activity was practically unheard of in 1995 in all the countries presented here (except for in Switzerland); however, by 2004 around a quarter of firms had included some element of the 360-degree approach.

A very striking result can be seen if we consider the 1999 data, and compare firms in Japan and Sweden. In Japan, 10 per cent of firms rely on employee input into the appraisal process, compared to 90 per cent in Sweden. This is likely a result of the very different national cultures in these two countries: the former having a very strong power distance, strongly reliant on hierarchy, and the latter having a low power distance, with a strong belief in individual empowerment and participation.

There appears to be a modest increase in the participation of subordinates in the appraisal process from less than 10 per cent in 1995 to round 25 per cent in 2004. It is probably too early to link conclusions to these findings. However, this might be a first indication of what is yet to come. The next phase in performance management might be to put increasing emphasis on the opinions of subordinates in the appraisal process. In the GHRRA research, one company is already using an HR dashboard with information about the leadership capabilities of all the front line managers from their subordinates. Red 'warning lights' against a front-line manager indicate poor evaluations by subordinates and a reason to take action. These actions might involve developmental interventions, but can also result in the replacement of the manager.

The final aspect of performance management considered here is the purpose of these appraisal processes (see Table 16.4). Four options were given to respondents: training, promotion, career planning and performance-related pay. Overall, identification of training needs remains the most popular outcome of the appraisal process. However, career planning has increased in popularity over this period too. Comparing between countries, we can see that Japan tells quite a different story to its European counterparts. Here, the long-term focus on the employment relationship is reflected in the emphasis on promotion resulting from the appraisal process. Firms in Japan are also the highest users of appraisal to determine performance-related pay.

SO WHAT DOES ALL THIS EMPIRICAL DATA TELL US?

Looking first at the case study data, these suggest that Guest and Conway's (1998) observed shift from content to process attention, from appraisal by the direct supervisor to joint evaluation (including employees' direct supervisors, peers and clients), from top-down evaluation to 360-degree feedback mechanisms, from a strong emphasis on performance-related pay to a strong focus on employee development, and from performance management being the property of the HR department to being the property of line management is still relevant and being confirmed by our case studies in contemporary multinational companies. However, based on the results, we observe an extension of Guest and Conway's (1998) observations within the MNCs.

- First, there is a global tendency to use performance management to support corporate values and to align the corporate goals with individual employee goals. Performance management has become a vehicle for culture management in many multinational companies.
- Second, there is an increasing tendency among MNCs to apply performance management for identifying, developing and rewarding talent. Performance management is often integrated with or part of the talent management programmes of an organisation.

Table 16.4 Percentage of firms where the appraisal system is used to determine the following outcomes

	1995				1999				2004			
	Training	Promotion	Career	PRP	Training	Promotion	Career	PRP	Training	Promotion	Career	PRP
Denmark	41	25	25	16	82	49	52	36	87	–	71	66
France	74	54	59	53	95	74	74	61	–	–	–	–
Japan	–	–	–	–	29	85	37	91	–	–	–	–
Spain	63	55	41	52	77	63	50	63	–	–	–	–
Sweden	93	49	52	35	98	48	54	41	79	–	66	86
Switzerland	91	70	59	53	98	74	55	60	96	–	91	76
Netherlands	71	59	66	52	83	69	80	63	88	–	92	75
UK	89	61	72	40	98	62	77	34	98	–	87	54

- Third, performance management is used for leadership development, for example reflected in performance management as part of succession planning or the search and development of the future leaders of an organisation.
- Fourth, there is increasing attention to applying performance management to distinguish good performers and bad performers.
- Fifth, the criteria used in the evaluation are linked to past performance, present performance and potential performance, the latter often measured through competency frameworks. Competency management and performance management often go hand in hand in the MNCs in this study.
- Sixth, performance management and 360-degree feedback mechanisms are often quite time consuming and expensive. However, when applied, the outcomes can serve as input for benchmarks and scorecards reflecting the relative position of an individual employee, a specific department, a business unit and/or an organisation in relation to other comparators.
- Finally, performance management and new technology in terms of new hardware, software and networks are interwoven. There is a strong tendency towards corporate standardisation and central control using new technology (for example embedded in ICT systems and used through shared service centres) affecting the performance management in MNCs.

In summary, performance management has developed further since Guest and Conway's (1998) observations with a stronger strategic linkage to areas of culture management, talent management, leadership development, competency management and technology.

Moving on to consider the results of the Cranet survey, these data show an overall increase in the application of appraisal systems in organisations, in particular for clerical workers and manual workers. Overall, this seems to reflect increased attention on job performance and the necessity to evaluate individual employees. These results might be in line with the case study findings of increased attention to using performance management to distinguish good and poor performers.

Secondly, the data show an increase in appraisal participation by people other than the direct supervisor. Other evaluators can be next level managers, the individual employee him or herself and subordinates, although the use of subordinates in the evaluation system is much lower than participation by the next level manager. Self-evaluation reveals the highest score here. Including multiple raters in the appraisal system increases the validity and reliability of the actual evaluation (Den Hartog et al., 2004).

For example, including the next level manager in the appraisal process potentially forces the direct supervisor to avoid poor evaluations of subordinates.

The reported Cranet data are mainly focused on the use or application of performance appraisal. Wright et al. (2008) present survey data, including appraisal practices, highlighting both the use of a practice and the effectiveness of it. Their findings suggest significant differences between the application of a practice and the effectiveness of that practice. It is therefore likely that not only the application of a 'best practice' itself is relevant but also the quality of the implementation of that practice.

Finally, the survey data show an increase in the application of appraisal systems aimed at determining the training and development needs of employees, promotion, career management and performance-related pay. It is interesting to note that training and development purposes have the highest scores. In other words, employee development is one of the most important elements of contemporary performance management. This also has important implications for new HR roles as underlined by Ulrich and Brockbank (2005). They emphasise the new role of Human Capital Developer based on their Global Human Resource Competence Survey. The Human Capital Developer role can help shape employee development within contemporary performance management.

SUMMARY CONCLUSIONS

The Global HR Research Alliance case study data and the Cranet survey data show some interesting findings with respect to performance management in contemporary organisations.

First, performance management is linked to or embedded in relevant areas of interest in practice such as (1) culture management, (2) talent management, (3) leadership development (succession planning), (4) competency management and (5) new technology.

Second, there is an overall increase in the use of appraisal systems, in particular for clerical workers and manual workers. There is also a shift towards 360 degree feedback system with an emphasis on self-evaluation. The appraisal system is mainly in place to determine career management, promotion and performance-related pay; however most emphasis is on training and development.

Third, there are few differences between regions in the case studies (probably because of their multinational nature), but there are also few differences between countries in the Cranet data on appraisal systems. Perhaps this is indicative of the increasing standardisation of performance management practices across the globe. If we look in a little more detail, there are some contextual differences that may affect performance management in different countries. The main driver of these differences between countries appears to be associated to cultural differences reflected in variance in leadership, communication and self-evaluation. In other words, the leadership styles, the nature of communication and information sharing, and the role of the individual in the appraisal procedure differ between countries when looking through the lens of performance management.

With these conclusions, we enter into the debate around the extent to which HRM practices can be standardised across different countries, or whether the national context has an overriding effect. Guest and Hoque (1996: 50) start with the premise that 'even in an increasingly global economy, where transnationals compete in similar markets, we find persistent variations in the approaches to the management of human resources'. Indeed there is substantial evidence for this statement. For example, national level characteristics (in this case, levels of spending on education and some aspects of national culture) have been found to affect the link between training and development practices and firm performance (Nikandrou et al., 2008). Equally, Parry et al. (2008) found evidence of certain HRM practices being more common within a specific type of market economy: firms in liberal market economies are more likely to use sophisticated selection techniques and have diversity programmes, whilst those in coordinated market economies are more likely to have trade union recognition and collective bargaining rights in place. This said, there is also some support for a more universalistic approach: Gooderham et al. (2008) argue that there is evidence of a link between calculative HRM practices (e.g. individual performance-related pay and individual bonuses) and firm performance in multiple countries, but that these practices need to be embedded at organisation level in a firm's strategic processes. However, none of the studies reported here are specific to performance management practices, about which recent research is scarcer.

Perhaps the debate can be clarified somewhat if we consider the type of organisation we are looking at. Focusing on the difference between MNCs and domestic firms, there is clear evidence that these two types of operation adopt different approaches to HRM within the same country setting (Farndale et al., 2008). This gives some support to our findings that in the case of performance management, it may well be that multinational firms are managing to implement standardised practices in many different country contexts, whilst the activities of domestic firms are more country-specific. The distinction between the 'best practices' and the 'best-fit' school of thought in the HR field (Boxall & Purcell, 2008) can be applied to this MNC debate. Brewster et al. (2000) make a distinction between two paradigms:

- the universalist paradigm
- the contextual paradigm

They argue that the universalist paradigm assumes the existence of best practices in HRM –

> careful and extensive systems for recruitment, selection and training; formal systems for sharing information with the individuals who work in the organisation; clear job design; local level participation procedures; monitoring of attitudes; performance appraisals; properly functioning grievance procedures; and promotion and compensation schemes that provide for the recognition and financial rewarding of high performing members of the workforce' (Brewster et al., 2000: 11)

– that can be applied by multinational companies successfully worldwide. In Europe, in particular, the contextual paradigm is more widespread (Brewster et al., 2000) building on the notion that there might be some general best principles in HRM (Boxall & Purcell, 2008), but the organisational context in the end determines the nature of the specific human resource practice. An illustration of the contextual paradigm in an IHRM perspective is the typical recruitment and selection of employees in much of southern Europe through the network of family and friends (Brewster et al., 2000). The debate may then shift to the level of implementation: the empirical field is still lacking in research which explores the extent to which a global HRM policy from headquarters is implemented as intended in all the different subsidiaries, or whether differences at national and individual manager levels mean that the practice is implemented substantially differently in each location. We explore this point further below.

Finally, even if we start to look at an even broader range of countries than presented here, we start to reach some similar conclusions. Performance management in the United States is based very strongly on the individualist culture and focuses primarily on linking individual performance to rewards. Performance management processes are also seen as organisational tools to avoid legal problems such as those covered under equal opportunities legislation (Pulakos et al., 2008). This US model of performance management was adopted in Mexico in the 1970s; however, a different culture and a lack of training of managers to carry out the systems has led to little progress in the development of sophisticated systems: the problems of implementing systems means they remain in an infancy stage of progress (Davilla & Elvira, 2008). Similar slow progress of development is being seen in Turkey – there is evidence of wide use of performance management systems, but also evidence of these systems still being highly ineffective (Aycan & Yavuz, 2008).

Looking to Asia, in India there is substantial variation in the degree of sophistication of performance management practices between companies. The notion of performance evaluation is also difficult in this culture where the line manager often takes on a paternal role, raising issues of how objective feedback can be (Sharma et al., 2008). Finally, looking at China, this country has a long history of performance management, initially being a mechanism for monitoring attendance and skills. It has been harder to introduce a more Western approach to evaluation due to the values ascribed to age and seniority in this context (Cooke, 2008). Nevertheless, there is evidence of merit-based performance appraisal systems emerging here too. In summary, this broader global picture still points to a certain degree of convergence in performance management practices, as concluded also by DeNisi et al. (2008: 258): 'as a country becomes more economically mature, [performance management systems] tend to move more closely towards the type of systems we find in the US and Western Europe'.

IMPLICATIONS FOR FUTURE RESEARCH

The findings in this chapter provide input for a future research agenda in performance management. First, there is little or no attention currently being paid to the enactment of performance management by line management, as suggested by Den Hartog et al. (2004). Other scholars emphasise the relevance of strategy implementation for creating organisational success (Becker & Huselid, 2006). One of the issues related to enactment is the role of the direct supervisor in the performance management process. HRM practices including internal promotion opportunities, employee development opportunities and pay increases are often closely linked to performance appraisal with a central role of the direct supervisor of the employee being evaluated. In general the role of the front line manager is neglected in HRM and this might also be the case in performance management.

Second, organisational justice literature shows that part of the performance management success is a result of employee involvement in the design of a performance management system (Colquitt et al., 2001). Future research could focus on other potential critical success factors. These factors might include top management support, good communication, appropriate training, and the right IT infrastructure in terms of hardware and software available to support the performance management system.

Third, several authors have suggested that performance management and HRM show several commonalities (Bach, 2000; Dewettinck, 2008), including the alignment of individual practices (human resource practices or performance management practices) into coherent and consistent bundles. Future research could focus on ideal performance management bundles targeted at achieving internal fit within these bundles and the linkage between the bundle as a whole to the organisational context (organisational fit).

Fourth, more attention could be paid in future research to the role of technology in controlling and standardising performance management systems. Management information systems (MIS) and HR information systems (HRIS) play a crucial role in the underlying performance management processes, for example with respect to data collection, storage, access, analysis, and reporting.

Finally, our empirical findings showed very little variance in general between multinationals in their performance management practices, irrespective of their country-of-origin. It is possible that these MNCs pay more attention to their own organisational culture than to the impact of national cultures of local subsidiary operations. Future comparative research should therefore make a distinction between performance management practices in MNCs and performance management practices in domestic companies – the latter potentially being more subject to the national context than the MNCs which impose their own organisational culture across national borders.

IMPLICATIONS FOR PRACTITIONERS/PRACTICE

Contemporary performance management is a potentially powerful instrument that can be used to help solve organisational challenges including strategy implementation, talent management (attraction and retention of valuable employees), leadership development and culture management aimed at creating a high performance culture based on strong corporate values. Performance management has become a vehicle for culture management in many multinational companies by emphasising the mission, goals and values of the corporation in the competencies and criteria which are being used in the performance appraisal and management process. In this respect it is important to note that performance management (should) include all employees (clerical workers, manual workers, management and professionals) and that it is a way to set organisational goals linked to individual goals.

It is also worthwhile noting that the alignment of individual practices (for example, appraisal, development, promotion, career development and reward) into a coherent and consistent performance management system will be more likely to be successful than the application of single performance management practices without linking these together. A coherent and aligned performance management system will unequivocally send consistent messages to all employees concerning relevant and effective behaviours for realising the stated goals at every level in the organisation.

Finally, it may be important to take into account international cultural differences (Brewster et al., 2004) that might affect the leadership style, the type of communication, the nature of rewards and the use of self-evaluation in the performance management approach. The differences between Japan (large power distance, strong hierarchy) and Sweden (small power distance, emphasis upon employee empowerment/participation) are illustrative in this respect and determine the (im)possibilities for feedback vis à vis leaders and the involvement of employees in that process. However, due to the influence of so-called best practices, as being promoted by the large MNCs and management consultancy firms, we expect that for the years to come performance management will continue in the direction of increased inclusion of subordinates in the appraisal system. Mobilising subordinates will then act as an important device for ensuring managers receive feedback on the different aspects of their leadership behaviour, which is indispensable for facilitating their learning process. In this respect it is interesting to note that employee development is one of the most important elements of contemporary performance appraisal and performance management.

NOTE

1. Spain shows a decrease in the use of appraisal systems across all employee groups; however, this is most likely due to a change in the translation of the questionnaire in 1999 whereby the word '*Evaluacion*' was used to translate appraisal rather than '*Valoracion*', which had been used previously, and has a more specific meaning.

REFERENCES

Aycan, Z. & Yavuz, S. 2008. Performance management in Turkey. In A. Varma, P. S. Budhwar & A. De Nisi (eds), *Performance Management Systems. A Global Perspective.* London: Routledge, pp.168–179.

Bach, S. 2000. From performance appraisal to performance management. In S. Bach & K. Sisson (eds), *Personnel Management.* Oxford: Blackwell.

Baron, A. & Armstrong, M. 1998. *Performance Management: The New Realities.* London: CIPD.

Baron, J. N. & Kreps, D. M. 1999. *Strategic Human Resource Management: Frameworks for General Managers*. Danvers, MA: John Wiley & Sons, Inc.

Becker, B. & Huselid, M. 2006. Strategic human resource management: where do we go from here? *Journal of Management*, **32**(6): 898–925.

Björkman, I. & Lu, Y. 1999. The management of human resources in Chinese–Western joint ventures. *Journal of World Business*, **34**(3): 306–325.

Boxall, P. & Purcell, J. 2008. *Strategy and Human Resource Management*, 2nd edn. Basingstoke, UK: Palgrave Macmillan.

Brewster, C., Mayrhofer, W. & Morley, M. 2000. *New Challenges for European Human Resource Management*. Basingstoke, UK: Macmillan Press.

Brewster, C., Mayrhofer, W. & Morley, M. 2004. *Human Resource Management in Europe: Evidence of Convergence?* Oxford: Butterworth-Heinemann.

Caligiuri, P. M. 2000. The big five personality characteristics as predictors of expatriate desire to terminate the assignment and supervisor-rated performance. *Personnel Psychology*, **53**(1): 67–88

Claus, L. & Briscoe, D. B. 2008. Employee performance management across borders: a review of relevant academic literature. *International Journal of Management Reviews*, **10**(2): 1–22.

Colquitt, J., Conlon, D., Wesson, M., Porter, C. & Ng, K. 2001. Justice at the millennium: a meta-analytic review of 25 years of organizational justice research. *Journal of Applied Psychology*, **86**(3): 425–445.

Cooke, F. L. 2008. Performance management in China. In A. Varma, P. S. Budhwar & A. De Nisi (eds), *Performance Management Systems. A Global Perspective*. London: Routledge, pp.193–209.

Davilla, A. & Elvira, M. M. 2008. Performance management in Mexico. In A. Varma, P. S. Budhwar & A. De Nisi (eds), *Performance Management Systems. A Global Perspective*. London: Routledge, pp.115–130.

Den Hartog, D. N., Boselie, P. & Paauwe, J. 2004. Performance management: a model and research agenda. *Applied Psychology: An International Review*, **53**: 556–569.

DeNisi, A. 2000. Performance appraisal and performance management: a multilevel analysis. In S. Kozlowski & K. J. Klein (eds), *Multilevel Theory, Research and Methods in Organizations*. San Francisco, CA: Jossey-Bass.

DeNisi, A., Varma, A. & Budhwar, P. S. 2008. Performance management around the globe: what have we learned? In A. Varma, P. S. Budhwar & A. De Nisi (eds), *Performance Management Systems. A Global Perspective*. London: Routledge, pp. 254–262.

Dewettinck, K. 2008. Employee performance management systems in Belgian organisations: purpose, contextual dependence and effectiveness. *European Journal of International Management*, **2**(2): 192–207.

Drucker, P. 1954. The practice of management. New York: Harper & Snow. *European Journal of International Management* (2008) **2**(Special issue on global performance management, guest edited by L. Claus & D. Briscoe): 132–227.

Farndale, E., Brewster, C. & Poutsma, E. 2008. Coordinated versus liberal market HRM: the impact of institutionalization on multinational firms. *International Journal of Human Resource Management*, **19**(11): 2004–2023.

Fletcher, C. 2001. Performance appraisal and management: the developing research agenda. *Journal of Occupational and Organizational Psychology*, **73**(4): 473–487.

Galang, M. C. 2004. The transferability question: comparing HRM practices in the Philippines with the US and Canada. *International Journal of Human Resource Management*, **15**(7): 1207–1233.

Gooderham, P., Parry, E. & Ringdal, K. 2008. The impact of bundles of strategic human resource management practices on the performance of European firms. *International Journal of Human Resource Management*, **19**(11): 2041–2056.

Guest, D. E. & Conway, N. 1998. Appendix 4, analysis of survey data in. In M. Armstrong, & A. Baron (eds), *Performance Management: The New Realities*. London: CIPD.

Guest, E. & Hoque, K. 1996. National ownership and HR practices in UK greenfield sites. *Human Resource Management Journal*, **6**(4): 50–74.

Lam, S. S. K., Chen, X. P. & Schaubroeck, J. 2002. Participative decision making and employee performance in different cultures: the moderation effect of allocentrism/idiocentrism and efficacy. *Academy of Management Journal*, **45**(5): 905–914.

Lunnan, R., Lervik, J. E., Traavik, L., Nilsen, S., Amdam, R. & Hennestad, B. 2005. Global transfer of management practices across nations and MNC subcultures. *Academy of Management Executive*, **9**(2): 77–80.

Nikandrou, I., Apospori, E., Panayotopoulou, L., Stavrou, E. & Papalexandris, N. 2008. Training and firm performance in Europe: the impact of national and organizational characteristics. *International Journal of Human Resource Management*, **19**(11): 2057–2078.

Parry, E., Dickmann, M. & Morley, M. 2008. North American MNCs and their HR policies in liberal and coordinated market economies. *International Journal of Human Resource Management*, **19**(11): 2024–2040.

Ployhart, R. E., Wiechman, D., Schmidt, N., Sacco, J. M. & Rogg, K. 2003. The cross-cultural equivalence of job performance ratings. *Human Performance*, **16**(1): 49–79.

Pulakos, E., Mueller-Hanson, R. & O'Leary, R. 2008. Performance management in the United States. In A. Varma, P. Budhwar & A. De Nisi (eds), *Performance Management Systems. A Global Perspective*. London: Routledge: pp. 97–114.

Roberts, I. 2001. Reward and performance management. In I. Beardwell & L. Holden (eds), *Human Resource Management: A Contemporary Approach*, 3rd edn. Edinburgh: Pearson, pp. 506–558.

Shadur, M. A., Rodwell, J. & Bamber, G. J. 1995. The adoption of international best practices in a Western culture: East meets West. *The International Journal of Human Resource Management*, **6**(3): 735–757.

Sharma, T., Budhwar, P. & Varma, A. 2008. Performance management in India. In A. Varma, P. Budhwar & A. De Nisi (eds), *Performance Management Systems: A Global Perspective*. London: Routledge, pp. 180–192.

Shen, J. 2004. International performance appraisals: policies, practices and determinants in the case of Chinese multinational companies. *The International Journal of Manpower*, **25**(6): 547–564.

Ulrich, D. & Brockbank., W. 2005. *The HR Value Proposition*. Boston, MA: Harvard Business School Press.

Wright, P., Holwerda, J., Stiles, P., Trevor, J., Stahl, G., Paauwe, J., Farndale, E. & Morris, S. 2008. Global survey of MNC HR practices. Technical report. Sanyo Global HR Research Consortium.

17 International perspectives on diversity and equal treatment policies and practices[1]

Alain Klarsfeld, Gwendolyn M. Combs, Lourdes Susaeta and María Belizón

Globalisation has brought many changes to the way organisations and societies attempt to address human resource management issues (Brewster, 2007; Sparrow, 2007). Flexibility in how work is accomplished and organisations are arranged requires permeable boundaries and work structures (Mor-Barak, 2005). Organisation–environment theories are often called on to explain why organisations adopt particular routines, policies and procedures. New institutional theory emphasises the regulatory constraints on organisational action embedded in organisational fields (Kostova et al., 2008). Regulative adoption, similar to the 'conformance to regulations' category (Sharma, 2000), involves adopting environmental practices as sanctioned by environmental regulations. Additionally, research on the ambiguities inherent in equal opportunity (EO) laws, and the weak structures for implementation, examines the adoption and diffusion of programmes, policies and procedures across organisations in response to anti-discrimination legislation. These studies propose that the influences of environments (country of operation) on the adoption of organisational EO policies and programmes may institutionalise a set of legitimate practices, even when these practices have limited influence on actual inequality results (Edelman, 1992; Dobbin & Sutton, 1998).

The overarching objective of EO policies is to guarantee equal access to employment opportunities by eliminating disparate treatment based on an individual's social group identity, such as their sex, race, age or disability. However, there is considerable variation in the nature and scope of EO policies across countries (Aslund & Skans, 2010). Such country variations should shape organisational perspectives in determining when and what type of workforce diversity policies are required. For global organisations, this decision may rest on the specific and general regulatory frameworks that are operative through particular country mandates and guidelines.

Managing and developing workplace diversity is on the political and business agenda in many countries. Diversity management has become an area of research, knowledge and practice in its own right (Kidder et al., 2004). Yet all too often, it is assumed to be a single concept, with uniform interpretation across cultures and countries. The diversity concept has its roots in the US context. The discussion of diversity as a positive force and influence on performance started in the United States with the publication of the Workforce 2000 (Johnston & Packer, 1987) report (Kelly & Dobbin, 1998; Thomas, 1990). For this reason, much of the diversity literature is written by US or Anglo-Saxon scholars. Some diversity researchers suggest that from both historical and conceptual standpoints diversity management represents a break or an 'alternative model' to equality and equal opportunities perspectives (Shen et al., 2009; Thomas, 1990; Thomas & Ely, 1996;). Diversity as a management tool and concept has been weakly studied from an international perspective. However, recently the European Commission (2005) promoted a study of 'the business case for diversity' which similarly advocates the benefits of diversity.

Our objective is to restore diversity management to its national contexts, and in particular to assess its relationship with equal employment legislation when such legislation exists. This chapter aims to analyse diversity management taking into account national environments and national business systems. We examine the similarities and differences between the legislation and constitutional prescriptions currently in force in the countries studied. As Brewster et al. (1994) recognise, there is a divergence between the US human resource management system and the European human resource management systems. On the other hand, there is a certain amount of convergence in the European human resource systems due to the common legislation formulated by the EU which affects the different labour markets and distinctive workforces in member countries. Later in this chapter we will consider further American, European, African and Asian diversity perspectives and international comparisons of equal employment and positive action policies.

The main contribution emanates from reports drawn from a large scale international research project originally involving 39 researchers[2] and covering 16 countries spanning four continents: Africa, North America, Asia and Europe. Countries covered by this project are Austria, Belgium, Canada, France, Germany, Spain, India, Italy, the Netherlands, Pakistan, Singapore, South Africa, Sweden, Switzerland, Turkey, the United Kingdom and the United States (Klarsfeld, 2010). After the completion of the initial research, additional countries (Botswana, Taïwan and Spain) and researchers were added to the project and the present chapter includes their work.[3] The work of Jain et al. (2003) is used in this chapter to include comparative information on Malaysia. This chapter therefore uses mostly secondary data as well as an extensive literature review.

At this stage of analysis our aim is to identify and sketch initial transverse 'lessons' to be gleaned from the different country approaches. This will provide a systematic comparative study similar to those commissioned by the International Labour Organization or the European Commission. In this chapter we introduce a typology for assessing and clustering the countries under study in terms of the parameters of their anti-discrimination and equity legislation, and their level of initiation and embracement of the diversity paradigm.

DIVERSITY DEFINED

A simple and complete definition of the term diversity that incorporates the perspectives of countries that have some type of inclusionary initiative would be difficult; and, to some degree, counter to the premise of this chapter and overarching research. However, prior to a comparative discussion of diversity management among targeted countries, it is useful to establish a framework for what is or may be meant by the term. While a definition is offered, it is important to recognise and respect different country connotations for the term and country specific conditions and situations.

Diversity in its purest and most generic sense was defined by Williams and O'Reilly (1998) as the set of attributes which make an individual different from others (Lillevik, Combs & Wyrick, 2010). This definition includes concepts such as gender (O'Reilly III et al., 1991; Shen et al., 2009), race (Riordan & Shore, 1997), age (Pelled, 1996), experience (Hambrick et al., 1996), education (Jackson et al., 1991), functional knowledge (Jehn et al., 1999) and civil status (Harrison et al., 2002). Other scholars have enlarged the concept of diversity to include dimensions that embrace cultural values and aspects (Cox, 1994; Ferner et al., 2006; Jehn et al., 1999; Shen et al., 2009; Wentling, 2004), affections (Barsade et al., 2000) or networking (Beckman & Haunschild, 2002). A definition of diversity that synthesises multiple perspectives could be 'the collective mixture of differences that exist between individuals, or the variation of social and cultural identities inclusive of but not limited to: race, colour, language, dialect, gender, geographic origin, abilities, religion, culture or age' (Chao, 2000; Cox & Blake, 1991; Thomas, 2005).

Research shows that regardless of the definition or focus of diversity, country-specific initiatives operate on the macro, meso, and micro levels of analysis where cultural and social influences impact the initiation and operationalisation of diversity practices (Bucher, 2009; Cox, 2001; DiTomaso et al., 2007; Kalev et al., 2006). Table 17.1 is a description of the general focus of diversity initiatives at these levels.

Table 17.1   The levels at which country-specific initiatives operate

MACRO	MESO	MICRO
Actions, policies, legislation and behaviour at the national or societal level	Interactions and dynamics at the sector level	Influences, values, beliefs and perceptions at the individual firm level

Similar to diversity researchers, and due to differences in main diversity issues, countries that demonstrate an interest in promoting and embracing diversity approach the definition of diversity in differing ways. For example, while gender inequality is the oldest and most widespread diversity issue worldwide, religion and ethnicity separate people in India and the Middle East (Shen et al., 2009). Also, India, with its population of over 1.2 billion people with 1.9 per cent growth yearly, 179 spoken languages with 544 dialects, several different major religions and stark socio-economic differences between population groups, is a good example of the issues surrounding diversity that countries can face (Budhwar, 2001; Haq & Ng, 2010). While there exists a comprehensive labour law in Iran, it is open 'to manipulation and distortion by those who enforce it' (Keep & Storey, 1989: 124) with the consequence of ineffective utilisation of all human resources or as Dickens (1995: 253) put it, 'wasted resources' (Soltani, 2010).

Across countries, the approach to accounting for and measuring levels of difference can also be multifaceted (Sparrow, 2007). For example, Sweden's diversity focus is ethnicity with goals of immigrant integration and social cohesion in inter-group interactions (Hamde, 2008). France, on the other hand, is struggling to institute change in its ability to classify French citizens or collect statistics on the number of ethnic minorities. Such a change in policy in efforts to fight discrimination and promote equality and access is counter to France's universalistic tradition (Bender et al., 2010; Fofana, 2009).

An examination of the laws, regulations, and other initiatives regarding diversity reveal differences in focus across organisational and country formulations of their rationale for promotion of diversity policies. Although variation exists in the methods and mechanisms used by countries to ensure inclusion and anti-discrimination, frameworks establishing the rationale for diversity initiatives tend to primarily fall within two specific categories. First, there is the social justice rationale which represents the moral imperative to provide opportunity for the active participation of all categories and classes of people within a country (Arai & Kibel, 2009). A focus on social justice includes morality in decision making and practice.

Attempts to bring diversity in line with this principle, moral issues of prejudice were transformed into social justice and legal concerns, which has resulted in a set of laws, regulations, and in some cases quotas. Diversity initiatives are methods to facilitate a just society that recognises that the rights and needs of all citizens should be considered and protected (Bell, 2007). This approach is reflected in the case of India and historically in the United States. In India reservations for specified tribes and castes are established to provide action for disadvantaged groups (Combs & Nadkami, 2005; Haq & Ojha, 2010). Similarly, in the United States and in South Africa, diversity initiatives continue to have a remedial and redistributive perspective (Bennett-Alexander & Hartman, 2009; Booysen & Nkomo, 2010; Gullett, 2000).

The second framework includes the evolutionary and global imperative rationale. From this position the level of global engagement of countries in terms of trade balances and cross-cultural workers signals that interactions with diversity are an inevitable reality and are here to stay. Therefore, countries and business organisations have no choice but to determine ways to make the most of the diversity faced in cultures, ethnicities, gender, religions, abilities, age and other socio-economic and cognitive dimensions. This position focuses on the ability of organisations to maximise profits while operating in a global and culturally diverse marketplace. This rationale correlates with the presumption that diversity is good for business and maximising profits. However, Syed and Kramar (2010) discuss scepticism about this theoretical rationale. They question whether the narrow capitalistic emphasis undergirding this approach ensures equitable outcomes for diverse employees (Syed & Özbilgin, 2009).

FROM EQUALITY TO DIVERSITY?

A question to examine is whether equal employment legislation and, specifically, diversity management exists across different countries, and whether diversity management represents a break from equality concepts such as equal opportunity and affirmative action. Such a break between diversity management and equality concepts has been argued for almost 20 years (Jain et al., 2003; Thomas, 1990; Thomas & Ely, 1996). The claim of a disassociation of concepts and movement from equality to diversity is salient in North America, particularly in the United States. This concept has been broadly assumed in industrialised countries of the West including the UK, Canada and Australia (Agocs & Burr, 1996; Jain & Verma, 1996; Liff, 1997; Teicher & Spearitt, 1996).

Analysis across countries suggests that the US-centric concept of diversity has not similarly emerged elsewhere. In countries where diversity has emerged, the differentiation and sequencing between diversity management and its antecedent concepts of equality, equal opportunity and affirmative action, is far from obvious. Noon (2007) suggests that 'the fatal flaw' of diversity 'quarrels that diversity is essentially a concept that marginalises the importance of equality and suppresses the significance of ethnicity in the workplace' (p. 780). This argument begs the question as to how diverse workforces of Middle Eastern and Asian countries have been managed so far (Soltani, 2010). For instance, in countries, such as India, Pakistan, Singapore and Turkey, diversity management appears undiffused, and un- or under-researched as an academic field (Chia & Lim, 2010; Haq & Ojha, 2010; Özbilgin et al., 2010). To a lesser extent, this has also been the case in the European Union. In many countries, diversity management appears strongly linked to equality and non-discrimination and/or affirmative action legislation, albeit in very country-specific ways.

For some authors, the link between diversity, compliance, and equality, is sometimes termed 'confusion'. The assumption is that diversity management should go beyond equality discourse (moral imperatives) and legislation (compliance), and more specifically focus on the business benefits inherent in the diversity management concept. This is the case for authors from Canada (Haq & Ng, 2010), South Africa (Booysen & Nkomo, 2010) and to a lesser extent the United States (Lillevik et al., 2010). Other authors do not carry similar assumptions and see diversity management as an ongoing vehicle for institutionalising equality and non-discrimination at work. This is also typical of European Union countries such as Sweden (Kalonaityte et al., 2010), Germany (Bruchhagen et al., 2010), France (Bender et al., 2010), and Italy (Murgia & Poggio, 2010). In these countries, diversity management is depicted as a mechanism for the diffusion of equality and non-discrimination policies and practices, rather than a radically distinct approach.

Notwithstanding limitations and important differences in context and adoption, diversity management and equal opportunities appear to be much more similar in content than suggested by early advocates of diversity management. Although attempts are made to divest the concept of diversity from the context of its historical equality predecessors (equal employment opportunity and affirmative action), the break has not been definitive or convincing. A clear example of this dichotomy can be found in the United States where the term 'diversity' was first coined. The management literature tried to couch or define diversity as being all inclusive of differences found in workers across a wide spectrum of demographics. To counter and disassociate diversity from the backlash and fire storm surrounding affirmative action, diversity was promoted as a concept that encompassed all differences beyond race, ethnicity and sex/gender (Thomas, 1990). However, given the historical context of equality efforts in the United States it was, and continues to be, difficult to maintain consistent and concise distinctions between the meaning and practice of diversity and other inclusionary methods such as affirmative action. Therefore, in the United States, where there are strong anti-discrimination laws and protracted work towards inclusion, diversity management practices have been labelled as 'old wine in new wineskins' by some scholars (Kelly & Dobbin, 1998). Additionally, further confusion exists and is perpetuated because diversity management and affirmative action often converge in the eyes of the general public (Lillevik et al., 2010). Moreover, in the specification of dimensions of diversity, researchers list demographics addressed by affirmative action and equal opportunity measures (race, ethnicity, gender, age, etc.) as primary dimensions of diversity programming (Loden, 1996).

However, this should not be interpreted as another normative assumption about diversity management since a few countries, such as Canada (Haq & Ng, 2010) and Belgium, at least as far as Flanders is concerned (Cornet & Zanoni, 2010), seem to have developed an approach to diversity management in line with the vision of the founders of this notion, that is, the search for a competitive advantage or other business-driven motives rather than compliance with anti-discrimination laws (Thomas, 1990; Thomas & Ely, 1996). For example, in Canada employers go beyond compliance with the law and use diversity management to be more inclusive (of the white male majority) and business driven. This approach seems to afford public acceptance of preferential treatment for designated groups (Haq & Ng, 2010). Again, this underscores the need for contextualising diversity management to country-specific contexts.

MAPPING LEGISLATION: AN ATTEMPT TOWARDS BUILDING A CONTINUUM FROM 'EQUALITY' TO POSITIVE ACTION

Contextualising diversity research and practice will assist organisations in better implementing diversity initiatives and enhance their awareness of potential pitfalls in addressing diversity, equal treatment or affirmative action, as 'natural' and self-evident concepts. Indeed, diversity management, equality and affirmative action are not universal concepts across or within countries. At the practitioner and policy-maker levels in Singapore (Chia & Lim, 2010), 'harmony' and 'fairness' prevail over the terms 'equal opportunities' and 'diversity'. In Germany, prior to the emergence of diversity, 'gender mainstreaming' was in the forefront (Bruchhagen et al., 2010).

In France (Bender et al., 2010) and Sweden (Kalonaityte et al., 2010), diversity has a strong relationship with the integration of immigrants and signals the rising awareness of addressing the place of immigrants and their descendants in respective societies. Canada's legislation and corporate practices insisted on multiculturalism and employment equity long before the advent of the concept of diversity in the 1990s (Haq & Ng, 2010).

Each country covered by this chapter has anti-discrimination legislation. In most countries, states have first introduced 'equality of rights' legislations prohibiting negative discrimination. Subsequently, to varying degrees, at various speeds and for different criteria, 'positive action' or 'affirmative action' legislation was enacted to introduce differential treatment for traditionally underprivileged population groups. Although this sequencing is typical, it is not generalisable to all countries. For example, India and Malaysia from the beginning included positive discrimination in their constitutions (Haq & Ojha, 2010; Jain et al., 2003). Given the differences found in countries regarding equal opportunities and diversity, we have attempted to summarise these differences in a topology showing a continuum of country perspectives on laws promoting inclusion. The continuum presented in Table 17.2 below extends from negative discrimination legislation at one end, to the strongest form of affirmative action policies that impose outcome-based quotas for jobs and educational opportunities for targeted groups at the other end, positive discrimination.[4] While the continuum is an evolving document, it is considered a starting point for comparative analysis.

Coverage of Equality Laws

In most countries under study, anti-discrimination laws, particularly those laws that prescribe positive action, do not comprehensively cover all organisations. Coverage generally varies according either to the public/private sector divide, and/or by company size. Generally, larger firms tend to be more covered than small firms. The public sector generally is covered by more extensive equality legislation than the private sector. For instance, in the United States and Canada, affirmative action was initiated primarily in the public sector and for federal contractors (Lillevik et al., 2010). Reporting on gender and origins of employees is compulsory for all employers with 100 employees or more. Similarly, in Canada, sectors covered by affirmative action (under the employment equity legislation) are the public sector, federal contractors based on level of contracts, and 'federally regulated' sectors generally comprising large undertakings such as banking and telecommunications (Haq & Ng, 2010). In the United Kingdom, only public bodies have to follow statutory duties and codes of

Table 17.2   A typology of equality and positive action legislations

Degree of constraint of positive action legislation	Definition
Negative discrimination Legal discrimination Laws provide against the criterion	Persons covered by the criterion are discriminated against under the laws of the country.
Legal vacuum No legal protection	The criterion is mentioned by neither equality nor positive action legislation. It might not even be discussed in public or academic debates.
Restricted quality of rights No reporting allowed	Equality of right is explicitly granted against discrimination based on the criterion. However, it is forbidden for employers to directly collect data and report figures on the criterion; action plans cannot target these criteria directly.
Equality of rights Allowed reporting	Equality of right is explicitly granted against discrimination based on the criterion. Collecting data and reporting on the criterion is possible. This remains at the discretion of employers, and might be, according to the country, highly controversial.
Encouraged voluntarism Positive action encouraged	Collecting data and reporting on the criterion is compulsory, but not the setting of outcome targets, which remain at the discretion of employers. Employers have a broad duty to act, such as to engage in collective bargaining.
Constrained process Positive action compulsory	Collecting data, setting targets, acting and reporting progress on the criterion is compulsory. Covered employers must demonstrate good faith action and progress. The target is remote and not binding on the short term. Sanction may apply if there is a lack of 'good faith' and progress.
Constrained outcome Positive discrimination	Strict targets (quotas) have to be met for the criterion. Sanction is imposed systematically when targets are not met.

practices which include equality schemes (Tatli, 2010). Amongst others, these equality schemes make ethnic monitoring of employment and service provision an obligation. However, case law in the UK makes such reporting desirable though not compulsory for private employers. In India, with its very diverse population, and strong affirmative action legislation in the public sector, diversity-labelled initiatives are scarce in the private sector, occurring mainly in subsidiaries of foreign-owned multinational corporations and in the IT sector (Haq & Ojha, 2010).

However, the relationship between coverage and belonging to the public sector may not systematically work one-way, that is, towards more legal provisions. For instance, in France, until recently, explicit age limitations used to apply to most public sector jobs, therefore creating a legal negative discrimination based on age, from which private sector jobs were exempt. These age restrictions have only very recently been removed, with some remaining exceptions. As regards discrimination based on nationality, still, up to the present day, public sector jobs in France can only be filled by members of the European Economic Area, this being regardless of the possession of a work permit by a national from another country, so in this respect, too, the French public sector is less inclusive than the private sector. Until recently, public sector jobs in France were actually set aside for French citizens only, and this changed only under pressure exerted by the European Union (Bender et al., 2010).

Criteria to which Legislations Apply

Things would be too easy if the above continuum could apply similarly to all discrimination criteria covered by the different countries. In fact, provisions regarding positive action tend to focus not only on a limited subset of organisations, but also to a limited subset of criteria. For instance, in the United States EEO-1 reports that employers with 100 employees or more have to file annually, concern gender and race/ethnic origin, but not other criteria such as age, disability or national origin (Lillevik et al., 2010). Criteria identified in the 19 countries presented in this chapter are as follows: gender, pregnancy status, family status, disability (physical or mental), health status, origin (with varied typologies according to the country), nationality, age, religion, belief (again, with varied declensions according to country), colour, sexual orientation, gender identity, genetic characteristics, life habits, looks, union affiliation, political opinion, bearing in mind that not all countries deal with all criteria in their respective legislations. Where many countries include strong remedial affirmative or positive action for the disabled, based on a 'constrained outcome' approach where people with disabilities are attributed a certain proportion of employment posts, only a small group of countries apply a similar approach to origin-related criteria such as ethnic group or castes. As for gender, approaches range from 'equality of right' to 'constrained process' according to the country.

Special mention must be devoted to origin, a highly contextual concept. According to the country, origin can be understood as race, colour,

Table 17.3   Clustering of countries according to intensity of affirmative action, relative precedence of gender and origin, maturity of legislation, and maturity of diversity management debates

	Intensity of existing affirmative action policies	Maturity of affirmative action policies	Relative precedence of gender and origin	Maturity of the diversity concept in country debates
Group 1 India Malaysia Singapore	Constrained outcome	Medium to high	Origin before gender	Low
Group 2 Canada South Africa UK United States	Constrained process	Medium to high	Gender and origin on a par	High
Group 3 EU countries Pakistan Turkey	Equality of rights with moves towards constrained process and outcomes	Low	Gender before origin	Low

ethnicity, tribe, caste, national origin, aboriginal status or 'visible minority'. For instance, while 'race' is used in Anglo-Saxon countries, 'caste' is used in India, colour is used in South Africa, national origin (targeting descendants of immigrants) is more relevant in mainland European Union states.

Clustering Countries Together

Based on previous international literature relative to diversity management (Jain et al., 2003; Klarsfeld, 2010), we propose clusters of countries (See Table 17.3) according to four criteria: intensity of affirmative action policies; the precedence granted to discrimination based on origin over gender or vice versa; the maturity of the equality regulation; and the use of the term 'diversity'. Because many countries stand on the edge of two clusters, we caution that the clusters should be seen as broad groupings. Additionally, it must be noted that some countries distance themselves from the 'majority' in the cluster on a few points.

In a first group of countries, consisting of India, Malaysia, and Singapore, affirmative action policies are present in their most intense version ('constrained outcome'), as they provide quotas for designated groups in employment and/or education (India, Malaysia) or housing (Singapore) (Chia & Lim, 2010; Haq & Ojha, 2010; Jain et al., 2003). In India, 22.5 per cent of jobs in the public sector are reserved for members of scheduled castes and scheduled tribes, and the proportion of jobs covered by reservation can total a maximum of 50 per cent on a state-by-state basis. In Malaysia, 80 per cent of public sector jobs are reserved for Bumiputras, or native Malays, and provisions also exist to ensure that Malays are found at all levels of the hierarchy in the private sector.

Singapore is somewhat of an 'outlier' in this first group as its ethnic quota policy affects housing but not employment and does not target just one ethnic group but all of them. Each ethnic group is granted a housing quota in each residential area in order to foster a mixing of diverse people and prevent the formation of ethnic enclaves (Chia & Lim, 2010). However, in employment, although Singapore does not have affirmative action provisions, it has adopted a distinctive non-legislated voluntary equality of rights approach with ethnic monitoring at the national level, particularly focusing on the native Malays. Emphasis on an equality of rights approach suggests a similarity with EU countries grouped in cluster 3. In all three countries precedence is given to addressing discrimination based on origin (race/ethnicity) over gender-based discrimination. Maturity of affirmative action legislation is medium to high with quotas for designated groups having been developed over a period of 20 to almost 60 years (since 1950 and 1957 for India and Malaysia respectively, 1989 in Singapore). However, diversity management as a business concern, with its distinct terminology and literature, is only very recent in this group of countries.

The second group of countries consists of the United States (Lillevik et al., 2010), Canada (Haq & Ng, 2010), South Africa (Booysen & Nkomo, 2010) and the UK (Tatli, 2010). Affirmative action policies are less binding than in the case of the countries in cluster one. There is an obligation (or a strong encouragement in the case of the UK) made for covered employers to engage in action plans with goals and timetables, and to report on inequalities and progress towards equality ('constrained process' or 'encouraged voluntarism' as far as the UK's public sector is concerned). However, quota systems granting systematic preferences are rejected as a source of reverse discrimination and are illegal. At present, these countries try to reconcile the need to enhance the standing of designated group members, with the requisite of treating everyone on an even basis, and have banned quotas. Additionally, in all of these four countries, gender-based measures, race/ethnicity and similar origin-based measures have grown in conjunction to one another, and are given the same type of affirmative action provisions. The maturity of legal provisions is high (as concerns the United States and the UK), that is, comprised between 40 and 50 years, to medium (Canada and South Africa) with provisions dating 15 to 25 years as of 2010. Diversity management as a concept distinct from equality and affirmative action has been given its earliest and highest interest in this group of countries, particularly in the United States.

The third cluster of countries includes mainland European Union countries (Bendl et al., 2010; Murgia et al., 2010), Switzerland (Nentwich et al., 2010), Pakistan and Turkey (Özbilgin et al., 2010), Botswana (Mpabanga, 2010), and Taïwan (Hsu, 2010; Hsu & Lawler, 2008). Affirmative action is not commonplace in these countries. These countries have a strong tradition of and preference for equal treatment, in other words, for an 'equality of rights' approach with or without allowed or facilitated reporting. Analysis shows that these countries are shifting more towards affirmative action and the inclusion of more criteria in their legislations. The idea that the origins of people can be registered and monitored under the form practised in countries belonging to groups 1 and 2, even for their own benefit, is generally traditionally unpopular,.

In the list of demographics eligible for affirmative action, gender has been given a longstanding precedence over origin (race/ethnicity), with the first laws targeting gender equality initiated as early as the 1940s in Sweden. This contrasts with a more recent preoccupation for discrimination based on origin. In the third country cluster the maturity of affirmative action is low, with only disability benefiting from 'constrained outcome' provisions. The term 'positive action' is preferred to that of 'affirmative action' in order to distance the approach from that used in groups 1 and 2. However, recent moves by a number of European Union countries and Pakistan regarding gender equality push towards the 'constrained process' and perhaps the 'constrained outcome' levels. For example, France, Norway and Spain have imposed quotas for women on boards of large companies. This practice is being considered by other European Union countries. As part of a larger regional interstate cooperation institution (the Southern African Development Community[5]), Botswana is covered by the recently signed SADC Protocol on Gender and Development (2008). This protocol provides that by 2015, the proportion of women in decision-making positions of public and private sector organisations should be 50 per cent in member countries. Pakistan adopted a 33 per cent quota for women at local elections in 2000 and a 5 per cent quota for non-Muslims in government jobs in 2009. Finally, 'diversity management' is a fairly recent expression and concern in this group of countries. Where the concept exists, rather than succeeding to equal opportunities and affirmative action policies as a new rationale for inclusiveness, diversity management grows in parallel to and in reinforcement of legal measures destined to intensify the fight against discrimination.

FROM EQUALITY OF RIGHTS TO AFFIRMATIVE ACTION: A ONE-WAY STORY?

A question of interest is whether the move along the continuum presented in Table 17.2 from 'negative discrimination' through 'equality of rights' to 'constrained process' and 'constrained outcome' is a deterministic one-way process or whether there is space for two-way developments. In other words, can there be a change of direction, as in any other field covered by political action? Critics of affirmative action contend that although affirmative action policies claim to be temporary, once in place, they tend to take on permanency (Calvès, 2008). Overall, affirmative action policies have proved enduring, even in the face of turbulence and threats to dismantle programmes in the United States (Kelly & Dobbin, 1998). This appears to be the case in all countries in groups 1 and 2. However, we would argue against the 'one-way' thesis.

For instance, the history of affirmative action policy in the United States has experienced ebbs and flows. On the one hand, resources granted to the agencies in charge of enforcing affirmative action programmes were curtailed during the Reagan administration in the 1980s (Kelly & Dobbin, 1998). On the other hand, leading organisations voluntarily engage in affirmative action and expend considerable resources on affirmative action programme implementation and maintenance. Additionally, the Supreme Court tends to interpret the notion of adverse impact more restrictively than in the past (Kelly & Dobbin, 1998; Lillevik et al., 2010). More strikingly, in 1994, the Netherlands introduced a 'constrained process' type of affirmative action legislation with an obligation placed on employers to report national origin, define goals and timetables. The Netherlands amended this legislation in 1998 and repealed it in 2004 following employer resistance (Bleijenbergh et al., 2010). On another note, India started from its very foundation, with a strong policy of quotas, without 'moving along the continuum' in Table 17.2. In some states in India, where Other Backward Classes (OBCs) are eligible demographic groups, quotas were introduced without evidence of an economic gap similar to the one suffered by members of scheduled tribes and scheduled castes, which suggests that sheer demographic weight, rather than actual injustice, sometimes makes the difference when it comes to the decision to introduce constrained outcome provisions. Actually, debates are now taking place in India, aimed at mitigating the caste-based affirmative action legislation with other criteria such as wealth, merit and place of residence (Haq & Ojha, 2010). All these examples suggest that political balance of power, rather than an objective measurement of discrimination, may have the final say in decisions to initiate, develop, maintain and dismantle affirmative action legislations. This suggests an uncertain future regarding which direction countries will move along the continuum.

Diversity, Equality and Managerial Discretion

As a subset of corporate social responsibility, the concept of diversity assumes that corporate discretion can only take place beyond the law, whereas such mandated concepts as equality and affirmative action are supposed to rest on a set of laws that leave little room for choice. Indeed, for many authors diversity management implies moving beyond compliance (Thomas, 1990; Thomas & Ely, 1996). This is also reflected in EU countries where diversity is promoted under the form of non legislated 'diversity charters'. Respecting the law is typically seen as a baseline where there is no room for voluntarism: you just 'have to' comply. Yet, various country-based studies show that in many areas, in many countries, simply following the law is far from obvious. Many firms choose not to align to legal requirements in various aspects of their business.

We would argue that in many countries equality laws are weak laws (in the sense of Kuznetsov et al., 2009) especially when one compares them to the more stringent laws governing tax collection. Kelly and Dobbin (1998) show that in the United States, where firms and people have a higher reputation for following laws than in 'transitional' economies, Civil Rights laws adopted in 1964 were supposedly compulsory. However, through the 1960s these laws received poor employer interest and response. Employer compliance with the law occurred only after a significant increase in the 1970s of the enforcement powers of the Equal Employment Opportunity Commission.

Similarly, Klarsfeld (2009) shows that in France the adoption of 'diversity' management practices deemed 'compulsory' by law is a kind of 'half-full/half-empty' situation, where in fact a significant proportion of firms choose not to follow the law or just ignore it. Only about half the firms which are required annually to report gender-disaggregated data do so. In the Netherlands, only a minority of firms – 20 per cent of those covered by the law – engaged in the monitoring of the national origin of their workforce between 1994 and 2004 even though this was supposedly compulsory during this period of time (Bleijenbergh et al., 2010). Likewise, Sweden, with its high profile regarding gender equality, still has not reached parity in salaries between men and women workers. Controlling for sector and occupation, women's' salaries are 92 per cent of that of men. Also, 95 per cent of top executive positions are held by men, a proportion which seems difficult to justify on the mere basis of merit or even career preferences (Kalonaityte et al., 2010). These suggestions of gender-based discrimination exist in spite of Sweden's globally vaunted gender equality policy.

Providing a better mapping of the degree to which countries adopt and enforce diversity and equality policies, certainly is a matter for improvement in future cross-country comparative research.

IMPACTS OF DIVERSITY RELATED PRACTICES

Impacts on Organisational Effectiveness

It is not the focus of this chapter to debate in depth the research results regarding the nexus between diversity management and organisational performance. An important consideration in discussions of the relationship between performance and diversity, is that much of the research in this areas was conducted in Western countries, particularly in the United States and Canada. Therefore, more research is needed in other national contexts, so as to assess the universality/contextuality of the findings and their applicability across a wide range of cultures. The increase in globalisation and the organisational need for a diverse workforce has made diversity an imperative issue for business worldwide (Cox & Beale, 1997). This organisational global mind-set coupled with the differences in diversity and equal opportunity laws and regulations across countries, increases the importance and timeliness of the examination and understanding of cross-country comparisons for the exploration of the link between diversity and performance.

In Germany, for instance, Schäffner et al. (2006) found that if the firm incorporates the normative assumption that diversity is an opportunity, then age diversity becomes a predictor of team innovativeness, but not otherwise. Kearney and Gebert (2006) found that diversity in age, nationality and functional background have a positive effect on team innovativeness in a high transformational leadership context, but no effect in a low one. It had already been established that failing to manage diversity properly or developing diversity per se leads to only mixed results (Bell, 2007; Klein & Harrison, 2007) but is this true universally? While research on diversity and performance has typically occurred at the organisational level, country level analyses of this relationship might inform our knowledge of the performance/diversity relationship. Therefore, more research is needed in other national contexts so as to assess the universality/contextuality of the findings and their applicability across a wide range of cultures.

Impacts on Social Acceptability

One of the main arguments against equal opportunity, affirmative action and diversity management, is that such policies may introduce elements of backlash or perceived reverse discrimination (Bell, 2007). Reverse discrimination claims emanate from persons categorised as 'privileged' (for example, white males in North America and Europe, the Brahmins in India, or the Chinese in Malaysia) expressing resentment of being stigmatised as perpetrators of past discrimination and denied opportunities when targeted protected groups are favoured. Indeed, the pursuit of diversity and equality must follow a narrow path which tries to reconcile progress towards more equality of outcomes (or at least, less inequality of outcomes), and equality of treatment, which implies treating persons equally. Research suggests that countries which have gone furthest along the introduction of quotas, namely India and Malaysia, face considerable internal criticism based on the perceived lack of fairness inherent in the systematic priority given to members of some groups over others (Haq & Ojha, 2010; Jain et al., 2003).

In the United States and Canada, affirmative action policies may face the same kind of criticism (Haq & Ng, 2010; Lillevik et al., 2010). The use of the term of diversity may be an answer to such criticism (Haq & Ng, 2010; Thomas, 1990; Thomas & Ely, 1996). However, there is a lack of comparative and reliable data to suggest that affirmative action policies followed in North America, which reject quotas as a recruitment and promotion tool, are better or worse perceived than caste-based quotas in India, or quotas for the disabled in Europe. The only indication presently is that quotas are categorically considered illegal in the United States, and that quotas for the disabled have achieved a certain consensus in the European Union and other countries such as Pakistan and Taiwan. The question here is: are these country differences in social acceptability linked to an objective general perceived equity/inequity of quotas versus goals and timetables; to the criterion (disability/gender/origin) itself; or to a certain political balance of power in the respective countries? Clearly, more comparative research is called for here, both within countries in order to compare the perceived fairness of a host of policies both within and between criteria, and then between countries in order to give evidence of transnational versus local patterns of acceptability of equality/ affirmative action/positive action/diversity policies.

FUTURE RESEARCH PERSPECTIVES

The research perspectives introduced in this chapter are numerous and multifaceted. Therefore, it is impossible in this limited space or medium to do justice to the richness of possibilities for the comparative analysis of country perspectives on equality and diversity. However, this chapter provides a good and solid beginning to this inquiry.

More research should be devoted to assessing the relevance of the continuum of legislations presented and its possible refinements, applications and limitations. For instance, there is debate among the research team for this project as to whether to expand this typology to include other potential country differences in implementing EO and diversity regulations. For example, in some countries diversity is not a consideration, so the bottom level of the typology continuum should reflect this stance. Even for existing categories, there is a debate, whether 'positive action encouraged' should not be conceptually differentiated from the notion of 'constrained reporting', as an obligation to report is but one among other possible encouragements to encourage positive action. In a similar vein, collective bargaining, widely used in European Union countries, could be granted a specific categorisation rather than being subsumed in the 'encouraged voluntarism' category. A point to include in future comparative efforts would therefore be the space devoted to trade unions, collective bargaining and works councils in national legislations, a trait which is distinctive of many EU countries given the role granted to social partners, consultation and collective bargaining under EU and national legislations. This also applies to Singapore and its tripartite model (Chia & Lim, 2010).

Beyond state legislations, research efforts should try to extend beyond strictly focusing on the laws at the state level and adapt this typology to other levels of policy formulation such as the industry and firm levels. Similar to states, industries (through collective bargaining in some countries) and firms (through collective bargaining and internal, voluntary rules such as corporate codes of conduct) regulate the management of their own diversity. At the supranational level, international institutions (such as the European Union) can put in place policies whose aim is to eliminate discrimination and develop and manage diversity. Research efforts should focus on parallels and differences that may apply across these different levels of regulation and policy making. Once a more refined typology in established, it will become possible to intensify comparative research at these various levels on antecedents and consequences of such policies. Particular focus could be efficacy in achieving organisational performance, together with distributive and procedural justice (Jain et al., 2003). Another interesting research perspective is to move beyond studying policies at one single level, in order to 'capture the relational interplay of structural- and agentic-level concerns of equality' (Klarsfeld, 2009; Syed & Özbilgin, 2009).

Other future research questions might include categories that are not legally protected. Examination of country consideration of discrimination against group demographics (e.g. level of obesity, (un)attractiveness, gay, lesbian, transgendered, etc.) may prove instructive to our understanding of comparative structures of diversity. For example, in India, it is well known that the 'Hijras' (an Indian equivalent to eunuch or hermaphrodite) community faces tremendous discrimination. Finally, future research on the level of backlash against equality legislation and diversity management practices may determine if there are predictors of backlash or if backlash is strictly a country-specific process.

NOTES

1. Special thanks to Annie Cornet, Rana Haq, Jacqueline Laufer, Eddy Ng, Mustafa Özbilgin, Marloes Van Engen, Patrizia Zanoni, for feedback about this chapter while it was still in progress.
2. Anne-Françoise Bender, Regine Bendl, Inge Bleijenbergh, Lize Booysen, Verena Bruchhagen, Audrey Chia, Gwendolyn M. Combs, Annie Cornet, Beliz Dereli, Jürgen Grieger, Rana Haq, Edeltraud Hanappi-Egger, Roswitha Hofmann, Viktorija Kalonaityte, Alain Klarsfeld, Iris Koall, Jacqueline Laufer, Brigitte Liebig, Waheeda Lillevik, Angeline Lim, Michael Meuser, Annalisa Murgia, Julia Nentwich, Eddy Ng, Stella M. Nkomo, Abhoy Ojha, Renate Ortlieb, Mustafa Özbilgin, Barbara Poggio, Pushkala Prasad, Barbara Sieben, Chris Steyaert, Jawad Syed, Ahu Tatli, Adiam Tedros, Ashley Terlouw, Marloes Van Engen, Cheryl Wyrick and Patrizia Zanoni.
3. Dorothy Mbpabanga, María Belizón, Lourdes Susaeta and Corwin I-Chieh Hsu.
4. The term positive discrimination is used here to be congruent with some national connotations and refers to both mandatory and voluntary programmes established to affirm the civil rights and privileges of designated classes of individuals by taking positive action to protect them from the lingering effects of historical and long-term actions resulting in the denial of equal opportunity in employment and other work relate outcomes.
5. Which originally included Angola, Botswana, Lesotho, Malawi, Mozambique, Swaziland, Tanzania, Zambia and Zimbabwe, and now also includes the Democratic Republic of Congo, Madagascar, Mauritius, Namibia, Seychelles and South Africa (Source: http://www.sadc.int).

REFERENCES

Agocs, C. & Burr, C. 1996. Employment equity, affirmative action and managing diversity: assessing the differences. *International Journal of Manpower*, **17**(4): 30–46.
Arai, S. & Kibel, B. D. 2009. Critical race theory and social justice perspectives on whiteness, difference(s) and (anti)racism: a fourth wave of race research in leisure studies. *Journal of Leisure Research*, **41**(4): 459–470.

Aslund, O. & Skans, O. N. 2010. Will I see you at work? Ethnic workplace segregation in Sweden, 1985–2002. *Industrial & Labor Relations Review*, **63**(3): 471–493.

Barsade, S. G., Ward, A. J., Turner, J. D. F. & Sonnenfeld, J. 2000. To your heart's content: a model of affective diversity in top management teams. *Administrative Science Quarterly*, **45**(4): 802–836.

Beckman, C. M. & Haunschild, P. R. 2002. Network learning: the effects of partners' heterogeneity of experience on corporate acquisitions. *Administrative Science Quarterly*, **47**(1): 92–124.

Bell, M. P. 2007. *Diversity in Organisations*. Mason, OH: Thomsen South-Western.

Bender, A. F., Klarsfeld, A. & Laufer, J. 2010. Equality and diversity in the French context. In A. Klarsfeld (ed.), *International Handbook on Diversity Management at Work: Country Perspectives on Diversity and Equal Treatment*. Cheltenham, UK: Edward Elgar.

Bendl, R., Hanappi-Egger, E. & Hofmann, R. 2010. Austrian perspectives on diversity management and equal treatment, regulations, debates, practices and trends. In A. Klarsfeld (ed.), *International Handbook on Diversity Management at Work: Country Perspectives on Diversity and Equal Treatment*. Cheltenham, UK: Edward Elgar.

Bennett-Alexander, D. & Hartman, L. 2009. *Employment Law for Business*. 6th edn. Burr Ridge, IL: McGraw-Hill.

Bleijenbergh, I., van Engen, M. & Terlouw, A. 2010. Laws, policies and practices of diversity management in the Netherlands. In A. Klarsfeld (ed.), *International Handbook on Diversity Management at Work: Country Perspectives on Diversity and Equal Treatment*. Cheltenham, UK: Edward Elgar.

Booysen, L. & Nkomo, S. 2010. Employment equity and diversity management in South Africa. In A. Klarsfeld (ed.), *International Handbook on Diversity Management at Work: Country Perspectives on Diversity and Equal Treatment*. Cheltenham, UK: Edward Elgar.

Brewster, C. 2007. Comparative HRM: European views and perspectives. *International Journal of Human Resource Management*, **18**(5): 769–787.

Brewster, C., Mayne, L. & Tregaskis, O. 1994. Employee communication and participation. In C. Brewster & A. Hegewisch (eds), *Policy and Practice in European Human Resource Management: The Evidence and Analysis from the Price Waterhouse Cranfield Survey*. London: Routledge.

Bruchhagen, V., Grieger, J., Koall, I., Meuser, M., Ortlieb, R. & Sieben, B. 2010. Social inequality, diversity, and equal treatment at work. The German case. In A. Klarsfeld (ed.), *International Handbook on Diversity Management at Work: Country Perspectives on Diversity and Equal Treatment*. Cheltenham, UK: Edward Elgar.

Budhwar, P. 2001. Doing business in India. *Thunderbird International Business Review*, **43**(4): 549–568.

Calvès, G. 2008. *La Discrimination Positive*. Paris: Que Sais-je, Presses Universitaires de France.

Chao, G. T. 2000. Multilevel issues and culture: an integrative view. In K. J. Klein & S. W. Kozlowski (eds), *Multilevel Theory, Research and Methods in Organisations*. San Francisco, CA: Jossey-Bass, pp. 308–344.

Chia, A. & Lim, A. 2010. Singapore: equality, harmony and fair employment. In A. Klarsfeld (ed.), *International Handbook on Diversity Management at Work: Country Perspectives on Diversity and Equal Treatment*. Cheltenham, UK: Edward Elgar.

Combs, G. M. & Nadkami, S. 2005. A tale of two cultures: attitudes towards affirmative action in the United States and India. *The Journal of World Business*, **40**(2): 158–171.

Cornet, A. & Zanoni, P. 2010. Diversity management in Belgium. In A. Klarsfeld (ed.), *International Handbook on Diversity Management at Work: Country Perspectives on Diversity and Equal Treatment*. Cheltenham, UK: Edward Elgar.

Cox, J. & Blake, S. 1991. Managing cultural diversity: implications for organisational competitiveness. *Academy of Management Executive*, **5**(3): 45–56.

Cox, T. 1994. *Cultural Diversity in Organizations: Theory, Research, and Practice*. San Francisco, CA: Berrett-Koehler.

Cox, T. 2001. *Creating the Multicultural Organisation: A Strategy for Capturing the Power of Diversity*. San Francisco, CA: Jossey-Bass.

Cox, T. & Beale, R. L. 1997. *Developing Competency to Manage Diversity: Readings, Cases and Activities*. San Francisco, CA: Berrett-Koehler Publishers.

Dickens, L. & Sisson, K. 1995. Wasted Resources? *Equal Opportunities in Employment. Personnel Management: A Comprehensive Guide to Theory and Practice*, 2nd edn. Oxford: Blackwell.

DiTomaso, N., Post, C. & Parks-Yancy, R. 2007. Workforce diversity and inequality: power, status, and numbers. *Annual Review of Sociology*, 33(1): 473–501.

Dobbin, F. & Sutton, J. R. 1998. The strength of a weak state: the rights revolution and the rise of human resources management divisions. *American Journal of Sociology*, 104(2): 441–476.

Edelman, L. B. 1992. Legal ambiguity and symbolic structures: organisational mediation of civil rights law. *American Journal of Sociology*, 97(6): 1531–1576.

European Commission. 2005. *The Business Case for Diversity*. Brussels: European Commission.

Ferner, A., Morley, M., Muller-Camen, M. & Susaeta, L. 2006. Workforce diversity policies. In P. Almond & A. Ferner (eds), *American Multinationals in Europe Managing Employment Relations Across National Borders*. Oxford: Oxford University Press, pp. 146–171.

Fofana, I. 2009. Black, blanc, beur: France debates counting its minorities. *Harvard International Review*, 11–12(31): 2.

Gullett, C. R. 2000. Reverse discrimination and remedial affirmative action in employment: dealing with the paradox of nondiscrimination. *Public Personnel Management*, 29(1): 107–118.

Hambrick, D. C., Cho, T. S. & Ming-Jer Chen. 1996. The influence of top management team heterogeneity on firms' competitive moves. *Administrative Science Quarterly*, 41(4): 659–684.

Hamde, K. 2008. The current debate on cultural diversity in Sweden. *Journal of Cultural Diversity*, 15(2): 86–92.

Haq, R. & Ng, E. 2010. Employment equity and workplace diversity in Canada. In A. Klarsfeld (ed.), *International Handbook on Diversity Management at Work: Country Perspectives on Diversity and Equal Treatment*. Cheltenham, UK: Edward Elgar.

Haq, R. & Ojha, A. 2010. Affirmative action in India: caste based reservations. In A. Klarsfeld (ed.), *International Handbook on Diversity Management at Work: Country Perspectives on Diversity and Equal Treatment*. Cheltenham, UK: Edward Elgar.

Harrison, D. A., Price, K. H., Gavin, J. H. & Florey, A. T. 2002. Time, teams, and task performance: changing effects of surface- and deep-level diversity on group functioning. *Academy of Management Journal*, 45(5): 1029–1045.

Hsu, I.-C. 2010. Equality and diversity in Taïwan, Unpublished manuscript.

Hsu, I.-C. & Lawler, J. J. 2008. Toward a model of gender diversity in the workplace in East Asia: preliminary evidence from manufacturing industries in Taiwan. In J. J. Lawler & H. G. S. (eds), *Advances in International Management*, Vol. 21. Bingley, UK: JAI Press, pp. 171–190.

Jackson, S. E., Brett, J., Sessa, V., Cooper, D., Julin, J. & Peyronnin, K. 1991. Some differences make a difference: individual dissimilarity and group heterogeneity as correlates of recruitment, promotions, and turnover. *Journal of Applied Psychology*, 75(5): 675–689.

Jain, H. C., Sloane, P. J. & Horwitz, F. 2003. *Employment Equity and Affirmative Action: An International Comparison*. New York: Sharpe.

Jain, H. C. & Verma, A. 1996. Managing workforce diversity for competitiveness. *International Journal of Manpower*, 17(4): 14–30.

Jehn, K. A., Northcraft, G. B. & Neale, M. A. 1999. Why differences make difference: a field study of diversity, conflict, and performance in workgroups. *Administrative Science Quarterly*, 44(4): 741–763.

Johnston, W. B. & Packer, A. H. 1987. *Workforce 2000, Work and Workers for the 21st Century*. Indianapolis, IN: Hudson Institute.

Kalev, A., Dobbin, F. & Kelly, E. 2006. Best practices or best guesses? Assessing the efficacy of corporate affirmative action and diversity policies. *American Sociological Review*, **71**(4): 589–617.

Kalonaityte, V., Prasad, P. & Tedros, A. 2010. A possible brain drain? Workplace diversity and equal treatment in Sweden. In A. Klarsfeld (ed.), *International Handbook on Diversity Management at Work: Country Perspectives on Diversity and Equal Treatment.* Cheltenham, UK: Edward Elgar.

Kearney, E. & Gebert, D. 2006. Does more diversity lead to more innovativeness? An examination of the critical role of leadership, IFSAM VIIIth World Congress, Track 16. Berlin.

Keep, E. & Storey, J. 1989. *Corporate Training Strategy: The Vital Component. New Perspectives on Human Resource Management.* London: Routledge

Kelly, E. & Dobbin, F. 1998. How affirmative action became diversity management: employer response to anti-discrimination law, 1961–1996. *American Behavioral Scientist*, **41**(7): 960–984.

Kidder, D. L., Lankau, M. J., Chrobot-Mason, D., Mollica, K. A. & Friedman, R. A. 2004. Backlash toward diversity initiatives: examining the impact of diversity programme justification, personal, and group outcomes. *The International Journal of Conflict Management*, **15**(1): 61–94.

Klarsfeld, A. 2009. The diffusion of diversity management: the case of France. *Scandinavian Journal of Management*, **25**(4), Special Issue on Diversity Management? Translation? Travel?: 363–373.

Klarsfeld, A. (ed.) 2010. *International Handbook on Diversity Management at Work: Country Perspectives on Diversity and Equal Treatment.* Cheltenham, UK: Edward Elgar.

Klein, K. J. & Harrison, D. A. 2007. On the diversity of diversity: tidy logic, messier reality. *Academy of Management Perspectives*, November: 26–33.

Kostova, T., Roth, K. & Dacin, M. T. 2008. Institutional theory in the study of multinational corporations: a critique and new directions. *Academy of Management Review*, **33**(4): 994–1006.

Kuznetsov, A., Kuznetsova, O. & Warren, R. 2009. CSR and the legitimacy of business in transition economies: the case of Russia. *Scandinavian Journal of Management*, **25**(1): 37–45.

Liff, S. 1997. Two routes to managing diversity: individual differences or social group characteristics. *Employee Relations*, **19**(1): 11–26.

Lillevik, W., Combs, G. M. & Wyrick, C. 2010. Managing diversity in the USA: the evolution of inclusion in the workplace. In A. Klarsfeld (ed.), *International Handbook on Diversity Management at Work: Country Perspectives on Diversity and Equal Treatment.* Cheltenham, UK: Edward Elgar.

Loden, M. 1996. *Implementing Diversity*. Burr Ridge, IL: McGraw-Hill Publishing.

Mor-Barak, M. E. 2005. Diversity management: paradigms, rationale and key elements. In M. E. Mor-Barak (ed.), *Managing Diversity*. London: Sage publications, pp. 207–223.

Mpabanga, D. 2010. Diversity management in Botswana, Unpublished manuscript.

Murgia, A. & Poggio, B. 2010. The development of diversity management in the Italian context: a slow process. In A. Klarsfeld (ed.), *International Handbook on Diversity Management at Work: Country Perspectives on Diversity and Equal Treatment.* Cheltenham, UK: Edward Elgar.

Nentwich, J., Steyaert, C. & Liebig, B. 2010. Diversity made in Switzerland: connecting the business case with the traditional and new plurality. In A. Klarsfeld (ed.), *International Handbook on Diversity Management at Work: Country Perspectives on Diversity and Equal Treatment.* Cheltenham, UK: Edward Elgar.

Noon, M. 2007 The fatal flaws of diversity and the business case for ethnic minorities. *Work, Employment and Society*, **21**(1): 773–784.

O'Reilly III, C. A., Chatman, J. & Caldwell, D. F. 1991. People and organizational culture: a profile comparison approach to assessing person-organization fit. *Academy of Management Journal*, **34**(3): 487–516.

Özbilgin, M., Syed, J. & Dereli, B. 2010. Managing gender diversity in Pakistan and Turkey:

a historical review. In A. Klarsfeld (ed.), *International Handbook on Diversity Management at Work: Country Perspectives on Diversity and Equal Treatment.* Cheltenham, UK: Edward Elgar.

Pelled, L. H. 1996. Demographic diversity, conflict and work group outcomes: an intervening process theory. *Organisation Science*, 7(6): 615–631.

Riordan, C. M. & Shore, L. 1997. Demographic diversity and employee attitudes: examination of relational demography within work units. *Journal of Applied Psychology*, 82(3): 342–358.

Schäffner, M., Gebert, D., Schöler, N. & Kirch, J. 2006. Diversity, its risk and chances for team innovativeness. IFSAM VIIIth World Congress, Track 16. Berlin.

Sharma, S. 2000. Managerial interpretations and organisational context as predictors of corporate choice of environmental strategy. *Academy of Management Journal*, 43(4): 681–697.

Shen, J., Chanda, A., D'Netto, B. & Monga, M. 2009. Managing diversity through human resource management: an international perspective and conceptual framework. *International Journal of Human Resource Management*, 20(2): 235–251.

Soltani, E. 2010. The overlooked variable in managing human resources of Iranian organisations: workforce diversity – some evidence. *International Journal of Human Resource Management*, 21(1): 84–108.

Sparrow, P. R. 2007. Globalisation of HR at function level: four UK-based case studies of the international recruitment and selection process. *The International Journal of Human Resource Management*, 18(5): 845–867.

Syed, J. & Kramar, R. 2010. What is the Australian Model for managing cultural diversity. *Personnel Review*, 39(1–2): 96–115.

Syed, J. & Özbilgin, M. 2009. A relational framework for international transfer of diversity management practices. *International Journal of Human Resource Management*, 20(12): 2435–2453.

Tatli, A. 2010. Discourses and practices of diversity management in the UK. In A. Klarsfeld (ed.), *International Handbook on Diversity Management at Work: Country Perspectives on Diversity and Equal Treatment.* Cheltenham, UK: Edward Elgar.

Teicher, J. & Spearitt, K. 1996. From equal employment opportunity to diversity management. *International Journal of Manpower.* 17(4): 109–133.

Thomas, D. & Ely, R. 1996. Making differences matter. *Harvard Business Review*, 74(5): 79–90.

Thomas, R. R. 1990. From affirmative action to affirming diversity. *Harvard Business Review*, 68(2): 107–117.

Thomas, R. R. 2005. *Building on the Promise of Diversity: How we Can Move to the Next Level in Our Workplace, Our Communities, and Our Society.* New York: AMACOM Division American Management Association.

Wentling, R. M. 2004. Factors that assist and barriers that hinder the success of diversity initiatives in multinational corporations. *Human Resource Development International*, 7(2): 165–180.

Williams, K. & O'Reilly, C. A. 1998. Demography and diversity in organisations: a review of 40 years of research. In B. M. Staw & R. Sutton (eds), *Research in Organisational Behaviour.* Greenwich: JAI Press, pp. 77–140.

18 A cross-national perspective on the intersection between information technology and HRM

Huub J. M. Ruël and Tanya Bondarouk

The intersection between information technology (IT) and human resource management (HRM) has resulted in a stream of research starting in the 1990s. Research on this intersection, in this chapter referred to as electronic HRM or, in short, e-HRM, has addressed questions regarding the implementation of e-HRM, the adoption of e-HRM and the outcomes of e-HRM usage. Organisations all around the world have invested in e-HRM in one way or another, be it the usage of online recruitment practices or e-recruitment, the automation of HRM administrative processes or the implementation of a competence management-based package as a way to link HRM policies and practices with strategic goals. Annual surveys conducted by international consultancy firms have shown a growth in e-HRM adoption and usage year after year since the 1990s (e.g. CedarCrestone's annual survey).

e-HRM as a research field, as Strohmeier (2007) puts it, is relatively new and intriguing and is an innovative, lasting and substantial development in HRM resulting in new phenomena and major changes. Scholars have worked hard to understand the phenomenon of e-HRM and its multi-level implications within and across organisations. One sign of this are the several special issues on e-HRM in international academic journals between 2004 and 2011 (e.g. *Human Resource Management*, 2004 and 2008; *Journal of Managerial Psychology*, 2009; *The International Journal of Human Resource Management*, 2009).

However, the field faces a number of major challenges, as Bondarouk and Ruël (2009) point out. The current state of the e-HRM field is characterised by its predominantly non-theoretical character, a broad range of different qualitative and quantitative approaches, lack of specification of levels of analysis, and a patchiness of topics covered. Strohmeier (2007) brings up an additional characteristic of the current state of the field, namely a lack of international comparative studies. This characteristic is the main stimulus for writing this chapter. e-HRM research needs 'to go international' in order to contribute to a full and comprehensive understanding of the phenomenon.

The goal of this chapter is to develop a model for comparative e-HRM research in an international context. In order to do so, we will review the existing literature on e-HRM with the intention of presenting a picture of what exactly is known about e-HRM in different national contexts. The conclusions drawn from this review will be linked to the convergence–divergence debate in international management and business studies. From there we will start to construct a model that can help to describe, understand and explain the differences and similarities in e-HRM between national contexts, which could be a starting point to improve our understanding of these differences and similarities.

FROM HRIS TO E-HRM

The first influence of the developments of automation in the area of HRM dates from the 1940s. At that time, companies started to mechanise their payroll activities and employee records. The developments continued, and new areas, like accounting and finance, were gradually mechanised (DeSanctis, 1986). The landscape of IT for HRM purposes really started to take shape with the beginning of automation within offices in the 1980s. At that time, cost reduction was seen as one of the main advantages of IT, because it could replace employees (Kovach et al., 2002). Nowadays, IT and HRM are indissolubly connected. Human resource information systems (HRIS), often integrated as a HRM module of an enterprise resource planning (ERP) system like SAP or Oracle, are used to improve HRM in administrative and analytical terms (Kanthawongs, 2004).

Over time, the definition of HRIS has not changed much. Walker (1982) defines it as: 'a systematic procedure for collecting, storing, maintaining, retrieving, and validating data needed by an organisation about its human resources, personnel activities, and organisation unit characteristics'. Tannenbaum (1990) defines it as: 'a system used to acquire, store, manipulate, analyse, retrieve, and distribute pertinent information about an organisation's human resources'. Boyett et al. (2001) define it as: the 'main intent of a Human Resources Information System (HRIS) is to keep an accurate, complete, updated database that can be used when needed for reports, recordkeeping and automating routines and tasks such as application tracking'.

In the middle of the 1990s, the influence of the internet became noticeable in the field of HRM. HRIS started to become more of an internet-based technology. The focus changed from mainly supporting the HRM department to targeting the effectiveness of managers and employees. The term e-HRM, which stands for electronic HRM, is used for labelling

HRM services provided through the use of internet technology. The term ESS, employee self-service, is also used to refer to web-based HRM technology. That e-HRM is not a temporary phenomenon is illustrated by a recent study that examined the adoption of e-HRM in Europe. The results show national adoption rates varying from less than 20 per cent to almost 90 per cent of organisations (Strohmeier, 2007). A study by Foster (2008) stated that at least 91 per cent of midsize and large US organisations use web-based HRM technology in some way. According to a survey in 2006, the most frequently used application is administrative e-HRM (62 per cent of the surveyed companies) followed by talent acquisition services (61 per cent) and performance management (52 per cent) (CedarCrestone, 2006).

Nevertheless, there is still little consistency or agreement on the definition of e-HRM (Bondarouk et al., 2009; Strohmeier, 2007). In a recent editorial, Bondarouk and Ruël (2009) state that after two years of debate with e-HRM researchers, the following definition represents the consensus-based understanding of e-HRM: 'an umbrella term covering all possible integration mechanisms and contents between HRM and Information Technologies aiming at creating value within and across organisations for targeted employees and management' (Bondarouk & Ruël, 2009: 507).

One of the functionalities of e-HRM is to provide employees with applications that allow them to modify and update their personal records and to enrol in benefit programs. It provides managers with information in the form of reports, tools to improve decision making, and the systems to ensure compliance with government regulations (Lukaszewski et al., 2008). The main reasons for implementing e-HRM are cost reduction, enabling employees to take responsibility and ownership of their personal information, improving the quality and timeliness of HRM service, and improving the overall organisational efficiency (Bell et al., 2006; Lukaszewski et al., 2008). The greatest benefits of implementation of HRIS are the quick response and access to information, and the greatest barrier is insufficient financial support (Ngai & Wat, 2006). However, this does not mean that all organisations are using HRIS and their functionalities to a similar extent and in similar ways. A study by Ball (2001) showed that there is a significant relation between the use of HRIS and the size of an organisation and which modules it adopts (like core personnel administration or data management). Based on a survey involving 115 organisations in the UK, she found that smaller companies (<500 employees) are less likely to implement HRIS, and if they adopt HRIS, they will mostly use core modules and no additional training and recruitment modules.

The use of e-HRM can also lead to a competitive advantage (Ruta, 2009). In today's organisations, creating, maintaining, measuring and leveraging intellectual capital are the main sources of competitive advantage.

It is hard to imitate, and therefore the focus is shifting more to creating and developing this. Providing employees with specific personalised applications through HRM portals means e-HRM can be a key method in the creation of competitive advantage through intellectual capital. Marler (2009) argues that although e-HRM has the capability to be strategic, few will realise its potential to create competitive advantage because in a competitive environment, companies will respond in the same way and won't allow competitive advantages to exist for too long.

Despite all the benefits of e-HRM, there are also some growing concerns about privacy and the potential to violate the employees' confidentiality. Bloom (2001) argues that systems like this may decrease employee satisfaction with the services provided by HRM departments. Individuals may be less likely to accept e-HRM when they perceive that these systems invade their privacy or reduce the level of HRM service provided. Therefore, acceptance by the employees is crucial in the success of the implementation of such a system (Lukaszewski et al., 2008).

In sum, in its path from HRIS to e-HRM, the integration of IT and HRM has been shown to progress from basic support for managing HRM data towards a new way of managing the workforce based on IT facilities.

e-HRM RESEARCH AND THE CROSS-NATIONAL FOCUS: A LITERATURE REVIEW

As noted earlier, over the past decade the number of pertinent journal articles, book chapters, and conference papers has grown impressively; in our view an indication of the significance and relevance of e-HRM as a research topic. In the context of this chapter, we conducted a systematic literature review with the purpose of characterising publications on e-HRM in terms of their contribution to our understanding of e-HRM in different national contexts. Our main questions for the literature review were: how many studies on comparative e-HRM have been published in academic journals, books, and conference proceedings? What are these studies telling us? Where are the data gathered that are used for studies on e-HRM, and what is the overall picture that emerges from these studies when it comes to convergence and divergence of e-HRM practices?

Studies concerning e-HRM were found using four online databases (Scopus, Picarta, Web of Science, and scholar.google.com) and covering a large variety of disciplines, from the social sciences to engineering. Fifteen different search terms were used including general terms such as e-HRM and HRIS and related terms such as e-recruiting and virtual teams. Citations of articles found through the databases were also utilised in order to find older literature, as suggested by Torraco (2005). Only papers in the English language were considered, as it is the largest and dominant academic language area. We applied a certain hierarchy to the publications: firstly, papers published in academic journals were taken into consideration, then book chapters and finally conference papers in officially published proceedings. An overview was made of the various papers, based on the concept matrix as outlined by Webster and Watson (2002). The matrix criteria included, among other things, the main topic of the paper, the findings, the level of analysis and the countries in which the research was performed.

Analysis of the publications allowed us to distinguish four groups related to research into e-HRM in a cross-national context: e-HRM studies with a cross-continental focus, e-HRM studies with a cross-national focus but limited to one continent, e-HRM studies with a cross-national focus but within one company, e-HRM studies within a specifically mentioned national context; and finally e-HRM studies with no explicit reference to a national context.

e-HRM Studies with a Cross-continental Focus

The number of research publications on cross-cultural or cross-continental e-HRM is limited. Let us first briefly describe their main findings. Beulen (2008) and Rao (2009a) focused on e-HRM activities in emerging economies. The researchers were interested in the role of internet recruitment methods in companies in emerging economies in Asia, South America and Europe. The case study performed by Beulen (2008) at global organisations' branches in Argentina, Brazil, China, India, Latvia and Slovakia explores 'how IT supports HR work and how it contributes to their efforts in the global war for talent' (Beulen, 2008: 215). Overall, organisations were standardising their HRIS in the 'war for talent'; however, some cultural factors influenced a particular division to divert from this standardisation. This was especially true for the outsourcing division in India, which deals with large numbers of résumés. The study suggests that strategic decision making at the corporate level will deal with the discrepancy between the need for standardisation and local needs.

In a conceptual paper, Rao (2009a, c) addressed the challenges of e-recruitment in the emerging economies of India and Mexico. The predominant challenges of e-recruitment in both India and Mexico are the poor telecommunication infrastructure and the importance of personal interaction because of the collectivist culture. An additional challenge in India is the large number of recruiters, while in Mexico employees fear a loss of confidentiality in submitting their resumes on the internet.

Williams et al. (2009) conducted a case study with project teams working in multinational organisations. The team members originated from the UK, United States, Germany and Canada. The purpose was to identify the HRIS skills and knowledge in global projects. The authors presented a framework, based on human capital theory. The framework included guidelines for the collection of employee details, personal attributes, employees' skills, firm-specific attributes.

Puck et al. (2006, 2009) focused on internet recruitment and included emerging as well as developed economies in their analysis. Fourteen different countries from three different continents were included in their study of the role of national culture on corporate website recruitment. In particular, they analysed the use of pre-selection and selection methods and the use of the information function of corporate websites. Based on Hofstede's model of national culture, seven hypotheses were formulated and tested. Results showed that national cultures do affect the use of the internet in corporate website recruitment, with several implications for the companies and the job applicants as well as for the companies developing corporate website recruitment software. Power distance as well as the level of individualism was negatively related to the comprehensiveness of information in corporate website recruiting. Additionally, firms in a culture with a high level of uncertainty avoidance made less integrative use of corporate website recruiting.

The study by Marler and Parry (2008) included a large number of countries, representing many regions. Based on the Cranet survey in which HRM professionals from 29 countries participated, they investigated the strategic role of e-HRM. It does not appear to be the direct linking mechanism between HRM strategy and elevating the HRM function into a strategic business partner. However, the relationship between e-HRM and strategic HRM operates indirectly through the company's HRM strategy. The study did not include cultural or national context as a control variable.

Harris et al. (2003) included the United States and Belgium in their research investigating privacy and attitudes towards internet-based selection systems. By means of a survey, four hypotheses were tested. The results showed some commonalities between the two countries as well as some cross-cultural differences; however, the relation with the cultural factors of the countries was not explored. In both countries the same amount of reluctance to submit employment-related data over the internet was observed, and higher self-rated knowledge of the internet led to less concern about employment-related data falling into the wrong hands. A main difference is that in Belgium there is a stronger belief among knowledge workers that companies have to get approval before releasing

Table 18.1   e-HRM studies including cross-continental data

Author	Region	Topic	Type of study
Beulen (2008)	Asia, Europe, South America	HRIS	Qualitative
Harris et al. (2003)	Europe, North America	e-selection	Quantitative
Marler and Parry (2008)	Africa, Asia, Australia, Europe, North America, South America.	e-HRM	Quantitative
Olivas-Luján and Florkowski (2009)	Europe, North America	HRIS	Quantitative
Puck et al. (2006)	Asia, Europe, North America	e-recruitment	Quantitative
Williams et al. (2009)	Europe, North America	virtual teams	Quantitative
Rao (2009c)	Asia, South America	e-recruitment	Literature study

information about a candidate, while in the United States, the dominant belief is the opposite.

Olivas-Luján and Florkowski (2009) investigated the diffusion of HRI technologies across English-speaking countries. They found that diffusion is stimulated more by internal influences from the information system of potential adopters than by external influences, except for integrated HRM suites and HRM intranets. The analysis showed no differences in diffusion between countries.

Overall, the number of studies with a cross-continental focus is very limited, especially those focusing on finding differences and similarities between countries (Table 18.1), and is clearly skewed towards the United States and Europe. Studies with a cross-continental focus do not go beyond concluding that culture seems to be important and a possible explanatory factor for the differences between continents and countries.

e-HRM with a Cross-national Focus but Limited to One Continent

Another group of studies on e-HRM is cross-national in focus, though still within one continent (Table 18.2). A good example of these kinds of studies is the investigation of the adoption of e-HRM in companies in 16 different European countries performed by Galanaki and Panayotopoulou (2009). They found some links with a nation's characteristics, such as internet penetration and the adoption of e-HRM. Their study showed a positive relationship between a company's characteristics and the level of usage of

Table 18.2   Cross-national, one-continent e-HRM studies

Author	Region	Topic	Type of study
Beamish et al. (2002)	Europe	e-learning	Qualitative
Galanaki and Panayotopoulou (2008)	Europe	e-HRM	Quantitative
Imperatori and de Marco	Europe	e-work	Qualitative
Ruël et al. (2004)	Europe	e-HRM	Qualitative
Strohmeier and Kabst (2009)	Europe	e-HRM	Quantitative

e-HRM, such as company size (mostly multinationals were included), the level of the strategic orientation of the HRM function, the level of education received by employees, and the level of innovation and service quality.

Beamish et al. (2002) investigated the deployment of e-learning in the UK and European corporate organisations. The managers who participated in the study were able to identify a series of benefits from e-learning, such as cost effectiveness, as well as barriers, usually based on cultural resistance and learner motivation. In general, managers supported the view that e-learning can have a role in strategy-led training. No attention was paid to culture as an explanatory factor.

Ruël et al. (2004a) explored e-HRM in large companies in the Netherlands, Luxembourg, Germany and Belgium. They conclude that the e-HRM goals of companies are cost reduction, service quality improvement and improving HRM's strategic focus. There is a 'gap' between available e-HRM functionalities and the real use of it; e-HRM implies a process of 'growth' in a company. Outcomes of e-HRM are a reduction of costs, an improvement of client satisfaction with HRM services and improved quality of communication. Cultural or national differences were not taken into account as an explanatory factor, but the study raises some interesting issues such as the role of language of the e-HRM applications in their adoption by users in foreign subsidiaries and the differences of communication styles between the United States and Western Europe in the case of a US-based multinational.

Imperatori and De Marco (2009) looked at the real labour transformation process related to the introduction of e-work projects in four different companies in the UK and Italy. The results confirm the alignment of the managerial discourse with organisational practices. Factors concerning

Table 18.3   Cross-national e-HRM research within one multinational
company

Author	Region	Topic	Type of study
Tixier (2004)	Europe	HRIS	Qualitative
Vaughan and MacVicar (2004)	Europe	e-learning	Quantitative

the design and implementation of technology-based work systems were evaluated, such as the organisational and employer viewpoint, the organisational culture and evaluation and monitoring phases during the project. Cultural and national differences were not included in their analysis.

Strohmeier and Kabst (2009) conducted a large-scale survey in 23 European countries and found that e-HRM is a common practice throughout Europe. Major determinants of e-HRM are size, work organisation and HRM configuration, according to their study. Interestingly, they found cross-national differences in e-HRM adoption: Eastern European post-communist countries are ahead of Western European countries. The study was not able to conclude about converging of adoption over time.

The overall picture that emerges from this overview of e-HRM studies with a cross-national focus but within the same continent is that all those studies are done in Europe. Hardly any of the studies aims at revealing cross-national differences. Only Strohmeier and Kabst (2009) partly include a cross-national focus in their analysis. However, no clear theory is applied to explain the differences and similarities in e-HRM adoption.

e-HRM with a Cross-national Focus but Within One Company

Some e-HRM studies include cross-national data, but they were collected within one company (Table 18.3). Beulen (2008) and Williams (2009) provide examples of this type of study, but as discussed earlier, the focus of the studies was to find cross-national differences rather than to focus on the company. Other international case studies focus on establishments in European countries. An example of this kind of research is the case study of Tixier (2004) at the Rexel group in four different European countries: Belgium, England, Portugal and Spain. She followed the implementation of HRIS and examined the influence of the local contexts on the implementation. The study included exogenous factors, industry and country/regional characteristics of the subsidiaries. Tixier identified two distinctive HRM practices in the different subsidiaries, which she called the management staff (with a focus on quantitative manpower and conflict resolution) and the human resource management system (with a focus on the utilisation of resources to achieve organisational goals). The author concluded that HRIS could support the harmonisation of the practices in a multinational company.

Vaughan and MacVicar (2004) studied the blended approach to e-learning of a large multinational banking organisation in the UK. The pre-implementation procedure and the perceptions of employees were investigated in subsidiaries in England, Ireland and Scotland. A qualitative investigation showed a low awareness of e-learning among the employees and that the attitudes of managers diverged from very supporting towards learning and the development of employees to not being supportive at all. The major barrier is the time spent on learning and development, while the major benefits of e-learning are its accessibility, relevance and user-friendliness.

The overall picture that is that cross-national e-HRM research conducted within one multinational company is Western-biased, exploratory in nature, and more importantly not explicitly contributing to the cross-national and cross-cultural body of knowledge on e-HRM.

e-HRM Research Within a Specifically Mentioned National Context

In Europe, Majó (2006) investigated the condition of e-recruitment in Hungary by studying the internet sites of 50 different companies. International trends, related to the diffusion of IT for recruitment purposes, can be observed in Hungarian companies, yet to a minor extent and with lower intensity. Parry and Wilson (2006) concentrated their study on online recruitment in the UK. Factors influencing the adoption of e-recruitment were relative advantage, difficulties and external compatibility for corporate websites, and relative advantage and compatibility for commercial websites. Fernándes-Sánchez et al. (2009) explored the recruitment process in Spanish firms. They noted that HRIS are being introduced steadily in Spanish firms; however, the presence of traditional information systems is still strong. Haunsdorf and Duncan (2004) investigated internet recruiting in Canada in relation to firm size. Large companies do have their own website more often and use more internet recruiters while small firms are less aware of internet recruitment. The adoption of e-HRM in large New Zealand organisations was the focus of Lau and Hooper's (2009) study, while Olivas-Luján et al. (2006) concentrated on the same topic in Mexico. In New Zealand the popularity of e-HRM is a growing phenomenon among large companies (Lau and Hooper, 2009). Olivas-Luján et al. (2006) identified several research gaps for e-HRM in Mexico. They also found that Mexican enterprises face a bigger challenge in implementing an e-HRM system as they are mainly production-oriented and, thus, have difficulties in justifying the investment.

Some studies were also performed in Asia. Hooi (2006) investigated the readiness for e-HRM in Malaysian small and medium-sized companies (SMEs). The author found that many organisations are still utilising traditional HRM instead of e-HRM. Financial resources and expertise seem to be the main barriers to e-HRM implementation. In Taiwan organisational support and HRIS effectiveness were higher in the case of a higher HRIS level, as measured by the usage of top managers and HRM staff (Lin, 1997). AbuZaineh and Ruël (2008) explored and compared the usage of e-HRM tools in SMEs in Kuwait and the Netherlands and found that the main objective in both countries was to reduce costs and time. The cultural context, especially the higher uncertainty avoidance tendency in Kuwait compared with the Netherlands, could help to explain the lag in adoption of e-HRM in Kuwaiti SMEs compared with the Netherlands. Jones (2007) also studied e-HRM in Kuwait. She addressed the challenges involved in implementing a management system for training and development. She highlighted the importance of a skilled senior management and HRM staff. In India, successful HRIS practices included internal job positioning, e-recruitment, learning communities and e-learning (2009c).

Among those who explicitly mentioned a national context in the title of the publication, but did not evidence any intention of linking the results to the characteristics of that particular context, we find Bondarouk and Ruël (2006) with their investigation of e-HRM in a Dutch ministry; Koopman and Batenburg (2008) focusing on employee self-service applications in the Dutch public sector; Farndale and Paauwe (2006) investigating HRM Shared Service Centres (SSC) in Dutch organizations; and Rahin and Sigh (2007) studying B2E (business-to-employee) systems in two Australian universities.

The studies in this category, we observe, hardly relate their findings to the specific characteristics of the national context in which the data were collected, although this context is included in the title of their paper (see Table 18.4).

Remaining e-HRM Studies with no Explicit Reference to National Context

Besides the publications specified above, there are, of course, a whole range of publications on e-HRM and e-HRM activities without any specific reference to the national or cultural context (Table 18.5). Topics that have been studied the most are e-recruitment and selection and e-learning. Empirical studies about recruitment and selection in the context of e-HRM have been studied mainly in North America (see e.g. Braddy et al.,

Table 18.4 e-HRM in a specifically mentioned national context

Author	Country	Topic	Type of study
AbuZaineh and Ruël (2008)	Kuwait	e-HRM	Qualitative
Bondarouk and Ruël (2006)	The Netherlands	e-HRM	Qualitative
Farndale and Paauwe (2006)	The Netherlands	SSC	Qualitative and quantitative
Fernándes-Sánchez et al. (2009)	Spain	e-recruitment	Quantitative
Haunsdorf and Duncan (2004)	Canada	e-recruitment	Quantitative
Hooi (2006)	Malaysia	e-HRM	Qualitative and quantitative
Jones (2007)	Kuwait	e-HRM	Qualitative
Koopman and Batenburg (2008)	The Netherlands	ESS	Qualitative
Lau and Hooper (2009)	New Zealand	e-HRM	Qualitative and quantitative
Lin (1997)	Taiwan	HRIS	Quantitative
Majó (2006)	Hungary	e-recruitment	Quantitative
Olivas-Luján et al. (2006)	Mexico	e-HRM	Qualitative
Parry and Wilson (2006)	UK	e-recruitment	Quantitative
Rahin and Sigh (2007)	Australia	B2E	Qualitative
Rao (2009b)	India	HRIS	Qualitative

2003; Chapman & Webster, 2003; Elgin & Claphan, 2004; Jattuso & Sinar, 2003; McManus & Fergson, 2003; Pearce & Tuten, 2001) and in Europe (see e.g. Dineen et al., 2004; Hoye van & Lievens, 2007; Strohmeier & Diederichsen, 2006). There are a few studies available from South America as well (e.g. Joia & Silva, 2009).

Another activity of e-HRM which has attracted much attention is e-learning; this is particularly the case for Europe (e.g. Macpherson et al., 2004; Oiry, 2006). More general studies on e-HRM originate from various regions around the world; the same applies for specific e-HRM practices, but by far the most research originates from Europe and the United States (see e.g. Bondarouk & Ruël, 2009; Foster, 2009; Reddington et al., 2006; West & Berman, 2001). Relatively few studies originate from non-Western countries. One example is Al-Ibraheem and Ruël (2009), who investigated in-house vs. off-the-shelf applications in Kuwait. Huang et al. (2004) measured satisfaction with B2E systems in Taiwan. Shwartz-Asher et al. (2009) investigated virtual teams in Israel.

Table 18.5   Remaining e-HRM studies: without reference to national or cultural context

Region	Topic	Authors
Asia	e-HRM	Al-Ibraheem and Ruël, 2009.
	B2E	Huang et al., 2004.
Australia	Virtual teams	Shwartz-Asher et al., 2009.
	HRIS	Deakins, 2009; Hawking et al., 2004.
Europe	e-HRM	Ball, 2001; Bondarouk and Ruël, 2008; Bondarouk et al., 2009a; Bondarouk et al., 2009b; Foster, 2009; Guiderdoni-Jourdain, 2006; Guiderdoni-Jourdain, 2007; Guiderdoni-Jourdain, 2009; Heikkilä and Smale, 2009; Imperatori and Bissola, 2009; Loijen and Bond
	HRIS	Oiry et al., 2008.
	e-recruitment and selection	Dineen et al., 2004; Furtmueller et al., 2009; Girard and Fallery, 2009; Holm, 2009; van Hoye and Lievens, 2007; Konradt et al., 2003; Parry and Tyson, 2009; Salgado and Moscoso, 2003; Strohmeier and Diederichsen, 2006; Wolters and Mackaaij 2006.
	e-learning	Hustad and Munkvold, 2005; Macpherson et al., 2004; Oiry, 2006; Oiry, 2007.
North America	e-HRM	West and Berman, 2001.
	HRIS	DeSanctis, 1986; Haines and Petit, 1997; Lukaszewski et al., 2008; Olivas-Luján and Florkowski, 2008.
	e-recruitment and selection	Braddy et al., 2003; Buckley et al., 2004; Chapman and Webster, 2003; Cober et al., 2004; Elgin and Claphan, 2004; Jattuso and Sinar, 2003; McManus and Fergson, 2003; Pearce and Tuten, 2001; Sinar et al., 2003.
South America	e-recruitment and selection	Joia and Silva, 2009.

Conclusion

Truly international comparative e-HRM research is scarce, something that clearly emerges from our literature review above. The comparative studies available are basically non-theoretical and do not refer to cultural or national contextual aspects as an explanatory factor. Most of the e-HRM research originates from the United States and from Europe, and multinational companies are the units of analysis. SMEs are under-represented. As such this picture can lead us to the following conclusion, however cautiously: Western-based multinationals lead the way in e-HRM adoption and usage, but multinationals from non-Western regions are quickly following suit. SMEs in Western countries are lagging behind but adopting e-HRM as well.

All the studies on e-HRM so far have not been suitable to conclude anything on whether e-HRM practices in Western countries and non-Western countries look similar or are developing similarly or not. In other words, no study to date has clearly addressed the basic issue underlying international comparative research, which is the convergence–divergence debate.

MANAGEMENT PRACTICES IN A COMPARATIVE PERSPECTIVE: THE CONVERGENCE–DIVERGENCE DEBATE

The main purpose of international comparative research is to identify and explain differences and similarities. This issue is referred to as the convergence–divergence debate; a debate that has been keeping researchers busy since the beginning of the twentieth century. Around that time the current debate started with Veblen's statement that developing countries have an advantage by adapting technologies that had been developed by the more mature countries (Elmslie, 1995). Nowadays, the debate on convergence–divergence is widespread in all kinds of research areas, for instance Baumol (1986), who initiated the debate on economic convergence.

The most quoted definitions of convergence and divergence are from Webber (1969). Based on his work Ralston (2008) describes convergence as a process in which: 'technological influence is the catalyst that motivates individuals to develop a values system that is consistent with the technology of their society, regardless of the socio-cultural influences'; and divergence as a process in which: 'socio-cultural influence is the driving force that will cause individuals from a society to retain the specific values system of the societal culture through time, regardless of other possible influences, such as technological, economic and political change' (p. 28–29).

Today's convergence–divergence debate in the area of organisation and management practices started in the mid-1980s, with the increase in globalisation. Economies have become more and more integrated. This integration has led to a spreading of global management structures and the adoption of similar operating techniques. Hence it can be argued that global organisations are converging (McGaughey & De Cieri, 1999). The following circumstances led to this convergence: the rise of the internet, which simplified the global communication process and data exchange, increased travelling and the deregulation of economic activities by governments (Doz & Prahalad, 1991; Levitt, 2006; McGaughey & De Cieri, 1999). However, opponents of the convergence hypothesis state that despite the structural and technological convergence, cultural differences remain (McGaughey & De Cieri, 1999). One of the first studies on the convergence–divergence theory was done by Adler et al. (1986). Because of the increasing shift in business from West to East, Adler studied the impact of cultural diversity on organisations in the Atlantic and the Pacific region. Douglas and Wind (1987) examined whether a global strategy for products and brands is the key to success, or whether adaption to the local situation leads to better results.

The debate on convergence–divergence was extended in 1993 with the crossvergence perspective (Ralston et al., 1993). The results of that study showed that the managerial values of a country are often influenced by both culture and the business environment. Therefore, they suggested a third perspective, a combination of convergence and divergence: crossvergence. In 1997 Ralston et al. broadened the definition of crossvergence: 'crossvergence advocates that the combination of socio-cultural influences and business ideology influences is the driving force that precipitates the development of new and unique values systems among individuals in a society due to the dynamic interaction of these influences' (Ralston et al., 1997: 183).

McGaughey and De Cieri (1999) developed a conceptual framework based on micro-, macro-, and meso-level organisational variables and processes, which offers four different types of convergence–divergence: assimilation, integration, separation and novelty. Assimilation takes place when an entity loses a part of its own characteristics by adopting norms from another entity. Integration is a combination of characteristics of two or more entities. Separation purposefully avoids integration of the characteristics of the other entity. Novelty does not maintain its own characteristics nor those from the other entity. In addition to convergence and divergence, McGaughey and De Cieri (1999) introduced 'maintenance' as a third option: keeping the level of similarity or dissimilarity as a possible direction.

In 2006 Spicer offered a new view on the debate. Instead of arguing that organisational logics are converging into one model or diverging into national types, he argued that organisational logics are transforming (Spicer, 2006). This means that when organisation logics move across space, they undergo a process of transformation. A remarkable aspect of the convergence–divergence debate is that the researchers did not try to extend each other's work; instead, it seems like they more or less ignored it.

Convergence–divergence in HRM

In the field of IHRM, Brewster probably is the most active researcher contributing to our understanding of the relationship between globalisation and HRM. In 2008 Brewster et al. examined if there was similarity, isomorphism or duality in the HRM policies and practices in host countries of multinational corporations (MNCs), based on three schools of thought: global homogeneity/ethnocentricity, local isomorphism, and duality theories. They found evidence for common global practices, but the duality theories provided the best explanation.

Wöcke et al. (2007) examined the differences between HRM practices of parent MNCs and affiliates. He concluded that there are several factors that influence the need for standardisation or localisation: variation in the business model, the need to accommodate national culture, and the type and role of organisational culture in the MNC. Additionally, the evolution of a MNC leads to a higher level of standardisation of HRM practices.

Standardisation–localisation

Linked to the convergence–divergence debate, the standardisation–localisation debate plays a role in the area of organisation and management practices (e.g. Porter, 1986; Prahalad & Doz, 1987). This debate is concentrated on the company or meso-level, while convergence–divergence is more focused on the macro-level (Pudelko & Harzing, 2007). Rosenzweig and Nohria (1994) defined standardisation–localisation as: to what extent subsidiaries of multinational companies are behaving as local firms (localisation) versus to what extent their practices are similar to those of the headquarters (standardisation). HRM plays an important role in this debate because it deals with the management of people and is therefore seen as least likely to converge across countries. MNCs are more likely to localise practices than to export country-of-origin practices (Pudelko & Harzing, 2007; Leat & El-Kot, 2007).

Over the years numerous studies examined cross-cultural comparisons of HRM. Some studies examined the transfer of HRM practices, while others focused on which HRM practices and issues are relevant for a certain country (Myloni et al., 2004). Laurent (1986) argued that HRM practices represent the values of national culture, and because of this an HRM system that is successful in one culture doesn't have to be successful in another. Rosenzweig and Nahria (1994) examined what the influence of national culture is on HRM policies and practices. Schuler et al. (1993) addressed the tension between integration and differentiation between inter-unit linkages and how to operate effectively in the local environment.

Lu and Björkman (1997) examined the tension between standardisation or localisation in joint China–Western ventures using five 'classical' HRM practices.

Recently, Pudelko and Harzing (2008) extended the debate. In their study they examined whether MNCs from different countries (Germany, Japan and the United States) put different emphases on the extent of standardisation versus localisation of the HRM practices of their foreign subsidiaries. Based on an international survey (mostly filled in by highly placed HRM managers), they concluded that the debate on standardisation and localisation needs a major extension. Their results showed that standardisation not only takes place towards the headquarters but can also take place towards global best practices, wherever they originate from. Based on these findings, they stated that in today's globalised corporate environment, ethnocentric approaches to management are no longer sustainable.

There are several factors that determine the degree of standardisation. Prahalad and Doz (1987) mention seven pressures for standardisation, like high technological intensity, the presence of multinational competitors, and cost reduction. Parry et al. (2008) mentions four reasons why companies are likely to standardise their processes: HRM practices are more likely to be transferred from the headquarters if they are regarded as superior; HRM policies and practices can be standardised in order to support their wider business strategy; ethical issues like minimum rights and precluding child labour can lead to international standardisation of practices; and finally, knowledge transfer, quality standards, and creating an international network can lead to the standardisation of HRM practices and policies. There are numerous factors which determine the degree of standardisation, like the relationship between the headquarters and the subsidiary, organisational culture, authority structures, market characteristics, work norms, etc. (Parry et al., 2008). Local factors that have an influence are unions, labour market, legal and political context (Brewster, 1995; Ngo et al., 1998).

TOWARDS A MODEL FOR CROSS-NATIONAL e-HRM RESEARCH

As noted earlier, based on our literature review, which reconfirmed Strohmeier's (2007) observation, e-HRM research has so far ignored the cross-national or cross-cultural focus. This chapter aims at developing a research model that can stimulate this kind of study; a model that can be used as a lens through which one can look at e-HRM in different national contexts and understand and interpret differences and similarities, as well as a framework that can be tested and advanced further; a model that can be used to guide research questions such as to what extent does e-HRM in different national contexts converge or diverge as well as questions that go beyond that focus and aim at studying how e-HRM converges or diverges in different contexts.

Building up the research model will take place in three steps. Firstly, as e-HRM emerged from the intersection between IT and HRM, or technology and organisation, the theoretical fundaments of the research model will be defined. Secondly, the content of the model, the variables, will be presented and discussed. Thirdly, the model will be positioned in the convergence–divergence debate.

Theorising Information Technology in Organisations

The study of the role of technology in organisations has a long tradition. Over the years, different views on technology have developed in parallel with theoretical perspectives on organisations: Orlikowski (2007) mentions, for example: contingency theory, strategic choice models, Marxist studies, symbolic interactionist approaches, transaction-cost economics, network analyses, practice theories, and structurational models. Nowadays, technology and organisations undergo rapid and radical changes in form and function. Therefore, researchers on technology are also using the ideas of innovation, learning, and improvisation for a better understanding of the implications of new technologies on organisations (Orlikowski, 2007: 405).

In an attempt to overcome the limitations of contingency theory in linking technology and organisational forms, a number of scholars in the mid-1980s started to use Giddens's (1984) theory of structuration (Schuessler, 2006b). This led to a new view on studying the interaction between technology and organisation, assuming that technology is dualistic in nature. Until that time, the dominating view was deterministic in nature (Orlikowski, 1992).

Barley (1986) was one of the first researchers to use Giddens's structuration theory in order to study the relation between technology and organisational structure. Based on this theory, he argued that technology can be constraining and enabling. Technology was considered to be social in nature rather than a physical object. Most interestingly, and opposing a deterministic view on technology, Barley's study showed that the organisations responded differently to the implementation of the same sort of technology. He concluded that 'technologies do influence organisational structures in orderly ways, but their influence depends on the specific historical process in which they are embedded' (p. 107).

Orlikowski (1992) takes Barley's point of view further and argues that in contrast to Barley's view that technology's physical form remains fixed across time, information technologies may vary with different users and contexts and with the same users over time. With this view, she takes a step away from social constructivism, which assumes the interdependence of social and individual processes in the co-construction of knowledge (Palincsar, 1998). Orlikowski states that technology may become routinised because of repeated use, but it cannot become stabilised. Technology is built with the intention of being modified in time. Software is continuously updated to improve its stability or to fulfil user needs. Orlikowski's practice lens (Orlikowski, 2007) does not make any assumption about the completeness of the technology or its stability.

DeSanctis and Poole (1994) adapted structuration theory to study the interaction of groups and organisations with advanced information technologies (AITs), like group decision support systems (GDSSs). They developed the adaptive structuration theory (AST). 'The AST examines the process from two positions: the type of structures that are provided by advanced technologies and the structures that actually emerge in human action as people interact with these technologies' (DeSanctis et al., 1994: 121). Or formulated differently, AST is focused on the rules and resources of advanced technologies and how users in small groups adapt to the rules and use the resources. The adaption can lead to different outcomes even in the same context because users can act differently when utilising the same technology.

An important aspect of AST is spirit: 'The spirit is the "official line" which the technology presents to people regarding how to act when using the system, how to interpret its features, and how to fill in gaps in procedure which are not explicitly specified' (DeSanctis et al., 1994: 126). Another central aspect of AST is the concept of appropriation. Appropriation in the context of information systems in organisations refers to the process of actively selecting 'structural features' of a given system or application and incorporating them in their daily work activities. From a large set of potentially applicable features, individuals actively choose the ones they judge as most useful and easy to use, though in the way individuals interpret those features. This implies that a similar set of structural features of an information system can be used in different ways and therefore have different expected or unexpected consequences.

As mentioned earlier, the rapid and radical changes in technologies and organisations have called for new concepts, like improvisation and emergence, for studying and understanding the use of technology in practice. With similar intentions, Orlikowski (2007) extended her view on technology as being an emergent structure, a process of enactment (to constitute/

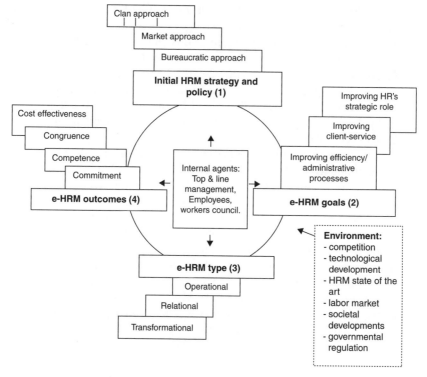

Source: Ruël et al. (2004b: 370).

Figure 18.1   The e-HRM model

perform). This view focuses on how humans enact structures that shape their emergent and situated use of the technology during the interaction with that technology in their daily life. This means that structures are not embedded in technology but enacted by users. There are three types of enactment: inertia – technology used to maintain the status quo; application – technology used to modify and improve (work) processes; and change – technology used to change the status quo considerably. By using this view, a better understanding of the recursive interaction between people, technologies and social action becomes possible (Orlikowski, 2007: 404).

The Variables of the Research Model

As the foundation of a research model, the framework of Ruël et al. (2004b) will be adopted (Figure 18.1). The framework was evaluated based on the findings from five large organisations that had had several years of experience with e-HRM. The framework of Ruël et al. distinguishes four 'phases' in e-HRM adoption in organisations. Each phase will be described and viewed through the perspective of structuration. This perspective is useful for information system (IS) research because it is able to connect two important aspects that play a role in the e-HRM context: firstly, how ISs are developed and physically shaped by the actions of the users and, secondly, how the organisation is influenced by the implementation of an IS (Schuessler, 2006a).

In the middle of the model are situated the internal agents who determine and influence the four phases. Orlikowski (1992, 2007), also inspired by structuration theory (Giddens, 1984), states that technology only comes into existence through human action. Ongoing maintenance by human action sustains the technology, and it is constituted through use. On its own, technology plays no role. Therefore, it seems legitimate to place internal agents in the middle of the model.

The internal agents and the four phases are situated in a context. The model distinguishes six factors that play a role: competition, technological development, the state of the art of HRM, labour market, societal developments, and government regulation. These are similar to the institutional properties Orlikowski (1992) refers to as influencing human agents in their interaction with technology. She described the following institutional properties: business strategy, ideology, culture, operating procedures, communication patterns, control mechanisms, expertise but also external forces like government regulation, competitive environment, vendor strategies, socio-economic conditions, and knowledge about technology (p. 409). These institutional properties can also be referred to as conditions and consequences (Orlikowski, 2007). Conditions can be subdivided into: interpretive conditions (the way that members of a community share meanings and understandings to make sense about their world including the technology they use), technological conditions (tools and data available), and institutional conditions (social structures that form part of the larger social system within which users work). Consequences can be subdivided into: process consequences (execution and outcomes of users' work practices), technology consequences (technological prosperity available to users), and structure consequences (structures that users enact as part of the larger social system in which they are participating) (Orlikowski, 2007: 421). We also include the three types of enactment noted above (inertia, application and change).

Additionally, we 'split' the research model into two parts. One side represents the part where institutional conditions are the dominant influential factors, phases one and four, and the other side represents the part where technological conditions are the dominant influential factors, phases two and three. The combination of the conditions and consequences can lead to the three different types of enactments.

Hence, the four phases of the model: the first phase, initial HRM strategy and policy, refers to the state of HRM in an organisation. When companies start with or invest further in e-HRM, there will be certain implicit or explicit HRM policy assumptions and practices already in use. Based on the classic work of Beer et al. (1985), three types of policies can be distinguished: bureaucratic policies, found in organisations that operate in a stable environment; market policies, found in organisations that have to respond rapidly to changes in the environment; and clan policies, found in organisations that rely heavily on delivering quality and innovation. Ruël et al. (2004b) assumes that within the context of an existing HRM policy type, internal agents select the role given to technology within the overall HRM strategy of the company.

The second phase refers to the goals of e-HRM. Goals are selected by internal agents within the existing HRM policy context (or internal institutional properties) in which they act, but intermediated by external institutional properties such as competition and technological developments. In terms of the work of Giddens's, Orlikowski, and DeSanctis and Poole's AST, the existing HRM policy is a set of 'structures' interpreted and applied by internal agents, in AST terms referred to as 'appropriation'. The e-HRM goals selected, whether implicitly or explicitly, are outcomes of that appropriation process.

In general terms, the outcome can be one or a combination of the following goals: to improve the strategic orientation of HRM; to reduce costs and/or increase efficiency; and to improve the quality of HRM service for management and employees. These goals are in line with the benefits/advantages of e-HRM found by Bell et al. (2006) and Lukaszewski et al. (2008) discussed earlier in this chapter.

These goals of e-HRM can be linked to what DeSanctis and Poole (1994) refer to as the spirit of technology. The spirit is concerned with questions like, 'what kind of goals are being promoted by this technology?' and 'what kind of values are being supported?' (DeSanctis et al., 1994: 127). For example, e-HRM applications can 'contain' the spirit of 'improving client services'.

From the e-HRM goals selected, an e-HRM type emerges as an outcome of deliberations by internal agents interpreting and applying e-HRM goals in day-to-day organisational practices. e-HRM types refer to a combination of selected technologies and their appropriation by internal agents. Therefore, it is not a static context with a technological application deployed in a technical sense. Rather, e-HRM types are a dynamic context, in which at a certain point in time there can be a huge gap between available technological functionalities and real usage of these functionalities by internal agents. Analytically, three types of e-HRM can be distinguished: operational e-HRM, meaning that the dominant usage consists of more traditional administrative services like salary administration and record-keeping; relational E-HRM, meaning that the dominant usage consists of executing HRM processes, like recruitment, compensation, and training and development; and transformational e-HRM, meaning that the dominant usage has a strategic character, such as knowledge management, strategic competence management, and organisational change.

From the appropriation of e-HRM applications, e-HRM outcomes emerge, intended and unintended ones. These outcomes should not be confused with the e-HRM goals described as phase two of the model. Ruël et al. (2004b) state that e-HRM is a way of carrying out HRM; it is a way of thinking about and implementing HRM strategies, policies, and practices aimed at achieving certain goals: improving the strategic role of HRM, improving the client services, and improving efficiency/administrative processes. Besides these goals, there are a number of overall HRM policy outcomes to which all e-HRM activities will be directed implicitly or explicitly. Beer et al. (1985) distinguish the following four: (1) commitment – the trust between management and employees; (2) competence – the ability of employees to learn and perform new tasks; (3) cost effectiveness – financial competiveness; and (4) congruence – structuring the internal organisation, the reward system, and the input-output of personnel in the interests of stakeholders. The e-HRM outcomes can be considered as interpretations by internal agents, applied and reflected in an organisation's HRM policy. The types of enactments described earlier can also be seen as types of outcomes and are added to the fourth phase of the model.

The Convergence–Divergence Dimension to the e-HRM Model

The variables of the research model as described can be taken as the point of departure for comparative research in different national contexts. However, as we believe that international comparative research only becomes meaningful when it contributes to the convergence–divergence debate, we will now place our model in this debate by theorising how converging and diverging forces affect the phases of e-HRM in organisations. The environmental factors in the model (Figure 18.1) can be categorised as being either an example of a source for business ideology features, or an example of a source for socio-cultural features.

Based on an initially small empirical study on e-HRM in four organisations in the Lebanon, we came up with assumptions about this issue. In the four organisations, three of them multinational companies (a bank, two telecom companies and a private university), we collected data by conducting semi-structured interviews with HRM and IT professionals. The guiding research question was: how does the deployment of IT for HRM purposes impact the convergence or divergence of HRM policies and practices in Middle Eastern companies? We expected to find that internal agents within an organisational context refer either to business ideology features or socio-cultural features in the ongoing interactions in an e-HRM implementation or upgrading project. This process of referring to either of these features results in converging, standardisation tendencies, in line with widely, internationally shared ideas, for example, regarding decision making about the sequential steps of a performance management system, or diverging, localisation tendencies, in line with local customs. Based on the outcomes of the study, we concluded that converging tendencies were indeed strongly reflected in phases one and two (the policy and goal defining stages) and that diverging tendencies predominantly emerged in phases three and four (the actual appropriation of the e-HRM applications by internal agents).

Earlier, we 'split' the research model into two parts. One side represents the part where institutional conditions are the dominant influential factors, phases one and four: the e-HRM system is part of a larger social system, and the social structures of the social system will influence the way the technology is designed. For example, the type of HRM policies will be influenced by the environment of the organisation. The other side represents the part where technological conditions are the dominant influential factors, phases two and three: agents will determine the goals of the technology and the type of e-HRM which eventually provides tools and data for the users. The combination of the conditions and consequences can lead to three different types of enactments (inertia, application, and change).

The full research model as explained above is visualised in Figure 18.2.

CONCLUSION AND IMPLICATIONS FOR CROSS-NATIONAL e-HRM RESEARCH

In this chapter we propose a research model for cross-national or cross-cultural e-HRM research. The model is based on a constructivist view of the relationship between technology and organisation, adopting the lines of thought of Orlikowski (1992, 2000) and DeSanctis and Poole (1994). The model identifies four phases of e-HRM in organisations, assuming

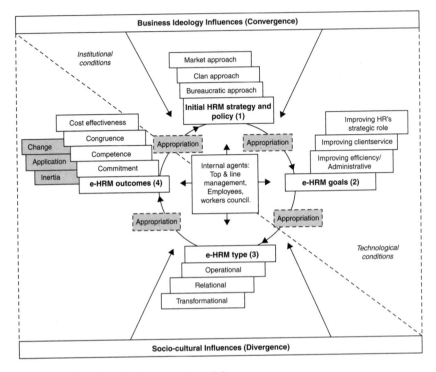

Figure 18.2   The final research model

these phases analytically as separate and sequential, though empirically they are overlapping.

The research model can be used as a framework for international comparative e-HRM research. It is suitable for this purpose as it tries to be all-encompassing, including the main focus areas of e-HRM research so far (goals, implementation, adoption, outcomes, HRM transformation), and therefore allows comparison of these areas and variables across borders in a multinational context. However, as we mentioned earlier in this chapter, comparative multinational research as such does not serve much of a purpose; it needs contextualisation.

The convergence–divergence debate is the relevant debate where international comparative e-HRM research should be positioned as it offers a relevant and rich explanatory ground for differences and similarities across national and cultural boundaries. The model proposed in this chapter is a stimulus for e-HRM studies that aim to contribute to this debate. In its current shape the model hypothesises that e-HRM in different national or cultural contexts will show predominantly converging tendencies during phases one ('reigning' HRM policy under which e-HRM decisions are taken in organisations) and two (explicitly or implicitly formulated e-HRM goals that most likely are to be chosen within the spirit of the business ideology). Diverging, socio-cultural specific tendencies will appear most likely during phases three (e-HRM types, reflecting the appropriation of e-HRM by internal agents) and four (e-HRM outcomes, reflecting the perceptions of internal agents regarding intended and unintended consequences of e-HRM appropriation).

The proposed model can be used for quantitative as well as qualitative research approaches and allows different additional theoretical lenses. For quantitative studies, the model triggers research questions such as: do converging forces have a dominant impact on how e-HRM is shaped in organisations in phases one and two? Do diverging forces have a dominant impact on how e-HRM is shaped in organisations in phases three and four? Do converging and diverging influences on the phases of e-HRM in organisations differ per national or cultural context? To what extent do different internal agents perceive converging and diverging influences differently related to different phases of e-HRM?

For qualitative studies, interesting research questions are, for example: how do internal agents appropriate business ideological and socio-cultural features in the different phases of e-HRM? How do internal agents among each other arrive at decisions on how to shape e-HRM in different national or cultural contexts? How are e-HRM outcomes perceived and interpreted by internal agents in different national and cultural contexts and 'translated' into the HRM policy? How do internal agents bring about change in e-HRM in different national and cultural contexts? How do converging and diverging influences 'interact' during an e-HRM change project?

In terms of additional theoretical perspectives, researchers can take political, behavioural, economic, as well as cultural lenses to shape and specify their research questions. Political lenses will help to understand the role of power and how power is exercised regarding e-HRM and how it results in converging or diverging tendencies. Behavioural lenses will contribute to revealing the role of individual actions and interpersonal interactions, and economic lenses may focus on quantifying costs and benefits of converging and diverging tendencies in shaping e-HRM in organisations. Finally, cultural lenses will help to understand how the cultural backgrounds of internal agents play a role in shaping e-HRM in organisations and how this results in either converging or diverging tendencies.

REFERENCES

AbuZaineh, T. & Ruël, H. 2008. e-HRM-user perceptions of e-HRM tools in Kuwaiti SMEs. In H. Ruël & R. Magalhaes (eds), *Proceedings of the Second International Workshop on Human Resource Information Systems.* Barcelona: INSTICC Press, pp. 124–135.

Adler, N., Doktor, R. & Redding, S. 1986. From the Atlantic to the Pacific century: cross-cultural management reviewed. *Journal of Management,* **12**(2): 295–318.

Al-Ibraheem, N. & Ruël, H. 2009. In-house vs. off-the-shelf e-HRM applications. In T. Bondarouk, H. Ruël, K. Guidedoni-Jourdain & E. Oiry (eds), *Handbook of Research on E-Transformation and Human Resources Management Technologies: Organizational Outcomes and Challenges.* New York: Hershey, pp. 92–115.

Ball, K. 2001. The use of human resource information systems: a survey. *Personnel Review,* **30**(6): 677–693.

Barley, S. 1986. Technology as an occasion for structuring: evidence from observations of CT scanners and the social order of radiology departments. *Administrative Science Quarterly,* **31**(1): 78–108.

Baumol, W. 1986. Productivity growth, convergence, and welfare: what the long-run data show. *The American Economic Review,* **76**(5): 1072–1085.

Beamish, N., Amistead, C., Watkinson, M. & Armfield, G. 2002. The deployment of e-learning in UK/European organisations. *European Business Journal,* **14**(3): 105–115.

Beer, M., Walton, R., Spector, B. & Mills, D. 1985. *Human Resource Management: a General Manager's Perspective: Text and Cases.* New York: The Free Press.

Bell, B., Lee, S. & Yeung, S. 2006. The impact of eHR on professional competence in HRM: implications for the development of HR professionals. *Human Resource Management,* **45**(3): 295–308.

Beulen, E. 2008. The enabling role of information technology in the global war for talent: Accenture's industrialized approach. *Information Technology for Development,* **14**(3): 213–224.

Bloom, N. 2001. In search of intelligent self-service. *International Association for Human Resources Information Management (IHRIM) Journal,* **5**(April–June): 53–61.

Bondarouk, T., Horst, V. & Engbers, S. 2009. Exploring perceptions about the use of e-HRM tools in medium sized organisations. In T. Bondarouk, H. Ruël, K. Guiderdoni-Jourdain & E. Oiry (eds), *Handbook of Research on E-Transformation and Human Resources Management Technologies: Organizational Outcomes and Challenges.* New York: Hershey, pp. 304–323.

Bondarouk, T. & Ruël, H. 2006. e-HRM effectiveness in a Dutch Ministry: results of survey and discursive exploration combined. *Proceedings of the First European Academic Workshop on e-HRM.* Enschede, the Netherlands: University of Twente, pp. 1–17.

Bondarouk, T. V. & Ruël, H. J. M. 2008. HRM systems for successful information technology implementation: evidence from three case studies. *European Management Journal,* **26**: 153–165.

Bondarouk, T. & Ruël, H. 2009. Electronic human resource management: challenges in the digital era. *The International Journal of Human Resource Management,* **20**(3): 505–514.

Boyett, T., Joseph, H., Henson, R. & Spirgi-Hebert, H. 2001. HR in the new economy. People Soft White Papers Series.

Bondarouk, T., Horst, V. & Engbers, S. 2009a. Exploring perceptions about the use of e-HRM tools in medium sized organisations. In T. Bondarouk, H. Ruël, K. Guiderdoni-Jourdain & E. Oiry (eds), *Handbook of Research on E-Transformation and Human Resources Management Technologies: Organizational Outcomes and Challenges.* New York: Hershey, pp. 304–323.

Bondarouk, T., Ruël, H. & van der Heijden, B. 2009b. e-HRM effectiveness in a public sector organization: a multi-stakeholder perspective. *The International Journal of Human Resource Management,* **20**(3): 578–590.

Braddy, P. W., Thompson, L. F., Wuensch, K. L. & Grossnickle, W. F. 2003. Internet recruiting: the effects of web page design features. *Social Science Computer Review*, **21**(3): 374–385.

Brewster, C. 1995. Towards an 'European' model of human resource management. *Journal of International Business Studies*, **26**(1): 1–21.

Brewster, C., Wood, G. & Brookes, M. 2008. Similarity, isomorphism and duality? Recent survey evidence on the HRM Policies of MNCs. *British Journal of Management*, **19**(4): 320–342.

Buckley, P., Minette, K., Joy, D. & Michaels, J. 2004. The use of an automated employment recruiting and screening system for temporary professional employees. *Human Resource Management*, **43**(2/3): 233–241.

CedarCrestone 2006. *Workforce Technologies and Service Delivery Approaches Survey*, 9th annual edn. Alpharetta, GA: CedarCrestone.

Chapman, D. S. & Webster, J. 2003. The use of technologies in the recruiting, screening, and selection processes for job candidates. *International Journal of Selection and Assessment*, **11**(2/3): 113–120.

Cober, R. T., Brown, D. J. & Levy, P. E. 2004. Form, content, and function: an evaluative methodology for corporate employment web sites. *Human Resource Management*, **43**(2/3): 201–218.

Deakins, E. 2009. Influence of job relevance, output quality, task technology fit, and privacy concerns on human resources information systems usage. In T. Torres-Coronas & M. Arias-Oliva (eds), *Encyclopedia of Human Resources Information Systems: Challenges in e-HRM, Volume II*. New York: Hershey, pp. 525–531.

DeSanctis, G. 1986. Human resource information systems: a current assessment. *MIS Quarterly*, **10**(1): 15-27.

DeSanctis, G. & Poole, M. 1994. Capturing the complexity in advanced technology use: adaptive structuration theory. *Organizational Science*, **5**(2): 121–147.

Dineen, B. R., Noe, R. A. & Wang, C. 2004. Perceived fairness of web-based applicant screening procedures: weighing the rules of justice and the role of individual differences. *Human Resource Management*, **43**(2/3): 127–145.

Douglas, S. & Wind, Y. 1987. The myth of globalization. *Columbia Journal of World Business*, **22**(4): 19–30.

Doz, Y. & Prahalad, C. 1991. Managing DMNCs: a search for a new paradigm. *Strategic Management Journal*, **12**(S1): 145–164.

Elgin, P. D. & Claphan, M. M. 2004. Attributes associated with the submission of electronic versus paper résumés. *Computers in Human Behaviour*, **20**: 535–549.

Elmslie, B. 1995. The convergence debate between David Hume and Josiah Tucker. *Journal of Economic Perspectives*, **9**(4): 207–216.

Farndale, E. & Paauwe, J. 2006. HR shared service centres in the Netherlands: restructuring the HR function. *Proceedings of the First European Academic Workshop on e-HRM*. Enschede, the Netherlands: University of Twente, pp. 18–29.

Fernándes-Sánchez, F. A., de Juana-Espinosa, S. & Valdés-Conca, J. 2009. Exploring the relation between the use of HRIS and their implementation in Spanish firms. In T. Torres-Coronas & M. Arias-Oliva (eds), *Encyclopedia of Human Resources Information Systems: Challenges in e-HRM*, Volume I. New York: Hershey, pp. 399–405

Foster, S. 2008. *An Exploratory Analysis of e-HRM in the Context of HRM 'Transformation'*. Hertfordshire: Business School University of Hertfordshire.

Foster, S. 2009. Making sense of e-HRM: transformation, technology and power relations. In T. Bondarouk, H. Ruël, K. Guiderdoni-Jourdain & E. Oiry (eds), *Handbook of Research on E-Transformation and Human Resources Management Technologies: Organizational Outcomes and Challenges*. New York: Hershey, pp. 1–19.

Furtmueller, E., Wilderom, C. & van Dick, R. 2009. Utilizing the lead user method for promoting innovation in e-recruitment. In T. Bondarouk, H. Ruël, K. Guiderdoni-Jourdain & E. Oiry (eds), *Handbook of Research on e-Transformation and Human Resources Management Technologies: Organizational Outcomes and Challenges*. New York: Hershey, pp. 252–274.

Galanaki, E. & Panayotopoulou, L. 2009. Adoption and success of e-HRM in European firms. In T. Torres-Coronas & M. Arias-Oliva (eds), *Encyclopedia of Human Resources Information Systems: Challenges in e-HRM*, Volume I. New York: Hershey, pp. 24–30.

Girard, A. & Fallery, B. 2009. e-Recruitment: new practices, new issues an exploratory study. In T. Bondarouk & H. Ruël (eds), *Proceedings of the Third International Workshop on Human Resource Information Systems*. Milan, Italy: INSTICC Press, pp. 39–48.

Guiderdoni-Jourdain, K. 2006. Assessment of an HR intranet through middle managers positions and uses: how to manage the plurality of this group in the beginning of an e-HR conception. *Proceedings of the First European Academic Workshop on e-HRM*. Enschede, the Netherlands: University of Twente, pp. 38–49.

Guiderdoni-Jourdain, K. 2007. Does the 'local universe' impact on representations, levels of utilisation of an HR intranet by the middle management user? In H. Ruël & R. Magalhaes (eds), *Proceedings of the First International Workshop on Human Resource Information Systems*. Funchal/Madeira, Portugal: INSTICC Press.

Guiderdoni-Jourdain, K. 2009. The enrichment of the HR intranet linked to the regulation's processes between HR actors. In T. Bondarouk, H. Ruël, K. Guiderdoni-Jourdain & E. Oiry (eds), *Handbook of Research on e-Transformation and Human Resources Management Technologies: Organizational Outcomes and Challenges*. New York: Hershey, pp. 289–302.

Giddens, A. 1984 *The Constitution of Society: Outline of the Theory of Structuration*. Berkeley: University of California Press.

Haines, V. & Petit, A. 1997. Conditions for successful human resource information systems. *Human Resource Management*, 36(2): 261–275.

Harris, M. M., van Hoye, G. & Lievens, F. 2003. Privacy and attitudes towards internet-based selection systems: a cross-cultural comparison. *International Journal of Selection and Assessment*, 11(2/3): 230–236.

Hawking, P., Stein A. & Foster, S. 2004. e-HR and employee self service: a case study of a Victorian public sector organisation. *Issues in Informing Science and Information Technology*.

Haunsdorf, P. A. & Duncan, D. 2004. Firm size and internet recruiting in Canada: a preliminary investigation. *Journal of Small Business Management*, 42(3): 325–334.

Heikkilä, J. P. & Smale, A. 2009. Implementing English language e-HRM systems: effects on user acceptance and system use in foreign subsidiaries. In T. Bondarouk & H. Ruël (eds), *Proceedings of the Third International Workshop on Human Resource Information Systems*. Milan, Italy: INSTICC Press, pp. 18–27.

Holm, A. B. 2009. Virtual HRM: a case of e-recruitment. In T. Bondarouk & H. Ruël (eds), *Proceedings of the Third International Workshop on Human Resource Information Systems*. Milan, Italy: INSTICC Press, pp. 49–58.

Hooi, L. W. 2006. Implementing e-HRM: the readiness of small and medium sized manufacturing companies in Malaysia. *Asia Pacific Business Review*, 12(4): 465–485.

Hoye van, G. & Lievens, P. 2007. Investigating web-based recruitment sources: employee testimonials versus word-of-mouth. *International Journal of Assessment and Selection*, 15(4): 372–382.

Huang, J. H., Yang, C., Jin, B. H. & Chiu, H. 2004. Measuring satisfaction with business-to-employee systems. *Computers in Human Behaviour*, 20(1): 17–35.

Imperatori, B. & De Marco, M. 2009. e-Work and labor processes transformation. In T. Bondarouk, H. Ruël, K. Guiderdoni-Jourdain & E. Oiry (eds), *Handbook of Research on e-Transformation and Human Resources Management Technologies: Organizational Outcomes and Challenges*. New York: Hershey, pp. 34–54.

Jattuso, M. L. & Sinar, E. F. 2003. Source effects in internet-based screening procedures. International *Journal of Selection and Assessment*, 11(2/3): 137–140.

Joia, L. A. & Silva, J. A. A. 2009. Assessing the use of internet in the recruiting process. In T. Torres-Coronas & M. Arias-Oliva (eds), *Encyclopedia of Human Resources Information Systems: Challenges in e-HRM*, Volume I. New York: Hershey, pp. 70–76.

Jones, S. 2007. The challenges of implementing an integrated web-based software system for managing training and development in a large organization: an example from the Middle East. In H. Ruël & R. Magalhaes (eds), *Proceedings of the first International Workshop on Human Resource Information Systems*. Funchal/Madeira, Portugal: INSTICC Press, pp. 40–47.

Kanthawongs, P. 2004. Does HRIS matter for HRM today. *BU Academic Review*, 3(1): 104–109.

Konradt, U., Hertel, G. & Joder, K. 2003. Web-based assessment of call center agents: development and validation of a computerized instrument. *International Journal of Selection and Assessment*, 11(2/3): 184–193.

Koopman, G. & Batenburg, R. 2008. User participation and involvement in the development of HR self-service applications within the Dutch government. In H. Ruël & R. Magalhaes (eds), *Proceedings of the Second International Workshop on Human Resource Information Systems*. Barcelona: INSTICC Press, pp. 16–29.

Kovach, K., Hughes, A., Fagan, P. & Maggitti, P. 2002. Administrative and strategic advantages of HRIS. *Public Personnel Management*, 28(2): 43–48.

Lau, G. & Hooper, V. 2009. Adoption of e-HRM in large New Zealand organisations. In T. Torres-Coronas & M. Arias-Oliva (eds), *Encyclopedia of Human Resources Information Systems: Challenges in e-HRM*, Volume I. New York: Hershey, pp. 31–41.

Laurent, A. 1986. The cross-cultural puzzle of international human resource management. *Human Resource Management*, 25(1): 91–102.

Leat, M. & El-Kot, G. 2007. HRM practices in Egypt: the influence of national context. *International Journal of Human Resource Management*, 18(1): 147–158.

Levitt, T. 2006. What business are you in? Classic advice from Theodore Levitt. *Harvard Business Review*, 84(10): 126–137.

Lin, C. Y. Y. 1997. Human resource information systems: implementation in Taiwan. *Research and Practice in Human Resource Management*, 5(1): 57–72.

Loijen, Y. & Bondarouk, T. 2009. Electronic HRM: from implementation to value creation. In T. Bondarouk & H. Ruël (eds), *Proceedings of the Third International Workshop on Human Resource Information Systems*. Milan, Italy: INSTICC Press, pp. 84–97.

Lu, Y. & Björkman, I. 1997. HRM practices in China–Western joint ventures: MNC standardization versus localization. *The International Journal of Human Resource Management*, 8(5): 614–628.

Lukaszewski, K. M., Stone, D. L. & Stone-Romero, E. F. 2008. The effects of the ability to choose the type of human resources system on perceptions of invasion of privacy and system. *Journal of Business Psychology*, 23(3/4): 73–86.

Macpherson, A., Elliot, M., Harris, I. & Hofman, G. 2004. E-learning: reflections and evaluation of corporate programmes. *Human Resource Development International*, 7(3): 295–313.

Majó, Z. 2006. Development of web-based human resource management: corporate practice of e-recruitment in Hungary. *Proceedings of the First European Academic Workshop on e-HRM*. Enschede, the Netherlands: U. of Twente, pp. 64–75.

Marler, J. H. 2009. Making human resources strategic by going to the Net: reality or myth? *The International Journal of Human Resource Management*, 20(3): 515–527.

Marler, J. H. & Parry, E. 2008. Which comes first e-HRM or SHRM? In H. Ruël & R. Magalhaes (eds), *Proceedings of the second International Workshop on Human Resource Information Systems*. Barcelona, Spain: INSTICC Press, pp. 40–50.

McGaughey, S. & De Cieri, H. 1999. Reassessment of convergence and divergence dynamics: implications for international HRM. *The International Journal of Human Resource Management*, 10(2): 235–250.

McManus, M. A. & Fergson, M. W. 2003. Biodata, personality, and demographic differences of recruits from three sources. *International Journal of Selection and Assessment*, 11(2/3): 175–183.

Myloni, B., Harzing, A. & Mirza, H. 2004. Human resource management in Greece: have the colours of culture faded away? *International Journal of Cross Cultural Management*, 4(1): 59–76.

Ngai, E. & Wat, F. 2006. Human resource information systems: a review and empirical analysis. *Personnel Review*, **35**(3): 297–314.

Ngo, H., Turban, D., Lau, C. & Lui, S. 1998. Human resource practices and firm performance of multinational corporations: influences of country origin. *The International Journal of Human Resource Management*, **9**(4): 632–652.

Oiry, E. 2006. e-Learning effectiveness: should we not take its effects on socialization into account? *Proceedings of the First European Academic Workshop on e-HRM*. Enschede, the Netherlands: University of Twente, pp. 101–112.

Oiry, E. 2007. e-Learning: which effects on socialization in a work team? In T. Bondarouk & H. Ruël (eds), *Proceedings of the First International Workshop on Human Resource Information Systems*. Funchal, Madeira (Portugal): INSTICC Press.

Oiry, E., Pascal, A. & Tchobanian, R. 2008. From IS to organisation: analysing the uses of a collaborative IS in a high-tech SME. In H. Ruël & R. Magalhaes (eds), *Proceedings of the Second International Workshop on Human Resource Information Systems*. Barcelona, Spain: INSTICC Press, pp. 30–39.

Olivas-Luján, M. R. & Florkowski, G. W. 2008. e-HRM and IT governance: a user department's perspective using diffusion of innovations (DOI) theory. In H. Ruël, & R. Magalhaes (Eds.), *Proceedings of the Second International Workshop on Human Resource Information Systems*. Barcelona, Spain: INSTICC Press, pp. 3–15.

Olivas-Luján, M. R. & Florkowski, G. W. 2009. The diffusion of HRITs across English-speaking countries. In T. Torres-Coronas & M. Arias-Oliva (eds), *Encyclopedia of Human Resources Information Systems: Challenges in e-HRM*, Volume I. New York: Hershey, pp. 242–247.

Olivas-Luján, M. R., Ramírez, J. & Zapata Cantú, L. 2006. e-HRM in Mexico: towards a research agenda. *Proceedings of the First European Academic Workshop on e-HRM*. Enschede, the Netherlands: University of Twente, pp. 113–124.

Orlikowski, W. 1992. The duality of technology: rethinking the concept of technology in organisations. *Organizational Science*, **3**(3): 398–427.

Orlikowski, W. 2007. Using technology and constituting structures: a practice lens for studying technology in organizations. In M. Ackerman, C. Halverson, T. Erickson and W. Kellog (eds), *Resources, Co-evolution and Artifacts in Theory in CSCW*. London: Springer-Verlag, pp. 255–305.

Palincsar, S. 1998. Social constructivist perspectives on teaching and learning. *Annual Review of Psychology*, **49**: 345–375.

Parry, E., Dickmann, M. & Morley, M. 2008. North American MNCs and their HR policies in liberal and coordinated market economies. *The International Journal of Human Resource Management*, **19**(11): 2024–2040.

Parry, E. & Tyson, S. 2009. What is the potential of e-recruitment to transform the recruitment process and the role of the resourcing team? In T. Bondarouk, H. Ruël, K. Guiderdoni-Jourdain & E. Oiry (eds), *Handbook of Research on E-Transformation and Human Resources Management Technologies: Organizational Outcomes and Challenges*. New York: Hershey, pp. 202–217.

Parry, E. & Wilson, H. 2006. Online recruitment within the UK: a model of the factors affecting its adoption. *Proceedings of the First European Academic Workshop on e-HRM*. Enschede, the Netherlands: University of Twente, pp. 133–145.

Pearce, C. G. & Tuten, T. L. 2001. Internet recruiting in the banking industry. *Business Communication Quarterly*, **64**(1): 9–18.

Porter, M. 1986. Competition in global industries. 8th edn. Watertown, MA: Harvard Business School Press.

Prahalad, C. & Doz, Y. 1987. *The Multinational Mission: Balancing Local Demands and Global Vision*. New York: The Free Press.

Puck, J., Holtbrügge, D. & Mohr, A. T. 2006. Applicant information and selection strategies in corporate web site recruiting: the role of national culture. *Proceedings of the First European Academic Workshop on e-HRM*. Enschede, the Netherlands: University of Twente, pp. 154–164.

Puck, J., Holtbrügge, D. & Mohr, A. T. 2009. Applicant information and selection strategies in corporate web site recruiting: the role of national culture. In T. Bondarouk, H. Ruël, K. Guiderdoni-Jourdain & E. Oiry (eds.), *Handbook of Research on E-Transformation and Human Resources Management Technologies: Organizational Outcomes and Challenges.* New York: Hershey, pp. 187–201.

Pudelko, M. & Harzing, A. 2007. Country-of-origin, localization, or dominance effect? An empirical investigation of HRM practices in foreign subsidiaries. *Human Resource Management,* **46**(4): 535–559.

Pudelko, M. & Harzing, A. 2008. The golden triangle for MNCs: standardization towards headquarters practices, standardization towards global best practices and localization. *Organizational Dynamics,* **37**(4): 394–404.

Rahin, M. & Singh, M. 2007. Understanding benefits and impediments of B2E e-business systems adoption: experiences of two large Australian universities. *Journal of Internet Commerce,* **6**(2): 3–17.

Ralston, D. 2008. The crossvergence perspective: reflections and projections. *Journal of International Business Studies,* **39**(1): 27–40.

Ralston, D., Gustafson, D., Cheung, F. & Terpstra, R. 1993. Differences in managerial values: A study of US, Hong Kong and PRC managers. *Journal of International Business Studies,* **24**(2): 249–275.

Ralston, D., Holt, D., Terpstra, R. & Kai Cheng, Y. 1997. The impact of national culture and economic ideology on managerial work values: a study of the US, Russia, Japan and China. *Journal of International Business Studies,* **28**(1): 177–207.

Rao, P. 2009a. e-Recruitment in emerging economies. In T. Torres-Coronas & M. Arias-Oliva (eds), *Encyclopedia of Human Resources Information Systems: Challenges in e-HRM,* Volume I. New York: Hershey, pp. 357–362.

Rao, P. 2009b. Identifying the 'best' human resource management practices in India: a case study approach. In T. Bondarouk & H. Ruël (eds.), *Proceedings of the Third International Workshop on Human Resource Information Systems.* Milan, Italy: INSTICC Press, pp. 69–83.

Rao, P. 2009c. The role of national culture on e-recruitment in India and Mexico. In T. Bondarouk, H. Ruël, K. Guiderdoni-Jourdain & E. Oiry (eds), *Handbook of Research on e-Transformation and Human Resources Management Technologies: Organizational Outcomes and Challenges.* New York: Hershey, pp. 218–230.

Reddington, M., Martin, G. & Park, R. 2006. Theorizing the links between e-HR and strategic HRM: a framework, case illustration and some reflections. *Proceedings of the First European Academic Workshop on e-HRM.* Enschede, the Netherlands: University of Twente, pp. 165–176.

Rosenzweig, P. & Nohria, N. 1994. Influences on HRM practices in multinational corporation. *Journal of International Business Studies,* **25**(2): 229–251.

Ruël, H. 2009. Studying human resource information systems implementation using adaptive structuration theory: the case of an HRIS implementation at Dow Chemical Company. In T. Bondarouk, H. Ruël, K. Guiderdoni-Jourdain & E. Oiry (eds), *Handbook of Research on e-Transformation and Human Resources Management Technologies: Organizational Outcomes and Challenges.* New York: Hershey, pp. 171–185.

Ruël, H., Bondarouk, T. & Looise, J. K. 2004a. e-HRM: innovation or irritation. An explorative empirical study in five large companies on web-based HRM. *Management Revue,* **15**(3): 364–380.

Ruël, H., Bondarouk, T. & Looise, J. K. 2004b. *e-HRM: Innovation or Irritation. An Explorative Empirical Study in Five Large Companies on Web-based HRM.* Utrecht, the Netherlands: Lemma Publishers.

Ruta, C. 2009. HR portal alignment for the creation and development of intellectual capital. *The International Journal of Human Resource Management,* **20**(3): 562–577.

Salgado, J. F. & Moscoso, S. 2003. Internet-based personality testing: equivalence of measures and assesses' perceptions and reactions. *International Journal of Selection and Assessment,* **11**(2/3): 194–205.

Schuessler, E. 2006a. Implementing e-HRM: a structural approach to investigating technological and organizational change. *Proceedings of the First European Academic Workshop on e-HRM*. Enschede, the Netherlands: University of Twente, pp. 177–188.

Schuessler, E. 2006b. Implementing e-HRM. A structurational approach to investigating technological and organisational change. Paper presented at the 'First European Academic Workshop on Electronic Human Resource Management', University of Twente, Netherlands.

Schuler, R., Dowling, P. & De Cieri, H. 1993. An integrative framework of strategic international human resource management. *Journal of Management*, 19(2): 419–459.

Shwartz-Asher, D., Ahituv, N. & Etzion, D. 2009. Improving virtual teams through swift structure. In T. Torres-Coronas & M. Arias-Oliva (eds), *Encyclopedia of Human Resources Information Systems: Challenges in e-HRM*, Volume II. New York: Hershey, pp. 510–517.

Sinar, E. F., Reynolds, D. H. & Paquet, S. L. 2003. Nothing but 'net? Corporate image and web-based testing. *International Journal of Selection and Assessment*, 11(2/3): 150–157.

Spicer, A. 2006. Beyond the convergence–divergence debate: the role of spatial scales in transforming organizational logic. *Organizational Studies*, 27(10): 1467–1483.

Strohmeier, S. 2007. Research in e-HRM, review and implications. *Human Research Management Review*, 17(1): 19–37.

Strohmeier, S. & Diederichsen, A. 2006. Electronic recruitment: does the internet displace conventional print media? *Proceedings of the First European Academic Workshop on e-HRM*. Enschede, the Netherlands: University of Twente, pp. 211–222.

Strohmeier, S. & Kabst, R. 2009. Organizational adoption of e-HRM in Europe: an empirical exploration of major adoption factors. *Journal of Managerial Psychology*, 24(6): 482–501.

Tannenbaum, S. 1990. HRIS: user group implications. *Journal of Systems Management*, 41(1): 27–32.

Tixier, J. 2004. Does the evolution of the human resources practices imply the implementation of an information system? For a contextualism of practices. *International Journal of Human Resources Development and Management*, 4(4): 414–430.

Torraco, R. J. 2005. Writing integrative literature reviews: guidelines and examples. *Human Resource Development Review*, 4(3): 356–367.

Vaughan, K. & MacVicar, A. 2004. Employees' pre-implementation attitudes and perceptions to e-learning. a banking case study analysis. *Journal of European Industrial Training*, 28(5): 400–413.

Walker, A. 1982. *HRIS Development: A Project Team Guide to Building and Effective Personnel Information System*. New York: Van Nostrand Reinhold Company.

Webber, R. 1969. Convergence or divergence. *Columbia Journal of World Business*, 4: 75–83.

Webster, J. & Watson, R. T. 2002. Analysing the past to prepare for the future: writing a literature review. *MIS Quarterly*, 26(2): xiii–xxiii.

West, J. P. & Berman, E. M. 2001. From traditional to virtual HR. Is the transition occurring in local government? *Review of Public Personnel Administration*, 21(1): 38–64.

Williams, H., Tansley, C. & Foster, C. 2009. HRIS project teams skills and knowledge: a human capital analysis. In T. Bondarouk, H. Ruël, K. Guiderdoni-Jourdain & E. Oiry (eds), *Handbook of Research on E-Transformation and Human Resources Management Technologies: Organizational Outcomes and Challenges*. New York: Hershey, pp. 135–152.

Wöcke, A., Bendixen, M. & Rijamampianina, R. 2007. Building flexibility into multinational human resource strategy: a study of four South African multi-national enterprises. *The International Journal of Human Resource Management*, 18(5): 829–844.

Wolters, M. J. J., & Mackaaij, I. 2006. The effectiveness of board internet recruitment. *Proceedings of the First European Academic Workshop on e-HRM*. Enschede, the Netherlands: University of Twente, pp. 235–245.

PART III

REGIONAL PERSPECTIVES

19 HRM practice and scholarship: a North American perspective
Susan E. Jackson, Randall S. Schuler, David Lepak and Ibraiz Tarique

Human resource management (HRM) in the United States and Canada, referred to here as the 'North American' perspective, has undergone dramatic change during the past 30 years.[1] Beginning in the 1980s, the focus of North American businesses began shifting from domestic to multinational to global. With the support of new technologies, the speed at which business was conducted increased dramatically. With these changes came the realisation that competitive advantage could be seized and sustained through the wise utilisation of human resources (Gupta & Govindarajan, 2001; Kanter, 1983, 1994; Porter, 1980, 1985). Reflecting these trends, both the practice of HRM within organisations and its study within academia have evolved accordingly.

Concurrently with these developments, business executives in some North American organisations began to view HRM professionals as potential business partners who should be involved in strategic decision making processes. Prior to the 1980s, an older 'personnel' model dominated in North America. Specialists who worked from a centralised department were responsible primarily for acquiring and motivating the firm's employees, and doing so within specified legal and cost constraints. Increasingly, however, HRM professionals are viewed as 'human capital' asset experts whose efforts are directed at creating competitive advantages for the firm (Barney & Wright, 1998; Gupta & Govindarajan, 2001; Pfeffer, 1994, 1998; Schuler & Jackson, 2007; Schuler et al., 2001).

In this chapter, we focus on the current state of North American HRM practice and scholarship in larger public and private sector organisations, while recognising that it will continue to evolve and change in response to dynamic business conditions. Our discussion begins with a broad overview of the context within which the practice of North American HRM occurs. Then we describe recent scholarship in the area of strategic HRM, which currently is the dominant paradigm for North American HRM scholarship. We conclude our discussion by considering several current issues that offer opportunities for future endeavours that address the practical interest of HRM professionals while incorporating the strategic HRM scholarship paradigm.

In our coverage of North American HRM practice and scholarship, we make no attempt to compare and contrast the North American HRM scene to other regions or countries. Nor do we consider issues that are unique to either the United States or Canada. Recent comparative studies have described North American HRM policies and practices as reasonably similar. Both have been characterised as: using an individualised approach to handling employment relations and communication; relying on sophisticated selection techniques; using individualised, performance-based rewards; emphasising training and development for the purpose of human capital accumulation; showing strong concern with diversity management; and adopting a rather ethnocentric approach to managing international operations on the belief that North American HRM policies and practices reflect a 'one-best way' (Fenton-O'Creevy et al., 2008; Parry et al., 2007: 2008). While there are some differences in HRM policies and practices between the United States and Canada, the North American approach reflects the liberal market economies found in both countries (Hall & Soskice, 2001) as well as the penetration of US multinationals into the Canadian economy (Dickmann & Muller-Camen, 2006; Parry et al., 2008).

THE PRACTICE OF STRATEGIC HRM

Among HRM professionals, the term 'strategic HRM' is used broadly to signal the view that HRM activities should contribute to business effectiveness. Included under the broad umbrella of HRM activities are the development and articulation of an HRM philosophy, the design of HRM policies that reflect the firm's overarching philosophy, as well as the implementation and evaluation of specific HRM practices (e.g. planning, recruitment, training, compensation, etc.).

For North American HRM professionals, the pursuit of strategic HRM typically implies that a key objective to be achieved through these HRM activities is improved firm performance. In addition, a strategic HRM approach recognises that an effective HRM system is influenced by and entwined with numerous contextual forces (Jackson & Schuler, 1990; 1995; Jackson et al., 2009; Schuler & Jackson, 1989; 1999; 2007).

Understanding the Context

In North America, the practice of human resource management has long been shaped by legal regulations, which provide to employees a variety of rights and protections against unfair and unsafe employment practices (see Elkins, 2007). Monitoring the legal and regulatory environment to ensure that a firm's HRM practices comply with legal requirements has long been one of the primary roles for North American HRM professionals. In addition, because an organisation's pay practices must take into account the pay practices of other organisations competing for the same labour, HRM professionals took responsibility for monitoring competitors' pay practices. Likewise, because an organisation's planning for future recruitment, staffing and development is affected by supply and demand in the external labour market, the traditional role of HRM professionals generally included tracking labour market conditions.

Strategic HRM also includes developing a comprehensive understanding of the environment's implications for the organisation. In his discussion of strategic job modelling (which evolved from traditional job analysis), Jeffery Schippmann states: 'perhaps the most useful thing a strategic job modeller can do is develop his or her own understanding and framework for thinking about the customer's [organisation's] problems. This means . . . working to understand the underlying issues and developing working hypotheses about what is important and what is relevant in a given context' (Schippmann, 1999: 37). HRM professionals who demonstrate a deep understanding of business issues and their implications are better able to develop HRM policies and implement HRM practices that recognise human resource management as a source of competitive advantage (Huselid et al., 1997; Lado & Wilson, 1994; Schuler & MacMillan, 1984; Wright et al., 1994).

HRM Systems

Integration and coherence among the parts are hallmarks of a strategically aligned HRM system. An example of how adopting a systems perspective can influence the practice of HRM is provided by Higgs et al. (2000). After noting that the traditional HRM perspective treats selection primarily within the context of hiring decisions, Higgs et al. describe how systems thinking is transforming the way some HRM professionals develop and manage selection processes. Adopting a systems view of selection reveals that many HRM policies and practices that previously were treated as distinct activities (e.g. hiring, training, performance evaluation, special assignments, career development) can all be considered selection processes that need to fit together. According to Higgs et al., competency modelling and managing against core values are two approaches North American organisations use to achieve systemic integration.

Competency modelling

Prior to the 1990s in North America, job analysis was firmly established as the only appropriate basis for developing HRM practices that meet legal requirements. While appropriate for that purpose, the results of job analysis were not as useful as a foundation for creating a coherent and integrated HRM system that is aligned with the organisation's strategic direction. Decreased job specialisation, increased job sharing and the increased prevalence of work teams are a few of the reasons why North American employers have begun to emphasise the competencies employees have over the tasks employees do in their jobs when designing HRM practices. The use of competency models is considered to be more consistent with the trend toward increased sharing of responsibilities across jobs and across levels in the organisation. Part of the appeal of competency modelling seems to be that it is more useful for identifying the common competencies and behaviours that are similar across all jobs in a department, business unit, or organisation. Competency modelling encourages more consideration of the organisation's future needs rather than focusing on the details of specific jobs as they are carried out in the present (Sackett et al., 2003; Schippmann, 1999). Thus, competency modelling can provide the foundation upon which to build an appropriate HRM architecture (cf. Lepak & Snell, 1999, 2003).

Vision and values

Declarations of the organisation's vision and values also guide the development of coherent HRM systems. Statements of organisational vision and values are sometimes derided as superficial. But when taken seriously, they provide direction and a set of implicit decision rules for evaluating the firm-specific appropriateness of various HRM practices. Regardless of whether vision and values statements are considered the foundation of, or reflections of, the organisation's culture, they provide a common understanding of what the organisation is striving to be – its desired identity. Thus, vision and values statements serve as touchstones for employees and HRM professionals alike (Pfeffer, 1998; see also Boswell & Boudreau, 2001).

Demonstrating the Effectiveness of HRM

Assessments of the 'effectiveness' of an organisation's HRM practices have traditionally been made using technical criteria established by the profession (e.g. validity and reliability) and embodied in legal regulations. More recently, HRM professionals have been called on to demonstrate the strategic effectiveness of HRM practices in monetary terms.

Monetary criteria

Thirty years ago, efforts to demonstrate the effectiveness of HRM practices in monetary terms usually employed utility analysis (e.g. Schmidt et al., 1979) or cost accounting (e.g. Cascio, 2000). Regardless of the technical merits of such approaches, they have not been widely adopted by North American firms. Instead, most firms continue to rely on subjective estimates and intuition when assessing the effectiveness of their HRM practices (Becker et al., 2001; Lepak, 2009).

During the past decade, there has been a growing desire to demonstrate the effectiveness of HRM practices using business-relevant metrics. Thus, HRM consultants now offer a variety of more sophisticated measures that estimate the economic value added (EVA) or return-on-investment (ROI) for HRM activities (e.g. see Becker et al., 2001; Fitz-enz, 2000). Such metrics place considerable emphasis on monetary costs and monetary returns, and reflect great deference to the financial interests of shareholders and other owners. This narrow approach to assessing HRM effectiveness is likely to change in the future, however, as organisations develop an improved understanding of the underlying drivers of long-term organisational success. For example, using the logic of balanced scorecards and strategy maps (Kaplan & Norton, 1996), some firms have begun to develop more sophisticated models of how HRM practices can contribute to achieving strategic objectives (Becker et al., 2001; Lepak, 2009; Rucci et al., 1998; Ulrich, 1998). Looking ahead, we anticipate that North American firms will continue to develop business-related approaches to evaluating the effectiveness of their HRM systems.

Satisfying multiple stakeholders

A more complete assessment of HRM effectiveness would evaluate the effects of an HRM system on the organisation's broad array of multiple stakeholders (Colakoglu et al., 2006; Hyland & Jackson, 2006; Tsui, 1990; see Figure 19.1). Certainly, the organisation itself is a primary stakeholder, so it is appropriate to assess the impact of the HRM system against objectives such as improving productivity, improving profitability, and ensuring the organisation's long-term survival. Increasingly, employers also recognise that organisational strategies that depend on total quality, innovation and customer service cannot be met unless employees are willing to strive for these same goals on the organisation's behalf. Thus, employees also are legitimate stakeholders whose concerns must be addressed, so 'soft' indicators of employees' feelings about the organisation (e.g. commitment, satisfaction, engagement) are being recognised as relevant indicators of effectiveness that are worthy of top management's attention (Boudreau, 2003; Boudreau & Ramstad, 1999; Macey & Schneider, 2008).

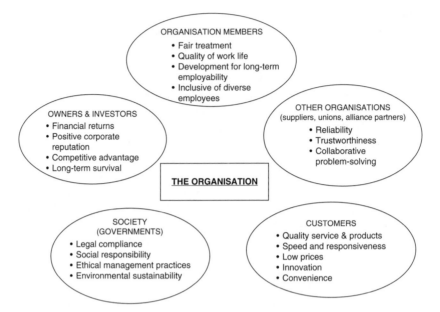

Source: Adapted from S. E. Jackson, R. S. Schuler and S. Werner, *Managing Human Resources*, 11th edn. Mason, OH: Cengage, 2012. Used with permission.

Figure 19.1   Stakeholders and their concerns

Some organisations also evaluate HRM effectiveness against its consequences for customers. An effective HRM system should influence the quality and variety of products available to customers, the price at which products can be profitably sold, the service customers receive, and so on. As the US economy evolved toward services, customers' expectations have been incorporated into job descriptions, their preferences have influenced criteria used to select new employees, their input is often sought to assess employee performance, and so on (White & Schneider, 2003).

Summary

Briefly, the practice of strategic human resource management in North America reflects the confluence of several unfolding trends, which include: development of a contextualised understanding of human resource management, emergence of a systems perspective to guide internally consistent and aligned HRM practices, and creation of new monetary metrics for assessing HRM effectiveness.

STRATEGIC HRM SCHOLARSHIP

In North America, the science and practice of strategic HRM are related, but not tightly coupled. Thus, we turn next to a description of strategic HRM scholarship in North America.

North American scholars have not adopted a common definition of 'strategic HRM,' but most would probably agree that it covers research intended to improve our understanding of the relationship between how organisations manage their human resources and their success in implementing business strategies (cf. Snell et al., 1996). As a focal topic for HRM scholarship, strategic HRM began to emerge approximately 30 years ago. Since then it has evolved to include several streams of theory and empirical research. Due to space limitations, our tour of this work is necessarily too brief to adequately compare and contrast the numerous conceptual frameworks proposed, or to examine the ongoing methodological debates. Instead, we simply attempt to summarise a few key issues of interest to strategic HRM scholars and to visit some emerging areas of research. More detailed reviews can be found elsewhere (e.g. see Becker & Huselid, 1998a; Gardey et al., 2004; Jackson & Schuler, 1995; Lengnick-Hall, 1988; McMahan et al., 1999; Schuler & Jackson, 2007; Wright & McMahan, 1992).

Best Practices and HRM Bundles (Configurations)[2]

One of the primary conceptual developments in strategic HRM research is to differentiate between studies that focus on (1) the direct effects of HRM practices and/or systems on relevant outcomes, and (2) studies that focus on various contingencies that impact the use and effectiveness of HRM practices. Many early strategic HRM scholars examined the impact of individual HRM practices in search of 'best practices' that positively influence various outcomes. For example, Terpstra and Rozell (1993) found a positive relationship between several staffing practices and annual profits. Russell et al. (1985) found that the use of several training practices was positively correlated with retail store sales volume and store image. Gerhart and Milkovich (1990) provided evidence that differences in compensation practices were related to financial firm performance.

Extending this approach, strategic HRM researchers shifted to consideration of HRM practice 'bundles', arguing that a defining element of strategic HRM is its focus on the entire HRM system. That is, HRM practices are assumed to operate in concert with each other. As noted by MacDuffie (1995: 198), 'an HR bundle or system must be integrated with complementary bundles of practices from core business functions'. When properly aligned, several practices together may reinforce each other; when mismatched, they may work against each other and interfere with performance (Delery, 1998; Lawler, 1992; Lawler et al., 1992). Alternatively, some practices may serve as substitutes for other practices (Ichniowski et al., 1996), such that only one or the other practice is needed. Such bundles of HRM practices have been referred to by various labels, including high performance work systems (Becker & Huselid, 1998b; Huselid, 1995), high involvement HRM systems (Guthrie, 2001), human capital enhancing HRM systems (Youndt et al., 1996), commitment-based HRM systems (Arthur, 1994), or innovative employment practices (Ichniowski et al., 1997).

Several empirical studies have shown that firms using bundles of so-called high performance HRM practices outperformed firms that used only a few of these practices (Becker & Huselid, 1998a). For example, Huselid (1995) found that high performance work systems were associated with lower employee turnover and higher labour productivity, which in turn, were associated with two financial indicators of firm performance. Batt (2002) found significant relationships between high involvement HRM practices and labour productivity and employee turnover rates for small companies and service companies. Similarly, Ichniowski et al. (1997) found a positive relationship between innovative work practices and labour productivity for steel-finishing lines.

However, as critics have pointed out, there has been some inconsistency in the specific practices that various authors consider to be among the preferred practices, making it difficult to draw general conclusions about which practices qualify as 'best practices' (e.g. see Becker & Gerhart, 1996). In order to continue moving forward with this line of research, more theory-driven research may be needed. The challenge is to trace the causal chain that explains how specific bundles of HRM practices influence intermediate outcomes such as motivation, productivity, turnover and how those outcomes, in turn, can influence specific indicators of financial performance (Becker & Huselid, 1998a; Boswell & Boudreau, 2001; Rogers & Wright, 1998; Wright & Gardner, 2002).

Research on best practices and HRM bundles is considered to fall within the realm of strategic HRM primarily because on the emphasis on predicting firm financial performance. That is, for some North American researchers, strategic HRM research is defined primarily by the outcome of interest – firm performance. Next we consider strategic HRM research that puts more emphasis on creating alignment between the HRM system and a firm's particular strategic imperatives.

Strategic contingencies

The emergence of the strategic contingencies perspective in HRM research can be traced to early efforts to bridge the fields of strategic management (also referred to as business policy) and human resource management. The earliest works addressed the question of whether the effectiveness of specific HRM practices might depend on the strategic objectives of the firm that adopted the practice (e.g., Miles & Snow, 1984; Schuler & Jackson, 1987).

Strategic contingency theory assumes that managers adopt strategies to compete in the specific environments they face (Lundy & Cowling, 1996). Two of the most well-known typologies for describing the alternative strategies available to firms are the defender–reactor–analyser–prospector typology proposed by Miles and Snow (1984) and the competitive strategies identified by Porter (1980). Following the logic of strategic contingency theory, the choice of human resource practices can be understood as a process of matching HRM practices to the strategies pursued by the organisation (Lundy & Cowling, 1996). For example, prospectors may look externally for people in order to bring in the cutting edge competencies needed for technological innovation. In contrast, an organisation pursuing a reactor strategy may value knowledge about the organisation's own internal processes over technological advances (Hambrick, 2003).

Drawing on Porter's work, Jackson et al. (1989) tested and found support for several hypotheses that specified the HRM practices that should be found in firms pursuing strategies that emphasised cost reduction, quality improvement, or innovation (see also Cappelli & Crocker-Hefter, 1996). Although the authors did not empirically test whether the use of strategically aligned HRM practices was more effective, their logic presumed that the HRM practices found in firms had evolved to fit the firms' strategies. More recently, this line of reasoning has evolved into the contingent configurational perspective. Scholars adopting the contingent configuration perspective focus on empirically examining the conditions under which various types of HRM systems are most valuable for achieving specific outcomes. In essence, the contingent configurational perspective embraces both a systems view and a contingency view. This complex approach attends to two issues: (1) the extent to which value is derived by having HRM practices that are aligned with each other (referred to as internal or horizontal alignment), and (2) the extent to which value is derived by having HRM practices should that are aligned with relevant contingencies (referred to as external or vertical alignment).

Theoretical Underpinnings

Throughout the many studies that comprise the body of research referred to as strategic HRM, one finds that a variety of theoretical arguments have been used to develop a supporting logic for the hypothesised effects (Jackson & Schuler, 2002; Jackson et al., 2006).

Human capital theory

Grounded in economics, human capital theory provides a partial explanation for the choices firms make in managing human resources. The crux of this theory is that people are of value to the organisation to the extent they make it productive (Becker, 1964; Becker & Huselid, 1998a; Lepak et al., 1999). Thus, organisations make decisions about investing in people just as they make decisions about investing in machinery, viewing them as a form of capital. Costs related to training, retraining, motivating and monitoring the organisation are viewed as investments in the human capital of the firm, just as maintenance of machinery would constitute an investment in the capital of the firm (Flamholtz & Lacey, 1981; Wright et al., 1994; Wright et al., 2001). Efforts to develop HRM metrics that establish the value of investments in HRM practices are firmly grounded in the logic of human capital theory.

Resource-based view

The resource-based view of the firm emphasises the need for resources as being primary in the determination of policies and procedures (Wernerfelt, 1984). Organisations are viewed as being able to succeed by gaining and retaining control over scarce, valuable, and inimitable resources (Barney, 1990; Porter, 1980). The application of this theory to human resource management has led to an array of new insights for understanding how effective organisations manage their employees (Gupta & Govindarajan, 2001).

Within the organisation, the HRM department can be viewed as controlling scarce resources to the extent that it controls access to the skills and motivation necessary for the achievement of strategic goals (Lepak & Snell, 2003). On a broader level, firms gain competitive advantage by using HRM practices – for example, an appealing remuneration scheme – to lure and retain top talent (Gomez-Mejia & Balkin, 1992). These competitive advantages are sustained through continued training, support of organisational culture, selection processes and other HRM practices.

The resource-based view has been invoked as the logic for explaining why coherent HRM systems lead to sustained competitive advantage: whereas it may be easy for competitors to copy or imitate any single HRM practice, it should be more difficult to copy an entire system of aligned practices (Lado & Wilson, 1994; Wright et al., 1994). Furthermore, even if competitors are able to copy an entire HRM system, they may find that the system is not as effective because it is not aligned with the organisation's specific strategy or other elements of its broader context.

Behavioural perspective

Grounded in role theory, the behavioural perspective focuses on the interdependent role behaviours that serve as building blocks for an organisational system. Schuler and Jackson (1987) used role theory to link HRM practice with the competitive strategies of organisations (Porter, 1980). They argued that different strategies require different role behaviours of the employees and thus require different human resource practices. Therefore, human resource management is effective when the expectations which it communicates internally and the ways in which it evaluates performance are congruent with the system's behavioural requirements (Fredericksen, 1986).

Recently, the behavioural perspective has been expanded into a newer area of research that examines the effects of so-called 'network building' HRM practices. There are many potential avenues by which HRM practices and systems can influence the pattern of social relationships and interactions among co-workers. For example, incentive systems and performance management practices can induce individuals to attend to the performance of their co-worker, but the effectiveness of such inducements may depend on the structure of social relationships among interdependent actors. Focusing on top management teams, Collins and Clark (2003) showed that several HRM practices seemed to improve firm performance by encouraging executives to build their internal and external social networks, which they could then leverage to improve their firm's financial bottom line. In other recent examples, Jackson and her colleagues have extended the behavioural perspective to describe how HRM practices might be used to encourage behaviours needed for knowledge-based competition (Jackson et al., 2003; Jackson et al., 2006). As noted by Subramaniam and Youndt (2005, p.459), 'unless individual knowledge is networked, shared, and channelled through relationships, it provides little benefit to organisations in terms of innovative capabilities'. Understanding how HRM practices and systems impact and combine with the existing social capital of organisations appears to be a rapidly emerging area of interest for North American strategic HRM scholarship.

Models of causal processes

Having established that HRM systems can influence the attainment of strategic objectives, North American researchers have begun to investigate the processes through which HRM practices and systems influence relevant outcomes. Included in this growing body of research are studies that consider the role of social exchange processes, employee attributions, and climate perceptions.

Social exchange Social exchange theorists (e.g. Gouldner, 1960) examine the exchanges that occur between employers and employees and the perceptions of reciprocity that are formed based on those exchanges. The norm of reciprocity suggests that employees feel obligated to respond equitably to treatments from others (including one's employer). HRM systems can be viewed as providing inducements that encourage employees to make valued contributions that are needed to realise a competitive advantage. From the perspective of social exchange theory, understanding the quality and type of exchange between the employer and employee is key to understanding employee performance. Two prominent streams of strategic HRM research on social exchanges consider employees' perceived organisational support and their psychological contract.

Wayne et al. (1997) argued that 'employees seek a balance in their exchange relationships with organisations by having attitudes and behaviours commensurate with the degree of employer commitment to them as individuals' (p. 83). In an empirical investigation Wayne et al. (1997) demonstrated that HRM practices that were developmental in nature were positively related to perceived organisational support. Perceptions of organisational support, in turn, were positively associated with affective organisational commitment and constructive suggestions (Eisenberger et al., 1990) as well as citizenship behaviours (Wayne et al., 1997), attendance (Eisenberger et al., 1990), and intentions to remain with one's current employer (Guzzo et al., 1994).

The process perspective also is used to explain the role of HRM systems in shaping employee's psychological contracts. As noted by Rousseau (1995), psychological contracts are 'individual beliefs, shaped by the organization, regarding terms of an exchange agreement between individuals and their organization' (p. 9). HRM practices are important because they shape these expectations and also influence judgments about whether or not these expectations have been met.

Attributions Attribution theory provides additional insights into the process through which HRM systems operate to influence employee behaviours. As noted by Nishii et al. (2008), employees make attributions about the extent of control their organisation maintains in implementing HRM policies. External attributions are made when events and outcomes are viewed as beyond the control of management, while internal attributions are made when events and outcomes are viewed as within the control of management. According to this attribution perspective, internal (rather than external) attributions are expected to have stronger influence on employee attitudes and behaviour. A key reason for this difference is that internal attributions reflect employees' beliefs about the motivations of their managers – and such motivations are something that employees interpret and respond to.

If an employee perceives that the reason for their company's HRM policies and practices is because it values the contribution of its employees, the employee may reciprocate by engaging in positive employee behaviours and attitudes. Conversely, when internal attributions for HRM policies and practices used are more negative – for example, the HRM practices are viewed as attempts to exploit the workforce – employees are likely to respond in a dramatically different and potentially negative manner. In an empirical investigation of employees of a large supermarket chain, Nishii and colleagues (2008) found that negative attributions about HRM practices were related to lower employee satisfaction, while positive attributions were associated with both affective commitment and employee satisfaction.

Climate An additional process explanation for how HRM systems operate is that HRM systems shape the atmosphere or 'climate' in which people work. An effective HRM system creates a setting in which employees' behaviours are directed toward achieving strategic targets (e.g. safety, customer service, etc.). The organisational climate reflects employees' collective views of what behaviours are expected and rewarded (e.g., Bowen & Ostroff, 2004).

An Integrative Framework: Contextualised and Dynamic

Suppose we accept the proposition that an HRM system that is effective in one context might be quite ineffective in another context. If that proposition is true, then one challenge that scholars face is how to explain and accurately predict which approaches are most suitable for which contexts. By any standard, the field of strategic HRM is still in its infancy. Nevertheless, there is an emerging consensus regarding the need to understand the interplay between human resource management systems and the broader context in which these systems are used. Because the internal and external environments are dynamic, the process of managing human resources also must be dynamic. Success requires meeting the present demands of multiple stakeholders while also anticipating their future

Source: Adapted from S. E. Jackson, R. S. Schuler and S. Werner, *Managing Human Resources*, 11th edn. Mason, OH: Cengage, 2012. Used with permission.

Figure 19.2   Contextualised, dynamic framework for strategic HRM

needs. Our interpretation of these essential elements of the emerging field of strategic HRM is illustrated in Figure 19.2.

CURRENT CONCERNS AND FUTURE DIRECTIONS

To date, scholars of strategic HRM have focused on trying to answer the design question, that is, what comprises the best HRM system in a given context? Looking ahead, it seems likely that the focus of academic work in the field of strategic HRM will evolve away from its current search for effective HRM system designs and toward understanding the processes through which HRM systems evolve and change in concert with their dynamic contexts. Also needed in the future is scholarship that more fully considers outcomes that reflect the varied concerns of multiple stakeholders. In addition to seeing scholarship aimed at gaining new insights into how HRM systems evolve in the context of environmental complexity, we expect North American HRM experts to also look for solutions to several immediate, more focused issues. In the remainder of this chapter, we consider a few current concerns that are attracting the attention of North American practitioners and scholars alike. As these examples illustrate, the central challenge to be addressed can often be traced to the conflicting interests of employers and employees.

Employee Privacy

Simply stated, the right to privacy is the right to keep information about ourselves to ourselves. Early in US history, Henry Ford faced no resistance from federal or local governments when he sent social workers to the homes of employees to investigate their personal habits and family finances. Since then, legislation that addresses employee privacy rights has been enacted in both Canada and the United States.

Access to electronic communications
The United States and Canada both have federal privacy laws that give individuals the right to verify information collected about them and used by federal agencies (not private employers) in employment decisions. What many North American employees don't understand is that employers have substantial rights, too. For example, most electronic documents can be considered business records, which employers may be obligated to preserve (Roberts, 2007; Smith, 2007). Personal e-mails sent on a company computer; e-mail messages typed on a company computer but never sent; personal web searches conducted on a company computer; personal instant or text messages sent to friends from a company device and text entered into a word-processing document that the employee later deleted all can be treated as business records (Zeidner, 2007).

Access to medical information
In addition to electronic communications, another privacy issue of concern is employer access to medical information (Eddy et al., 1999; Lane, 2004; Saton & Network, 2000). In the United States (but not in Canada, where healthcare is a service provided by the government), employer-provided health insurance is the norm. In recent years, health insurance costs have

grown so dramatically that many employers feel pressure to do whatever is necessary to reduce them. One way to lower costs is to employ people who make little use of healthcare services, because insurance for such employees is less expensive. Information about lifestyles and genetic makeup could help an employer determine who is likely to need extensive and expensive health care.

Managing Workplace Diversity

During the past decade, two types of workplace diversity have been of particular concern to North American employers: demographic diversity within the domestic workforce and international diversity within the increasing global operations of large firms. Left to work out their differences on their own, diverse teams and work units often experience a variety of negative consequences, including interpersonal conflict and dissatisfaction. On the other hand, when appropriately leveraged, diversity can also lead to beneficial outcomes such as improved decisions and greater creativity (Jackson & Joshi, 2010; Jackson et al., 2003; Van Knippenberger & Schippers, 2007).

Diversity training
Training initiatives are among the most common HRM initiatives used to address the issue of workplace diversity. Domestic diversity training programmes often seek to raise cultural awareness among participants. Typically, these programmes are designed to teach the participants about how their own culture differs from the cultures of other employees with whom they work. In this context, the term culture is used to refer very broadly to the social group to which a person belongs. Ethnic background is one aspect of culture, but so are one's age, socioeconomic status, religion, and so on. (For a review of research on cross-cultural training, see Bhawuk & Brislin, 2000).

Diversity awareness training   Diversity awareness training often seeks to help people understand how the stereotypes they hold about various groups can influence the way they treat people – often in subtle ways that they may not be conscious of. A typical diversity awareness programme is conducted over the course of one or two days. The hope is that raising awareness about differences will lead to attitudinal and behaviour changes. Based on a review of 20 studies conducted in organisational settings, Kulik and Roberson (2008) concluded that diversity awareness training results in sustained improvements in overall attitudes toward diversity. However, attitudes toward specific demographic groups (e.g. defined by ethnicity, gender, age) appear to be more resistant to change and may even be at risk of a backlash effect (e.g. Alderfer, 1992).

Diversity skills training   Another approach to diversity training focuses more specifically on developing the behavioural competencies needed to work effectively in organisations characterised by diversity. With diversity skills training, the objective is to change behaviours that are needed to work effectively with dissimilar others. Among the skills identified as relevant for working in diverse teams are communications, conflict management, behaving in ways that reflect sensitivity to cultural differences, as well as other skills that are generally useful for teamwork.

Improving diversity climate
Diversity climate refers to employees' perceptions of the degree to which all members of the organisation are integrated into the social life of the organisation practices (Mor Barak et al., 1998). Diversity climate perceptions have been shown to predict behavioural outcomes such as attendance (Avery et al., 2007) and turnover (McKay et al., 2007). Given that training alone does not achieve behavioural change, other HRM practices may also need to change before employees notice a difference in the organisation's diversity climate (Rynes & Rosen, 1995).

Evaluating diversity initiatives
As is true for most HRM initiatives, North American employers believe that programmes aimed at effectively managing workplace diversity are justifiable in part because they promise to reduce labour costs and improve productivity. In a comprehensive study of diversity management practices, Kalev et al. (2006) sought to determine whether the use of diversity initiatives improves organisational outcomes such as diversity among top executives or firm performance. Based on data from 708 private sector establishments, the authors concluded that diversity practices aimed at reducing managerial bias (e.g. diversity training) were the least effective in increasing the proportion of white women and black men and women. Practices aimed at reducing social isolation (e.g. mentoring) were modestly effective. Practices aimed at increasing accountability for meeting diversity goals were the most effective.

Performance Management

During the past decade, North American HRM professionals have adopted the term performance management to refer a set of HRM practices that includes performance measurement, performance feedback and performance-based rewards. While there are many current trends that might be discussed here, we focus on two specific issues that characterise the North American perspective, namely the widespread adoption of multi-rater performance evaluation and feedback and performance-based pay.

Multi-rater (360-degree) performance evaluation and feedback

Many North American companies assume that supervisors know more than anyone else about how well subordinates perform their jobs, so they give supervisors all the responsibility for measuring employee performance and providing feedback. Supervisors produce more reliable and useful performance judgments than other sources, perhaps because they have knowledge about several aspects of employees' performance (Smither et al., 2005; Viswesvaran & Schmidt, 1996). Nevertheless, increasingly, North American employers understand the need to ensure that a variety of perspectives are considered when making employment decisions (Lawler, 1992; Walker & Smither, 1999).

Performance-based pay

Employers have always recognised the importance of rewarding employees for good performance. For the past several decades, most North American employers relied on merit pay to achieve this objective. According to one survey, 80 per cent of US employers offer performance-based bonuses. For non-executive white-collar employees, variable pay accounts for more that 11 per cent of employees' total compensation (White, 2006). For non-executive employees, performance-based pay is typically tied to individual performance, but for executives, performance of their business unit or the organisation as a whole are the most important performance indicators.

Following the financial crisis of 2008, many people expressed substantial ethical concerns about the aggressive use of performance-based pay within the financial services industry. But ethical concerns about the use of performance-based pay are not really new. Because of its powerful motivating ability, performance-based pay is recognised as a potential explanation for unethical behaviour by employees in a variety of jobs and industries. Poorly designed pay practices can lead to employee behaviours that maximise the performance being measured, yet are detrimental to the interests of the employer and/or customers and/or the broader society.

Widespread use of performance-based pay has also contributed to increasing pay disparities between high-level executives and rank-and-file employees. CEO pay levels in the United States are widely perceived as unfair (Makri & Gomez-Mejia, 2007). CEOs of US companies are paid more than 400 times what their employees earn, on average (Lublin, 2007).

While public concern about unfair CEO pay is the norm, HRM professionals have generally done little to address this issue, and HRM scholars
have done little to examine the consequences of these perceived inequities.

Looking ahead, we expect the issue of performance management to continue to attract attention within North America. Concerns over the role
that some HRM practices have perhaps played in creating greater income
disparities and tempting employees to engage in unethical behaviour will
likely challenge HRM experts to consider new approaches to monitoring
and rewarding employee performance. Furthermore, to the extent that
societal unease with corporate executives persists after current economic
conditions have moderated, it is likely that HRM scholars and practitioners will be called upon to pay greater attention to the HRM systems used
to manage high-level executives in particular.

International HRM Issues

Within North America, the growth of international HRM (IHRM)
has been a significant development during the past 30 years (Briscoe
et al., 2009). Due to economic globalisation, many firms compete on a
worldwide basis rather than on the regional basis that predominated
previously (Gupta & Govindarajan, 2001). For North American firms,
human resource management in this new international context requires
developing an understanding of the issues facing multinational enterprises
(MNEs).

Whereas managing expatriates had been the dominant and most active
area of IHRM practice and scholarship in North American during the
1980s and into the 1990s, it is now just one of many topics attracting
attention. As the pace of globalisation quickened, and as the costs associated with the growing numbers of expatriates came under scrutiny,
North American firms reduced their reliance on expatriates. Like other
global firms, they turned to third-country and host-country nationals to
staff both non-managerial and managerial positions. In the twenty-first
century, North American MNEs are fully engaged in managing a global
workforce comprised of all employees, at all levels and in all locations of
the firm's international operations (Tarique et al., 2006).

Global talent management
As North American firms first began expanding their international operations, they often assumed that the HRM practices of the parent country
could and would be adopted worldwide. Consistent with this perspective,
they staffed senior management positions in their foreign operations with
expatriates from the United States, creating a senior management cadre

for international locations. By staffing foreign operations with expatriates, the North American parent sought to exercise control over their foreign operations (Tarique & Caligiuri, 2004).

Increasingly, however, the efforts of North American international HRM staff have been redirected toward managing local-nationals, global staffing, integration of worldwide HRM policies, management development, and other topics considered to be of strategic value (Tarique & Schuler, 2010). Recognising that there is now an extensive body of knowledge that should be mastered by HRM professionals with international responsibilities, the Society for Human Resource Management's HRM Certification Institute recently introduced specialised testing and certification for the title of Global Human Resource Professional (GPHR).

Managing cross-border alliances
For most North American firms, the process of internationalising involved expanding slowly from a domestic base into progressively distant areas. But for other North American firms, establishing cross-border alliances has been the preferred means for expanding internationally. Ideally, this approach enables a firm to learn how to operate in a new location prior to investing heavily to establish a presence in that location (Luo, 2002). Two common types of cross-border alliances are international mergers and acquisitions and international joint ventures. While international mergers and acquisitions have the tendency to reduce the number of companies in a market, international joint ventures typically increase the number of companies in a market. In both cases, costs can be reduced, profits enhanced, speed of market entry increased and risks managed.

Research suggests that many of the problems that arise in managing cross-border alliances are due to ineffective human resource management (Schuler et al., 2004). Research intended to improve our understanding of how to manage cross-border alliances is still in its infancy. Nevertheless, there is a growing volume of scholarship devoted to developing testable, theoretically grounded frameworks that can serve as guides to new empirical research while also providing new insights to practising HRM professionals (Inkpen & Beamish, 1997).

CONCLUSION

Human resource management in North America is evolving rapidly as firms focus on the new strategic challenges of the twenty-first century.

Increasingly, HRM issues are recognised as integral elements in strategic planning and strategy implementation – for domestic firms as well as MNEs. With the objective of providing an overview of HRM in North America, we have briefly commented on a few major developments, including the importance of analysing and interpreting the impact of context, responding to the concerns of multiple stakeholders for HRM, the use of empirical data and theoretical frameworks that contribute to advances in HRM practice and scholarship, several current issues that provide opportunities for HRM practitioners and scholars to collaborate in future research, and the challenges of international HRM.

As we write this chapter we see the dynamics of the global economy and global labour markets becoming increasing important forces that shape human resource management in North America. These dynamics appear so powerful that attempting to draw a distinction between domestic and international HRM may become an obsolete exercise. Almost all large North American firms have operations and/or strategic partners located in other countries. To the extent that large firms set the norms and standards for workforce management, small and medium-sized firms also are influenced by the increasing globalisation of economic activity within North America. Thus, for HRM practitioners and scholars alike, the pressing challenge now is to develop contextualised and dynamic frameworks for understanding and effectively managing human resources in organisations that span the globe and compete in an increasingly integrated economic system.

NOTES

1. A geographic definition of North America would include the countries of Central America, also. The countries of Central America, however, share more cultural similarities with South American countries than they do with the United States and Canada, and thus often are included within a cultural grouping referred to as Latin America. For discussion of HRM in Latin America, see Elvira and Davila (Elvira, M., & Davila, A. 2005. Emergent directions for human resource management research in Latin America. *International Journal of Human Resource Management*, **16**: 2265–2282.) and other chapters in this volume.
2. Generally, North American research on strategic HRM has not draw a sharp theoretical or measurement distinction between organisations' formal HRM policies and the specific ways in which those policies are implemented by managers. Here we use the term HRM practices as a general term that can refer to formal policies as well as the actual practices found in organisations, which reflects the use of this term in the literature we discuss in this section.

REFERENCES

Alderfer, C. P. 1992. Changing race relations embedded in organizations: report on a long-term project with the XYZ corporation. In S. E. Jackson (ed.), *Diversity in the Workplace: Human Resource Initiatives*. New York: Guilford Press, pp. 138–166.

Arthur, J. 1994. Effects of human resource systems on manufacturing performance and turnover. *Academy of Management Journal*, 4: 670–687.

Avery, D. R., McKay, P. F., Wilson, D. C. & Tonidandel, S. 2007. Unequal attendance: the relationships between race, organizational diversity cues, and absenteeism. *Personnel Psychology*, 60: 875–902.

Barney, J. B. 1990. Firm resources and sustained competitive advantage. *Journal of Management*, 17: 99–120.

Barney, J. B. & Wright, P. 1998. On becoming a strategic partner. The role of human resources in gaining competitive advantage. *Human Resource Management*, 37: 31–46.

Batt, R. 2002. Managing customer services: human resource practices, quit rates, and sales growth. *Academy of Management Journal*, 45: 587–597.

Becker, B. & Gerhart, B. 1996. The impact of human resource management on organizational performance: progress and prospects. *Academy of Management Journal*, 39: 779–801.

Becker, B. & Huselid, M. 1998a. High performance work systems and firm performance: a synthesis of research and managerial implications. *Research in Personnel and Human Resource Management*, 16: 53–101.

Becker, B., Huselid, M. & Ulrich, D. 2001. *The HR Scorecard: Linking People, Strategy, and Performance.* Boston: Harvard Business School Press.

Becker, B. E. & Huselid, M. A. 1998b. High performance work systems and firm perform-ance: a synthesis of research and managerial implications. In G. Ferris (ed.), *Research in Personnel and Human Resources Management*. Greenwich, CT: JAI Press.

Becker, G. S. 1964. *Human Capital.* New York: National Bureau of Economic Research.

Bhawuk, D. P. & Brislin, R. W. 2000. Cross-cultural training: a review. *Applied Psychology: An International Review*, 49: 162–191.

Boswell, W. R. & Boudreau, J. W. 2001. How leading companies create, measure and achieve strategic results through 'line of sight'. *Management Decision*, 39: 851–859.

Boudreau, J. W. 2003. Strategic knowledge measurement and management. In S. E. Jackson, M. A. Hitt & A. S. DeNisi (eds), *Managing Knowledge for Sustained Competitive Advantage*. San Francisco: Jossey-Bass, pp. 360–398.

Boudreau, J. W. & Ramstad, P. M. 1999. Human resource metrics: can measures be strate-gic? *Research in Personnel and Human Resources Management*, 4: 75–98.

Bowen, E. & Ostroff, C. 2004. Understanding HRM-firm performance linkages: the role of the 'strength' of the HRM system. *Academy of Management Review*, 29: 203–221.

Briscoe, D. R., Schuler, R. S. & Claus, L. 2009. *International Human Resource Management*, 3rd edn. London: Routledge.

Cappelli, P. & Crocker-Hefter, A. 1996. Distinctive human resources are firms' core compe-tencies. *Organizational Dynamics*, 24(3): 6–22.

Cascio, W. F. 2000. *Costing Human Resources.* Mason, OH: South-Western College.

Colakoglu, S., Lepak, D. P. & Hong, Y. 2006. Measuring HRM effectiveness: consider-ing multiple stakeholders in a global context. *Human Resource Management Review*, 16: 209–218.

Collins, C. J. & Clark, K. D. 2003. Strategic human resource practices, top management team social networks, and firm performance: the role of human resource practices in creat-ing organizational competitive advantage. *Academy of Management Journal*, 46: 740–751.

Delery, J. E. 1998. Issues of fit in strategic human resource management: implications for research. *Human Resource Management Review*, 8: 289–309.

Dickmann, M. & Muller-Camen, M. 2006. A typology of international human resource man-agement strategies and processes. *International Human Resource Management Journal*, 17: 580–601.

Eddy, E., Stone, D. & Stone-Romero, E. 1999. The effects of information management policies on reactions to human resource information systems: an integration of privacy and procedural justice perspectives. *Personnel Psychology*, **52**: 335–358.

Eisenberger, R., Fasolo, P. & Davis-LaMastro, V. 1990. Perceived organizational support and employee diligence, commitment, and innovation. *Journal of Applied Psychology*, **75**: 51–59.

Elkins, T. J. 2007. New HR challenges in the dynamic environment of legal compliance. In S. Werner (ed.), *Managing Human Resources in North America*. London: Routledge.

Elvira, M. & Davila, A. 2005. Emergent directions for human resource management research in Latin America. *International Journal of Human Resource Management*, **16**: 2265–2282.

Fenton-O'Creevy, M., Gooderham, P. & Nordhaug, O. 2008. Human resource management in the US subsidiaries in Europe and Australia: centralization or autonomy? *Journal of International Business Studies*, **39**: 151–167.

Fitz-enz, J. 2000. *The ROI of Human Capital*. New York: Amacom.

Flamholtz, E. G. & Lacey, J. M. 1981. *Personnel Management, Human Capital Theory and Human Resource Accounting*. Los Angeles: Institute of Industrial Relations, University of California.

Fredericksen, N. 1986. Toward a broader conception of human intelligence. *American Psychologist*, **41**: 445–452.

Gardey, G. S., Alcazar, F. M. & Fernandez, P. M. R. 2004. Strategic human resource management: integrating the universalistic, contingent, configurational and contextual perspectives. *International Journal of Human Resource Management*, **16**: 633–659.

Gerhart, B. & Milkovich, G. T. 1990. Organizational differences in managerial compensation and financial performance. *Academy of Management Journal*, **33**: 663–691.

Gomez-Mejia, L. & Balkin, D. B. 1992. *Compensation, Organizational Strategy, and Firm Performance*. Cincinnati: South-Western.

Gouldner, A. W. 1960. The norm of reciprocity. *American Sociological Review*, **25**: 161–178.

Gupta, A. & Govindarajan, V. 2001. Converting global presence into global competitive advantage. *Academy of Management Executive*, **15**: 45–58.

Guthrie, J. 2001. High-involvement work practices, turnover, and productivity: evidence from New Zealand. *Academy of Management Journal*, **44**(1): 180–190.

Guzzo, R. A., Noonan, K. A. & Elron, E. 1994. Expatriate managers and the psychological contract. *Journal of Applied Psychology*, **79**: 617–626.

Hall, P. & Soskice, D. 2001. *Varieties of Capitalism: the Institutional Foundations of Comparative Advantage*. New York: Oxford University Press.

Hambrick, D. C. 2003. On the staying power of defenders, analyzers and prospectors. *Academy of Management Executive*, 17: 115–118.

Higgs, A. C., Papper, E. M. & Carr, L. S. 2000. Integrating selection with other organizational processes and systems. In J.F. Kehoe (ed.), *Managing Selection in Changing Organizations*. San Francisco: Jossey-Bass.

Huselid, M. A. 1995. The impact of human resource management practices on turnover, productivity, and corporate financial performance. *Academy of Management Journal*, **38**: 635–672.

Huselid, M. A., Jackson, S. E. & Schuler, R. S. 1997. Technical and strategic human resource management effectiveness as determinants of firm performance. *Academy of Management Journal*, **40**: 171–188.

Hyland, M. A. & Jackson, S. E. 2006. A multiple stakeholder perspective: implications for measuring work–family outcomes. In M. Pitt-Catsouphes, E. E. Kossek & S. Sweet (eds), *The Work and Family Handbook: Multi-disciplinary Perspectives and Approaches*. Mahwah, NJ: Lawrence Erlbaum, pp. 527–549.

Ichniowski, C., Kochan, T., Levine, D., Olson, C. & Strauss, G. 1996. What works at work: overview and assessment. *Industrial Relations*, **35**(3): 299–333.

Ichniowski, C., Shaw, K. & Prennushi, G. 1997. The effects of human resource management practices on productivity: a study of steel finishing lines. *The American Economic Review*, **87**: 291–314.

Inkpen, A. & Beamish, P. 1997. Knowledge, bargaining power and the instability of international joint ventures. *Academy of Management Review*, **22**: 177–202.

Jackson, S. E., Chuang, J., Harden, E. & Jiang, Y. 2006. Toward developing human resource management systems for knowledge-intensive teamwork. In J. Martocchio (ed.), *Research in Personnel and Human Resource Management*, Vol. 25. Oxford: Elsevier, pp. 27–70.

Jackson, S. E., Hitt, M. A. & DeNisi, A. S. 2003. *Managing Knowledge for Sustained Competitive Advantage*. San Francisco, CA: Jossey-Bass.

Jackson, S. E. & Joshi, A. 2010. Work team diversity. In S. Zedeck (ed.), *APA Handbook of Industrial and Organizational Psychology*, Vol. II. Washington, DC: APA.

Jackson, S. E. Joshi, A. & Erhardt, N. L. 2003. Recent research on team and organizational diversity: SWOT Analysis and Implications. *Journal of Management*, **29**: 801–830.

Jackson, S. E. & Schuler, R. S. 1990. Human resource planning: challenges for industrial/organizational psychologists. *American Psychologist*, **45**: 223–239.

Jackson, S. E. & Schuler, R. S. 1995. Understanding human resource management in the context of organizations and their environments. *Annual Review of Psychology*, **46**: 237–264.

Jackson, S. E. & Schuler, R. S. 2002. Managing individual performance: an individual perspective. In S. Sonnentag (ed.), *Psychological Management of Individual Performance*. New York: John Wiley and Sons, pp. 371–390.

Jackson, S. E., Schuler, R. S. & Rivero, J. C. 1989. Organization characteristics as predictors of personnel practices. *Personnel Psychology*, **42**: 727–786.

Jackson, S. E., Schuler, R. S. & Werner, S. 2012. *Managing Human Resources*, 11th edn. Mason, OH: Cengage.

Kalev, A., Dobbin, F. & Kelly, E. 2006. Best practices or best guesses? Assessing the efficacy of corporate affirmative action and diversity policies. *American Sociological Review*, **71**: 589–617.

Kanter, R. M. 1983. Frontiers for strategic human resource management. *Human Resource Management*, **22**: 85–92.

Kanter, R. M. 1994. Change in the global economy: an interview with Rosabeth Moss Kanter. *European Management Journal*, **12**: 19.

Kaplan, R. S. & Norton, D. P. 1996. *Translating Strategy into Action: The Balanced Scorecard*. Boston, MA: Harvard Business School Press.

Kulik, C. T. & Roberson, L. 2008. Diversity initiative effectiveness: what organizations can (and cannot) expect from diversity recruitment, diversity training, and formal mentoring programs. In A. P. Brief (ed.), *Diversity at Work*. Cambridge: Cambridge University Press, pp. 265–317.

Lado, A. A. & Wilson, M. C. 1994. Human resource systems and sustained competitive advantage: a competency-based perspective. *Academy of Management Review*, **19**: 699–727.

Lane, F. S. 2004. *The Naked Employee*. New York: AMACOM.

Lawler, E. E. 1992. *The Ultimate Advantage: Creating the High Involvement Organization*. San Francisco, CA: Jossey-Bass.

Lawler, E. E., Mohrman, S. A. & Ledford, G. E. 1992. *Employee Involvement in America: An Assessment of Practices and Results*. San Francisco, CA: Jossey-Bass.

Lengnick-Hall, C. A. 1988. Strategic human resource management: a review of the literature and proposed typology. *Academy of Management Review*, **13**: 454–470.

Lepak, D. & Snell, S. 1999. The human resource architecture: toward a theory of human capital allocation and development. *Academy of Management Review*, **24**: 31–48.

Lepak, D. P. 2009. The John Lovett Memorial Lecture. Advances in HR systems and their impact on performance. Presented at the University of Limerick, Ireland.

Lepak, D. P. & Snell, S. A. 2003. Managing the human resource architecture for knowledge-based competition. In S. E. Jackson, M. A. Hitt & A. S. DeNisi (eds), *Managing Knowledge for Sustained Competitive Advantage*. San Francisco, CA: Jossey-Bass, pp. 127–154.

Lublin, J. S. 2007. The pace of pay gains, a survey overview. *The Wall Street Journal*, R1.

Lundy, O. & Cowling, A. 1996. *Strategic Human Resource Management*. New York: Basic Books.

Luo, Y. 2002. Capability exploitation and building in a foreign market: implications for multinational enterprise. *Organizational Science*, **13**: 48–63.

MacDuffie, J. 1995. Human resource bundles and manufacturing performance: flexible production systems in the world auto industry. *Industrial & Labor Relations Review*, **48**(2): 197–221.

Macey, W. H. & Schneider, B. 2008. The meaning of employee engagement. *Industrial and Organizational Psychology*, **1**: 3–30.

Makri, M. & Gomez-Mejia, L. R. 2007. *Executive Compensation: Something Old, Something New, Managing Human Resources in North America: Current Issues and Perspectives.* London: Routledge.

McKay, P. F., Avery, D. R., Tonidandel, S., Morris, M. A., Hernandez, M. & Hebl, M. R. 2007. Racial differences in employee retention: are diversity climate perceptions the key? *Personnel Psychology*, **60**: 35–62.

McMahan, G. C., Virick, M. & Wright, P. M. 1999 Alternative theoretical perspectives for strategic human resource management revisited: progress, problems and prospects. *Research in Personnel and Human Resources Management*, **4**: 99–122.

Miles, R. E. & Snow, C. C. 1984. Designing strategic human resource systems. *Organization Dynamics*, **16**: 36–52.

Mor Barak, M. E., Cherin, D. A. & Berkman, S. 1998. Organizational and personal dimensions of diversity climate: ethnic and gender differences in employee perceptions. *Journal of Applied Behavioral Sciences*, **31**: 82–104.

Nishii, L. H., Lepak, D. P. & Schneider, B. 2008. Employee attributions of the 'why' of HR practices: their effects on employee attitudes and behaviors, and customer satisfaction. *Personnel Psychology*, **61**: 503–545.

Parry, E., Dickmann, M. & Morley, M. 2008. North American MNCs and their HR policies in liberal and coordinated market economies. *International Journal of Human Resource Management*, **19**(11): 2024–2040.

Pfeffer, J. 1994. *Competitive Advantage Through People: Unleashing the Power of the Workforce.* Boston, MA: Harvard Business School Press.

Pfeffer, J. 1998. *The Human Equation.* Boston, MA: Harvard Business School Press.

Porter, M. E. 1980. *Competitive Strategy: Techniques for Analyzing Industries and Competitors.* New York: Free Press.

Porter, M. E. 1985. *Competitive Advantage.* New York: Free Press.

Roberts, B. 2007. Avoiding the perils of electronic data. *HR Magazine*, **27**: 72–77.

Rogers, E. W. & Wright, P. M. 1998. Measuring organizational performance in strategic human resource management research: problems, prospects, and performance information markets. *Human Resource Management Review*, **8**: 311–331.

Rousseau, D. M. 1995. *Psychological Contracts in Organizations: Understanding Written and Unwritten Agreements.* Thousand Oaks, CA: Sage Publications.

Rucci, A. J., Kirn, S. P., & Quinn, R. T. 1998. The employee–customer–profit chain at Sears. *Harvard Business Review*, **76**(1): 83–97.

Russell, J. S., Terborg, R. S. & Powers, M. L. 1985. Organizational performance and organizational level training and support. *Personnel Psychology*, **38**: 849–863.

Rynes, S. L. & Rosen, B. 1995. A field survey of factors affecting the adoption and perceived success of diversity training. *Personnel Psychology*, **48**: 247–270.

Sackett, P. R., Laczo, R. M. & Lippe, Z. P. 2003. Differential prediction and the use of multiple predictors: the omitted variables problem. *Journal of Applied Psychology*, **88**: 1046–1056.

Saton, D. & Network, W. 2000. *Workplace Privacy: Real Answers and Practical Solutions.* Toronto: Thompson.

Schippmann, J. S. 1999. *Strategic Job Modeling: Working at the Core of Integrated Human Resources.* Mahwah, NJ: Lawrence Erlbaum.

Schmidt, F. L., Hunter, J. E., MacKenzie, R. & Muldrow, T. 1979. The impact of valid selection procedures on workforce productivity. *Journal of Applied Psychology*, **64**: 627–670.

Schuler, R. S., & Jackson, S. 1989. Determinants of human resource priorities and implications for industrial relations. *Journal of Management*, **15**: 89–99.

Schuler, R. S. & Jackson, S. E. 1987. Linking competitive strategy with human resource management practices. *Academy of Management Executive*, **3**: 207–219.

Schuler, R. S. & Jackson, S. E. 1999. *Strategic Human Resource Management: A Reader*. London: Blackwell Publishing.

Schuler, R. S. & Jackson, S. E. 2007. *Strategic Human Resource Management: A Reader*, 2nd edn. London: Blackwell.

Schuler, R. S., Jackson, S. E. & Luo, Y. 2004. *Managing Human Resources in Cross-border Alliances*. London: Routledge.

Schuler, R. S., Jackson, S. E. & Storey, J. 2001. HRM and its link with strategic management. In J. Storey (ed.), *Human Resource Management: A Critical Text*. London: Thomson Learning, pp. 114–130.

Schuler, R. S. & MacMillan, I. C. 1984. Gaining competitive advantage through human resource management practices. *Human Resource Management*, **23**(3): 241–255.

Smith, A. 2007. Federal rules define duty to preserve work e-mails. *HR Magazine*, **27**: 36.

Smither, J. W., London, M. & Reilly, R. R. 2005. Does performance improve following multisource feedback? A theoretical model, meta-analysis, and review of empirical findings. *Personnel Psychology*, **58**: 33–66.

Snell, S. A., Youndt, M. A. & Wright, P. M. 1996. Establishing a framework for research in strategic human resource management: merging resource theory and organizational learning. *Research in Personnel and Human Resource Management*, **14**: 61–90.

Subramaniam, M. & Youndt, M. A. 2005. The influence of intellectual capital on the types of innovative capabilities. *Academy of Management Journal*, **48**: 450–463.

Tarique, I. & Caligiuri, P. 2004. Training and development of international staff. In A. W. Harzing & J. Van Ruysseveldt (eds), *International Human Resource Management*. Thousand Oaks, CA: Sage Publications.

Tarique, I. & Schuler, R. 2010. Global talent management: literature review, integrative framework, and suggestions for further research. *Journal of World Business*, **45**: 122–133.

Tarique, I., Schuler, R. & Gong, Y. 2006. A model of multinational enterprise subsidiary staffing composition. *International Journal of Human Resource Management*, **17**: 207–224.

Terpstra, D. E. & Rozell, E. J. 1993. The relationship of staffing practices to organizational level measures of performance. *Personnel Psychology*, **46**: 27–48.

Tsui, A. S. 1990. A multiple-constituency model of effectiveness: an empirical examination at the human resource subunit level. *Administrative Science Quarterly*, **35**: 458–483.

Ulrich, D. 1998. *Delivering Results: A New Mandate for Human Resource Professionals*. Boston, MA: Harvard Business School Press.

Van Knippenberger, D. & Schippers, M. C. 2007. Work group diversity. *Annual Review of Psychology*, **58**: 515–541.

Viswesvaran, C., Ones, D. S. & Schmidt, F. L. 1996. Comparative analysis of the reliability of job performance ratings. *Journal of Applied Psychology*, **81**: 557–574.

Walker, A. J. & Smither, J. 1999. A five-year study of upward feedback: what managers do with their results matters. *Personnel Psychology*, **52**: 393–423.

Wayne, S. J., Shore, L. M. & Liden, R. C. 1997. Perceived organizational support and leader-member exchange: a social exchange perspective. *Academy of Management Journal*, **40**: 82–111.

Wernerfelt, B. 1984. A resource-based view of the firm. *Strategic Management Journal*, **5**: 171–180.

White, E. 2006. Employer's increasingly favor bonuses to raises. *The Wall Street Journal*, Vol. (August 28): B3.

White, S. & Schneider, B. 2003. *Service Quality*. Mahwah, NJ: Lawrence Erlbaum.

Wright, P. M., Dunford, B. B. & Snell, S. A. 2001. Human resources and the resource-based view of the firm. *Journal of Management*, **27**: 701–721.

Wright, P. M. & Gardner, T. M. 2002. Theoretical and empirical challenges in studying the HR practice-firm performance relationship. In D. Holman, T. Wall, C. Cleff, P. Sparrow

& A. Howard (eds), *The New Workplace: A Guide to the Human Impact of Modern Working Practices.* Chichester: John Wiley and Sons.

Wright, P. M. & McMahan, G. C. 1992. Theoretical perspectives for strategic human resource management. *Journal of Management*, **18**: 295–320.

Wright, P. M., McMahan, G. C. & McWilliams, A. 1994. Human resources and sustained competitive advantage: a resource-based perspective. *International Journal of Human Resource Management*, **5**: 301–326.

Youndt, M. A., Snell, S. A., Dean, J. W. & Lepak, D. P. 1996. Human resource management, manufacturing strategy, and form performance. *Academy of Management Journal*, **39**: 836–866.

Zeidner, R. 2007. Employees don't 'get' electronic storage. *HR Magazine*, January: 36.

20 Latin American HRM models

Anabella Davila and Marta M. Elvira

Developing a Latin American model of human resources management (HRM) implies using novel theoretical approaches. Though HRM practices differ across country, organisation and industry lines in Latin America, evidence suggests that traditional models of management and organisation offer only partial explanations for HRM complexity in this region where contextual elements challenge the use of a single disciplinary approach. To understand HRM in Latin America's distinct environment of economic, political and social instability, interdisciplinary views are required. Such views would help account for key contextual elements such as the role of the enterprise as a social institution, the value of the individual within society, and the pragmatic character of governmental public policies.

Recent research, based on culturally sensitive frameworks and in-depth qualitative studies of firms in Latin America, highlights the explanatory value of stakeholder theory (Davila & Elvira, 2009). This theory allows examination of the impact of HRM systems on an organisation's multiple stakeholders, including those specific to particular societies. In this chapter we aim to extend stakeholder theory to understand how effective HRM systems meet the diverse demands of stakeholders in Latin America such as employees, unions and relevant community members.

Because in Latin America business organisations play a key role as social institutions (Elvira & Davila, 2005b), their environment includes stakeholders seeking social integration regardless of their legitimacy or power. HRM practices appear to perform best when including multiple stakeholders, both powerful and silent ones. Acknowledging a horizontal relationship organisation–stakeholder, instead of a hierarchical relationship of subordination, is a step toward a more comprehensive stakeholder theory of HRM (Davila & Elvira, 2009). From this perspective, HRM systems would be most effective when strengthening the horizontal relationship organisation–stakeholder that facilitates social inclusion of diverse Latin American groups.

To illustrate this theoretical approach we advance a framework based on analyses of Latin American stakeholders, their needs and demands. Recognising diverse stakeholders and weighting their demands should guide reflection on how HRM systems could be best designed and managed.

After reviewing existing literature, our analysis focuses on identifying both loud and silent stakeholders involved in business organisations in Latin America. We then discuss critical HRM issues that local and international researchers investigate in the region. Different weights apply in evaluating the salience and value of HRM by various stakeholders. Although some issues are viewed as important by either researchers or popular business media, they might be perceived as less relevant by other stakeholders. Our inductive approach in this chapter aims to identify the extension to which managers use HRM practices and resources to satisfy stakeholder's demands in Latin America.

STAKEHOLDER MANAGEMENT THEORY

Stakeholder theory is considered an alternative to the traditional input-output model (Donaldson & Preston, 1995) or to the shareholder model (Kaler, 2009) for managing organisations. It has been used to describe organisations and the various interests of internal or external corporate constituencies, as well as the specific connections between an organisation and salient individuals or groups of stakeholders relative to performance from a strategic viewpoint (Clarkson, 1995). Stakeholder theory has also served to interpret the purpose of a corporation regarding its moral obligations, with a strong emphasis on ethics and corporate social responsibility (CSR) (Clarkson, 1995; Donaldson & Preston, 1995; Freeman, 1984).

Several well-established frameworks of stakeholder theory exist (e.g. Clarkson, 1995; Donaldson & Preston, 1995; Fassin, 2009), with research addressing two central questions: (1) who key stakeholders are, and (2) how organisations interact with them.

To start, consider Freeman's classic definition: 'A stakeholder in an organisation is any group or individual who can affect or is affected by the achievement of the organisation's objectives' (1984: 46). In this view, a typical stakeholder model includes those groups that provide resources for the firm or those groups to whom the firm offers products or services, such as shareholders, suppliers, employees and clients. Other stakeholders include government institutions and the community in general (Freeman, 1984). Some scholars argue that this definition may have limited applicability to determine the salience of various stakeholders. They propose, instead, to consider attributes such as power, legitimacy or urgency in the demands of different groups (Mitchell et al., 1997) that potentially influence firm executives' values, perceptions, and actions (Agle et al., 1999).

Other stakeholder classifications derive mainly from managerial or legal interpretations of the stakeholder concept (Fassin, 2009). The managerial perspective usually considers stakeholder groups as those that might 'influence' the organisation, which in turn should develop diverse strategies to deal with stakeholder relationships. By contrast, the legal perspective typically addresses contractual requirements, assuming that stakeholders have a legitimate role to 'claim' or 'demand' the fulfilment of their needs or rights (Fassin, 2009). For our purpose, both perspectives consider stakeholders as salient and instrumental to the organisation's survival. Moreover, a social perspective underlies these approaches as they examine the structural nature of interactions between a firm and its stakeholders. Yet a broader social perspective, inclusive of international views, could help further understand organisations' role in context. That is, despite research progress in stakeholder theory, defining who the stakeholders are ends up surrounded by ambiguity and attributed to a context-specific situation (Hall and Vredenburg, 2005; cited in Fassin, 2009).

Regarding stakeholders per se, researchers typically assume intergroup heterogeneity (Donaldson & Preston, 1995; Mitchell et al., 1997). Yet recent studies suggest that heterogeneity could also exist within a stakeholder category, because of its members' diverse interests or roles (Fassin, 2008; Wolfe & Putler, 2002). Much work has examined what motivates stakeholder groups to develop common priorities with respect to a given issue. Empirical evidence suggests that homogeneity depends as much on individuals' self-interest as on symbolic politics or predispositions that influence attitudes towards a specific issue. This approach helps understand the existence of different interests or needs and, therefore, types of demands from members of the same stakeholder group, as well as to identify groups of individuals based on their priorities (Wolfe & Putler, 2002.

The importance given to identifying who the stakeholders are and what their interests, needs or demands require, indicates that stakeholder theory is overly concerned with potential conflict emerging from diverse views on resource dependency or control issues (Frooman, 1999). Therefore, searching for strategies that avoid or mitigate such conflicts turns researchers' attention toward the organisation–stakeholder relationship. How organisations relate or interact with stakeholders is another substantive concern for stakeholder theory. Studies addressing this question take different approaches. Mainstream approaches examine a hierarchical relationship where the organisation plays the central role when interacting with stakeholders (Donaldson & Preston, 1995; Mitchell et al., 1997). Alternative propositions suggest that stakeholders could also play a central role when organisations have a high dependence on the type of resources stakeholders possess (Frooman, 1999). Stakeholders are also central in building alliances with other stakeholders to set rules targeting organisational membership, governance or implementation monitoring of target organisations (Fransen & Kolk, 2007). Further, stakeholders become key players when directly contributing to the economic functioning of a business. Kaler (2009) proposes the contributing principle for classifying stakeholders. According to this contributory principle, stockholders and employees become primary stakeholders because of their accountability in providing resources and knowledge for businesses. Customers, suppliers or lenders would be secondary stakeholders because of their complementary role in providing capital beyond that from shareholders (Kaler, 2009).

A focus on this interactional structure is the foundation of a network perspective for studying organisation–stakeholder relationships (Rowley, 1997). This view aims to identify the level at which such relationships actually occur: at the senior management level of the company with the leading group of the stakeholder, not the organisation as a whole (Fassin, 2008).

This said, we surmise that research on the organisation–stakeholder relationship takes an instrumental view of stakeholder management, whether from the firm or the stakeholder's standpoint. That is, a stakeholder is defined as such when possessing something that the organisation needs or vice versa. Though this managerial approach has produced valuable findings, we argue that there exist more than instrumental goals to stakeholder management. The salience of specific stakeholders might depend of factors beyond managerial value preferences, resource dependency or contractual actions.

An international view of this theory could provide further insight on which stakeholders matter and how and why they interact with organisations. Here we focus on the Latin American region through the lens of HRM practices.

STAKEHOLDER MANAGEMENT IN LATIN AMERICA AND HRM

Our approach to studying stakeholder management in Latin America builds on Brewster's (1999) contextual paradigm 'of what is contextually unique and why' in international HRM (p. 215). This view accepts that different constituencies (such as societies, governments or regions) can affect strategic human resources management (SHRM) practices, not just firms. Two important assumptions are that an organisation's objectives are not necessarily optimal for either the organisation or the society, and that the interests of all stakeholders in an organisation are not necessarily the same. This seems to fit the reality of Latin American HRM where employees, organised labour, managers and other stakeholders often have differing interests and, therefore, demands or expectations (Elvira & Davila, 2005b).

Kochan (1999) adds to this contextual view the institutions that underlie the social contract as contextually critical for HRM. In doing so, he shifts (1) the unit of analysis from one of the organisation to one of the employment relationships and (2) the role of the HRM professional from one of creating and implementing organisational HRM policy to one of contributing to societal policy related to workers, or other constituencies.

Focusing on the social contract could help identify both who the salient stakeholders are and how to interact with them, meeting their expectations for social development. Social contracts can be defined as the 'mutual expectations and obligations that employees, employers, and members of society in general hold for work and employment relationships' (Kochan, 1999: 201). In Latin America, the countries' economic opening and political adjustments have impacted the social contract including demands for security in employment, decreased inequality, and search for trust of employers.

Because in Latin America companies play a major role not only in economic but also in social development (Elvira & Davila, 2005b), organisational stakeholders might not at first present the usual attributes discussed in the literature. The attributes of power, legitimacy or urgency seem more applicable to organisational stakeholders possessing economic or social resources that could be capitalised as a 'stake', thereby engaging organisations in satisfying their claims. Yet relevant stakeholders in the region may lack resources to represent their interests and be seldom considered by business organisations (Tavis, 1994). Even if organisations ignore the potential effects of such stakeholders' claims or the legitimate role they play in society, they impact an organisation's ability to reach its objectives.

For example, in places such as Latin America, indigenous groups' demands turn often into valid and long-term relationships that originally lack such legitimacy or power. Consider land ownership disputes between multinational corporations and indigenous people, which happen often in colonised countries. In Australia, for example, acknowledging the legitimisation of an indigenous stakeholder group and its land claims depends more on the coloniser economic and political elite than a natural social process of granting ancestral land property rights (Banerjee, 2000). In Latin America, diverse stakeholders also coexist with organisations, and desire to achieve social integration. It is appropriate to ask to what extent business organisations should consider stakeholders that have been marginalised by economic development systems and, therefore, lack of socio-political representation. Tavis (1994) analytical framework parallels our view of stakeholders as including a broad segment of the Latin American society. He argues that when local public-government institutions are incapable or unwilling to represent some segments of society, those segments are largely dependent upon the decisions and actions of firms for their wellbeing.

In Latin America, some social groups present unique characteristics because of historical and cultural reasons. Workers' families, for example, become constituents of business organisations and HRM performs best when including practices that benefit them (Elvira & Davila, 2005b). Grupo San Nicolas illustrates this case. The Group is a pharmaceutical manufacturer and drug store distributor from El Salvador in Central America. Operating during a prolonged civil war and experiencing the consequences of a severe earthquake in the 1980s, the Group's owners took on the responsibility of personally investing the company's economic and material resources to protect the well-being of employees and their families (Leguizamon et al., 2009). The demonstration of solidarity with employees in times of dramatic misfortune surpassed potential claims that a legitimate stakeholder – in the traditional theoretical view – could demand.

Besides re-examining who key stakeholders are, knowing what both stakeholders and organisations care about in Latin America matters. Ponder, for instance, the case of conflict-ridden Colombia, where the business environment has been severely tested by violence and political and economic instability. The cases of two agribusiness companies show how working closely with workers produced a respect for property rights otherwise difficult to achieve, while simultaneously aligning workers' interests with the organisations' objectives. Property rights, in turn, established a structural foundation for developing HRM practices potentially unique for such environments, such as providing protection and guaranteeing peace in the area where the companies operate (Andonova et al., 2009). Property rights – via a co-operative formed by workers – were also used as a bridge to close the gap produced by social and economic distance between company owners/managers and workers – a reflection of the social differences formed in Colombia after its economic opening in the 1990s. HRM practices that work effectively in this environment include extensive technical and administrative training for employees (now co-owners in the co-operative) and, specifically, education in workers' rights and personal development. In these circumstances, designing a socially responsible corporate strategy to satisfy indigenous stakeholders' needs fell short, requiring also the sharing of control rights and ownership-related privileges with employees. Yet these practices resulted in effectively preventing vulnerable workers from joining other non-strictly-business organisations to produce damage through violent conflict.

Other groups of silent stakeholders emerge during economic or political crises, as happened in Aracruz Celulose's case (Osland et al., 2009). An award-winning Brazilian company, the firm produces bleached eucalyptus pulp for paper manufacturing, and owns 279 000 hectares (including 154 000 hectares of native forest reserves) in Brazil. Local indigenous groups, landless and in poverty, recently claimed 11 000 additional hectares for their reservation, in a conflict lasting from 1993 to 2007, when the company was legally forced to grant away the land. Although indigenous groups such as those in Aracruz's case could be considered situational stakeholders, that is, an interest group emerging in particular situations, one can argue that they belong among the silent stakeholders: they lack legitimate claim, power or urgent needs (judging by the 11 years it took their claims to be noticed). From an HRM perspective, the company was unprepared to deal with the conflicts provoked by those local groups. Yet corporate social responsibility standards create new responsibilities on human resource departments, which in Latin America are often accountable for managing stakeholders' demands.

These illustrations suggest that the role of human resources departments is crucial when national and local institutions fail to enforce basic property rights, or to provide protection and security. In such circumstances employment conflicts tend to escalate into wider social, political and economic clashes. Therefore, attending to the broad employment relationship becomes much more important than has traditionally been recognised in HRM research.

This view of organisational stakeholders could be particularly valuable in times of environmental crisis or conflict. These circumstances mostly characterise Latin American countries' economic and political environment, which in turn affect business organisations and their managerial practices. Economic action is embedded in a concrete and dynamic social system (Granovetter, 1985). In times of crisis, particularly, trust plays a key role as calibrator of economic exchange. Trust is socially nurtured; it does not derive from a structured legal framework or a general moral behavioural approach (Granovetter, 1985).

Considering the evidence just discussed, we observe that organisations and stakeholders in Latin America tend to interact not so much on the basis of a strict dependency relationship or contributing principle of their accountability in providing resources and knowledge for businesses, but on a social contract infused by trust (or lacking it). Naturally, an exchange system based on social relationships reaches a limit for member participation or integration. In particular, in Latin America, social groups are closed and tied to long-term kin relationships, potentially seeking self-interested group behaviour and, in the long run, possibly corrupting the system and its values.

From Latin America, as perhaps no other region, one learns important lessons for stakeholder management in times of crisis. For instance, saving employment becomes the number one priority not only for governments but also for business organisations and union representatives. The cases discussed above show how employment relationships were nurtured by training programmes and shared ownership with workers to a greater extent than by a simple exchange on demands. In addition, the 'silent' stakeholders are members of the local community. Thus, when an organisation implements corporate social responsibility (CSR) initiatives through HRM practices, the returns directly benefit its workers' community. This is an important distinction in corporate social responsibility for stakeholder management in Latin America.

This stakeholder management perspective on organisations operating in emerging economies substantively differs from prior research that usually assumes a normative approach (e.g. Reed, 2002; Tavis, 1994). Normative views address the obligations of multinational corporations (MNCs) towards immediate stakeholders in terms of ethics, morality and legitimacy of foreign subsidiaries. However, empirical research shows that MNCs place importance on global CSR issues (e.g. general environment conservation), over country-specific social-economic needs (e.g. job creation, natural habitats). It is the product or market driven MNC that is more likely to pay attention to local needs (Husted & Allen, 2006) and, therefore, their stakeholders' representatives.

Further, to approach the Latin America HRM model from a stakeholder management perspective one should understand not only business organisations' role in the socio-economic arena, but also how well HR practices satisfy the interests of those groups that lack specific attributes to be generally considered as stakeholders.

In sum, using a contextual lens illuminates idiosyncratic characteristics for stakeholder management in Latin America. Research evidence presents numerous instances where acknowledged and accepted HRM practices were applied differently depending on a people's circumstances. Though this application might appear inconsistent or even economically 'irrational', it makes sense when considered in the context of the cultural antecedents of HRM in Latin America, antecedents that give precedence to people's needs over system consistency. HRM policies that may not appear economically rational (e.g. keeping employees and protecting workers' families) make cultural sense and can lead to increased worker loyalty and productivity. Thus, tightening the link between HRM practices and financial performance may appear as a secondary goal. This produces yet another paradox: by attending to the cultural context in implementing HRM practices, performance may ultimately be enhanced.

KEY STAKEHOLDERS: EMPLOYEES IN LATIN AMERICA

Applying a contextual lens to stakeholders in Latin America, (Brewster, 1999; Hall and Vredenburg, 2005; cited in Fassin, 2009), one can identify groups with differing priorities (Wolfe & Putler, 2002). As mentioned above, the contextual view also recognises an organisation's institutional environment in which salient or silent stakeholders emerge and the arrangements involved in a social contract with the firm.

Latin American businesses seem to have taken on responsibilities formerly placed on the communities. Firms are involved in people's lives as well as their work and thus provide for their social and economic needs. Nevertheless, formerly strong paternalistic labour laws have weakened with market liberalisation and no longer offer the benevolent protections of the past. The result is that employees are now less trusting of their employers. This tension presents a challenge for Latin American firms that were scarcely focused on performance until recently and which due to competitive pressures now need to focus also on meeting business objectives. In this context, HRM's role becomes crucial to help companies achieve both their financial and social/employment goals.

HRM research has focused mainly on understanding managerial perspectives of HRM practices effectiveness. This research is criticised by stakeholder management researchers arguing that employees are not typically given voice in evaluating HRM practices, despite their being the beneficiaries or recipients. In fact, managers and employees tend to differ in their ratings of HRM's importance and HRM practices implementation effectiveness (Geare et al., 2006). In this section, we turn to some illustrations of companies' success in aligning their HRM practices with multiple, including silent, stakeholders with diverse demands.

In general, we see that HRM policies cater to Latin American stakeholders mainly through three mechanisms that might be specific to this region. These mechanisms include:

1. Investment in employees – salary and benefits levels as well as education, training and development.
2. Efforts to operate within a co-operative labour relations framework.
3. Community-centred CSR practices.

HRM Practices Showing Investment in Employees

Contemporary stakeholder theory stresses that employees depend upon one firm for employment and often for their entire income (Kaler, 2009). As argued elsewhere (Elvira & Davila, 2005b), companies in Latin America work on survival as a key measure of financial success. The same principle might apply also to employees. Companies appear to understand that survival depends on employee loyalty and design HRM practices accordingly.

Take the example of *Unilever Mexico*, Home and Personal Care division, a subsidiary of Unilever that manufactures and markets personal hygiene and household products. In Latin America, the company is known for its best practices in terms of human resources. HRM's stated objective is to have motivated workers with the necessary skills to provide quality service and products. To enhance HRM systems, the firm works especially on staffing and training. Compensation policies consider a context of reduced purchasing power, due to devaluations, inflationary growth and age. For these reasons, Unilever tries to keep wages at acceptable levels: for example, currently the lowest base salary paid by the company corresponds to temporary workers, yet is equivalent to three times Mexico's minimum wage. The second lowest wage, paid to machinists, equals four times the minimum wage in Mexico, and is designed to cover an average family's basic food needs. In addition, Unilever is known for always paying punctually, on schedule and for all hours worked, which is often not the case for companies operating in Mexico.[1]

Another case illustrating concern for employees as key stakeholders is Zanzini Móveis, a medium size family-run business in the furniture manufacturing industry. Located in the city of Dois Córregos, state of São Paulo (Brazil), it was ranked ninth in the 2008 Great Place to Work Institute. Oliver Zanzini and his wife Palmyra Benvenuto founded the company in 1965. From a small workshop, the firm expanded its commercial presence in Brazil and in the South Cone's region. It is considered one of the finest Brazilian furniture manufacturers, employing about 200 workers (Zanzini Móveis, 2009), and respected for its management system and CSR activities.

In terms of HRM practices, Zanzini Móveis illustrates the positive working climate encouraged by top management and through an employee-training programme. The company stresses skill development for its workers aiming to facilitate high job satisfaction. In addition, top management has installed several tools such as team workshops focusing on communication, identifying work needs and keeping a team's work in harmony with individual and business interests (Zanzini Móveis, 2009).

The company's philosophy holds that improving workers' educational level is the first step in improving their quality of life of workers' families. Given the low average educational level in Brazil, the company is taking actions to enhance workers' technical skills (Downie, 2007). When Zanzini's managers realised that even employees with a high-school education could not interpret graphs or follow the manuals to manufacture furniture, the company set aside a room on its shop floor to use as an impromptu classroom whenever a worker needs help (Downie, 2007).

Besides educational services, Zanzini Móveis provides other *special* benefits to its workers such as: (1) sports and leisure in a private country club; (2) health care services with medical and orthodontist services via agreements with local health establishments and workplace medical programmes; (3) a basic food package supplement; (4) programmes for family and organisational integration; and (5) productivity and results-based bonuses (Zanzini Móveis, 2009).

The type and diversity of benefits granted to employees by Unilever and Zanzini might be considered unusual for firms outside Latin America, yet can be understood from the viewpoint of employees' critical importance as firm stakeholders. Investing in employee education through training and development, assuring satisfaction and quality of life through compensation according to employees' purchasing power, and expanding the boundaries of this satisfaction through salaries that cover employees' family basic food needs, all exemplify HRM practices that are centred around individuals

HRM Efforts to Operate Within a Co-operative Labour Relations Framework

A third company case illustrates effective HRM practices. FEMSA, the largest beverage company in Latin America has its roots in Monterrey (Mexico). FEMSA is well-known for a philosophy framed by two main goals: to generate economic and social value (FEMSA, 2009). In Mexico, the firm was considered a pioneer of policies focused on the employee such as health and pension fund benefits. It also contributed to community development by introducing an affordable housing system for all workers, and developing environment-conscious strategies.

Here we focus specifically on Coca-Cola FEMSA Colombia, which employs over 2000 workers in six plants. The company has permanent relationships with multiple Colombian unions, including the largest in the country representing bottling plant workers. To work at FEMSA candidates must be at least 18 years old. Wages and work hours are regulated by national law and reinforced in collective bargaining agreements. All workers – permanent employees and contractors alike – are paid at least 30 per cent above the nation's minimum wage. In a country where violence against union members has deterred all but 4 per cent of workers from unionising, 31 per cent of the employees of the Coca-Cola Colombian bottling company belong to unions (Coke Facts, 2009). FEMSA and bottling partners respect the rights of employees, including those who choose third-party representation. In fact, FEMSA has effective relationships with multiple unions, with which it currently has collective bargaining agreements covering wages, benefits and working conditions.

Besides policies concerning employees, FEMSA has also invested in Colombia's political infrastructure and people's well-being, in alliance with other international organisations aiming to strengthen peace and stability in the region. Through both collective bargaining agreements and their own initiative, Colombian bottling partners are working with unions and the government to provide emergency cell phones, transportation to and from work, secure housing and other measures to protect employees. Thus, FEMSA has established the successful management model developed originally in Mexico and has adapted it to the current reality of Colombia (Coke Facts, 2009). This effective integration of policies is likely due to FEMSA's close relationship with multiple stakeholders.[2]

HRM Targeting Community-centred CSR Practices

The case of Mexico's Grupo Bimbo illustrates the potential benefits of understanding Latin American work values in order to implement HRM practices that are both culturally acceptable and effective (Elvira & Davila, 2005a). Bimbo is a large multinational organisation with operations in the United States and 14 countries in Europe, Latin America and Asia. It is one of the world's most important baking companies in brand and trademark positioning, sales, and production volume. The company has been labelled as an 'entirely human' organisation (Flores-Vega, 1995). One of the person-centred policies Bimbo adheres to is avoiding employee layoffs even during downturns. Though costly, this commitment to employees has endured the test of time. In return, Bimbo benefits from increased employee loyalty and sustained financial success, which executives attribute to this and other similarly humanistic policies. This very public commitment to its people also enhances the firm's reputation for corporate ethics, social responsibility, and altruism (Elvira & Davila, 2005a). From our perspective, Bimbo understands the importance of employees as key stakeholders and commitment to long-term employment in Latin America and has been able to make this practice beneficial to long-term firm performance.

TOWARD A STAKEHOLDER ANALYSIS OF HRM IN LATIN AMERICA

HRM practices in Latin America are better understood by using a stakeholder management approach. Based on the contributing principle of their accountability in providing resources and knowledge for businesses (Kaler, 2009), employees' attributes qualify them as primary stakeholders. In addition, a social perspective highlights their silent attribute, because of organisations' role in individual, family, and community development.

Because of this social role granted to business organisations, HRM practices target not only salient but also silent stakeholders that are unique to the region's context. The relationship 'organisation–stakeholder' is based on trust and respect for the social contract, taking on a horizontal character of social inclusion versus a hierarchical, power-centred relationship around the organisation.

Our overview of research and case studies on HRM practices depicts a set of companies catering to diverse stakeholders who seek social integration yet often hold relatively low legitimacy or power. Interestingly, top-performing companies are perceived simultaneously as leading economic and social development and as satisfying self-interested demands. The cases also illustrate how stakeholder management strategies are grounded in local and country-driven needs rather than universal corporate social responsible objectives.

Developing common evaluation criteria for a general HRM model applicable to Latin America implies that all stakeholders have similar needs or demands. However, given the diversity among and within stakeholder groups we are inclined toward recognising these differences through a contextual approach in this particular region (Brewster, 1999). In Table 20.1, we present a simple way of evaluating stakeholder demands based on the research described. A positive (+) weight applies to those issues that are critically important and, thus, valued by salient as well as silent stakeholders. The absence of a sign applies to those issues that appear important to specific stakeholders according to research or popular business media but are not valued by other stakeholders.

We identify two emerging strategies underlining HRM practices in conflict and uncertainty-laden environments: sharing control rights and ownership-related privileges with employees. These strategies are consistent with our theoretical proposition that HRM systems perform best when promoting a horizontal organisation–stakeholder relationship that facilitates social inclusion (Davila & Elvira, 2009). We also identify other strategies that companies use to generate commitment, loyalty and good working climate, and this not only from their employees but also from their

Table 20.1 Stakeholder analysis for evaluating needs and demands

Stakeholder	Emerging evidence from a silent-stakeholder analysis					Emerging evidence from a salient-stakeholder analysis	
	Attention to Property Rights	Ownership-Related Privileges	Benefits for Worker's Family	Employee Development	Forms of Union-Cooperative Organizations	Compensation	Positive working climate
Employees		(+)	(+)	(+)		(+) According to local purchasing power	
Union Representatives					(+)		
Indigenous People	(+)						
Media Rankings							(+)
HRM Research						(+)	

surrounding communities. The region's strengths include a serious and effective commitment to the individual and his or her job; a willingness to provide social benefits to employees via the company, since governments have limited resources or are poorly managed; and a culture in which managers transform companies into centres for community development. Ultimately, it is the community who grants organisations a social licence to operate (Andonova et al., 2009).

Our analysis of selected stakeholders serves as the foundation for an inductive model of HRM in Latin America. Such model would first consider salient as well as silent stakeholders and their primary needs and demands. Second, it should also consider differences among diverse stakeholders groups and within the same group. On this basis, HRM policies would serve as a bridge for closing the gap between the organisation, the employees and their communities.

NOTES

1. At the time of closing this chapter, Unilever Mexico ranked third in *Super Empresas 2009*, the Top Companies list of *Expansion*, a major business magazine in Mexico. Rankings are based on employees' views of HRM practices.
2. The authors would like to thank Bruce Delloye, Alexandre Cabon, Guéret Louis-François International Students at EGADE Business School, Tecnologico de Monterrey for researching the Unilever, Zanzini Móveis, FEMSA cases, respectively.

REFERENCES

Agle, B. R., Mitchell, R. K. & Sonnenfeld, J. A. 1999. Who matters to CEOs? An investigation of stakeholder attributes and salience, corporate performance, and CEO values. *Academy of Management Journal*, **42**(5): 507–525.

Andonova, V., Gutierrez, R. & Avella, L. F. 2009. The strategic importance of close employment relations in conflict-ridden environments. Three cases from Colombia. In A. Davila & M. M. Elvira (eds), *Best HRM Practices in Latin America*. Oxford: Routledge, pp. 25–36.

Banerjee, S. B. (2000) Whose land is it anyway? National interest, indigenous stakeholders, and colonial discourses. *Organization & Environment*, **13**(1): 3–28.

Brewster, C. (1999). Different paradigms in strategic HRM: questions raised by comparative research. In P. M. Wright, L. D. Dyer, J. W. Boudreau & G. T. Milkovich (eds). *Strategic Human Resource Management in the Twenty First Century. Research in Personnel and Human Resource Management*, Supplement 4. Stamford, CT: JAI Press pp. 213–238.

Clarkson, M. B. E. 1995. A stakeholder framework for analyzing and evaluating corporate social responsibility. *Academy of Management Review*, **20**(1): 92–117.

Coke Facts. 2009. Available at: http://www.femsa.com/en/social/global-vision/colombia.htm.

Davila, A. & Elvira, M. M. 2009. Theoretical approaches to best HRM in Latin America. In A. Davila & M. M. Elvira (eds), *Best HRM Practices in Latin America*. Oxford, UK: Routledge.

Donaldson, T. & Preston. 1995. The stakeholder theory of the corporation: concepts, evidence, and implications. *Academy of Management Review*, **20**(1): 85–91.

Downie, A. 2007. Back to school. *Time Magazine*, Apr. 12. Available at: http://www.time. com/time/magazine/article/0,9171,1609790,00.html.

Elvira, M. M. and Davila, A. (2005a). Emergent directions for human resource management research in Latin America. In M. M. Elvira and A. Davila (eds). *Managing Human Resources in Latin America: An Agenda for International Leaders*. Oxford: Routledge, pp. 235–252.

Elvira, M. M. & Davila, A. 2005b. Emergent directions for human resource management research in Latin America. *International Journal of Human Resources Management*, **16**(12): 2265–2282.

Fassin, Y. 2008. Imperfections and shortcomings of the stakeholder model's graphical representation. *Journal of Business Ethics*, 80: 879–888.

Fassin, Y. 2009. The stakeholder model refined. *Journal of Business Ethics*, **84**(1): 113–135.

FEMSA. 2009. Available at: http://www.femsa.com/en/.

Flores-Vega, E. (1995). Bimbo la multiplicación de los panes [Bimbo the multiplication of bread]. Expansión, Seccion Principal, Ed. No. 677. Available at: http://www.cnnexpan sion.com/expansion/2011/09/14/bimbo-la-multiplicacin-de-los-panes.

Fransen, L. W. & Kolk, A. 2007. Global rule-setting for business: a critical analysis of multistakeholder standards. *Organization*, **14**(5): 667–684.

Freeman, R. E. 1984. *Strategic Management: A Stakeholder Approach*. Lanham, MD: Pitman.

Frooman, J. 1999. Stakeholder influence strategies. *Academy of Management Review*, **24**(2): 191–205.

Geare, A., Edgar, F. & Deng, M. 2006. Implementation and consumption of HRM: stakeholder differences. *Research and Practice in Human Resource Management*, **14**(2): 34–48.

Granovetter, M. 1985. Economic action and social structure: the problem of embeddedness. *American Journal of Sociology*, **91**(3): 481–510.

Husted, B. W. & Allen, D. B. 2006. Corporate social responsibility in the multinational enterprise: strategic and institutional approaches. *Journal of International Business Studies*, **37**(6): 838–849.

Kaler, J. 2009. An optimally viable version of stakeholder theory. *Journal of Business Ethics*, **86**(3): 297–312.

Kochan, T. A. (1999). Beyond myopia: human resources and the changing social contract. In P. M. Wright, L. D. Dyer, J. W. Boudreau & G. T. Milkovich (eds), *Strategic Human Resource Management in the Twenty First Century: Research in Personnel and Human Resource Management*, Supplement 4. Stamford, CT: JAI Press.

Leguizamon, F. A., Ickis, J. C. & Ogliastri, E. 2009. Human resource practices and business performance: Grupo San Nicolás. In A. Davila & M. Elvira (eds), *Best HRM Practices in Latin America*. Oxford: Routledge, pp. 85–96.

Mitchell, R. K., Agle, B. R. & Wood, D. J. 1997. Toward a theory of stakeholder identification and salience: defining the principle of who and what really counts. *Academy of Management Review*, **22**(4): 853–886.

Osland, A., Osland, J. S., Tanure, B. & Gabrish, R. 2009. Stakeholder management: the case of Aracruz Celulose in Brazil. In A. Davila & M. M. Elvira (eds), *Best HRM Practices in Latin America*. Oxford: Routledge, pp. 10–24.

Reed, D. 2002. Employing normative stakeholder theory in developing countries. *Business and Society*, **41**(2): 166–207.

Rowley, T. J. 1997. Moving beyond dyadic ties: a network theory of stakeholder influences. *Academy of Management Review*, **22**(4): 887–910.

Tavis, L. 1994. Bifurcated development and multinational corporate responsibility. In W. M. Hoffman, J. B. Kamm, R. E. Frederick & E. S. Petry (eds), *Emerging Global Business Ethics*. Westport, CT: Quorum Books, pp. 255–274.

Wolfe, R. A. & Putler, D. S. 2002. How tight are the ties that bind stakeholder groups? *Organization Science*, **13**(1): 64–80.

Zanzini Móveis. 2009. Available at: http://www.zanzini.com.br/es/empresa.asp.

21 The practice of HRM in Africa in comparative perspective
Christine Bischoff and Geoffrey Wood

The body of research on HRM in Africa remains limited, reflecting the peripheral position of the continent in academic discourse, with the bulk of existing work focused on the case of South Africa. Yet it is incorrect to conclude that economic marginalisation simply means that, in most African countries, there is a general lack of attention to people management at all, or that in most cases there is nothing more to people management than simply labour repression. This chapter aims to provide an overview of the key concerns of the existing literature, current debates and practices, and likely future trends.

CROSS-CULTURAL APPROACHES TO UNDERSTANDING HRM IN AFRICA

Much of the literature on HRM in Africa has been influenced by cultural accounts (Jackson, 2002; Karsten & Illa, 2005; Swartz & Davis, 1997). Many of these accounts, influenced by the work of Hofstede (1991), see variations as in line with distinct cultural communities that are shared across clusters of nations within specific regions, which may be defined against a general standard. Culture is seen as a given: countries may develop their social capital, but it is not possible to depart from established ways of doing things (Fukuyama, 1995). Spector et al. (2002) argue that in dealing with HRM issues, the impact of cultural variations on beliefs about participation and control need to be taken into account: it would be inappropriate to simply impose Western models on non-Western contexts.

Studies on HRM in Africa have focused on the communitarian dimensions in African culture, the challenges this poses for organisations, and the extent to which this may be harnessed to promote optimal HRM, and wider organisational outcomes. For example, Ghabadamosi (2003) argues that a systematic and human orientation, and a tendency to view practice in relation to an ideal, are culturally embedded values shared by many African managers. This would suggest the need to develop a broader HRM management philosophy based on African values (p. 279).

Swartz and Davis (1997: 290–291) argue that central dimensions of such a philosophy could incorporate the notion of 'ubuntu', solidarity or brotherhood amongst the historically disadvantaged, the persistence of both positive and negative spirits in organisational life, the need to take account of persistent fears, the ongoing evolution of organisation and that, in the absence of collective support, any initiative will fail (cf. Karsten & Illa, 2005). At the same time, two caveats are in order. Firstly, any cultural dimension incorporates internal contradictions (Swartz & Davis, 1997: 293). Secondly, the above-mentioned dimensions may not be applicable in all – or even most – African contexts (p. 294): cultural diversity can be encountered at a range of levels.

A limitation of such approaches is that given assumptions of the persistence of distinct cultural traditions, poor economic performance within specific regions may be blamed on cultural shortcomings, which are not easily resolved. Making assumptions as to which cultures are functional or dysfunctional to specific organisational forms, and types of economic activity, may, at worst, descend into racism, and discounts the possibility that firms – and countries – may radically reinvent themselves; examples of the latter would be Botswana's transformation from a poor backwater to a developed nation or, conversely, the descent of Ivory Coast from prosperity to civil conflict. Indeed, Anakwe et al. (2000) argue that there is a pressing need for research that recognises the common aspects in many cultures, despite superficial differences. Similarly, Karsten and Ghebregiorgis (2005: 145) note that it is simply wrong to conclude that Western HRM practices cannot be adopted in Africa on account of allegedly insurmountable cultural differences.

An alternative way of exploring the impact of culture on HRM has been to focus on the effects of the myths different groupings hold about each other. For example, Jackson (2002) points to the effects of negative stereotypes on HRM in theory and practice. Even if based on false premises, myths and stereotypes mould decision-making and values in organisations, and inform approaches to communication (Hansen, 2003: 17). Indeed, individuals entrusted with human resource development tend to frame their interventions in terms of how they viewed the local cultural setting. Whatever their origins, in fact, fiction, or in the distant past, myths influence expectations of behaviour (pp. 17–18). Within organisations, 'myths' become a means by which groups of individuals may impart meaning to activities: the nature of group formation in turn will reflect existing cleavages, on ethnicity, occupation (or gender or skill), within the organisation. Based on a comparative study, involving interviews with German, US and Ivorian managers, Hansen (2003: 25) found that non-Ivorian nationals working in Ivory Coast tended to make claims as to the 'sabotaging' effects of the local culture, steeped with clan loyalties and nepotism. In contrast, Ivorian managers felt that they were forced to micro-manage, as they were likely to be blamed for any shortcomings on the behalf of their subordinates; this contributed to feelings of a loss of control.

INSTITUTIONAL APPROACHES: HRM IN THE AFRICAN BUSINESS SYSTEM

An alternative approach to understanding HRM in Africa has been through the use of business systems theory. Originally developed by Whitley (1999), business systems theory identifies three defining features of national business systems: variations in ownership co-ordination, in non-ownership co-ordination and in employment relations. Whitley originally identified six archetypes (or clusters of countries) associated with particular practices, encompassing the economies of the developed world. Using business systems theory, a further archetype has been identified by Wood and Frynas (2006), the segmented business system, based on the experience of East Africa; however, this archetype is useful to understanding the practice of HRM across tropical Africa. The segmented business systems' key characteristics are summarised in the Table 21.1, which is contrasted with two archetypes from the developed world. The segmented business system has many distinct characteristics. It does not represent a hybrid form of business systems encountered in the developed world (Wood & Frynas, 2006). Whilst the segmented business system may be functional in terms of the concerns of elites, it has proven dysfunctional as a basis for sustainable growth (see Table 21.1).

A key aspect of HRM in such economies is an underlying dualism. On the one hand, there are relatively large organisations, such as subsidiaries of foreign MNCs and many in the public sector, characterised by formalism in systems and procedures. This may include a degree of pluralism in employment relations, including collective bargaining. On the other hand, there are smaller and/or family owned firms, which make up the bulk of the indigenous private sector (Baruch & Clancy, 2000: 794). Such firms are mostly unitarist in HRM orientation, with decision making being concentrated in the hands of managers, and employees being firmly subordinated (Wood & Frynas, 2006). Whilst job security is likely to be poor, and state regulation weak, employers may be drawn into informal peasant based networks of support, with employees being granted informal loans or handouts in the case of financial setbacks, or special occasions, such as weddings and funerals (Hyden, 1983). Recruitment is likely to be informal

Table 21.1   The segmented business system versus two successful business systems

Characteristics	Business system type		
	Segmented business system	Compartmentalised (typical of Anglo-Saxon countries)	Highly co-ordinated (typical of Japan)
Ownership co-ordination			
Owner control	Direct/Mixed	Market	Alliance
Ownership integration of production chains	Mixed	High	Some
Ownership integration of sectors	Low	High	Limited
Non-ownership co-ordination			
Alliance co-ordination of production chains	Marketers and end-users dominate production chains	Low	High
Collaboration between competitors	Highly adversarial competition in informal sector Tendency to oligopolistic relations in export-orientated sectors	Low	High
Alliance co-ordination of sectors	Deep variation in practices between sectors	Low	Some
Employment relations			
Employer/ employee interdependence	Some	Low	High
Delegation to employees	Low	Low	Considerable
Source	Authors	Whitley (1999)	Whitley (1999)

Source: Wood and Frynas 2006; Whitley 1999.

and centre on the use of existing staff to find new ones from amongst their friends and relatives (Wood & Frynas, 2006).

What both areas of economic activity are likely to have in common is a durable paternalism, with hierarchical lines of authority and clear divisions of labour; if unions are present, the latter are likely to be in a relatively weak position, owing to high levels of unemployment (Wood & Frynas, 2006). MNCs may be under some pressure from lobby groups in their country of origin to uphold basic labour standards, although evidence would suggest that, in most cases, cost concerns will take priority (Mellahi & Wood, 2003).

What many tropical African countries have in common is that unions have a relatively narrow social base. The bulk of the working age population are employed in agriculture and the informal sector, with unions being confined to manufacturing, public services and, in some cases, mining (Manda et al., 2001). Also, during the 1960s and 1970s, when most tropical African states were under one party or military rule, unions were firmly subordinated to the government (Tordoff, 1984). With a general move back towards multi-partyism across the continent in the late 1980s and early 1990s, most national union movements regained their autonomy, but faced the challenges of coping with large-scale job losses as a result of ruinous neo-liberal reforms. Whilst unions had more room to express alternative political views, their bargaining position was weakened as a result of the evaporation of large components of their constituency (Bracking, 2003; ILO, 1997); they had regained some power and arguably lost much more at the same time. Moreover, as Williams (1994: 222) notes, the marketisation of social services raised the cost of the reproduction of labour power at the same time as real wages stagnated or declined. Faced with a loss of formal bargaining power, in many cases the only protests open to workers entailed a return to informal mechanisms of resistance, ranging from deliberately low productivity to sabotage or the theft of company resources (cf. Cohen, 1994).

The increased importance of informal livelihoods opened up further challenges for unions. Across the continent, unions have generally failed to unionise informal or semi-formal sector workers: this would reflect hardline employer attitudes (often prompted by the very marginal nature of the enterprise itself) and the high attrition rate amongst such enterprises. Moreover, the general lack of union success in organising such workers could reflect an inability to take account of the specific needs posed by the sector, and an inattention to gender issues: many areas of informal sector work are dominated by women (Anonymous, 1999).

Wood and Frynas (2006) summarise the nature of employment relations in segmented business systems as follows, drawing on Whitley's

Table 21.2   Employment relations in segmented business systems

Employment Relations	Export and State Sectors	Indigenous Sector
Employer/employee interdependence	Low	Some
Delegation to employees	Low	Low

Source: Wood and Frynas 2006.

(1999) classification of the defining features of work and employment relations (Table 21.2).

Wood and Frynas (2006) conclude that HRM in segmented business systems is characterised by authoritarian management, weak communication and a tendency to over-rely on low cost, unskilled labour. Such strategies are likely to result in low productivity and poor quality control, locking firms into the 'sweatshop trap' (Wood & Frynas, 2006). Firms are simply not able to move beyond low cost, low value added activity: should they significantly reinvest in plant or staff skills, competitors that do not do so will use the opportunity to exploit their own short term cost advantages.

In an extensive study of Mozambican industrial relations, Webster et al. (2006) found that the practice of HRM in Mozambique followed a distinct, path-dependent trajectory, as suggested by business systems theory (Webster et al., 2006). They argued that Mozambican employment relations could not be simply dismissed as yet another manifestation of an emerging global bleak house model characterised by full-scale labour repression. Rather, they found that Mozambican work and employment relations represented a manifestation of path dependency, reflecting the opportunities and distortions posed by national institutional realities. But, what form did such work and employment relations assume? Webster and Wood (2005) found that a consistent strand stretching back to the colonial era was that of 'durable informalism'. A survey of employers found that many openly admitted to breaking collective agreements and making widespread usage of redundancies; there is also much evidence that Mozambican employment law is often 'honoured in the breach rather than the observance'. However, employment relations are also characterised by direct and personal contact between managers and employees, the use of informal recruitment and selection techniques, giving preferential access to the relatives and friends of existing staff, and the extension of informal credit mechanisms. Hence, the resulting model is more paternalist (albeit of the authoritarian variety) than an anonymous 'bleak house' model would imply (Webster & Wood, 2005).

Based on a comparative survey of Nigerian organisations, Okpara and Wynn (2008) found that the focus of HRM managers tended to be primarily on training and development, the latter in part due to limitations in the wider training system. At the same time, this led to other key areas of the HRM function, ranging from compensation and benefits to health and safety, being neglected. Moreover, a wide range of external pressures – ranging from wider political instability to the demands placed by extended kin-based networks – often precluded managers from operating effectively. Again, Nigerian HRM tended to follow a path-dependent trajectory that had many common features with that of Mozambique, and, indeed, many other states across the continent.

More recent extensions and developments to business systems theory argue that firms will modify and experiment with old ways of doing things, and try new ways as well (Morgan, 2007). This means that whilst HRM in tropical African countries remains path dependent, some adjustments to practices will take place at firm, regional, sectoral and national levels; what defines HRM in Africa may be still evolving on an episodic and uneven basis.

DIFFERENCES AND SIMILARITIES ACROSS THE CONTINENT

Both cross-cultural and institutional accounts have highlighted similarities in regions, and in countries with similar historical experiences. Does this mean HRM is similar across the continent? Two recent edited collections on industrial relations practice in different countries across the continent, Wood and Brewster's work, *Industrial Relations in Africa* (2007) and a 2008 special issue of the journal *Employee Relations* (see Wood, 2008) bring together detailed country studies, mostly by scholars working at African universities across the continent. A few themes emerge from this work. Firstly, it is evident that in many tropical African anglophone countries – such as Kenya, Uganda, Zambia and Malawi – 'labour rights that were lost during the one party era(s) were recovered' (Dzimbiri, 2007: 63). This has led to a return to freedom of union organising, and the expansion of the individual rights of employees. At the same time, what can only be described as vandalistic structural adjustment policies imposed by the IMF led to the wholesale destruction of jobs, greatly weakening the bargaining power of employees. Such policies also weakened the capacity of the state to enforce the law. This pattern – job destruction and the weakening of state capacity – was similarly encountered in many francophone and lusophone states. However, what sets the latter apart are differences in legal traditions (cf. Croucher, 2007: 204). Both francophone and lusophone countries have common law legal traditions, which tend to circumscribe owner rights, and give employees more clearly delineated rights under the law. However, any advantage this accords has, in most cases, been more than offset by political authoritarianism, and, again, the destruction of much economic activity by predatory structural adjustment (Croucher, 2007; Essaaidi, 2007). Other differences imposed reflect the specific political traditions of countries. For example, in Eritrea, a tradition of civil involvement in economic reconstruction has made for hybrid patterns involving both cooperation and authoritarianism (see Ghebregiorgis & Karsten, 2007). In Uganda, the depredations of the Amin and Obote II dictatorships have posed particularly severe challenges in terms of institution rebuilding (Kiringa, 2007).

Two African states represent particularly exceptional cases. South Africa is by far Africa's largest economy. An excellent infrastructure and a large industrial sector have both weathered neo-liberal reforms. Mostly organised under the umbrella of the Congress of South African Trade Unions (COSATU), unions are the strongest on the continent, and are supported by a generally labour-friendly body of labour law. However, once more, the bargaining position of organised labour has been greatly undercut by very high levels of unemployment, as much as 45 per cent in some estimates. Mass immigration from across tropical Africa and China, and, to a lesser extent, South Asia and Eastern Europe, have provided the country with new skills and entrepreneurial capabilities; however, intense competition for jobs led to periodic outbreaks of xenophobic riots. COSATU has historically been aligned to South Africa's ruling party, the African National Congress (ANC); it is too soon to tell how the formation of a new breakaway political party, the Congress of the People, will affect union–government relations. More detail on the South African situation is provided later in the chapter.

Nigeria is by far Africa's most populous country. Oil revenues have not contributed to sustainable development, but, rather, a predatory elite and personalised politics. Within such a context, unions remain weak, and vulnerable to political currents. Despite democratisation, the political system remains unstable and inconsistent, greatly reducing the chances for 'normal' industrial relations (Fajana, 2007: 160–161).

Finally, there is the issue of corruption. Hyden (1983) ascribed corruption to pre-modern forces, with extended peasant-based networks of support interpenetrating the state and commercial activity; whilst providing a means for survival this may also serve as a basis for corruption. This, and similar accounts of the failure of the state, concluded that modernisation would gradually weaken such ties. Given the role of the state in supporting corrupt networks, neo-liberals within the IMF concluded that the simplest remedy would be to do away with the state as a site of corruption (cf. Hoogevelt, 2005). In practice, the resultant policy prescriptions weakened the capacity of the state to enforce social order and provide basic services. Forced and over hasty privatisations simply led to state assets being handed over to well connected elites, worsening endemic corruption. In addition, there have been numerous corruption scandals implicating foreign companies – for example, the activities of the British arms firm, BAE, in South Africa and Tanzania. A peculiar lopsided morality invariably leads to local politicians shouldering the blame, with the briber being left free to continue its activities across the continent.

What does all this mean for the practice of HRM? Firstly, flows of corruptly obtained monies to tax havens has meant that less money is available for local investment; this means that local firms often face difficulties of chronic under-capitalisation. Secondly, a culture of corruption can easily contaminate large areas of social life, increasing transaction costs in any exchange relationship.

HRM IN PRACTICE: EMERGING TRENDS AND ISSUES

In view of the above, a number of key issues emerge. Firstly, whilst many African countries have extensive bodies of labour law – of either the common or civil law variety – evidence points to uneven enforcement, reflecting both limitations in government capacity and a lack of political will (Wood & Brewster, 2007). As Eronda (2004) notes, there is 'widespread ambiguity surrounding the rule of law'. The latter reflects the unwillingness – and inability – of national governments to protect either their citizens or local firms in the face of global competition (Greider, 1997).

Secondly, owing to similar capacity shortfalls, it is likely that, faced with intense adversarial competition, firms will battle to adopt longer-term policies that require reinvestment in plant or people (Hoogevelt, 2005). To put it another way, firms cannot afford to move much beyond labour repression.

Thirdly, and despite this, African HRM is less simply a bleak house model than, often, an autocratic and low-wage low-skill model ameliorated by a kind of paternalism that incorporates conceptions of personal and family based ties, rights and obligations (Ovadje & Ankomah, 2001; Wood & Brewster, 2007). The overwhelming managerial focus is likely to be on control, emphasis tested processes and hierarchies, founded on either pre-colonial notions of chieftanship (Beugre, 2002) and/or colonial despotism (Jackson, 2002). Low wages may be offset through ad hoc financial assistance, and the willingness of firms to countenance wage adjustments in response to unexpected increases in living or transport costs (Beugre, 2002). However, it is likely that older male managers may play a patriarchal role, women are likely to be marginalised, and informal recruitment will be on the lines of existing patronage mechanisms, excluding outsiders (Ovadje & Ankomah, 2001: 183–5).

Fourthly, what bargaining power unions had is likely to have been undercut by the large-scale job losses that have universally accompanied destructive structural adjustment policies (Hyman, 2003).

Fifthly, risk aversion and close supervision, and a concentration of decision making at the centre, may make for low productivity and morale (Jackson, 2002: 1006). This is compounded by imbalances in knowledge as to the potential and challenges of specific HRM situations, in turn reflecting limits in skills, knowledge and existing enquiry (Kamoche et al., 2003).

Sixthly, training tends to be informal and on the job, linked to the notion of a 'community concept of management', with employment not being seen so much as a formal, fixed contract, but rather as part of a set of reciprocal informal obligations (Eronda, 2004: 6; cf. Beugre, 2002). As many firms have been forced to focus on cost, rather than quality and, in the export sector, on primary products, the need for training may in any event be constrained (Jackson, 2002: 999). The limited resources most firms have at their disposal means that it would be difficult for them to invest in formal training systems even if they wanted to (p. 1000).

Seventhly, as Harvey (2002) notes, critical to understanding HRM in Africa is that not only laws, but formal rules are often ignored or bent, reflecting limitations both in the state, and the constrained nature of civil society (cf. Webster & Wood, 2005). In part, this may allow firms a greater degree of room for manoeuvre than would otherwise be the case. At the same time, this is likely to make for lower levels of systemic trust, given the greater difficulty in enforcing both implicit and explicit contracts: in turn, this will raise transaction costs relating to the operationalisation of the employment contract, and reduce overall organisational effectiveness (cf. Marsden, 1999).

What this body of literature has in common is view that a large body of existing practices have translated into poor outcomes (Budhwar & Debrah, 2001; Kamoche, 2002; Kamoche et al., 2003; Mellahi & Wood, 2003; Wood & Frynas, 2006). This would represent, at least in part, a product the limited capacity of many African states, both to support the development of human resources and to enforce existing labour laws. Uneven growth (reflecting volatile primary commodity prices) and poor terms of trade, and often inappropriate and misdirected foreign aid, have worsened things. Poor outcomes also represent the product of the embeddedness of authoritarianism and patriarchy both within and the beyond the workplace. In turn, this would make it difficult to introduce and maintain advanced HRM paradigms (Kamoche, 2002: 993–5; cf. Hyden, 1983).

Finally, there is the role of international organisations to be considered. Kamoche et al. (2003: xvi) rather optimistically suggest that foreign firms have a vital role to play in developing human capital and diffusing knowledge. However, while they may 'have a responsibility to act responsibly', many clearly do not. A lack of commitment to a specific locale other than as a supply of cheap raw materials, cheap labour or a market for low cost goods is too often the norm. Whilst it could be argued that political instability may deter many multinationals from greater investment in people and communities across much of Africa, this instability is itself at least partially a product of unequal terms of trade and an inability to move to higher value added production paradigms. Contrary to Kamoche et al. (2003), we would suggest that a greater problem than a lack of ideas and skills is a lack of willingness by international players to systematically commit to developing them. Too often private or non-private international organisations are excessively short-termist in their orientation, with little attention being given to sustainability. The 2008 global depression appears to have worsened such tendencies, and has resulted in greatly reduced inward capital flows across the continent.

WAYS FORWARD?

Recent studies have pointed to the internal limitations within organisations and the need for more effective usage of non-financial incentives, particularly given widespread limitations in organisational resources (Mathauer & Imhoff, 2006). Whilst financial incentives are important, failings even in basic internal organisational communication may prove severely counterproductive. Trans-Africa research has revealed (as with studies elsewhere) imparting dignity in working life, and a recognition of the worth of employees' vocations can be highly effective HRM interventions.

Brigaldano (1996: 438) notes that a lack of access to capital (itself a product of low savings rates), poor terms of trade and weak infrastructure mitigate heavily against the competitiveness of firms and nations in tropical Africa: no matter how effective management is, an adverse external context makes it very difficult for firms to succeed. Gender imbalances also play a role: the greater the divide between men and women in human resource indicators, the lower the national GDP (p. 439). Sustainable industrialisation depends on indigenous capabilities, including the development of human capital and infrastructure.

This focus on practical issues and constraints is echoed by Anakwe et al. (2000), who argue that the main factors moulding HRM policy within the organisation are socio-economic, rather than perceived cultural variations. At the same time, it is necessary to take a critical approach towards the former: it has become commonplace for politicians and those in the conservative community to mouth platitudes on 'good governance' or 'bridging the digital divide', when it is necessary to take account of the long time horizons needed, and the need to devote resources to incrementally developing sustainability (Helleiner, 2002: 532). And, the solutions prescribed – totally open regimes regarding foreign investment, open markets and minimal state intervention – have time and again proven ineffective in promoting the competitiveness of firms based in poor regions of the world.

Karsten and Ghebregiorgis (2005: 145) argue that although the view that great cultural differences preclude the adoption of Western-type HRM practices is incorrect, the successful diffusion of new paradigms depends in part on adaption in the light of local social, cultural and economic circumstances. Research drawing on the Eritrean experience pointed to a greater degree of local expertise than might have been presumed by incoming Western organisations: in other words, there was a real risk of ignoring local capabilities. Similarly, Kamoche (1997) argues that the internal capabilities of African organisations are often discounted, when there is a real need to move beyond 'dependency' approaches. Indeed, the diverse nature of workforces within many African organisations can be a real source of competitive advantage, owing to the wide range of life experiences and perspectives.

A caveat is in order here: as noted earlier there is considerable diversity within Africa. For example, research by Karsten and Ghebregiorgis (2005) points to a relatively high degree of consultation and workplace egalitarianism within Eritrean organisations. Hence, it would be simply wrong to conclude that all tropical African workplaces are authoritarian environments. Institutions may mould strategic choices, but real alternatives remain even in unpromising circumstances, even if most firms seek to remain with tried and trusted tools and techniques (Harvey et al., 2002).

SOUTH AFRICAN EXCEPTIONALISM?

As noted above, studies on HRM and its relationship to the wider social context in South Africa should be seen as falling in a distinct category, on account of the country's very much more developed economy and supporting infrastructure. Two relevant strands of literature are worth exploring in more detail here.

The first strand explores the economic effects of South Africa's political transformation, and the firm level implications thereof (see, for example, Carmody, 2002; Smith & Wood, 1998). Such studies highlight the extent to which the phased reduction of protective tariffs and associated subsidies has forced firms to become more competitive, necessitating more sophisticated HRM policies; relatively strong unions made, in many cases, outright labour repression an unviable option. Under high apartheid, many firms relied on cheap and, in many respects, coerced labour. In the post-apartheid era, firms have often been forced to use labour more intelligently (although large islands of labour repression may be found on the rural periphery), with a stronger emphasis on skills development and the adoption of more capital-intensive production paradigms (Wood & Sela, 2000; Smith & Wood, 1998). Wood and Els (2000) found that organisations were gradually moving towards more sophisticated HRM strategies, involving team working, quality circles and a greater investment in people. At the same time, the take-up of new production paradigms was uneven. Moreover, the adoption of 'modern' HRM systems has gone hand-in-hand with wholesale job shedding (Smith & Wood, 1998; Wood & Els, 2000). In turn, this has both weakened the position of organised labour, and contributed to the expansion of an underclass locked in poorly paid and insecure informal sector work (Webster, 2004).

A second focus on the literature relating to HRM in South Africa has been affirmative action and Black Economic Empowerment (BEE). Currently, inequity in the South African labour market is the result of past statutory discrimination in the workplace, as well as interventions by the colonial and apartheid regimes in other policy realms (see Buhlungu et al., 2008).

Labour markets in the South African context are complex and were historically segmented along the lines of race, gender, class and geography and to date still are, despite a vastly different political, social and economic regime since 1994. Certain pieces of legislation have been enacted to attempt to reconfigure both the formal and informal characteristics of labour market functioning; that is they seek to eliminate unfair discrimination in terms of access to workplace resources such as employment itself, promotions, training and workplace benefits as well as eliminating prejudice, intolerance and discrimination within the workplace (Buhlungu et al., 2008).

The authors of the 'Black Economic Empowerment Commission' state that due to South Africa's colonial and apartheid policies, the development of black human capital in the country has been severely stunted.

The most heinous crime of all was the deliberate neglect of the country's majority population and this was propped up by the delivery of an inferior education during this period.

The continued imbalance in the attainment of skills presents a formidable challenge to the possibility of equitable growth. South Africa is in a crisis as the country does not possess, as yet, the human capital required to attain sustained, high levels of economic growth at a time when global competitiveness is not simply based on the mass production of standardised goods, cheap raw material inputs and low-skill, low-wage labour (Black Economic Empowerment Commission).

As Buhlungu et al. (2008) note, the quality of labour supplies is at least partially dependent on education. There have been considerable improvements in the schooling, with the percentage of people with no schooling having almost halved from the 1996 to 10 per cent in 2007. Across the board, there has been a general increase in access to schooling, although women and blacks are still proportionately under-represented, especially at the tertiary level.

Such work points to abiding inequality on racial lines, the over-representation of white males in management, and potential policy options. In turn, this inequality represents both a product of past injustices, and present imbalances in training, and skills shortfalls (Horwitz et al., 2002; 2003). Horwitz et al. (2002; 2003) argue that diversity management is closely related to HRD, and, has 'hard' (recruitment, planning, performance awards) and 'soft' (awareness raising) dimensions.

Currently the challenge in South Africa remains to design and implement an Integrated Human Resources Development (HRD) strategy. This will aid the country to plan its HRD requirements for the twenty-first century in the face of formidable obstacles identified in its educational system but also in the face of one more worrying factor: the HIV/AIDS pandemic. This poses a threat and promises to significantly derail the attempts to substantially increase the country's human capital. Estimates are that the overall prevalence of HIV will reach almost 25 per cent in the general population by 2010. After that, life expectancy is expected to fall from the 68.2 years anticipated in the absence of the AIDS epidemic to 48 years (Black Economic Empowerment Commission).

RESEARCH ON HRM IN AFRICA: UNDER-REPRESENTED AND MARGINALISED?

Africans writing on work and employment relations issues in Africa is under-represented in major international journals (Wood & Dibben,

2006); there is a similar under-exposure of topics relating to HRM in Africa in such journals (De Cieri et al., 2007). Indeed, Özbilgin (2004) goes so far as to conclude that, based on a general lack of coverage both in terms of printed articles and the composition of journal editorial boards, Africa represents a 'blind spot' in studying about HRM. This is particularly the case when South Africa is removed from the equation. Based on an extensive survey of academic journals in the sub-field of industrial relations, Wood and Dibben (2006) found that not only was the number of papers published on Africa-related topics disproportionately small, but it was gradually declining. This would reflect both the limited resources available to African scholars and the marginalisation of Africa in wider debates. However, they found no relationship between an Africa-focus and the quality of journal outlet in terms of various journal rankings: African scholars were not ghettoised to the lowest ranked journals (Wood & Dibben, 2006). This would suggest that what research is coming out of Africa is often of good quality. Encouragingly, African scholars are reasonably well represented in two established journals, *International Journal of Human Resource Management* and *Employee Relations*. Finally, as Kamoche (1997) notes, much of the literature on HRM in Africa has focused on the concerns and needs of multinational companies, rather than the needs of organisations and individuals based in Africa.

CONCLUSION

Across much of tropical Africa, people management tends to be characterised by authoritarian, paternalist and personal management, with informal recruitment networks based on existing family and personal ties, informal on the job training and the use of informal credit to ameliorate job insecurity, and often poor wages and working conditions. However, HRM on the continent should not be seen as monolithic. Firstly, there are many variations reflecting different historical legacies (Jackson, 2002: 1008).

Secondly, at firm level, experimental innovations, adaptions and changes will always take place (cf. Morgan, 2007).

Thirdly, and related to the second, there are pockets of best practice to be found, practices that make optimal use of recent advances in Western HRM and the specific challenges of the local. Examples of the latter would include the export orientated motor industry in South Africa and mining in Botswana. There are many barriers to the further diffusion of such practices. Whilst it could be concluded that the general prospects for higher value added HRM paradigms across the continent are bleak, the slow institutionalization of multi-partyism in many African countries provides a basis for greater pluralism not only in the polity, but also the workplace.

REFERENCES

Anakwe, U., Igbaria, M. & Anandarajan, M. 2000. Management practices across cultures: the role of support in technology usage. *Journal of International Business*, **31**(4): 653–666.

Anonymous. 1999. Gender and informal sector. *International Labour Review*, **138**(3): 340.

Baruch, Y. & Clancy, P. 2000. Managing AIDS in Africa: HRM challenges in Tanzania. *International Journal of Human Resource Management*, **11**(4): 789–806.

Beugre, C. 2002. Understanding organizational justice and its impact on managing employees. *International Journal of Human Resource Management*, **13**(7): 1091–1094.

Black Economic Empowerment Commission, n. d. Available at: http://www.foundation-development-africa.org/africa_black_business/index.htm.

Bracking, S. 2003. Regulating capital accumulation: negotiating the imperial 'frontier'. *Review of African Political Economy*, **30**(95): 11–32.

Brigaldano, G. 1996. Africa's economic renewal under the spell of globalization. *Review of African Political Economy*, **23**(69): 437–442.

Budhwar, P. & Debrah, Y. A. 2001. *Human Resource Management in Developing Countries*. London Routledge.

Buhlungu, S., Bezuidenhout, A., Lewins, K. & Bischoff, C. 2008. Tracking progress on the implementation and impact of the employment equity act since its inception. Report, Sociology of Work Unit, University of the Witwatersrand.

Carmody, P. 2002. Between globalisation and (post) apartheid: the political economy of restructuring in South Africa. *Journal of Southern African Studies*, **28**(2): 255–275.

Cohen, R. 1994. Resistance and hidden forms of consciousness amongst African workers. In E. Webster et al. (eds), *Work and Industrialisation in South Africa*. Johannesburg: Ravan.

Croucher, R. 2007. Industrial relations in francophone Africa: the case of Niger. In G. Wood & C. Brewster (eds), *Industrial Relations in Africa*. London: Palgrave.

De Cieri, H., Cox, J. W. & Fenwick, M. 2007. A review of international human resource management. *International Journal of Management Reviews*, **9**(4): 281–302.

Dzimbiri, L. 2007. Industrial relations in Malawi. In G. Wood & C. Brewster (eds), *Industrial Relations in Africa*. London: Palgrave.

Eronda, E. 2004. Effective management: a key factor in sustainable development in sub-Saharan African economies. Working paper. Hempstead, New York: Frank. G. Zarb School of Business, Hofstra University.

Essaaidi, M. 2007. Industrial relations in an emerging Morocco. In G. Wood & C. Brewster (eds), *Industrial Relations in Africa*. London: Palgrave.

Fajana, S. 2007. The development of industrial relations in Nigeria: 1900–2006. In G. Wood & C. Brewster (eds), *Industrial Relations in Africa*. London: Palgrave.

Fukuyama, F. 1995. *Trust: Social Virtues and the Creation of Prosperity*. New York: Free Press.

Ghabadamosi, G. 2003. HRM and the commitment rhetoric: challenges for Africa. *Management Decision*, **41**(3): 274–280.

Ghebregiorgis, F. & Karsten, L. 2007. The dynamics of industrial relations in Eritrea: 1991–2006. In G. Wood & C. Brewster (eds), *Industrial Relations in Africa*. London: Palgrave.

Greider, W. 1997. *One World, Ready or Not*. Harmondsworth, UK: Penguin.

Hansen, C. 2003. Cultural myths about human resource development: analyzing the cross-cultural transfer of American models to Germany and Cote d'Ivoire. *International Journal of Training and Development*, **17**(1): 16–30.

Harvey, M. 2002. Human resource management in Africa: Alice's adventures in Wonderland. *International Journal of Human Resource Management*, **13**(7): 1119–1145.

Harvey, M., Myers, M. & Novicevic, M. 2002. The role of MNCs in balancing human capital books between African and developed countries. *International Journal of Human Resource Management*, **13**(7): 1060–1076.

Helleiner, G. 2002. Marginalization or participation: African in today's global political economy. *Canadian Journal of Africa Studies*, **36**(3): 531–550.

Hofstede, G. 1991. *Cultures and Organizations*. London: McGraw-Hill.

Hoogevelt, A. 2005. Postmodern intervention and human rights. *Review of African Political Economy*, **32**(106): 595–599.

Horwitz, F., Bowmaker-Falconer, A. & Searll, P. 2003. Human resource development and managing diversity in South Africa. International *Journal of Manpower*, **17**(4/5): 134–151.

Horwitz, F., Browning, V., Jain, H. & Steenkamp, A. 2002. Human resource practices and discrimination in South Africa: overcoming the apartheid legacy. *International Journal of Human Resource Management*, **13**(7): 1105–1118.

Hyden, G. 1983. *No Shortcuts to Progress*. London: Heinemann.

Hyman, R. 2003. An emerging agenda for trade unions, Labournet. Available at: www.labournet.de/diskussion/gewerkschaft/hyman.html.

ILO. 1997. Press Kit: World Employment Relations Report 1996–7. Geneva: ILO.

Jackson, T. 2002. Reframing human resource management in Africa. *International Journal of Human Resource Management*, **13**(7): 998–1018.

Kamoche, K. 1997. Managing human resources in Africa. *International Business Review*, **6**(5): 537–558.

Kamoche, K. 2002. Introduction: human resource management in Africa. *International Journal of Human Resource Management*, **13**(7): 993–997.

Kamoche, K., Debrah, Y. A., Horwitz, F. M. & Muika, G. N. 2003. Preface. In K. Kamoche, Y. A. Debrah, F. M. Horwitz & G. N. Muika (eds), *Managing Human Resources in Africa*. London: Routledge.

Karsten, L. & Ghebregiorgis, F. 2005. Human resource management practices in Eritrea: challenges and prospects. *Employee Relations*, **28**(2): 144–163.

Karsten, L. & Illa, H. 2005. Ubuntu: a key African management concept. *Journal of Managerial Psychology*, **20**(7): 607–620.

Kiringa, J. 2007. Contemporary issues in industrial relations: Uganda. In G. Wood & C. Brewster (eds), *Industrial Relations in Africa*. London: Palgrave.

Manda, D. K., Bigsten, A. & Mwabu, G. 2001. Trade union membership and earnings in Kenyan manufacturing firms. Working Papers in Economics No.50. Goteburg: Goteborg University.

Marsden, D. 1999. *A Theory of Employment Systems*. Oxford: Oxford University Press.

Mathauer, I. & Imhoff, I. 2006. Health worker motivation in Africa: the role of non-financial incentives and human resource management tools. *Human Resources and Health*, **4**(24): 1–17.

Mellahi, K. & Wood, G. 2003. From kinship to trust: changing recruitment practices in unstable political contexts: the case of Algeria. *International Journal of Cross-Cultural Management*, **3**(3): 393–405.

Morgan, G. 2007. Globalization, institutions and multinationals. Working Paper. Coventry: University of Warwick.

Okpara, J. & Wynn, P. 2008. Human resource management practices in a transition economy: challenges and prospects. *Management Research News*, **31**(1): 57–76.

Ovadje, F. & Ankomah, A. 2001. Human resource management in Nigeria. In P. Budhwar & Y. Debrah (eds), *Human Resource Management in Developing Countries*. London: Routledge.

Özbilgin, M. 2004. International human resource management. *Personnel Review*, **33**(2): 205–221.

Smith, M. & Wood, G. 1998. The end of apartheid and the organization of work in South Africa's Eastern Cape Province. *Work, Employment and Society*, **12**(3): 479–495.

Spector, P., Cooper, C. L., Sanchez, J. I. & O'Driscoll, M. 2002. Locus of control and well-being at work: how generalizable are Western findings? *Academy of Management Journal*, **45**(2): 453–466.

Swartz, E. & Davis, R. 1997. Ubuntu. The spirit of African transformation management: a review. *Leadership and Organization Development Journal*, **18**(6): 290–294.

Tordoff, W. 1984. *Government and Politics in Africa*. London: Macmillan.

Webster, E. 2004. New forms of work and the representational gap: a Durban case study. In G. Wood & M. Harcourt (eds), *Trade Unions and Democracy*. Manchester: Manchester University Press.

Webster, E. & Wood, G. 2005. Human resource management practice and institutional constraints. *Employee Relations*, **27**(4): 369–385.

Webster, E., Wood, G. & Brookes, M. 2006. International homogenization or the persistence of national practices? The remaking of industrial relations in Mozambique. *Relations Industrielles/Industrial Relations*, **61**(2).

Whitley, R. 1999. *Divergent Capitalisms*. Oxford: Oxford University Press.

Williams, G. 1994. Why structural adjustment is necessary and why it doesn't work. *Review of African Political Economy*, **21**(60): 214–225.

Wood, G. 2008. Introducing employment relations in Africa. *Employee Relations*, **30**(4): 329–332.

Wood, G. & Brewster, C. 2007. Introduction: comprehending industrial relations in Africa. In G. Wood & C. Brewster (Eds.), Industrial Relations in Africa. London: Palgrave.

Wood, G. & Dibben, P. 2006. Coverage of African related studies in international journals: greater exposure for 'public intellectuals' in sociology and industrial relations. *African Sociological Review*, **10**(1): 180–192.

Wood, G. & Els, C. 2000. The making and remaking of HRM: the practice of managing people in the Eastern Cape Province, South Africa. *International Journal of Human Resource Management*, **11**(1): 112–125.

Wood, G. & Frynas, G. 2006. The institutional basis of economic failure: anatomy of the segmented business system. *Socio-Economic Review*, **4**(2): 239–277.

Wood, G. & Sela, R. 2000. Making human resource development work. *Human Resource Development International*, **3**(4): 451–464.

22 Human resource management in the Middle East

Pawan Budhwar and Kamel Mellahi

An attempt is made in this chapter to provide an overview regarding the scenario of human resource management (HRM) in the Middle East. Given both the geographical vastness of the Middle East and scarcity of reliable information on many countries of the region and in order to put things into perspective, we initially describe the Middle East context and then present an analysis of relevant literature related to the developments in the field of HRM specific to the region. While doing the latter, we point out the main determinants of HRM in the region, any emerging HRM model(s)/approach(es) relevant to it and conclude by highlighting the main challenges for HR in the Middle East and an indicative way forward.

Before we describe the geographical, socio-economic, political and business context of the Middle East it is important to clarify the terminology used to denote the region. The literature highlights the interchangeable usage of terms such as 'Middle East', 'Near East', 'Middle East–North Africa (MENA)', 'Southwest Asia', 'Greater Middle East', 'Arabian-peninsula' or the 'Arab World' in a very general sense (i.e. it is applied for a group of nations existing in the region) by both academics and policy makers. However, it is important to acknowledge that despite some commonalities, each nation in the region has an independent set of socio-economic components which differ from one another in content, arising inevitably from the interplay of social relations unique to themselves. Hence, it would be sensible to look at the HRM phenomena as a part and parcel of the distinctive political, socio-economic, cultural and institutional system of a given country in the region (Budhwar & Debrah, 2001; Morishima, 1995). This is further complicated by the fact that countries in the Middle East region are at different stages of industrialisation and economic and political development. Such variations should be kept in mind while analysing HRM systems of the region.

Given the infancy of developments in HRM in most countries in the region (see Budhwar & Mellahi, 2006; 2007), it is important to define HRM in the broadest sense. This is sensible as several HR approaches can exist within firms in different countries, each of which depends (along with a number of other factors, such as different institutions and national culture) on a number of distinct 'internal labour markets' (Boxall, 1995; Budhwar & Sparrow, 2002; Osterman, 1994). Within each labour market, HRM incorporates a range of sub-functions and practices which include systems for work force governance, work organisation, staffing and development and reward systems (Begin, 1992). For this chapter, HRM is concerned with the management of all employment relationships in the firm, incorporating the management of managers as well as non-management labour.

THE MIDDLE EAST CONTEXT

As indicated above, the term Middle East is loosely defined and perhaps refers to a cultural area with no precise borders. There are different versions of what should be included under the Middle East region (see Encyclopaedia – Answers.com 2010). In the broadest sense it is the geographic region where Europe, Africa, and Asia meet. Sometimes it is referred to as an area with its centre in the eastern Mediterranean basin. The most limited version of the region only includes Syria, Lebanon, Israel, Palestine and Jordan. Another version also includes Cyprus, Turkey, Iraq and Egypt, while a yet broader version of the Middle East includes Iran, Kuwait, Saudi Arabia, Bahrain, Qatar, United Arab Emirates, Oman and Yemen. Further, in some cases, the Middle East region is extended to include countries in North Africa with clear connections to Islam, like Libya, Tunisia, Algeria, Morocco, Mauritania and Sudan, Eritrea, Djibouti and Somalia. For this chapter, the last interpretation of Middle East is used.

Islam is the main religion of the Middle East with approximately 95 per cent of the total population following it. Apart from Islam, it is also the birthplace of Judaism and Christianity with Turks and Arabs as its largest population groups, followed by Kurds and Jews. The dominating languages are Turkish, Arabic, Kurdish, English, French and Hebrew respectively (Encyclopaedia of the Orient, 2009). With approximately 65 per cent of the world's known oil reserves, the Middle East has occupied a position of primary strategic importance since World War II. Initially, in the 1950s it exhibited one of the lowest levels of economic development in the world. However, in the 1960s and 1970s, many countries in the region experienced a strong economic growth mainly due to discovery of oil. Still, in 1990s (with the exception of Israel, Egypt, Turkey and Lebanon), the GDP growth per worker in the region was roughly 1 per cent per year (almost half the rate of other developing countries) and there has been a regular decline in total factor productivity (World Bank, 2009).

A variety of factors are responsible for a slow economic development in the Middle East. These range from structural imbalances, the so-called 'curse of natural-resource abundance' (over-dominance of the oil sector), underdeveloped financial markets, deficient political systems and political reforms, lack of privatisation, slow integration into the global economy, dominant public sectors, growing unemployment, government systems (such as traditional sheikhdoms, absolute monarchies, military or auto-cratic regimes) in the region to conditions of war and conflict (for details see Abdelkarim, 2001; Abed, 2003; Budhwar & Mellahi, 2006; Kuran, 2004; Looney, 2003; Shaban et al., 1995; Yousef, 2004).

Nevertheless, due to the continuous rise in oil prices between 2004 and 2008 the economic growth in the oil-rich countries of the region has been phenomenal (for details see World Bank, 2009). The non-oil producing countries (such as Israel, Egypt, Tunisia, Morocco) also experienced an improved growth over the years; however, due to recent global economic crisis, the economic growth in the region has obviously slowed down. Indeed, serious concerns for security lie over the forecast of both kinds of economies in the region (EIU ViewsWire, 2009). Such concerns have serious implications for foreign direct investment in the region, especially in the non-oil producing economies which tend to rely heavily on sectors such as tourism, agriculture and merchandise exports.

The existing information on the region clearly indicates that most countries in the Middle East are now emphasising the development of their human resources (see Mellahi & Budhwar, 2006). The countries with rich oil resources in the region want to reduce their dependence on it and develop other sectors which need skilled human resources. Similarly, the non-oil producing countries tend to rely on an efficient human resources bank for sustained economic growth. Most countries in the region also tend to overly rely on a foreign workforce and, given the rapidly increas-ing indigenous population and unemployment in the region, there is an increased emphasis on the development of 'locals' and reducing the number of 'foreigners' from the workforce, for example by Saudi Arabia, UAE and Oman. Indeed, issues related to the creation of right kind of employable skills in the region and to change the mindset of locals to work in private sector and lower levels positions is proving to be a major chal-lenge. Such developments have serious implications for the HR function in the region (also see Murphy, 2002; Mellahi & Budhwar, 2006).

DEVELOPMENTS IN HRM IN THE MIDDLE EAST

As indicated above, we still have little literature available related to the field of HRM for most of the countries in the Middle East. There are even fewer works which can provide an overview of the HRM in the region.

Lately, Budhwar and Mellahi (2006; 2007) have created a couple of useful volumes on HR-related issues in a number of Middle East countries. In this section, we initially summarise the main HR-related works in the region and then present the key messages emerging from the same.

A number of scholars have attempted to provide a country-specific HRM overview: see for example the works of Namazie and Tayeb, 2006 and Namazie and Frame (2007) on Iran; Al-Hamadi and Budhwar (2006) and Al-Hamadi et al. (2007) on Oman; Suliman (2006) on UAE; Ali and Al-Kazemi (2006) on Kuwait; Mellahi and Wood (2004) and Mellahi (2006) on Saudi Arabia; Abdalla (2006) on Qatar; Branine and Analoui (2006) on Jordan; Aycan (2006) on Turkey; Baruch et al. (2006) and Tzafair et al. (2007) on Israel; Leat and Al-Kot (2007) on Egypt; Hatem (2006) on Sudan; Yahiaoui and Zoubir (2006) on Tunisia; Branine (2006) on Algeria; and Benson and Al Arkoubi (2006) on Morocco. These scholars present the nature and emerging patterns of HRM systems along with their key determinants in respective countries.

Also, depending on the economic development of a given country in the region, studies covering specific aspects of HRM have been conducted. For example, effects of regulations on HRM in the Saudi Arabia private sector by Mellahi (2007), on employment policy in Kuwait by Al-Enizi (2002; human resource development (HRD) in Oman by Budhwar et al. (2002), impact of HRM practices and corporate entrepreneurship on firm performance in Turkish firms by Kaya (2006), HRM and organisational effectiveness in Israel by Bamberger et al. (1989), transformation in HRM in Israel by Sagie and Weisberg (2001) and management in Israel by Baruch (2001) and Dale (1978), management and international business issues in Jordan by El-Said and Becker (2003), impact of cultural value orientations on preferences for HRM by Aycan et al. (2007), challenges for employment in the Arab region by Shaban et al. (1995), rise and demise of participative management in Algeria by Branine (1994) and management in Arab Middle East by Weir (2000). There are a few studies that examine women in management-related issues in the Middle East countries (see for example, Aycan, 2004, for Turkey; Izraeli, 1987, for Israel; Metcalfe, 2006, for Bahrain, Jordan and Oman; and Metle, 2002, for Kuwait). Also, there are publications which debate the transfer of HRM from overseas to the region (such as Al-Husan and James, 2009, for Jordan; and Mellahi and Frynas, 2003, for Algeria). We acknowledge that this is not an exhaustive list of different studies in the region but certainly a good indicator about the kind of HR-related analysis being carried out in the recent past.

A thorough analysis of the existing literature highlights the emergence of a number of key HR-related themes. Perhaps the dominant theme is the one that highlights the influence of Arab culture and values on its management systems (see Al-Faleh, 1987; Ali & Al-Shakis, 1985; Aycan, 2006; Bakhtari, 1995; Elsayed-Elkhouly & Buda, 1997; Hunt & At-Twaiijri, 1996; Mellahi, 2003; Yasin, 1996). Also a number of scholars (see Tayeb, 1997; Ali, 1992; 2004; Robertson et al., 2001) highlight the immense impact of Islamic values, Islamic work ethics and Islamic principles on the management of human resources in the Islamic countries of the region (see Ahmad, 1976; Budhwar & Fadzil, 2000; Mellahi & Budhwar, 2006; Rosen, 2002). As expected, due to socio-cultural similarities, a number of countries (such as Egypt, Morocco, Turkey, Kuwait and Qatar) tend to be similar in various aspects of cultural value orientations such as high on group-orientation, strong on hierarchical structures, high on masculinity, strongly following the Arab traditions and low on future orientation (see Kabasakal & Bodur, 2002). Similarly, in the Turkish context, Yucelt (1984) found that managers in traditional public sector organisations tend to lean toward a benevolent-authoritarian system and less toward participative style.

Mellahi and Budhwar (2006) report a strong impact of high power distance on managers' perception towards the delegation of authority to lower level of employees and interaction with them in countries like Kuwait, Saudi Arabia, Morocco and Egypt. As a result of this, managers in such countries practise centralised decision-making processes, are less willing to delegate responsibility and discourage active employee participation. In such circumstances and socio-cultural and traditional set-ups, loyalty to one's family and friends is expected to override loyalty to organisational procedures and this often results in the use of inequitable criteria in recruitment, promotion and compensation. Ali and Al-Kazemi (2006) and Mellahi (2006) further highlight the influence of Islamic values and principle of Shura, i.e. consultation, social harmony and respect, which is manifested in consensus decision-making styles, respect for authority and age, and concern for the well-being of employees and society at large in countries like Kuwait and Saudi Arabia. Ali and Al-Kazemi (2006) reveal that several ideal Islamic values such as equity and fairness are often not adhered to in practice. This explains the widespread adoption of some HRM practices in the Middle East that are not compatible with Islamic values, such as the use of nepotism in recruitment and compensation, known as 'wasta' in Gulf Co-operation Council (GCC) countries and 'piston' in North African countries.

Due to significant differences (such as sociological, economic, legal, political, etc.) between the Middle East and other parts of the world (West, in particular), it is recommended that a foreign element is, at best, not conducive to the development of sound management practices in the region (Ali, 1995; Ali & Camp, 1995; Anwar, 2003; Neal & Finlay, 2008; Yavas, 1998). An analysis by Saleh and Kleiner (2005) indicates that if

American companies want to be successful in the Middle East then they should develop an understanding of the local culture, politics and people of the region. Similarly, Hill et al. (1998) highlight the problems of transferring technology designed and produced in developed countries to the Arab region. As technology is culturally biased in favour of developed countries, this creates cultural and social obstacles while transferring it to developing countries.

A related theme clearly evident in the literature is that of 'human resource development' where issues related to the impact of Arab management styles on the effectiveness of cross-cultural negotiations and organisational development activities in the region (see Ali, 1996) along with relationship between management education and its impact on managerial effectiveness (see Analoui & Hosseini, 2001; Ali & Camp, 1995; Atiyyah, 1991; Anastos et al., 1980) and the need for and mechanisms of management development in the Arab world (for details see Agnala, 1997; al-Rasheed & al-Qwasmeh, 2003; Budhwar et al., 2002). Atiyyah (1991, 1996) emphasises the usefulness of cultural training and acculturation in the adjustment of expatriates to the region. Al-Rajhi et al. (2006) reveal the challenges for HRM in the region regarding the adjustment of impatriates. Contributions from Elmuti and Kathawala (1991), Fiegenbaum and Lavie (2000) and Marriot (1986) further confirm the need for foreign firms and employees to be strongly responsive/adaptive to the local requirements in order to be successful in the Middle East context. This is important given the significant cultural diversity of the foreign workforce in the Middle East where it is crucial for managers to recognise, understand and acknowledge the cultural differences of subordinates and accordingly adopt a relevant leadership style. Given the high power distance nature of most Middle East nations, an employee-orientated approach tends to be more successful than others (see al-Rasheed, 2001; Badawy, 1980; Enshassi & Burgess, 1991).

In the absence of awareness, an outsider might believe there are strong similarities among nations of the Middle East (especially due to the dominance of Islam, with the exception of Israel, and the stereotype that all countries in the region are oil-rich); however, there remains considerable variation across countries in the Middle East that the above cultural factors cannot explain. It is now well-established in the literature that the management of human resources in a given set-up is influenced by a combination of national factors (such as the above mentioned cultural and institutional factors), different contingent variables (such as size, age, nature of an organisation) and the kind of policies and strategies an organisation pursues (see Budhwar & Sparrow, 2002). Many such factors and variables are shaping the HRM function in the Middle East region as well. The remaining part of this section further highlights the main determinants of the HRM policies and practices of Middle East.

Over the past couple of decades, countries such as Iran, Jordan, Turkey, Egypt, Algeria and Tunisia have been actively pursuing the process of privatisation (see Mellahi & Budhwar, 2006; Murphy, 2001). Such countries are also pursuing liberalisation of their economic systems as a result of which the central government control over HRM practices has been greatly reduced and such developments have serious implications on HRM systems of these countries. Some of the obvious impacts are on job security in the public sector (which is now eroding fast) and downsizing and closure of poorly performing firms. The growing high level of unemployment has had a strong impact on employment relations in Tunisia, Egypt, Algeria and Morocco in the form of decline in union membership, decrease in their bargaining power and accordingly reduction in trade union militancy.

The variation in HRM practices based on size and nature/ownership of the firm (private, public or a multinational) is also evident from an analysis of HRM in countries such as Iran, Turkey, Morocco, Algeria, Kuwait, Saudi Arabia and Egypt. Benson and Al Arkoubi (2006) highlight that in Morocco multinational firms in comparison to both public and privately owned firms tend to apply equitable HRM practices for recruitment and selection, pay on average higher salaries and provide more training for their employees. Expectedly, they also put more pressure on employees to perform. Interestingly, large private sector organisations, notably in Algeria, Morocco and Egypt, tend to pay higher salaries than public sector organisations, but job security is low in private sector firms as compared to public sector organisations (in countries like Algeria, Morocco and Egypt). In GCC countries (i.e., Oman, UAE, Kuwait, Saudi Arabia and Qatar), however, public sector organisations pay higher salaries than most private sector organisations and job security is still relatively high in the public sector (for more details see Mellahi & Budhwar, 2006).

There is also evidence that in many Middle Eastern countries (such as Oman, UAE, Egypt, Algeria, Saudi Arabia, Morocco and Iran) the respective national governments are emphasising the development of human resources and accordingly giving organisations freedom in HRM matters, though within the legal framework. As a result, the names and nature of traditional personnel departments are changing to emphasise the development of effective HRM systems to help firms compete at home and abroad. However, in the absence of skilled HR professionals in most Middle Eastern countries (perhaps with the exception of Israel), HR managers have been muddling through, often relying on 'trial and error', to cope with the impact of market liberalisation and severe international competition. In order to cover such skill gaps many countries like Algeria, UAE, Oman, Jordan, Kuwait, Saudi Arabia, Israel and Iran are heavily investing in the development of their human resources. A number of inherent problems with these countries such as lack of a vocation-based education system, the supply and demand imbalance, negative perception of locals working in the private sector or in lower positions and the lack of participation of women in the main workforce are proving to be the main bottlenecks (see Heeti & Brock, 1997; Diyen, 2004; Mellahi, 2006; Rugh, 2002; Shaw, 2002). Further, the strong emphasis on localisation (i.e. giving priority to local nationals while offering jobs and promotions) is not helping either the private sector or multinational firms to achieve rationalisation of their HRM systems (see Ahmad, 2004; Rees et al., 2007).

Based on the above analysis, it can be concluded that there is a scarcity of literature on different aspects of HRM systems in the Middle East, as a result of which it is difficult to draw a conclusive and comprehensive picture of the scene. Also, we cannot confidently say whether there is such a thing as a 'Middle Eastern HRM model', i.e. a single HRM model with distinct Middle Eastern characteristics. Perhaps due to a number of reasons related to diversity within the region (historical contexts, institutional, geographical, cultural, political, legal, social, development stage of nations, support of relevant agencies, national wealth, poverty, national priority, issues related to terrorism, role of unions, reliance on foreign labour, etc.), it seems that organisations in the Middle East use a whole range of different HRM policies and practices and the professionalisation of HRM functions is at different stages in different countries.

CHALLENGES FOR THE FUTURE OF HR IN THE MIDDLE EAST

Based on the above we can say that HRM policies and practices throughout the Middle East are changing, both in terms of the contexts within which they operate, and in terms of the HRM function. There is emerging evidence about major HR related changes in the region. A number of forces are contributing in this regard, such as changes in the business environment, globalisation, and increased interest in the region both because of oil and on-going conflicts. For example, Aycan (2006), Branine (2006), Benson and Al Arkoubi (2006) and Hatem (2006) highlight a move towards individualisation in HRM policies such as rewards and promotion in Turkey, Algeria, Morocco and Egypt, respectively. These scholars also indicate the efforts being made in most Middle Eastern countries for firms to move away from relationship-based practices and use more performance-based criteria in recruitment, selection, rewards and promotion (also see Mellahi & Budhwar, 2006). In order to make such changes widespread and reap their real benefits, there are massive challenges for the HR function in the region. The first is to convince all concerned about the need to bring such changes. The second is to ensure these changes take place both quickly and effectively. One of the major hurdles in this regard is changing the mindset of top managers whose beliefs are embedded routines and old ways of doing things (see Mellahi, 2003).

Related to changing the mindset of top managers, the creation of a more strategic image and status of the HR function in the region is another major challenge. Mellahi and Budhwar (2006) conclude that the HRM function in most Middle Eastern countries suffers from low status and is often relegated to 'a common sense' function that, according to top management, does not require professional skills. To a great extent this is an outcome of the poor development of HR managers who are not fully capable and ready to manage change and meet current and future challenges. Given some of the above raised inherent problems within the Middle East, such as increasing unemployment, deficiency of employable skills in the available job candidates, pressure to survive, the right size firms in the present difficult times and reducing over-reliance on the oil economy, it is high time that the HR function in the region is given the freedom to make the required changes and accordingly make useful contributions towards organisations' performance, as has happened in many other parts of the world. In this regard, there is a need to not only overhaul the educational and vocational courses and training provided by different institutions in the region but also be open and receptive to adopting some more of the successful systems of other parts of the world (indeed with the required modifications), as is happening in many emerging markets, resulting in crossvergence of HRM systems (see Budhwar & Debrah, 2009).

In order to achieve some of the above-indicated changes, it is important to move away from the inequitable relationship-based HRM policies such as 'wasta' and 'piston' towards a competence- or merit-based approach. This is now becoming a serious issue given the aggressive localisation programmes pursued by many countries of the region, on the one hand, while, on the other, firms in the region are being pushed into global economic integration in order to survive and flourish. The absence of skilled local human resources and open discrimination against overseas skilled employees might result in serious skill gaps in the region which will have massive economic implications when many nations in the region are making serious attempts to move to new sectors and reduce their over-reliance on oil-related products. The HR function in the region has then serious tasks at hand to determine how such a transition (towards localisation) can take place and also to ensure that talent is not pushed out of the region haphazardly, creating skills gaps and increasing the cost of attracting, acquiring and retaining talent. Organisations in the Middle East then have much to sort out and learn.

This is further aggravated by the problems created by both high unemployment levels and rapidly increasing population in most Middle Eastern countries (Harry, 2007). In future this may be a major destabilising factor for economic development in the region. Indeed many governments of different countries in the Middle East, along with the private sector, are trying to develop schemes whereby the government contributes towards the cost of training locals to encourage private sector firms to recruit more local workers (this is happening, for example, in Saudi Arabia, Oman and the UAE). Dealing with such major issues then not only poses major challenges to national governments but also has serious implications for HR functions. In the present imperatives of a global dynamic business environment and the need for global competitiveness, it is expected that social protection and welfare provisions would be weakened in favour of more liberal and market oriented socio-economic development (see Richards, 2001; Rivlin, 2001). We also expect a significant variation on this front between oil-rich nations of the region, such as Qatar and UAE (which might continue to provide support to less efficient public sector organisations) and less rich nations such as Morocco, Sudan and Egypt. Also, one would expect that trade unions in the Middle East, consistent with the global trend, will continue to decline and lose more power, and will be excluded or marginalised from the process of setting future HRM policies and practices (for more details see Mellahi & Budhwar, 2006).

Given that little is researched and published on HRM in the region, clearly, there is a need for more research to develop a clear view about the key factors that shape the HRM function and determine the performance thereof. But this raises another set of challenges such as in the absence of established research culture, how can researchers conduct meaningful research? Also, given the socio-cultural context of the Middle East and the emerging evidence about the need to adopt and modify Western HRM practices in the region, one needs to be careful while adopting western HRM constructs, items, measures and methodologies to conduct investigations in the region. For example, the Chinese context over the past decade or so, where a lot of work is being carried out on the development of context-specific constructs, measures and methodologies, is a way forward for the Middle East context as well. As reported above, indeed some work has been conducted in the past on Arab and Islamic work values and management styles and systems. This can be further developed specifically for the HRM function. In particular, future research should seek to identify and classify the unique region-specific aspects of national culture and other variables, political institutions and other possible external factors that influence HRM in the Middle East.

Apart from the above, there is a need for both HRM practitioners and researchers to work on issues related to diversity management, psychological contracts, HRM and performance, emerging dominant HRM approaches and systems of the Middle East, the kind of internal labour markets suitable for firms operating in the region, tackling nepotism and corruption, ensuring a robust legal framework that works properly to safeguard both local and overseas employees, the creation of relevant employment relations and how to encourage sharing of evidence-led best practices available with certain case companies in the Middle East. The emphasis should be to further highlight successful indigenous HRM practices as well as practices developed elsewhere which can be adopted in the region (e.g. high performance work systems (HPWS); organisational structures/systems that bundle together innovative work practices, skills, people and technology into an internally coherent configuration that enhances organisational performance; specific types of participatory work practices that are successful in high power distance societies; comparisons of the effectiveness of participatory work practices with the current paternalistic approaches being practised in the region).

Dealing with the above raised challenges will never be easy as it needs macro-level changes at the country level and also at an individual-level a change of mindset, one which is deeply rooted in the socio-cultural milieu of the region. Also, it is important to acknowledge that to conduct HR research in most parts of the Middle East is and will continue to be a challenging task in an environment where access to reliable data and organisations is very demanding. However, reports like this one and indeed others help us to identify the factors that shape and reshape HRM in the Middle East, and perhaps better understand the mechanisms by which they do so, and also guide us in what we need to do in future and how best to do it.

REFERENCES

Abdalla, I. A. 2006. Human resource management in Qatar. In P. Budhwar & K. Mellahi (eds), *Managing Human Resources in the Middle East*. London: Routledge, pp. 121–145.

Abdelkarim, A. 2001. UAE Labour Market and Problems of Employment of Nationals. D. P. Series, Vol. No. 4. TANMIA.

Abed, G. T. 2003. Unfulfilled promise. *Finance and Development*, **40**(1).

Agnala, A. A. 1997. Management development in the Arab World. *Human Resource Management International Digest*, **5**(5): 38–41.

Ahmad, A. 1976. *Islam: Its Meaning and Message*. London: Islamic Council of Europe.

Ahmad, M. 2004. When does final mean final? *Arab News*, 4 November 2004.

Al-Enzi, A. 2002. Kuwait's employment policy: its formulation, implications, and challenges. *International Journal of Public Administration*, **25**(7): 885–900.

Al-Faleh, M. 1987. Culture influence on Arab management development: a case study of Jordan. *The Journal of Management Development*, **6**(3): 19–34.

Al-Hamadi, A. B. & Budhwar, P. 2006. HRM in Oman. In P. Budhwar & K. Mellahi (eds), *Managing Human Resources in the Middle East*. London: Routledge, pp. 40–58.

Al-Hamadi, A. B., Budhwar, P. & Shipton, H. 2007. Managing human resources in the Sultanate of Oman. *International Journal of Human Resource Management*, **18**(1): 100–113.

Al-Husan, F. B. & James, P. 2009. Multinationals and the process of post-entry HRM reform: evidence from three Jordanian case studies. *European Management Journal*, **27**(2): 142–153.

Al-Raji, I., Altman, Y., Metcalfe, B. & Roussel, J. 2006. Managing impatriate adjustment as a core HRM challenge. *Human Resource Planning*, **29**(4): 15–24.

Al-Rasheed, A. M. 2001. Feature of traditional Arab management and organization in the Jordan business environment. *Journal of Transnational Management Development*, **6**(1–2): 27–39.

Al-Rasheed, A. M. & Al-Qwasmeh, R. M. 2003. The role of the strategic partner in the management development process: Jordan Telecom as a case study. *International Journal of Commerce & Management*, **13**(2): 144–156.

Ali, A. 1992. Islamic work ethic in Arabia. *Journal of Psychology*, **126**(5): 507–520.

Ali, A. 1995. Cultural discontinuity and Arab management thought. *International Studies of Management and Organization*, **25**(3): 1–15.

Ali, A. 1996 Organizational development in the Arab World. *Journal of Management Development*, **15**(5): 4–21.

Ali, A. 2004. *Islamic Perspectives on Management and Organization*. Cheltenham: Edward Elgar.

Ali, A. & Al-Kazemi, A. 2006. Human Resource Management in Kuwait. In P. Budhwar & K. Mellahi (eds), *Managing Human Resources in the Middle East*. London: Routledge, pp. 79–96.

Ali, A. & Al-Shakis, M. 1985. Managerial value systems for working in Saudi Arabia: an empirical investigation. *Group & Organization Studies*, **10**(2): 135–152.

Ali, A. & Camp, R. C. 1995. Teaching management in the Arab World: confronting illusions. *The International Journal of Educational Management*, **9**(2): 10–18.

Analoui, F. & Hosseini, M. H. 2001. Management education and increased managerial effectiveness: the case of business managers in Iran. *The Journal of Management Development*, **20**(9/10): 785–795.

Anastos, D., Bedos, A. & Seaman, B. 1980. The development of modern management practices in Saudi Arabia. *Columbia Journal of Business*, **15**(2): 81–90.

Anwar, S. A. 2003. Globalisation of corporate America and its implications for management styles in an Arabian cultural context. *International Journal of Management*, **20**(1): 43–52.

Atiyyah, H. S. 1991. Effectiveness of management training in Arab Countries. *The Journal of Management Development*, **10**(7): 22–30.

Atiyyah, H. S. 1996. Expatriate acculturation in Arab Gulf Countries. *Journal of Management Development*, **15**(5): 37–47.

Aycan, Z. 2004. Key success factors for women in management in Turkey. *Applied Psychology*, **53**(3): 453–471.

Aycan, Z. 2006. Human resource management in Turkey. In P. Budhwar & K. Mellahi (eds), *Managing Human Resources in the Middle East*. London: Routledge, pp. 160–179.

Aycan, Z., Al-Hamadi, A. B., Davis, A. & Budhwar, P. 2007. Cultural orientations and preference for HRM policies and practices: the case of Oman. *International Journal of Human Resource Management*, **18**(1): 11–32.

Badawy, M. K. 1980. Styles of Middle Eastern managers. *California Management Review*, **22**(2): 51–58.

Bakhtari, H. 1995. Cultural effects on management style: a comparative study of American and Middle East management style. *International Studies of Management & Organization*, **25**(3): 97–119.

Bamberger, P., Bachrach, S. & Dyer, L. 1989. HR management and organizational effectiveness: high technology entrepreneurial start-up firms in Israel. *Human Resource Management*, **28**(3): 349–366.

Baruch, Y. 2001. Management in Israel. In M. Warner (ed.), *IEMB Management in Europe*. London: Thompson International Press, pp. 267–273.

Baruch, Y., Meshoulam, I. & Tzafrir, S. 2006. Human resource management in Israel. In P. Budhwar & K. Mellahi (eds), *Managing Human Resources in the Middle East*. London: Routledge, pp. 180–198.

Begin, J. P. 1992. Comparative HRM: a systems perspective. *International Journal of Human Resource Management*, **3**(3): 379–408.

Benson, P. & Al Arkoubi, K. 2006. Human resource management in Morocco. In P. Budhwar & K. Mellahi (eds), *Managing Human Resources in the Middle East*. London: Routledge, pp. 273–290.

Boxall, P. F. 1995. Building the theory of comparative HRM. *Human Resource Management Journal*, **5**(5): 5–17.

Branine, M. 1994. The rise and demise of participative management in Algeria. *Economic and Industrial Democracy*, **15**(4): 595–631.

Branine, M. 2006. Human Resource Management in Algeria. In P. Budhwar & K. Mellahi (eds), *Managing Human Resources in the Middle East*. London: Routledge, pp. 250–272.

Branine, M. & Analoui, F. 2006. Human resource management in Jordan. In P. Budhwar & K. Mellahi (eds), *Managing Human Resources in the Middle East*. London: Routledge, pp. 145–159.

Budhwar, P., Al-Yahmadi, S. & Debrah, Y. 2002. Human resource development in the Sultanate of Oman. *International Journal of Training and Development*, **6**(3): 198–215.

Budhwar, P. & Debrah, Y. 2009. Future research on human resource management systems in Asia. *Asia Pacific Journal of Management*, **26**(2): 197–218.

Budhwar, P. & Debrah, Y. A. 2001. Rethinking comparative and cross national human resource management research. *The International Journal of Human Resource Management*, **12**(3): 497–515.

Budhwar, P. & Fadzil, K. 2000. Globalisation, economic crisis and employment practices: lessons from a large Malaysian Islamic institution. *Asia Pacific Business Review*, **7**(1): 171–198.

Budhwar, P. & Mellahi, K. 2006. Introduction: HRM in the Middle-East context. In P. Budhwar & K. Mellahi (eds), *Managing Human Resources in the Middle East*. London: Routledge, pp. 1–19.

Budhwar, P. & Mellahi, K. 2007. Human resource management in the Middle East. *International Journal of Human Resource Management*, **18**(1): Special Issue.

Budhwar, P. & Sparrow, P. 2002. An integrative framework for determining cross national human resource management practices. *Human Resource Management Review*, **12**(3): 377–403.

Dale, Z. 1978. Management in Israel. *Business Horizons*, **21**(4): 36.

Diyen, H. 2004. Reform of secondary education in Morocco: challenges and prospects. *Prospects*, **34**(2): 211–222.

Economists Intelligence Unit ViewsWire. 2009. Middle East economy: 25 March, 2009. Available at:http://viewswire.eiu.com/index.asp?layout=VWChannelVW3&region_id=43 0000443&country_id=&channel_id=190004019.

Elmuti, D. & Kathawala, Y. 1991. An investigation of the human resources management practices of Japanese subsidiaries in the Arabian Gulf region. *Journal of Applied Business Research*, **7**(2): 82–89.

El-Said, H. & Becker, K. 2003. *Management and International Business Issues in Jordan*. London: International Business Press.

Elsayed-Elkhouly, S. & Buda, R. 1997. A cross-cultural comparison of value systems of

Egyptians, Americans, African and Arab Executives. *International Journal of Commerce & Management,* **7**(3–4): 102–120.

Encyclopaedia: Answers.com. 2009. Available at: http://www.answers.com/topic/middle-east.

Encyclopaedia of the Orient. 2009. Middle East. Available at: http://lexicorient.com/e.o/middle_east.htm.

Enshassi, A. & Burgess, R. 1991. Managerial effectiveness and the style of management in the Middle East: an empirical analysis. *Construction Management and Economics,* **9**(1): 79–93.

Fiegenbaum, A. & Lavie, D. 2000. Strategic management of MNCs' entry into foreign markets: experience of Israel in the 1990s. *European Management Journal,* **18**(1): 93–102.

Harry, W. 2007. Employment creation and localization: the crucial human resource issues for the GCC. *International Journal of Human Resource Management,* **18**(1): 132–146.

Hatem, T. 2006. Human resource management in Egypt. In P. Budhwar & K. Mellahi (eds), *Managing Human Resources in the Middle East.* London: Routledge, pp. 199–218.

Heeti, A. G. A. & Brock, C. 1997. Vocational education and development: key issues, with special reference to the Arab world. *International Journal of Educational Development,* **17**(4): 373–389.

Hill, C. E., Loch, K. D., Straub, D. W. & El-Sheshai, K. 1998. A qualitative assessment of Arab culture and information technology transfer. *Journal of Global Information Management,* **6**(3): 29–38.

Hunt, D. M. & At-Twaiijri, M. I. 1996. Values and the Saudi manager: an empirical investigation. *The Journal of Management Development,* **15**(5): 48–56.

Izraeli, D. N. 1987. Women's movement into management in Israel. *International Studies of Management & Organization,* **16**(3–4): 76–108.

Kabasakal, H. & Bodur, M. 2002. Arabic cluster: a bridge between East and West. *Journal of World Business,* **37**(1): 40–54.

Kaya, N. 2006. The impact of HRM practices and corporate entrepreneurship on firm performance: evidence from Turkish firms. *The International Journal of Human Resource Management,* **17**(12): 2074–2092.

Kuran, T. 2004. Why the Middle East is economically underdeveloped: historical mechanisms of institutional stagnation. *Journal of Economic Perspectives,* **18**(3): 71–90.

Leat, M. & Al-Kot, G. 2007. HRM practices in Egypt: the influence of national context. *The International Journal of Human Resource Management,* **18**(1): 147–158.

Looney, R. 2003. The Gulf co-operation council's cautious approach to economic integration. *Journal of Economic Cooperation,* **24**(2): 137–160.

Marriot, R. G. 1986. Ads require sensitivity to Arab culture. Religion. *Marketing News,* **20**(9): 3–5.

Mellahi, K. 2003. National culture and management practices: the case of GCCs. In M. Tayeb (ed.), *International Management: Theory and Practices.* London: Prentice-Hall, pp. 87–105.

Mellahi, K. 2006. Human resource management in Saudi Arabia. In P. Budhwar & K. Mellahi (eds), *Managing Human Resources in the Middle East.* London: Routledge, pp. 97–120.

Mellahi, K. 2007. The effect of regulations on HRM: private sector firms in Saudi Arabia. *The International Journal of Human Resource Management,* **18**(1): 85–99.

Mellahi, K. & Budhwar, P. 2006. HRM challenges in the Middle East: agenda for future research and policy. In P. Budhwar & K. Mellahi (eds), *Managing Human Resources in the Middle East.* London: Routledge, pp. 291–301.

Mellahi, K. & Frynas, J. G. 2003. An exploratory study into the applicability of Western HRM practices in developing countries: an Algerian case study. *International Journal of Commerce & Management,* **13**(1): 61–73.

Mellahi, K. & Wood, G. 2004. Human resource management in Saudi Arabia. In P. Budhwar & K. Mellahi (eds), *Managing Human Resources in the Middle East.* London: Routledge, pp. 135–151.

Metcalfe, B. 2006. Exploring cultural dimensions of gender and management in the Middle East. *Thunderbird International Business Review,* **48**(1): 93–108.

Metle, M. K. 2002. The influence of traditional culture on attitudes towards work among Kuwati women employees in the public sector. *Women in Management Review*, **17**(5–6): 245–262.

Morishima, M. 1995. Embedding HRM in a social context. *British Journal of Industrial Relations*, **33**(4): 617–640.

Murhpy, T. E. 2002. Market forces and the Middle East's new interest in HRM. *Business Horizons*, **45**(5): 63–71.

Murphy, C. E. 2001. The state and the private sector in North Africa: seeking specificity. *Mediterranean Politics*, **6**(2): 1–28.

Namazie, P. & Frame, P. 2007. Development in human resource management in Iran. *The International Journal of Human Resource Management*, **18**(1): 159–171.

Namazie, P. & Tayeb, M. 2006. Human resource management in Iran. In P. Budhwar & K. Mellahi (eds), *Managing Human Resources in the Middle East*. London: Routledge, pp. 20–39.

Neal, M. & Finlay, J. L. 2008. American hegemony and business education in the Arab World. *Journal of Management Education*, **32**(1): 38–49.

Osterman, P. 1994. Internal labor markets: theory and change. In C. Kerr & P. D. Staudohar (eds), *Markets and Institutions*, Vol. 303–339. Cambridge, MA: Harvard University Press.

Rees, C. J., Mamman, A. & Braik, A. B. 2007. Emiratization as a strategic HRM change initiative: case study evidence from a UAE petroleum company. *The International Journal of Human Resource Management*, **18**(1): 33–53.

Richards, A. 2001. The political economy of economic reform in the Middle East: the challenge to governance. Working paper. Santa Monica, CA: Rand.

Rivlin, P. 2001. *Economic Policy and Performance in the Arab World*. Boulder, CO: Lynne Rienner.

Robertson, C., Al-Habib, M., Al-Khatib, J. & Lanoue, D. 2001. Beliefs about work in the Middle East and the convergence versus divergence of values. *Journal of World Business*, **36**(13): 223–235.

Rosen, L. 2002. *The Culture of Islam: Changing Aspects of Contemporary Muslim Life*. Chicago: The University of Chicago Press.

Rugh, W. A. 2002. Education in Saudi Arabia: choices and constraints. *Middle East Policy*, **9**(2): 40–55.

Sagie, A. & Weisberg, J. 2001. The transformation in human resource management in Israel. *International Journal of Manpower*, **22**(3): 226–234.

Saleh, S. & Kleiner, B. H. 2005. Issues and concerns facing American companies in the Middle East. *Management Research News*, **28**(2/3): 56–62.

Shaban, A. R., Asaad, R. & Al-Qudsi, S. 1995. The challenges of employment in the Arab region. *International Labour Review*, **134**: 65–82.

Shaw, K. E. 2002. Education and technological capability building in the Gulf. *International Journal of Technology and Design Education*, **12**(1): 77–91.

Suliman, A. M. T. 2006. Human resource management in the United Arab Emirates. In P. Budhwar & K. Mellahi (eds), *Managing Human Resources in the Middle East*. London: Routledge, pp. 40–58.

Tayeb, M. 1997. Islamic revival in Asia and human resource management. *Employee Relations*, **19**(4): 352–364.

Tzafair, S. S., Meshoulam, I. & Baruch, Y. 2007. HRM in Israel: new challenges. *The International Journal of Human Resource Management*, **18**(1): 114–131.

Weir, D. T. H. 2000. Management in the Arab Middle East. In M. Tayeb (ed.), *International Business, Theories, Policies and Practices*. Upper Saddle River, NJ: Pearson Education Limited, pp. 501–510.

World Bank. 2009. Global economic prospects 2009: Middle East and North Africa regional outlook. Washington, DC: World Bank.

Yahiaoui, D. & Zoubir, Y. H. 2006. Human resource management in Tunisia. In P. Budhwar & K. Mellahi (eds), *Managing Human Resources in the Middle East*. London: Routledge, pp. 233–249.

Yasin, M. 1996. Entrepreneurial effectiveness and achievement in Arab culture. *Journal of Business Research*, **35**(1): 69–78.

Yavas, U. 1998. The efficacy of US business education in the transfer of management technology: the case of Saudi Arabia. *Journal of Education for Business*, **71**(1): 50–54.

Yousef, T. M. 2004. Development, growth and policy reform in the Middle East and North Africa since 1950. *The Journal of Economic Perspectives*, **18**(3): 91–114.

Yucelt, U. 1984. Management styles in the Middle East: a case example. *Management Decision*, **22**(5): 24–36.

23 European human resource management: a contextualised stakeholder perspective

Wolfgang Mayrhofer, Paul Sparrow and Chris Brewster

THE IMPORTANCE OF CONTEXT FOR HRM

Human Resource Management (HRM) is always HRM in context. How HRM works, what it covers, what is regarded as good HRM, who is an important player in HRM, what role legal regulations and cultural values play, etc. – all this depends heavily on the respective context. Context in this sense includes the internal context of organisations, e.g. organisational size, structure, demography, and strategy, as well as the external context. The latter covers, for example, national culture and values; elements of the institutional environment such as legal regulations, the respective industry and the type of economy; economic factors such as amount and speed of economic growth, degree of foreign direct investment in the respective country and structure of the industries prominent in the country; and societal characteristics such as population structure and growth/decline, educational system and level, and political system (Mayrhofer et al., 2011).

Discussing European approaches to HRM inevitably has to address matters of context because, as we argue in this chapter, European HRM unfolds in a unique context, conceptually has developed some unique characteristics, in particular compared to more universalist assumptions of other HRM approaches as prevalent in North America or in the Far East, and shows some unique patterns at the level of policies and practices which, at the same time, reflect the conceptual specifics and the internal variety of European HRM. In a first step, we further characterise the contextual uniqueness of Europe relevant for European HRM.

EUROPE: A UNIQUE CONTEXT

Europe offers a mix of hetero- and homogeneity leading to a unique context for organisational decision makers. Covering roughly the same area as the United States, Europe displays a picture of heterogeneity. For example, the Council of Europe covers 47 nation states; the European Union (EU) alone has 23 official languages and more than 60 indigenous regional or minority language communities.[1] A centuries-old and often belligerent relationship between European countries creates a tradition of tension and rivalry which is true for large European states like the UK, France, Spain, Germany or Italy as well as smaller states or ethnic groups, e.g. Hungarian minorities in Slovakia and Romania or conflicts in Northern Ireland, Bosnia or the Basque region. Significant cultural differences exist between cultural clusters – e.g. a Nordic, an Anglo-Saxon, a Romanic and a Germanic cluster – (see, e.g. Hofstede, 1980; Trompenaars, 1994) as well as between closely related countries such as, e.g. Germany and Austria (Brück, 2002), indicating deep rooted cultural specifics at the level of values/norms and basic assumptions. Economically, countries with a comparatively high GDP per person employed such as France (55 052 dollars) or the UK (51 697 dollars) are a stark contrast to countries of comparable size such as Turkey (26 187 dollars) or Poland (24 553 dollars), not to mention countries like Romania (11 644 dollars) or the Ukraine (11 134 dollars; source: World Bank Data, all figures for 2008[2] and constant 1990 purchasing power parity). Institutionally, great heterogeneity is present, too. This ranges from labour law, especially in the area of protection of employees, via a widely varying degree of resistance against corruption – e.g. Denmark as a global #2 in the perceived level of public-sector corruption in a country or territory; Russia and the Ukraine as a shared #146 out of 180 ranks (Source: Corruption Perception Index, 2009[3]) – to different basic systems of law and jurisdiction, e.g. common law in the UK and Ireland versus civil law in the rest of Europe. It is no surprise that many of the key studies in varieties of capitalism (see Chapter 4; Hall & Soskice, 2001; Maurice et al., 1986; Whitley, 1999) have been written by scholars from Europe and focused on this region.

Despite all these differences, there is also remarkable homogeneity. Major drivers for this include, for example, global rationality myths as emphasised in institutionalist approaches such as the world polity view (Meyer et al., 1997), globally operating media conglomerates providing similar information and entertainment to vast numbers of people, the information available through the internet or emerging political entities going beyond single nation states.

In Europe, the latter plays an especially important role through the rise and the enlargement of the European Union. Currently 27 European countries are members of the EU, with 16 countries sharing the Euro as joint currency. Linked to, but separate from, the EU are Norway and Switzerland, part of the geographical concept of Europe and also following the European Union Social Policy. The EU is an historically unique attempt to bring together long-established independent nations to accept, by treaty rather than conquest, the same legislation and markets. Tying together formerly sovereign states into a more coherent and, in some areas such as competition regulation or consumer protection, heavily interdependent union, the EU has created a more unified context that organisations have to operate in. Arguably, the four freedoms, i.e. the freedom of movement of goods, persons, services and capital, exemplify this best and have direct implications for HRM. Both the freedom of movement of goods and of services have, among others, increased business across national borders with consequences for the kind, number and geographical location of employees that organisations need. Free movement of persons created new options for labour market mobility and affects HRM, especially in areas such as recruitment, career planning or compensation. The freedom of movement of capital increased European competition, changing the strategic outlook for companies formerly operating at a national level only, which, in turn, creates new demands for human resources in terms of mobility and qualifications. Beyond the four freedoms, the EU also makes deliberate efforts to invest in the human capital available for organisations. Maybe most typical in this respect are programmes such as SOCRATES, Leonardo da Vinci or TEMPUS which are investments in human capital, on the surface supporting the exchange of people within Europe, but also creating an informal network of understanding and contacts.

At least four global mega-trends have a specific European meaning and relevance for HRM. First, globalisation as a widely debated 'all-pervasive' phenomenon (see e.g. Giddens, 2000; Michie, 2003; Stiglitz, 2002) is linked to Europe's struggles to keep its role in the world (Laqueur, 2006). Among others, this raises the issue of competitiveness and performance at the organisational, national and regional levels and the role human capital plays in this process. Second, diversity and gender issues are prevalent in practical action and theoretical debate in Europe and in EU legislation. For example, as the workforce of companies becomes more diverse in terms of gender, ethnicity, age, physical ability, age, religion, sexual orientation and so forth, HRM has to ask itself whether this is adequately reflected in practical action at the political and organisational level as well as in its research agenda. Third, virtualisation, in itself affecting all parts of life (Sichler, 2006: 26f.), allows new forms of work and careers (Mayrhofer et al., 2002a). The decoupling of processes/actions and the underlying material basis, especially through the means of information technology in combination with the relatively small geographical distances in Europe, raises new issues for HRM practice and research. Examples include dealing with different forms of working in a unified Europe and handling the work/non-work interface against the backdrop of European policy issues supporting the participation and reintegration of women in the labour market. Fourth, demography in Europe shows a two-sided picture. Taken to extremes, Europe is an ageing and dying continent, at least if you look at current reproduction rates (see e.g. Beets, 2007). In many countries in Europe, the reproduction rate is well below the required figure for keeping the population stable, which is roughly a birth rate of 2.1 per female (2004 EU-25 average birth rate 1.5; Poland 1.23; Spain 1.32; Germany 1.37; source: EUROSTAT as cited in Höhn et al., 2006: 18). At the same time, however, other countries, such as Turkey, show a rapidly growing population. This has consequences for a great number of issues relevant for HRM in Europe ranging from labour market policies to regulations of retirement age or immigration restrictions.

Beyond the factual level, Europe also has a unique methodological heritage, thus providing alternatives to the classical objective, deductive perspective with a focus on the world as a 'given' entity that can be looked at and analysed without referring to subjective interpretation. Beyond constructivists' (see e.g. Hejl, 2000) or constructionists' (see e.g. Gergen, 2002) epistemology, there is a wide range of inductive reasoning ranging from dialectics as interpreted by Hegel (1807) to social phenomenology by Schütz (1981 (Original 1932)) or Feyerabend's 'anything goes' (1978).[4] Altogether, this heritage influences the research landscape by encouraging questioning and looking for reasons behind the facts rather than mere description.

Against this backdrop, 'European' in this chapter does not implicate a monolithic European context. On the contrary, both commonalities and differences do play a role. A telescope analogy (Brewster, 1995) is helpful here: changing the focus on a telescope provides the viewer with ever more detail and the ability to distinguish ever-finer differences within the big picture than can be seen with the naked eye. Vice versa, zooming-out provides a broad overall picture. None of the chosen perspectives are wrong or inaccurate, but some are more useful for some purposes than for others. For some purposes, speaking of Europe as if it were, by and large, 'one' does make sense, for example, when analysing effects of the EU on European mobility and its consequences for the labour market. However, studies about effects of different national institutions on, for example, the role of women in the labour force and the respective reactions of HRM require a much more fine-grained understanding.

EUROPEAN HRM: THE CONCEPTUAL LEVEL

Given these European specifics, it is little wonder that a more contextual as opposed to a universalistic perspective dominates the academic discussion of HRM in Europe. A contextual perspective focuses on understanding the differences between and within HRM in various contexts and the causes of these differences. Factors such as culture, ownership structures, management decision processes, labour markets, the role of the state and trade union organisation become critical.

Consequently, the notion of 'European HRM' as a conceptually distinct approach emerged, arguably as a reaction to the hegemony of US conceptions of HRM (see, e.g. Brewster, 1993; Sparrow & Hiltrop, 1994; Brewster et al., 2000). The specifics of this concept of European HRM do not relate to the core tasks and basic function of HRM. Of course, supplying organisations with the right number of people with the right qualifications at a specified time and location is still a key characteristic of HRM. However, there are arguments about how this can and should be done and what 'right' means in this context. Specifically, in the discussion about European HRM some of the basic assumptions behind the US version of HRM are questioned and it is argued that they are not or only partly applicable in Europe. We argue that foundations of a distinctive European approach lie in its approach to 'stakeholders' rather than 'shareholders'. In addition and combined with the importance of the unique context, three additional elements are cornerstones for the emerging conceptual stance in HRM: the role of the state; a belief that people have 'rights' in and to their jobs; an acceptance that consultation is proper; and a more critical and less 'managerialist' agenda going beyond the mere HRM-organisational performance link. Though none of these elements is unique on its own, the specific combination in Europe leads to conceptual distinction.

Stakeholder Rather than Shareholder Approach

When conceptually changing from personnel to human resource management (Guest, 1987, takes a critical perspective here), one of the major characteristics was the stronger emphasis on strategic aspects, in particular linking HRM, contextual developments and the contribution of HRM to the overall performance of the organisation. Particularly in the United States, the assumption that underlies HRM is that its purpose is to improve the operation of the organisation: understanding HRM is especially valued because this improves the way that human resources are managed strategically within organisations, with the ultimate aim of increasing organisational performance, as judged by its impact on the organisation's declared corporate strategy (Fombrun et al., 1984; Huselid, 1995), the customer (Ulrich, 1989) or shareholders (Huselid, 1995; Becker & Gerhart, 1996; Becker et al., 1997). Thus, the widely cited definition by Wright and McMahan states that strategic HRM is 'the pattern of planned human resource deployments and activities intended to enable a firm to achieve its goals' (1992: 298). In the US context, this leads to giving primacy to the interests of the shareholders.

The stakeholder debate challenges this view. Instead of purely looking at shareholders' interest, the stakeholder view acknowledges the greater array of actors within and outside the organisation that are of relevance for survival as well as for economic success. Agency theory (for an overview see Eisenhardt, 1989) already acknowledges two groups with potentially conflicting interests: owners ('shareholders') and managers. A further enlargement identifies additional groups who have a legitimate stake in the organisation, e.g. employees, customers, trade unions, creditors, or NGOs. The basic argument of the stakeholder approach (Freeman, et al., 2010; for a European angle, see Bonnafous-Boucher & Pesqueux, 2005) is that such groups have a collective interest in the organisation, e.g. regarding decisions about employment, keeping the environment clean or acting as a good corporate citizen in the local environment.

By and large, HRM in Europe is leaning more towards a stakeholder approach. Going beyond owners and managers, HRM takes into account a great variety of groups. In some countries, some of these groups have a legal basis for influencing organisational decisions. For example, in the Germanic countries co-determination is comparatively strong and legally regulated. Therefore, it is not only works councils and trade unions that play a role at the organisational level. Under specific circumstances, employee representatives are part of the supervisory board and have a strong vote when appointing one member of the board of directors who is responsible for labour issues within the company.

The Role of the State

'The major difference between HRM in the US and in Western Europe is the degree to which [HRM] is influenced and determined by state regulations. Companies have a narrower scope of choice in regard to personnel management than in the US' (Pieper, 1990: 82). This remains an accurate assessment (see also Blanchard, 1999) and could equally well be made with many other countries and regions besides the United States. Not only has the state a higher involvement in underlying social security provision and a more directly interventionist role in the economy, it also provides far more personnel and industrial relations services and is a more substantial employer in its own right by virtue of a more extensive government-owned sector. For example, most European countries have a substantial share of the 18–24 age group in higher education and, in addition, provide substantial support to employers through state-aided vocational training programmes. Equally, in most European countries much higher proportions of GDP are spent by the state on labour market programmes. This includes training, retraining and job transition support, job creation schemes and programmes to help younger people and the long-term unemployed get into the labour market. Substantial proportions of employment (up to 50 per cent in some countries) are in the public sector (Brewster, 1995).

This has consequences in terms of the basic approach to HRM and its scope. In a country like the United States where 'freeing business from outside interference' is seen as a broadly approved objective, it makes sense to develop a vision of HRM which focuses on the policies and practices of management. From a European perspective, this excludes much of the work of HRM specialists and many of the issues that are vital for the organisation such as trade union relationships and dealing with government, for example. Europeans are also more likely to assume that HRM can apply at a variety of levels and cannot be restricted to the organisational or sub-organisational level. For example, in Europe there are discussions of the strategic human resource management policies of the European Union as a distinct body, of particular governments or sectors. Even specific regions within a country may have HRM policies and practices, e.g. raising training standards to attract inward investment, establishing local employment opportunities, etc. All these levels, which might be seen as exogenous factors impinging upon HRM in the universalist paradigm, are seen in Europe as within the scope of HRM.

The state plays a larger role in HRM partly by being a larger employer than is the case in many other world regions and partly by taking a more controlling and/or supporting role in employment practices. With the state as an employer, a number of basic parameters for HRM change. The time horizon for HRM activities is different, with less pressure for management in general and HRM in particular to take a very short-term view of investments and results. In addition, the education and training infrastructure put in place by the state and still mainly state provided in most European countries, has a significant impact on organisational HRM (Boxall, 1995; Mabey, 2004). Although human resource development practices vary considerably by country in Europe (Mabey & Ramirez, 2005), in world comparative terms the provision is extensive and of good quality. State support for post-education training is also high and gives these countries an advantage in country level competitiveness.

People's Rights in and to their Jobs

By and large, the state in Europe accepts and guarantees people's rights in and to their jobs. Legislation is not independent of national values

(Hofstede, 1980) and it is no surprise therefore to find that the United States, which is characterised by high levels of individualism and comparatively low levels of uncertainty avoidance, has overall comparatively less legislative control over (or interference from, or support for) the employment relationship than is found in most of Europe. Pieper (1990), making this point, included the greater regulation of recruitment and dismissal, the formalisation of educational certification and the quasi-legal characteristics of the industrial relations framework in comparison to the United States. Paauwe and Boselie (2007), for example, have noted the influence of legislation and the government in Europe particularly. We could also include, or specify, legislative requirements on pay, on hours of work, on forms of employment contract, rights to trade union representation, requirements to establish and operate consultation or co-determination arrangements – and a plethora of other legal requirements. These are all additional to those few areas, such as the legislation on equality or health and safety, which intrude on the employment relationship on both sides of the Atlantic.

Moreover, the EU is unique in the world in having 27 countries committed to a supra-national level of legislation on a considerable range of aspects of the employer–employee relationship. The European Union, particularly through the Social Charter and its associated Social Action Programme, is having an increasing legislative influence on HRM. Whilst there is a clear trend to reduce the restrictions imposed by legislation at the national level, there is an equally clear trend to extend the influence of the supranational regulations. A prominent example is the introduction of European Works Councils where employee representatives meet with senior managers on a regular basis to debate a series of subjects laid down in the legislation. According to data from the European Trade Union Institute, 908 European Works Councils were active in 2009, primarily in large transnational corporations.[5] Also the effect of social and legislative requirements on pay and conditions of work shows marked differences. For example, reports show that the kind of legal regulations about paid holidays and vacation do have an effect on the average hours worked and, consequently, 'annual hours worked in Europe have fallen relative to hours in the US' (Altonji & Oldham, 2003).

The Importance of Consultation and Collective Representation

In Europe there is a frequent shared understanding that businesses need to be controlled and to treat their employees in a socially responsible way. Consequently, key questions in HRM are about communication and consultation with the workforce. Employee representation or 'voice' (Hirschman, 1970) may take individual or collective forms.

The collective forms include both union-centred and non-union mechanisms. In Europe, these tend to be complementary (Brewster et al., 2007). The range and type of employee representation and involvement is a defining feature of different national business systems, as demonstrated in the extensive literature on the varieties of capitalism (see Chapter 2 and Amable, 2003; Hall & Soskice, 2001; Whitley, 1999). Legislation in countries such as the Netherlands, Denmark and, most famously, Germany has for a long time required organisations to have two-tier management boards, with employees having the right to be represented on the more senior Supervisory Board. In all European Union countries the law requires the establishment of employee representation committees in all organisations except the smallest. These arrangements give considerable (legally backed) power to the employee representatives.

Individually, effective communication, it could be argued, is at the heart of effective human resource management. It might, therefore, be expected to be increasingly common everywhere. There are, however, good reasons to suppose that cultural differences, in particular the influence of hierarchy (Hofstede, 2001; House et al., 2004), will have an impact on the way that managers communicate to their workforce, so that the drive for greater efficiency, which might lead to convergence, will be counteracted to some degree by the national cultures. It is certainly going to be influenced by the institutional and legislative issues noted above. There is now clear evidence that organisations across Europe are increasing the amount of communication and consultation in which they involve those employees (Mayrhofer et al., 2004, 2011). The EU's Works Council Directive and the desire of organisations to use as many communications channels as possible have ensured that although there has been a growth in the use of individual channels of communication, the collective channels are still widely used amongst larger employers at least.

The legislative status and influence accorded to trade unions is a further core feature of European states. Europe is the continent with the strongest independent trade unions. The definition, meaning and reliability of union membership figures vary between countries. However, it is quite clear that, in general, the European countries are more heavily unionised than most other areas of the world. Although trade union membership varies considerably by country and has declined over the past decades, it is always significant. Recent figures on trade union density (European Foundation for the Improvement of Living and Working Conditions, 2009: 23; for 2008 or most recent year for which data are available) show that the EU15 and Norway have an overall trade union density of about 35 per cent and the new member states of about 23 per cent. Yet, there are considerable differences between countries in Europe.

Table 23.1   Labour union density (in %)

Country	2008
Sweden	68.3
Denmark	67.6
Finland	67.5
Norway	53.3
Belgium	51.9
Luxembourg	37.4
Italy	33.4
Ireland	32.3
Austria	28.9
United Kingdom	27.1
Greece	24.0
Portugal	20.4
Netherlands	18.9
Switzerland	18.3
Slovak Republic	16.8
Hungary	16.8
Poland	15.6
Spain	14.3
France	7.7
Turkey	5.8
United States	11.9

Note: Labour union density figures are prone to a number of different calculation methods and databases; hence, you find partly varying figures for the same country. Nevertheless, the basic message – substantial variation within Europe; higher union density than in the United States – consistently holds up.

Source: OECD.Stat extracted on 26 February 2011.

The unions in many countries are supported by legislation and, at the European Union level, unions, management and governments, the 'social partners' as they are called, are required to consult with one another.

Of course, even within in Europe the unions are very different between countries and perform different roles. The unions may be industrially or occupationally based, as in the UK, or split on regional lines, (Belgium, Spain) or on religious or political lines (France, Italy). The unions may have very high membership figures (Nordic countries) or low ones (France), though their coverage in collective bargaining is nearly always greater than their membership. The unions may take the view that what the employer has is wealth that their members have created and of which they deserve a greater share, or they may, as do most of the Nordic unions, take the view that their best interests are served by their employers being as successful as possible. Whatever their nature, independent trade unions play a larger role in HRM in Europe than in most other world regions.

More Critical View

Europeans have been at the forefront of criticism of the rhetoric of HRM (for critical views see, for instance, Guest, 1990; Legge, 2005). In Europe, the academic field of human resource management tended to develop from the field of industrial relations. As trade union membership and influence declined in many countries over the past quarter of a century (Katz & Darbishire, 2000; Rigby et al., 2004), academics in those disciplines tended to turn towards the management side of the topic and to embrace HRM. One effect, as noted in Chapter 1, has been that the industrial relations tradition of assumptions of national embeddedness and awareness of national differences was transferred to human resource management, leading in turn to the development of work on comparative HRM.

More than two decades ago, Beaumont (1991) argued that much of the US literature is prescriptive – discussing what should happen even though, perhaps, it does not happen that way in practice. Given the critical view on HRM as a concept and perhaps partly as a result of some of the unique European combinations of circumstances, studies of HRM in Europe tend to take a more critical view of the topic than is common elsewhere (Brewster, 2007). At the level of the organisation (not firm – public sector and not-for-profit organisations are also included) the organisation's objectives (and therefore its strategy) are not necessarily assumed to be 'good' either for the organisation or for society. There are plenty of recent examples where this is clearly not the case. Nor, in this paradigm, is there any assumption that the interests of everyone in the organisation will be the same or any expectation that an organisation will have a strategy that people within the organisation will support. Employees and the unions have a different perspective to the management team (Keenoy, 1990; Purcell & Ahlstrand, 1994). Even within the management team there may be different interests and views.

Rather than analysing the management of people as a contributor to finding more cost-effective ways to ensure that the top management's organisational objectives are met, commentators in Europe are more likely to analyse critically the way human resources are managed. This leads to challenging the declared corporate strategy and approach to HRM laid down by senior management – asking whether these have deleterious consequences for individuals within the organisation, for the long-term health of the organisation and for the community and country within which the organisation operates.

In addition, European academic studies are less focused on the policies of a small number of 'leading edge' major multinationals and are more likely to study the practices of smaller businesses, public sector organisations and local workplaces. Here, the objective is less likely to be about achieving the organisation's objectives than about understanding the impact of the practices on the various stakeholders involved. The HRM/ performance linked literature is a good example. Most of the critique of that literature from US researchers has been concerned with weaknesses in the empirical or statistical data (Cappelli & Newmark, 2001; Gerhart, 2005). The critiques of the concept within Europe have tended to be more wide-ranging, examining the assumptions of universalism, of the inevitable 'goodness' of the link and the effects on those other than managers in the system (Guest et al., 2003; Marchington & Grugulis, 2000; Paauwe & Boselie, 2005). Overall, in Europe HRM is, as a concept, a more contested notion than it is elsewhere.

EUROPEAN HRM: THE LEVEL OF POLICIES AND PRACTICES

Regional Clusters

The generalisations made so far have not been able to avoid noting that there are many variations within Europe. Thus researchers have distinguished HRM in northern Europe from that found in southern Europe (Apospori et al., 2008; Brewster & Larsen, 2000); have linked differences in HRM to main cultural groupings within Europe (see Chapter 3), finding 'three clusters: a Latin cluster [which includes Spain, Italy, France]; a central European cluster . . . and a Nordic cluster' (Filella, 1991: 14); focused on the presence or absence of communitarian infrastructures, finding the Anglo cultures distinct from the rest of Europe (Hollingsworth & Boyer, 1997a); emphasised the importance of the role of the state and differences between countries such as the UK, Ireland and the Nordic countries in which the state has a limited role in industrial relations and the Roman-Germanic countries such as France, Spain, Germany, Italy, Belgium, Greece and the Netherlands where the opposite is true (Due, Madsen & Jensen, 1991: 90). Other researchers have used the institutional literature (see Chapter 2 and Brewster et al., 2007; Farndale et al., 2008; Goergen et al., 2009; Tregaskis & Brewster, 2006) to find differences between the UK and Ireland, the Nordic countries, the central continental

European countries, sometimes separating out the flexicurity countries of Denmark and the Netherlands, and the Mediterranean countries.

Areas of Practice

HRM in Europe not only varies in terms of the general approach, but also at the level of HRM practices. Due to space limitations, it is not possible to systematically cover all the areas of practice in detail. Still, we would like to highlight three major issues, i.e. the role distribution between HRM specialists and line managers, flexible working practices and communication within the organisation (see also Brewster & Mayrhofer, 2011).

HRM department and role distribution between HRM specialists and line managers

There is a widely shared understanding that HRM is a joint effort between HRM specialists, usually institutionally organised in a specialised department, and line managers who are in direct and day-to-day contact with the workforce. Among others, this raises at least two issues: how is the HRM department integrated into the organisational decision making processes and how is the role distribution between HRM specialists and line managers in various areas of responsibility?

Especially in the light of the debate about strategic HRM, the importance of knowledge as a production factor, and the rhetoric of people being the most valuable resource of organisations, many commentators argue that HRM has become more important to organisations in the last two decades. Consequently, we should expect to see the influence of the human resource function on corporate decision increasing over time (e.g. Pfeffer, 1998; Ulrich & Brockbank, 2005). Arguably, where the human resource function is represented at the key decision-making forums of the organisation and becomes closely involved in strategic decision making, awareness of the problems or opportunities that effective HRM might provide will be raised and the decision making in increasingly knowledge-reliant organisations consequently will be improved. Yet, one perceptive commentator on HRM made the point some time ago that the rhetoric of integration of the HRM specialist function at board level and its position of influence has outpaced the reality (Legge, 1995). In terms of membership of the board, the Cranet research data show considerable stability over time set alongside large variation between countries (Brewster et al., 1997; Mayrhofer & Brewster, 2005). France, Spain and Sweden, for example, consistently report seven or eight out of ten organisations having an HRM director on the main decision-making body of the organisation (the board in shareholder companies). Many other European countries,

including the UK and Germany, show a little less than half of the organisations with HRM departments being directly represented at the top
decision-making level. In the Netherlands and Germany employees have
rights to have representatives at the supervisory board level: presumably
the employee representatives ensure that the HRM implications of corporate strategy decisions are taken into account. Germany is a particularly
interesting case, as it is one of the few countries where HRM representation on the board has increased significantly over the rounds of the study,
and at a time that human resources have become more critical for organisations and the function itself has become less administrative in focus. In
terms of HRM influence on the corporate strategy, there is more uniformity: in most countries the personnel departments are involved from the
outset in strategy formulation in approximately half of the organisations.

Not only the structural integration of the HRM department, but also
its size matters (Brewster et al., 2006). Again, given the strong emphasis
on outsourcing, the pressure to reduce overheads, and the proclaimed
shift towards line management taking over more HRM responsibilities,
one would expect that the relative size of HRM departments, i.e. their
headcount relative to the overall number of employees in the organisation,
would have decreased over the past decades. While there is comparatively
little empirical evidence of this, one study on HRM in various European
countries comes to the conclusion that the relative size of HRM departments hardly changed at all during 1990s and early 2000s (Mayrhofer et
al., 2011).

In line with the shift from personnel to human resource management,
the role of the line managers for managing human resources became more
important. The notion is that people can only be managed cost-effectively
and well when their immediate superiors have a substantial responsibility for that management. Looking at Europe during the 1990s, there was
a visible reduction of the extent to which HRM departments control or
restrict line management autonomy in various areas of HRM (Brewster et
al., 1997). However, in more recent years, this development has reversed.
A recent analysis of HRM in larger private sector firms in 13 European
countries between 1992 and 2004 comes to the conclusion that overall the
responsibilities of the HRM specialists have increased. A more detailed
analysis shows that various countries within this sample show different
developments, For example, in Denmark the overall devolution of HRM
to line management is quite strong. Yet, over time there is a development
of re-assigning more responsibilities back to HRM specialists. In a similar
vein, countries with a medium amount of responsibilities given to line
management such as the UK, Germany, or Spain show a comparable
trend. Conversely, countries such as Switzerland or Sweden, again with a

medium degree of devolvement, show a trend towards giving more responsibility to line managers (Mayrhofer et al., 2011).

Flexible working practices
Providing organisations with some flexibility in labour patterns in order to adapt to changing market demands is a critical issue in HRM. Data from a variety of sources such as national labour market statistics (European Commission Eurostat, 2008) and workplace level data (Kersley et al., 2006) show the extensive use of flexible working across Europe.

Specifically looking at flexibility in European working practices from an HRM angle, Tregaskis & Brewster (2006) show that across Europe flexible working practices are growing in both extent and coverage regardless of sector, organisational size and form or origin of ownership, and differing legal, cultural and labour traditions. They also demonstrate that there is only a minority of organisations where these forms of flexibility cover the majority of their workers. Furthermore, the increase in the use of flexible contracts tends to be significantly higher among those organisations already making comparatively high use of such contracts. For example, the Netherlands and the UK with a substantial proportion of part-time contracts amongst their workforce (more than 25 per cent) tend to increase usage; countries with very few part-timers continue to have very few. Different countries also prefer different kinds of flexibility and no country or organisation makes extensive use of the full range of flexible labour patterns. Thus, Spain combines a high level of short-term employment with lower levels of part-time work. Countries such as Austria, the Netherlands, Sweden and the UK have a third or more of organisations with over 5 per cent of the workforce on temporary contracts with most of the other countries in Europe having far fewer. Conversely, the Netherlands, Sweden and the UK all have more than a quarter of their working population employed in part-time jobs.

Despite common trends and similarities, the situation is unique in each of the countries. The specific interplay between cultural and institutional forces, expressed in factors such as national cultural values, history, legal framework, role of works councils and trade unions, or national approaches to management are responsible for this.

Communications
Communication within organisations is vital for organisational success. Yet, both content and form of effective communication are up to debate and vary by country. Given the overall trend of deregulation and the changing role of collective representation, one would assume that there is an increase in individualised forms of communication while collective

forms of communication, relying to a great extent on formal bodies such as trade unions or works councils, become less important.

Empirical research in European companies shows that over time there have been increases in all forms of communication: through representative bodies (trade unions or works councils), as well as through direct verbal and written communication (Brewster et al., 2004). The latter two channels have expanded considerably. When upward communication is examined, the two most common means, by a considerable margin, are through immediate line management and through the trade union or works council channel. The evidence tends to support the analyses of those researchers (Hollingsworth & Boyer, 1997b) who focus on the presence or absence within countries of communitarian infrastructures that manifest themselves in the form of strong social bonds, trust, reciprocity and co-operation among economic actors.

Convergence

Globalisation is regarded as an all-pervasive phenomenon and has been extensively debated (e.g. Michie, 2003). This underlines that the convergence debate has become a key feature of much social science theorising (Rojek, 1986).

Looking at convergence at the organisational level, two rather different theoretical lines of enquiry come to discrepant conclusions. On the one hand, various theoretical schools of thinking underline the forces towards the emergence of reasonably similar organisational structures and processes. This includes rational actor models which assume that under conditions of globalisation, in particular with rationality, cost effectiveness, flexibility and the existence of best-practice models being central characteristics of a capitalist society, firms develop similar structures and processes when realising their economic goals. Sociological neo-institutionalism (see Meyer & Rowan, 1977; DiMaggio & Powell, 1983) builds on the assumption that institutions are central for understanding organisational structures, processes and outcomes because legitimacy in the respective environment is central for the survival of organisations (Havemann, 1993; Kostova & Roth, 2002). Hence, in a globalised economy, convergence and isomorphic developments are to be expected. To be sure, some of these approaches challenge the globalisation thesis per se (Hirst & Thompson, 1999). On the other hand, theories of comparative institutionalism in the varieties of capitalism literature (Hall & Soskice, 2001; Whitley, 1999) build on the notion of differences due to national boundaries: 'Nation states constitute the prevalent arena in which social and political competition is decided in industrial capitalist societies' (Whitley, 1999: 19).

Differences between nation states and respective economic arrangements will remain or even deepen because of the different institutional arrangements at national level.

In addition to the variety in terms of theoretical foundations, there is also a variety in terms of conceptual clarity about what convergence/divergence actually means. While we suggest speaking of similarity and difference if we compare in a cross-sectional studies two units of analysis at the same point in time, we suggest two major types of convergence (Mayrhofer et al., 2002b). Final convergence occurs if a variable in different units of analysis points towards a common end point, that is, the differences between countries decrease. We speak of directional convergence when development tendencies of variables in units of analysis go in the same direction, regardless of their initial starting level.

In addition to the debate about the convergence of HRM across the globe towards the US model there is also some discussion about the emergence of a more homogeneous model within Europe. Despite the significant national differences, the European Union and the resulting changes in the areas of the free flow of goods, services, capital and persons provide a strong source of potentially homogenising HRM across Europe. Overall, there is scarce empirical evidence on this matter. A trend study analysing the development in 13 European countries comes to the conclusion that there are clear signs that countries remain distinctive in the way that they manage their HRM (Mayrhofer et al., 2011). In terms of final convergence, no empirical support was found when looking both at HRM configuration, i.e. the role distribution between line management and HRM specialists, and the relative size of the HRM department, and HRM practices, i.e. employee development, reward and communications. Regarding directional convergence, three trends have been observed: flexible patterns of employee reward and the range of groups included in internal communication have strongly increased and, to a lesser extent, HRM responsibilities have been directed more towards the HRM specialists. In all the other areas, no changes were observed.

CONCLUSIONS

The early attempts to distinguish European versions of HRM (Brewster & Burnois, 1991; Thurley & Wirdenius, 1991) have led on to a considerable literature drawing on cultural and institutional theories and, on rare occasions, combining them. Key to understanding this literature is to appreciate the different levels of analysis that different authors have adopted. However, there is clearly a necessity for more research into HRM in Europe both at the conceptual and empirical level (Larsen & Mayrhofer, 2006). Clarity about the research paradigm and the perspective from which HRM is being addressed can only help our understanding of the notion and meaning of human research management. Further work on HRM in Europe will undoubtedly make a serious and significant, and perhaps more critical, contribution to the subject.

NOTES

1. http://ec.europa.eu/education/languages/languages-of-europe/index_en.htm; accessed October 14 2010.
2. http://data.worldbank.org/indicator/SL.GDP.PCAP.EM.KD?cid=DEC_SS_WBGDataEmail_EXT; accessed 27 September 2010
3. http://www.transparency.org/policy_research/surveys_indices/cpi/2009/cpi_2009_table: accessed 27 September 2010.
4. To be sure, rationalism did leave its traces on Europe's scientific maps; see e.g. the contributions to positivism of methodological falsificationism and objective knowledge by Popper (1972).
5. http://www.worker-participation.eu/European-Works-Councils/Facts-Figures, accessed 25 February 2011.

REFERENCES

Altonji, J. G. & Oldham, J. 2003. Vacation laws and annual work hours. *Economic Perspectives*, **Q3**: 19–29.
Amable, B. 2003. *The Diversity of Modern Capitalism*. Oxford: Oxford University Press.
Apospori, E., Nikandrou, I., Brewster, C. & Papalexandris, N. 2008. HRM and organizational performance in Northern and Southern Europe. *International Journal of Human Resource Management*, **19**(7): 1187–1207.
Beaumont, P. B. 1991. The US human resource management literature: a review. In G. Salaman (ed.), *Human Resource Strategies*. Milton Keynes: The Open University, pp. 20–37.
Becker, B. & Gerhart, B. 1996. The impact of human resource management on organizational performance: progress and prospects. *Academy of Management Journal*, **39**(4): 779–801.
Becker, B., Huselid, M., Pickus, P. & Spratt, M. 1997. HR as a source of shareholder value: research and recommendations. *Human Resource Management Journal*, **36**(1): 39–47.
Beets, G. 2007. EU demographics: living longer and reproducing less. *Pharmaceuticals Policy & Law*, **9**(1/2): 29–40.
Blanchard, O. 1999. European unemployment: the role of shocks and institutions. Unpublished working paper: Massachusetts Institute of Technology.
Bonnafous-Boucher, M. & Pesqueux, Y. (eds) 2005. *Stakeholder Theory: A European Perspective*. Basingstoke, UK: Palgrave Macmillan.
Boxall, P. 1995. Building the theory of comparative HRM. *Human Resource Management Journal*, **5**(5): 5–17.
Brewster, C. 1993. Developing a 'European' model of human resource management. *International Journal of Human Resource Management*, **4**(4): 765–784.

Brewster, C. 1995. Towards a 'European' model of human resource management. *Journal of International Business Studies*, **26**(1): 1–21.

Brewster, C. 2007. Comparative HRM: European views and perspectives. *International Journal of Human Resource Management*, **18**(5): 769–787.

Brewster, C., Brookes, M., Croucher, R. & Wood, G. 2007. Collective and individual voice: convergence in Europe? *International Journal of Human Resource Management*, **18**(7): 1246–1262.

Brewster, C. & Bournois, F. 1991. Human resource management: a European perspective. *Personnel Review*, **20**(6): 4–13.

Brewster, C. & Larsen, H. H. (eds). 2000. *Human Resource Management in Northern Europe*. Oxford: Blackwell.

Brewster, C., Larsen, H. H. & Mayrhofer, W. 1997. Integration and assignment: a paradox in human resource management. *Journal of International Management*, **3**(1): 1–23.

Brewster, C. & Mayrhofer, W. 2011 Comparative human resource management. In A.-W. Harzing & A. Pinnington (eds), *International Human Resource Management*, 3rd edn. London: Sage Publications, pp. 47–78.

Brewster, C., Mayrhofer, W. & Morley, M. 2000. The concept of strategic European human resource management. In C. Brewster, W. Mayrhofer & M. Morley (eds), *New Challenges for European Human Resource Management*. London: Macmillan, pp. 3–33.

Brewster, C., Mayrhofer, W. & Morley, M. (eds). 2004. *Human Resource Management in Europe. Evidence of convergence?* Oxford: Elsevier/Butterworth-Heinemann.

Brewster, C., Wood, G., Brookes, M. & van Ommeren, J. 2006. What determines the size of the HR Function? A cross-national analysis. *Human Resource Management*, **45**(1): 3–21.

Brewster, C., Wood, G., Croucher, R. & Brookes, M. 2007. Are works councils and joint consultative committees a threat to trade unions? A comparative analysis. *Economic and Industrial Democracy*, **28** (1): 53–81.

Brück, F. 2002. *Interkulturelles Management. Kulturvergleich Österreich-Deutschland-Schweiz*. Frankfurt a. M.: IKO–Verlag für Interkulturelle Kommunikation.

Cappelli, P. & Newmark, D. 2001. Do 'high-performance' work practices improve establishment level outcomes? *Industrial and Labour Relations Review*, **54**(4): 737–775.

DiMaggio, P. J. & Powell, W. W. 1983. The iron cage revisited: institutional isomorphism and collective rationality in organizational fields. *American Sociological Review*, **48**: 147–160.

Due, J., Madsen, J. S. & Jensen, C. S. 1991. The social dimension: convergence or diversification of IR in the Single European Market? *Industrial Relations Journal*, **22**(2): 85–102.

Eisenhardt, K. 1989. Agency theory: an assessment and review. *Academy of Management Review*, **14**(1): 57–74.

European Commission Eurostat 2008. *Europe in Figures: Eurostat Yearbook 2008*. Luxembourg: Office for Official Publications of the European Communities.

European Foundation for the Improvement of Living and Working Conditions. 2009. *Trade union membership 2003–2008*. Dublin, Ireland: European Foundation for the Improvement of Living and Working Conditions.

Farndale, E., Brewster, C. & Poutsma, E. 2008. Co-ordinated versus liberal market HRM: the impact of institutionalisation on multinational firms. *International Journal of Human Resource Management*, **19**(11): 2004–2023.

Feyerabend, P. 1978. *Against Method: Outline of an Anarchistic Theory of Knowledge*. London: Verso.

Filella, J. 1991. Is there a Latin model in the management of human resources? *Personnel Review*, **20**(6): 14–23.

Fombrun, C. J., Tichy, N. & Devanna, M. A. 1984. *Strategic Human Resource Management*. New York: Wiley.

Freeman, R. E., Harrison, J. S., Wicks, A. C., Parmar, B. L. & de Colle, S. (eds). 2010. *Stakeholder Theory: The State of the Art*. Cambridge: Cambridge University Press

Gergen, K. J. 2002. *Konstruierte Wirklichkeiten: eine Hinführung zum sozialen Konstruktionismus*. Stuttgart: Kohlhammer.

Gerhart, B. 2005. Human resources and business performance: findings, unanswered questions and an alternative approach. *Management Revue*, **16**: 174–185.

Giddens, A. 2000. *Runaway World: How Globalization is Reshaping Our Lives*. New York: Routledge.

Goergen, M., Brewster, C. & Wood, G. 2009. Corporate governance regimes and employment relations in Europe. *Relations industrielles/Industrial Relations*, **64**(4): 620–640.

Guest, D. E. 1987. Human resource management and industrial relations. *Journal of Management Studies*, **24**(5): 503–521.

Guest, D. E. 1990. Human resource management and the American dream. *Journal of Management Studies*, **27**(4): 377–397.

Guest, D. E., Michie, J., Conway, N. & Sheehan, M. 2003. Human resource management and performance in the UK. *British Journal of Industrial Relations*, **41**: 291–314.

Hall, P. A. & Soskice, D. (eds). 2001. *Varieties of Capitalism. The Institutional Foundations of Comparative Advantage*. Oxford: Oxford University Press.

Havemann, H. A. 1993. Ghosts of managers past: managerial succession and organizational mortality. *Academy of Management Journal*, **36**(4): 864–881.

Hegel, G. W. F. 1807. *Phänomenologie des Geistes*. Frankfurt a. Main: Suhrkamp.

Hejl, P. M. 2000. Konstruktion der sozialen Konstruktion: Grundlinien einer konstruktivistischen Sozialtheorie. In H. Gumin & H. Meier (eds.), *Einführung in den Konstruktivismus*, Vol. 5. Aufl. München: Piper, pp. 109–147

Hirschman, A. O. 1970. *Exit, Voice and Loyalty: Responses to Decline in Firms, Organizations, and States*. Cambridge, MA: Harvard University Press.

Hirst, P. & Thompson, G. 1999. *Globalization in Question: The International Economy and the Possibilities of Governance*. Cambridge: Polity Press.

Hofstede, G. 1980. *Culture's Consequences. International Differences in Work-Related Values*. Newbury Park, CA: Sage Publications.

Hofstede, G. 2001. *Culture's Consequences. Comparing Values, Behaviors, Institutions and Organizations Across Nations*, 2nd edn. London: Sage Publications.

Höhn, C., Ette, A. & Ruckdeschel, K. 2006. *Kinderwünsche in Deutschland. Konsequenzen für eine nachhaltige Familienpolitik*. Stuttgart: Robert Bosch Stiftung.

Hollingsworth, J. R. & Boyer, R. (eds). 1997a. *Contemporary Capitalism*. Cambridge: Cambridge University Press.

Hollingsworth, J. R. & Boyer, R. 1997b. Coordination of economic actors and social systems of production. In J. R. Hollingsworth & R. Boyer (eds), *Contemporary Capitalism*. Cambridge: Cambridge University Press.

House, R. J., Hanges, P. J., Javidan, M., Dorfman, P. W. & Gupta, V. (eds). 2004. *Culture, Leadership, and Organizations: The GLOBE Study of 62 Societies*. Thousand Oaks, CA: Sage Publications.

Huselid, M. A. 1995. The impact of human resource management practices on turnover, productivity, and corporate financial performance. *Academy of Management Journal*, **38**(3): 635–672.

Katz, H. C. & Darbishire, O. 2000. *Converging Divergences: Worldwide Changes in Employment Systems*. Ithaca, NY: Cornell University Press.

Keenoy, T. 1990. HRM: a case of the wolf in sheep's clothing. *Personnel Review*, **19**(2): 3–9.

Kersley, B., Alpin, C., Forth, J., Bryson, A., Bewley, H., Dix, G. & Oxenbridge, S. 2006. *Inside the Workplace: Findings from the 2004 Workplace Employment Relations Survey*. London: Routledge.

Kostova, T. & Roth, K. 2002. Adoption of an organizational practice by subsidiaries of multinational corporations: institutional and relational effects. *Academy of Management Journal*, **45**(1): 215–233.

Laqueur, W. 2006. *Die letzten Tage von Europa. Ein Kontinent verändert sein Gesicht*. Berlin: Propyläen.

Larsen, H. H. & Mayrhofer, W. 2006. European HRM: on the road again. In H. H. Larsen & W. Mayrhofer (eds), *Managing Human Resources in Europe. A Thematic Approach*. London: Routledge, pp. 259–270.

Legge, K. 1995. HRM: rhetoric, reality and hidden agendas. In J. Storey (ed.), *Human Resource Management: A Critical Text*. London: Routledge, pp. 33–59.

Legge, K. 2005. *Human Resource Management. Rhetorics and Realities*. Houndmills, UK: Palgrave Macmillan.

Mabey, C. 2004. Developing managers in Europe: policies, practices, and impact. *Advances in Developing Human Resources*, 6(4): 404–427.

Mabey, C. & Ramirez, M. 2005. Does management development improve organizational productivity? A six-country analysis of European firms. *International Journal of Human Resource Management*, 16(7): 1067–1082.

Marchington, M. & Grugulis, I. 2000. 'Best practice' human resource management: perfect opportunity or dangerous illusion? *International Journal of Human Resource Management*, 11(6): 1104–1124.

Maurice, M., Sellier, F. & Silvestre, J. 1986. *The Social Foundations of Industrial Power*. Cambridge, MA: MIT Press.

Mayrhofer, W. & Brewster, C. 2005. European human resource management: researching developments over time. *Management Revue*, 16(1): 36–62.

Mayrhofer, W., Brewster, C., Morley, M. J. & Ledolter, J. 2011. Hearing a different drummer? Convergence of human resource management in Europe: a longitudinal analysis. *Human Resource Management Review*, 21(1): 50–67.

Mayrhofer, W., Meyer, M., Steyrer, J., Iellatchitch, A., Schiffinger, M., Strunk, G., Erten-Buch, C., Hermann, A. & Mattl, C. 2002a. Einmal gut, immer gut? Einflussfaktoren auf Karrieren in 'neuen' Karrierefeldern. *Zeitschrift für Personalforschung*, 16(3): 392–414.

Mayrhofer, W., Morley, M. & Brewster, C. 2004. Convergence, stasis, or divergence? In C. Brewster, W. Mayrhofer & M. Morley (eds), *Human Resource Management in Europe. Evidence of Convergence?* Oxford: Elsevier/Butterworth-Heinemann, pp. 417–436.

Mayrhofer, W., Müller-Camen, M., Ledolter, J., Strunk, G. & Erten, C. 2002b. The diffusion of management concepts in Europe: conceptual considerations and longitudinal analysis. *Journal of Cross-Cultural Competence & Management*, 3: 315–349.

Meyer, J. W., Boli, J., Thomas, G. M. & Ramirez, F. O. 1997. World society and the nation-state. *The American Journal of Sociology*, 103(1): 144–181.

Meyer, J. W. & Rowan, E. 1977. Institutionalized organizations: formal structure as myth and ceremony. *American Journal of Sociology*, 83: 340–363.

Michie, J. (ed.). 2003. *The Handbook of Globalisation*. Cheltenham, UK: Edward Elgar.

Paauwe, J. & Boselie, P. 2005. Best practices . . . in spite of performance: just a matter of imitation? *International Journal of Human Resource Management*, 16(6): 987–1003.

Paauwe, J. & Boselie, P. 2007. HRM and societal embeddedness. In P. Boxall, J. Purcell & P. M. Wright (eds), *The Oxford Handbook of Human Resource Management*. Oxford: Oxford University Press, pp. 166–184.

Pfeffer, J. 1998. *The Human Equation: Building Profits by Putting People First*. Cambridge, MA: Harvard Business School Press.

Pieper, R. (ed.). 1990. *Human Resource Management: An International Comparison*. Berlin: de Gruyter.

Popper, K. 1972. *Objective Knowledge. An Evolutionary Approach*. Oxford: Clarendon Press.

Purcell, J. & Ahlstrand, B. 1994. *Human Resource Management in the Multi-Divisional Firm*. Oxford: Oxford University Press.

Rigby, M., Smith, R. & Brewster, C. 2004. The changing impact and strength of the Labour Movement in Europe. In G. Wood & M. Harcourt (eds), *Trade Unions and Democracy: Strategies and Perspectives*. Manchester, UK: Manchester University Press.

Rojek, C. 1986. Convergence, divergence and the study of organizations. *Organization Studies*, 7(1): 25–36.

Schütz, A. 1981[1932]. *Der sinnhafte Aufbau der sozialen Welt. Eine Einleitung in die verstehende Soziologie*, 2nd edn. Frankfurt a.M.: Suhrkamp.

Sichler, R. 2006. *Autonomie in der Arbeitswelt*. Göttingen: Vandenhoeck & Ruprecht.

Sparrow, P. & Hiltrop, J. M. 1994. *European Human Resource Management in Transition*. Hempel Hempstead, UK: Prentice Hall.

Stiglitz, J. E. 2002. *Globalization and its Discontents*. London: Penguin.

Thurley, K. & Wirdenius, H. 1991. Will management become 'European'? Strategic choices for organisations. *European Management Journal*, **9**(2): 127–134.

Tregaskis, O. & Brewster, C. 2006. Converging or diverging? A comparative analysis of trends in contingent employment practice in Europe over a decade. *Journal of International Business Studies*, **37**(1): 111–126.

Trompenaars, F. 1994. *Riding the Waves of Culture. Understanding Diversity in Global Business*. Chicago, IL: Irwin.

Ulrich, D. 1989. Tie the corporate knot: gaining complete customer commitment. *Sloan Management Review*, Summer: 19–28.

Ulrich, D. & Brockbank, W. 2005. *The HR Value Proposition*. Cambridge, MA: Harvard Business School Press.

Whitley, R. 1999. *Divergent Capitalisms: The Social Structuring and Change of Business Systems*. Oxford: Oxford University Press.

Wright, P. & McMahan, G. C. 1992. Theoretical perspectives for strategic human resource management. *Journal of Management*, **18**(2): 295–320.

24 The transition states of Central and Eastern Europe and the Former Soviet Union

Michael J. Morley, Dana Minbaeva and Snejina Michailova

Since the fall of the Berlin Wall and the attenuation of socialism, two words have become synonymous with the economies of Central and Eastern Europe (CEE) and the Former Soviet Union (FSU), namely 'transition' and 'transformation'. While these terms are sometimes mistakenly used interchangeably as if they signalled the equivalent development, both do call attention to the latent dynamics and complex changes characterising this part of the world. Inherent in the discourse is the notion of an ideological, political, economic and socio-cultural shift. This is not in question. What are, of course, more contested are the nature, speed and substance of the shift and what the eventual outcome might be. Changing economies is complex and not all organisations within a country alter radically or consistently when this country goes through radical changes (Whitley, 1990: 240–241). Waves of progress towards change on some indicators can mask negative consequences on others. For example Kiriazov et al. (2000) demonstrated in their analysis that East European political reforms aimed at improving productivity had in many instances caused decreased output, reduced wage rates, and resulted in more downsizing and increased layoffs.

Lane (2007) argues that transition states can be divided into three categories: middle income; low income; and very low income: the former (including for example Hungary and Slovakia) are closest to continental European capitalism, reflecting the pressures associated with joining the European Union and the need to form institutional arrangements that are complementary to their closest developed trading partners. Other states, such as for example Bulgaria and Romania, are less developed and have moved closer to liberal market type arrangements (see also Bandelj, 2009; Buchen 2007; Crowley, 2005). The divergent developments and distinctive trajectories that have occurred in the transition economies have led some to argue that what we may be witnessing is 'a new variety of capitalism' (Amable 2003). Martin (2006) suggests that capitalism in CEE can be segmented into at least three types: managerial capitalism, entrepreneurial capitalism and international capitalism with each form of capitalism having a particular pattern of employment relations. There is little doubt that these societies are now characterised by a rising economic heterogeneity and a rapidly changing socio-cultural context, underscored by waves of restructuring, privatisation, increasing foreign direct investment and emerging individualism. Because the development trajectory that they have experienced could not be considered uniform, similarly, the notion of a model of HRM explaining unifying aspects of people management practices in the transformation states of CEE and FSU is perhaps a stretch too far, given the inexorable link between the state of HRM and the developmental trajectory and business culture. The consequence is that charting the landscape of HRM in the complex terrain that is contemporary CEE and FSU is a difficult task.

This geographic territory is not historically well documented in the management and human resources literature and contemporary developments occur against the backdrop of large scale political, economic and socio-cultural shifts. Several analyses have called attention to the lack of detailed knowledge of HRM in this area (Jankowicz, 1998; Kahancová & van der Meer, 2006; Kase & Zupan, 2005; Zupan & Kase, 2005). Michailova et al. (2009), through a review of journal publications and books, reveal that there has been relatively limited specialised and systematic research dedicated to HRM in the CEE region and that 'a closer review of the literature reveals most studies to be rather general, fragmented and subordinate to the Western European studies' (Michailova et al., 2009: 7). They also note that if the notion of 'European HRM' was developed arguably in reaction to the hegemony of US conceptions of HRM, further independent and systematic analyses into the HRM issues in the transition economies are now needed in light of the transitions experienced by many of the economies of CEE and FSU. The appropriateness of a blanket approach to the transposition of human resource and industrial relations models and the simple importation of system elements from developed to developing economies remains in question (Morley et al., 1996).

OVERVIEW OF THE CHAPTER

Against the backdrop of ancient cultures, a socialist legacy and eventual institutional atrophy, many of the societies of CEE and FSU have pursued aggressive development trajectories since the early 1990s, though, as has become apparent, with rather divergent outcomes (Morley et al., 2009). While the socialist platform from whence these economies spring is not in doubt, the anatomy of that which might emerge is much less clear. As Buciuniene et al. (2010: 147) recently noted, 'whilst it is clear what they are transitioning from, it is not clear exactly what they are transitioning to'. An important question that has emerged in this context is the extent to which US and Western Europe-dominated HRM theories and practices can be applied to the CEE and FSU countries, whether there is evidence of a unique approach to HRM emerging in this region or whether there is evidence of a hybrid system drawing upon Western imported features fused with ethno elements. This is a question that deserves serious research attention, given the potential significance of many of these emerging economies.

In pursuing this agenda, while an increasing number of research papers have recently treated the issue of the emergence of new and distinctive HRM in the transitioning economies, scholars do not have easy access to a systematic mapping of existing research on HRM in the transitioning economies. In this chapter we seek to provide such a mapping and identify under-researched issues that future investigation in this field must deal with. We reviewed (mainly) empirical studies examining HRM in CEE and FSU countries. We conducted article title, abstract and introduction searches in the most influential IHRM journals (Caligiuri, 1999; Hoobler and Johnson, 2004). We supplemented this search with additional journals in situations where the focus of the research was on specific HRM practice(s) neglected in previous research (e.g. outsourcing in Smith et al., 2006), where the research offered a focus on a country not well covered by earlier efforts (e.g. Serbia in Milikic et al., 2008) or where the research offered the possibility of particular insight because of the unique research methods employed (e.g. Gurkov, 2002). The question of how best to build understanding of human HRM across territories, or indeed for that matter any other socially derived, institutionally embedded phenomena characterised by internal (ethno) as well as external (global) influences, is an open one, something that becomes obvious when one looks at the diversity of approaches employed in research on transition economies to date.

In order to bring some systematics to this body of work and to provide a route map for the reader through this complex and diverse literature, we drew upon the universalist/contextual paradigm to organise the results of our search and create a taxonomy of the reviewed studies. More specifically, we examine whether these studies build knowledge underscored by the basic nomothetic assumptions of the universalistic approach to HRM or provide more idiographic, contextual knowledge linked with national and institutional difference arguments as they apply to transition economies. Through this approach, this chapter therefore landscapes some key idiosyncratic features of HRM in CEE and FSU and unearths elements of commonality across countries in the region, along with identifying distinctive elements.

NOMOTHETIC INFORMED ENQUIRY ON HRM IN CEE AND FSU

It was only after the fall of the socialist regimes throughout CEE and FSU that HRM, as we have come to understand it, started taking hold in the discourse of management thinking and in emerging practice (Morley et al., 2009). This provided an important opportunity for scholars to observe whether and how core tenets of HRM are therefore embraced as part of a new beginning, given that its earlier emergence has been a source of intense debate with respect to its theoretical pedigree, empirical foundations and practical implications in the Western context. In the transition economies context, the Soviet model of management was centralised with a strong emphasis on rules. The people management function followed a similar pattern with a heavy emphasis on departmentalisation, centralisation and rule making. While there is evidence of significant variation in personnel/ HRM practices within CEE and FSU countries, largely explained by different levels of economic and social development, cultural and political factors and the willingness of people to change (Erutku & Valtee, 1997), the transformation that has taken place has essentially been a move from a unitarist to a more pluralist system. This development and how it has begun to become institutionalised must be considered as something significantly different from the historical 'Cadre Department' that was commonplace in organisations during the socialist era. In the socialist times, this function mainly performed administrative, ideological and social roles. Letiche (1998) noted that the 'personnel office' in communist companies seems to have limited itself to administrating the payroll. The department of 'personnel and organisation', which one often finds in north-western European companies, whose tasks include recruitment and selection, organisational problem solving and conflict resolution, training and development, appraisal and evaluation, did not exist in communist Europe. Writing in the Russian context, Gurkov and Zelenova (2009) note that in a large enterprise often there could be up to five units responsible for personnel issues, with the local Communist Party committee often having the final say in promotions. In this system, they describe how the personnel department dealt with routine functions such as paperwork relating to hiring and firing, the trade union took responsibility for organising sports and social events, along with decisions regarding the allocation of housing to those working in the enterprise, the salary department focused on wages administration and a unit overseen by the plant engineer dealt with work design and work safety. This fragmented approach resulted in the absence of clearly articulated human resource strategy at enterprise levels (Gurkov & Zelenova, 2009). Many of these functions were prerogatives of management, and were a means of earning and exchanging of favours (*blat*, see Ledeneva, 1998). Such a system was not conducive to the growth of more sophisticated, value adding, activities, with the result that there was always going to be significant ground to be made up if the emerging, transitioning economies of CEE and FSU were going to be able to support, sustain and expand a developmental trajectory based on free market principles (Garavan et al., 1998).

As late comers to internationalisation, the development trajectory in many of these economies has been based on the premise that it is necessary to compete not only in the domestic but also in the regional and global marketplace. As a result, the emergence and development of the modern conception of HRM in CEE and FSU can be traced to the broader development of the sustainable, competitive market economy, operating in an era of globalisation. While the fall of the Berlin Wall brought with it great expectations of political and economic revolution for the economies, much of this early expectation has been characterised in retrospect as wishful thinking (cf. Martin, 1999). Earlier research had suggested that some citizens of these countries preferred the old communist system to the new reformed one (Luthans et al., 1995), something which could clearly be seen to have implications for HRM in these counties. Kiriazov et al. (2000) have argued that employees in these countries are attached to characteristics of the old centralised economy such as job security, guaranteed pay and highly structured jobs. Other employees pine for the benefits of nepotism and a black market system that they understood and of which they were part. The consequence is that companies were likely to find resistance to introducing performance related pay, for example, as employees, particularly older ones, remained wedded to a culture which supported guaranteed wages and bonuses. These companies were also likely to find lower levels of motivation among employees as they have witnessed a large number of business failures among newly investing MNCs, and thus they are likely to view new ventures sceptically. This, combined with a tradition of periodic job changes as a means of gaining pay rises and promotion in these states, may limit levels of motivation among employees. On the other hand however it is important to note that MNCs have been facilitated in introducing innovative HRM practices by the absence of a strong trade union presence on the shop floor (Martin and Cistescu-Martin, 2004).

Central to these interests over the past two decades has been the increased concern to achieve a closer alignment between strategy and

HRM, and more recently in evaluating the impact, if any, of HRM practice on organisation performance. It is important to say at the outset that there are those who take the view that we would do well to exercise some caution in assuming any automatic connection between HRM practices and organisational performance (Paauwe, 2009). Modest progress in developing theory (Chadwick & Dabu, 2009; Fleetwood & Hesketh, 2008) and on-going methodological limitations in research (Wall & Wood, 2005), aside, this is a literature that is now well established and its proponents generally contend that there is a 'best' way to manage HRM in firms (Harrell-Cook, 2002). This type of nomothetic enquiry seeks to identify HRM practices 'whose adoption generally leads to valued firm-level outcomes' (Huselid, 1995: 643). The findings of empirical studies on this subject are similar: either across industries or within a specific sector, the more high performance HRM practices used, the better are the various performance measures, such as productivity, labour turnover and financial indicators (see for example, Delaney & Huselid, 1996; Huselid, 1995; Huselid et al., 1997). The strength of the approach, it is argued, is that good research based upon it tends to have a clear potential for theoretical development, it can lead to carefully drawn research questions, the research tends to be easily replicable, the research methodologies are sufficiently sophisticated, and there is a coherence of criteria for judging the research (Mayrhofer et al., 2000).

Our search revealed a tranche of studies in this genre in CEE and FSU which, at their core, explore aspects of the HRM-performance question in several of the transition economies. From early in the transition process, the performance question, albeit in different guises, has formed a central policy agenda and an important aspect of academic enquiry with the emergence and institutionalisation of new approaches to workforce management being bound up in the overall economic transition process. This is hardly surprising. As Koubek and Brewster (1995) noted, the countries in transition faced similar difficulties in terms of the endurance of socialist practices where there was an unwillingness to decide anything without approval of some superior authority and where responsibilities were ambiguous, the result of which meant that the performance question needed serious tackling at many different levels.

Nomothetic-led research in CEE and FSU has been tackling the performance question in at least three distinguishable ways. First, some have set themselves the task of analysing the characteristics, attitudes and values of the specialist charged with people management, along with the fundamental architecture of the specialist function that they lead. Key lines of enquiry in this regard have included, for example, who are the specialists and what are their responsibilities, the latter providing insight into what is considered to be legitimate HRM activity. In at least one interpretation, this work can be seen to be trying to unravel the extent to which there has been a break with the past as a result of the transition, or as part of it, or conversely the extent to which there remains an underlying attitudinal and behavioural continuity with the earlier command system. Second, a deal of work has sought to examine the state of HRM and its contribution to business in CEE and FSU testing the receptivity of local indigenous firms in these transition economies to particular HRM tools and techniques that did not form part of the professional toolkit heretofore. Here, the underlying cultural and institutional framework, the network of rules within which these firms operate and the extent to which these may be evaluated to be changing have proven illuminating. Third, several research teams have focused on foreign multinational companies' subsidiaries that have established in host locations in CEE and the former Soviet Union and concentrated on examining the systems and techniques employed in these subsidiaries, relative to sister subsidiaries in Western, more advanced economies, or to indigenous firms in their respective host locations. We shall attend to all three approaches below.

The Attitudinal Legacy and the Architectural Shift

Milikic et al. (2008) examine Serbian companies and characterise them as having only recently established formal HRM departments, many of which still perform relatively limited functions, notably mostly administrative tasks required under the Serbian Labour Code. Lack of competences among HRM professionals represented an underlying problem. Several factors were thought to account for this including a long tradition of performing rather old-style administrative inherent in the communist era, a lack of appropriate education and development programmes within the education system, a preponderance of lawyers and clerical staff within the specialist function and a belief among managers that the main role of the specialist department is to ensure legal compliance and observance of the labour code. The latter is consistent with findings from other transition economies where, for example, the underlying managerial mind-set presents an important determinant of divergence in HRM practices, especially in terms of the absence of a more profound strategic involvement of the HRM function (Minbaeva et al, 2007; Zupan & Kase, 2005). Reflecting on the overall extent of change, Milikic et al. (2008) conclude that their findings are relatively congruent with the 'crossvergence' hypothesis reflecting aspects of change, as part of the transition process, side-by-side with elements of continuity. They argue that in all likelihood aspects of the management system in transition economies, like Serbia, will change in some areas because of a strong need to adjust to standard managerial technology common in a functioning market economy. Conversely, it is argued that in some areas management systems and practices in transition countries will remain unchanged because of the influence of existing values and traditions derived from a national culture, values and traditions which are not likely to be jettisoned in the short term.

The attitudinal and structural legacy of communism and its capacity to act as a constraint on significant change is also tracked by Gurkov (2002). He draws upon longitudinal data from among surveys of Russian CEOs between 1998 and 2000 and concludes that despite the drive towards some modern instruments of HRM, most innovations are implemented on a trial and error basis, often without reference to international practices. Gurkov and Zelenova (2009) point to HRM systems being unsystematic, with a general underlying concern to simply follow and mimic what other players and competitors are doing. Reflecting on the situation in the intervening years they note that after the fall of the central planning system and the significant rise in new HRM challenges, most especially in the Russian context, the lack of appropriately qualified professionals meant that HRM departments do not appear well positioned to play a key strategic role (Gurkov & Zelenova, 2009).

One possible response to this dilemma has been the option of considering outsourcing HRM activity to specialists better trained and equipped to deliver the services required. Smith et al. (2006) examined this issue in the Russian context in the initial stages of transition. They note that many believe that the cost of outsourcing is prohibitive and that acts as a significant deterrent. In addition, it was observed that oftentimes the actual identification of purely outsourcable tasks or activities is not as straightforward as it might look at first glance. From an attitudinal perspective, the low incidence of outsourcing could be linked to an underlying belief that fundamentally it causes a loss of control. However, against the backdrop of transition developments in Russia, Smith et al. (2006) postulate that outsourcing will likely grow, with a particular shift to more strategic, priority areas.

Karoliny at al. (2009) present evidence on HRM developments in Bulgaria, the Czech Republic, Estonia, Hungary, Slovakia and Slovenia. Based on large-scale comparative survey evidence, they identify a number of developments that appear to characterise contemporary HRM in this part of CEE. In the area of staffing, they find that managerial selection relies heavily on internal resources, with the internal labour market being highly significant in the filling of these positions. Interestingly, in the area of performance appraisal, they find that it is used the least often in the case of manual workers, despite the fact that before the start of transition this tool (or rather its predecessor, referred to as 'attestatsiya') was almost exclusively used to evaluate the performance of this staff category. With regard to compensation, survey respondents indicated that local establishments have the strongest role in determining basic pay. Finally, in terms of a pluralism shift, they find that the proportion of respondents who do not employ trade union members is high, with establishment level union figures and the relative power and influence of the trade union having dropped sharply. Many of these developments, the authors argue, stem from the market pressures to develop an underlying competitiveness, to hold that competitiveness through performance efficiencies and to emerge as an attractive host location for multinational companies' foreign direct investments, which in turn become conduits to the dissemination of particular HRM practices. In this sense they can be seen to be relatively 'culture free', with underlying economic and developmental exigencies determining the path of these countries. On the other hand, it is argued that it would be a mistake simply to consider them completely permissive, receptive economic regimes. They are beset by the constraints of several old institutional factors and ideational legacies that have explanatory power in accounting for commonalities and differences. It is precisely the interplay between the old and the new dynamics which, the authors suggest, draws attention to both the path dependent feature of changes and the path creation phases of it.

Ideational and structural legacies also represent an important thread in academic work on HRM in Slovenia. Zupan and Kase (2005) concentrate on the issue of the emergence of a more strategic orientation. The period between 1996 and 1998 is viewed as being unsuccessful in developing the architecture of the HRM function as a strategically important one. Drawing upon survey data, they observe the prevalence of conservative or administrative models, but with the emergence of some professional and strategic HRM models, the latter mostly being observed in those companies competing in international markets and subsidiaries of foreign multinationals located in Slovenia. New, more flexible forms of employment did not appear to be commonplace. While a deal of training appeared to be taking place, its effectiveness was rarely measured with little or no evidence of systematic evaluation of such interventions taking place. This led to the question of whether this training was making any contribution to preparing these companies for the challenges of the future. In terms of the overall function, Zupan and Kase (2005) characterise it as having relatively low power, with HRM specialists often having a dearth of core competencies necessary to bring the function more centre stage. The result was a HRM function which was best regarded as administrative, playing an often marginal role in business activity and not well positioned to impact, or be seen to impact business performance. The architectural shift demanded in response to the competitive, post-communist landscape was less than anticipated.

Lucas et al. (2004) in their analysis of the transition in Slovakia found that there had been a move away from the traditional rigid socialist type of personnel management, but it had not been fully replaced by what could be described as a systematic approach to HRM. Of particular note, they did observe the emergence of performance-related pay and more diversified remuneration systems, along with a greater emphasis on recruitment, selection of staff, and training. However, provision of training was not satisfactory, given the competitive challenges being faced, and there was an absence of a strategic approach to HRM development. Interventions designed to enhance employee satisfaction and engagement in the workplace such as job rotation, enrichment and enlargement had been introduced, but they were at best sporadic phenomena rather than commonly used widespread practices.

Buck et al. (2003) in their analysis of developments in Ukraine explore the relations between governance, HRM strategies and performance and in this context examine the extent to which HRM policies are changing, or remain wedded to historical institutional influences. In their work they develop and dimensionalise three bundles of HRM strategies and their constituent elements, namely a Traditional Social Welfare model, a Cost Minimization model and a Human Resource Investment model. This analysis in the Ukrainian context corroborates Fey and Björkman's (2001) study in Russia in that the implementation of the HRM investment bundle is again seen to be positively related to firm performance. This study goes behind strategic choice and finds that the degree of insider ownership is positively and significantly associated with this strategy, and is negatively associated with cost-cutting strategies and downsizing. Buck et al. (2003) find no significant relationship between the pursuit of the Traditional Social Welfare model and performance. Cost-cutting HRM strategies are, in turn, associated with weaker firm performance.

Receptivity to New Tools and Techniques

Welsh et al. (1993) study the extent to which the use of US-based behavioural theories and techniques might be helpful in meeting the performance challenges facing HRM in Russia. They examined the impact of US-based behavioural and participative approaches on factory workers in a textile plant in Russia. The findings confirmed that extrinsic rewards and behavioural management interventions have a positive impact on the performance of Russian textile workers. However, the institutionalisation and impact of participative management as an approach to enhancing performance proved more challenging. The participative intervention seemed to have a counterproductive effect on the Russian workers' performance. The authors argue that the failure of the participative intervention does not indicate so much that this approach just won't work across cultures, but rather that historical and cultural values and norms characterising the host context need to be recognised and overcome for such a relative sophisticated theory and techniques to work effectively (Welsh et al., 1993: 75). In a study of the role of participation and empowerment in Russian companies Michailova (2002), too, concluded that these HRM techniques had a counter-productive effect in the Russian context in the late 1990s and beginning of 2000s. She emphasised that one-man authority, anti-individualism and dependence, tightly-coupled hierarchies, lack of knowledge sharing and double-bind situations are important dominating factors that act against the logic of participation and empowerment and if foreign managers were to be respected by Russian managers and employees, they had to utilise alternative HRM instruments.

Costigan et al. (2005) in an analysis of Russia, Poland and the United States examined the extent to which cultural dimensions, such as in-group collectivism, power distance and performance orientation moderate the relationship between performance management techniques and employee behaviour. The results showed that the correlations between a performance–management composite and these two behavioural measures are significant, but that national culture did not moderate these relationships in the three countries.

Shekshnia (1998) tackles the performance question through a chronicling of the characteristics of firms that could be adjudged to have successful HRM in Russia as a result of embracing new tools and new approaches. Several features were identified which could be seen to have some explanatory power. First, concerted efforts were made directly to link business objectives, strategy and people management practices. The establishing of a HRM strategy designed to support business objectives was a chief concern. HRM was taken seriously, something which was reflected in the level of investment in bringing about and institutionalising HRM practices. On the whole, it was observed that firms that pursued imported practices, most often introduced with Russian nationals acting as the drivers and custodians, were more successful than those that favoured remaining with the conventional domestic approach. Fey et al. (1999: 69) similarly concluded that successful companies tend to use Western 'high performance' HRM practices but adjust them to fit with the Russian environment. The key challenge is in trying to understand what adjustments are needed.

Western companies often tend to react negatively to existing knowledge and HRM practices that have been institutionalised in socialist times and so they tend to implement knowledge and practices that countervail the existing ones (Björkman et al., 2007; Michailova, 2000), an approach that has not worked particularly well. Peiper and Estrin (1998) in an analysis of the emerging situation in Poland, Hungary, Czech Republic, Slovenia, Romania and Russia report practice developments in three major areas. Firstly, they observed a modernisation of practices and tools in the areas of recruitment, in training and HRM development, with accompanying altered skill patterns and changed patterns of work. They also observed a tightness in the talent pool, with consequential skill shortages and salary and benefit adjustments and they examined the role of expatriate managers working in these transition economies and the shift from employing expatriates to relying on locals. Despite differences among countries in reform and economic performance, the authors found these particular changes to be surprisingly common across the countries studied. They included rapid rises in salary and benefit levels, narrowing of some skill gaps, shifts to more sophisticated methods of recruitment and an overall move towards Western management practices, tools and techniques.

It has to be noted that the receptivity of local firms to Western HRM tools varies in terms of their in-country location, especially in geographically large countries such as Russia. For example, Moscow and St. Petersburg regions are educational centres in Russia with 12 top universities (based on the number of applicants) located there (http://rating.rbc. ru/). Companies operating in those regions already reported noticeably improved labour quality at the end of the 1990s (Shekshnia, 1998). In those regions, number of job offers for qualified candidates (those with diploma from a recognisable university, knowledge of foreign languages, additional functional training and work experience) increased in 2005 by three times compared to the previous year. Those were only about 14 per cent of all graduates. Hence a qualified candidate may have two or three offers at the same time and will not consider any offers coming from the regions. In this way local and regional labour market dynamics caused a boom in recruitment and pushed local companies operating in the regions to adopt more long-term attraction and retention strategies. At the same time, these regions attract most of inward foreign direct investment (FDI) to Russia (Broadman and Recanatini, 2003). Due to spillover-effects, growing supply and demand, in the largest urban regions we find a large number of local organisations practice advanced Western-style HRM practices, such as rigorous recruitment and selection processes, career management, succession planning, etc. The probability that a high number of organisations located in more rural parts of Russia adopt such practices is significantly lower.

Multinational Companies' Subsidiaries and the Limits to Transfer

A third very prominent theme in nomothetic-led enquiry on HRM in CEE and FSU relates to the experience of foreign multinational subsidiaries established in these locations and the extent to which these economies represent liberal regimes, allowing for the adoption of foreign policies and practices.

Given the power and economic dominance of multinational corporations, it is not surprising that there has been significant debate in recent years as to whether they act as 'nation-less organisations' (Ohmae, 1990) vis-à-vis the extent to which they 'are embedded in larger and wider societal collectivities' (Sorge, 2004: 118) and thus must organise their activities in the context of the multiple institutional environments in which they operate. Indeed it has been argued that globalisation is redefining the role of the nation state in managing the economic fortunes of nations (cf. Boyer and Drache, 1996) and further that multinationals may also play a part in constructing the environment in which they operate (cf. Williams and Geppert, 2004). There are few locations in which this could be truer than in the transition economies which, as late comers to internationalisation, have pursued the attracting of mobile foreign direct investment as a fundamental plank of their economic policy transition agenda. While traditionally foreign direct investment flows have been concentrated in developed countries, recent years have heralded a shift in location of such investments toward new destinations, including CEE and the former Soviet Union.

Guglielmo (2006) argued that due to their weakly organised industrial relations systems, many of these economies provide a permissive environment allowing multinational companies to unilaterally implement their home HRM strategies. Any opposition that does arise is informal employee resistance aimed at trying to limit employer freedom. Similarly McCann and Schwartz (2006) point to efforts towards the establishment of the most benign environment possible for the expansion of capital, entailing the augmentation of managerial prerogative and 'low-road' employment practices. In their analysis, emerging forms of management are tending towards the subordination of the work systems to a neoliberal form of world capitalism.

Weinstein and Obloj (2002) draw upon data from 303 state-owned, domestic private and foreign-owned subsidiaries located in Poland to test how strategic and environmental variables are related to the diffusion and adoption of HRM innovations. In this analysis they argue that in many instances, theoretical models of HRM developed to describe the experiences of advanced industrial democracies are useful in understanding the early experiences of countries in transition from a planned to a market economy and that the underlying concerns to achieve economic efficiency, the desire to match the preferred HRM approach to the overall business strategy and surrounding competitive pressures, in combination, contribute to the decision to introduce new HRM policies, practices and approaches. Their analysis revealed that the predominant mechanisms by which HRM innovations diffuse are a combination of the free flow of management personnel from foreign to domestic firms, the benchmarking of competitors' management practices, the influence of HRM consultants and the rise of Western management education availability in the transition economy.

Taylor and Walley (2002) examine emerging HRM practices in Croatia. They draw on 21 diverse company case-study experiences in this country to review emerging HRM practices and assess the relevance of Western management models. The results suggest that subsidiaries of multinational corporations are leading the way towards the advancement of more sophisticated HRM practices and are acting as innovators in this regard. Young Croatian managers broadly welcomed new HRM practices and identified with most of the broad objectives and philosophy of HRM. In contrast to the emergence, diffusion and institutionalisation of new style practices among MNC subsidiaries, the authors also point to evidence which suggests what they describe as the 'hijacking' of HRM amongst some Croatian companies by old style traditional forces in an attempt to maintain the status quo, representing what might be classified as a strong ideational legacy.

Björkman et al. (2007) found that employees in Russia-based MNC subsidiaries received considerably more training[1] than employees in US and Finnish subsidiaries. They also found that multinational corporations operating in Russia use performance-based compensation and performance-based appraisal systems to a greater extent than units located in the United States, and that they also pay more attention to merit in promotion decision making. This, the authors suggest, may be on the basis that multinationals react against what is seen as a negative heritage from the Soviet period, or what we have earlier referred to as an underlying ideational legacy, by implementing practices that countervail what has been traditionally used in the Russian context. Similarly, Minbaeva et al. (2007) describe how in promotion decisions HR managers of foreign subsidiaries in Kazakhstan rated personality and professionalism higher than the seniority that should be important given the Kazakh culture, emphasising respect for age. In addition to the ideational legacy, this could be explained by the fact that foreign subsidiaries usually attract younger employees (in the sample of Minbaeva et al., 2007, the average age of the workforce in the studied organisation was 35.5 years). Regardless, the authors argue that certain local-cultural conditions will necessitate the significant adaptation of such context-specific HRM practices as performance appraisal. Although some form of performance appraisal is practised in foreign subsidiaries, the 360 degree feedback favoured in many western organisations is not in use due to local socio-cultural conditions. This is in line with the previous research indicating that multi-source feedback requires low power distance (Fletcher and Perry, 2001).

In a series of earlier investigations (Fey & Björkman, 2001; Fey et al., 2000) on Russia strong support for the existence of a positive relationship between HRM practices and the performance of Russian subsidiaries of Western corporations was unearthed. The evidence appeared largely consistent with results obtained in studies of the HRM-firm performance link conducted in other geographical areas. However, the results pointed to the necessity to pursue different HRM bundles for managerial and non-managerial employees because, while a focus on collective responsibility and group-based bonuses appeared to work well for non-managerial employees, a stronger focus on individual responsibility taking and rewards based on individual performance was more effective for the managerial category. Further differential configurations for managerial and non-managerial employees were also in evidence. The provision of non-technical training and high salaries were found to be positively associated with HRM outcomes for managers, while job security was a strong predictor of HRM outcomes for non-managerial employees. In addition, there was a direct positive relationship between managerial promotions based on merits and firm performance in the Russian context.

Recently, two contextual moderators were identified as potentially affecting the adaptation of the HRM practices employed in foreign subsidiaries located in transition economies compared to their sister subsidiaries in Western, more advanced economics. The first one is the attractiveness of the acquiring firm vis-à-vis the acquired firm (Minbaeva & Muratbekova-Touron, 2011). This factor could be linked to the degree of economic development of the acquirer's country of origin but may also be related to the stereotypes of the acquirers formed historically and shared by the local employees (see also Koveshnikov, 2011). This is especially the case for acquisitions taking place along the developing–developing country axis (as opposed to developed-to-developed and developed-to-developing; see Braga Lacombe et al., 2007).

Another factor is the state of local HRM development at the time of acquisition. At the beginning of the transition, all companies acquired by foreign MNCs were being acquired for the first time. As Uhlenbruck (2004) explains, given their recent establishment and limited resources, the subsidiaries in transition economies were unlikely to take significant initiative and hence passively followed the acquirer. For example, in Kazakhstan, the underdeveloped state of local HRM coupled with the necessity to satisfy individual physiological needs provided very 'fat land' for North American HRM (Minbaeva & Muratbekova-Touron, 2007). Over time, when the subsidiaries experience second or third consecutive acquisitions, their market and managerial capabilities have evolved, they have experienced how to deal with the foreign acquirers and, most probably, they have developed certain expectations with regard to the acquirer's behaviour during the post-acquisition stage. The later entrants are dealing not only with more dynamic but also more institutionalised labour markets. Over the 1990s, the need for rapid structural adjustment of the transitional economies after the introduction of economic and social reforms was reflected in profound amendments to national employment protection legislation at the start of economic and social reforms. Still, in the majority of countries in transition, the labour laws were not a primary concern of policy makers. For example, in Kazakhstan, despite the rapid growth of the economy the Labour Law of the 1970s (pre-transition) was only replaced in 2001. Labour regulations in Russia and Slovenia are still regarded as strict compared to Hungary and Poland, which are amongst the most flexible for regular employment.

IDIOGRAPHIC ACCOUNTS OF HRM IN CEE AND THE FORMER SOVIET UNION

The relative size, importance and performance of the CEE states differs enormously (McCann & Schwartz, 2006), something which impacts the nature of HRM. Distinct developmental trajectories, coupled with differentiated levels of development, result in issues being viewed differently and done differently in these different countries resulting in differences in the way HRM is conceptualised, institutionalised and practised (Brewster et al., 2010). Obvious country specific differences are omnipresent, something which may be accounted for by the path dependent nature of change and by significant ideational legacies, many of which are not easily jettisoned (Morley, 2004). In this sense, CEE countries since 1989 have represented a form of test laboratory for HRM, which is central to the strategic directions and competitive advantage of the firms operating there (Taylor & Walley, 2002). Perhaps because of their heterogeneity, and distinct developmental trajectories since the transition process commenced in the late 1980s, they have proven the object of much academic enquiry in the contextual, or more idiographic tradition, in addition to the idiographic investigations outlined above. In contrast to these idiographic studies rooted within the universalist paradigm presented earlier, those anchored in contextualism provide a different kind of evidence on the state of HRM in the transition economies and what is distinct and different about it. Referred as an exercise in 'landscaping' (Michailova et al., 2009), in the HRM field it often involves a focus on understanding what is different between and within approaches to HRM in various contexts and what the antecedents of those differences are. These studies stress the importance of focusing on national differences in understanding HRM in specific countries. Thus this approach to researching HRM explores the importance of such factors as culture, ownership structures, labour markets, the role of the state and trade union organisation as aspects of the subject rather than external influences upon it. The scope of HRM goes beyond the organisation.

Mills (1998) explores the emerging paradigms of HRM in the Czech Republic. Here the emphasis is on linking the external environment to the organisation through the advancing of a stakeholder analysis and appropriate HRM models. In furthering the contextual debate, it is argued that the influence of external stakeholders will shape a paradigm characterised by government intervention and an insider model of corporate governance. Tung and Havlovic (1996) also explore macro-environmental variables (political-economic and socio-cultural) that have a major bearing on a firm's HRM practices and policies. In their evaluation of the transition process in both the Czech Republic and Poland, they note that despite the fact that they operated under the communist model for nearly four decades, their HRM policies and practices have already evolved down quite different paths in their transition to free-market economies. In particular, the authors suggest that each country seems to be wedded to a framework which is more consistent with their socio-cultural heritage and stage of economic development/transition to a free-market economy. They note that most likely because of its closer link with west Europe, its higher level of industrialisation and more robust economy, the Czech Republic has tended to exhibit characteristics which are more in line with those of the industrialised West.

Minbaeva et al. (2007) examine the development of HRM in Kazakhstan and establish the extent to which practices and policies were reflective of their countries of origin, older-style Soviet or post-Soviet practices, or an emerging Kazakhstan model and approach to HRM. The analysis points to an emerging model of HRM and

Table 24.1   A comparison of Kazakh, Soviet, American and European HRM practices

	Old Soviet model	American model	European model	Emerging Kazakhstani model
HR Role	Administrative back-up	Strategic partner	Strategic buffer	Strategy implementer
HR Objectives	Bureaucratic	Organisational objectives	Social concern and organisational objectives	Organisational objectives
Relations with the Environment	Top down legal restrictions	De-regulated	Negotiated legal framework	Deregulated
Relations with Employees	State level unions	Non-union	Mainly unionised	Non-union
Relations with Line Managers	None	Specialist as support to line	Specialist/line liaison	Specialist/line liaison

Source: Minbaeva et al., 2007.

employee relations practices as a hybrid of old style Soviet practices and Western European and US approaches (see Table 24.1). The reasons for the emergence of a new HRM style are (1) increasing government regulation of employment practices (new labour law; profound amendments to national employment protection legislation); (2) changes in individual preferences (i.e. the shift from group-oriented values to individualism) driven by an increase in the strength of certain individual 'needs' (usually those which emphasise status and achievement – which corresponds to an existing cultural emphasis on status, albeit often other than financial) and (3) availability and quality of human capital (i.e. a highly competitive and very dynamic labour market, at least in central cities).

Soulsby and Clark (2006), employing a case study approach, explore changing patterns of employment in post-socialist organisations in CEE and seek to develop a 'ground-up' mode of explanation of unemployment dynamics which starts with the examination of the real decision-making practices and processes of socially embedded enterprise managers. Through this approach, they advance an alternative theoretical framework to the dominant 'top-down' macro-economic and institutional views that have been so significant in many of the investigations of the post-socialist economies heretofore. The authors argue that in order to understand economic outcomes more fully, researchers need to adopt a theoretical approach that combines the sociological reasoning of institutionalism with micro-processual arguments that theorise employment and unemployment as outcomes of everyday social construction: enterprise restructuring has not been a uniform or monocausal process, emphasising once again the significance of contextual influences on transition process outcomes.

Woldu et al. (2006) in a comparative analysis examined the cultural value orientation of employees (managers and non-managers) working in three categories of organisations (professional, technical and local services) in India, Poland, Russia and the United States. Referring to Russia, they observed that the traditional collective and hierarchical value system of Russian managers was seen to be diminishing. In the managerial sub-sample of their data-set from both Poland and Russia, they found that the national cultural differences between both countries were modest, but the differences reappeared on a significant number of cultural dimensions when they compared their respective non-managerial level respondents. On balance, they suggested that employees who work for similar organisations in relatively similar positions show a degree of cultural convergence in value orientations. Tixier (1995) observed the evolution in styles of management and to the reduction of cultural differences between those concerned through an examination of the operation, dynamics and intermingling of culturally mixed management teams with executives from France, Romania and Bulgaria, among others. The acquiring of new or distinctive values and behaviours among local managers and employees in CEE was also observed by Cyr and Schneider (1996). Data were collected through interviews, questionnaires and field observation in East–West joint ventures located in Poland, Hungary and the Czech Republic. In particular, the authors sought to integrate strategic aspects of HRM, international joint ventures and transition economies and investigate how HRM policy and practice contributes to the accomplishment of the ventures' strategic objectives in the transition economy context. The findings pointed to several conditions necessary to encourage employee performance, satisfaction and learning in joint ventures in transition context including the sharing of responsibility between local and foreign managers, an emphasis on how to develop a new corporate culture that focuses on quality and results, the value of a training effort in contributing to the acquiring of new values and skills, and the structuring and institutionalisation of a rewards system that provide incentives for new behaviour.

CONCLUSIONS

In their 20-year review of research on the management of HRM in comparative and international perspective Clark et al. (1999) concluded that many of the articles examined displayed similar shortcomings to those noted in earlier reviews of cross-national management/organisation studies, with in particular an over-reliance on a small number of primarily Anglo-Saxon countries, a lack of a longitudinal perspective, a loose specification of culture, an ethnocentric bias and a frequent failure to explain observed differences and similarities. What this signals is that charting the landscape of HRM in different socio-cultural contexts and diverse geographic territories is challenging social science research and is an endeavour paved with many potential pitfalls. It certainly would be a mistake to think of the process as a neat adoption of Western practices, because in reality the riddle of interpretation is complex, most especially in the context of the transition economies. The 'transition' from state socialism in CEE and the FSU has been judged to be one of the most significant economic and social processes in recent history (McCann & Schwartz, 2006) underscored by complex political, economic and social dynamics. Early in the transition process, it was realised that there was a basic need for effective HRM systems in the post socialist economies (Kovach, 1994), as these countries sought new beginnings.

Broadly, two types of explanatory contextual factors have been previously identified in the literature: cultural and institutional. The former argues that national values are deeply embedded in a society and have a direct impact on the way one does business. At the institutional level, business system theory takes as fundamental the view that it is nationally based institutions that determine the nature of employment practices. Brewster (2007) suggests considering cultures and institutions as reciprocally constituted and using both cultural and institutional factors as explanatory factors of formation and implementation of the employment practices may be important in this effort. The notion of contextualisation as a necessity in international business research (Michailova, 2011) and as a useful paradigm for understanding HRM across countries (Grønhaug & Nordhaug, 1992; Osland et al., 2005; Von Glinow et al., 2002) has been gathering momentum in recent years. Studies in this genre are often quite descriptive in their nature. In the context of CEE and FSU, the usual aim is to examine the development of HRM in the specific country by cataloguing and describing the nature of HRM practices in common usage and identifying the extent to which practices and policies resemble so called 'Western' HRM or are ethnocentric practices or are a hybrid representing elements of both the etic and the emic. There have also been attempts to advance more macro comparisons of countries against other emerging markets such as China and India and against more advanced economies, typically the United States and Western Europe.

In terms of what typifies the research to date, a number of characteristics are discernible. First of all, the dominant universal and contextual paradigms have inspired a deal of nomothetic and idiographic led enquiry predominantly concerned with examining the core tenets of HRM in this post socialist period and the evidence for a new epoch. Inevitably, the HRM issues in the region that have been examined are inexorably bound up in the economic transition and the phenomenal transformations that have taken place in the region, and the HRM-performance question has proven significant. At the functional level, there have been studies concerned with specific HRM practices like training and development, selection and recruitment, performance management, and compensation issues. Some also explored HRM issues at the strategic level, while other studies have probed into both HRM strategies and functions. Multinational corporations' subsidiaries locating in the region have proven especially important as both a context for and the object of enquiry. In addition, and arising from the diversity of geographical and cultural coverage in the region and the dearth of much previous contextual knowledge in the literature, a considerable amount of the prior research has extensively utilised case studies. At a more macro level a number of studies present general, within country descriptions of HRM, while others have engaged in comparative analysis.

On the whole though, it is plausible to conclude that our knowledge bank of specialised and systematic research dedicated to HRM in CEE remains circumscribed. There have only been a small number of journal special issues, among them Jankowicz (1998), Pocztowski (2008) and Buciuniene et al. (2010) which focused on a limited number of countries. Valuable as these thematic special issues have been in further advancing our understanding of HRM in CEE, it is evident that further independent and systematic analyses into the HRM issues in these countries are needed. The results of the efforts to date have, in combination, given us insights into important aspects of transition dynamics, but there remain several gaps in our knowledge on HRM in the region. The state of theorising is limited and few conceptual frameworks, with explanatory power exist. As Brewster (2007: 84) notes 'In many areas of comparative HRM we lack adequate theory to explain the complexity of the differences between the meaning, policies and practices of HRM in different countries'. The overall dearth of theory has knock-on consequences for the overall empirical effort and how we might rate it. The number of studies to date is limited, and much of the work, whether of necessity or otherwise, is exploratory in nature. As a consequence, if we are to fully chart the landscape of HRM in this region, move beyond mere description and provide a springboard for more complete and nuanced empirical accounts dealing with important research questions, we have much to do.

NOTE

1. In many cases foreign investors are obliged to provide training for local employees by the host country legislation (e.g. laws around inward FDI). For example, the government of the Republic of Kazakhstan implemented a workforce nationalisation policy which included the required investment of one percent of operating capital to be allocated to training of national workforce.

REFERENCES

Amable, B. 2003. *The Diversity of Modern Capitalism.* Oxford: Oxford University Press.

Bandelj, N. 2009. The global economy as an instituted process: the case of Eastern and Central Europe. *American Sociological Review,* **74**(1): 128–149.

Björkman, I., Fey, C. & Parks H. J. 2007. Institutional theory and MNC subsidiary HRM practices: evidence from a three-country study. *Journal of International Business Studies,* **38**(3): 430–446.

Boyer, R. & Drache, D. 1996. *States Against Markets: The Limits of Globalisation.* London, Routledge

Braga Lacombe, B., Tonelli, M. and Caldas, M. 2007. IHRM in developing countries: does the functionalist versus critical debate make sense south of the equator? Conference Paper, EGOS Conference, Sub-theme 33: Critical Approaches to IHRM

Brewster, C. 2007. Comparative HRM: European views and perspectives. *International Journal of Human Resource Management,* **18**(5): 769–787

Brewster, C., Buciuniene, I. & Morley, M. 2010. The reality of human resource management in Central and Eastern Europe. *Baltic Journal of Management,* **5**(2): 145–155.

Broadman, H. & Recanatini, F. 2003. Is Russia restructuring? *Journal of Corporate Ownership and Control,* **1**: 21-32.

Buchen, C. 2007. Estonia and Slovenia as Antipodes. In D. Lane and M. Myant (eds), *Varieties of Capitalism in Post-Communist Countries.* London: Palgrave.

Buciuniene, I., Brewster, C. & Morley, M. 2010. The reality of human resource management in Central and Eastern Europe. *Baltic Journal of Management,* **5**(2): 145–287.

Buck, T., Filatotchev, I., Demina, N. & Wright, M. 2003. Insider ownership, human resource strategies and performance in a transition economy. *Journal of International Business Studies,* **34**(6): 530–549.

Caligiuri, P. 1999. The ranking of scholarly journals in international human resource management. *The International Journal of Human Resource Management,* **10**(3): 515–519.

Chadwick, C. & Dabu, A. 2009. Human resources, human resource management, and the competitive advantage of firms: toward a more comprehensive model of causal linkages. *Organization Science,* **20**(1): 253–272.

Clark, T., Grant, D. & Heijltjes, M. 1999. Researching comparative and international human resource management. *International Studies of Management & Organization,* **29**(4): 6–23.

Costigan, R., Insinga, R. Berman, J., Ilter, A., Kranas, G. & Kureshov, V. 2005. An examination of the relationship of a western performance-management process to key workplace behaviors in transition economies. *Canadian Journal of Administrative Sciences,* **22**(3): 255–267.

Crowley, S. 2005. Welfare capitalism after communism: labor weakness and post-communist social policies. In L. Hanley, B. Ruble & J. Tulchin (eds.), *Becoming Global and the New Poverty of Cities*. Washington, DC: Woodrow Wilson Center Press.

Cyr, D. & Schneider, S. 1996. Implications for learning: human resource management in East–West joint ventures. *Organization Studies*, 17(2): 207–226.

Delaney, J. T. & Huselid, M.A. 1996. The impact of human resource management practices on performance in for-profit and nonprofit organizations. *Academy of Management Journal*, 39: 949–969.

Erutku, C. & Valtee, L. 1997. Business start-ups in today's Poland: who and how? *Entrepreneurship and Regional Development*, 9: 113–26.

Fey, C. and Björkman, I. 2001. The effect of human resource management practices on MNC subsidiary performance in Russia. *Journal of International Business Studies*, 32(1): 59–75.

Fey, C. F., Björkman, I. & Pavlovskaya, A. 2000. The effect of human resource management practices on firm performance in Russia. *International Journal of Human Resource Management*, 11(1): 1–18.

Fey, C., Engström, P. & Björkman, I. 1999. Doing business in Russia: effective human resource management practices for foreign firms in Russia. *Organizational Dynamics*, 28(2) 69–79.

Fletcher, C. & Perry, E. 2001. Performance appraisal and feedback: a consideration of national culture and a review of contemporary research and future trends. In N. Anderson, D. Ones, H. Kepir-Sinangil & C. Viswesvaran (eds), *Handbook of Industrial, Work and Organizational Psychology*, Vol. 1. London: Sage Publications, pp. 127–145.

Fleetwood, S. & Hesketh, A. 2008. Theorising under-theorisation in research on the HRM–performance link. *Personnel Review*, 37(2): 126–44.

Garavan, T., Morley, M., Heraty, N. Lucewicz, J. & Schudolski, A.1998. Managing human resources in a post command economy: personnel administration or strategic human resource management? *Personnel Review*, 27(3): 200–213.

Grønhaug, K. & Nordhaug, O. 1992. International human resource management: an environmental perspective. *International Journal of Human Resource Management*, 3(1): 1–14.

Guglielmo, M. 2006. Multinationals' heaven? Uncovering and understanding worker responses to multinational companies in post-communist Central Europe. *International Journal of Human Resource Management*, 17(8): 1366–1378.

Gurkov, I. 2002. Innovations and legacies in Russian human resource management practices: surveys of 700 chief executive officers. *Post-Communist Economies*, 14(1): 137–144.

Gurkov I. & Zelenova O. 2009. Human resource management in Russia. In M. Morley, N. Heraty & S. Michailova (eds), *Managing Human Resources in Central and Eastern Europe*. London: Routledge.

Harrell-Cook, G. 2002. Human resources management and competitive advantage: strategic perspective. In G. Ferris, M. Buckley & D. Fedor (eds), *Human Resource Management: Perspectives, Context, Functions and Outcomes*. New Jersey: Prentice Hall.

Hoobler, J. & Johnson, N. 2004. An analysis of current human resource management publications. *Personnel Review*, 33(6): 665–676.

Huselid, M.A. 1995. The impact of human resource management practices on turnover, productivity, and corporate financial performance. *Academy of Management Journal*, 38: 635–672.

Huselid, M. A., Jackson, S. E. & Schuler, R. S. 1997. Technical and strategic human resource management effectiveness as determinants of firm performance. *Academy of Management Journal*, 40(1): 171–188.

Jankowicz, A. D. 1998. Issues in human resource management in central Europe. *Personnel Review*, 27(3): 169.

Kahancová, M. & van der Meer, M. 2006. Coordination, employment flexibility, and industrial relations in Western European multinationals: evidence from Poland. *The International Journal of Human Resource Management*, 17(8): 1379–1395.

Karoliny, Z., Farkas, F. & Poór, J. 2009. In focus, Hungarian and Central Eastern European characteristics of human resource management: an international comparative survey. *Journal for East European Management Studies*, **14**(1): 9–47.

Kase, R. & Zupan, N. 2005. HRM and firm performance in downsizing: evidence from Slovenian manufacturing companies. *Economic and Business Review for Central and South-Eastern Europe*, **7**(3): 239-262.

Kiriazov, D., Sullivan, S. & Tu. H. 2000. Business success in Eastern Europe: understanding and customizing HRM. *Business Horizons*, **43**(1): 39.

Kovach, R. (1994). Matching assumptions to environment in the transfer of management. *International Studies of Management and Organization*, **24**(4): 83–100.

Koveshnikov, A. 2011. The effects of cultural stereotypes on decision-making processes in Western MNCs in Russia. Conference paper, Academy of International Business, Rio-de-Janeiro, Brazil.

Koubek, J. & Brewster, C. 1995. Human resource management in turbulent times: HRM in the Czech Republic. *International Journal of Human Resource Management*, **6**(2): 223–247.

Lane, D. 2007. Post state socialism: a diversity of capitalisms? In D. Lane and M. Myant (eds), *Varieties of Capitalism in Post-Communist Countries*. London: Palgrave, pp. 13–39.

Ledeneva, A. 1998. *Russia's Economy of Favours: Blat, Networking and Informal Exchange*. Cambridge: Cambridge University Press.

Letiche, H. 1998. Transition and human resources in Slovakia. *Personnel Review*, **27**(3): 213–226.

Lucas, R., Marinova, M., Kucerova, J. & Vetrokova, M. 2004. HRM practice in emerging economies: a long way to go in the Slovak hotel industry? *International Journal of Human Resource Management*, **15**(7): 1262–1279.

Luthans, F., Patrick, R.R. & Luthans, B.C. 1995. Doing business in Central and Eastern Europe: political, economic, and cultural diversity. *Business Horizons*, Sept–Oct: 9–16

Martin, R. 1999. *Transforming Management in Central and Eastern Europe*. Oxford: Oxford University Press.

Martin, R. 2006. Segmented employment relations: post-socialist managerial capitalism and employment relations in Central and Eastern Europe. *The International Journal of Human Resource Management*, **17**(8):1353–1365.

Martin, R. & Cristescu-Martin, A.M. 2004. Consolidating segmentation: post-socialist employment relations in Central and Eastern Europe. *Industrial Relations Journal*, **35**(6): 629–646.

Mayrhofer, W., Brewster, C. & Morley, M. 2000. The concept of strategic European human resource management. In C. Brewster, W. Mayrhofer & M. Morley (eds), *New Challenges for European Human Resource Management*. London: Macmillan, pp. 3–37.

McCann, L. and Schwartz, G. 2006. Terms and conditions apply: management restructuring and the global integration of post-socialist societies. *The International Journal of Human Resource Management*, **17**(8): 1339–1352.

Michailova, S. 2000. Contrasts in culture: Russian and Western perspectives on organizational change. *Academy of Management Executive*, **14**(4): 99–112.

Michailova, S. 2002. When common sense becomes uncommon: participation and empowerment in Russian companies with western participation. *Journal of World Business*, **37**(3): 180–187.

Michailova, S. 2011. Contextualizing in international business research. Why do we need more of it and how can we be better at it? *Scandinavian Journal of Management*, **27**(1): 129–139.

Michailova, S. Heraty, N. & Morley, M. 2009. Studying human resource management in the international context: the case of Central and Eastern Europe. In M. Morley, N. Heraty and S. Michailova (eds), *Managing Human Resources in Central and Eastern Europe*. London: Routledge, pp. 1–24.

Milikic, B., Janicijevic, N. & Petkovic, M. 2008. HRM in transition economies: the case of Serbia. *SEE Journal*, November: 75–88.

Mills, A. 1998. Contextual influences on human resource management in the Czech Republic. *Personnel Review*, **27**(3): 177–199.

Minbaeva, D., Hutching, K. & Thomson, B. 2007. Hybrid human resource management in Post-Soviet Kazakhstan. *European Journal of International Management*, **1**(4): 350–371.

Minbaeva, D. & Muratbekova-Touron, M. 2011. Experience of Canadian and Chinese acquisitions in Kazakhstan. *International Journal of Human Resource Management*, doi:1 0.1080/09585192.2011.606120.

Morley, M. 2004. Contemporary debates in european human resource management: context and content. *Human Resource Management Review*, **14**(4): 353–364.

Morley, M., Brewster, C., Gunnigle P. & Mayrhofer, W. 1996. Evaluating change in European industrial relations: research evidence on trends at organisational level. *International Journal of Human Resource Management*, **7**(3): 640–657.

Morley, M., Heraty, N. & Michailova, S. 2009. *Managing Human Resources in Central and Eastern Europe*. London: Routledge.

Ohmae, K. 1990. *The Borderless World: Power and Strategy in the Interlinked Economy*. New York: Harper.

Osland, A. & Osland, J. 2005. Contextualization and strategic international human resource management approaches: the case of Central America and Panama. *International Journal of Human Resource Management*, **16**(12): 2218–2236.

Paauwe, J. 2009. HRM and performance: achievements, methodological issues and prospects. *Journal of Management Studies*, **46**(1): 129–152.

Peiper, M. & Estrin, S. 1998. Managerial markets in transition in Central and Eastern Europe: a field study and implications. *International Journal of Human Resource Management*, **9**(1): 58–78.

Pocztowski, A. 2008. From the editor. *Human Resource Management*, **60**(1), 7–9.

Shekshnia, S. 1998. Western multinationals' human resource practices in Russia. *European Management Journal*, **16**(4): 460–466.

Smith, P. C., Vozikis, G. S. & Varaksini, L. 2006. Outsourcing human resource management: a comparison of Russian and US practices. *Journal of Labor Research*, **27**(3): 305–321.

Sorge, A. 2004. Cross national differences in human resources and organisations. In A.W. Harzing & J. van Ruysseveldt (eds), *International Human Resource Management*, 2nd edn. London: Sage Publications.

Soulsby, A. & Clark, E. 2006. Changing patterns of employment in post-socialist organizations in Central and Eastern Europe: management action in a transitional context. *The International Journal of Human Resource Management*, **17**(8): 1396–1410.

Taylor, D. & Walley, E. 2002. Hijacking the Holy Grail? Emerging HR practices in Croatia. *European Business Review*, **14**(4): 294–298.

Tixier, M. 1995. Trends in international business thought and literature. Mixed management teams: how west European businesses approach central and eastern Europe. *International Executive*, **37**(6): 631–644.

Tung, R. & Havlovic, S. 1996. Human resource management in transitional economies: the case of Poland and the Czech Republic. *International Journal of Human Resource Management*, **7**(1): 1–19.

Uhlenbruck, K. 2004. Developing acquired foreign subsidiaries: the experience of MNEs in transition economies. *Journal of International Business Studies*, **35**(2): 109–123.

Von Glinow, M., Drost, E. & Teagarden, M. 2002. Converging on IHRM best practices: lessons learned from a globally distributed consortium on theory and practice. *Human Resource Management*, **41**(1): 123–140.

Wall, T. & Wood, S. 2005. The romance of human resource management and business performance, and the case for big science. *Human Relations*, **58**(4): 429–462.

Weinstein, M. & Obloj, K. 2002. Strategic and environmental determinants of HRM innovations in post-socialist Poland. *International Journal of Human Resource Management*, **13**(4): 642–659.

Welsh, D., Luthans, F. & Sommer, S. 1993. Managing Russian factory workers: the impact of US-based behavioral and participative techniques. *Academy of Management Journal*, **35**(1), 58–79.

Whitley, R. (1999) *Divergent Capitalisms: The Social Structuring and Change of Business Systems.* Oxford: Oxford University Press.

Williams, K. & Geppert, M. 2004. Employment relations in the socio-political construction of transnational social spaces by multinational companies and their subsidiaries in Germany and the UK. Paper presented at International Conference on Multinationals and the International Diffusion of Organizational Forms and Practices: Convergence and Divergence in the Global Economy, IESE, Barcelona, 15–18 July 2004.

Woldu, H, Budhwar, P. & Parkes, C. 2006. A cross-national comparison of cultural value orientations of Indian, Polish, Russian and American employees. *International Journal of Human Resource Management*, 17(6): 1076–1094.

Zupan, N. & Kase, R. 2005. Strategic human resource management in European transition economies: building a conceptual model on the case of Slovenia. *International Journal of Human Resource Management*, 16(6): 882–906.

25 Human resource management in the Indian subcontinent
Pawan Budhwar and Arup Varma

In this chapter we provide an overview of the nature, pattern and determinants of human resource management (HRM) functions and systems in the Indian subcontinent. Given the acknowledged usefulness of the need to examine HRM in a given context in order to conduct a meaningful analysis (e.g. Schuler et al., 2002), the next section presents the geographical and socio-economic context of the Indian subcontinent. This is followed by an analysis of the existing HRM literature of the region. Within this analysis, we highlight the core aspects of the HRM function in the main countries of the subcontinent. Finally, we present the key challenges facing the HRM function in the region and avenues for future research.

THE INDIAN SUBCONTINENT CONTEXT

The Indian subcontinent is a peninsula that extends towards the south from the rest of Asia like an enormous arrowhead. It is called a subcontinent because of its distinct landmass and also, perhaps, because it is not large enough to be considered as a continent. The Indian subcontinent is bounded by the Himalayas in the north and east, and the Arabian Sea, Indian Ocean and the Bay of Bengal to the south (see Ganeri, 2005). It includes countries such as India, Bangladesh, Pakistan, Sri Lanka, Nepal and Bhutan (when the Maldives and Afghanistan are also included then the more commonly used term is South Asia). The region covers about 4 480 000 km² or 10 per cent of the Asian continent and approximately 40 per cent of its population (see Wikipedia, 2009). The GDP of the region grew by an average annual rate of 5.4 per cent during 1990–2003, which is considerably more than most other regions of developing countries. This is mainly due to the strong economic performance by the Indian economy. Despite an impressive economic growth, the region scores very low on the human development index (including nutrition, education and health). It is home to 23 per cent of the world's population but as much as 39 per cent of the world's poor (Reddy, 2006). Despite of the economic developments,

Table 25.1 *Basic indicators of human development in the Indian subcontinent*

Country	GDP per capita[a]	Life expectancy (years at birth)	Adult literacy (% of 15 years and over)	Infant mortality (per 1000 live births)
Bangladesh	1770	62.8	41.1	46
Bhutan	1969	62.9	47.0	70
India	2892	63.3	61.0	75
Maldives	4798	66.6	97.2	55
Nepal	1420	61.6	48.6	61
Pakistan	2097	63.0	48.7	81
Sri Lanka	3778	74.0	90.4	13

Note: a. Purchasing-power parity (PPP) in US$ at current international prices.

Source: UNDP, Human Development Report 2005; Reddy (2006).

the gap between rich and poor is increasing. The section of society that most benefits from the economic growth is the booming middle class. The subcontinent is not a homogenous region and a lot of variation exists between its countries in terms of religion and culture (Islam dominating in Pakistan and Bangladesh; Hinduism in India and Nepal; and Buddhism in Sri Lanka and Bhutan), political systems, forms of government, political stability, the law and order situation in the region, and industrial growth. Table 25.1 presents key human development indicators for the main countries of the Indian subcontinent (see also Bhattacharya et al., 2004; Budhwar & Singh, 2007).

Like most developing parts of the world, the countries of the Indian subcontinent also pursued a state regulated economic system after their independence, which hindered innovation and strong economic growth. The main economic development in the region was initiated from 1980s onward when the markets of Sri Lanka and later on India, Pakistan and Bangladesh were de-regulated and opened to foreign investors (see Budhwar, 2001; Chandrakumara & Budhwar, 2005; Khilji, 2004a). Nevertheless, a strong development of the social sector (such as education and health) in Sri Lanka (from the 1970s onward) in comparison to other countries in the region is clearly responsible for its high performance on most human development indicators. Economic growth in the region is due to specific sectors in each of the countries. For example, both in Bangladesh and Sri Lanka it is due to the garment industry; in India it was initially because of the software sector and then information technology enabled services (ITeS) and business process outsourcing (BPO) along with few other emerging sectors such as pharmaceuticals. In Nepal and Bhutan it is perhaps due to the tourism industry (for more details see Reddy, 2006).

In order to enhance intra-regional economic cooperation, in 2004 the national governments in the region outlined a plan to create a South Asian Free Trade Area (SAFTA) by 2016. The intention behind such an initiative is to create a South Asian Customs Union and eventually a South Asian Economic Union – similar to the European Union. To a great extent the success of such ambitions depend on how countries in the region deal with internal strife, conflicts, terrorism and natural disasters. The Indian subcontinent (with the exception of Bhutan) has suffered from widespread armed conflict (such as the civil war in Sri Lanka; growing conflicts between certain factions of society within Pakistan; the significant intrusion of the Taliban in north-west Pakistan in 2009–2010; Kashmir and militancy-related conflict between India and Pakistan; the increasing terrorist attacks both in India and Pakistan; the increasing conflict between government and Maoist rebels in Nepal; and serious internal security threats by both Maoist and Naxalite rebels in the south-east of India) and natural disasters (for example, the tsunami of 26 December 2004; the 2005 earthquake mainly on the Pakistan side of Kashmir; yearly monsoon-related floods in parts of Bangladesh; and the 2010 floods in Pakistan).

For the past 6–7 decades, there has been a regular movement of people both within and outside the region, which seriously impacts its economies and has implications for HRM in issues such as recruitment and retention (see also Ramaswamy, 2003). Both legal and illegal migration from Nepal and Bangladesh to India has been substantial. This mainly involves low-wage and unskilled migrants. On the other hand, there has been large emigration of semi-skilled and skilled migrants from India and Pakistan initially to the Middle East and then of highly skilled migrants from India to North America and Western Europe. Similarly, in the 1980s lots of unskilled and semi-skilled migrants from Bangladesh and Pakistan went to Western Europe. From Sri Lanka, the migration has been mainly due to the internal war, which began in the 1980s lasting until 2009, and also for economic reasons such as many female domestic workers moving to West Asia. Also, there has been a regular and significant influx of migrants from the Indian subcontinent to the United Arab Emirates and adjoining countries. This mainly constitutes low-skilled people (see Reddy, 2006). Also, a significant number of students migrate from the Indian subcontinent, initially to study overseas both in the west (mainly the United States and UK) and east (primarily to Australia, Singapore, Hong Kong and New Zealand) and many of them try to stay there and succeed in doing so (see

Baruch et al., 2007). Those who come back (still a significant number) are trained in the Western-established ways of management education, which they try to implement and practise on their return. Similarly, management schools in the Indian subcontinent adopt a similar syllabus to the United States and UK, which also results in the creation of a Western managerial mindset. This certainly is useful for foreign firms to practise global human resource (HR) policies, but creates a challenge to working with the local employees.

Such movement of people results in skills shortage and has serious implications for human resource development (HRD). On the other hand, remittances from migrants from the region working in West Asia, North America and Western Europe make a significant contribution to the economies of India, Pakistan, Bangladesh and Sri Lanka. For example, according to the World Bank estimates in 2007, an estimated 5.7 million Indian workers abroad sent home $27 billion, making India the top recipient of remittances in the world (with China and Mexico in second and third places). In the same year, Pakistan and Bangladesh were the fourth and seventh highest recipients of remittance incomes in the world, respectively, and such remittances in Sri Lanka were equivalent to 7 per cent of its GDP (also see Reddy, 2006). Apart from skills shortages, the region also suffers from serious imbalance between rich and poor, a significant proportion of the population living below the poverty line, high levels of corruption affecting businesses, population pressure (India and Pakistan have the second and seventh largest populations in the world, respectively), poor infrastructure, less effective economic reforms, political instability, internal national security issues and increasing competition from East Asian countries. Despite these problems, the region has a lot to offer to businesses in the global context, such as India's contributions in the above-mentioned sectors. Along with other factors, effective and efficient management of human resources can play a significant role in the economic development of the region (Budhwar, 2004; Budhwar & Singh, 2007; Debrah et al., 2000; Ramaswamy, 2003).

DEVELOPMENTS IN HRM IN THE INDIAN SUBCONTINENT

In comparison to many other parts of the world, the Indian subcontinent has less literature related to HRM available. Given the variation in the economic developments in different countries of the region, an analysis of the existing literature indicates that the majority is on HRM is on India, followed by Sri Lanka and Pakistan, with even less on the other countries of the subcontinent. Perhaps a sensible way of analysing the HRM-related scenario in the region would be to look at the kind of work being published in the field, and the key messages emerging from it, and then to propose a possible way forward for the HRM function in the region. In order to draw any meaningful HRM comparisons between the countries of the region, where possible, an attempt is made to highlight the historical developments in the field of HRM, key determinants of HRM, and sector and ownership based HRM variations in each of the countries of the subcontinent.

At this stage of analysis, it is important to note that the information used in this chapter along the above-mentioned topics and issues is mostly based on and is relevant for the organised sector in the subcontinent, which is small and on which only scant research evidence is available. The unorganised or the informal sector is big in countries like India for which hardly any information it available, but it still is relatively more in comparison to other subcontinent countries. For example, the total workforce of India is over 400 million, out of which nearly 90 per cent or more are engaged in the activities of the unorganised sector (including the so-called informal sector) and remaining 10 per cent of the workforce is employed in the organised sector. About 55 per cent of the workforce is engaged in agriculture and the remaining in the non-agriculture sector. Of the non-agriculture sector employment, the unorganised workforce is 80 per cent and the remaining 20 per cent belongs to the organised segment. Only about 12 to 15 per cent of the total workforce in the country is estimated to fall in the category of wage/salary employment. Such employees constitute 6 per cent of the workforce in the rural areas and about 40 per cent of the workforce in the urban. It is estimated that only about 5 per cent of the workforce in the age group of 20–24 years has acquired some kind of a formal vocational training (see Budhwar, 2009a; Datt & Sundram, 2009). Such statistics are not readily available for other countries of the Indian subcontinent, but they are expected to be worse in comparison to India.

Also, like most parts of the world, the SMEs (small and medium enterprises) in the subcontinent contribute significantly to the region's economic growth. Research clearly highlights significant differences in the pattern of HRM systems between SMEs and medium and large-scale industries. The evidence used in this chapter is mainly based on the latter as information is not available on the former.

In India, there is no legal or policy concept of SME or medium enterprise. The popular concept is the small-scale industry (SSI) sector; this is different from the SME sector in other countries. Thus, apart from SSI, the concept of 'tiny unit' (having an investment of less than a million Rupees, £1 = 80 Rupees approximately) is also important to note; for these units are an important part of the informal sector in India. A considerable part of Indian manpower works in this sector. A large proportion of tiny enterprises are of the own-account manufacturing enterprises type (OAMEs). An OAME in India is defined as one which does not hire any worker on a regular basis and does not maintain any accounts. In addition to OAMEs, India's informal manufacturing sector consists of Non-Directory Manufacturing Enterprises (NDMEs) and Directory of Manufacturing Enterprises (DMEs). The former category employs fewer than six hired workers and in the latter more than six hired workers are employed (see Datt & Sundram, 2009). The HRM systems of both the SME/SSI and OAME in comparison to medium and large units are very different. In fact, the former do not have a HR department, a dedicated HR manager, or formal HR policies. They tend to recruit only locals from where they are based, have a range of informal, unstructured and highly indigenous work systems, which have significant regional differences (for details see Saini & Budhwar, 2008). It is safe to assume the existence of a similar situation and nature of work for similar units in other Indian subcontinent countries.

HRM in India

The existing literature on the organised sector confirms that formalised personnel functions in Indian organisations have existed for many decades (see Budhwar, 2009b). Their origin can be traced back to the colonial 1920s with the concern for labour welfare in Indian factories. The Trade Union Act of 1926 gave formal recognition to workers' unions. Similarly, the recommendations of the Royal Commission on Labour gave rise to the appointment of labour officers in 1932 and the Factories Act of 1948 laid down the duties and qualifications of labour welfare officers. These developments all formed the foundations for the Personnel Function in India and seem to parallel the initial developments of the British Personnel Function (Budhwar & Khatri, 2001; Sparrow & Budhwar, 1997). Provisions similar to those provided by Cadbury in the UK were initially provided by J. R. D. Tata (one of the most prominent entrepreneurial figures of India) in the early 1920s in India (see Budhwar, 2009a).

In the early 1950s, two HRM-related professional bodies were set up in India: the Indian Institute of Personnel Management (IIPM) formed at Calcutta and the National Institute of Labour Management (NILM) at Bombay. During the 1960s, the Personnel Function began to expand beyond its welfare origins with the three areas of Labour Welfare, Industrial Relations and Personnel Administration developing as the constituent roles for the emerging profession. In the 1970s, the thrust of the personnel function shifted towards the need for greater organisational 'efficiency' and by the 1980s personnel professionals began to talk about new concepts such HRM and HRD. The two professional bodies of IIPM and NILM were merged in 1980 to form the National Institute of Personnel Management (NIPM) based in Bombay. The status of the personnel function in India has therefore changed over the years (see Budhwar, 2009a). However, presently it is changing at a much more rapid pace than ever, mainly due to the pressures created by the liberalisation of economic policies initiated in 1991. To summarise, looking at the evolution and developments in the Indian HRM function we can say that its status has changed from that of 'clerical' in 1920–30s, to 'administrative' in 1940–60s, to 'managerial' in 1970–80s, to that of 'executive' in 1990s and towards the 'strategic partner' in the present decade. Accordingly, its emphasis has changed from statutory, welfare, paternalism to regulatory conformance to human resource development and how it can help to improve organisational performance (for more details, see Budhwar, 2009a).

Within these developmental phases, certainly the increased emphasis on HRD in 1990s has been the dominant topic in the broad area of the personnel function. To a great extent, this was an outcome of the pressures created by foreign firms (due to deregulation of the Indian economy) on Indian firms to significantly improve the contribution of their HRM function towards organisational performance (see Saini & Budhwar, 2007). In fact, in the late 1990s in India, HRD became a more often used term to denote the personnel function than HRM (Budhwar, 2004). HRD in India has been seen as a continuous process to ensure the planned development of employee competencies and capabilities, the motivation and exploitation of inner capabilities for organisational development purposes, and the pursuit of dynamism and effectiveness (see Rao et al., 1994). It also emphasised the provision of tools and techniques to the line managers who encourage its philosophy.

The changes in response to the pressure created by economic reforms on the traditional Indian personnel management system are now clearly noticeable in the way organisations are managed in India, especially in the modern and organised sectors (software, IT, business process outsourcing (BPO)) and the ones that are managed professionally (see Budhwar et al., 2006a, b). This also applies to the majority of the foreign firms operating in India (see Björkman & Budhwar, 2007). In most of such organisations, the HRM function is seen as well structured and rationalised. The proportion of Indian organisations operating in such a way is still in a minority, but certainly is on the increase. Since the traditional Indian HRM system was developed over a long time period, understandably, it will take some time to change. However, the symptoms of change are quite prominent as HRM is playing a noticeable role in bringing about changes in Indian organisations and more and more Indian organisations are now creating a separate HRM/HRD department. Accordingly, there has been a significant increase in the level of training and development of employees (Budhwar & Sparrow, 1997; Saini & Budhwar, 2007). There are also indications of a movement towards performance-related pay and promotions (Bordia & Blau, 1998). Indeed such developments have already matured in the modern industrial sectors such as business process outsourcing (see Budhwar et al., 2006a).

Similarly, in comparison to the public sector, the internal work culture of private enterprises now places greater emphasis on an internal locus of control, future orientation in planning, participation in decision making, effective motivation techniques and obligation towards others in the work context (Saini & Budhwar, 2008). The existing research evidence also reveals the significant influence of different contingent variables (like age, size, sector) and indeed national factors such as national culture and institutions on the HRM systems of Indian firms (see Budhwar & Khatri, 2001). Overall, it would be appropriate to say that the HRM function in India is in a phase of rapid transition. A collective effort is now required from both practitioners and researchers to support each other and share the on-going developments in the field with different audiences.

The emerging evidence also suggests that researchers are pursuing investigations on a variety of HRM related topics in India such as evolution of the personnel function (Balasubramanian, 1994; 1995); the role of unions and industrial relations in the new economic environment (Seth, 1996; Sharma, 1992; Sodhi, 1994; Venakata Ratnam, 1998), factors determining HRM and organisational commitment (Budhwar & Sparrow, 1997; Bhatnagar, 2007), HRM in multinationals (Amba-Rao, 1994; Björkman & Budhwar, 2007; Björkman et al., 2008; Venakata Ratnam, 1998), HRM, culture and organisational performance (Agarwala, 2003; Budhwar & Sparrow, 1997; Chand & Katou, 2007; Singh, 2003), talent management and organisational learning capability (Bhatnagar, 2007; Bhatnagar & Sharma, 2005), innovative HRM (Som, 2008), employee relations (Budhwar, 2003), comparative HRM in public and private sector organisations (Budhwar & Boyne, 2004; Bordia & Blau, 1998), HRM in SMEs (Saini & Budhwar, 2008), emerging patterns of HRM in the business outsourcing sector (Budhwar et al., 2006a; Budhwar et al., 2006b; Budhwar, 2009a), applicability of western HRM models in India (Budhwar & Khatri, 2001; Björkman & Budhwar, 2007), HRD (Rao et al., 1994; Sparrow & Budhwar, 1997) and training (Yadapadithaya, 2000), and comparative HRM between India and other countries (Budhwar

& Sparrow, 1997; Kuruvilla, 1996; Sparrow & Budhwar, 1997). Also, a number of researchers have examined various aspects of organisational behaviour and organisational dynamics (see for example, Aryee et al., 2002, 2004; Kakar, 1971; Sahay & Walsham, 1997) and the influence of national culture of Indian HRM (see Sharma, 1984; Budhwar & Sparrow, 2002). With a rapid increase in the number of expatriates moving to India, some scholars have initiated investigations related to their adjustment (e.g. Thite et al., 2009; Varma et al., 2006). These examples, give a clear indication about the kind of HRM issues explored in the Indian setting. However, it is important to note that this is not an exhaustive list of works published on India (for details, see Budhwar & Bhatnagar, 2009).

HRM in Pakistan and Bangladesh

Both Pakistan and Bangladesh, being part of India prior to separation in 1947 (during partition India was divided into India and Pakistan with Bangladesh as part of Pakistan called Eastern Pakistan, until 1971 when it became independent), also inherited a number of management systems from the English. Hence, we can expect a number of similarities in the nature of HRM systems of the three countries, especially during the decades of 1950–70s. Nevertheless, due to the variations in economic growth of the three countries, along with the growing importance of certain institutions in them contributing to both uniqueness and differences over the past few decades, we can see differences regarding both the developments and nature of HRM function in these countries, with India perhaps having more developed HRM functions (at least in certain sectors and more professionally run firms) followed by Pakistan and Bangladesh. For both these countries of the Indian subcontinent there is scant HRM literature available.

Both Pakistan and Bangladesh are predominantly Muslim countries (with, respectively, approximately 95 per cent and 85 per cent of the population following Islam), with a very high density of population (Pakistan and Bangladesh being the sixth and seventh most populous countries in the world), high illiteracy and unemployment rates and agriculture being the dominating sector for both contributing towards GDP and employment. For Pakistan, perhaps Khilji's (Khilji, 2002; 2003; 2004a; 2004b; Khilji & Wang, 2006) work is most comprehensive. She has researched and written on various aspects of people management in Pakistan starting from evolution of HRM functions, factors determining HRM policies and practices, comparative HRM in local and foreign firms, HRM and firms' performance, and the challenges facing the HRM function in Pakistan.

Khilji (2004a: 110–111) presents a comprehensive analysis of the impact of main national factors on various aspects of HRM in Pakistan. Under the factor of national culture she highlights how the social and hierarchical set-up of the Pakistani society, marked by high power-distance, having a strong inheritance of British class systems and influences of the American management systems, impacts on most spheres of HRM from recruitment, rewards, appraisals (who knows whom), decision making (more centralised) and training. Similarly, she highlights how the competitive business environment is impacting on an increased emphasis on training; national instability and political uncertainty are contributing to a lack of trust amongst the key actors of employment system. Trade unions (as in India) seem to have been a significant influence on HRM in Pakistan (on such issues as termination, dismissals and safety and health). The impact of Islam in the workplace is also evident in Pakistan (see Khilji, 2004a; Syed, 2008). For example, prayer rooms, extended lunch breaks on Fridays and less working time during the fasting months are provided in most organisations. Due to the existence of the unique business and institutional set-up (characterised by increasing impact of Islamic principles on work systems, increasing levels of red-tapism, strong relationship- and caste-based social set-ups, corruption and discontentment in society at large due to poor economic growth, economic and national security related instability, and scarcity of resources to share with the rapidly increasing population) and the strong impact of the same on HRM in Pakistan, multinational firms are required to modify their HRM practices to suit such a context (see Khilji, 2003). For example, provision of flexible working to support employees for Friday prayers and during the fasting months, a more localised approach to HRM practices (e.g. a word-of-mouth and referral-based recruitment). It is important to realise the complex dynamic within which foreign firms operate in developing countries like Pakistan. On the one hand, they directly employ staff from the host country for whom they adopt a mixture of global HR policies and local context-specific practices (such as to recruit, motivate, communicate and retain talent). On the other hand, multi-national corporations (MNCs) tend to rely on local SMEs for the supply of goods and services, who many a time resort to questionable practices such as employment of child labour, violation of labour standards such as denial of minimum wage and other minimum-work conditions. Overall, the status of HRM in Pakistan is still low in comparison to other functions. This is evident from the absence of an established HRM professional body or many business schools offering HRM degrees in Pakistan (see Khilji, 2004a).

The available literature on Bangladesh is primarily on the management of the public sector and on governance issues. Zafarullah (2006) analyses new tools and practices in public governance in both Pakistan and Bangladesh. Sarker (2005, 2006) explores the factors influencing the success and failure of new public management initiatives in Bangladesh and Singapore. Zafarullah and Rahman (2008) blame successive governments for politicising administrative services in Bangladesh. Along with it, they also point to the significant contribution of corruption and nepotism towards inefficiency and the failure of the state machinery in formulating and implementing sound policies. Similarly, Zafarullah (2006) highlights the need of better relationship between governance and socio-economic outcomes, and accountability, transparency and participation as important ingredients for effective management developments in a developing country like Bangladesh. Due to the economic, social and cultural positions of women in that society, perhaps a clear difference is evident when it comes to the movement of females to higher positions in Pakistan and Bangladesh (see Andaleep, 2004; Aston, 2008; Lucy et al., 2008) and India (see Budhwar et al., 2005) where, perhaps due to religious institutional constraints, there are less females in key positions in the former.

HRM in Sri Lanka, Nepal and Bhutan

According to World Bank (2006), Sri Lanka was one of the first developing countries to understand the importance of investing in human resources and promoting gender equality. As a result, it has a fairly well developed human resource base and achieved human development outcomes more consistent with those of higher income countries: for example, on indices such as the human development index (0.665), literacy rate (92 per cent), pupils completing primary school (97 per cent) and life expectancy (71 years), Sri Lanka stands higher than all other nations in South Asia. Foreign investors have noted that the Sri Lankan labour force is highly trainable.

Recent developments in the field of HRM bear witness to the fact that both the Sri Lankan government and private sector organisations have recognised the importance of the role HRM plays in the nation's growth and in achieving a sustainable competitive advantage in the global market place. There are several examples:

1. The formation of a Human Resource and Education (HR&E) Sub Committee (June, 1999) by the Ceylon Chamber of Commerce in order to bridge the country's human resource development gap, with the collaboration of private sector organisations and Sri Lankan universities;
2. The formation of the Association of HR Professionals (AHRP), having recognised the pivotal role that HRM plays in the present

global and regional environment, in order to give due recognition to HRM, which will benefit the professional as well as the whole country, to share knowledge and experience among HRM managers and to establish strategic alliances with other institutions in order to carry out research projects on HRM in collaboration with academic institutions; and

3. The establishment of the Commercial Mediation Centre (CMC) of Sri Lanka by an act of parliament in order to act as a viable alternative to litigation when dealing with business disputes and conflicts, besides helping the parties save face and continue their existing employment relationships (for more details, see Chandrakumara & Budhwar, 2005).

The existing literature reveals an increasing number of HRM research investigations being pursued in the Sri Lankan context. For example, the study by Chandrakumara and Sparrow (2003) highlights the nature of work and people management practices in Sri Lanka. The analysis is based on the responses of CEOs and HR managers of both local and foreign-invested manufacturing companies. The main aspects of work and people management practices include the existence of a moderate level of HRM planning and empowering system; performance-based rewards systems with business driven training; functional perspectives on job-person fit; and job and behaviour-related competence and rewards. A closer analysis highlights differences between domestic and foreign firms (either fully owned multinationals or joint ventures). For example, in comparison to domestic firms, foreign firms tend to adopt a more structured, formal and rationalised approach to all the above-mentioned HRM practices.

Akuratiyagamage (2005, 2006) has examined issues related to management development in different ownership firms in Sri Lanka. She found similarity of management development practices across the three forms of firm ownership – local, foreign and joint ventures. Along the same lines, Mamman et al. (2006) looked at the managerial perceptions towards the role of the HRM function in the development of organisational strategy processes in Sri Lankan organisations. Their results reveal no significant differences between local and foreign firms. Wickramasinghe and Jayabandu (2007) examine issues related to 'flexitime' such as employees' attitudes towards it, their level of satisfaction with it, various hindrances in the adoption of flexitime, and the extent to which flexitime can be effectively used to attract and retain employees. Their findings reveal that flexitime allows employees autonomy to harmonise work and non-work demands and enables them to balance work/life commitments. It is also evident that large companies offer more flexitime initiatives in comparison to small firms. Further, employees see flexitime as an important feature to have in their future workplaces. Not surprisingly, those employees who have not experienced flexitime are not yet convinced about its benefits. Chandrakumara (2007) provides empirical evidence on the impact of HRM fit on citizenship and task performance of employees in seven manufacturing companies and a survey of 433 employees and managers in Sri Lanka. His findings confirm the thesis of a positive relationship between HRM fit and performance, more for citizenship performance than for task performance.

Chandrakumara and Sparrow (2004) reveal a significant impact of meaning and values of work orientation as an element of national culture in predicting HRM policy-practice design choices. Their investigations reveal that the four dominant clusters of HRM design choices (i.e. planned and open career and empowering system, qualifications and performance based reward system, generic functional perspectives of job-person fit, and job-related competence and rewards) are influenced by eight factors of meaning and values and work orientations (i.e. individual growth/ humanistic beliefs oriented work norms, organisations and positions oriented work ethics and beliefs, status and security oriented upward striving, extrinsic value orientation, external work locus of control, work centrality, working defined as a burden and constraint, and working defined as a social responsibility and contribution). Wickramasinghe (2006) investigated the validity of training objectives in the Sri Lankan context. In another analysis, she found that in the private sector companies place a higher weighting on the external labour market in recruitment and the use of objective criteria in selection (see Wickramasinghe & Jayabandu, 2007). Further, an important role of interviews, written examinations, psychometric tests and assessment centres is being highlighted within the selection methods. The above evidence reveals the existence of a more professional approach to HRM in the Sri Lankan context. A comparative analysis of the Indian subcontinent countries highlights Sri Lanka (along with India) as a more attractive place for investors. Some of the main factors in this regard include its position as a regional trading hub; a provider of strategic access to South Asian markets (through bilateral free trade agreements); the presence of a highly literate and cost-competitive labour force; the existence of an open economy; the presence of free trade zones and industrial parks; the existence of a reliable infrastructure; and a relatively high quality of life (see Chandrakumara & Budhwar, 2005). Nevertheless, Sri Lanka has had its own share of internal disturbances over the past three decades led by the LTTE (Liberation Tigers of Tamil Eelam).

Lately, some scholars have also initiated research in HRM related issues in Nepal. Adhikari and Mueller (2004) provide a good summary regarding the scene of HRM in Nepal and the significant impact of the business environment, national culture and national institutions on Nepali HRM. Gautam et al. (2005) examine the constructs of organisational citizenship behaviour and organisational commitment in the Nepalese context. Further, Gautam and Davis (2007) investigate the constructs of strategic integration of HRM in terms of the corporate strategies and devolvement of responsibility for HRM to line managers in 26 commercial banks and insurance companies operating in Nepal. The results indicate a relatively higher level of integration of HRM into the corporate strategy in comparison to devolvement of responsibility for HRM to line. The partial level of devolvement is more out of a necessity in the absence of a strong HRM function. Such investigations are useful in revealing that Western HRM constructs are making inroads into more developed aspects of the Nepalese business. It also highlights how the socio-economic and cultural context of the nation is influential in shaping the devolvement of HRM mechanisms in Nepal and the extent to which a real transfer of Western constructs is possible in such a context (also see Pant et al., 1996). The existing literature highlights a scarcity of managerial skills in Bhutan and there is an absence of any reliable HRM-related literature (see McWeeney, 1998; Rice, 2004).

A few conclusions can be drawn from the above analysis: (1) There is a scarcity of HRM research on the Indian subcontinent (though strongly emerging in the Indian context); (2) There is very little evidence regarding the kind of methodologies that might be suitable for conducting useful research in the region. At present many of the above mentioned researchers have adopted Western constructs and measures to examine HRM in the region and have found some interesting results. Given the heterogeneity of the countries within the region and obvious differences from the West, and knowing the limitations regarding the applicability of Western constructs/measures elsewhere, it is important to further develop more region specific instruments and conduct investigations using the same (Budhwar, 2004; Budhwar & Debrah, 2009; Pant et al., 1996); (3) There is little HRM research evidence for SMEs in the region. They recruit a significant proportion of the population, contribute to the economic growth of the region and also strongly support MNCs operating in the region. SMEs employ a range of indigenous work and management practices which reveal the nature of the society, which perhaps is not reflected in the above presentation. Indigenous systems are characterised by unique internal labour markets based on ones social connections, high level of power distance, informality, and lack of rationalisation; (4) All countries of the Indian subcontinent, apart from Bhutan, regularly experience serious disturbance from terrorists, banned groups or unsupportive local political parties. This significantly disturbs business in general and has implications for HRM. For example, the opposition political party in the state of West Bengal forced Tata Motor Manufacturers to discontinue their operations to build the one-lakh Rupee (less than 2500 dollar) car – the Nano – and move it to the state of Gujarat. Similarly, the intrusion of Taliban into north-west Pakistan forced the population to flee from the area and schools to close; (5) In order to reveal the region and context-specific nature of HRM policies and practices there is a strong need to identify the main aspects of indigenous management systems relevant to each country of the subcontinent and also the main factors and variables which might be determining the same.

CHALLENGES FOR HRM AND THE WAY FORWARD IN THE INDIAN SUBCONTINENT

The economic liberalisation being pursued by most countries in the Indian subcontinent along with many related attractions for foreign investors, such as availability of cheap and talented human resources offer, on the one hand, immense opportunities for businesses but, on the other hand, issues related to instability, security, uncertainty, corruption, nepotism, lack of enough skilled human resources and so on. These pose massive challenges for overseas firms to enter the Indian subcontinent markets and flourish there. Given the evolutionary phase of the HRM function in many of the countries in the region and the economic developments in dynamic business circumstances there are massive challenges before the HRM function of firms operating in the region.

It is clear that HRM systems in these countries are now rapidly evolving and are in a state of flux, the traditional mechanisms of managing human resources in the present dynamic business era are being challenged though still strongly prevalent in SMEs, the validity of established Western or Eastern management systems in the Indian subcontinent is questionable, the establishment of 'best-practices' model(s) to suit the subcontinent context is still emerging and will take a while to become reliable, and the pace of change is phenomenal (especially in India) as a result of which it is difficult to pin-point the dominant and perhaps more successful ways of managing human resources in the subcontinent.

In such circumstances, perhaps the main challenge before the HRM function in the Indian subcontinent is to change the traditional mindset of top decision makers and make them realise the useful contribution HRM can make towards achieving organisational objectives. This is certainly happening in countries like India, Sri Lanka and in large firms and MNCs in Pakistan. The way forward for other countries is perhaps to learn from these two countries and companies and initiate HRM-related initiatives in the form of new academic programmes, develop HRM professional bodies and amend their dated labour legislation which is creating difficulties in bringing about the required changes. Apart from updating of the legislation, there is a strong need to strengthen its implementation part. Corruption of different types (such as personal preferences and favours at work based on social connections) is perhaps the main hindrance in this regard.

Perhaps one of such changes needed for places like India is the downsizing of organisations in order to tackle the problem of surplus labour, especially in public sector organisations. Both the existing legislation and the existence of pressure groups (in the form of unions and vested interests of politicians and other leaders) resist such changes and create a massive challenge for the HRM function to tackle such difficult issues. The experience of China and also a few cases in India suggests that it will only happen with the help of visionary decision making, and pressure created by private and foreign firms on public sector firms to perform, rationalise and professionalise their HRM systems.

The analysis also highlights the important influence of social contacts, the caste to which one belongs, ones financial position and political affiliation on most HRM practices (also see Budhwar & Khatri, 2001) in the region. This not only restricts optimum use of talent but many times simply ignores it, which results in nepotism and corruption at the workplace. This poses a major challenge for the HRM function in the subcontinent (indeed in many other developing countries around the world as well) to stay efficient and effective. It is interesting to witness that many organisations in India are now successfully pursuing a formal, structured, rationalised and professional approach to HRM in some sectors in the traditional set-up. It is now evident that most foreign firms and firms operating in the business process outsourcing sector in India are able to pursue such modern HRM systems (see Budhwar et al., 2006a, b, 2009). To a great extent, the demands of the sector make this possible (in the BPO sector most performance indicators are quantifiable and most systems are based on objective indices). A number of firms are now rapidly learning from such successful examples and are modifying their HRM systems. It is believed that growing competition, along with increased awareness about the benefits of such systems, will encourage other firms to adopt such systems. However, it is also clear that such developments will vary significantly between countries of the region that may vary depending on their economic development, stability, growth of professional management institutes and the will of top decision makers.

In the new sectors such as BPO, software and IT and also working in foreign firms, employees in the Indian subcontinent are experiencing a move away from traditional employment practices and established internal labour markets, which might constitute a violation of their traditional psychological contracts. Thus, the challenge for HR managers is how to deal with the outcome of employees' response to the perceived violation of the psychological contract – such as reduced effort on the job or output and reduced contributions in the form of loyalty and commitment (DeNisi & Griffin, 2001). We might assume that it is in the new sectors where problems relating to psychological contract and job stress are now becoming prominent. For example, in the case of India, a majority of call centre employees after a while discover the dark side of the 'rosy' picture and then their level of morale declines considerably. This often results in high attrition. To a great extent, the lack of talent development initiatives and the lack of clear career structure are held responsible for this (see Budhwar et al., 2006a). Such emerging trends pose challenges to HR managers regarding both their recruitment and retention policies and practices.

Yet another challenge for HR managers is the issue of diversity management, especially that related to gender, caste and religion based diversity. The cultural constraints in the region (especially in Muslim countries) regarding the acceptance of females into the workforce, and certainly in key positions, are a massive challenge for the HRM function. It is evident that there are glass-ceiling problems in subcontinental organisations. Perhaps, there it would be useful to learn from the successful examples of the BPO sector in India, which not only has about a 50 per cent female workforce, but also pushed the Indian government to amend its Factories Act under which females were not allowed to work on night shifts. However, this will be a major problem in Muslim countries where there is even evidence that female students are not even allowed to attend schools.

Nevertheless, it seems that the status of the personnel function in many sectors in India and Sri Lanka has improved over the last two decades or so. The number of personnel specialists moving to the position of CEO has increased over the last few years (see Saini & Budhwar, 2007). On the other hand, it seems that Indian firms are witnessing a significant devolvement of responsibility of HRM to line managers (see Budhwar & Sparrow, 2002). However, if a strategy of devolvement is not associated with a closer integration of HRM into the business planning processes, it may create a situation of chaos in organisations as they attempt to cope with the HRM implications of liberalisation. Hence, the way forward is the adoption of a more strategic approach to HRM. To pursue such an agenda it is important that the foundations of the HRM function are sound. Perhaps this agenda is already on the move and is being put in practice in many Indian organisations (see Agarwala, 2003; Singh, 2003). This also seems to be happening in Pakistan, but every time the momentum is disturbed by either an internal security threat or by a natural disaster. In other countries this is certainly is not the case and it is a direction to follow.

A further challenge is in the form of how best to manage the 'new-employee' – the expatriate in the Indian subcontinent context. In countries like India, the number of expatriates (self-initiated or others) is now increasing rapidly. Given the unique context of the subcontinent, we do not have established approaches for managing expatriates. Perhaps, this should not only be seen as a challenge but also an opportunity to learn and accordingly improve management systems in the region.

Another challenge revolves around the quality of HRM research in the Indian subcontinent context. It seems that too much of the research effort has been limited to simplistic comparisons, correlational analyses providing no insight into underlying processes, and skewed, idiosyncratic sampling. Such research, it is argued, does not contribute significantly to theory development. There is then a strong need to increase both rigour and relevance of HRM research efforts in the Indian subcontinent context. The focus of research should also be to develop constructs that can help to study local and global issues and enable the development and validation of new constructs so as to get into the depth of issues more relevant to the region.

To summarise, the challenges facing HRM in the Indian subcontinent are clearly complex and daunting. The majority of these challenges have emerged due to the changes in the economic environment. In particular, globalisation and international competitiveness have brought to the fore the need for organisations to adopt appropriate HRM practices in their quest for competitive advantage. In this globalised era, competitive pressures have laid bare the limitations of the traditional models of management in all the countries of the region. Clearly, there is some indication that HRM is undergoing transformation in the region but it is unclear what the outcome of this transformation would be. Early indications from India at least are that a move towards a more professional approach to HRM is evolving in certain sectors. However, it is too early to see a clear model or approach emerging. Possibly, a hybrid system (based on a mixture of both traditional Asian characteristics and Western rationalised system) will emerge. However, it is important that any HRM system that emerges in the subcontinent should be context based.

REFERENCES

Adhikari, D. R. & Mueller, M. 2004. Human resource management in Nepal. In P. Budhwar & Y. Debra (eds), *Human Resource Management in Developing Countries*. London: Routledge, pp. 91–101.

Agarwala, T. 2003. Innovative human resource practices and organizational commitment: an empirical investigation. *International Journal of Human Resource Management*, 14(2): 175–198.

Akuratiyagamage, V. M. 2005. Identification of management development needs: a comparison across companies of different ownership: foreign, joint-venture and local in Sri Lanka. *International Journal of Human Resource Management*, 16(8): 1517–1533.

Akuratiyagamage, V. M. 2006. Management development practices: empirical evidence from Sri Lanka. *International Journal of Human Resource Management*, 17(9): 1606–1624.

Amba-Rao, S. 1994. US HRM principles: cross-country comparisons and two case applications in India. *International Journal of Human Resource Management*, 5(3): 755–778.

Andaleep, S. S. 2004. Participation in the workplace: gender perspectives from Bangladesh. *Women in Management Review*, 19(1/2): 52–61.

Aryee, S., Budhwar, P. & Chen, Z. X. 2002. Trust as a mediator of the relationship between organizational justice and work outcomes: test of a social exchange model. *Journal of Organizational Behaviour*, 23(3): 267–285.

Aryee, S., Chen, Z. X. & Budhwar, P. 2004 Exchange fairness and employee performance: an examination of the relationship between organizational politics and procedural justice. *Organizational Behavior and Human Decision Processes*, 94(1): 1–14.

Aston, J. 2008. Why Bangladeshi and Pakistani women face cultural and practical barriers to work. *People Management*, 14(1): 46.

Balasubramanian, A. G. 1994. Evolution of personnel function in India: a re-examination. Part 1. *Management and Labour Studies*, 19(4): 196–210.

Balasubramanian, A. G. 1995. Evolution of personnel function in India: a re-examination. Part II. *Management and Labour Studies*, 20(1): 5–14.

Baruch, Y., Budhwar, P. & Khatri, P. 2007. Brain drain: the inclination of international students to stay abroad after their studies. *Journal of World Business*, 42(1): 99–112.

Bhatnagar, J. 2007. Predictors of organizational commitment in India: strategic HR roles, organizational learning capability and psychological empowerment. *International Journal of HRM*, 18(10): 1782–1797.

Bhatnagar, J. & Sharma, A. 2005. The Indian perspective of strategic HR roles and organizational learning capability. *International Journal of Human Resource Management*, 16(9): 1711–1739.

Bhattacharya, M., Smyth, R. & Vicziany, M. 2004. *South Asia in the Era of Globalization: Trade, Industrialisation and Welfare*. Hauppauge, NY: Nova Science Publishers.

Björkman, I. & Budhwar, P. 2007. When in Rome. . .? Human resource management and the performance of foreign firms operating in India. *Employee Relations*, 29(6): 595–610.

Björkman, I., Budhwar, P., Smale, A. & Sumelius, J. 2008. Human resource management in foreign-owned subsidiaries: China versus India. *International Journal of Human Resource Management*, 19(5): 964–978.

Bordia, P. & Blau, G. 1998. Pay referent comparison and pay level satisfaction in private versus public sector organizations in India. *The International Journal of Human Resource Management*, 9(1): 155–167.

Budhwar, P. 2001. Doing business in India. *Thunderbird International Business Review*, 43(4): 549–568.

Budhwar, P. 2003. Employment relations in India. *Employee Relations*, 25(2): 132–148.

Budhwar, P. 2004. Introduction: HRM in the Asia-Pacific context. In P. Budhwar (ed.), *Managing Human Resources in Asia-Pacific*. London: Routledge, pp. 1–15.

Budhwar, P. 2009a. HRM in the Indian context. In P. Budhwar, & J. Bhatnagar (eds.), *Changing Face Of People Management in India*. London: Routledge, pp. 3–19.

Budhwar, P. 2009b. Managing human resources in India. In J. Storey, P. Wright & D. Ulrich (eds), *Companion to Strategic HRM*. London, NY: Routledge, pp. 435–446.

Budhwar, P. & Bhatnagar, J. 2009. *Changing Face of People Management in India*. London: Routledge.

Budhwar, P. & Boyne, G. 2004. Human resource management in the Indian public and private sectors: an empirical comparison. *International Journal of Human Resource Management*, **15**(2): 346–370.

Budhwar, P. & Debrah, Y. 2009. Future research on human resource management systems in Asia. *Asia Pacific Journal of Management*, **26**(2): 197–218.

Budhwar, P. & Khatri, P. 2001. HRM in context: the applicability of HRM models in India. *International Journal of Cross Cultural Management*, **1**(3): 333–356.

Budhwar, P., Luthar, H. & Bhatnagar, J. 2006a. Dynamics of HRM systems in BPOs operating in India. *Journal of Labor Research*, **XXVII**(3): 339–360.

Budhwar, P., Saini, D. & Bhatnagar, J. 2005. Women in management in the new economic environment: the case of India. *Asia Pacific Business Review*, **11**(2): 179–193.

Budhwar, P. & Singh, V. 2007. Introduction: people management in the Indian subcontinent. *Employee Relations*, **29**(6): 545–553.

Budhwar, P. & Sparrow, P. 1997. Evaluating levels of strategic integration and devolvement of human resource management in India. *The International Journal of Human Resource Management*, **8**(4): 476–494.

Budhwar, P. & Sparrow, P. 2002. Strategic HRM through the cultural looking glass: mapping cognitions of British and Indian HRM managers. *Organization Studies*, **23**(4): 599–638.

Budhwar, P., Varma, A., Malhotra, N. & Mukherjee, A. 2009. Insights into the Indian call centre industry: can internal marketing help tackle high employee turnover? *Journal of Services Marketing*, **23**(5): 351–362.

Budhwar, P., Varma, A., Singh, V. & Dhar, R. 2006b. HRM Systems of Indian call centres: an exploratory study. *The International Journal of Human Resource Management*, **17**(5): 881–897.

Chand, M. & Katou, A. 2007. The impact of HRM practices on organizational performance in the Indian hotel industry. *Employee Relations*, **29**(6): 576–594.

Chandrakumara, A. 2007. Does HRM fit really matter to citizenship and task performance? Sri Lanka manufacturing sector experience. *Employee Relations*, **29**(6): 595–610.

Chandrakumara, A. & Budhwar, P. 2005. Doing business in Sri Lanka. *Thunderbird International Business Review*, **47**(1): 95–120.

Chandrakumara, A. & Sparrow, P. 2003. The impact of work and values orientations on HRM policies and practices in domestic and foreign invested companies in Sri Lanka. Paper presented at the 7th Annual Conference of the International Journal of Human Resources Management. Limerick, Ireland.

Chandrakumara, A. & Sparrow, P. 2004. Work orientation as an element of national culture and its impact on HRM policy-practice design choices: lessons from Sri Lanka. *International Journal of Manpower*, **25**(6): 564–589.

Datt, R. & Sundram, K. P. M. 2009. *Indian Economy*. New Delhi: S. Chand & Company Ltd.

Debrah, Y., McGovern, I. & Budhwar, P. 2000. Complementarity or competition: the development of human resources in a growth triangle. *The International Journal of Human Resource Management*, **11**(2): 314–335.

DeNisi, A. S. & Griffin, R. W. 2001. *Human Resource Management*. Boston, MA: Houghton Mifflin.

Ganeri, A. 2005. *Indian Subcontinent*. Mankato, MN: Black Rabbit Books.

Gautam, D. & Davies, A. 2007. Integration and devolvement of human resource practices in Nepal. *Employee Relations*, **29**(6): 711–726.

Gautam, T., Van Dick, R., Wagner, U. & Upadhyay, N. 2005. Organizational citizenship behavior and organizational commitment in Nepal. *Asian Journal of Social Psychology*, **8**(3): 305–314.

Kakar, S. 1971. Authority pattern and subordinate behaviours in Indian organization. *Administrative Science Quarterly*, **16**(3): 298–307.

Khilji, S. 2004a. Human resource management in Pakistan. In P. Budhwar & Y. Debra (eds), *Human Resource Management in Developing Countries*. London: Routledge, pp. 102–120.

Khilji, S. 2004b. Whither tradition? Evidence of generational differences in HR satisfaction from Pakistan. *International Journal of Cross-Cultural Management*, **4**(2): 141–157.

Khilji, S. E. 2002. Modes of convergence and divergence: an integrative view of multinationals in Pakistan. *The International Journal of Human Resource Management*, **13**(2): 232–253.

Khilji, S. E. 2003. To adapt or not to adapt? Exploring the role of national culture in HRM. *International Journal of Cross-Cultural Management*, **3**(2): 121–144.

Khilji, S. E. & Wang, X. 2006. 'Intended' and 'implemented' HRM: the missing linchpin in strategic human resource management research. *The International Journal of Human Resource Management*, **17**(7): 1171–1189.

Kuruvilla, S. 1996. Linkages between industrialization strategies and industrial relations/ human resource policies: Singapore, Malaysia, the Philippines and India. *Industrial and Labor Relations Review*, **49**(4): 634–657.

Lucy, D. M., Ghosh, J. & Kujawa, E. 2008. Empowering women's leadership: a case study of Bangladesh microcredit business. *S.A.M. Advanced Management Journal*, **73**(4): 31–40.

Mamman, A., Akuratiyagamage, V. W. & Rees, C. J. 2006. Managerial perceptions of he role of the HR function in Sri Lanka: a comparative study of local, foreign-owned and joint venture companies. *International Journal of Human Resource Management*, **17**(12): 2009–2026.

McWeeney, M. 1998. Management accountancy in Bhutan. *Management Accounting*, **76**(10): 60–62.

Pant, D. P., Allinson, C. W. & Hayes, J. 1996. Transferring the Western model of project organisation to a bureaucratic culture: the case of Nepal. *International Journal of Project Management*, **14**(1): 53–57.

Ramaswamy, K. V. 2003. *Globalization and Industrial Labor Markets in South Asia: Some Aspects in a Less Integrated Region*. East–West Center, Honolulu: University of Hawaii Press.

Rao, T. V., Silveria, D. M., Shrivastava, C. M. & Vidyasagar, R. 1994. *HRD in the New Economic Environment*. New Delhi: Tata McGraw-Hill Publishing Company Limited.

Reddy, C. M. 2006. Globalization and human development in South Asia. In *South Asia 2006: Europa Regional Surveys of the World*. London: Routledge.

Rice, M. 2004. Bhutan gets with the program. *Intheblack*, **74**(9): 13.

Sahay, S. & Walsham, G. 1997. Social structure and managerial agency in India. *Organization Studies*, **18**(3): 415–444.

Saini, D. & Budhwar, P. 2007. Human resource management in India. In R. Schuler & S. Jackson (eds), *Strategic Human Resource Management*. Oxford: Blackwell Publishing, pp. 287–312.

Saini, D. & Budhwar, P. 2008. Managing the human resource in Indian SMEs: the role of indigenous realities in organizational working. *Journal of World Business*, **43**(4): 417–434.

Sarker, A. E. 2005. New public management, service provision and non-governmental organizations in Bangladesh. *Public Organization Review*, **5**(3): 249–267.

Sarker, A. E. 2006. New public management in developing countries: an analysis of success and failure with particular reference to Singapore and Bangladesh. *The International Journal of Public Sector Management*, **19**(2): 180–204.

Schuler, R. S., Budhwar, P. & Florkowski, G. W. 2002 International human resource management: review and critique. *International Journal of Management Reviews*, **4**(1): 41–70.

Seth, N. R. 1996. We, the trade unions. *Indian Journal of Industrial Relations*, **32**(1): 1–20.

Sharma, B. R. 1992. *Managerialism Unionism: Issues in Perspective*. New Delhi: Shri Ram Centre for Industrial Relations and Human Resources.

Sharma, I. J. 1984. The culture context of Indian managers. *Management and Labour Studies*, **9**(2): 72–80.

Singh, S. 2003. Strategic orientation and firm performance in India. *The International Journal of Human Resource Management*, **14**(4): 530–543.

Sodhi, J. S. 1994. Emerging trends in industrial relations and human resource management in Indian industry. *Indian Journal of Industrial Relations*, **30**(1): 19–37.

Som, A. 2008. Innovative HRM and corporate performance in the context of economic liberalization in India. *International Journal of HRM*, **19**(7): 1278–1291.

Sparrow, P. & Budhwar, P. 1997. Competition and change: mapping the Indian HRM recipe against world-wide patterns. *Journal of World Business*, **32**(3): 224–242.

Syed, J. 2008. Pakistani model of diversity management: rediscovering Jinnah's vision. *The International Journal of Sociology and Social Policy*, **28**(3/4): 100–113.

Thite, M., Srinivasan, V., Harvey, M. & Valk, R. 2009. Expatriates of host-country origin: 'coming home to test the waters'. *International Journal of Human Resource Management*, **20**(2): 269–283.

Varma, A., Toh, S. M. & Budhwar, P. 2006. A new perspective on the female expatriate experience: the role of host country national categorization. *Journal of World Business*, **41**(2): 112–120.

Venakata Ratnam, C. S. 1998. Multinational companies in India. *The International Journal of Human Resource Management*, **9**(4): 567–589.

Wickramasinghe, V. M. 2006. Staffing practices in the private sector in Sri Lanka. *Career Development International*, **12**(2): 108–122.

Wickramasinghe, V. M. & Jayabandu, S. 2007. Towards workplace flexibility: flexitime arrangements in Sri Lanka. *Employee Relations*, **29**(6): 554–575.

Wikipedia. 2009. http://en.wikipedia.org/wiki/Indian_subcontinent.

World Bank. 2006. Sri Lanka: strengthening social protection. Available at: http://siteresources.worldbank.org/INTSOUTHASIA/Resources/Strengthening_Social_Protection.pdf.

Yadapadithaya, P. S. 2000. International briefing 5: training and development in India. *International Journal of Training and Development*, **4**(1): 79–89.

Zafarullah, H. 2006. Shaping public management for governance and development: the cases of Pakistan and Bangladesh. *International Journal of Organization Theory and Behavior*, **9**(3): 352–378.

Zafarullah, H. & Rahman, R. 2008. The impaired state: assessing the state capacity and governance in Bangladesh. *The International Journal of Public Sector Management*, **21**(7): 739–747.

26 HRM and Asian socialist economies in transition: China, Vietnam and North Korea

Ngan Collins, Ying Zhu and Malcolm Warner

In East Asia, there are three so-called 'socialist countries', namely the People's Republic of China (henceforth to be referred to as China), the Socialist Republic of Vietnam (Vietnam) and the Democratic People's Republic of Korea (DPRK; North Korea). These three countries have experienced very different political, economic and social changes. China, the most populous of the three by far, started its economic reform and 'Open Door' policy in the late 1970s and it has become one of the largest economies and an influential political power in international affairs. Vietnam developed a relatively moderate reform agenda labelled as '*Doi Moi*' a little later, as its route to economic renovation. Now, Vietnam has emerged as one of the leading economies among the ASEAN group in Southeast Asia. Both China and Vietnam claim their economies as 'socialist market economies'. However, North Korea had adopted a rather slow and careful strategy regarding reform and they still follow their former 'Great Leader' Chairman Kim Il Sung's approach with its characteristics of top-down socialist planning and political self-reliance. It started to learn from its 'socialist brothers' of China and Vietnam late in the day and has built a small number of special economic zones and industrial parks. But due to lack of foreign investment and technological and management 'know-how', as well as tension between north and south from time to time, these economic reform initiatives have not to date proved to be very successful.

In this chapter, we aim to illustrate the tasks and processes of economic reform and development in these countries, their changing political, ideological and economic systems and the impact of reform on the changing relationship between government, market and firms as well as the influence on management in general and on HRM in particular. In order to achieve these aims, we develop the following structure within this chapter: section two reviews the economic transition and management changes; section three provides the background information regarding the reform in general and reforming people-management system in particular; section four illustrates the employment relations (ER) and industrial relations

(IR) systems in the three countries; section five explores the pattern of transformation of human resource management (HRM) policies and practices at enterprise level; sections six, seven, eight and nine examine the changing relationship and interaction between government and enterprises; section ten concludes the chapter by highlighting the implications for socialist economies in transition.

ECONOMIC TRANSITION AND MANAGEMENT CHANGES

China and Vietnam have a number of similarities in terms of their economic, political and social systems as well as their people-management models, although this is very much less the case with North Korea. China and Vietnam constitute the main subject of this chapter – as they have undergone decades of transformation into transitional economies but we also make some limited comparisons with the less reformed third economy in the grouping. As neighbouring countries, they have, however, very similar histories and cultures and share a background of Confucian values. These traditional values of harmony and collectivism, which were introduced into Vietnam by the Chinese emperor in 111 BC (Warner, 2005) still remain as key social values in modern Vietnam as well as in Chinese societies, both on the mainland and amongst overseas Chinese (*Nanyang*). Additionally, both Koreas, North and South, have a Confucian legacy going back centuries (Flake, 2002: 4579)

Since the late 1970s in the case of China and the 1980s in the case of Vietnam, both countries claim to have transformed themselves into 'socialist market economies'; however, North Korea has been seen, by contrast, as the last bastion of 'Stalinism' (Lankov, 2006). The fundamental cause of these reforms was that both Chinese and Vietnamese governments realised that their traditional system of running a country was no longer adequate for maintaining economic and political stability. Economic reform was essential to the State's and Party's survival. Through the economic transition, the governments aimed to attract foreign capital and bring in up-to-date technology to achieve their goal of building a 'socialist' nation with a modernised and industrialised economy, hence the 'Open Door' (*kaifang*) and 'Four Modernisations' (*sige xiandaihua*) policies in China in the years after 1978. As China became inexorably linked to the international economy and increasingly faces the challenges of globalisation, for example, its enterprises and their managers have not only had to adapt to external market pressures, international norms and so on, but at the same time have needed to respond to internal institutional pressures.

The tension between these factors, external as well as internal, provides an arena in which managers, as well as workers, now have to cope, perform and survive. The government's goal of reform in transitional economies is to ensure that those economic benefits help reduce political instability and enable the State to retain its power and eventually realise the purpose of national development.

Economic transition in the two main cases we consider, China and Vietnam, is unlike the process that took place in Eastern Europe (see Warner, 2005). There was no immediate blue-print at hand. China had to learn its economic reform approach, therefore gradualism was chosen for this reform. The Chinese leadership described the reform process as, in Deng Xiaoping's' phrase 'crossing the river by feeling for the stones' (*mo zhe shitou guohe*). In Vietnam too, the reform process unfolded gradually and largely in the economic sphere. There was no accompanying reform of the political system. Both countries refer to their economies as transferring from a 'planned socialist economy' to a 'socialist market economy'. The Communist Party remains the only political organisation in all three countries and holds authority to decide on policies affecting the nation.

Both governments, in China and Vietnam, clearly stated that the characteristic of these processes was to be pragmatic as well as gradualist, beginning with micro-economic reform, then to be followed by macro-economic reforms but with only limited political reform. They have been assessed as following a 'third way' (as described in Fahey, 1997), separate from the 'shock therapy' or 'big bang' approaches on the one hand – and the traditional top-down planning system, on the other. The North Korean economy was, however, stuck with the Soviet model and remains to this day a highly authoritarian State-planned entity.

Chung (2003) suggests that North Korea, because it is a latecomer, may now be more able to choose a more advantageous path to development: 'To this end, North Korea needs to adapt a pragmatic economic policy similar to China's "White Cat, Black Cat Theory," which places priority on economic utility' (2003:102). Much depends on China acting as a broker in the efforts to resolve the nuclear issue and create security and stability in the peninsula, as a recent Rand Corporation working paper has argued (see Wolf & Levin, 2008).

Despite the many similarities between the two transitional economies, there is a difference between reform in China and Vietnam in that, during the pre-reform period, state-owned enterprises (SOEs) in China were more developed and operated on a larger scale than in Vietnam. The Chinese government governs a huge population of one and one-third billion, and has always been firm in its leadership, so that its reform policies have been seen as very determined and decisive (Forde & De Vylder, 1996). It is even prepared to employ the army internally to enforce its objectives, as in 1989. On the other hand, the Vietnamese government may be less willing to resort to violence in the name of reform because it leads what was a divided country and its authority is weaker, so it needs to be more cautious in its leadership of reform. With the long history of involvement in wars, Vietnam's economy has depended heavily on foreign aid, especially from the Soviet Union and China. During the economic reforms, the role of foreign investment in Vietnam has been even more prominent than in China. In addition, economic reform in China occurred several years before Vietnam and therefore China is a step further along the road to reform. Vietnam often looks over its shoulder at the Chinese experience when it put into place its reforming processes; so, learning about change in China is important for Vietnam. By contrast, North Korea appears to be last in line for economic reform.

Economic reforms have achieved great successes in the more advanced reforming countries, namely China and Vietnam (see Table 26.1). China has become an 'economic superpower'; its economy ranked second in the world, after the US, and its GDP per capita has grown dramatically since 1978. In Vietnam, income per head has about tripled from the early days and the Vietnamese people's standard of living has increased markedly. These are now the top two fastest growth economies in Asia. Living standards for most of their populations have improved greatly in recent years. The unevenness of development between urban and rural areas has however mitigated the benefits. The urban population so far has done better than those in rural areas. As the economic reform process has brought in wealth for many social groups, there was the birth of a 'new middle class' in the urban centres such as in Beijing and Shanghai, as well as Ho Chi Minh City and Hanoi. Furthermore, there has been a large increase in income inequality between different groups of earners. The income gaps between different groups of Chinese and Vietnamese societies have become much bigger, compared with the pre-reform period. Together with these new economic phenomena brought in by the reforms, there has been a shift of social culture, as well as ideology. Even though the general culture of these societies is based on collectivism and harmony, as mentioned earlier, there has been a rise of individualism and competitiveness within the societies, especially among the younger generation. Less, however, is known about North Korea, with much lower incomes per head than in the other two economies, although a 'new rich' stratum has been emerging since the limited reforms were introduced in 2002.

Table 26.1 provides an overview of the three countries' profiles. It is obvious that China is the giant among the group in terms of the size of area, population, GDP level, trade value and the size of the labour force.

Table 26.1   Country profiles

	China	Vietnam	N. Korea
Area	9.5 m. sq km	0.3 m. sq km	0.1 m. sq km
Population	1.3 b.	85 m.	23 m.
Population growth rate	0.6%	1%	0.8%
Infant mortality rate	2.2%	2.4%	2.3%
Life expectancy	72.9	71.1	71.9
Male	71.3	68.2	69.2
Female	74.8	74.1	74.8
Literacy	90.9%	90.3%	99.0%
Male	95.1%	93.9%	99.0%
Female	86.5%	86.9%	99.0%
GDP 2007	$7.043 tr.	$222.5 b.	$40 b.
(purchasing power parity)			
GDP 2007	$3.249 tr.	$66.4 b.	$2.22 b.
(at official exchange rate)			
GDP per capita 2007(PPP)	$5300	$2600	$1900
GDP composition			
Agriculture	11.7%	19.4%	23.3%
Industry	49.2%	42.3%	43.1%
Services	39.1%	38.3%	33.6%
Labour force	803.3 m.	45.73 m.	20 m.
Exports	$1,221 tr.	$48.3 b.	$1.47 b.
	(f.o.b. 2007)	(f.o.b. 2007)	(f.o.b. 2006)
Imports	$917.4 b.	$60.75 b.	$2.88 b.
	(f.o.b. 2007)	(f.o.b. 2007)	(c.i.f. 2006)
Democracy Index	112/125	11/125	120/125
Management Index	67/125	6/125	122/125
Market Econ. Index	51/125	9/125	122/125

Source: Miscellaneous: Bertelsmann Stiftung, 2008; CIA World Factbook, 2008; UNDP Human Development Report, 2007/2008.

Interestingly, those three so-called socialist economies had relatively lower rates of infant mortality, longer life expectancy and higher rates of literacy compared with other developing countries with similar levels of per capita income. China had a much higher GDP level, as well as GDP per capita level, based on the calculation of purchasing power parity (PPP) compared with Vietnam and North Korea. In terms of composition of GDP, China had a relatively lower proportion of agriculture, and a higher proportion of industry and services. Vietnam is second to China in these proportions and North Korea ranks third. In addition, China generated a huge trade surplus but both Vietnam and North Korea experienced trade deficits in recent years. In the Bertelsmann Stiftung's indices of democracy, management and market economy, the latter nation lags far behind (see Table 26.1). North Korea has its unique system that has a number of aspects similar to the former socialist planning system existed in the former Soviet Union and pre-reform China but is still fundamentally distinct (ibid.). In addition, some traces of the South Korean and Japanese systems could be found, but North Korea has created a society that is different from our understanding of 'normal' societies as well as our common sense (Bertelsmann Stiftung, 2008).

BACKGROUND

Background in China

Under the former command economy model in China in the period 1949–78, its SOEs implemented a form of personnel management (*renshi guanli*) to administer their employees. It was a template partly borrowed from their Soviet counterparts (see Kaple, 1994; Warner, 1995). The enterprise-based employment system, known as the 'iron rice bowl' (*tie fan wan*), had been de rigueur in the SOE sector (see Bian, 2005) and possibly even a paternalistic hangover from pre-communist times and the Japanese Occupation (see Warner, 1995). It was characterised by what were called the 'three old irons', (*jiu santi*), that is, the pillars of life-time employment (the 'iron rice bowl', *tie fan wan*), centrally administered wages (the 'iron wage', *tie gongzi*), and ministry-based appointment and promotion of managerial staff (the 'iron chair', *tie jiaoyi*) (see Ng & Warner, 1998). Since Deng's economic reforms were introduced in the 1980s, this enterprise-based system of 'lifetime employment' and 'cradle-to-grave' mini-welfare state (*xiao shehui*) has been gradually cut back: in 1986, for example, the authorities experimented with the introduction of labour contracts for new workers (see Korzec, 1992; Zhu, 2005). In 1992, another important step was the 'three personnel reforms' (*san gaige*); this inaugurated labour contracts, performance-linked rewards systems, and contributory social insurance (Warner, 1995). *Pari passu*, access to health-care, eventually became less and less equitable. By this time, the system had already become a 'hybrid' one, mixing what remained of the old one with the newer features (see Warner, 2009; Warner, 2011). The new demarche was to be known as '*renli ziyuan guanli*', quite literally meaning 'labour force resources management', having the same characters in Chinese as in Japanese, being used as a synonym for (what is in effect) 'HRM'.

Another important area is related to the rural workforce migration to the urban areas through the engagement in urban development and industrial production. In fact, the rural workforce has since the late 1970s been in a process of transformation (Webber & Zhu, 2006). The transformation began in the late 1970s, when the central government sanctioned the de-collectivisation of agriculture, approved the household responsibility system and raised agricultural prices (Carter et al., 1996; Findlay et al., 1993). By the mid-1980s, the key elements of the new system of management were in place. Evidently, universal access to land among the peasants provides a floor below which incomes from labour cannot fall and guards against the emergence of purely commodity labour within the countryside (McKinley, 1996; but see Hinton, 1990). In China, therefore, the social relations of work within the countryside are being transformed much more through the market, and looking for better income through job seeking in the urban areas became one of the key elements for migrant workers under the relaxation of the *hukou* (household registration) system. This means that more and more rural workers are entering the commodity labour markets of China's cities. Their pay and working conditions are lower than the urban workforce, but higher than their previous work in the countryside.

Another step forward was the Labour Law of 1994, implemented in 1995, which put the emerging labour market at its heart, legalised individual contracts (*geren hetong*) as well as collective contracts (*jiti hetong*) and the like (Warner, 1996). The All-China Federation of Trade Unions (ACFTU) (*Zhonghua quanguo zonggong hui*), with its over 150 million members, 15 industrial unions and 1.2 million local branches, greatly influenced this legislation (see Warner, 1996, 2008; Warner & Ng, 1999).

The implementation of these new legal steps led to what might be described as recognisable 'industrial relations' or what became known as 'labour relations' (*laodong guanxi*) in Chinese parlance (see Taylor et al., 2003). Nonetheless, there is currently no 'right to strike' in the Chinese constitution. There have been many openly 'wild-cat' outbreaks and unofficial labour protests, mostly about unpaid wages and pensions, downsizing or factory closures. Officially recognised disputes can be sent to arbitration and many hundreds of thousands have been dealt with since the 1994 labour law was enacted; the new 2007 follow-up legislation may further help contain grievances. On paper, at least, the system appears to be preserving social peace but strikes are increasing in frequency, especially in areas like the Shenzhen Special Economic Zone, for instance. More recently, the Labour Contract Law in 2007 extended worker protection (*The Economist*, 2007). The new law makes it mandatory for employers to offer written contracts to workers, restricts the use of temporary labour and makes it harder to lay-off employees. It was opposed by many foreign-invested corporations. Additionally, a new Mediation Law was introduced in early 2008.

Background in Vietnam

Vietnam began its economic reform process, known as *Doi Moi*, in 1986. The adoption of changes to Vietnam's economic system accompanies and is in part a response to globalisation. The introduction and adoption stages of HRM, to replace the old personnel management system, have followed the economic reform process in order to ensure that competitive advantage is gained through organisational level management reforms (Collins, 2005). With the economy in a serious downturn after a long period of war, economic reform was necessary for Vietnam's survival. The government of the time realised that the economy could not depend solely on traditional capital sources for its development. In addition, a number of factors prompted the government to recognise the importance of external relations to its economic well-being. The collapse of socialist regimes in the Soviet Union and former socialist countries in East Europe left Vietnam isolated economically and politically. Popular demonstrations in the Mekong Delta region had also reminded the authorities how economic problems could result in political instability. Arguably, *Doi Moi* originated in Vietnam to maintain the power of the Communist regime. Throughout the transition, the Vietnamese government aimed to attract foreign capital and bring in up-to-date technology to provide the foundation to achieve its goal of building a 'socialist nation' with a modernised and industrialised economy, as in the case of its more populous neighbour.

The *Doi Moi* policy gave Vietnam the chance to join with the international community after a long period of isolation. The economic restructuring led to changes in government policy and enterprise level management practices regarding labour and human resources. Changes also occurred in the trade union structure. As in China, the General Confederation of Labour (*Tong Lien Doan Lao Dong*) is the only union permitted. The SOEs were given greater autonomy, a new union charter was drawn up, employment contract systems were introduced, and a Labour Code was implemented. Reforms were also made to working life issues, such as wages and working hours. These steps can be seen as the interaction between political–economic reform in the society and the human resources transformation at enterprise level.

Background in North Korea

The people-management template in North Korea was originally derived from the Soviet one, now defunct, and the Chinese state-owned enterprise 'iron rice bowl' (*tie fan wan*) model, now on the wane (see Warner, 2005). In so far as it has undertaken a very limited degree of reform, this nation lags far behind both China and Vietnam in this respect. The original post-war management mode was called the '*Taean*' system, introduced in the 1960s after experiments in the Taean Heavy Equipment Plant near the capital Pyongyang. It was allegedly modelled on Maoist Chinese practice, as a Brookings Institution visiting fellow (Mansourov, 2003) put it as the DPRK's leadership appeared to follow the CCP's (Chinese Communist Party's) ideological demarche and emulated Chinese methods of labour mobilisation, e.g., the *Ch'ollima* ('Flying Horse') movement copied from the Maoist 'Great Leap Forward' and the *Soktojon* ('speed battle'). North Korea also took on some Chinese-like forms of organisation of industrial and agricultural production processes called the *Taean* system. After Deng Xiaoping launched economic reforms in China in 1978, Kim Il Sung set out to imitate the Chinese example by bringing in the Joint Venture Law and an innovative self-accounting system in the mid-1980s (Mansourov, 2003).

The *Taean* system entailed on-site collegial management control of the enterprise by the Party officials, with limited autonomy for top managers, and has lasted for many decades. Executives had very few rights to hire and fire. But the system was phased out in the controversial, limited reforms of 2002, with results as yet to be seen. But this had more than just symbolic meaning, as the previous system had been the flagship policy of the late 'Great Leader'. It signalled that the 'primacy of politics' over economics might possibly be coming to an end.

Wages and living standards remain very low in the DPRK; experts estimate that rewards run to around two dollars per month per worker. Kim (2006) reports that state-enterprise employees get between 2000 to 3000 won per month and 800 won of this goes on rice, with a month's salary needed to buy meat for a meal. Due to the economy almost imploding in the late 1990s, many North Koreans have been close to starvation or have actually died of lack of sustenance. An estimated 10 per cent of the population died during a prolonged famine; the economy was mired in inertia (see Chung, 2003). The outside world sent food aid, as the rationing system did not work; today, many survive due to the opening up of limited private market activity but this is often shut. Migrants, however, still illegally pour across the Tumen River into China, driven by hunger and deprivation; if caught the penalties for them are harsh, including penalties for innocent family members (Demick, 2010).

EMPLOYMENT RELATIONS, INDUSTRIAL RELATIONS AND HRM SYSTEMS IN TRANSITION

Since the transition of the economies in China and Vietnam, many new institutions underlying their employment relations (ER) systems were gradually established and fused with a new pattern of such relations. These changes influenced the industrial relations (IR) and human resources management (HRM) policies at national level, which we subsume under the ER rubric. The establishing of a Foreign Investment Law launched the birth of multi-sectoral economies – where the emergence of non-State sectors including Wholly-Owned Enterprises (WOEs) and Domestic Private Enterprises (DPEs) were established, along with older SOEs (see Warner, 2005). The introduction of a Labour Code was also necessary, to become the basic legal framework for many important policy reforms at macro-level, such as the experimentation with an individual labour-contract system in 1986 in China and in 1993 in Vietnam. This element was the beginning of the end of a 'life-time employment' system in these Socialist planned economies, particularly the 'iron rice-bowl' (*tie fan wan*) system in the PRC and 'permanent job' (*bien che*) in Vietnam. The wage-system liberalisation has in turn allowed SOEs to have full control over establishing their own wage and payment methods. The relationship between the party and union in the new environment has also undergone significant changes. During the pre-reform period, trade unions in both China and Vietnam were, on paper, supposed to represent the workers' interests but were simultaneously agents for Party control. Economic reform since 1978 in China has encouraged trade unions in part to pursue sectional interests among the enterprises but the contradiction of 'dual functioning' unions has prevented them from achieving their potential as an alternative centre of power at a national level; a similar process unfolded in Vietnam, if a little later.

Little has shifted in North Korea in this respect. Since there has been some attempt to develop special economic zones in North Korea in concert with their southern compatriots, there has also been a corresponding effort to codify its labour laws, at least in these locations, although this has been on a limited scale; workers are not paid directly by the foreign partners but by a joint venture (JV) or a State agency and with substantial deductions. Managers have been promised more leeway and more training but results have been unimpressive thus far (see Flake, 2002).

THE ENTERPRISE LEVEL: HRM PRACTICES IN TRANSITION

The authors have conducted a series of research studies on the transformation of people-management systems in both China and Vietnam during the period of the economic reforms. Their research has been largely at enterprise level and focused on the relationships between differences in HRM practices, using different criteria: type of ownership, location, market orientation, labour intensiveness and employee size. So far, the empirical research in China has some general implications. For example, the study by Ding et al. (2002) shows that multinational corporations (MNCs) and some joint ventures both adopted more international standardised HRM policies and practices in the Chinese case. In contrast, SOEs remained more conservative regarding changes with their 'iron rice bowl' (*tie fan wan*) policies. In addition, township and village enterprises (TVEs) and other domestic private enterprises (DPEs) had much more autonomy in their people-management compared with SOEs. Regarding the changes of HRM in SOEs, Benson and Zhu's (1999) research identifies three models of transition: (1) a minimalist approach, where organisations have made little attempt to adopt a HRM approach; (2) a transitional stage between the old and the new forms of people-management; (3) an innovative attempt to adopt the HRM paradigm. The fact is that liberalisation of the economy and the introduction of foreign investment have created the opportunity for Chinese domestic enterprises to adopt some of the widely used Western and Japanese HRM practices. The SOEs that are involved in JVs or contracting arrangements with foreign companies are more likely to have adopted the 'new' HRM. Therefore, globalisation, more business-oriented beliefs and a stronger customer-oriented strategy are crucial determinants whether enterprises engage in HRM practices (Benson & Zhu, 1999).

Overall, the major changes started in the mid-1980s when the 'labour contract system' was introduced in China (Warner & Ng, 1999). Two important aspects are associated with the introduction of the 'labour contract system': (1) adopting individual labour contracts with fixed-term (one to five years) to replace the old 'life-time' employment system; (2) 'individual' contracts were supplemented by 'collective' contracts in the mid-1990s, and that provided opportunity for trade unions to be involved in signing 'collective' contracts at firm-level and set up a 'framework agreement' for the myriad individual contrasts in the enterprise (Warner & Ng, 1999). It must be made clear, however, that this contract is not fully equivalent to Western-style collective bargaining – as there are no independent unions. In addition, there is an increasing autonomy of management on issues such as the rights to hire and fire, performance evaluation, managerial decision on performance standards and the way of conducting evaluations, performance related matters, such as pay and promotion (Warner & Ng, 1999).

Since China joined the World Trade Organization (WTO) in 2002, it has added an international dimension to the complicated domestic employment relations systems (Zhu & Warner, 2004). There was also increasing pressure from international governing bodies, such as the International Labour Organization (ILO) and international trade unions like the International Confederation of Free Trade Unions (ICFTU), with regard to the issues of labour rights, the role of unions and labour standards, as well as broader, more controversial concerns about human rights, social protection and political reform in China. The empirical study of Zhu and Warner (2004) regarding firms' responses to WTO accession identifies an increasing number of firms that have an active response through innovative strategies and new HRM practices. The following are more likely to have proactive HRM responses: enterprises with foreign ownership, those that have transformed from SOEs to joint stock enterprises (JSEs), those that are located in the coastal region, those have weaker links with the traditional State planning system, those have experienced modern management systems and internationalisation, and those in high-value-added sectors (Zhu & Warner, 2004).

Clearly, at present, there is no a homogeneous model of HRM in Chinese enterprises, or indeed in Vietnamese ones. Individual enterprises are reforming their HRM systems differently – on the basis of their existing conditions and the impact of the economic reforms. In addition, relevant empirical research projects on Vietnam have been of great interest and include those of Kamoche (2001), Zhu (2002, 2005) and Thang and Quang (2005). Kamoche's (2001) research explores the business environment and the reform process and their implications for skill formation and the development of managerial expertise. It examines some specific HRM practices in four organisations in Hanoi, two SOEs and two MNCs. The research shows that SOEs have fairly conservative policies with traditional welfare paternalism rather than formal HRM practices. It is mainly MNCs that are striving to introduce Western practices into traditional management systems (Kamoche, 2001).

Zhu's (2002) work examines a number of organisations with different ownerships in Ho Chi Minh City, which has a more market-oriented economic environment than Hanoi. Three key variables – ownership, size and market-orientation – are used to test the transformation of HRM in Vietnam. The research finds that there are variations of HRM practices between different ownership forms, with JVs and MNCs normally using more advanced technology and more international standards of HRM policies than local organisations. However, there is a tendency for localisation of MNCs' behaviour among the cases. In addition, the reformed and equitised SOEs that have become Joint Stock Companies (JSCs) have transformed their practices into more formalised HRM practices. Another interesting finding is that the adoption of HRM is not only related to ownership, but is also associated with sector (high-tech versus labour intensive), size (large versus small) and market-orientation (export versus domestic orientation) as in China (see Ding et al., 2002). Generally speaking, high-tech, large and export-oriented organisations have been more likely to adopt more formal HRM practices.

Based on these findings, Zhu (2005) introduces the notions of numerically flexible strategies and functionally flexible strategies in order to illustrate the changes in people-management in recent years, in particular since the Asian financial crisis. The data suggest that labour flexibility strategies were not fully adopted by the sample companies. Political, cultural, legal and economic factors make labour flexibility in Vietnam different from that in other countries (Zhu, 2005). For instance, companies are not able to adjust the number of regular employees due to the constraints of legislation. In addition, Vietnamese cultural traditions, that place great emphasis on organisational and personal commitment, and harmonious working environments prevent the full deployment of functional flexibility (Zhu, 2005).

Thang and Quang's (2005) research examines Vietnamese HRM practices in five areas: the functions of HRM departments, recruitment and selection, training and development, performance appraisal and compensation. Overall, foreign-invested enterprises are somewhat more likely to have developed HRM practices than SOEs, which is consistent with the argument made by institutional theory about social entities seeking approval for organisational performance, and using HRM to gain legitimacy (Jackson & Schuler, 1999). In addition, local private companies are often less receptive to adopting HRM practices than SOEs. Transforming SOEs into equitised companies has brought about no significant changes in this regard, which is inconsistent with the resource dependence approach using HRM practices to reflect a more complicated power distribution (Thang & Quang, 2005).

Our most recent research project (Zhu et al., 2008) was based on 32 enterprises from four key ownership type: WOEs, SOEs, DPEs and JVs in two main locations Ho Chi Minh City and Hanoi (see the details in later section). There are a number of important results arising from these studies showing the interrelationships between the economic transition process, governments' and enterprises' interests during the reform in both

China and Vietnam. Research on HRM in North Korea has however been problematic and there are no comparable studies. The reason for this stems from the very nature of the North Korean authoritarian, closed and secretive regime (see Eberstadt, 1999).

INTERACTION BETWEEN ECONOMIC REFORM PROCESS, GOVERNMENTS AND ENTERPRISES

The interaction between governments and enterprises since the economic reforms in China and Vietnam has been more complex than previously, because government policies are no longer the sole determinant of enterprises' HRM practices. The interests of enterprises and of the State are no longer the same, because the former's interests have changed with market reform, yet the State's desire for dominance over the economic and political systems remains largely unchanged. The role of the State in the reform process remains strong and the Party still retains the reins of power. The State's desire for stability is the reason for promoting different economic policies on different time-lines or applying different policies for different regions and for different types of business ownership. This fact helps to explain the determining factors behind two further characteristics, namely the correlation of HRM practices with location and with ownership type.

Whilst the State wants to gain economic development advantages for political proposals, it also needs strong support from the grassroots, involving enterprise management as well as workers. Therefore, the State–enterprise relationship is typified by a desire to find compromise between these frequently conflicting interests. This ability to compromise is responsible for the HRM practices being broadly in line government policy. In other words, the HRM functions encouraged by government policy are generally applied in areas like training and development. They also promote the 'unitarist' model of trade unions. In contrast, some HRM functions such as building a corporate culture or individual wage determination are not yet well-applied.

GOVERNMENTAL PERSPECTIVES

From its own perspective, the State sometimes feels the need to compromise with enterprises, mainly due to its desire to minimise discontent and promote economic growth. It has succeeded in that so far economic development in both China and Vietnam has encouraged these nations to support their socialist governments. Due to this pragmatic approach, when the government recognises that a policy is not working well, it tries to act quickly to adjust the policy to minimise enterprises' grievances. When firms have needed more flexibility in recruiting and training workers, for example, the government has boosted reforms in these areas to give the enterprises more freedom.

In addition, enterprise leaders have been allowed to gain a great deal more power and freedom during the 'Open Door' period, in China and Vietnam, but very much less so in North Korea. They are now free to manage their own affairs and are less strictly supervised than before the reforms in these two transitional economies. Enterprise leadership now has greater scope to attain their business targets and also has the authority to achieve individual goals made possible by their leadership position. Therefore, enterprise leaders, even low-paid SOE leaders, work to pursue their individual interests, not to serve the collective ones.

ENTERPRISE PERSPECTIVES

From the enterprises' point of view in China and Vietnam, firms are more likely to fully comply with government policy and even compromise their economic interests – if and when the cultural or ideological values embodied in the policy match their own beliefs. This juncture is clearly the case with the view of many enterprises on the role of trade unions. The historical background of these trade unions has been linked with the history of the Communist Party in fighting against 'capitalist exploitation' in China, 'Western domination' in Vietnam, and 'imperialism' in North Korea. The unions, therefore, on paper at least, share the State's view vis-à-vis the role of a socialist government in protecting working class interests from 'capitalist exploitation' (see Warner, 2008). Even in the new business environment, union leaders' ideological beliefs still remain the same, so they do not see any need to replace the traditional union model and are happy to co-operate with the government, as is the case with the All-China Confederation of Trade Unions (ACFTU) or its Vietnamese counterpart the General Confederation of Labour (GCL). In addition, management has found that the 'socialist' union-structure serves the business well in terms of maintaining harmony and minimising conflict and bargaining at the workplace. It in turn makes the labour force easier to control. They therefore support this type of union structure and role and as a result this is the structure practised in both China and Vietnam's enterprises. Less is known about the role played by unions in North Korea, although they did play an integral part in the post-1950s factory-management model, known as the '*Taean*' system, described earlier. Trade union representation in North Korea is largely token, via a Leninist top-down 'transmission-belt' model, through the General Federation of Trade Unions of Korea (GFTUK) covers mostly State firms.

Conversely, most enterprises in China and Vietnam, especially domestic ones, choose to retain the traditional model for wage determination and labour-management relations. Moving to an HRM approach for these functions might not fit in with the government's principle of socialism, and it goes against enterprise management's cultural values of collectivism in decision making and harmony. Change could be harmful to their business by breaking the harmony of the working environment. Individual bargaining is not yet well received in either country, because it creates a sense of jealousy between employees and has a negative impact on business. 'Collective consultation' is now de rigueur in China and it has received a boost from the new Labour Contract Law, as noted above; in Vietnam, the labour contract is mainly a document used to enforce the responsibilities of the employers and employees (see Collins & Zhu, 2003).

The government's emphasis on reducing conflict in the workplace in both China and Vietnam is supported by the high value that enterprise management and workers still place on harmony and collectivism. The latest Chinese government policy is to achieve the so-called 'harmonious society' (*hexie shehui*). The philosophy behind this is an attempt by the current Chinese dual-leadership of President Hu Jintao and Premier Wen Jibao, to rectify perceived inequities in the economy and society, particularly wealth and income inequalities. If taken seriously, it may in turn have an influence on how Chinese enterprises implement their human resource management policies. The Party leaders have become more and more aware of emergent social tensions arising from the less egalitarian implications of their policies; so, they want to consolidate social harmony, appeasing the 'losers' somewhat, without penalising the 'winners' too much (see Warner, 2008).

This reality also reflects the national history of each 'socialist system', which cannot be separated from current practices. A reason for the frequent ideological match between the State and enterprises is that both are linked to the historical background of enterprise leaders in all three countries. Most local managers in China and Vietnam come from SOE backgrounds, including those leading DPEs, JVs and even some WOEs. This background and experience has strongly influenced the way they operate their current enterprises.

THE NATURE OF ECONOMIC TRANSITION: NEGOTIATION PROCESS BETWEEN GOVERNMENTS AND ENTERPRISES

The compromise between the State and business in the Asian socialist economies under discussion is made easier by both government ministries and enterprises leaving many HRM policies very vague. Whilst this may partly be unintentional, some policies are purposely ambiguous. Needing to find a way of resolving the conflict between satisfying the political demands of the State and operating profitably in a global market environment, enterprises take advantage of the vagueness to find loopholes in the laws that suit their commercial interests. By doing so, they can often find a way to comply with government policy while still maximising their competitiveness. For some dimensions, enterprises also take advantage of the State's inability to enforce their policies by avoiding implementation of policies with which they disagree.

However, enterprises vary in the extent to which they seek to exploit loopholes or avoid implementation of government policy to maximise their commercial interests. Their doing so is dependent on two factors: their willingness to find ways around the policies and their ability to exploit them. These in turn are dependent on their relative cultural and/or ideological differentiation from government and their freedom from strict enforcement of government regulations. The combination of these two factors can be used to explain one of the most significant findings of the previous research of the present authors: the correlation between HRM, ownership-type and enterprise location (see Zhu et al., 2008).

Foreign-influenced JVs and WOEs, in the cases we studied in both China and Vietnam, practise more recognisably 'Western' HRM functions than domestic-influenced DPEs and SOEs do, principally due to the cultural and ideological gap between these enterprises and the governments. The gap serves the purpose of increasing their commitment to practising the HRM model and reducing their willingness to compromise with government policy. Consequently, they more commonly look for loopholes in, or ways of avoiding, government policies that prohibit or discourage practice of some HRM functions. Of the local enterprises, DPEs practise more HRM functions than SOEs and DPEs, as they are subject to less government control and are more driven by market forces.

The relation between location and practice of HRM functions can partly be explained by similar reasons. Our research regarding context factors' influence on the people-management systems (Zhu & Warner, 2005) indicated that coastally located enterprises are more likely to implement formal HRM practices. Our evidence shows that enterprises located in the developed coastal region are under more pressure to innovate in order to be able to compete and survive, and adopting a formal HRM system appears to be part of their strategy for achieving the goal. However, enterprises located in the inland areas, remote from competition and the influence of globalisation, are less concerned about formal HRM practices.

In Vietnam, cities such as Ho Chi Minh City and Hanoi are also more amenable to new ideas and approaches, such as implementing the HRM model. When the government introduces a new policy, it often does not introduce the policy evenly across the countries. In some cases, the large cities are used to experiment with the new reform policy before it is implemented throughout the country. Sometimes these policies need testing before they are embedded in these locations as they are still vague and open to interpretation. With their background making them more open to the new practices than in other places, the enterprises in big cities can take advantage of the laxer controls to choose models and find loopholes in the policies in order to bring greater profits to their business. The policy experiments conducted are an example of State–enterprise interaction in general. For any given policy, the State and enterprises engage in a form of indirect negotiation to establish a policy that each side can accept. In this negotiation, the State introduces the policy as a trial (either overtly or by implication) and leaves it vague enough for enterprises to take some individual initiative to deal with the policy in the way that suits them best. The State observes how enterprises deal with the policy and adjusts it accordingly through tightening the regulations or, more commonly, further compromise. Although the process of change is undoubtedly gradual, these findings indicate that economic transition and particularly the HRM reform in China and Vietnam are neither 'bottom-up' nor 'top-down' and as such do not match the transition theories posited by previous studies.

Examples of this 'experiment' and 'adjustment' approach can be found in the new employment policies introduced in China and Vietnam. Throughout the process the governments learned and adjusted their policy with the hope of satisfying both business interests and their own interests. Such was the case with the introduction of the Labour Codes in the two nations, a key part of employment policy. This was the first time the governments had created such an important legal framework and they did not have much experience with them. As with many other policies, government was continually in the process of studying and improving the codes. Now that they have had time to trial the codes, they have amended them, following feedback from the business community. As mentioned above, political interests and ideology meant that some aspects of the codes were detrimental to businesses. However, the amended Codes formalised a number of issues that reflected enterprise demands. All business sectors, including foreign invested enterprises, can now recruit freely from the labour market. This step is a great relief for foreign-invested enterprises, because until the amended codes arrived, in both countries, they still needed to recruit through government labour agencies, which took a long time, were more expensive and offered fewer choices, and in many cases the applicants did not fulfil the job requirements.

The State in both countries acknowledges that policy reforms are necessary but does not give the interests of enterprises top priority when forming new policies. They take other factors into consideration, of which the most important factor is self-interest, such as budgetary constraints and their own political role. The policies are only suitable to the enterprises' interests if those interests coincide with or are similar to the State's interests.

Policies relating the reform process and HRM implementation occur along mainly the lines intended by the State in these transitional economies (see Warner et al., 2005). However, because enterprises operate in a rapidly changing market-oriented environment, policies are only introduced after there is already a clear demand for them. This criterion necessitates that the enterprises deal with the situation before the States recognises it and is able to introduce new policies. While awaiting the new policies, the enterprises continue to implement the old policies, but only in a way that serves their own interests. If it is not politically expedient, then the State's amended policies may only partially satisfy business requests, leading to enterprises continuing not to implement the policies fully as intended and a new cycle of negotiation between enterprises and the governments is needed.

The enterprises in such transitional societies look for loopholes in the law to allow them to operate profitably. They bend the policies to suit their circumstances or find a way of getting around the policies without upsetting the State. Their activities continue to be contrary to the State's objectives – until they develop to a level where they can no longer be tolerated. At that time, the State introduces new policies to deal with the undesirable activities. Consequently, the reform of HRM in both China and Vietnam's enterprises can now take place semi-independently of the State and enterprises' actual implementation of new models never completely corresponds with the State's policies.

The interaction between government and enterprises shows that any study of the transformation of HRM in transitional economies such as China and Vietnam cannot be isolated from changes at macro level and the business environment. This discussion also shows strong evidence that reform to HRM in these countries is the process of integration between a number of key actors, including socio-political, economic and enterprise practices. In other words, the practices and reform of HRM at enterprises cannot be separated from the surrounding environment. Enterprises' HRM strategies first need to fit in with their business strategies, and second, need to be well integrated with overall government policy, ideology and cultural norms.

The results of our studies into transitional economies show a strong interaction between three main forces responsible for determining the reform process and HRM practices, particularly in China and Vietnam. These are, in turn: first, the interrelation of the transition process, second, the government interests of supporting the new practices for its political purposes and third, the demands of business operation from enterprises. None of the three forces can be considered separately in this transformation process. The findings from our China and Vietnam studies also show that without serious investigation of these three relationships, the transition of HRM in these Asian socialist economies cannot be fully understood and research cannot make a solid contribution to the world of knowledge. We know even less about North Korea and perhaps, one day, it will be open to Western scholars to conduct empirical research.

CONCLUDING REMARKS

The reform of the economies in general and people-management in particular in China and Vietnam has presented a two-way, interactive relationship of national State political interests and wider business activities (see Warner et al., 2005). In this reform process, the various forces are continually negotiating a compromise to their sometimes conflicting interests. At the enterprise level, the extent to which functions of HRM are adopted depends on the relative strengths of the communist and nationalist ideological contexts and political influences on the one hand, and market economic influences on the other. These differences provide a unique context to HRM practices in China and Vietnam (see Zhu et al., 2008). Less interaction has been noted in North Korea, where the State still just imposes any change in policy.

Within this context, enterprises' overall HRM practices have changed from a traditional socialist model to a new model combining aspects of some socialist, traditional and HRM approaches in varying degrees, the so-called 'hybridisation' process noted in detail elsewhere (see Warner, 2009) during reform in China and Vietnam, although only a minor shift has been seen in North Korea. The actors in the transitional economies do share some common goals and, in some cases, common culture and ideology with the government, but there remain also significant differences between government and business interests. The 2008 world economic crisis will no doubt shape the fate of these three systems in significant ways but it is still too soon to predict the outcomes.

REFERENCES

Benson, J. & Zhu, Y. 1999. Markets, firms and workers: the transformation of HRM in Chinese state-owned enterprises. *Human Resource Management Journal*, **9**(4): 58–74.

Bertelsmann Stiftung. 2008. North Korea Country Report.

Bian, M. L. 2005. *The Making of the State Enterprise System in Modern China: The Dynamics of Institutional Change.* Cambridge, MA: Harvard University Press.

Carter, C. A., Zhong, F. N. & Cai, F. 1996. *China's Ongoing Agricultural Reform.* San Francisco, CA: 1990 Institute.

Chung, Y. H. 2003. The prospects of economic reform in North Korea and the direction of its economic development. *Vantage Point*, **26**(5): 43–53.

CIA World Factbook, 2008. Available at: https://www.cia.gov/library/publications/the-world-factbook/.

Collins, N. 2005. Economic reform and unemployment in Vietnam. In J. Benson & Y. Zhu (eds), *Globalisation and Unemployment in Asia.* London: Routledge, pp. 176–193.

Collins, N. & Zhu, Y. 2003. Vietnam's labour policies reform. In G. Frost & E. Shepherd (eds), *Asia Pacific Labour Law Review: Workers' Rights for the New Century.* Hong Kong: Asia Monitor Resource Center Ltd, pp. 375–388.

Demick, B. 2010. *Nothing to Envy: Real Lives in North Korea.* London: Granta.

Ding, D., Goodall, K. & Warner, M. 2002. The impact of economic reform on the role of trade unions in Chinese enterprises. *International Journal of Human Resource Management*, **13**(3): 431–449.

Eberstadt, N. 1999. *The End of North Korea.* Washington, DC: American Enterprise Institute.

Fahey, S. 1997. Vietnam and the third way: the nature of socio-economic transition. *Journal of Economic and Social Geography*, **88** (Special issue: The Dynamics of the Asian Pacific Rim): 468–480.

Findlay, C., Martin, W. & Watson, A. 1993. *Policy Reform, Economic Growth and China's Agriculture.* Paris: OECD Development Centre.

Flake, G. 2002. Management in North Korea. In M. Warner (ed.), *The International Encyclopedia of Business and Management*, Vol. 5, 2nd edn. London: Thomson, pp. 759–766.

Forde, A. & De Vylder, S. 1996. *From Plan to Market: The Economic Transition in Vietnam.* Boulder, CO: Westview Press.

Hinton, W. 1990. *The Great Reversal: The Privatization of China 1978–1989.* New York: Monthly Review.

Jackson, S. E. & Schuler, R. S. 1999. Understanding human resource management in the context of organizations and their environments. In R. S. Schuler & S. E. Jackson (eds), *Strategic Human Resource Management.* London: Blackwell, pp. 4–28.

Kamoche, K. 2001. Human resource in Vietnam: the global challenge. *Thunderbird International Business Review*, **43**(5): 625–650.

Kaple, D. 1994. *Dream of a Red Factory: The Legacy of High Stalinism.* Oxford: Oxford University Press.

Kim, Y. J. 2006. . Current wage per month in North Korea is one dollar: the survey of North Korean prices in January 2006, Daily NK (20 January): 1.

Korzec, M. 1992. *Labour and the Failure of Reform in China.* London: Routledge.

Lankov, A. 2006. The natural death of North Korean Stalinism. *Asia Policy*, **1**: 95–121.

Mansourov, A. 2003. *Giving Lip Service with an Attitude: North Korea's China Debate.* Washington, DC: Brookings Institute.

McKinley, T. 1996. The *Distribution of Wealth in Rural China.* New York: M. E. Sharpe.

Ng, S. H. & Warner, M. 1998. *China's Trade Unions and Management.* Basingstoke, UK: Macmillan St Martins Press.

Taylor, W., Chang, K. & Li, Q. 2003. *Industrial Relations in China.* Cheltenham, UK: Edward Elgar.

Thang, L. C. & Quang, T. 2005. Antecedents and consequences of dimensions of human resource management and practices in Vietnam. *International Journal of Human Resources Management,* **16**: 48–64.

The Economist 2007. Red flag. *The Economist,* 28 July: 74.

UNDP Human Development Report, 2007/2008. Available at: http://hdr.undp.org/en/reports/global/hdr2007-2008/.

Warner, M. 1995. *The Management of Human Resources in Chinese Industry.* Basingstoke, UK: Macmillan St Martin's Press.

Warner, M. 1996. Economic reforms, industrial relations and human resources in the People's Republic of China: an overview. *Industrial Relations Journal,* **27**(3): 195–210.

Warner, M. 2005. *Human Resource Management in China Revisited.* London: Routledge.

Warner, M. 2008. Trade unions in China: towards the harmonious society. In J. Benson & Y. Zhu (eds), *Trade Unions in Asia.* London: Routledge.

Warner, M. (ed.) 2009. *Human resource management with Chinese characteristics.* London: Routledge.

Warner, M. (ed.) 2011. *Confucian HRM in Greater China.* London: Routledge.

Warner, M. & Ng, S. H. 1999. Collective contracts in Chinese enterprises: a new brand of collective bargaining under 'market socialism'. *British Journal of Industrial Relations,* **37**(2): 295–314.

Webber, M. & Zhu, Y. 2006. Primitive accumulation, transition and unemployment in China. In G. Lee & M. Warner (eds.), *Unemployment in China.* London: Routledge, pp. 17–35.

Wolf, C. J. & Levin, N. D. 2008. *Modernizing the North Korean System: Objectives, Method and Application.* Santa Monica: Rand Corporation.

Zhu, Y. 2002. Economic reform and human resource management in Vietnamese enterprises. *Asia Pacific Business Review,* **8**(3): 115–134.

Zhu, Y. 2005. The Asian crisis and the implications for human resource management in Vietnam. *International Journal of Human Resource Management,* **16**(7): 1262–1277.

Zhu, Y., Collins, N., Webber, M. & Benson, J. 2008. New forms of ownership and human resource practices in Vietnam. *Human Resource Management,* **47**(1): 157–175.

Zhu, Y. & Warner, M. 2004. The implications of China's WTO accession for employment relations. *European Business Journal,* **16**(2): 47–58.

Zhu, Y. & Warner, M. 2005. Changing Chinese employment relations since WTO accession. *Personnel Review,* **34**(3): 354–369.

27 Japan, Korea and Taiwan: issues and trends in human resource management

Philippe Debroux, Wes Harry, Shigeaki Hayashi, Huang Heh Jason, Keith Jackson and Toru Kiyomiya

The three countries discussed here, although very different in ethnic and cultural backgrounds, share some common factors. The three are at the periphery of the Asian landmass – South Korea on a peninsula and the other two in groups of islands. These countries had a shared history, at least for a time, when Korea and Taiwan (then Formosa) were occupied by Japan for much of the first half of the twentieth century. During the second half of that century the three countries successfully embraced capitalism, with government support and under the influence of the United States of America, and in so doing recovered fairly rapidly from the devastation of the Pacific War – in contrast to their neighbours in North Korea and the People's Republic of China which in the 1940s adopted the Communist economic model (as discussed in Chapter 27).

In this chapter we draw attention to the aspects of HRM that may be little understood by foreigners even those who are resident in the region for many years. Although much has been written by foreigners about the economic miracles of these East Asian states the impressions gained by outsiders may not reflect the realities of hard work, dedication, ability and innovation of the citizens nor the uncertainly, exploitation and health risks also experienced by these citizens. As we are concentrating on the HRM aspects of these countries we have omitted general discussions of the business environment (for the reader who wishes to understand the background we recommend Tselichtchev & Debroux, 2009). The authors undertook the writing of this chapter as a collaborative effort applying and sharing knowledge together and in the process hope that we have introduced the reader to greater understanding of the changes in the means of managing Human Resources in these Asian States.

JAPAN

Background to HRM Issues

Although it appears to outsiders that Japan has accepted, and very success-fully applied, Western management techniques, the modern Japanese still learn from ancient history in order to apply their cultural heritage to current management and organisation issues. The Japanese have a strongly held view that management relies on people more than other available resources such as raw materials, finance and capital. The patriarchal relationship in classic Japanese management that embraces Confucianism became domi-nant in the social order of Japanese society in ancient times, and continued into modern Japanese society. Confucianism and Buddhism still strongly influence people's lives, and many business leaders embrace these value systems (Kotter, 1997; Yui, 2008) so that cultural and religious factors are embodied in the Japanese form of Human Resources Management (HRM).

HRM development creates continuity of moral principle in the work-place. For example, spiritual principles are embodied in '5S' activities; *Seiri* (storing), *Seiton* (straightening), *Seiso* (cleanliness), *Seiketsu* (sani-tary care) and *Shitsuke* (sustaining discipline) involved in daily work life. Many modern Japanese companies emphasise moral discipline and as such the HRM function is a key part of continuing this tradition and allows the HRM department, apparently, to have more power than is generally found in Western organisations.

After the trauma of World War II the Japanese adopted what has been called 'welfare corporatism' in which employers and employees work jointly to facilitate production and services, for example, Total Quality Management (TQM) and team-based work systems. Under these systems, employment (at least for core workers) is assumed to be stable and progres-sion (generally) by seniority was the norm for many (but not all) employees of large organisations. Other aspects of the welfare corporatism system were low wage differentials, top management financial sacrifice in times of crisis, endeavours to find alternative positions for surplus core employees and a generally paternalistic style of management. These systems incor-porated the traditional spiritual approach to work and to workers. Thus, Japanese HRM systems and practices were the result of Japanese culture and history. However, much is changing in Japan and in Japanese HRM.

Recruitment and Selection

In the past two decades recruitment and selection systems have changed radically in Japan. The Japanese 'recruitment for life' model, often cited by Westerners, was always mainly restricted to large organisations but in the spirit of moral principles and people-centred management, most employers did try to create long-term employment within the 'family' of the organisation for 'core' workers. Meanwhile, females and those working on the periphery were not considered for long-term employment relationships. Increasingly, temporary and dispatch (agency) workers are more commonly employed as a means of reducing the high labour costs associated with long-term employees. Such temporary workers also help the Japanese firm deal with the more volatile economic environment of recent decades. Highly skilled and specialist workers are also employed on temporary contracts for specific tasks and projects as even the largest corporations realise that they cannot justify the expense of developing and retaining a wide range of expertise which may be rarely used. The temporary workers in Japan, as in most economies, give flexibility to the organisation transferring 'uncertainty' (and often hardship) to these workers on the periphery.

The downsizing increasingly found in Japanese industry has impacted upon traditional Japanese recruitment methods, which included the system of employing all new graduates together each April. According to a survey conducted by the Ministry of Health, Labour and Welfare (MHLW), 25 per cent of companies now hire new employees year-round although 53 per cent of them keep to the traditional annual recruitment (Ministry of Health Labour and Welfare, 2007a). There has been a shift in HRM strategies whereby recruitment has moved towards more flexible forms of employment – such as part-time workers and outsourcing jobs and tasks. As a result, the Japanese workplace has become more complicated in composition with not only regular employees but also temporary staff, dispatched workers from the outsourcing companies and part-time workers

The seniority systems (usually associated with the Japanese model of employment) do not work well under dynamic labour market conditions even if long-term employment is still the preference in most Japanese organisations. According to a White Paper (Ministry of Health Labour and Welfare, 2007b), while companies are interested in attracting recruits who have high levels of expertise and professional knowledge with a sense of responsibility and of duty, they seek candidates who can be immediately effective, which leads to greater interest in mid-career recruitment of capable and immediately productive employees. As mid-career recruits have already inculcated the culture of previous organisations the potential employer spends much time seeking to match candidates with their existing corporate culture. The selection process involves a series of interviews with a mix of individual and group interviews. For Japanese organisations in the twenty-first century mid-career and first time recruitment are both valued.

Training and Development

After the World War II there was a great shortage of labour, and especially of skilled workers, so employers built a successful system making use of Japanese traditions, such HR development and in-house training that created skills and abilities. This system did not rely on seeking and directly hiring a talented individual or elite groups of professionals – since these individuals and groups were scarce until recently. In this sense, Japanese management systems have been sustained by human resources development that emphasises skill-development by on-job training (OJT) and moral education (as mentioned above). According to the MHLW, the core of Japanese HR development is both planned OJT and off-the-job training (OffJT), but the investment in employee development declined by an annual rate of 100 billion Japanese Yen (US$2 billion/Euro 1.8 billion) in the previous 10 years (Ministry of Health Labour and Welfare, 2005). Aoshima (2005) points out that companies have been reluctant to invest in the human resources of R&D and production because this investment does not show a return in the short-term. After the collapse of the bubble economy, HRM strategies placed less emphasis on employee development and emphasised short-term outcomes and a reduction of labour costs. Both lack of time and lack of trainers were additional reasons for a reduced focus on HR development.

However, many Japanese employees still have a strong motivation to develop their own capabilities (Ministry of Health Labour and Welfare, 2005). Now, however, we find a mix of de-skilling and up-skilling among Japanese workers with OffJT becoming much more important, including for 'blue collar' workers. This increasing importance of training and developing blue collar workers and their inclusion in mixed project teams with 'white collar' workers is a new feature in Japan. Companies are willing to invest in training, of core employees no matter what their level, if this leads to higher performance.

Reward and Managing Performance

Traditional Japanese HRM faced serious problems in the 1990s, after the bubble economy (of asset inflation) burst. These serious problems have driven the transformation of Japanese HRM. In particular, HRM paid attention to *Seika-shugi* (a performance-based or merit-based system) which has become widely adopted, because of the promised reduction in current and future labour costs and consequently has created problems with many companies in which management and employees had expected continuation of the people-centred traditions. *Seika-shugi* is similar to the merit-based or performance-based pay systems of Western HRM. In fact, this system has been adopted from the Western style of HRM, which emphasises the results of performance and individual competition. *Seika-shugi* as practised in Japan links performance results and appraisal to increase or decrease pay (monthly salary with bonus) and to determine promotion. Some Japanese appreciate this system because they are able to generate the good performance which is rewarded, whereas under the traditional seniority-based HRM systems 'good performance' would not generally lead to pay increases or to career advancement.

It is instructive to consider factors that changed traditional Japanese HRM and brought *Seika-shugi* to Japanese companies. Hierarchal positions in the corporate ladder collapsed in large part because of the rapid aging of the population of Japan with fewer youngsters entering the workforce to replace those retiring or moving up the organisation on the basis of seniority. The clear hierarchical structure worked well in the rapid economic growth in the 1960s and 1970s and was partly a useful method of attracting and retaining workers in the period of severe shortages of young men as a result of the destructive effect of World War II. In the twenty-first century, the potential promotion opportunities in middle age no longer motivate younger employees. In traditional HRM, employees (especially in larger organisations) expected to be promoted on the basis of age irrespective of performance – although there was always, in practice, several career tracks (fast, average and slower) for those with recognised abilities and connections or who were viewed as being below standard in performance. A major difference in the twenty-first century is that whereas in the past those on the 'slow' career path could expect to keep a job and status as a *salariiman*, now they may find themselves unemployed and unemployable – except in the most menial of temporary jobs.

Seika-shugi is not only adopted because of the negative impacts arising from the demanding economic environment and demographic change. Companies actively intend to make their organisation more competitive through changing HRM systems and therefore they attempt to strengthen employee motivation and competitiveness in the market. Traditional HRM systems emphasise stable labour forces with slow career development, which are no longer viable in the early twenty-first century. In order to overcome some disadvantages of the traditional approaches, *Nouryoku-shugi* HRM (which is similar to the Western knowledge- or competency-based pay) developed, and emphasises improvement and strengthening of individual capability. Individual performance appraisal is undertaken to examine not only the results of performance attained but also the abilities that contribute to performance. As such this *Nouryoku-shugi* system is compatible with the traditional seniority system as it holds employees for a minimum number of years at each step on the corporate ladder and consequently less rapid promotion – even for the good performers who resent the 'unfairness' to them. Broad-banding of salary scales and job types have helped to keep employees from progressing too quickly – whilst appearing to keep to the spirit of *Nouryoku-shugi*. However, there are substantial changes taking place. There has been an increase in the pay differential with a matching decline in the broad equity in distribution of profits (which was the norm in the second part of the twentieth century) meaning that in practice high performance is recognised and rewarded while poor performance is likely to lead to a search for a new job instead of years of being a member of the 'window tribe' (looking out the side without work to do) which was the 'traditional' way of dealing with poor performance or a surplus core jobholders.

Employee Relations

As Abegglen (1958) showed, Japanese industrial relations and corporate HRM systems have been typically illustrated as three pillars, namely – life-long employment, seniority system and enterprise unionism – which were developed and maintained for a long time after the end of World War II. However, following the bursting of the 'Japanese bubble economy', the 1990s was what is often called the 'Lost Decade' and the Japanese economic environment was fundamentally changed during this period. At the same time as a loss of economic certainty, the structure of the Japanese population has changed with a rapidly aging society (Ministry of Economy, Trade and Industry, 2006). These environmental changes caused a shift in the traditional Japanese HRM systems. In particular, the Japanese custom of life-long employment has collapsed with drastic downsizing in human resources in many traditionally patriarchal companies. Some companies that have faced serious cost reduction have undertaken large-scale lay-offs, often called *risutora* (restructuring), going against the system of people-centred tradition and the expectation of human resources being at the core of the organisation. Due to these political and economic trends, the numbers of trade unions and their members have been decreasing. Workers, at least those with skills that are in demand, are now less reliant on the protection of trade unions and are much more concerned with their employability and individual capability. The increasing size and complexity of the external labour market means that people are willing (or have no choice but) to take charge of their own careers.

Generally, trade unions have lost power in negotiation against management. On the other hand, the position of union leader is still one of the career paths to climb the corporate ladder to the executive, especially in big companies. In many cases, unions are under the control of companies; enterprise unionism – called *goyou-kumiai*. Although Japanese unions historically had strong power with high unionisation rates; more than 50 per cent membership in 1950 (Ministry of Health, Labour and Welfare (MHLW), 2009), the rates rapidly decreased in the late 1950s to 35 per cent. The decline of unionisation rate continued to reach 18 per cent in 2009. The *Syunto* (Spring Offense) is a typical Japanese negotiation event between enterprise unions and their employers. During the recent weak economy, Japanese unions are not able to succeed in gaining wage increases and improvement of employment conditions. Therefore unions have emphasised security of employment for their members rather than wage increases.

Likely Future Trends

Although many Japanese companies have adopted *Seika-shugi* HRM (because of its impact on strengthening employees' motivation and flexibly at work while dealing with the external environment) this new system is not appreciated by many Japanese employees. As can be expected, some employees lose their motivation under the new system. One company, studied by two of the authors, conducted a survey on employee satisfaction in which it was found that there is a clear distinction between real mangers and nominal mangers (specialists with a manager title) in terms of the level of satisfaction. Specialists (who should do better from the *Seika-shugi* system) are less satisfied in their jobs and work environments so it seems that the system is not successful in terms of improving the motivation of many younger good performers. These potentially good performers are not satisfied with performance evaluation and feel that this system treats them unfairly. However it is difficult to see how the aspirations of these nominal managers can be satisfied within organisations' existing structures where high performers have their rewards and career progression is shared with those whose current performance is not so high.

A further of disadvantage in *Seika-shugi* HRM is more serious and creates more potential problems. This new system emphasises 'management-by-objective' (MBO) and a more rigid distribution of performance outcomes. *Seika-shugi* HRM strengthens differentiation of the performance appraisal and its results. The relative evaluation is determined by rigid forced distribution rules along with quantitative benchmarks for evaluation. In general, *Seika-shugi* is used for creating and enlarging differentiation of human resources in terms of salary, bonus, and promotion. In particular, the promotion opportunities are complicated as there are so few vacancies available – currently perhaps only 20 per cent of good performers are able to gain promotion.

The more companies stress individual goals and department goals, the more the internal competition is escalated among individual employees as well as between departments. As a result, collaborative relationships can collapse; and excessive competition damages harmony in the organisations. Examples of the deterioration of organisational culture found by two of the present authors, in the company studied above, include statements that 'this is not my job', and lack of initiative such as 'could you ask my boss first and follow the formal procedure'. Such inflexibility and distrust appears along with employees tending to avoid extra tasks and to protect their own arena of job responsibilities have become symptoms of *Seika-shugi* HRM systems. Employees tend to avoid challenging goals that seem difficult to achieve while avoiding clients who are tough to deal with. *Seika-shugi* HRM emphasises short-term outcomes, whereas the traditional HRM emphasises the process and long-term relationships that link HR development. In this respect, under *Seika-shugi* HRM, supervisors are not interested in developing human resources because it takes a long time and does not link with their own personal goals. *Seika-shugi* leads to organisational cultures in which employees tend to be ego-defensive and individualistic. This has shaped a new negative spiral of organisational problems.

The episodes recounted in the previous paragraph illustrate the harmful results of Seika-shugi HRM which can be characterised as (1) withdrawal from organisational learning and ability (problems in information- and knowledge-sharing), (2) hesitation to challenge (problems in goal setting), and (3) avoidance of collaboration and altruistic behaviours (problems of selfishness). Thus, *Seika-shugi* HRM negatively impacts on social capital in general, and these problems are identified in various business-activities and workplace attitudes.

Japanese companies are currently contending with amendment of *Seika-shugi* HRM systems that are more consistent with Japanese HRM traditions. Literature criticising *Seika-shugi* HRM has proliferated in the past decade (Takahashi, 2004). It is necessary to consider how Western styles of performance-based HRM fit within the Japanese context, because of the changing economy and population structures in Japan. In an historical sense, we observed that an American business style of neo-liberalism has proven to be not a perfect model – especially in banking and financial services. Japanese companies initially planned to take advantage of American HRM, and *Seika-shugi* HRM was expected to bring positive outcomes.

However, *Seika-shugi* HRM has actually led to harmful results, which are linked with materialism, market egoism and individual competition. Japanese traditions of harmony and altruistic behaviours are declining. On the one hand, the transformation of Japanese HRM led by *Seika-shugi* makes organisations pay attention to short-term outputs and competition but, on the other hand, it causes Japanese organisations to lose the advantage of collaborative approaches. As a result, *Seika-shugi* HRM has not been able to overcome disadvantages of the seniority systems, while Japanese organisations currently struggle with creating new HRM systems that combine both a Western style and Japanese traditional ways of organising work.

To give immediate reward to today's high performers with *Seika-shugi* HRM risks harming the spirit and trust which has been the basis of much of Japan's success in the past 60 years. To follow the path which led Western economies to the financial crisis that started in 2007 (and which is seen as being caused by a short-term orientation) is unlikely to be attractive to Japanese employers or employees. Recognising the importance of contingent relationships in Japanese organisations it is likely that *Seika-shugi* will continue to be an important aspect of HRM in Japan. Along with hard work, flexibility and a large degree of pragmatism it is likely that the Japanese, employers and employees, will find a way of continuing to succeed with a mixture of traditional and modern ways of managing human resources.

KOREA

Background to HRM Issues

Korea (for the purposes of this chapter we use 'Korea' to be the Republic of Korea, also known as South Korea) has seen the permeation of Confucian values to every part of society for many centuries. Although Korean culture has been changing since the Korean War, this Confucian heritage remained strong during the last few decades of the twentieth century. To some extent it could be said that cultural traits contributed to how firms organised and enabled developmental policies to be implemented successfully. The Confucian and collective-minded Korean companies organised around principles of respect for order and hierarchy, on the one hand, and benevolence and paternalism, on the other (Miles, 2008). In the 1950s the country was weak in technology, material and financial resources. Since the coup d'état in 1961 until the end of the 1980s, income redistribution was not given any priority at the state level.

There had been few significant social policies linked to economic growth or policies for labour relations during the all period of rapid economic growth up until the end of the 1980s. Comforted by the support of the state against trade union activities companies did not work collaboratively with the unions.

Conversely, *chaebols* provided opportunities to improve standards of living, albeit not equally for all categories of workers. Women's economic activities were reduced to ancillary production work and unpaid labour at home. During the whole period from the 1950s to the 1990s, production workers had to work long hours for low wages. The large companies offered a long-term job guarantee to their permanent workers but the female and temporary workers had no guarantees. Wages, salaries and promotion were largely based on seniority. Up until the 1990s under regulatory and social constraints large companies rearranged work, and cut back on bonus and dividends rather than dismiss those in the permanent workforce. However, it has to be noted that the internal labour market principle was better used in Korean SMEs than in Japanese equivalents. High labour mobility between firms was always the norm in Korea among the majority of the workforce (Hwang, 2006).

Companies invested in training and most white-collar employees had reasonable prospects of entering a managerial track. Corporate culture was constantly reinforced and the close bonds – group harmony – and emphasis on consensus and co-operation created strong dynamics. Subordinates were obedient but superiors were expected to take care of them beyond purely instrumental working relationships. Centralised decision making was counterbalanced by the possibility of developing informal interactions between subordinates and superiors (Miles, 2008). There was no place for entrepreneurial start-ups in the business system but Korea became an entrepreneurial economy of a kind through the *chaebols*. As a result of their rapid expansion and diversification managers were given a certain amount of freedom regarding policy implementation. This fitted with the kind of pattern of employees' loyalty traditionally found in Korean organisations that is said to go more to an individual than to the organisation (Miles, 2008).

The situation changed in the 1990s. The democratisation period after 1987 had seen the removal of government' regulations in industrial relations and Korea had become member of the International Labour Organization (ILO) in 1991. Production workers' started actions and obtained significant wages increase. Added to rising costs of energy and material these wage increases made labour-intensive industries less competitive because of the rigid pay system in a period where Korea was still unable to rival Western countries and Japan on technology, quality and design. With the advent of the World Trade Organization companies could no longer depend on government protection. Pressure increased further from the International Monetary Fund, after the Asian financial crisis of the mid 1990s, requesting a more hands-off and market-driven public policy in labour issues. Long-term job guarantees had to be curtailed and more flexible wage-setting policies had to be adopted.

Companies transferred work to lower labour cost countries and restructured HRM in Korea. With legalisation of mass redundancies the companies gained flexibility and with the support of the State started to dismiss workers in large numbers. Now, after a decade of liberalisation of the labour market, companies have developed multipronged HRM strategies. The shift toward knowledge-related industries requires HRM strategies attuned to the needs of knowledge workers in terms of autonomy and involvement in management, fair recognition of their contribution and importance given to work/life balance. Optimising their talents and creating synergetic effects require an environment with high levels of cooperation and coordination. The *chaebols* have the best access to tangible and intangible assets, giving them an edge to satisfy those conditions and attract the first class talents (Tselichtchev & Debroux, 2009) while non-permanent workers, who amount to about 50 per cent of the total of employees (Hemmert, 2009), have declining advantages from work. A different work organisation and a legal contract expertise are required to treat fairly and motivate employees working with different statuses and pay systems. Dismissal of workers is more casual than before but companies try to avoid straight retrenchment. They devise short-term contracts, outplacement and retraining schemes for their redundant workers.

Korea has one of the lowest fertility rates in the world. It does not face imminent problems of labour shortage but thinks about immigration in a longer-term perspective. It is a very culturally and racially homogeneous country where large-scale immigration is considered difficult. Foreign people account for 2 per cent of current population and the number is unlikely to increase significantly. So, transfer of labour-intensive jobs (to lower wage countries) is bound to continue and Korea counts on robotics to cover part of the basic production needs in the medium term. Korea is more interested in attracting small numbers of specialised workers. For the time being, the inflow remains small, though, and it would require a significant upgrading of working conditions and changes in the management style of Korean companies to attract first class international personnel. Therefore, Korea will most likely have to find solutions in making the most of its own human resources including making more worthwhile work and careers available to females.

Recruitment and Selection

The Korean external labour market is expanding with growing job mobility but recruitment of new graduates remains at the centre of HRM policy. Companies are aware of the need for more human resource diversity so they recruit more broadly, even outside of renowned universities and put more emphasis on specific skills, abilities and attitudes. Korean people have always been individual achievers in contrast to most Japanese and Taiwanese. This tendency has grown further since the 1990s. Employees become more individualistic and more willing to take charge of their own careers. They are not so moved anymore by slogans, songs, flags, and other manifestations of corporate culture (Pucik & Lim, 2001). Companies now put emphasis on job content, career opportunities and material reward. Many companies have a signing-on bonus system and an explicit fast track for the most talented. But Korean people are also worried about their career prospects. Companies cannot promise a long-term stable career with regular promotion to the majority of their employees. So, they have to offer something else, for example, training assuring employability or an attractive work environment.

Cultivation of relationships with universities is important to have access to the best students, especially in natural sciences. Large companies have high expectations concerning the qualifications of the new recruits. The recruitment of permanent employees is increasingly formalised with use of internal tests and assessment centres. Recruitment of some types of the non-permanent employees involved in routine jobs is more casual. However, companies have also strict selection criteria for those whose individual or group performance may impact on company performance.

Reward and Managing Performance

A uniform yearly increase of basic pay regardless of performance or ability levels used to be the norm, but it is now considered unsustainable in most industries. High costs of middle-aged employees are still a major hindrance but the seniority element is losing importance in pay and career paths. Performance-related pay (PRP) and promotion systems have been adopted in many large companies although offer of stock options and other profit sharing schemes is not widespread. Annualised remuneration schemes with salary based on individual performance or ability are popular. Management by objective and competencies frameworks are also adopted in relation of remuneration although they are mainly utilised for development purpose. Korean companies still seem to have difficulties mixing appraisal and reward flexibility with the internal market logic (Hwang, 2006). PRP systems motivate employees on the fast track, but companies are said to often end up creating a culture of narrow individualism and short-termism (Miles, 2008). In many companies the employees are not strongly involved in the development of the new systems, raising issues of equity and fairness of the reward frameworks and procedures. The most successful companies adopt evaluation systems mixing appraisal and reward of individual and group performance. It remains difficult to create a too high wage/salary differential. But managers are less hesitant to give different evaluation marks to those they perceive are good or bad performers. The overall differential remains relatively small in most companies but with a higher spread of the evaluation marks.

Only about 15 per cent of the total business sector employees work in large companies. The majority are employed in small and medium size enterprises (SMEs) with less than 300 employees. Although wages and salaries in large *chaebol*-related firms have increased significantly since the 1990s and working conditions have improved, this is not the case in the SMEs. Wages and salaries, in SMEs, remain much lower and working conditions have not improved much during the last decade. Most Korean SMEs are still concentrated in low profitability sectors in the domestic market (Hwang, 2006) despite the increase of export-oriented ventures.

Training and Development

Traditional respect and esteem is attached to educational attainment and efforts for self-improvement are pervasive in the whole society. Driven by the necessity of upgrading manpower productivity and the need of knowledge industries companies devote important resources to training. Large companies often have well-equipped learning facilities (Hemmert, 2009). For the core workers training is linked to the promotion of values such as trust, credibility, excellence and responsibility. The use of foreign nationals as trainers has increased – for languages, but also for technical and management skill transfers and cultural familiarity (Kim & Bae, 2004). Foreign trainers are invited but companies also dispatch trainees to overseas subsidiaries or to universities, research centres and business schools for MBA and MOT programmes. At the same time, companies are active in university–business partnerships in Korea and abroad. Organisations finance research projects giving their employees the opportunity to work in different environments. There are also examples of exclusive MBA programmes developed in collaboration with universities.

Employment Relations

A tripartite system has existed at the state level since the 1990s and at company level bargaining autonomy of the two parties has gradually replaced state regulations. Multiple unions are now allowed in one workplace. Mediation provided by the Labor Relations Commission is compulsory before starting any industrial action. Companies with more than 30 full-time employees must set up a labour-management consultation council (Dessler & Tan, 2009). The tripartite system does not yet operate optimally. At company level, employee participation through formal mechanisms is still limited. The unitarist tradition makes companies uneasy in engaging with the trade unions. Unions have problems penetrating the new industries and attracting young workers. There are doubts about the benefits of a confrontational trade union strategy among their members. The position of the state is ambiguous. It has imposed affirmative action in favour of female workers on large companies while pushing for better working conditions of the non-core workers. But the State is criticised for keeping restrictions on the rights of freedom of association, collective bargaining and strikes. Moreover, in taking strong legal actions against a number of union activists the State has shown that it wants to dissociate from radical policies that it believes are detrimental to the Korean economy.

Likely Future Trends

Contingent convergence of HRM practices with world standards is likely to continue in terms of appraisal and reward systems. Continuation of recruitment of contingent (temporary, agency and despatch) types of human resources can also be expected. But there is a need to question what cultural changes are likely to arise from these policy changes, in terms of contributing to sustainable social and economic growth pattern. Sharp differences between categories of employees continue. There is a growing inequality and a decline in job security leading to the marginalisation of some segments of population, especially women and old people. This creates a loss of a sense of community and trust in society. Further liberalisation of the labour market is only possible if the feeling of social security and fairness is restored. Korea still has a limited safety net and, in view, of its demographic profile and public debt it cannot become a European-style welfare state. Any solution necessarily supposes involvement of private business. Yet, the *chaebols* are still expected by government and society at large to fulfil social responsibilities.

A remaining dark point remains the low integration of female labour, especially of highly qualified women. In this respect, despite progress in some companies, Korea is still an outlier similar to Japan among OECD countries. A return to patriarchal values is perceived as unworkable and to keep women in ancillary positions is just wasteful and ethically unacceptable. A long-term solution goes beyond state regulations and requires a complete change of work patterns and organisation. Therefore, significant results cannot be expected in the short-term.

In fact, the modernity of the values of Confucianism as life ethics, and the social and spiritual role it could play in business are debated in the whole Eastern Asian cultural area. If class and mystical elements are removed the Confucian conception of management based on a humanistic, value-based, self-cultivating form of leadership striving towards social harmony may be more attuned that the Western conception to Asian business cultures. Confucianism always puts emphasis on modesty, perseverance, thrift and trust while also insisting on the fact that people decide themselves of their destiny. This could fit with the kind of management style Korean people are thought to prefer as managers and entrepreneurs and offer a moral foundation for modernity that does not necessarily mean a return to patriarchal values.

TAIWAN

Background to HRM Issues

While Taiwan has become an important source for a variety of products and services in the global markets, it has faced keen competition from other developed and developing countries. Companies on the island have to demonstrate their dynamic capabilities to maintain agility, flexibility, self-renewal, while learning to meet new commercial development. HRM's history as a major profession in Taiwan is not long, but Taiwanese firms have increasingly recognised and emphasised HRM's importance in meeting their objectives. As winning the 'talent war' has become a critical issue of survival, many well-trained HRM professionals have moved from foreign-invested companies to local firms. This movement has accelerated the diffusion of HRM knowledge and practices within the Taiwanese business society. In the meantime, some leading universities such as the National Sun Yat-Sen University and National Central University established academic institutes of HRM in the 1990s. They offer master and doctorate programmes and are an important source of HRM professionals to Taiwanese firms.

Confucianism is the main value system in Taiwan. This value system strongly emphasises education, diligence, frugality, family obligation and patriarchal orientation. In Taiwanese business organisations, decision making is very often guided by family influence – especially in long established organisations. The employees' attachment and loyalty towards their organisations are very important, while the management feels that companies should do as much as possible to look after the welfare of their employees. However, the external environment has changed dramatically in the first decade of the twenty-first century and the influence of traditional values seems to be declining. For example, in July 2001, Acer (Taiwan's best-known company) undertook a reorganisation which involved a massive layoff to cut 7 per cent of its Taiwan-based work force (*Economic Daily News*, 5 March 2001, p. 5). This action, by Acer, was a radical change in business philosophy for the company and a shock to most of the population of Taiwan.

Taiwan had enjoyed a low unemployment rate for decades because of its rapid growth in gross domestic production (GDP) and fairly equitable distribution of the fruits of prosperity. However, the economic conditions have changed in recent years. Being heavily dependent on exports, Taiwan's economy has been battered by global economic crises as local factories in the export sector cut production and carried out layoffs due to shrinking overseas markets in the West. The jobless rate peaked in August 2009 at 6.13 per cent (*Taipei Times*, 23 October, 2009b, p. 12) – the highest since the government began compiling jobless statistics in 1978. Although the overall deterioration of the employment situation slowed down after August 2009, unemployment among the middle-aged and elderly (aged between 45 and 64) continued to worsen. Involuntary job losses among this age group have particular importance because they are often the main breadwinners in the household.

Farh (1995) found that there were wide differences in HRM practices across different types of firms in Taiwan. He categorised Taiwanese companies into five groups: the small and family-owned, the moderate-to-large private enterprises, the subsidiaries of Western multinationals, the subsidiaries of Japanese multinationals and the government-owned enterprises. Each group has developed its own organisational cultural and management practices based on its situation. Some of the Western concepts and practices, such as merit pay, management by objectives, performance appraisal and so forth were introduced to Taiwan and have been emulated by Taiwanese companies, for example, the system of performance management. However, many companies find difficulties in reconciling the cultural differences when transplanting such Western management practices.

In recent years, the increasingly deep involvement of Taiwan in mainland China's economy has been a key development for HRM. As economic exchange across the straits became routine, labourers in Taiwan began to lose their jobs to cheaper labour in China. As a result, the government has campaigned to attract highly skilled labour to high-tech and service industries (where qualifications and capability can be leveraged) targeted to be Taiwan's future competitive stronghold. However as will be discussed below even highly skilled technical jobs may be lost to mainland Chinese. These important changes have had a lasting impact on HRM issues in Taiwan.

Recruitment and Selection

Prior to the emergence of the internet, as a means for applicants/candidates to find career opportunities, job seekers in Taiwan relied on newspapers for jobs. Newspaper employment advertisements are very expensive and did not necessarily attract the most suitable candidates. Thanks to the internet, companies seeking recruits can now find, for a relatively low cost, a wide range of job-bank services, such as the provision of regular updates regarding qualified applicants, recruitment of high-level or specialised applicants and offers to provide outsourced and temporary employees.

Recruiting at university campuses is common, especially for entry-level managerial and professional positions. For middle and senior level positions, headhunting has become increasingly popular. In almost all recruitment relationships, personal networking in Taiwan is important for job seekers. A cross-national comparison of personnel selection practices showed that Taiwan and Japan were the only two countries where firms listed 'a person's ability to get along well with others already working here' as one of the three most important criteria for selection (Huo et al., 2002). As in China and Hong Kong, personal networking in Taiwan is important in employee selection. It is noteworthy that Taiwanese tend to be more accustomed to a paternalistic culture. While assertiveness is generally a desired trait in the West, it is much less so in Taiwan society.

The key factor in facilitating the transformation of Taiwan's high-tech industrial development is the availability of sufficient numbers of talented candidates. However, the pace of development toward high-tech industrial production cannot be met by the corresponding adjustment of HR training within the rigid education system. Thus, university graduates had difficulty finding suitable jobs, while industries also have problems hiring the right staff. For example, despite many efforts attempted by the government, a survey of 100 multinational corporations (MNCs) in Taiwan showed a serious deficiency staff with information, communication and technology (ICT) skills (Hu et al., 2007).

With the increased development and deployment of HRM techniques

Taiwan has moved, to an extent, to systematic methods of selecting and recruiting employees. Hsu and Leat (2000) found that some, but certainly not all, decision making was shared between HRM and line management but that the cultural sensitivity of recruitment and selection practices meant that even foreign owned companies adjusted their systems to meet Taiwanese requirements – especially in relying upon networks, social standing and educational background.

Training and Development

As continuing technological advancement moved the Taiwanese economic structure from a labour-intensive to a more technology and/or capital-intensive marketplace, companies gradually began to realise they could not compete in world markets without maintaining competent human capital. Consequently, companies have become more willing to invest in people. Generally speaking, Taiwan employers are more pragmatic and emphasise skills training. The investment in people has led to the highest performing companies allocating an average of 3.3 per cent of payroll costs to training and development (Fei, 1990).

In a study of the high technology firms, which Taiwan aims to develop further, Lin (1996) found that training and development was usually recommended by supervisors (rather than HRM professionals), was usually on-the-job training and that Taiwanese- and Japanese-owned firms in Taiwan emphasised employee development much more than US-owned enterprises; in fact, she found that American companies were characterised by a focus on short-term profit rather than the stability and growth favoured by Taiwanese organisations. Lin also found that foreign firms, which did not understand the Taiwanese desire for long term career development and harmonious working relationships, experienced severe problems in attracting and retaining the most talented candidates in the labour market.

Reward and Managing Performance

Taiwan implemented a minimum wage system in 1984. The minimum wage, from January 2011, is NT$17880 per month or NT$98 per hour. A survey in August 2008 released by the Council of Labor Affairs (CLA) *Taipei Times*, 24 Aug 2009a, p. 2) showed that the average worker in Taiwan earns a monthly salary of NT$36564, while employees in 'managerial or supervisory' positions earned NT$59960, about 1.64 times as much as the average worker's salary.

In Taiwan, bonuses are a significant part of compensation, the most important being the Chinese New Year Bonus paid in late January or February. Bonuses range from one to six months' salary, and are given by both local and foreign firms. In addition, there is also a separate bonus known as the 'earning distribution' whereby public companies are required to distribute a percentage of their profits to their employees – a type of 'share in success' bonus. However, since 2008, the earning distribution bonus has been stated, in company accounts, as an expense instead of an earnings distribution. This new regulation has affected companies, especially the high-tech companies, which had made such a bonus an incentive compensation scheme to motivate and retain excellent employees. Previously, some high-tech companies in Taiwan had granted huge bonuses to their employees by giving shares instead of giving a cash distribution. At the same time, investors raised concerns about the adverse impact of this accounting treatment (*Asian Wall Street Journal*, 18 July 2002, p. 1).

Salter et al. (2006) found that, compared to their US counterparts, Taiwanese employers, even with a merit pay system, tend to reward most workers (including failing employees) to promote group harmony. TSMC, the world's biggest contract chipmaker, experienced serious problems which led Chairman Morris Chang to apologise in May 2009 (*Taipei Times*, 25 May 2009, p. 12) for the company's mishandling of its annual performance management and development (PMD) employee appraisal, saying that TSMC would invite all of its 800 laid-off workers back to work. Under the company's PMD system, the 5 per cent of its workers with the lowest performance evaluation scores were to be dismissed.

Employee Relations

Low-wage workers tend to be temporary or part-time workers whose work usually does not require a high level of skills and who are easily replaced or whose work can be moved to another location with little effort. In recent years, Taiwanese enterprises have increasingly hired temporary workers from manpower dispatching agencies, as they can save labour expenses and enhance flexibility. There are now over 200 000 dispatched workers in Taiwan (out of a workforce of 10.3 million), who are employed, in name, by manpower dispatching agencies, but actually work for enterprises which pay the agencies directly. Dispatched workers are paid much less than the regular workers, although they undertake almost the same job duties. Worrying about the downside of the practice, the government labour authorities plan to revise the Labor Standards Law to block some high-risk or highly specialised businesses from hiring dispatched workers; such businesses include healthcare, security, aviation, navigation, public transportation drivers and mining.

The Labor Standards Law (LSA) adopted in 1984 is the basic labour law in Taiwan. The LSA regulates every aspect of the employment relationship, including: minimum wage, overtime pay, work hours, work rules, labour contracts, leave of absence, women workers and child workers, retirement age and pensions, compensation for occupational accidents and labour–management negotiations. Since December 1998, the law has been extended to cover all employer–employee relationships, with very few exceptions. From 1 January 2001, the maximum number of work hours is 44 regular hours per week, and no more than 84 hours every two weeks.

The Employment Services Act (ESA), enacted in 1992, guarantees equal job opportunities and access to employment services, with the objective of balancing the manpower supply and demand, efficiently using human resources, and establishing an employment information network. To protect workers' rights during times of economic slowdown, the ESA stipulates that the central government should encourage management, labour unions, and workers to negotiate work hour reductions, wage adjustments, and in-service training to avoid layoffs. Under the ESA, employment discrimination evaluation committees have been established in Taipei, Kaohsiung and most counties and cities. These committees, formed by government, labour, management representatives, scholars and experts, ensure equal employment opportunities and determine whether discriminatory actions have been taken by an employer against an employee.

The Taiwan Labor Insurance Act (LIA) guarantees retirement, disability, death and unemployment benefits to Taiwanese workers. The insurance is funded by a combination of contributions from employees, employers, and the government. The Act was amended in 2004. Since then, instead of a lump sum payment upon retirement, annuity payments have been required. Under the LIA, all companies with at least five employees are required to participate. Foreign employees in Taiwan are also covered by the Labor Insurance Act.

In Taiwan, many categories of workers, including teachers and doctors, are not allowed to form a labour union. Collective agreements are still rare, and it is hard to hold a legal strike. In the case of labour problems and conflicts, the Labor Union Law and the Law on Settlement of Labor Disputes stipulate general procedures for reaching an employer/workers agreement. Failing an agreement, a long procedure must be followed prior to calling a strike. Workers may approach the government authorities in the event of a violation of their rights or in the event of labour disputes. In 2008, there were 24 540 events of this type which involved 65 274 people (Council of Labor Affairs, 2009)

Likely Future Trends

Taiwan is an export-dependent economy subject to the rise or fall in global trade which eventually affects the inflow and outflow of human resource at various levels. Many foreign workers want jobs in Taiwan because of its relatively high minimum wages. The number of foreign workers peaked at 374 000 in July 2008 before the recent financial turmoil. In the meantime, however, more and more Taiwanese work in Mainland China. For example, the American Chamber of Commerce in Taipei (2007) estimated that nearly 5 per cent of Taiwan's people live and work in China with the majority of these workers are aged between 24 and 50 years. There are particular opportunities for mid-career level professionals in the companies which expand to China. Expatriation to China is often seen as a shortcut to promotion for those lower-level managers.

The ties between China and Taiwan have improved dramatically in recent years. A noteworthy change in policy is that Taiwan Ministry of Education (MOE) has decided to recognise diplomas conferred by 41 prestigious universities in China. This policy change had been under heated debate for years not only because education and credentials are regarded as the most instrumental means for upward mobility in Chinese society (Huang & Cullen, 2001), but also because education plays an important role in the formation of national identity, a sensitive issue in Taiwan and the People's Republic of China.

Despite the protests from critics, the MOE is intending to allow Mainland Chinese graduate students to pursue master's degree courses at Taiwan's public universities, while local private universities will be permitted to enrol college students from China. It is believed that a shift in policies will also encourage even more Taiwanese students to seek their higher education in China. Those Taiwanese who have previously received diplomas from Chinese universities (estimated to be about 18 000) can now seek accreditation and find attractive jobs in Taiwan. Taiwan is well-placed when competing with foreign countries in trade with China due to a common language and cultural similarities. If Taiwan succeeds in improving economic co-operation with China, this will have a major impact on HRM on both sides of the Taiwan Straits.

The beginning of the second decade of the twenty-first century will be a pivotal point for change in Taiwan's development of human resources as well as for its economy. Taiwan signed an economic co-operation framework agreement (ECFA) with Mainland China in June 2010. However, Taiwan is increasing its efforts to seal free trade agreements (FTAs) with other countries on the ground that, now that an ECFA has been signed, other countries will be more willing to sign FTAs with Taiwan because China's opposition will be less.

FINAL OVERVIEW

In the discussions of HRM in Japan, Korea and Taiwan we have seen how these countries are meeting the demands of changing economic circumstances and coping with the social consequences of declining certainty and predictability in business and finance. The importation of Western methods of managing human resources in search of means of tackling these changes has led to the reduced use of seniority systems for promotion and the introduction of individual performance management, greater use of temporary workers and a widening gap between the large and small companies. Many individual workers and smaller firms have been badly hit by competition from China and South-East Asia where the larger companies have outsourced production.

Each country is facing severe problems on the status, access to social security, pension, and social support of the atypical workers who have suffered most from cost cutting and outsourcing production. These same atypical (who could within a decade or so become typical) workers miss out on training, career development and protection of the HRM policies that are given to regular workers. Among the 'atypical' workers in traditional organisations are the female workers who are seen as temporary workers (with little more security than agency/dispatch workers). From society's viewpoint, particularly where the available citizen workforce is declining, the neglect of the human capital present in the female population is a great waste of human resources.

It is possible, however, that is among those whom outsiders consider are the 'typical' workers, that less obvious but just as damaging changes are taking place. The motivation of these typical workers has been severely damaged by the uncertainty around career progression and employment stability. Younger workers are increasingly reluctant to accept punishing work schedules and regimes in the expectation that as they rise in the organisation their interests and aspirations will be protected. The disillusionment now felt by the employees in many Japanese, Korean and Taiwan organisations is likely to lead to issues around quality of output, cover-up of malpractice, workplace stress (leading to higher rates of psychological problems and higher levels of suicide) and declining trust in established powers and order within societies. The working together which was such a strength for these organisations may have been severely damaged by the introduction of Western management techniques which focused on the individual and the short term at the cost of the group, society and long-term prosperity.

On a more optimistic note, Hofstede's recent publication (Hofstede & Minkov, 2010) concerning the long-term orientation of various nation states showed that the countries with the highest scores were Korea 100, Taiwan 93 and Japan 88. So perhaps this long-term orientation will be a more sustainable economic model than the more short term orientation of the Western countries whose HRM policies and practices many employers in these three East Asian states had been tempted to adopt.

REFERENCES

Abegglen, J. 1958 *The Japanese Factory: Aspects of its Social Organization.* Glencoe IL: Free Press.

American Chamber of Commerce in Taipei. 2007. White Paper. Available at http://www.amcham.com.tw.

Aoshima, Y. 2005. The mobility of R&D Workers and the technical performance. *The Japanese Journal of Labour Studies,* **47**(8): 34–48.

Asian Wall Street Journal 2002. 18 July, p. 1.

Council of Labor Affairs. 2009. http://statdb.cla.gov.tw/statis/.

Dessler, G. & Tan, C.-H. 2009. *Human Resource Management: An Asian Perspective.* Singapore: Pearson Education.

Economic Daily News 2001. 5 March, p. 5.

Farh, J. L. 1995. Human resource management in Taiwan, the Republic of China. In L. F. Moore & P. D. Jennings (eds), *Human Resource Management on the Pacific Rim: Institutions, Practices and Attitudes.* Berlin: Walter de Gruyter.

Fei, T. Y. 1990. Training as a long term planning. *Management Magazine,* **194**: 168–171 (in Chinese).

Hemmert, M. 2009. Management in Korea. In H. Hasegawa & C. Noronha (eds), *Asian Business and Management, Theory, Practice and Perspectives.* London: Palgrave, pp. 241–255.

Hofstede, G. & Minkov, M. 2010. *Cultures and Organizations: Software of the Mind,* revised and expanded 3rd edn. New York: McGraw-Hill.

Hsu, Y.-R. & Leat, M. 2000. A study of HRM and recruitment and selection policies and practices in Taiwan *The International Journal of Human Resource Management,* **11**(2): 413–435.

Hu, M. C., Zheng, C. & Lamond, D. 2007. Recruitment and retention of ICT skills among MNCs in Taiwan. *Chinese Management Studies,* **1**(2): 78–92.

Huang, H. J. & Cullen, J. B. 2001. Labour-flexibility and related HRM practices: a study of large Taiwanese manufacturers. *Canadian Journal of Administrative Sciences,* **18**(1): 33–39.

Huo, P., Huang, H. J. & Napier, N. 2002. Divergence or convergence: a cross-national comparison of personnel selection practices. *Human Resource Management Journal,* **41**(1): 31–44.

Hwang, S.-K. 2006. *Wage Structure and Skill Development.* Korea: Korea Labor Institute.

Kim, D.-O. & Bae, J. 2004. *Employment Relations and HRM in South Korea.* Aldershot, UK: Ashgate.

Kotter, J. 1997. *Matsushita Leadership.* New York: The Free Press.

Lin, Y. Y. 1996. Training and development practices in Taiwan: a comparison of Taiwanese, American and Japanese firms. *Asia Pacific Journal of Human Resources,* **34**(1): 26–43

Miles, L. 2008. The significance of cultural norms in the evolution of Korean HRM practices. *International Law and Management*, **50**(1): 33–46

Ministry of Economy Trade and Industry 2006. White Paper on international economy and trade 2006. Tokyo.

Ministry of Health Labour and Welfare 2005. White Paper on the labour economy. Tokyo.

Ministry of Health Labour and Welfare 2007a. Survey on recruitment 2007 in the enterprise. Tokyo.

Ministry of Health Labour and Welfare. 2007b. White Paper on the labour economy 2007. Tokyo.

Ministry of Health Labour and Welfare. 2009. Basic survey on labour union 2009. Tokyo.

Pucik, V. & Lim, J.-C. 2001. Transforming HRM in a Korean chaebol: a case study of Samsung. *Asia Pacific Business Review*, 7(4): 137–160.

Salter, S. B., Brody, R. G. & Lin, S. 2006. Merit pay, responsibility, and national values: a US–Taiwan comparison. *Journal of International Accounting Research*, **5**: 63.

Taipei Times 2009. 25 May.

Taipei Times 2009a. 24 August, p. 2.

Taipei Times 2009b. 23 October, p. 12.

Takahashi, N. 2004. *Kyomou no seikashugi* [Illusion of Performance-Based Management]. Tokyo: Nikkei BP.

Tselichtchev, I. & Debroux, P. 2009. *Asia's Turning Point.* Singapore: John Wiley & Sons.

Yui, T. 2008. The significance of management philosophy Shibusawa Eiich Left. In *keiei Tetsugaku no Jissen* [Practice of Management Philosophy]. Tokyo: Bunshindo, pp. 3–22.

28 Models of human resource management in Australia and New Zealand
Peter Boxall and Steve Frenkel

The goal of this chapter is to compare and contrast models of HRM in Australia and New Zealand and to locate these models within the wider world of HRM. We start with an outline of the unique contexts of Australia and New Zealand, highlighting important similarities and differences between the two countries, and relating them to other Anglophone countries. We then examine what is known about distinctive models of HRM in the Antipodes, summarising studies of management practice and of workers' perceptions of how they are managed. Only a few studies of HRM are directly comparable across the Tasman, so in each country we use the most interesting and relevant empirical research available. In New Zealand's case, this means we explore the small-business character of HRM and the less formal and relatively empowering ways in which workers are managed. In Australia's case, where organisations are typically larger than in New Zealand, we discuss recent research on the role of HRM specialists and their interactions with line managers. Overall, this approach enables us to paint a picture of both small-firm and large-firm HRM in the Antipodes. We draw together the key lessons in our conclusions.

THE CONTEXT OF HRM IN AUSTRALIA AND NEW ZEALAND

What are the main features of the historical, geographical, economic and socio-political context of HRM in the Antipodes? This section offers a summary of the main similarities and contrasts. Much fuller reviews of the HRM context of each country can be found in Mylett and Zanko's (1999) report for APEC on Australia, and Boxall's (2003) report for APEC on New Zealand. In terms of comparative studies of the management of work and employment in the two countries, there is a small but valuable industrial relations literature. We refer readers to Barry and Wailes's (2004) review of this literature and its arguments.

Australia and New Zealand, located some 2000 kilometres apart in the south-western Pacific, are logically grouped together in a chapter like this: they share much in common and are increasingly integrated in terms of their economic activities. Colonised by the British during the maritime expansion of European influence in the Pacific in the eighteenth and nineteenth centuries, they are Anglophone societies with small ratios of people to space. New Zealand, with a population in 2008 of 4.23 million people, is slightly larger geographically than the densely populated UK, while Australia, with 20.61 million people, is closer in territorial size to the much more populous United States.[1]

The two countries were, however, colonised in different ways. In New Zealand, the British Crown signed a treaty with the Maori chiefs in 1840, the Treaty of Waitangi. The Treaty did not prevent war erupting in New Zealand in the mid-nineteenth century but it has enabled a major programme of settling historical grievances over land sales and confiscations, and has provided the constitutional basis for an evolving bicultural partnership between Maori – who comprise around 15 per cent of the population[2] – and other New Zealanders. Both English and Maori are official languages in New Zealand. In Australia, the indigenous people – Aborigines and Torres Strait Islanders – suffered social and legal discrimination over many years. Their numbers were reduced by disease and organised violence, so that they currently comprise less than 3 per cent of Australia's population (ABS, 2002b). Since 1967, these groups have had the vote and some legal redress in regard to land rights was conferred on them in 1988. However, this has not substantially altered their experience of poverty and social discrimination. Thus, the life expectancy at birth for indigenous Australians born in the period 1996–2001 is estimated to be about 17 years less than that for non-indigenous Australians (ABS, 2007a).

On the other hand, an important similarity between New Zealand and Australia is that the workforce of both is now very heterogeneous in regard to country of origin. Some 23 per cent of the New Zealand workforce in 2007 was born outside the country,[3] the corresponding figure for Australia being 33.8 per cent.[4] Both countries have historically attracted large numbers of migrants from Europe. While the UK and Ireland have been the primary source, Australia is home to a more diverse European population than New Zealand, which has been a much more important destination for Polynesian migrants. Now, in both countries, migrants from China and other Asian countries have become increasingly important.

Like the UK and the United States, Australia and New Zealand are developed economies with first-world infrastructure. New Zealand, characterised by higher rainfall levels and a more mountainous terrain, is dominated by its food processing industries (dairy, meat, horticulture, wine and fish) and by its tourism sector. Australia is much the larger economy with a GDP in 2006 of US$782 billion compared with US$102 billion in New Zealand. It has substantial rural, manufacturing and tourism sectors but, critically for its productivity performance and overall living standards, has internationally significant mining industries with high capital intensity. On the other hand, both countries share a feature of most advanced societies – a large service sector. In New Zealand, nearly 71 per cent of the workforce is employed in private and public service, a figure very similar to Australia where close to 76 per cent of employees work in this sector (New South Wales Government, 2008).

The trans-Tasman free trade agreement, Closer Economic Relations (CER), continues to foster a high level of economic and regulatory integration. The extent of trans-Tasman trade was recently summarised by New Zealand's Ministry of Economic Development as follows:

> Since the introduction of CER, the percentage of New Zealand exports to Australia has risen from 13% in 1983 to 20% currently. In the past ten years, trans-Tasman trade has increased annually by an average of 9%, exceeding both countries' annual international trade growth rates. The growth has been particularly strong in the New Zealand–Australia direction, contrary to early predictions. Australia is New Zealand's biggest export market, and New Zealand is Australia's equal second market (with the US) for manufactured goods.[5]

The liberalisation of trade and capital flows between the two countries has naturally had greater consequences for New Zealand, given Australia's much larger economic size and higher rate of saving and investment. Many New Zealand enterprises, including almost the entire banking sector and large parts of the retail sector, are now Australian owned. Data for New Zealand indicate that, in 2006, 41 per cent of equity was held by foreign companies or individuals[6] while in Australia the figure for 2004 was 30 per cent, this being higher for non-financial corporations (37.6 per cent) (ABS, 2004). Both countries have a shareholder-centred model of corporate governance but the New Zealand share market is much the thinner. There are many more corporate headquarters located in Australia than in New Zealand although people in both societies feel subject to 'foreign control' exerted by firms in the world's largest economies.

Australia and New Zealand share an Anglo-American democratic and legal tradition with strong property rights. As in Britain, the judiciary (the court system) is independent of the executive (elected government). Given its small population and geographic size, New Zealand has no state parliaments. There are simply two layers of government: the national parliament and local authorities (city and district councils), whereas Australia has three tiers of government (the national or 'commonwealth' government, state governments, and local authorities). Another point of difference lies in the simple structure of the New Zealand Parliament: unlike Australia, there is no upper house (i.e. a 'unicameral legislature'). As a generalisation, government in New Zealand is less layered, less bureaucratic and more amenable to fast-paced reform.

Australia and New Zealand have similar forms of education, vocational training and occupational registration, making transfer across the Tasman for educational and work purposes relatively straightforward. The Trans-Tasman Mutual Recognition Arrangement (TTMRA) facilitates movement in those occupations requiring some form of licensing: someone registered to practise such an occupation in Australia can typically practise the equivalent occupation in New Zealand, and vice versa. The ease of movement of labour across the Tasman has enabled firms in each of the Australian states to treat New Zealand workers as part of their recruitment pool, much as they do with workers from other Australian states. Promotion opportunities, managerial careers and money wages are all typically greater in Australia than in New Zealand.

Working hours in both countries – which average around 44 hours per week for full-time workers – are slightly higher than in other OECD countries (OECD, 2004a). The proportion of people working part-time (27.1 per cent) in Australia in 2006 was the second highest in the OECD, higher than in New Zealand (21.3 per cent), which is also above the OECD average (OECD, 2008).[7] Of the full-time employees in Australia, nearly three in ten (28.7 per cent) would like to reduce their working hours. This issue is particularly acute among professionals and managers who work longer hours and who claim to have the least control over this aspect of their work life (van Wanrooy et al., 2008: 58–61, 78).

Although there is an ongoing debate in the New Zealand media over whether real income and work–life balance are better in Australia, there is much greater skilled migration from New Zealand to Australia than the reverse. In the year to September 2008, some 47 200 people left New Zealand for Australia while 13 200 migrated the other way.[8] In the international labour market, of course, both countries are small and suffer from an international 'diaspora' of skilled workers seeking greater opportunities. It is estimated that around half a million New Zealanders (one in nine) live outside the country while around one million (one in twenty) Australians are living abroad.[9]

In both countries, the ten or so years prior to the 'credit crunch' of 2008 were years in which employers had real difficulty recruiting. From a peak of nearly 11 per cent in late 1992, unemployment in Australia declined almost continuously from the mid-1990s to slightly over 4 per cent in mid-2007 (compared with an even greater drop in New Zealand to around 3.4 per cent). Despite immigration into Australia making the largest contribution to population growth in recent years and skill-stream migrants accounting for over 40 per cent of recent settler arrivals (ABS, 2008a), skill shortages have consistently been reported by the Australian Chamber of Commerce and Industry (ACCI) as one of the most significant barriers to investment in Australia (EWRERC, 2003: 12). In addition, the Business Council of Australia has noted that the increasing average population age has necessitated a range of training measures to minimise a widespread skills shortage (EWRERC, 2003: 12–13). Data from the official monthly Skilled Vacancy Index shows that skill shortages have been most acute in accounting, finance and management, food, hospitality and tourism, and among labourers, factory and machine worker categories (DEWR, 2008 and online). The same concerns have been constantly echoed in New Zealand by employer associations.[10]

Besides the extent to which they operate as a common market for skilled labour, Australia and New Zealand fit within the more liberal Anglo-American model of labour market regulation (Freeman et al., 2007). Employer–employee relations are substantially decentralised: employment contracting typically takes place at enterprise, workplace or individual levels. While both countries established state-controlled systems of compulsory arbitration at the turn of the twentieth century, these modes of labour regulation have been disestablished and replaced with the more typical forms seen in the Anglophone world (Barry & Wailes, 2004; Freeman et al., 2007). Laws on union recognition, collective bargaining, health and safety in employment, minimum employment conditions and equal employment opportunity are important in this pattern but there is significantly less labour market regulation than in the co-ordinated market economies of continental Europe. At times, the role of unions has been challenged (for example, in New Zealand in the early 1990s and in Australia between 1995 and 2007 when the country was governed by a conservative Federal administration) but union recognition and collective bargaining remain important social norms in both societies and those who challenge them face major political risks.[11] On the other hand, this does not mean that unions enjoy high participation levels. Union density has been declining in both countries and unions currently cover around one in five employees, with much higher density in the public sector than in the private (Boxall et al., 2007a).[12]

STYLES OF HRM IN NEW ZEALAND

A comparative analysis of HRM styles needs to focus on overall patterns in the management of work and people. We adopt an approach in this section and the next which is based on identifying a country's 'dominant models of HRM' and analysing their implications for its workplace outcomes (Boxall, 1995). In doing so, it helps to look at models for managing managers and then at models for managing the non-managerial workforce.

Boxall and Gilbert's (2007) typology of company styles in the management of managers is a framework which examines how such factors as organisational size and socio-cultural differences affect the ways firms try to recruit, develop, reward and extract value from managers. The typology traverses five major styles: 'elite', 'elite-development', 'emergent', 'emergent-development', and 'transnational-hybrid'. In the elite model, managerial talent is identified early, based on social status or membership of an elite cadre, as in the French grande-école system. Those who successfully come through this defining group are channelled into a career path that gives significant responsibility from the outset. In the 'elite-development' model, characteristic of Germany and Japan, the managerial pool is also identified early but those recruited are put through an intense and structured development programme, which ultimately involves a competitive tournament based on performance against certain criteria for advancing to senior management ranks. The 'emergent' model, on the other hand, is characteristic of small firms almost everywhere which out-grow family resources and need to turn to external labour markets for managers. The 'emergent-development' model is the implicit model of medium to large Anglo-American firms. In the most prestigious firms, there are often attempts to recruit 'the cream' from elite educational institutions but experienced managers are also recruited to various levels from the external labour market and the identification of managerial potential is based more on demonstrated performance than on elite background. The 'transnational-hybrid' model is characteristic of multinational firms with a global governance structure of some kind and a need to manage the tension between global strategy and local adaptation in HRM. While corporate headquarters may seek to impose one style, such firms may, within their global operations, have elements of all the other types.

Unsurprisingly, Gilbert and Boxall's (2009) empirical study of major New Zealand companies suggests that the management of managers in New Zealand typically falls into the emergent pattern: New Zealand companies are heavily dependent on recruiting the managerial talent they need from the external labour market. Leaders of firms complain of talent shortages and feel they are at a major disadvantage in recruiting and retaining managers of sufficient calibre. This inevitably affects the ability of New Zealand companies to perform in the international environment and constrains their rate of growth. It is not, however, all bleak. New Zealand's smaller, less bureaucratic companies can be more flexible in how they deploy individuals across functions, can provide greater autonomy in how individuals do their work, and often offer individuals earlier responsibility and escalated career development. However, the degree of managerial responsibility and professional development is naturally limited in a country with no indigenous companies listed in the Fortune Global 500.[13] The more international, more extensive and more highly paid managerial and professional jobs are to be found in places such as the UK, the United States and Australia. Only a few large New Zealand firms have developed the kind of internal labour markets and management development structures seen in the world's largest corporations.

What is true of dominant styles of HRM for the management of managers is true more generally in terms of managing the non-managerial New Zealand workforce. There are, of course, large private-sector firms and public sector organisations with traditions of formal, bureaucratic HRM of the kind seen in large US or UK firms. In the largest New Zealand organisations, one does see such practices as formal job analysis, specialised work organisation and formal systems of recruitment, performance appraisal and internal development. In these organisations, such practices are often evolved within a framework of collective bargaining and joint consultation (Boxall, 1997). However, the dominant model of HRM for the New Zealand operating workforce reflects the fact that the average enterprise is a small to medium-sized company. Compared with Australia, the United States and the UK, a smaller percentage of New Zealand workers is employed in firms with at least 100 employees (44.8 per cent in New Zealand compared with 64.4 per cent in the United States and 60.2 per cent in the UK) (Mills & Timmins, 2004).[14]

Models of HRM in New Zealand therefore tend towards the less formal styles typical of small firms (Boxall & Purcell, 2008). Small employers do not adopt the HR planning, job analysis and career development procedures of the large and multinational employers and rely heavily on the external labour market for relevant skills (Marchington et al., 2003). This is illustrated by the fact that New Zealand firms are heavy users of recruitment agencies (Dakin & Smith, 1995). An active recruitment consultancy industry is not surprising given the fact that some 55 per cent of employment in New Zealand occurs in firms with less than 100 employees, which generally do not employ HRM specialists in-house. Small employers are also less able to afford large training budgets. Most employee development takes place on the job through coaching and mentoring (Macky & Johnson, 2000).

As with managerial labour, employers have long expressed a high degree of concern over skill shortages. An added twist is that literacy and numeracy are seen as major problems at the lower end of the labour market.[15] In an international study of adult literacy reported by the OECD (2000), New Zealand ranked seventh among 22 OECD nations – with very similar average levels of prose literacy as Canada and Australia but behind the leaders in Northern Europe (Sweden, Finland, Norway and the Netherlands). While the performance of the average adult seems good, the distribution includes 40 per cent of New Zealand adults whose prose literacy is 'very poor' or 'weak'. New Zealand's position is lower in terms of adult numeracy ('quantitative literacy'), ranking 15th among the OECD nations in this study. Some 50 per cent of adults are 'very poor' or 'weak' in numerical ability. Given high levels of employment in New Zealand, there is no doubt that the literacy/numeracy problem among less skilled workers is a constraint on workplace productivity growth (New Zealand Treasury, 2008). While the overall level of skills in New Zealand is consistent with a developed economy, that group of workers in the New Zealand workplace who have difficulty reading, writing or applying mathematical logic is less likely to participate effectively in teamwork, contribute to innovation, or show the skills needed for quality improvement. This inevitably affects workplace performance.

This brief sketch emphasises the small-business character of HRM in New Zealand but does not tell us how New Zealand workers perceive the way they are managed. Recent studies of employee perceptions of, and responses to, management practices help us build a more rounded picture of employer strategies and behaviour. Surveys of employee responses to work practices conducted by Macky and Boxall (2007, 2008a, 2008b), which are based on large national samples of employees (around 1000), measure worker well-being, and examine the extent to which workers can exercise influence on the job, feel well informed, consider themselves well rewarded, and experience good training opportunities. While some workers report high levels of work intensification and stress, the surveys reveal a workforce that, on average, perceives high levels of job influence and reports healthy levels of well-being. The overall picture is one of 'a fairly egalitarian workplace in terms of allowing individuals, of varying skill levels, to exert control over decisions in their day-to-day work' (Macky & Boxall, 2008a: 13).

These surveys confirm the picture of high levels of employee influence and job satisfaction, and a generally consultative management style found in the New Zealand Worker Representation and Participation Survey (NZWRPS) (Boxall et al., 2007b; Haynes et al., 2005). In that study, also based on a large-scale survey of New Zealand workers, nine out of ten workers said that they were satisfied with their jobs, eight out of ten said they trusted their employer, and 85 per cent agreed that relations between employees and management were good. In this respect, they rated relationships between management and workers nearly 20 per cent better than US workers and 15 per cent better than British workers (Diamond & Freeman, 2002; Freeman & Rogers, 1999).

There are, of course, nuances in this picture (Macky & Boxall, 2008a, b). There is evidence of both 'low-road' (work intensifying) and 'high-road' (high-skill/empowering) production strategies and a range of employee experiences across different contexts. For example, employees in the private sector feel better rewarded for their performance than public sector workers and also perceive themselves as having better chances of promotion from within the organisation. Professionals, technicians, and associate professionals in the private sector feel much better informed than their public sector counterparts. Employees in larger firms see themselves as having a better internal labour market. Those in unionised firms perceive better opportunities for training and development but report higher levels of stress and work-life imbalance (Macky & Boxall, 2009).

Overall, then, the evidence suggests that HRM in New Zealand workplaces is typically based on an informal, relatively empowering and consultative management style. This is not surprising given the average workplace size is small and direct communications between employee and employer are much more possible than in the large bureaucracies seen in much bigger countries. Within this general context, a range of contingent variables produce a nuanced set of models of HRM and worker experiences, as is observed everywhere: such variables include employer industry and production strategies, organisational size, unionisation, and employee occupation, among others. In terms of workplace outcomes, the most important issues facing employers are concerned with skill shortages and mismatches, at both managerial and operating levels, and their impact on productivity and enterprise growth.

STYLES OF HRM IN AUSTRALIA

It seems more than likely that small Australian firms share much the same style of HRM as their New Zealand counterparts. Larger firms, however, are somewhat different. In regard to managing managers, the most common models are the 'emergent-development' variant in locally owned firms and the 'transnational-hybrid', particularly in global IT and mining industry firms. In relation to managing non-managerial employees in large firms, there are two variants of what is, in effect, a large-firm model.

Before discussing these, it is helpful to explain what is known about HRM specialists in Australia. Apart from Hunt and Boxall's (1998) study of senior HR managers, there has been more research in Australia than in New Zealand on the role of HRM specialists but the results of the Australian research are very relevant to New Zealand because so many of the HRM specialists in the latter are employed by Australian firms. The educational qualification of entrants into the specialist HRM role has increased over time so that, according to a recent survey of practising members of the Australian Human Resource Institute, 46 per cent of respondents in 2005 were university graduates compared to 23 per cent in 1995. One third of these managers commenced work in the HRM function, with the second most popular starting point being Marketing and Sales (Sheehan et al., 2006). The importance of tertiary qualifications is more pronounced in larger firms. Thus, in an exploratory study of ten large firms, Frenkel and Gollan found that of 51 HR managers, 32 had undergraduate degrees and a further 12 had master's degrees. The remaining 5 managers had diplomas or equivalent while two managers had no tertiary qualifications.

The specialist HRM function in Australia is an occupation where women predominate and are increasingly occupying senior roles. It seems that Australian HR managers are exercising more influence in their organisations. This contrasts with their US counterparts, whose power and status may be lower relative to their aspirations (Kochan, 2007).[16] According to Sheehan et al. (2006), in 1995, 56 per cent of HR managers claimed that the HRM department was represented in the senior management group of their company. Ten years later, the comparable figure had grown to 68 per cent. This influence differs according to the two variants of the large-firm model summarised in Table 28.1.

The first variant, labelled bureaucratic-service, applies mainly to medium-sized and large locally owned firms whose market is almost entirely national. The large retailers, retail banks, building materials suppliers, and transport companies are in this category. These are organisations whose frame of reference is the Australian institutional context. The second, networked, value-adding variant, is characteristic of larger firms that are either wholly or partly UK- or US-owned, or who earn a significant amount of their revenue through exports. These firms have a more international perspective that includes adoption of HRM strategies pioneered overseas. Typical examples are the largest accounting and consulting organisations, alcoholic beverage and food companies and five-star hotels.

The bureaucratic-service variant is typically characterised by a matrix structure with a corporate HRM function guiding HRM units that are

Table 28.1   Two variants of HRM in large Australian firms

HRM model variants / HRM dimensions	Bureaucratic-Service	Networked, value-adding
HR managers' roles	HRM generalists with some specialist services (e.g. training) and some strategic capability	HRM transactional services combined with business partner generalists, specialists and strategists
HRM organisation	Centralised with divisional support	Networking between shared services, service-line business partners, and specialists, co-ordinated by senior strategists
HR management style	Reactive; mainly service providers with some strategic advice to the line; limited employee support	More equal relationship with the line; provides strategic and operational advice, tools and training for line leadership

decentralised to product divisions and which also report to divisional line management (McGraw, 2004). Policies and programmes are usually 'rolled-out' from corporate HQ with varying degrees of adaptation according to divisional needs. Recruitment, performance management, promotion and other HR policies devised at corporate level are often formalised with HR specialists assisting line managers to interpret and apply these at lower organisational levels. Where divisions serve very different markets, management devises distinct business strategies which allow their HRM specialists to do the same, albeit within the confines of corporate strategy set at the highest reaches of the local corporation.

HR managers in Australia view their role mainly as service providers to line management. They assist in interpreting employment law and advise on issues such as remuneration, health and safety, and human resource planning (Kulik & Bainbridge, 2006). In addition, HR managers address workforce problems such as employee turnover, skill shortages, and leadership development. Devolution of operational HRM activities to line managers has grown and, overall, intra-management relations are regarded by HRM specialists as 'respectful' and 'amicable'. However, tension exists in some organisations where much of the HRM function has been outsourced and the HRM department has been reduced to overseeing external consultants or where HRM specialists have been marginalised in the interests of cost reduction. In general, HRM managers perceive the trend to devolving policy implementation to line managers as having positive organisational consequences. However, line managers are generally more sceptical (Kulik & Bainbridge, 2006). Differences are most significant in regard to communication and interaction between line and HR managers. Line managers express concern over insufficient training in HRM. HR managers are significantly more inclined to the view that employee satisfaction has increased on account of devolution and more likely to want to continue the process so that they can focus on 'strategic issues' (Kulik & Bainbridge, 2006: 246–248).

According to the networked, value-adding variant, the HRM function assumes a more influential place in the corporation and roles are more specialised. Because of the global talent shortage, in particular, occupations needed by these companies (e.g. forensic accountants, genome engineers and nanotechnologists), HR managers are sensitive to the need to develop more effective HRM strategies, policies and practices. Wherever possible, HRM specialists seek to base their activities on research evidence, and try to ensure their roles are supported with sophisticated IT systems.

Routine policy execution is administered by a group of transactional experts for all employees. These are the shared-service personnel. Typically, much of this administration (e.g. queries about leave, pay and transfers) is handled initially on a self-service basis using the corporate intranet. In addition, line managers are supported by internal HRM consultants ('business partners') who have a sound knowledge of the business and are able to work with their line counterparts in providing tools and advice for improved people management. Then there are other HRM specialists who provide advanced services to the company or the local subsidiary. Learning and development is a key area, while organisational change is another. These are experts whose identity is often with their sub-discipline rather than with 'HRM' as a specialist profession (Wright, 2008). At the co-ordinating centre is a small group of senior HRM professionals who work closely with other senior managers to develop HRM strategy and a corporate culture that assists in realising the company's business objectives. They also allocate the HRM budget and often encourage the development of HRM practice groups, which focus on particular issues (e.g. knowledge management or employee engagement) and include shared-service personnel, business partners and strategic experts.

With the exception of shared-service employees, HR managers in the networked value-adding variant are typically either highly qualified, having a master's degree in an HRM-related discipline, and/or they are experienced practitioners in the business they are advising. They typically have close, egalitarian relationships with line managers to whom they seek to transfer information and knowledge about new HRM techniques and tools. These HRM specialists typically have a good understanding of the business units in which they are embedded, which helps them to provide valuable operational advice and to generate the trust necessary to influence strategic decisions relating to such issues as organisational change and succession planning. However, in the absence of a strong centralised leadership, organisations characterised by this network form tend to fragment into competing fiefdoms as managers in the different business units seek to dominate decision making at the local and regional levels in their companies.

Employee Perceptions of HRM Practice in Australia

As noted above, until the recent international recession, Australian employers were affected by a tight market for skilled labour. They have also been working in a legislative context that has been significantly redesigned to enable them to conduct relations with employees with less union involvement and with less regulation of pay and conditions. While legislative reforms have enabled some employers to hire at the lower end of the labour market to take advantage of employees (see Peetz, 2006), the behaviour of larger employers has been more strongly influenced by the labour market than by legislation. In short, large companies have generally been careful to relate to employees positively and fairly. For their part, workers have been aware of global competition and see their managers having to work longer and harder. Relevant information in this regard comes from a recent survey conducted by van Wanrooy et al. (2008: 60), which found that 17.6 per cent of managers (n = 711) strongly agreed and a further 39.2 per cent agreed that 'more and more is expected of me for the same amount of pay' compared with 16.9 per cent and 36.5 per cent of employees (n = 4825) answering the same question. And, as noted earlier, on average, managers work longer hours than other employees.

These numbers also indicate that non-managerial workers have been under increased pressure at work. In a 2001 official survey of nearly six million employees who had been with their current employer for at least one year, the most commonly reported changes at work over the previous 12 months were 'more responsibility' (41 per cent) and 'new, different or extra duties' (38 per cent) (ABS, 2002a). In short, some factors have been present that might be expected to promote increasing disaffection with management (coercive legislation and greater pressure at work) while others appear to have acted in a countervailing direction (tight labour markets and management that includes a higher proportion of better educated, professional HR managers). What, then, is the evidence regarding Australian employee attitudes to the way they are managed?

Data comes from two main sources, the van Wanrooy survey referred to above and a 2003–2004 large-scale employee survey (Teicher et al., 2007). The latter source provides brief but useful information regarding the incidence of consultative mechanisms in the Australian workplace. Eighty-three per cent of employee respondents reported an open-door policy to discuss problems with management, and 60.1 per cent reported the presence of regular staff meetings. Joint consultative committees were said to be present in half the workplaces surveyed. Of nearly half the sample of joint consultative committees that did not involve a union, nearly 80 per cent of respondents claimed these to be effective. This is similar to the findings regarding New Zealand consultative committees (Teicher et al., 2007: 139). The preliminary conclusion emerging from these data is that HRM, as in New Zealand, is now conducted in a more consultative way in Australia. Table 28.2 below, excerpted from van Wanrooy et al. (2008: 32), confirms this impression.

Table 28.2 indicates that 73.8 per cent of employees in 2008 perceived management to consult with employees over issues affecting them, up from 70.7 per cent in 2007. And close to 70 per cent of employees in 2008 agreed or strongly agreed with the statement that 'managers at my workplace can be trusted to tell things the way they are' (the equivalent figure in New Zealand, as noted above, is eight out of ten). Finally, in terms of fair treatment, over three-quarters of respondents agreed that 'I feel employees are treated fairly at my workplace.' In sum, there is strong evidence that most Australian companies have responded to the tighter labour market of the last decade with a more consultative, responsive style of HRM and did not take advantage of recent legislation to reduce employees' pay and conditions.

CONCLUSIONS

What, then, characterises HRM in the Antipodes? There is much about Australia and New Zealand that fits within typical Anglo-American patterns of HRM and employment relations: firms depend heavily on the external labour market for talent, and regulatory requirements and trade union involvement are lower than they are in the coordinated market economies of continental Europe. Labour market regulation has been through controversial periods in both countries but both seem to have settled into a decentralised pattern of employment contracting which

Table 28.2   Australian employees' attitudes toward management, 2007 and 2008, per cent

	2007 (n = 5628)	2008 (n = 4878)
Managers in my workplace consult employees about issues affecting staff		
Strongly agree	19.5	18.3
Agree	51.2	55.5
Neither agree nor disagree	6.6	7.0
Disagree	15.7	14.0
Strongly disagree	5.5	4.3
Can't choose	1.5	0.9
Managers can be trusted to tell things the way they are		
Strongly agree	18.2	17.0
Agree	52.2	52.6
Neither agree nor disagree	7.9	9.5
Disagree	15.0	15.3
Strongly disagree	5.8	5.0
Can't choose	0.9	0.6[a]
I feel employees are treated fairly at my workplace		
Strongly agree	19.7	17.9
Agree	58.3	60.5
Neither agree nor disagree	7.3	8.3
Disagree	11.1	10.4
Strongly disagree	3.2	2.5
Can't choose	0.4	0.3
Total	100.0	100.0

Note: a.   Estimate not reliable. Weighted according to labour force estimates for each year.

Source: Excerpted from van Wanrooy et al. (2008: 32)

preserves trade unionism and collective bargaining, where it is wanted by workers. On the New Zealand side of the Tasman, small business styles of HRM dominate: people are managed in relatively informal and empowering ways, which most find appealing. However, career development opportunities are fewer than in Australia and much fewer than elsewhere, making New Zealand more vulnerable than Australia in the international labour market for highly skilled workers. The greater average size of Australian firms brings both greater career development opportunities and a higher level of bureaucracy than is true in New Zealand. There are, correspondingly, greater roles for in-house HRM specialists in Australia and we see signs of a maturing 'partnership' between line and HR managers in developing responses to a more complex, more diverse workforce. The current international recession aside, the key issue for both countries in HRM is about skill development and skill matching: how to ensure that each country attracts and develops the kind of human capital that will underpin productivity growth; that organisations can find the labour they need when they need it; and that they become more adept at internal employee development and at building greater work/life balance. The Antipodes do provide a fine setting for achieving a balance between work and the personal life – something for which they are world-famous – but the studies we have noted suggest that this cannot be taken for granted, especially among managers and professionals. The ongoing challenge will be for management to become more creative in thinking about the recruitment, development and retention of skilled employees against sophisticated international competitors. This is needed to ensure that Australasian businesses can grow and take advantage of the international opportunities that are offered by the scarce resources and high-quality environment that characterise the Antipodes. Skills in strategic HRM planning, and a senior management which imputes significance to managing human capital, will become increasingly important.

NOTES

1. For statistical comparisons in this section, we rely on Statistics New Zealand. See http://www.stats.govt.nz. Accessed 11 January 2012.
2. http://www.tpk.govt.nz/en/in-print/our-publications/fact-sheets/beyond-2020-population-projections-for-maori/page/2/. Accessed 15 October 2010.
3. http://www.stats.govt.nz/Census/2006CensusHomePage/QuickStats/quickstats-about-a-subject/national-highlights/cultural-diversity.aspx. Accessed 11 January 2012.
4. See ABS 2008b. *Yearbook 2008*, p. 224.
5. From www.med.govt.nz, 2010 website, but no longer available on-line.
6. http://www.nzinstitute.org/Images/uploads/Magnetic_economy_080906.pdf. Accessed 15 October 2010.
7. Women workers (around 45 per cent of the workforce) in Australia are much more likely to work part-time than men. In 2006 nearly 46 per cent of female workers worked part-time compared to close to 15 per cent of men (see ABS, 2007a). Corresponding data for New Zealand (2007) indicate that women comprise 46 per cent of the workforce with 41.2 per cent of females working part-time compared to 16.6 per cent of males. The OECD averages are 25.8 per cent and 6.5 per cent for women and men respectively, see OECD, 2004b. Women at Work. http://www.oecd.org/dataoecd/36/7/17652667.pdf. For excessive working hours in Australia compared with other OECD countries, see ILO, 2008. http://www.ilo.org/wcmsp5/groups/public/dgreports/dcomm/documents/publication/wcms_082838.pdf; ILO. 2008. http://www.ilo.org/wcmsp5/groups/public/dgreports/dcomm/documents/publication/wcms_082838.pdf. Accessed 15 October 2010.
8. http://www.nzherald.co.nz/nz/news/article.cfm?c_id=1&objectid=10539016. Accessed 11 January 2012.

9.   Sources: For New Zealand, see the NZ Treasury Report: http://www.treasury.govt. nz/publications/research-policy/wp/2004/04-13/twp04-13.pdf. Accessed 15 October 2010. For Australia, see http://en.wikipedia.org/wiki/Australian_diaspora. Accessed 15 October 2010.
10.   See, for example, http://www.businessnz.org.nz/print/1507. Accessed 15 October 2010.
11.   Industrial relations was a key election issue in the 2007 Australian general election. The successful Labor party under Kevin Rudd translated its pledges into practice by passing the Fair Work Act 2008, which has re-introduced collective bargaining, and restored some of the rights that had been withdrawn from unions and workers under the previous government's legislation whose objective was to increase the power of employers, promote individual 'bargaining', and facilitate flexible employment contracts (see Peetz, D. 2006. *Brave New Workplace: How Individual Contracts are Changing our Lives.* Sydney: Allen & Unwin).
12.   In Australia, union density was over 50 per cent in the mid-1970s, declining to 20 per cent in 2006 with the private sector attracting far fewer members (density 15.2 per cent) compared to 42.6 per cent for the public sector (ABS, 2008b. *Yearbook 2008*). Australians may be more favourably disposed to unions than New Zealanders although survey responses may be strongly influenced by the prevailing political-economic context. Thus, according to a 2005 international survey, 65 per cent of Australian respondents agreed with the statement: 'Without trade unions, the working conditions of employees would be much worse than they are' while 55 per cent also agreed that 'trade unions are very important for the job security of employees'. The corresponding figures for the New Zealand respondents were 51 per cent and 41 per cent respectively (see van Wanrooy et al., 2008. *Working Lives: Statistics and Stories.* Sydney, Workplace Research Centre www.australiaatwork.org.au, pp. 47–48).
13.   Australia, by contrast, has eight companies in the Global Fortune 500. See http:// money.cnn.com/magazines/fortune/global500/2010/countries/Australia.html. Accessed 15 October 2010.
14.   A comparable figure for Australia is not readily available. However, a very small number of firms (<1 per cent) employ 200 or more employees. These companies employ a relatively large proportion of the workforce, perhaps as much as a third.
15.   See comments by Business New Zealand: http://www.businessnz.org.nz/file/1585/ Workforce%20Skills%20&%20Tertiary%20Education%20BusinessNZ.pdf. Accessed 11 January 2012.
16.   Annual salary surveys by the Australian Institute of Management indicate that over the 1997–2006 period, HRM senior executives were paid less than their counterparts in marketing and finance. This pattern of results is repeated for corresponding middle level managers and the same findings apply when we look at total remuneration. However, the rate of change of both HRM senior executives and HR managers' salaries and total remuneration was similar to their finance and marketing counterparts. These findings suggest that although HR managers are less valued than their finance and marketing colleagues, they have not declined in status over the past decade.

REFERENCES

ABS. 2002a. Career Experience, November 2002 Cat. No. 6254.0.
ABS. 2002b. National Aboriginal and Torres Strait Islander social survey. 4714.0. Canberra.
ABS. 2004. *Yearbook 2004*, updated. Belconnen, Australia: ABS.
ABS. 2007a. Deaths Australia, 2006, ABS 3302.0.
ABS. 2007b. *Yearbook: Employed People.* (cat. no. 3101.0). Belconnen, Australia: ABS. http://www.abs.gov.au/ausstats/ABS@.nsf/bb8db737e2af84b8ca2571780015701e/4143359 0903656DECA257236000146CB?opendocument.

ABS. 2008a. Migration, Australia (cat.no. 3412.0): make: http://www.abs.gov.au/AUS STATS/abs@.nsf/second+level+view?ReadForm&prodno=3412.0&viewtitle=Migration, %20Australia~2009-10~Latest~16/06/2011&&tabname=Past%20Future%20Issues&prod no=3412.0&issue=2009-10&num=&view=&.

ABS. 2008b. *Yearbook 2008*. Belconnen, Australia: ABS.

Barry, M. & Wailes, N. 2004. Contrasting systems? 100 years of arbitration in Australia and *New Zealand. Journal of Industrial Relations*, **46**(4): 430–447.

Boxall, P. 1995. Building the theory of comparative HRM. *Human Resource Management Journal*, **5**(5): 5–17.

Boxall, P. 1997. Models of employment and labour productivity in New Zealand: an interpretation of change since the Employment Contracts Act. *New Zealand Journal of Industrial Relations*, **22**(1): 22–36.

Boxall, P. 2003. New Zealand. In M. Zanko & M. Ngui (eds), *The Handbook of Human Resource Management Policies and Practices in Asia-Pacific Economies*, Vol. 2. Cheltenham, UK: Edward Elgar, pp. 228–284.

Boxall, P. & Gilbert, J. 2007. The management of managers: a review and conceptual framework. *International Journal of Management Reviews*, **9**(2): 1–21.

Boxall, P., Haynes, P. & Freeman, R. B. 2007. Conclusion: what workers say in the Anglo-American world. In R. B. Freeman, P. Boxall & P. Haynes (eds), *What Workers Say: Employee Voice in the Anglo-American Workplace*. Ithaca, NY: Cornell University Press, pp. 206–220.

Boxall, P., Haynes, P. & Macky, K. 2007. Employee voice and voicelessness in New Zealand. In R. B. Freeman, P. Boxall & P. Haynes (eds), *What Workers Say: Employee Voice in the Anglo-American Workplace*. Ithaca, NY: Cornell University Press, pp. 145–165.

Boxall, P. & Purcell, J. 2008. *Strategy and Human Resource Management*, 2nd edn. Basingstoke, UK: Palgrave Macmillan.

Dakin, S. & Smith, M. 1995. Staffing. In P. Boxall (ed.), *The Challenge of Human Resource Management: Directions and Debates in New Zealand*. Auckland: Addison Wesley Longman, pp. 112–149.

DEWR 2008. Vacancy Report.

Diamond, W. & Freeman, R. B. 2002. *What Workers Want from Workplace Organizations: A Report to the TUC's Promoting Trade Unionism Task Group*. London: Trades Union Congress.

EWRERC. 2003. (2003) *Bridging the Skills Divide*. Canberra: Employment, Workplace Relations and Education References Committee, Department of the Senate, pp.12–13.

Freeman, R. B., Boxall, P. & Haynes, P. 2007. Introduction: the Anglo-American economies and employee voice. In R. B. Freeman, P. Boxall & P. Haynes (eds), *What Workers Say: Employee Voice in the Anglo-American Workplace*. Ithaca, NY: Cornell University Press, pp. 1–24.

Freeman, R. B. & Rogers, J. 1999. *What Workers Want*. Ithaca, NY: ILR Press.

Gilbert, J. & Boxall, P. 2009. The management of managers: challenges in a small economy. *Journal of European Industrial Training*, **33**(4): 323–340.

Haynes, P., Boxall, P. & Macky, K. 2005. Non-union voice and the effectiveness of joint consultation in New Zealand. *Economic and Industrial Democracy*, **26**(2): 229–256.

Hunt, J. & Boxall, P. 1998. Are top human resource specialists 'strategic partners'? Self-perceptions of a corporate elite. *International Journal of Human Resource Management*, **9**(5): 767–781.

ILO. 2008. http://www.ilo.org/wcmsp5/groups/public/dgreports/dcomm/documents/public ation/wcms_082838.pdf.

Kochan, T. 2007. Social legitimacy of the HRM profession: a US perspective. In P. Boxall, J. Purcell & P. Wright (eds), *The Oxford Handbook of Human Resource Management*. Oxford: Oxford University Press, pp. 599–620.

Kulik, C. & Bainbridge, H. 2006. HR and the line: the distribution of HR activities in Australian organisations. *Asia Pacific Journal of Human Resources*, **44**(2): 240–256.

Macky, K. & Boxall, P. 2007. The relationship between high-performance work practices and employee attitudes: an investigation of additive and interaction effects. *International Journal of Human Resource Management*, **18**(4): 537–567.

Macky, K. & Boxall, P. 2008a. Employee experiences of high-performance work systems: an analysis of sectoral, occupational, organisational and employee variables. *New Zealand Journal of Employment Relations*, **33**(1): 1–18.

Macky, K. & Boxall, P. 2008b. High-involvement work processes, work intensification and employee well-being: a study of New Zealand worker experiences. *Asia Pacific Journal of Human Resources*, **46**(2): 38–55.

Macky, K. & Boxall, P. 2009. Employee well-being and union membership, New Zealand. *Journal of Employment Relations*, **34**(3): 14–25.

Macky, K. & Johnson, G. 2000. *The Strategic Management of Human Resources*. Auckland: McGraw-Hill.

Marchington, M., Carroll, M. & Boxall, P. 2003. Labour scarcity and the survival of small firms: a resource-based view of the road haulage industry. *Human Resource Management Journal*, **13**(4): 3-22.

McGraw, P. 2004. Influences on HRM practices in MNCs: a qualitative study in the Australian context. *International Journal of Manpower*, **25**(6): 535–546.

Mills, D. & Timmins, J. 2004. Firm dynamics in New Zealand: a comparative analysis with OECD countries. In New Zealand Treasury Working Paper, 04/11.

Mylett, T. & Zanko, M. 1999. Australia. In M. Zanko & M. Ngui (eds), *The Handbook of Human Resource Management Policies and Practices in Asia-Pacific Economies*, Vol. 1. Cheltenham, UK: Edward Elgar.

New South Wales Government. 2008. For most recent information see http://www.business.nsw.gov.au/invest-in-nsw/about-nsw/people-skills-and-education/employed-persons-by-industry.

New Zealand Treasury 2008. Working smarter: driving productivity growth through skills. NZ Treasury Productivity Paper 08/06.

OECD. 2000 *Literacy in the Information Age*. Paris: OECD.

OECD. 2004a. http://www.oecd.org/dataoecd/42/49/33821328.pdf.

OECD. 2004b. Women at Work, http://www.oecd.org/dataoecd/36/7/17652667.pdf

OECD. 2008 *Economic, Environmental and Social Statistics*. Paris: OECD.

Peetz, D. 2006. *Brave New Workplace: How Individual Contracts are Changing our Lives*. Sydney: Allen & Unwin.

Sheehan, C., Holland, P. & De Cieri, H. 2006. Current developments in HRM in Australian organisations. *Asia Pacific Journal of Human Resources*, **44**(2): 2–22.

Teicher, J., Holland, P., Pyman, A. & Cooper, B. 2007. Australian workers: finding their voice. In R. Freeman, P. Boxall & P. Haynes (eds), *What Workers Say: Employee Voice in the Anglo-American Workplace*. Ithaca, NY: Cornell University Press.

van Wanrooy, B., Jakubauskas, M., Buchanan, J., Wilson, S. & Scalmer, S. 2008. Working lives: statistics and stories. Sydney, Workplace Research Centre, http://www.australiaat-work.org.au/assets/Australia%20at%20Work%20W2%20Working%20Lives.pdf.

Wright, C. 2008. Reinventing human resource management: business partners, internal consultants and the limits to professionalization. *Human Relations*, **61**(8): 1063–1086.

Index